condensed computer encyclopedia

other reference works of interest

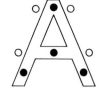 

Philip B. Jordain

Associate, Evans Research and Development Corporation
Associate, Artronic Information Systems, Inc.

assistant editor **Michael Breslau**

Supervisor, Scientific Programming, ITT Data Services

condensed computer encyclopedia

new york **McGRAW-HILL BOOK COMPANY**

san francisco   toronto   london   sydney

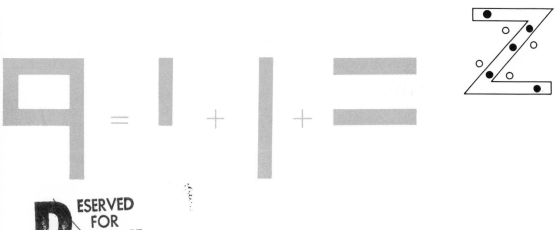

condensed computer encyclopedia

33038

1234567890 MAMM 754321069

Ronald Cullen *Systems Programmer, International Business Machines, New York, N. Y.*
(OPTICAL CHARACTER RECOGNITION)

Norman Cresswick *Technical Research Scientist, Thomas J. Lipton, Englewood Cliffs, N. J.*
(DELAY LINES)

M. Sheila Hollihan *Vassar College, Poughkeepsie, N. Y.*
(BIOGRAPHIES)

Raymond Kurland *Programming Manager, Datex, Englewood Cliffs, N. J.*
(IPL-V, INDEXING PROGRAM)

Alan Nuss *Senior Specialist Market Development, General Electric, Bethesda, Md.*
(TIME-SHARING)

Alan Schafler *President, Thompson-Starret, New York, N. Y.*
(ELECTRONIC DATA PROCESSING CENTERS)

Bohdan O. Szuprowicz *Market Development, Computer Usage, New York, N. Y.*
(APT, COGO, STRESS)

The avowed purpose of this book is easily stated: to define computer terms clearly and meaningfully for the nonspecialist.

Computer usage is relentlessly growing in business, industry, utilities, government, colleges.   Usually, if questionably, computerization begins in the accounting department, and from there spreads inexorably throughout the organization, often over strenuous if tacit departmental objections.   As with a rising tide, the impact of computer usage is at first imperceptible: obvious troughs—traditional fields of application—are filled immediately, and crests—those activities believed to be too complex—are at first spared.   But as the eye wanders about and returns, some crests are gone, other crests form the next obvious troughs, and the new crests single themselves out in apparently unperturbed isolation.   And the manager, whose department has just been discovered as a natural for computerization, is sent to a three-day seminar at a computer manufacturer's homestead.

At such seminars the businessman learns everything about GIGO, bits, linear programming, and how computers can solve all his problems (but beware GIGO).   Steeled by his new knowlege, he walks into *his* computer center.   His connoisseur's eye ignores the familiar computer and rests on the operator (the operator can always be identified by the punched cards sticking out of his shirt pocket and by the rubber bands around the palms of his hands).

"Hi!" says the manager to put the operator at ease: "How's the program running?"

"This is not a program, just a core dump."

"?" The manager smiles to put himself at ease: "Pretty good piece of hardware, huh!"

"It sure is: these new pluggable core stacks have an access time less than half the cycle time."

"?"

"And that's only part of it." The operator walks to a tape unit and dexterously flips on a tape, twirling it with uncanny precision: "It's the full range of option that gives it its flexibility." The operator's fingers fly over the console; and printer, reader, tapes seem to work all at once: "Those parity check circuits are really something, and they've gone overboard with their sequential address registers!" The operator riffles through a deck of cards with the expertise of a Mississippi gambler: "But that memory retention! And the read, modify, write-mode voltage margin switch! And the special interfacing. . . ."

The manager backs out, finds the door, returns to his office in a daze. His initial feeling of a week ago had been right: this electronic monstrosity should be in somebody else's basement. Oh, for the good old days of hunches, meetings, committees, guesswork, and even slide rules with their C and D scales (or was it A and B?).

A natural reaction for the manager. With the advent of the computer, a new language was born. And if some languages may be learned in three days, computerese is decidedly not one of them.

True, some men will turn to a computer dictionary. But consider the case of ADDRESS COMPUTATION, probably the single most important concept in computers, the concept that permits the computer to modify its program. A standard definition will read: "The process of machine creation, or modification by calculation of the address portion of the instruction." Chances are, the businessman will wearily give up and go out for a game of golf rather than go through a 500-page manual on programming in search of a simple illustration of ADDRESS COMPUTATION.

Conciseness is admirable, but sometimes insufficient when knowledge is sought, and for that reason, the *Condensed Computer Encyclopedia* attempts to place itself somewhere between the dictionary and the extensive manual, avoiding the mysteries of the former and the irrelevancies of the latter (while, undoubtedly, creating pitfalls of its own: but more of that later).

The *Condensed Computer Encyclopedia* is addressed to the businessman who has to (or wants to) deal with computers, to the student who must (or wants to) use a computer, and to the junior programmer who, fresh out of his programming course, is about to embark on his professional career. And because their requirements are not those of a professional programmer, or of a professional systems analyst, or of a computer designer, this book has been designed in a special way.

It would have been awkward if not impossible to make each entry self-sufficient: elementary terms could have been handled in a normal amount of space, but more complex terms would have required so much space that this work would have filled a bookshelf by itself. And who would have read a thousand pages of concepts already known to get at the meat of the subject? Consequently, a two-pronged approach to the problem was followed.

In the first place, computer terms were divided into three classes:

1. Generic terms, such as COMPUTER, MAGNETIC TAPE, PROGRAM

2. Specific terms, such as BINARY-CODED DECIMAL, MULTIPLEXOR, SYNCHRONOUS COMPUTER

3. Specialized terms, such as ADDRESS MODIFICATION, OR GATE, ZERO-LEVEL ADDRESS

Entries dealing with generic terms use mostly everyday English words, entries dealing with specific terms use generic and specific terms, and entries dealing with specialized terms use freely generic, specific, and specialized terms.

In the second place, each entry is structured from a simple and short definition to more advanced concepts whenever possible by the use of meaningful illustrations.

Consequently, the user of the *Condensed Computer Encyclopedia* need read only as much of an entry as he wants. Each paragraph will add to his knowledge of the item, but the whole entry is not essential for quick understanding.

Some entries will include one or more paragraphs written in smaller type than that used in the main body of the entries. Akin to footnotes, but embedded in the text, these paragraphs are included only when an entry warrants, beside the usual treatment, more technical information for the use of student programmers. Such smaller-type paragraphs may be omitted by the general reader with no loss of understanding of the basic concept.

The temptation to use mathematical examples has been resisted victoriously in all but hopeless cases. Programming examples are for the most part based on compound interest, a concept as familiar to businessmen as entropy is to physicists.

Because some terms are best explained in the course of a discussion of broader terms, and because too many repetitions would have increased the size of this volume to unwieldy proportions, some computer terms were not given an entry of their own but were defined within the entry for a related term. It is therefore suggested that the user go to the index whenever he cannot locate a word in the main text. The number of page references given in the index for any one term has been kept down to a useful minimum.

Whether the goal set forth in planning the *Condensed Computer Encyclopedia* has been achieved, only time and readers will tell. Encyclopedias seldom awaken an enthusiastic response from readers: to the layman, subjects are often too abstract; to the specialist, the treatment is always too elementary. A *condensed* encyclopedia should thus create even more displeasure among purists, and when the subject of a condensed encyclopedia happens to be a field as new as the field of computer science, where irreconcilable views are held by many leaders in the field, the uproar should be gratifying. No branch of science has moved ahead which evoked only indifference. It is high time that businessmen had their say too in a field which is becoming theirs, and for them and for that purpose also this book has been written.

I have made considerable and constant use of other people's knowledge. Their names and contributions appear elsewhere in the book.   To my contributors and especially to my friend and paraphrast, Michael Breslau, I do express my deep-felt gratitude for their patience, understanding, and participation.

This work is dedicated to

SIDNEY J. POLLACK

without whose prompting it would never have been started and, to

MY WIFE BETTY

without whose forbearance it would never have been completed.

Philip B. Jordain

acknowledgments

The author expresses his thanks to the computer manufacturers, colleges and universities, research companies, and consulting firms whose extensive and intensive publications on computers and computer applications have contributed so much in making this work possible. The author's gratitude is also expressed to the many computer and EDP magazines and journals whose contribution to the field are immeasurable and to which the author owes so much.

contents

abnormal statement   An element of FORTRAN V (UNIVAC) which specifies that certain function subroutines must be called every time they are referred to.   Abnormal declarations enable the compiler to optimize the calling of all other (nonabnormal) function subroutines.

On large-scale computers a compiler may include optional facilities to produce extra-efficient machine-language coding.   These optimizing routines examine the program for redundant expressions and other recognizably inefficient coding.   Thus the expression:

$$Y = (A + B * Z) + C/(A + B * Z)$$

is seen to contain the subexpression $(A + B * Z)$ twice.   The optimizer will cause this common subexpression to be evaluated once and saved, instead of requiring its evaluation to be repeated.   In effect, the statement is transformed into:

$$TEMP1 = A + B * Z$$
$$Y = TEMP1 + C/TEMP1$$

If the common subexpression contained a nonabnormal function call, such as SIN (X),

$$Y = (A + B * SIN (X)) + C/(A + B * SIN (X))$$

the common expression $(A + B * SIN (X))$ need be evaluated only once, a 50 percent time savings.

In effect:

```
TEMP1 = SIN (X)
TEMP2 = A + B * TEMP1
Y = TEMP2 + C/TEMP2
```

With the pseudo-random number generator function RAND (X), which is an abnormal function, the similar construction

$$Y = (A + B * RAND (X)) + C/(A + B * RAND (X))$$

cannot be so optimized. RAND (X) returns a different value every time it is used, and the programmer has indicated that it is to be called twice. However, in these cases it may be necessary for the programmer to specify explicitly the order of evaluation he wants, in order to avoid misunderstanding. Thus he should write

```
Y = A + B * RAND (X)
Y = A + B * RAND (X) + C/Y
```

Here Y is used first for temporary, and then for more meaningful storage.

If no abnormal statement is given, all functions will be treated as abnormal in order to agree with other FORTRAN compilers. Thus a dummy abnormal statement (designating a function not called by the program) may be used to trick the compiler into optimizing all function subroutine calls.

abrasiveness   The quality or characteristic of being able to scratch, abrade, or wear away another material.

In character recognition an important consideration of a transparent plastic or glass window through which appears the input document to be read. The accumulation of dust particles and/or any scratching on the surface of a read screen might affect the reading process. In character readers that employ such read screens a large input reject rate might be directly traceable to abrasiveness.

absolute address   The numerical identification of each storage location which is wired permanently into the hardware by the computer manufacturer. Such numerical identifications form a unique set of patterns of characters which are recognized by the computer without further translation. Consequently, each register, storage location, or component of a computer has a code number, and these code numbers form an integral part of the internal circuitry of a computer. Such code numbers are also called machine addresses.

Say a programmer wishes to refer to a specific component of the computer system (for instance, he wants to read a number written on a given magnetic tape): He can refer to the component by stating in the instruction the code number of that component, or he can refer to that component by means of a mnemonic word. In the first instance he would be using the absolute address of that component; in the second he would be using a symbolic address for the same component. In the latter case a computer program will first translate the symbolic address into the absolute address, and then carry out the corresponding instruction.

Although symbolic address programming requires more computer time than does programming with absolute addresses, practical consideration in programming ease will lead the programmer to favor symbolic addresses in most instances. See ABSOLUTE CODING.

absolute coding A programmer uses absolute coding when the addresses in his program are written exactly as they will appear when the instructions are executed by the control circuits. Such addresses are called absolute addresses.

In absolute coding each instruction is preceded by the actual location number of the storage unit in which the instruction will be placed. When the program is fed into the computer, the programmer knows exactly where each instruction of the program is located. However, this type of programming can lead to a large number of errors, regardless of the care a programmer may have taken in preparing his work. The errors arise mainly when the programmer either has to consider relatively many jump instructions or adds or deletes instructions to or from a finished program. In the first instance, filling in jump addresses left in blank always offers the possibility of inverting two or more digits in the address. In the second, each instruction following the break caused by an addition or deletion of instructions gets a different location number, and jump instructions must therefore be adjusted: the opportunity for error mentioned above is again present.

To minimize errors most programs are thus written with symbolic address (i.e., with addresses represented by programmer-assigned mnemonics).

This symbolic coding must be translated to absolute coding (by an extra processing step called assembly) before it can be executed by the computer.

absolute error The value of the error without regard to its algebraic sign. If two quantities P and Q are equal to 100 and 200, respectively, but through miscalculation are found to be 96 and 204, respectively, they are said to have the same absolute error, namely, an absolute error of 4.

absolute programming   The writing of a program in which all addresses are referred to by their actual code numbers within the computer system. Absolute programming is also called absolute language programming. It is the second of five steps involved in using a computer to solve a problem, the five steps being numerical analysis, programming, coding, debugging (or check-out), and production.

Programming involves preparing a block diagram and planning the memory allocation. There is no clear distinction between programming and coding inasmuch as the programmer is responsible for the maintenance of careful records of the work done during coding.

Suppose that two numbers P, Q have to be added and the sum is to be placed in memory location (or address) 300. The coder decides to use locations 100, 101, 102 to get the job done. He knows that P and Q are in memory locations 298 and 299. He then proceeds to write the instructions in the form of a detailed flowchart (very much expanded here). The actual translation of these instructions into machine language, or coding, is the next step. The memory location, or address, referred to in the instruction, such as memory location 298, represents a physical part of the computer with that actual code number. Such a program is called an absolute program, and the writing is called absolute coding.

Most programs are now written in procedure-oriented programming languages such as FORTRAN, COBOL, etc. (which are artificial languages imitating algebraic formulas or basic business languages), or else in symbolic languages where instructions are represented by means of symbolic or mnemonic operation codes and addresses.

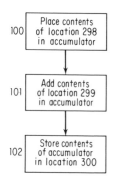

100 | Place contents of location 298 in accumulator

101 | Add contents of location 299 in accumulator

102 | Store contents of accumulator in location 300

absolute value   Quantity whose magnitude is acknowledged by the computer but whose sign is ignored.

It may be desired to work with the size or magnitude of a particular quantity without regard for its algebraic sign. For example, the difference between two numbers (each an estimate of the same quantity) is a measure of the discrepancy between the two numbers. A computer can take the absolute value of a number by retaining every digit of that number and forcing a positive sign onto the new numeral. This action can be produced by one or more computer instruction, for example:

SET SIGN + (in accumulator)
or
LOAD ABSOLUTE MAGNITUDE (of memory location contents into designated register).

Certain types of instructions contain signs that may indicate something about the address, or could form part of the operation code. In such cases address modifications require special considerations: When the instruction is brought into the accumulator, the instruction is considered by the computer as a number preceded by an algebraic sign. Consequently, if a quantity is to be added to the address part of the instruction, care must be exercised to neutralize the sign of the instruction. This can be done in two ways: (1) by taking the sign of the instruction into consideration (that is, subtracting from the instruction); (2) by taking the absolute value of the instruction when bringing the instruction into the accumulator (in which case only the address part of the instruction should be stored back in memory in order to avoid storing back the instruction with an incorrect sign). Such considerations are automatically taken care of by the computer when the programmer uses any of the procedure-oriented languages now available for computer work.

absorbency   In optical character recognition (OCR), an important property of paper resulting from the distribution of fibers within a given sheet, which ultimately affects a document's readability.

Absorbency affects a printed or handwritten image as laid down, for instance, its gloss. Also absorbency influences the likelihood of impairment immediately after transcription due to smudging, or in printing with liquid inks, to "setting off" onto an adjacent sheet in the delivery stack.

Usually absorbency is considered in conjunction with the properties of the printing ink, and with regard to the formation of the paper, i.e., the evenness of distribution of fibers in the sheet. However, we can generally state that there should be uniformity of absorbency over a sheet and between successive sheets.

acceleration time   The time required for a magnetic tape or any mechanical device to attain its operating speed. With magnetic tape several milliseconds are needed to start the tape in motion and to position it to read or write the first word of the record. Consequently, when an instruction is given to transfer a word of information between storage location and input/output unit, the execution of the first instruction is automatically delayed to compensate for the acceleration time. Depending on the computer, a certain amount of this acceleration time may be used by the processor for computation purposes. The amount of time available varies with the computer since it depends not only on the magnitude of the acceleration time but equally on the logical structure of the equipment.

access   See RANDOM ACCESS, SERIAL ACCESS.

access method   An access method is the programmer's software link between the program and the data that the program must transfer into or out of memory.

An access method is defined by both the data-set organization (file structures) that it uses and the programming language elements that the programmer may use to move the data.

A basic access method is elementary and close to the hardware level of coding. As such it permits greater flexibility for unusual requirements, but on the other hand it demands more detailed attention from the coder. All basic-access-method names begin with the letter B, and the fundamental operations of any basic access method are READ and WRITE.

A queued access method is much easier to use since it automatically handles details of blocking, unblocking, buffering, and overlap of I/O with processing. Queued access methods, however, are not available for every type of I/O, as buffering and blocking are basically incompatible with unpredictable access data sets (such as telecommunication and random access). The fundamental operations for any queued access method are GET (input) and PUT (output). The name of any queued access method starts with a Q.

The access methods of the IBM 360 Operating System (OS) can be listed in tabular form (see TABLE OF ACCESS METHODS). Some IBM

Data-set organization	Basic	Queued	Comments
Sequential	BSAM	QSAM	Magnetic tape and equivalent
Partitioned	BPAM		Program libraries
Indexed Sequential	BISAM	QISAM	Indexed Sequential
Direct	BDAM		Random access
Telecommunication	BTAM	QTAM	Conversational and transmissions
Graphic	BGAM		CRT, microfilm, plotter, etc.

Table of access methods.

360 operating systems do not provide all the access methods shown in the table, and some do not even use the access-method concept.

By support of an access method is meant providing the operating-system routines that are required at run time to execute the programs using the access method. Some access methods are supported by every operating system (BSAM, BPAM). On the other hand, some access methods are optional, and some installations may elect not to include such subroutines in their operating systems. These are system generation options (for instance BTAM, BGAM). Thus, if a center has no plotter or graphical display device, it need not use up space with unrequired BGAM routines. A program using an optional access method cannot run under an operating system that does not support the access method.

The totality of all access methods is called data management. See DATA MANAGEMENT.

access mode A clause that must be used when referring to a random-access device in COBOL. By means of this clause a specific record may be obtained from, or placed into, a file located in a mass storage device.

The access-mode clause tells the compiler how the data on the mass storage device will be handled: if access-mode sequential is specified, the data are read, or written, sequentially as they would be with a magnetic tape, even though a random-access device is being used; if access-mode random is specified, any datum may be referred to at any time. In the latter case data are said to be randomly accessed, or singly referenced.

access time The access time can be considered as the fundamental machine cycle, that is, the time required by the central processing unit to transmit or receive a word of information to or from the core storage. The amount of time required to receive a word of information from the core storage is known as the read time, and the amount of time required to transmit a word of information into the core storage is known as the write time.

Access time is often used as a means of rating computers, much as cars may be rated by their horsepower to the exclusion of all other characteristics.

accounting machine Any machine whose sole function is to produce tabulations or accounting records of unvarying format. Data for such machines are entered either through a keyboard or by means of cards or tapes.

Originally accounting machines referred to adding machines, billing machines (combination of typewriter and desk calculator to prepare monthly bills), or bookkeeping machines (similar to billing machines, but able to prepare customer statements, accounts payable records, cash-received records, cost sheets, etc.). Today the term accounting machine describes a host of types from the very simple to the highly complex.

Accounting machines differ from computers in that their program is fixed and cannot be altered without altering the accounting machine itself.

accumulated total punching Control device used to ensure that no item has been dropped from a file. Thus, if a deck of cards is to be used repeatedly, the contents of the cards are summed up each time, and the total obtained is matched against the original total. If the totals differ, the operator knows that a card either has been dropped, or has not been read by the machine. This total, or accumulated total punching, is sometimes called hash total, that is, a total that has no other physical meaning than that of arithmetically summing all data keypunched on cards.

accumulator A specific register, found in the arithmetic unit of a computer, in which the result of an arithmetic or logic operation is formed. It is in this register that numbers are added or subtracted and that certain operations such as sensing, shifting, and complementing are performed.

The number of accumulators available to the programmer and the manner in which they are used may vary.

For example, in the GE 400 series, the programmer has instructions that specify the location in core and the length of the accumulator. The accumulator (hardware) is not actually in memory, but its contents are stored in this location after every instruction and loaded from this location whenever it is moved. Thus, MOVE ACCUMULATOR, is equivalent to LOAD ACCUMULATOR, and every operation implies STORE ACCUMULATOR. The ability to change apparent accumulator size permits selection of arithmetic accuracy.

The simplest common arrangement has an accumulator and an accumulator extension which is used in multiplication, division, and some shifting operations. For example, in division the quotient may appear in the accumulator and the remainder in the extension (or vice versa). In multiplication a double-precision product usually fills both registers with the least significant digit in this extension. On multiple-accumulator machines odd- and even-numbered accumulators may be paired together similarly for multiplication and division operations.

In some computers there is only one accumulator, which is cleared each time it is used. In this case the accumulator is never referenced directly; instead, the programmer specifies an address in main memory as one of the operands in the instruction. The contents of the accumulator are automatically placed in this area when the arithmetic operation is completed.

On other designs the result of an operation remains in the accumulator and is available there to the programmer until it is intentionally changed. Computers using this concept sometimes have multiple accumulators.

The capacity of accumulators also varies. On word-oriented machines the size of an accumulator is generally a multiple of the word length. In character-oriented machines the computer designer is less limited; the standard parameters of cost and complexity are the main considerations.

Since there is a limit to the number of digits that an accumulator can hold, the execution of certain arithmetic operations, such as addition or multiplication, may result in a number of digits exceeding the accumulator capacity. The programmer is made aware of this overflow condition by means of light indicators on the console of some machines. Also, some instructions enable the program to sense the overflow condition during the computer run, and the programmer may take corrective action such as preserving some of the overflow if he so wishes.

On computers that do not appear to have accumulators, the programmer may set aside certain locations or areas in memory to hold working totals, subtotals, etc. Programmers of these computers sometimes call these areas accumulators because no ambiguity is thereby introduced.

accumulator jump instruction Instruction that permits a computer to ignore the established program sequence depending on the status of the accumulator at the time the accumulator jump instruction is executed.

There are many types of accumulator jump instructions, as for instance: (1) If the accumulator content is zero, take the next instruction sequence, if not, go to instruction N. (2) If the accumulator is positive, take the next instruction in sequence; if not go to instruction N. (3) If the accumulator content is smaller than the content of storage location N, take the next instruction in sequence; if it is equal to the content of storage location N, take the second instruction in sequence; if it is greater than the content of storage location N, take the third instruction in sequence.

Since the structure of a computer is absolutely logical, certain accumulator jump instructions must be used carefully. For example, in the accumulator jump instruction type (3) a positive zero will be considered greater than a negative zero.

accumulator shift instruction   A computer instruction that causes the contents of a register to be displaced a specified number of digit positions to the left or to the right.

The most common kind of shift moves the contents of a register and simply loses or drops any information shifted beyond the limits of the accumulator. Some kinds of shift preserve the algebraic sign and shift only digits (arithmetic shift). Others cause bits moved out of one end to be reinserted at the other end of the accumulator (circular shift). Still others couple two or more adjacent registers and treat them logically as one (long shift). Finally (as on IBM 7070), some instructions permit shifting part of the contents of the accumulator and preserving the original form of the remainder (split shift).

Examples:

	Accumulator 1	*Accumulator 2*
ORIGINAL FORM	+01234567	
AFTER LEFT SHIFT 2	+23456700	
AFTER RIGHT SHIFT 3	+00001234	
AFTER CIRCULAR LEFT SHIFT 2	+23456701	
AFTER SPLIT RIGHT SHIFT	+01230045	
AFTER LONG RIGHT SHIFT 5	+00000012	+34567000

accumulator transfer instruction   See ACCUMULATOR JUMP INSTRUCTION.

accuracy   The degree of freedom from error, not to be confused with precision which refers to the number of significant digits maintained in an operation.

A common fallacy in using computers is to consider a 10-digit result as accurate when this number is the result of operations involving a number of initial factors accurate to two or three places. Generally such a result will indicate an order of magnitude only, and depending on the operations involved, should be rounded after the first or second digit.

accuracy control system   An error-detection and control system. Since a considerable part of a computer's circuitry is assigned to error detection and control, concern for accuracy should start away from the computer, beginning with the generation of data, and continuing throughout the process of gathering and transforming the data into a form suitable for computer use. Random sampling, verification, double control, and squaring are some of the methods used in such systems, but there is no known method that will ensure 100 percent accuracy at all times. Striving for improvement in accuracy control systems should be a permanent assignment.

acoustical treatment   Structural and surface modifications required by floor, doors, walls, and ceiling of a computer center to retard vibrations and suppress noises caused by mechanical units such as card machines, printers, and blowers. The construction of walls from floor to base ceiling with soft surface or dropped ceiling with porous surface, special substructure of the floor, and characteristics of seals on doors and surface joints will vary with the size of the room. Since overhead ducts may very well carry the sound to remote areas, it is advisable to hire an acoustical consultant for that work, before the arrival of the hardware, but only after the area for the computer center and the type of computer have been decided on.

acoustic delay line   An acoustic delay line is a device used for cyclic storage of digital information in the form of a train of sound pulses.

In general, this device will have the form of either liquid transmission path (such as mercury) or a solid transmission path (such as quartz).

Before the extensive use of magnetic-core memories (about 1959), mercury delay lines were used for high-speed internal storage. This form of storage is not particularly well suited for large words with many bits because of the complexity of support equipment needed for its operation, and problems of maintaining a constant temperature environment for the acoustic medium. In EDVAC for example, 11 electronic tubes were needed for each thousand-digit line.

Acoustic delay lines operate by causing sound pulses, at frequencies of the order of 1 megahertz (1,000,000 cycles per second), to propagate through an acoustically transparent medium. Both liquids and solids are used with some preference being given to liquids. When sound waves propagate through liquids, the compressional wave mode predominates. In solids, transverse waves as well as other modes tend to render the design of such delay lines more difficult than the liquid equivalent. Compressional waves in liquids travel at the rate of about 1400 meters (or 4600 feet) per second, which results in a delay of approximately 18 microseconds per inch. The corresponding figure for solids is of the order of 6 to 10 microseconds per inch. Because of the inherent delay, or time of transit, through the acoustic medium, digital information can be stored as a series of pulses propagating through such a medium.

An acoustic delay line usually consists of:

1.   A piezoelectric transmitter which converts the normal electrical form of digital information into an acoustic wave

2.   The acoustic transmission path

3.   A piezoelectric receiving unit which converts the delayed acoustic data back into their original form

In addition to these main units, amplifiers and gates are also required.   The amplifiers are used to drive the piezoelectric transmitter and to make up for the inherent losses of the transmission path.   Read in, read out, and clear functions are handled by gates.

active master file   A master file the items of which are relatively active.   It should be noted that there does not exist a class of inactive items in the absolute meaning of the word: Such an inactive item would be represented by, for instance, the price of a pound of salmon in a file concerned with inventory records of tractor parts.   Such an absolutely inactive item would simply be erased.   What exists is a graduation of activity.   Usage data are required to determine whether an item is to be considered active or inactive.   When the distinction between active and inactive items becomes significant, it may be more economical to have two master files, the file holding the relatively active items becoming the active master file.

active master item   The relatively most active items on a master file, as determined by usage data.   See ACTIVE MASTER FILE, ITEM.

actual key   A clause in COBOL which permits using a data item as a hardware address.   This data item indicates the actual machine address of a logical record to be read from, or written onto, a random-access mass storage device.   When, in COBOL, a mass storage device is to be accessed, the hardware address of the next mass storage location to be used must be indicated by the program.   In order to do this, the programmer writes an ACTUAL KEY clause in COBOL, and this clause associates a data item with a particular file of information on the random-access device.   Every time the program reads, or writes, a logical record from, or on, the file, the computer looks up the ACTUAL KEY data item to determine which hardware address is to be used.   This implies that the program must store the correct address in the data item before each read or write is performed.   No ACTUAL KEY is required if the mass storage device is operated in access-mode sequential, for in this mode the logical records follow each other in predetermined locations on the mass storage device. See ACCESS MODE.

acyclic feeding In character recognition, a system employed by character readers in which the sensing of the trailing edge of the preceding document triggers the automatic feeding of the following document. Acyclic feeding thus minimizes and standardizes the physical gap that exists between successive documents on the document transport; in so doing, it maximizes the effective throughput rate.

Acyclic feeding is a special feature which allows manufacturers to provide character recognition of varying-sized documents. This is an improvement over the original timed feeding systems (cyclic feeding) which did not afford any extra efficiency for shorter-length documents.

Manufacturers usually provide on request a simple formula from which prospective users can derive throughput rates for the document sizes they have in mind.

adapting See SELF-ADAPTING.

addition file See FILE MAINTENANCE.

addition item An item that is to be inserted in its proper place in a file. If the file is a master file, the item should be properly called addition master item.

addition table A shorthand representation of addition. An addition table represents for addition what a multiplication table does for multiplication. In the binary system the table would appear as

	0	1
0	0	1
1	1	0*

where 0* stands for 0 + 1 carry.

address The number, or name, that uniquely identifies a register, memory location, or storage device.

It is useful to consider an address as a means of identifying the location in which a number may be stored. One may think of pigeonholes in an old-fashioned desk, each pigeonhole having an identification tag which does not necessarily indicate anything about the content of that pigeonhole. See ABSOLUTE ADDRESS, BASE ADDRESS, CONTENT-ADDRESSED STORAGE, DIRECT ADDRESS, EFFECTIVE ADDRESS, FOUR-PLUS-ONE ADDRESS, IMMEDIATE ADDRESS, INDIRECT ADDRESS, MACHINE

ADDRESS, MULTIADDRESS, N-LEVEL ADDRESS, ONE-LEVEL ADDRESS, ONE-PLUS-ONE ADDRESS, RELATIVE ADDRESS, SYMBOLIC ADDRESS, THREE-PLUS-ONE ADDRESS, ZERO-LEVEL ADDRESS.

address computation   Modification of an address within an instruction by the computer.

The possibility of modifying instructions is the central feature of stored program computers.   Such a possibility, which gives computers their flexibility, can be used in a number of ways, such as limiting the number of instructions required in performing a sequence of identical operations with different quantities; jumping to different out-of-sequence parts of the program, depending on the value of a computer parameter; writing general-purpose programs, that is, programs that will solve specific problems regardless of the problem size (within machine capacity); etc.

Consider, for instance, an example involving loop and jump instructions.   Assume a program in which, at a certain point, a block of memory must be cleared to zero before the program can continue: locations numbered 15000 through 15999 must each contain zero. Assume further that the computer has an accumulator register (AC) and a multiplier-quotient register (MQ), the program itself being stored in memory from location 600 through section 1400.   Moreover the number 1 has been stored in location 9990, and the MQ (multiplier-quotient register) has been cleared, that is, contains only zeros.

The set of instructions in the program required to clear the memory could appear as follows:

Location of instruction	Instruction
1000	Place in AC contents of location 1001.
1001	Place MQ contents in location 15000.
1002	If address portion of AC is equal to 15999, go to location 1006; if not, proceed to location 1003.
1003	Add contents of location 9990 to AC.
1004	Store contents of AC in location 1001.
1005	Jump to location 1001.
1006	Proceed with the program.

Location 1000 contains the instruction PLACE IN AC CONTENTS OF LOCATION 1001:   thereupon, the computer stores PLACE MQ

CONTENTS IN LOCATION 15000 in the AC. This is the only action that the computer takes since the content of the AC is not at this time an instruction for the computer, but just so many characters that had to be moved from location 1001 to the AC.

The computer proceeds to the next instruction in sequence, that is, to location 1001. The computer now does the following: location 1001 contains the instruction PLACE MQ CONTENTS IN LOCATION 15000; the computer thus stores zeros in location 15000, and this instruction being completed, the computer goes to the next instruction in sequence, that is, to location 1002: We assume that instruction 1002 does not destroy the contents of the AC.

Location 1002 contains the instruction IF ADDRESS PORTION OF AC IS EQUAL TO 15999, GO TO LOCATION 1006; IF NOT, PROCEED TO LOCATION 1003; the first time around, the address portion of the AC contains 15000: hence the computer takes the next instruction in sequence; that is, it goes to location 1003.

Location 1003 contains the instruction ADD CONTENTS OF LOCATION 9990 TO THE AC; the number 1 of location 9990 is added to the AC, and the AC now contains the characters PLACE MQ CONTENTS IN LOCATION 15001. We assume that the instruction image in the AC is a positive number; else a subtraction would be required to increment the address. The ADD instruction does not know (or care!) that the AC contains an instruction and not a data word. The computer now proceeds to the next instruction in sequence; that is, it goes to location 1004.

Location 1004 contains the instruction STORE CONTENTS OF AC IN LOCATION 1001; the computer erases the original contents of location 1001 and stores there the characters: PLACE MQ CONTENTS IN LOCATION 15001. Note that nothing has been altered in the MQ or AC. The computer proceeds next to location 1005, the next instruction in sequence.

Location 1005 contains the instruction JUMP TO LOCATION 1001. This instruction causes the computer to go back to location 1001 for the next instruction. The computer repeats instructions 1001, 1002, 1003 (where it transforms 15001 into 15002), 1004, 1005, and back to 1001. This is done continually until the address in location 1001 contains the number 15999. At this time, after executing the instruction contained in location 1001 (put zeros in location 15999), the computer will reach location 1002 where, as instructed, finding 15999 equal to 15999, it will immediately jump to location 1006 and proceed with the rest of the program.

It is clear that this program destroys forever the original contents of location 1001. If the computer had to repeat this sequence of operation later in the program, location 1001 would begin with an address content of 15999, and the loop would terminate at once.

To avoid this, the instruction orginally in location 1001 could be duplicated somewhere else, say in location 9998. Then, by having instruction 1000 load the AC register with the contents of location 9998, this sequence of instructions could be repeated as many times as necessary throughout the program.

The difference between destructive and nondestructive address computation must be kept in mind by the machine-language programmer. In some computers (e.g., IBM 650, SDS SIGMA 7), the high-speed registers AC, MQ, or their counterparts are addressable; that is, the program may refer to them as though they were extension of memory. Thus, an instruction residing in a register could be executed from that register. This technique is uncommon, but results in extremely fast execution of small loops of instructions.

In some computers (e.g., IBM 360, CDC 6600), the address part of an instruction usually resides in some indicated high-speed register (the instruction contains a 3- or 4-bit register designator instead of a 15- or 18-bit address). On these computers, address computations (or address modifications) may be performed conveniently and at high speed, using the arithmetic instructions: storage of addresses into memory is therefore rarely required.

address constant   An address constant, or ADCON, is a value, or its expression, used in the calculation of real or virtual storage addresses.

In the IBM 360 System and similar computers, a program or part of a program may be easily modified to run or to be loaded in any of a large number of locations. The only modification required consists in correctly setting the few ADCON's in the program unit.

In most computers, such a relocation would involve modifying the address parts of every instruction in the program text. In the IBM 360 System, however, the addresses reside principally in the general-purpose registers and not in the address part of the instructions. Thus, by simply changing the contents of the base registers, the entire program can be relocated. The base registers are loaded by the program segment with contents of word-size areas containing the address constants. Consequently, changing the contents of the ADCON's automatically modifies the addresses referred to by all the instructions of the program.

Since there may be anywhere from 5 to 50 ADCON's in a block of 2000 instructions, it is obviously much faster for the loader to modify the address constants than it would be to modify all the instructions individually as required in conventional computers.

Some computers bypass this problem entirely by loading a hardware register with the starting address of the program segment. Each segment is coded as though it began at location zero, and all memory references are automatically incremented by the content of this special register. Base register ADCON construction is not essential for easy program relocatability.

address conversion The translation of symbolic or relative addresses into absolute addresses either by manual methods or by using the computer and an assembly program. Conversion to absolute addresses can become fairly involved. The simplest method consists in letting the programmer assign an absolute address origin to the first statement in the program. The assembler will then assign an absolute address to each succeeding instruction and to symbolic addresses within the instructions. The programmer may, if he so wishes, retain a greater control of his program by assigning absolute address origins to the various segments of the program. However, were the programmer to assign absolute addresses, he would then have to take great care not to overlap storage areas (by allowing for enough storage space for one segment) or, conversely, not to waste storage space (by the judicious spacing of the program segments).

address format The address format describes the number of addresses included in a computer instruction. Most modern computers use one-address instructions, but some constructions still range from zero to five addresses per instruction.

The addresses that indicate operands determine the "power" of an instruction. Thus, a MULTIPLY BY Y instruction (one operand address) is less powerful than a MULTIPLY X BY Y AND STORE IN Z instruction (three operand addresses). An instruction may also indicate the address of the next instruction to be executed (as on the IBM 650). This type of address does not increase the "power" of the instruction, and thus is separately indicated by the tag "-plus-one."

address modification See ADDRESS COMPUTATION.

address of address Programming technique used principally in dealing with subroutines.

Consider, for instance, a program in which every time a value of X is determined, the hyperbolic cosine of X must be calculated. Rather than compute cosh X each time (which would considerably increase the size of the program), a subroutine for the calculation of cosh X is written once and for all.

When a point of the program is reached where a new value for X is found, the computer jumps to the subroutine, calculates cosh X, and returns to the main program. Schematically, such a program may appear as on the illustration entitled "Example of Address of Address."

Main program	
Instruction location	Instruction
....	....
1440	PLACE CONTENTS OF 1440 IN ACCUMULATOR.
1441	JUMP TO 5280.
1442	(LOCATION OF X IN ADDRESS PART OF INSTRUCTION)
1443	(MAIN PROGRAM SEQUENCE)
....	....

Subroutine	
Instruction location	Instruction
5280	(DETERMINE ADDRESS OF X: 1440 + 2.)
....	....
5640	(DETERMINE RETURN ADDRESS: 1440 + 3.)

Example of address of address.

Instruction 1440, which places itself in the accumulator, enables the subroutine to calculate the location 1442 (N + 2), and thus the location of X, and to calculate the location 1443 (N + 3) at which point reentry will be made into the program once cosh X has been calculated. Instruction 1441 is the actual jump instruction to the subroutine once the stage has been set. Instruction 1442 is not an instruction really, and therefore is not executed as an instruction. Its function is to carry the location of X in its address part. Thus, 1442 is the address of the address of X. The sequence 1440 to 1442 is known as the calling sequence. See INDIRECT ADDRESS.

address part The part of a computer instruction which contains the address of the operand. A computer instruction specifies an elementary action to be performed by the computer. The instruction is basically divided into two parts: the operation part (e.g., multiply, divide, add, etc.), and the address part. The address part specifies the location of the data that are to be used, or the location in which the result of the operation is to be stored.

In variable-instruction-length computers (e.g., IBM 1401, Honeywell 200), an instruction may have no address part, one address part, or two or more address parts. For instance, PAUSE (no address needed), BRANCH or TRANSFER to _____ (one address), MOVE CHARACTERS from _____ to _____ (two addresses).

In fixed-instruction-length computers, where an instruction is usually one word long, a fixed area within the word is designated to be the address part of the instruction. Most fixed-instruction-length computers (e.g., IBM 7070, IBM 7094, etc.) have one address per one instruction, but two-address format instructions are sometimes used (e.g., IBM 650).

It is common to speak of the address part of the word to designate this fixed subfield within the word, even when the word contains data and not an instruction. Thus, the address part of a word may contain a small data item while the remainder of the word contains bits identifying and/or modifying the item.

address register A register in which an address is stored. An address register is a part of the hardware of a computing system and is usually located in the central processing unit (CPU). This register is used for very high speed storage of address information.

The address register may contain the address of data to be fetched or stored, or the address of the instruction to be executed next in sequence, or then the location to which control will be transferred when a subroutine is finished processing.

An address register may be accessible to the program for modification (as in CDC 6600, Honeywell 200), or it may only be inspected by the computer program, as in some IBM 1401's, or it may be completely inaccessible to the program (as in other IBM 1401's).

adjacency In character recognition, a condition in which two consecutively printed or handwritten characters are separated by less than a specified distance.

Most manufacturers, in addition to imposing real or imaginary character boundaries, also specify that a minimum lateral distance must be obtained between consecutive characters. (Exceptions to this requirement can be found in character readers employing character masks which are designed along the lines of a particular type font. Hence, even extreme cases of adjacency such as touching characters, allow recognition to be accomplished providing the characters concerned remain coincident with their corresponding masks.)

While adjacency results when a minimum lateral distance is not achieved, there exists a converse condition which generates the machine-equivalent representation of a blank character whenever the maximum space between characters has been exceeded.

ADP Automatic data processing. ADP, as a generic term, includes, and goes beyond electric accounting machines (EAM) and electronic data processing equipment (EDP).

EAM is characterized by being card-oriented and having relay logic; EDP is characterized by tubes and solid-state logic. However, it should be noted that the clear-cut distinction between EAM and EDP has been diffused by equipment such as the UNIVAC 1004 card processor with its EAM features of being card-oriented and having only wired-plugboard programming available, and its EDP features of solid-state circuitry and core memory.

ADP covers equally the early all-mechanical analog computers (such as the MIT differential analyzer) and the modern nonelectronic pneumatic digital computers. However, ADP does not include desk calculators which must be hand-guided step by step.

advance feed tape Paper tape so punched that the leading edges of the feed holes line up with the lead edges of the data holes.

Normal punched paper tape has feed holes whose centerlines line up with the data holes. The problem is that it is easy to confuse the beginning of the tape with the end of the tape, and data may be read or transmitted backward by mistake. One could mark the beginning of the tape differently from the end, but errors still happen.

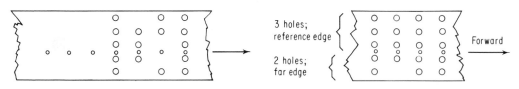

Five-level tape.   **Five-level advance feed tape.**

(One cannot confuse the top of the tape with the underside of the tape, for all punched tape formats have three rows of data holes between one edge and the feed holes: 6-level tape is therefore not used since this distinction would perforce disappear.)

Advanced feed tape has the feed holes moved forward. This provides a built-in directional indication, obvious by inspection. The price of the fool-proof format is possible incompatibility with conventional paper-tape readers. See PAPER TAPE.

ALGOL An algorithmic and procedure-oriented language used principally in the programming of scientific problems. ALGOL is an acronym for ALGOrithmic Language.

Devised in 1958 as an international mathematics language, ALGOL was revised in 1960. It is a powerful language, more widely used in Europe than in America. But, although not employed as frequently as FORTRAN for computational purposes in the United States, ALGOL is often chosen as the reference and publication language by programmers (ALGOL is the language used in the publication of algorithms in the *Communications of the Association for Computing Machinery*). ALGOL is also used frequently as a model, or starting point, for the invention of new artificial languages (see JOVIAL, NELIAC), and has played a leading role in the development and streamlining of compiling techniques.

Although it is elegantly mathematical as a language, ALGOL's elementary concepts can be described in nonmathematical terms. In ALGOL, an identifier is a group of letters and or numbers, but beginning with a letter, such as JOB, Y2, or PROFIT. A statement, denoting an action to be taken, is made up of symbols, identifiers, and, sometimes, numbers. Statements are separated by semicolons. For instance,

PROFITS : = SALES − COSTS;

is a statement indicating that COSTS must be subtracted from SALES, and the result assigned to PROFITS. A program is a set of statements.

It is possible to label a statement such as the preceding one in order to refer to it directly. For instance, the statement could be labeled FINANCIAL and could thus appear as

FINANCIAL : PROFITS : = SALES − COSTS;

During the course of a program, a jump instruction would permit that statement to be reached out of sequence. For instance:

GO TO FINANCIAL;
REDINK: LOSS : = COSTS − SALES;
FINANCIAL : PROFITS : = SALES − COSTS;

The jump instruction GO TO FINANCIAL will cause the statement labeled FINANCIAL to be the next statement to be handled in sequence, the statement labeled REDINK being thus bypassed. The instruction GO TO FINANCIAL is an unconditional jump instruction. Had a conditional jump instruction been used, the program could have been written

```
IF MONTH = 6 THEN GO TO FINANCIAL;
REDINK : LOSS : = COSTS − SALES;
GO TO NEXT;
FINANCIAL: PROFITS : = SALES − COSTS;
```

In this case, if the month value is 6 (or June), the statement FINAN-CIAL is the next in sequence. Otherwise, the statement REDINK is the next in sequence, GO TO NEXT being a necessary uncondi-tional jump required to bypass FINANCIAL which must not be performed if the MONTH is not June. Notice the difference made between the symbols := and =. The symbol := is an assignment: PROFITS will be given the value of the difference SALES − COSTS. But the symbol = is a proposition which may be true or false: the MONTH may be June.

Compound statements are groups of statements bracketed by the words BEGIN and END which, in a sense, act as beginning and end of a paragraph within which a certain context is true.

Repetitive operations, such as the multiplication of two sets of numbers one by one, can be programmed as follows:

```
FOR I := 1 STEP 1 UNTIL 100 DO TAKEHOME(I) :=
SALARY(I) * .75;
```

With this instruction, 100 salaries called SALARY(I) with I taking on the values 1 through 100 will be taxed at 25 percent, and the results called TAKEHOME(I). If only a sequence of salaries were to be so taxed, for instance the 1st, 2nd, 13th, 22nd through 36th, 54th, and 88th through 96th, the instruction would read:

```
FOR I := 1, 2, 13, 22 STEP 1 UNTIL 36, 54, 88 STEP 1 UNTIL
96 DO TAKEHOME(I) := SALARY(I) * .75;
```

An important concept in ALGOL is that of the PROCEDURE which, in a sense, serves the purpose of subroutines in ordinary ma-chine coding. For instance, the TAKEHOME pay calculated above could have been programmed as

```
PROCEDURE TAX(Z);
BEGIN Y := Z * .75 ; PRINT(Y) END;
START : READ (SALARY);
TAX(SALARY);
GO TO START;
```

All salaries presented to the computer will be then handled in the sequence they are in.

Consider, for instance, the calculations involved in determining capital growth at interest compounded quarterly. This program

has been made long so as to cover some of the many aspects of
ALGOL.

ALGOL program	Commentaries
REAL PROCEDURE VALUE (PRIN, RATE, NYRS); REAL PRIN, RATE, NYRS;	Actual values of PRIN, RATE, NYRS will be supplied from outside this program. The answer, VALUE, will be returned as a real number.
COMMENT THIS PROCEDURE EVALUATES THE WORTH OF A SUM PRIN INVESTED AT RATE PERCENT INTEREST COMPOUNDED QUARTERLY FOR NYRS YEARS.;	Comments are freely interspersed to improve readability of program by user. Aids in making programs self-documenting. N Y R S stands for n years.
BEGIN REAL INC, INCL; INTEGER M, N;	BEGIN and END act as left and right parentheses. The variables INC, INCL, M, and N are internal to this block and cannot be referred to from outside.
INC: = NYRS; INCL: = (1 + RATE/400) ↑ 4; N: = NYRS;	INC is given the true value of NYRS, N is given the value of the integer part of NYRS. INCL is the ratio of value at end of 1 year/ value at start of 1 year. The ↑ denotes exponentiation, or repeated multiplication.
IF NYRS < 1 THEN GO TO FINISH;	Skip next sequence if no whole number of years available.
FOR M: = 1 STEP 1 UNTIL N DO	Repeat the following N times.
BEGIN PRIN: = PRIN × INCL; INC: = INC − 1; END	Calculate increase for each year. INC measures amount of increase not yet calculated.
FINISH: M: = IF INC > 0 THEN 4 × INC ELSE 0;	A conditional assignment statement: M is the number of interest periods remaining.

ALGOL program	Commentaries
VALUE: = PRIN × (1 + RATE/400) ↑ M; END VALUE	Final computation—remaining interest periods, if any. The answer is assigned to VALUE so that it may be returned to the calling program. The final END marks the end of the procedure and also closes the BEGIN which follows the COMMENT.

Example of ALGOL program.

This example merely serves to illustrate some of the basic features of ALGOL. Were such a program actually required, it could be written more compactly as follows: VALUE: = PRIN x (1 + RATE/400) ↑ ENTIER (4 x NYRS); where ENTIER is a standard function meaning "largest integer not exceeding."

There are two kinds of words in all computer languages: "reserved words" which have a specific meaning or function defined by the language, and "optional words" which the programmer chooses for names of data items, mnemonic designations for section of memory, etc. Words such as REAL, PROCEDURE, COMMENT, BEGIN, END are reserved words in ALGOL and may not be used by the programmer for any purpose other than that defined by the language.

algorithm   The solution to a type of problem reduced to a uniform procedure for solving a specific problem.   Contrast with HEURISTIC.

algorithmic language   A language in which a procedure or scheme of calculations can be expressed with accuracy.

Programs written in machine language are readily accepted by the computer. Such programs, however, are tedious to write and offer the programmer many possibilities of committing errors. To shorten a programmer's task, a number of languages have been created: symbolic or assembly languages (e.g., FAP, AUTOCODER) which have algorithmic capabilities but are too machine-oriented and detailed to be classified as algorithmic languages; algorithmic languages which in turn can be subdivided into algebraic languages (e.g., ALGOL, FORTRAN), business languages (e.g., COBOL), and symbol manipulation languages (e.g., SNOBOL, IPL-V); and problem-oriented languages which describe problems to be solved without giving details of the procedures required for solving these problems (e.g., STRESS for structural engineering problems, COGO for civil engineering and surveying-geometrical layout problems).

The most common algorithmic languages today are FORTRAN and ALGOL. Others, such as SIMSCRIPT, JOVIAL, and MAD, are also in use on a more restricted scale. These languages share the ability to express arithmetic operations concisely and to deal with several kinds of arithmetic (such as floating point and integer). Algorithmic languages also have conditional (decision-making or testing) facilities and (except possibly for ALGOL) input/output specifying statements. Some languages, notably PL/1, combine the arithmetic power of algorithmic languages with more general or flexible data processing capabilities.

alias   An alternate entry point at which program execution can begin.

Normally, a unit of code has one unique name and one regular entry point: aliases may be used to provide additional names and entry points for the module.

When different functions are sufficiently similar (such as sine and cosine), it may be useful to combine them in a single subroutine. If, within this subroutine, each function has its own name and entry point, it is possible to refer to each function individually.

Aliases are used when the additional names are entered in the proper indexes and they are referred to the proper module and entry address.

Programs calling for sophisticated operating systems can be automatically degraded when running on simpler systems by providing the names of the complex support routines as aliases for the simpler, but functionally compatible, service routines in the simpler systems. The alias will cause the simpler routine to be automatically substituted for the more complex one without having to change the program in any way. This permits a degree of configuration independence to be obtained by all programs under the operating system.

allocation   The process of specifying memory locations during the execution of a program. A computer characteristic is that the introduction of a number or word in memory destroys whatever number or word existed there previously. To ensure that no information be lost during a computer run, a method must be devised which will specify (and keep track of) the memory locations for the program, the results calculated by the program, and all by-product information relevant to the execution of the program. See DYNAMIC STORAGE ALLOCATION, RELOCATE, STORAGE ALLOCATION.

alphabet   Any ordered set of unique graphics called characters, such as the 26 letters of the roman alphabet. Which of the character representation is to be called alphabetic is an arbitrary decision made by the computer manufacturer. The IBM 360 has 29 alphabetic characters as \$, @, and # are considered to be alphabetic characters: this offers compatibility with languages having up to 29 graphics.

In binary computers the maximum number of possible characters that can be represented by n bits is given by the formula 2^n. For example, $2^6 = 64$ (e.g., IBM 1401, IBM 7094), $2^8 = 256$ (e.g., IBM 360); in decimal computers, characters are represented by two digits, giving thus a maximum number of 100 characters. All the non-alphabetic characters must either be numerics, special characters, or undefined.

alphameric See ALPHANUMERIC.

alphanumeric In general, alphanumeric refers to all characters used by a computer including letters, numerals, blank, and characters such as \$, @, #, etc. For instance, the keyboard of a typewriter defines a set of alphanumeric characters (the spacing bar defines the "blank" character).

IBM uses the term alphameric to refer to a set of characters including only letters and numerals.This is a useful distinction which, unfortunately, is not followed by everyone.

A storage area is said to contain alphanumeric text when it is understood to contain any machine-representable characters in a printable way. For example, an area 30 characters long could contain THIS IS ALPHANUMERIC TEXT. -?+ or any other 30-character message. It is normally impossible to perform meaningful arithmetic upon alphanumeric information, but simple operations (like comparing for equality of content) can be defined.

analog The characteristic of a process A which is similar to a process B insofar as the proportional relationships are kept constant over a specified range. As a noun, analog denotes a thing (or process) which is used to represent another thing (or process) by virtue of some similarity in behavior.

The analog may be similar to the original (e.g., a model airplane in a wind tunnel), or completely different in form from the original (e.g., a resistor network to find the liquid-carrying capacity of a pipeline system).

As an adjective, analog describes something which employs an analog representation (e.g., analog computer): A broadcasting station transmits the electrical analog of a sound signal; the fuel gauge of a car displays the analog of the liquid volume of the gas tank.

analog computer A device capable of measuring the numerically defined variables of an abstract system in terms of some physical system. The speedometer of a car is an example of an elementary special-purpose analog computer which measures the voltage of a generator mechanically connected to the driving shaft: the voltage values are suitably translated in miles per hour on the meter face which may be considered as the analog display. The precision of the numerical answers, dependent on physical measurements, is limited. The odometer is another analog computer within an automobile. It integrates the product speed multiplied by distance and calculates the distance traveled in real time. A slide rule is another analog computer in common use.

analysis   A method of discovering the nature of a process or procedure which involves breaking down the complex entity into its constituent parts and examining these parts and their relationships (contrast with synthesis). In the computer field, analysis is associated with considerations of accuracy, error, solvability, and feasibility.

analyst   A person who defines a problem, determines exactly what is required in the solution, and defines the broad outlines of the machine solution; generally, an expert in the application. Analysis is one of the many functions brought to the fore with the advent of computers. See EDP CENTER.

analyzer   See DIFFERENTIAL ANALYZER, DIGITAL DIFFERENTIAL ANALYZER, NETWORK ANALYZER.

AND   In logical algebra, an operation on statements $P, Q, R, \ldots$ such that the operation is true if all the statements $P, Q, R, \ldots$ are true; and the operation is false if at least one statement is false. The AND operation is also called logical multiplication, or conjunction. AND is similar to the multiplication operator for two binary digits. If either digit is zero, or both are zero, the product is zero; if both are one, the product is one. If T stands for true and F for false, then:

Table 1

	A	
	T	F
B T	T	F
F	F	F

Table 2

	A	
	1	0
B 1	1	0
0	0	0

where A and B stand for statements in Table 1, and for the binary digits in Table 2. This similarity is sometimes used to simulate AND in languages which do not have logical operator facilities.

annotation Any comment or note included in a program or flow-chart to clarify a point. A most useful device in programming. See DOCUMENTATION.

antisetoff powder In optical character recognition (OCR), finely powdered limestone or starch applied to a sheet of paper immediately after printing. The powder is employed to reduce any unintentional transfer of ink (offset) occurring between successive sheets in a delivery stack.

Antisetoff powder allows for a more optically acceptable document. However, its use is not advocated indiscriminately, as it may affect the paper's coefficient of friction, an important consideration in document transportation.

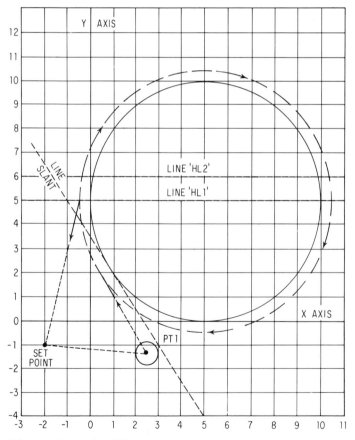

Reference diagram for APT program.

APT An acronym for Automatically Programmed Tools, APT is an aid to the part programmer.

Part programming evolved upon the introduction of numerically controlled machine tools. Part programming consists of writing numerically coded instructions which are followed by the machine control system to cause the machine to produce the desired part. As this programming must be precise, and is very intricate, a high-level compiler was conceived, and when written became known as APT.

APT is for the part programmer what COBOL is to a machine language programmer. APT performs most of the intricate mathematical operations necessary to part programming. The programmer simply defines the part he wishes to create in terms of its geometric components. For example: circles, straight lines, ellipses, etc. He then describes these components in English-language-type statements. Then, making reference to the various components, and referencing intersections of these various components, he instructs APT to move the cutting tool from place to place until the desired part is completed. The output from an APT run is a punched paper tape which can go directly to the numerically controlled machine.

To illustrate the working of APT, the following program instructs a machine tool to cut a 10-inch circle in a metal plate.

APT	
REMARK A 10 INCH CIRCLE	Remarks may be freely interspersed.
CUTTER /1	This statement indicates that the diameter of the cutting tool is 1 inch; thus APT automatically compensates for this, allowing the proper cutter offset.
TOLER / .001	The APT system uses a series of straight lines to approximate a curve. This statement means that a tolerance of not more than .001 in. deviation is allowed when computing cutter path.
FEDRAT / 50	This means that the maximum cutter speed is 50 inches per minute. APT may decrease the feed rate if its calculations indicate an excessive overshoot.

FROM / (SETPT = POINT / −2, −1, 0)	The very first cutter movement must begin somewhere. The FROM statement defines the start point. In this example, the start point is at location X = −2, Y = −1, Z = 0. SETPT is a symbolic label being assigned to the starting point. Hereafter in the program, the starting point may be referred to as SETPT.
PT1 = POINT /3, −1	This is a symbolic definition of a point at X = 3, Y = −1. PT1 may be used hereafter to refer to this point.
C1 = CIRCLE / 5, 5, 5	This is a symbolic definition of a circle whose center is located at X = 5, Y = 5, and which has a radius of 5 inches. C1 may be used to refer to this circle.
INDIRP / PT1	This is another first-time statement. It tells APT that the first cutter movement, *when initiated*, should move in the direction of point PT1 from the FROM point already defined. At this time, APT knows from what point, in what direction the first cutter movement will be. Now we must actually tell it to move.
GO TO / (SLANT = LINE / PT1, LEFT, TANTO, C1)	This tells APT to move the cutter from the FROM point, toward the INDIRP point (already defined) up to a line called SLANT, then stop. This statement also defines the line called SLANT. It is a line which passes through the point PT1, and is tangent to the circle C1. Since there are two such lines possible, LEFT indicates that looking from the point toward the circle, the line passes to the left of the circle. The

	cutter is now to the left of the line SLANT with its cutting extremity just touching point PT1.
TLLFT, GOLFT / SLANT	This says, keeping the cutting tool on the left side of line SLANT, turn left and proceed along line SLANT. This leaves the cutter proceeding along the left side of the SLANT with its cutting extremity actually at SLANT.
HL1 = LINE / 0, 5, 5, 5	This defines a line, HL1, which passes through points X = 0, Y = 5, and X = 5, Y = 5.
GOFWD / C1, ON, (HL2 = LINE / PARLEL, HL1, YLARGE, 1)	This says: when you reach circle C1, go forward around the circle until reaching line HL2. Line HL2 is defined as a line that is parallel to line HL1, and is 1 inch higher on the Y axis.
GOFWD / C1, ON, 2 INTOF, HL1	This tells the computer to move the cutter around the circle until the second intersection of line HL1, then stop. This leaves the cutter at approximately point —1/2, 5. The circle is complete.
GO TO / SETPT	This instructs the cutter to return to the start point.
STOP	This halts machine motion.
FINI	End of APT program.

area See CLEAR AREA.

argument The value of an independent variable for which the values of a function are tabulated: for instance, the number for which a logarithm is sought is the argument that enables the user to enter the table and get the required logarithm.

An argument is a quantity that must be supplied before a desired result can be obtained. A function requires an argument in order to yield an answer: for instance, cosine x as a function remains numerically undefined as long as the argument x is not given a specific value.   In this case we can say that cosine $x = y$, but cosine $60° = \frac{1}{2}$. Some subroutines must also be supplied with arguments to operate properly: such arguments are sometimes called parameters.

arithmetic shift   The shift of a number within the register containing it in such a way that the sign is not itself displaced.   In the binary system a shift of one to the left is equivalent to a multiplication by 2.   The arithmetic shift is frequently used to multiply by 10 (one shift to the left in the decimal system).   It is also commonly used to align the decimal—or binary—point of a number before addition or subtraction, or multiplication or division.

Shifts to the right are similarly used for division by 2^N (binary) or by 10^N (decimal).

arithmetic unit   That portion of the central processor of a computer which handles the execution of all arithmetic and logic operations.

The arithmetic unit consists of one or more accumulators, logic, shifting, and sequencing circuitry, plus a specific number of registers used for temporary storage of intermediate results.

Among the operations implemented by the arithmetic unit are addition, subtraction, multiplication, division, shifts, comparisons, certain types of conditional jumps, and Boolean logic operations.

As can be seen from the above list, the arithmetic unit performs the bulk of the internal processing commands of a computer.   Because of its important role, the design of the arithmetic unit has a major influence on the total processing power of a computer.

The simplest arithmetic units may be found on character- or digit-oriented computers such as the IBM 1620 or the Honeywell H-200 series.   These can form the sum or difference of one pair of digits at a time.   The addition of two multiple-digit numbers requires many memory cycles to fetch operands and store results on a digit-by-digit basis.   Multiplication and division are performed by repeated addition or subtraction and test, and are (relatively) very slow.   Indeed, in some extreme cases, desk calculators are faster than a 1620.   An example of a fast arithmetic unit of this class is that in the IBM 360/30, which requires 2421 microseconds to multiply two 10-digit numbers.

A common arithmetic unit organization on machines of moderate power contains one single-word-sized accumulator and an accumulator extension.   Addition, subtraction, and shifting are performed by circuits "built in" to the registers themselves.   Additional circuitry permits multiplication and division by iterated addition, subtraction, and testing at high speed. In this class, a good example is the IBM 360/50, which can multiply the same numbers mentioned above in 256 microseconds.

Still more powerful computers have multiple "accumulator" registers which only hold operands. Separate hardware is provided for addition/subtraction, shifting/testing, and multiplication/division. When an operation is to be performed, the operands are moved from the registers to the appropriate hardware, and the results are delivered to the appropriate accumulator register. This is cheaper than duplicating the arithmetic and logical facilities as an integral part of each register, and by separation of functional units permits specialized, efficient design of each hardware element. Also, accumulators that only hold data can be built at low cost. The 360/65, which falls in this class, can perform the example operation in 56.6 microseconds.

The CDC 6600 carries this concept a step further. It has eight 60-bit accumulators which hold only data, and multiple multipliers, shifters, dividers, adders, etc. Supervisory logic permits simultaneous execution of arithmetic, logical, and shifting operations (on unrelated operands) so that the total throughput is greatly increased. No operation must wait for an earlier instruction if its operands and functional hardware become available. This instruction could finish before the completion of an earlier instruction. Naturally, the hardware must assure that no paradoxes occur. Because of this simultaneity, it is impossible to state an exact time requirement for the example problem. However, given an average sequence of instructions, the 6600 might require an average of about 3 microseconds to execute this example if the time requirement were prorated among all the instructions being executed at that time.

artificial intelligence The characteristic of a machine capable of reasoning and learning, functions normally associated with human intelligence. Artificial intelligence is intimately related to machine learning.

In most cases, when a device or mechanism is able to mimic the behavior or performance of a human intelligence, the behavior or performance is preplanned by the designer of the device or mechanism, and as such is, in principle, fully predictable. An important class of artificial intelligence devices is of the learning or adaptive type. Such devices (either specially built hardware, or highly sophisticated programs) modify their behavior with acquired experience (this includes trial and error). Such devices will exhibit a behavior that cannot be predicted, and in some instances, may even surpass the performance of their designers. However, this class of devices can only learn in the manner and to the degree set down by their designers.   There would seem to be many modes of knowledge that cannot be directly imitated by a computer as, for example, perception, which appears to be a complicated process shaped by a mind interacting with senses and providing a subjective image of phenomena highly interlocked in their parts.

artificial language   A language based on a set of preestablished rules.

A language designed in a systematic and unified manner for a specific purpose is usually limited in applicability although free from the ambiguities and redundancies of a natural language.   A natural language offers a wide choice of equivalent expressions (which make poetry possible) but which make it poorly suited for exact rendering of meaning required by science.

From a user's point of view, the best language is the one that is best in formulating his problem, transforming his problem into a program, and running his program: such a language will help the user crystallize his thinking and reduce problem formulation time, and the program becomes both a documentation and means for communication.

From a designer's point of view, the best language will be the one that uses the least amount of memory space and will run in the least possible time: to achieve these objectives (which are of practical necessity), the designer introduces restrictions and conventions that are considered burdensome by the ultimate user.   These mutually conflicting points of view are at the root of the proliferation of languages in the computer world.

ASCII   American Standard Code for Information Interchange.   Now called USASCII.

assemble   The automatic translation of a program written in symbolic language into machine language.   After assembly, symbolic operation codes are written in absolute codes, and symbolic addresses are replaced by absolute or relocatable addresses.   A program written in a symbolic computer-dependent language cannot be run on a computer as such: a computer can run only machine-language programs. Consequently, a symbolic program is loaded in a computer together with a machine-language program called the assembler.   The assembler translates (or assembles) the symbolic program into a machine program which can then be run on the computer.

The word assemble is not used when programs are written in FORTRAN, COBOL, RPG, etc.   To prepare a machine-language program from such problem-oriented or procedure-oriented languages is known as compilation. See ASSEMBLER.

assembler A program designed to convert symbolic instructions into a form suitable for execution on a computer. In making this conversion the assembler also provides error messages and other diagnostic information to the programmer to help him develop an operational program.

An assembler may have the power to handle macro's, or macroinstructions (a macroinstruction being a special type of instruction equivalent to a sequence of machine instructions) which are programmer-defined models for sections of computer codes: A macrofacility permits a programmer to create a pseudolanguage to meet his needs and still retain complete control over the computer operations to be performed. An assembler may have the capability of executing a program immediately after assembly. Macro's and assemble-and-go features are seldom found on small-size computers.

A typical two-pass assembler would perform in the following manner:

An initial or first pass is made over the entire program text. The original text and intermediate derived data are either saved in main memory or written out on a temporary file. During the first pass, the symbolic name, location, and size of every programmer-defined symbolic area (data area or instruction) are recorded in a name table. Preliminary assignments of storage address are made during pass 1 as far as possible. In addition, macro's (if any) are expanded (converted to symbolic instructions in line in the program), and certain errors are detected such as bad input format, illegal characters, and omitted arguments. (In general, any error obvious from examination of one line of text is detected during pass 1).

The second pass over the program generates all the output. During pass 2 the mnemonic instructions are replaced with actual machine-format instructions. The correct absolute or relocatable addresses are substituted for symbolic addresses. A listing is prepared showing the instructions generated by each input statement, and also showing the detected errors. In pass 2 it is possible to detect many errors that could not be detected in pass 1, e.g., undefined symbolic addresses. A machine-language output is almost always produced even if the input program had many errors. This permits sophisticated programmers to work beyond the conventional limits of the assembly language.

It is possible to write one-pass assemblers which operate faster than two-pass assemblers but are more restricted in their capability. In addition, some three- and four-pass assemblers are known, but these are rare. Normally a simple assembler is the first program written for a newly designed computer.

associative storage   A memory device in which a location is identified by its content.

By associative storage is understood a memory capable of matching an item supplied to it with items stored in it, and returning related data from its storage. Normally a memory is addressed by hardware location (e.g., GO TO LOCATION 15726, READ FROM LOCATION 11007, etc.) and issues one word or character or whatever is stored in the indicated location. An associative memory is addressed by presenting a data item (e.g., JOHN SMITH) and returns either a related data item (e.g., 9 BRINKERHOFF AVE., TEANECK, N.J.), or the hardware address of the related data item (e.g., LOCATION 11007). The application of the associative storage concept to information retrieval is evident. It is of equally fruitful use in implementing new concepts in programming digital computers.

Associative storage plays an important role in time-sharing and multiprogramming computers by relating an actual hardware address with a program or instruction address. This permits each program to be written as though the entire computer were reserved for it. Every memory address of such a program will be converted by the associative storage to an address in a section of the computer that is reserved for that specific program. This technique is used, for instance, in the IBM 360/67 and SDS SIGMA 7 time-sharing computers. Synonymous with CONTENT ADDRESSED STORAGE and PARALLEL SEARCH STORAGE.

asynchronous computer   A computer in which an operation is initiated as soon as the preceding operation is completed. An asynchronous computer begins each operation at the earliest possible time. It is designed to check the availability of each functional unit required before beginning an operation, and will signal completion of each operation by restoring the availability indicators for the devices utilized. Although this type of computer offers the fastest possible execution of a program, it is seldom built in practice. Most computers are synchronous, the timing of each operation, or suboperation, being governed by an internal clock. This clock emits equally spaced pulses every so many micro- or nanoseconds to fetch the next operand, to execute the first part of the instruction, etc. As a consequence, all instructions must perforce begin and end at times that are integral multiples of the cycle time of the clock. Thus, instructions that could be executed very rapidly are delayed in execution time while waiting for the next pulse to take place. Synchronous computers are used more than asynchronous computers despite this handicap because they allow for simpler design of hardware and logic, and thus allow for cheaper computers.

attached support processor (ASP)   A system that utilizes multiple computers to increase the efficiency of processing numerous short-duration jobs.

Usually two computers are used, the support processor being a medium-scale computer which schedules the work to be done and handles all the low-speed input/output operations, and the main processor being a large-scale computer that is devoted entirely to high-speed computation and associated high-speed input/output operations. The computers are connected via channel-to-channel adapters, so that each computer appears to the others as a very high-speed input/output device. ASP achieves high productivity by division of effort, with each processor in the system performing those functions for which it is best suited.

In a typical configuration, the support processor has 250,000 characters of main memory, three printers, two card readers, one card punch, four disks, a few magnetic tapes, and a typewriter console. All punched-card operations and printing for the entire system will be performed by this computer. All card input is read and stored on magnetic disks until needed for processing. Output (print or punch) records are received as generated by the main processor, and are similarly stored on magnetic disks until they can be output properly. A large portion of main memory is devoted to a common buffer pool. Images of records going to and from disk, to and from the main processor, and to or from the input/ouput devices are stored here. Programs in the support processor keep track of every record in the buffer pool and every set of records on disk storage. Other routines keep track of the status of jobs not yet processed, or partially processed on the main processor. These routines schedule jobs for processing and supervise the workload of the main processor. Still other programs in the support processor monitor the progress of the card equipment and printers and see to it that no unit is idle while work is available for it.

The main processor for this system will have a larger, faster memory (perhaps 500,000 characters). There will be enough high-speed tape drives and magnetic disks and magnetic drums to meet the computational needs of the installation. This computer processes one job at a time, although multiprogramming is theoretically possible if required.

Each job running on the main processor may require specific tape reels or disk packs to be mounted on tape drives or disk drives for the duration of its run. The support processor keeps track of all such requirements and keeps a record of the usage and availability of all drives on the main processor. Before a job is initiated on the main processor, the support processor types a message to the operator, giving specific mounting instructions.

This enables mounting of tapes and disks on unused drives before they are needed. Similarly, dismounting of tapes and disks is supervised by the support processor. A job that requires little or no mounting operations may be run while tapes and disks are being mounted for a later job. In this way, waiting for operator intervention is all but eliminated.

Some main processors can function in two or more modes, for example, emulation of another computer, and operation in its own natural language. ASP can handle jobs for both modes of operation intermixed. For example, a 360/65 main processor with 7094 emulation feature can run OS/360 and 7094 (or 7044) programs intermixed under ASP. This requires that both OS/360 and the emulation program be modified to enable each to initiate the other under support processor control. In exceptional cases, 360, 7090, and 7040 programs could be intermixed by this technique.

The support processor can support data communications facilities to allow remote input of jobs. In addition to card input/output and printing adjacent to the computer itself, it is possible to have remote satellite computers perform card reading and transmit these data to the support processor. Data associated with these remotely entered jobs are stored on support processor disk storage and intermixed with the locally generated work. Output from remote jobs is transmitted back to the satellite computers for printing and punching.

The programs on the support processor may not fully utilize the capacity of that computer. The support programs may be run in multiprogramming mode, enabling other functions also to be performed on the same computer at the same time.

Jobs residing within the system have priorities associated with them, usually denoting order of submission to the system. This priority may be changed by the operator to expedite or retard selected jobs. In addition, the printing and punching phases of a job may be given priorities different from that of the processing step.

The efficiency of ASP systems is based on the following techniques:

1. Prescheduling of jobs with mounting and dismounting operations overlapped with processing of other jobs

2. The main processor seeing only high-speed I/O devices, the normally slow input/output operations being replaced by exceptionally fast memory-to-memory transfers

3. Emulation and nonemulation jobs or jobs for different operating systems being intermixed, with minimal environment-change overhead time being lost in transitions

4. The support processor being multiprogrammed to serve other non-ASP functions

ASP is a direct descendant of DCS, or direct-coupled system. Under DCS a 7040 with fast card and print devices was attached to a 7094. The 7094 was devoted to computation, while the attached 7040 was used for scheduling and input/output operations. ASP is an enlargement and extension of the DCS concept.

attribute   A characteristic required for defining or specifying something.

For data items, attributes could include location (if assigned), length (which may be null), and type of data represented (long, short, floating point, character string, packed decimal, etc.). If all the attributes of an item are known, then all manipulations of the item can be correctly performed. The actual information content of the item is not an attribute, and can be known only at run time.

At execution time, every job, task, data set, etc., has associated with it a control block in which the attributes of the item are listed in a condensed and formalized format. The operating-system routines interpret these control blocks which allow them to coordinate and function correctly according to the needs of the job.

In the macrofacility of BAL (basic assembly language of the IBM 360 System), a macro can test the attributes of each of its parameters, so as to be able to include, modify, or omit sections of code as the circumstances dictate. This ability to test attributes at macroexpansion time is one of the most powerful and flexible features of the macrocapability.

automatic carriage   Any mechanism such as the one found in the electric typewriters by means of which the paper is automatically spaced.

In EDP, most automatic carriages are designed to feed continuous forms through some kind of printing or writing device, e.g., line printer, typewriter, plotter. In almost every case the carriages are provided with sprockets that fit into uniformly spaced holes in the margins of the forms. This pin-feed principle allows precise registration of paper in the device, even when paper velocities over 100 inches per second are employed. In line printers, it is common to have a carriage control tape (continuous closed loop of perforated tape) attached to the automatic carriage. This control tape performs in the vertical direction as the adjustable tab stops of an office typewriter perform in the horizontal direction; i.e., the control tape allows rapid spacing to predefined positions, such as head of form, bottom of form, etc.

automatic check   An error-detecting procedure performed as an integral part of the normal operation of a device. Automatic checking usually requires no attention on the programmer's part until an error is actually detected. For instance, if while performing a multiplication, the computer finds that the product is too large to be contained in the space allocated, an error condition (called the overflow) will be signaled. The hardware provides some means of bringing this to the program's attention, and the experienced programmer will have made some provision in his program for the program to take the necessary corrective action at this time. In some cases the program is not made aware of error conditions, and the operator is expected to take the required corrective steps (such as a check for end of paper supply in a printer is a sign for the operator to load new paper stock and continue).

automatic coding The computer-assisted preparation of a machine-language program. The computer assigns actual locations to data and instructions, converts the instructions from symbolic form to machine language, and translates the symbolic addresses used by the programmer into the actual locations assigned earlier. If a small change is made to a symbolic language program which requires the reassignment of many addresses, the computer will perform the re-assignment rapidly: were the same program written in machine language, the programmer would have to rewrite this program almost entirely. See ASSEMBLER, COMPILER.

automatic computer Loosely, a computer that can carry out a special set of operations without human intervention. A computing device that is guided operation by operation by a human operator is known as a calculator. However, a device that functions without step-by-step guidance by a human operator but is not a computing device is called a robot, or, more usually, an automaton. It is usually required that a computer be capable of making tests (or comparisons), and choose between alternative courses of action depending upon the outcome of the tests (or comparisons). Calling a device without this capability a computer is erroneous.

automatic data processing Generic term loosely used to qualify certain types of equipment. See ADP.

automatic programming The preparation of a machine-language program by means of a computer. In general, automatic programming refers to the computer preparation of a computer-language program from an equivalent program written in a higher-level language (machine-oriented or procedure oriented). The term automatic programming is sometimes used to include automatic coding, but it should be reserved for those instances in which the computer actually chooses the machine operations required to obtain the indicated results. It is possible to increase markedly the production rate of operating programs by using automatic programming, but this is

usually done at the cost of program compactness and speed. See
COMPILER.

automation   Loosely, the mechanization of a process. Automation
equally refers to the act of making a process more automatic than
before.

Automation usually involves the integration of four types of devices: (1) sensors which detect the state of the system under control
(e.g., thermocouple, electric eye, remote scale); (2) computing elements which compare the observed measurements with the desired
state of the system and determine what corrective actions, if any,
should be taken (e.g., digital or analog logic elements); (3) actuators
which perform the control actions as directed by the computing elements (e.g., remote valves, switches, solenoids); (4) operational units
which comprise the system and actually carry out the desired process:
this is the part that would have to exist even if no automation were
involved (e.g., rolling mill, furnace, refinery, blender, machine tool).
The central feature of automation is the feedback of observed state
data to the regulatory process for automatic correction of error. A
common example is the thermostat in the temperature control of a
house.

auxiliary operation   An operation that is performed by hardware not
under continuous control of the central processing unit. An auxiliary
operation may be a computation, an input or output operation, or
some other operation performed under the internal control of the
device involved.

auxiliary storage   A memory device that supplements another
memory device. Generally, auxiliary storage refers to any data-
storing device that supplements the main memory of a computer.
Auxiliary storage is used to hold programs and data which otherwise would exceed the capacity of the main memory. It is more
economical to add auxiliary storage to a computer than to increase
the size of the main memory. Some common devices used are
high-speed core, low-speed core, magnetic drum, magnetic disk, magnetic tape, magnetic card, paper tape, card. Broadly speaking, the
cost per bit of information stored is highest with high-speed core,
lowest with punched card; the access time is smallest with high-speed
core, and longest with paper tape; and the physical volume required
for the equivalent amount of stored data is smallest with high-speed
core and largest with cards. Other auxiliary devices not too frequently in use are loops of magnetic tape, photoelectric systems (including lasers), acoustic delay lines, and electrostatic storage tubes.

See CARD, MAGNETIC DISK, MAGNETIC DRUM, MAGNETIC TAPE, PUNCHED TAPE.

availability   A ready-for-use condition of a system, subsystem, or program which results when it is both
1.   Operationally ready, and
2.   Not currently in use.
The term availability is often applied to data channels and input/output devices.   These usually operate asynchronously (time-independently) of the main program, and so a test for availability of the required output (input) equipment must be made before an I/O command is given.   Attempting to start I/O with unavailable equipment will result in delay of all further processing until the devices become available and I/O actually begins.   This could waste a great amount of computer time.

In a multiprogramming environment, a program (not reenterable) is available if it is loaded properly into main memory, and not currently in use by some job.   Many of the routines of an operating system fall into this category, and the operating system must test them for availability before each attempt to use them.

average-edge line   In optical character recognition (OCR), an imaginary line which traces and smoothes the shape of a handwritten or printed character that has been inputted for optical recognition.

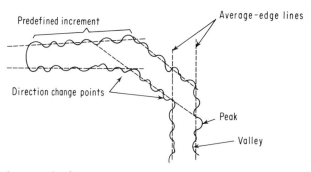

Average-edge line.

This average-edge line averages out the peaks and valleys in order to convey the intended form of the character.   Although imaginary, the average-edge line is similar to the line actually read by an optical scanner in that the scanner senses and ignores extraneous bulges and depressions on the edge of a character to the degree that is specified in the hardware limitations.

The direction of the line at a given point is determined by the average peaks and valleys along a predefined increment of the character stroke. A relatively uniform width is represented by two parallel lines; whereas if the width of the line appears tapered, the average-edge lines are tapered and not parallel.

The average-edge line is the base for measurement of character width, and is contrasted with voids and breakthroughs which are concerned with character length. See NORMALIZE.

B

Babbage, Charles Charles Babbage (1792–1871), English mathematician and mechanical engineer, who clearly understood in the nineteenth century all the fundamental principles embodied in the modern digital computers.

Machines that could perform one arithmetic operation at a time had existed since Pascal's calculator of 1642, but these machines saved neither time nor error, as the entering of numbers into the machine and the carrying out of a series of operations were almost as laborious and uncertain as performing the entire calculation by hand. Babbage's innovation was the development of a mechanical apparatus which would generate an entire numerical sequence according to the law of any given series, thus taking away the former uncertainty in calculating the elements of a mathematical table.

Babbage completed a small working model of his machine in 1822, the Difference Engine, based on difference tables of the squares of numbers. (The method of differences is the method of generating an arithmetic series by repeated addition of a common difference to fundamental numbers.) Babbage then proposed to build a difference engine on a greatly enlarged but overambitious scale—the new engine would be able to accommodate numbers of 20 places with sixth-order differences, the results to be printed out on a typewriter-like mechanism; however, because of the lack of precision in machine technology and Babbage's stormy dealings with his financial supporters, this project was never completed.

In 1835, during an impasse in the work on this giant difference engine, Babbage grasped the idea of an entirely new invention, the Analytic Engine. This machine was designed to tabulate the value of any function and to print out the results; the innovation was not that it was an accurate digital calculator which could perform the operations of addition, subtraction, multiplication, and division, but that it combined arithmetic processes with continual logic decisions based on the results of its own computations. In effect, the Analytic Engine would control itself: as answers were computed, they would be fed back to form the data in the various steps of a complex problem, the foundation of the modern feedback principle.

The chain of perforated cards to control the threads in looms when weaving complex patterns had been invented by J. M. Jacquard (1752–1834); Babbage quickly realized the utility of these cards for his Analytic Engine. Two sets of cards were used, one set with the punch-coded data to be operated on, and the second set with the sequence of operations to be carried out. The engine itself was made up of two principal components, the storage unit with a memory device consisting of groups of 50 counter wheels which could store 1000 figures of 50 digits each, and the arithmetic desk-calculator section, the mill. The perforated cards served as control unit: plungers passing through holes in the cards operated mechanisms for transferring numbers from the storage memory to the data processing mill.

Babbage also recognized that enough computations involve iterative processes, and that efficiency could be achieved by treating such cycles, or loops, as single operations. This realization was the forerunner of today's concepts of subroutines and automatic programming.

The Analytic Engine proposed by Babbage in the mid-nineteenth century was thus the world's first universal digital computer, and in its plans Babbage envisioned the principles of sequential control and programming, the feedback principle, looping, branching, an arithmetic unit and storage memory unit, and automatic printout. Although he was able to construct only a part of his Analytic Engine, Babbage nevertheless prepared detailed drawings from which the machine might have been constructed by skilled technicians.

In fact, Charles Babbage's engines were forgotten until Howard Aiken of Harvard University rediscovered his writings in 1937.

background In time-sharing and multiprogramming: the conventional, nonreal-time, nonconversational, lower-priority work done by a computer whenever high-priority or quick-response programs are inactive.

Foreground/background operation involves one or more small, fast high-priority programs sharing computer facilities with conventional, non-real-time work. As multiprogramming and time-sharing evolved into more complex forms (for example, conversational or multiaccess systems), the term background continued to apply to conventional, unglamorous, but necessary problems which were run in available time to minimize waste and increase total throughput. A background program may use any or all unoccupied memory and all spare peripheral devices remaining after foreground priority program needs are met. In general, background programs need not be specially tailored for multiprogramming; indeed, "they are not even aware" that they are being so processed. This means that existing programs may continue to be run while converting to multiprogramming. See FOREGROUND, TIME-SHARING, MULTIPROGRAMMING.

background reflectance In optical character recognition (OCR), the relative brightness of the background material on which a printed or handwritten character has been inscribed.

In order for raw paper to be acceptable to an optical scanner, it must achieve a certain minimum brightness. Although the appearance of an OCR character will reduce the brightness in a particular area, that area must still contain adequate background reflectance in order that the character be properly defined, that is, properly outlined. Touching characters, smudges, etc., might reduce this background reflectance to an unacceptable level.

In this regard it is noteworthy to mention that the inked area itself must also meet certain reflectance requirements. For example, one manufacturer cautions that the light reflected from the inked area which forms the printed character must be less than 50 percent as much as that reflected from the surrounding background paper.

band Any circular or otherwise cyclic segment of an auxiliary storage device such as magnetic drums, disks, or tape loops. A band is composed of tracks, each of which is a circular, or cyclic, sequence of bits of information being read entirely by a single recording or playback head in a fixed position. Also called a cylinder.

base The address of the starting location defining the beginning of a set of data or instructions.

Also, the number of distinct digits required by a positional system of numeric notation: for instance, the decimal system with base 10 (0, 1, 2, 3, 4, 5, 6, 7, 8, 9), the octal system with base 8 (0, 1, 2, 3, 4, 5, 6, 7), the binary system with base 2 (0, 1).

Also the origin or most fundamental point of a tree structure, more usually called the root.

base address A quantity that serves to derive absolute addresses from relative addresses.

When a computer instruction is executed, it must specify exactly the true location of its operands: this is achieved by giving the absolute address of each operand's location. It is, however, more convenient to use relative addresses in the instructions, the relative addresses specifying the operand location relative to some base address. Merely by changing the value of the base address, it then becomes possible to relocate the program's operands to a different area of main memory without having to rewrite the program to take into account the new operand locations. Thus, the base address is used to define the starting address of the memory area affected by a program.

An absolute address is usually obtained from a relative address by adding to it the value of the base address using modulo arithmetic. In any digital computer, a fixed number of digits is used to represent addresses in memory. Consequently, when base address and relative address are added to give the absolute address, only this number of digits is retained, high-order carry and overflow digits being ignored. This prevents too large a number becoming a valid address. For instance, assume a memory with 1000 memory locations numbered 000 through 999; if the base address is 255 and the relative address is 800, the absolute address will be:

$$800 + 255 = 055$$

There are two common methods of performing the conversion from relative addresses to absolute addresses:

1. A relocating loader can adjust addresses during the loading of a program into a computer, using programmed logic and the ordinary arithmetic capability of the computer, or

2. The base address can be placed in a hardware register, and the address modification can then be performed by hardware as an automatic prelude to the execution of each instruction.

Other methods, such as having each program relocate itself during execution, are less commonly used.

See ABSOLUTE ADDRESS, ADDRESS PART, RELATIVE ADDRESS.

BASIC An acronym for Beginner's All-purpose Symbolic Instruction Code, BASIC is a procedure-level computer language, well suited for conversational mode on a terminal usually connected with a remotely located computer.

BASIC was developed by Dartmouth College under the direction of Professors J. G. Kemeny and T. E. Kurtz, and supported by a grant from the National Science Foundation. The BASIC language compiler and the necessary executive routines were developed for the GE 235 and the Datanet 30 (a GE stored-program data communications processor).

BASIC is probably one of the easiest computer languages to learn (a matter of hours) and to master (a matter of days). Each line of the program begins with a number (the line number) which serves to identify the line and specifies the order in which the statements are to be performed by the computer. The statements may be fed to the computer in any order as the computer sorts out the program before running it. Thus, the program

```
10   LET A = 10
20   LET B = 20
30   LET C = A + B
40   PRINT C
50   END
```

will result in the computer printing 30 as an answer. However, the program could have been fed in the following way:

```
30   LET C = A + B
50   END
10   LET A = 10
40   PRINT C
20   LET B = 20
```

and the computer would still proceed to print out the correct answer.

It should be noted that spaces are ignored by the computer (except in a specific case), and are observed in writing the program only for ease of reading by the programmer. Thus:

```
30   LET C = A + B
```

might just as well have been written as

```
30LETC = A + B
```

The specific instance where spaces are meaningful is in a PRINT statement in quotation marks. For instance, the instruction

```
10 PRINT "HOW DO YOU DO?"
```

will cause the computer to print

HOW DO YOU DO?

respecting the spaces indicated by the programmer between the quotation marks.   For instance, to pretty up the first program, the PRINT statement number 40 could have been written

40 PRINT "C IS EQUAL TO" C

and the computer would have printed

C IS EQUAL TO 30

Addition and subtraction are indicated by + and −, multiplication by *, division by /, and exponentiation by ↑.

BASIC has a powerful set of matrix instructions such as

MAT K = INV(L)

which automatically inverts matrix L.

An advantage of BASIC over some implementations of languages such as FORTRAN and ALGOL consists in the possibility of mixed expressions.   For instance:

20 PRINT   .076 * 2 ↑ 7.6

is permissible in BASIC.

Although far from being as powerful as ALGOL or FORTRAN, BASIC is a language more than adequate for most of the problems that can be handled in the time-sharing mode.

The following example will illustrate some of the characteristics of BASIC: Suppose that the sum of 1000 is to be invested for 47 months at a yearly rate of 4 percent compounded quarterly (no interest earned in less than a quarter).   Assume, moreover, that the number of months may be subject to variations, and consequently the programmer may wish to decide just before running time what time period to indicate.   The program could be written in the following way:

BASIC program	Comments
50 PRINT "NUMBER OF MONTHS" ;	This statement causes the computer to print: NUMBER OF MONTHS? and the programmer will have to type 47 before the computer will proceed with the run.

BASIC program	Comments
60 INPUT N	The typed number 47 is assigned to location N; that is, N is set equal to 47.
70 LET R = .04 80 LET A = 1000	Statements 70 and 80 define the constants R (rate) and A (initial amount) as being equal to 4 percent and $1000.
90 LET B = N	Statements 90 to 190 ascertain whether N is an integral multiple of 3, since there is no interest earned in less than a quarter.
100 GO TO 130	This is an unconditional jump to statement 130.
120 LET B = B − 3	During the course of analysis of the number of months, B is reduced by 3 each time (the contents of location B are reduced by 3 and restored in location B).
130 LET T = B	This substitution permits B to be tested, by testing T, without destroying B.
140 LET T = T/3	T is divided (/) by 3.
150 IF T > 1 THEN 120	A test instruction: if T is greater than 1, the computer returns to statement 120. (Note that T greater than 1 means that B is greater than 3.) If T is not greater than 1, then the computer goes to the next instruction in sequence, that is, to instruction 160.
160 IF T = 1 THEN 190	Another test instruction: if T = 1, then N is an integral multiple of 3, and the calculation of the final amount may proceed without any further ado. If T is not equal to 1, then it must be smaller than 1.

BASIC program	Comments
	Therefore, B must be smaller than 3, and the computer goes instead to the next instruction in sequence, that is, to instruction 180.
180 LET N = N − B	This operation equates N to an integral multiple of 3, eliminating odd months which do not earn interest.
190 LET C = A * (1 + R/4)	The first sum, principal plus interest, is calculated, thereby establishing an initial value for C.
210 FOR I = 1 TO N/3 − 1	This instruction sets up a loop ending at 230: the instructions within this loop will be evaluated N/3 − 1 times.
220 LET C = C * (1 + R/4)	Each time this operation is carried out, the latest value of C is assigned to C on the right-hand side. This value is then stored in location C.
230 NEXT I	This instruction tests the value of I (or contents of location I). If not equal to N/3 − 1, the value of 1 is added to I, and the computer starts again, in this case at location 220.
240 PRINT "CAPITAL AFTER "N;" MONTHS = " C	This PRINT instruction will actually print CAPITAL AFTER as it appears between quotation signs; the value of N will then be printed out; the (;) reduces the space which will exist between 47 and the words MONTHS = which will follow; the value of the capital is then printed out.
250 END	ALL BASIC programs must end with the word END.

Note that this program could have been written

10   PRINT 1000*1.01 ↑ 15
20   END

and the same result, namely 1160.97, would have been obtained.

It will be observed that the line numbers do not have to follow a strict numerical sequence. It is sufficient that the line number corresponding to a statement be numerically greater than the line number of the logically antecedent statement.

basic access method (BAM)   An access method in which each input/output statement causes a corresponding machine input/output operation to be performed.

There are two distinct types of access methods, the basic access method which is close to machine language in its simplicity and directness, and the queued access method which provides great sophistication but cannot be used for all types of I/O.

In normal processing, a READ macroinstruction is used with a basic access method to perform a single input operation. A physical record is read into memory at the indicated location. The READ does not (by itself) cause overlap of processing with input, nor does it perform unblocking of blocked records. The READ macroinstruction does account for the individual properties of the hardware, record format, and data-set organization being used; and does perform error checking/correcting, end-of-volume sensing, end-of-data-set sensing, etc.

Similarly, a WRITE macroinstruction commands a single output operation to be performed. Blocking and padding, and the provision of control characters, are the programmer's responsibility (i.e., not provided automatically by the basic access method service routines). WRITE does account for end-of-volume or end-of-allocated-space sensing and hardware error checks.

Before processing data with a BAM, a DCB (Data Control Block) must be constructed describing the data set so that the service routines may correctly manipulate it. An OPEN macroinstruction causes automatic completion of DCB information, and also performs label checking. After being OPENed, a data set is ready for use by the program. When processing is completed, a CLOSE macroinstruction performs final label processing, optionally rewinds or unloads the volume, and disconnects the data set (and its associated service routines and control blocks) from the program.

After a READ, the program may continue with any processing that does not depend on the completion of the input operation. When the new data are required to permit any continuation of processing, a CHECK macroinstruction causes the program to wait upon completion of the operation, and check the validity of the transfer.

In exceptional cases, a WAIT macroinstruction may be used to delay until an operation is complete without causing an automatic verification of accuracy. Programmer-specified error checks may then be performed. See ACCESS METHOD, DATA MANAGEMENT.

batch processing   A technique that uses a single program loading to process many individual jobs, tasks, or requests for service. Often confused with stacked job processing.

In batch processing a program is loaded into memory and activated, and processes several unrelated jobs sequentially, without having to be reloaded or reinitialized for each job. A common example is a payroll program, which processes every employee individually in one continuous operation.

In many applications, where the complexity of the processing is too great to permit accomplishing the entire operation in one pass through the computer, a program is divided into phases. Each phase is loaded when the previous phase finishes, until the last phase completes the job. In batch processing every job is run through the first phase, then the second phase is loaded, and every (partially processed) job is run through it, etc.

Compare batch and stacked operation in a compiler that operates in three phases. If the phases are called A, B, C, and four jobs 1, 2, 3, 4 are to be processed, then in batch processing we have the operations

$$(A, \ 1), \ (A, \ 2), \ (A, \ 3), \ (A, \ 4), \ (B, \ 1), \ (B, \ 2), \ (B, \ 3), \ (B, \ 4),$$
$$(C, \ 1) \ . \ . \ . \ (C, \ 4)$$

whereas with stacked processing we have

$$(A, \ 1), \ (B, \ 1), \ (C, \ 1), \ (A, \ 2), \ (B, \ 2) \ . \ . \ . \ . \ . \ . \ , \ (B, \ 4),$$
$$(C, \ 4)$$

Both techniques require 12 individual processing steps, and both techniques require the same amount of data I/O. Yet the batch technique is faster, for it requires only 3 program loadings whereas stacked processing requires 12 program loadings. Note that this distinction essentially vanishes if only a single program phase is required, thus creating the confusion between batch and stacked.

baud   A unit of signaling speed equal to the number of signals events per second. For example, one baud equals one bit per second in a sequence of binary signals, and 70 bits per second in a TWX paper-tape transmission. Loosely speaking, a baud is a means of rating a data transmission line by measuring the information flow per unit of time. Bauds are increasingly being replaced by the expression "bits per second."

B box   A hardware element which holds a number that can be added to (or, in some cases, subtracted from) the address portion of a computer instruction to form an effective address.

The address modification is only performed at the discretion of the programmer, and never modifies the instruction itself; only the location of the operand is affected.

A computer may have no, one, a few, or a great many B boxes. The B boxes may be separate hardware (accessible only by special index-register instructions), or they may be selected arithmetic registers (accessible also by ordinary arithmetic instructions), or they may be preassigned locations in main (or core) memory (accessible by store/fetch instructions).

The in-core (or hardware) B boxes cost less than arithmetic index registers, but they are slower at execution time, since they require additional memory cycles. Synonymous with INDEX REGISTER.

benchmark problem   A standard problem that is used to evaluate the performance of computers relative to one another. An installation considering the acquisition of a computer system can prepare a set of benchmark problems to represent a typical mix of jobs. Running these problems on various computers under consideration will help determine the relative advantages of price and running speed. Although such a method may be profitably used by an organization with experience in computer use, it may turn out to be a misleading test if used by an organization with little or no computing experience: typical jobs have yet to be defined.

bias   The algebraic difference between the average of a set of numbers and a reference number. The uniform tendency of some data to come out too high or too low relative to an expected reference value. The numerical difference between observed average and expected average is called the bias. Bias may be compared to the error incurred in setting the zero on a bathroom scale: all weights tend to be off by the amount of the zero-setting error.

bidirectional flow   The flow that can be extended over the same flowline in either direction in a flowchart. Generally any connecting line with an arrowhead at each end indicates bidirectional flow:

the possibility of transmission or travel in either direction. It may be desirable to differentiate between flow in both directions at different times and simultaneous flow in both directions. The terms half duplex and full duplex are used to that end in characterizing transmission lines. In computer programming, the sequential nature of most computers prevents bidirectional flow: this limitation is being removed with the advent of multiprocessing equipment.

binary   Pertaining to a characteristic of a selection, choice, or condition involving only two possibilities. More generally, pertaining to the numeration system with the base 2. Binary is used as an adjective to characterize a number of things. For instance: (1) any state of affairs having only two possible outcomes: yes/no, on/off, zero/one, etc.; (2) the number system to the base (or radix) 2, and the arithmetic with such a system; (3) digital computers performing arithmetic in binary representation (as contrasted with decimal computers which use binary codes to represent the digits zero to nine and which perform arithmetic in a decimal form); (4) a magnetic tape written with internal representation of numbers usually with odd parity (as contrasted with a binary-coded decimal tape which is written with binary-coded decimals or alphanumeric data, usually with even parity). It should be noted that the distinction between binary tapes and binary-coded decimal tapes is normally made only by users of binary computers. See COLUMN BINARY, ROW BINARY.

binary cell   A storage cell or register, of one binary digit capacity. A hardware element capable of being in only one of two states: off or on. Hence, any memory element having either a 0 or a 1 but not both.

binary code   A code that makes use of exactly two distinct characters, 0 and 1. In general, a means of representing data other than binary numbers by binary numbers which, by convention, will have an equivalent meaning.

Most components of automatic data processing equipment can be in one of two states: off or on. These states can be represented by 0 or 1. The 2 bits (BInary digiTS) 0, 1 may be used in pairs to represent four unique combinations: 00, 01, 10, 11. To represent the number system 0, 1, 2, 3, 4, 5, 6, 7, 8, 9 would require codes 4 bits long. Of the available 16 combinations, only 10 would be used for the 10 digits. If the code were extended to include the alphabet and special characters such as (,), /, $, +, −, at least 42 combinations should be available. This would require 6 bit combinations. For instance, the following code could be established:

Binary code	Alphanumeric equivalent
000000	0
000001	1
000010	2
000011	3
000100	4
000101	5
000110	6
000111	7
001000	8
001001	9
001010	A
001011	B
....	....
100011	Z
100100	+
100101	−
etc.	etc.

See REFLECTED BINARY.

binary-coded decimal A decimal notation in which the individual decimal digits are each represented by a group of binary digits. Thus, in the 2-4-2-1 binary-coded decimal notation, the number 38 is represented as 0011 1110 whereas in binary notation, 38 is represented as 100110. The binary-coded decimal is one of a number of schemes for representing the 10 decimal digits by means of binary digit codes. For instance:

Decimal	2-4-2-1 code	8-4-2-1 code	Excess-3 code
0	0000	0000	0011
1	0001	0001	0100
2	0010	0010	0101
3	0011	0011	0110
4	0100	0100	0111
5	1011	0101	1000
6	1100	0110	1001
7	1101	0111	1010
8	1110	1000	1011
9	1111	1001	1100

As an extension, such a scheme can be made to include digits, letters, and special characters such as (,), \$, @. It is common for such schemes to represent 64, 128, or 256 unique characters by using combinations of 6, 7, or 8 bits, respectively. Binary-coded decimal is frequently abbreviated to BCD.

binary digit A character representing one of the two digits in the numeration system with a base of 2. Abbreviated BIT (from BInary digiT). A bit is one of the *only* two possible digits in arithmetic to the base (or radix) 2: usually, these digits are represented by zero and one. A binary number is written as a sequence of binary digits, with the value of each digit indicated by the number of positions between it and the binary point. In all existing digital computers, the ultimate representation of data is in binary digits. See EQUIVALENT BINARY DIGITS.

binary number A representation of a number by using a sequence of binary digits. A number is an abstract mathematical concept, whereas a numeral is a representation of a number using some system of notation. Because numerals have all the properties of numbers, the two terms are often used interchangeably when mathematical rigor is not required. In binary numbers the value of each digit is indicated by the number of positions between the binary digit and the binary point. See BINARY NUMERAL.

binary numeral A representation of a number in the positional notation using the base (or radix) 2, that is, a number represented by a series of binary digits. The value of each digit is indicated by the number of positions between it and the binary point:

Number	Decimal number	Binary number
One	1	1
Two	2	10
Three	3	11
Four	4	100
Five	5	101
One-half	½	.1
One-quarter	¼	.01
Three-quarters	¾	.11
Twelve and one-eighth	12⅛	1100.001
Two hundred fifty-five	255	11111111.
(pi)	3.14159	11.01011111100011011111

binary search A search in which an ordered set of items is divided into two equal parts, one part being rejected, and the process repeated on the accepted part until those items with the desired property are found. A binary search procedure assumes, initially, a set of items ordered in some logical sequence, for instance, a numerically increasing sequence of numbers. The number sought is compared to the midpoint of the set: unless this is the number sought, this number will be found in either the right-hand or the left-hand half of the set.   The number sought is compared to the midpoint of the correct half: if not equal to the midpoint, it is then in either the right-hand or the left-hand half of that portion of the set, that is, in one of the two quarters of the set.   This procedure is carried out until the number is found.   For example, assume a box of envelopes, each envelope bearing a number on its flap, and assume that these envelopes are ordered numerically, from the lowest to the highest number.   A check bearing a number must be placed in the envelope with the corresponding number: the envelope must be pulled out for its number to be seen.   Let us say that the number required is 27, and the envelopes are arranged as follows:

2   3   4   8   10   17   18   27   30   31   56

The midpoint envelope is pulled out and found to bear the number 17.   The correct envelope will thus be in the right-hand half of the set:

18   27   30   31   56

The midpoint envelope of that subset is pulled out and found to have the number 30.   The correct envelope will thus be found in the left-hand half of this subset:

18   27

In this case, the midpoint falls between two envelopes.   It is a matter of luck to pull number 27 out before number 18:   in either case, the search is ended.   It is a matter of interest that if we define "pulling out an envelope" as "asking a question," relatively few questions are needed to pinpoint a specific item in a large-size population. For instance, no more than 20 questions are required to identify uniquely a number in a set of one million numbers.   The number N of questions to be asked is equal to the exponent of 2 such that 2^N is just larger than or equal to the number of items to be searched.   Thus, if 1000 items must be searched to find one specific number, there will be 10 questions to be asked since $2^{10} = 1024$ ($2^9 = 512$ which is smaller than 1000).   Binary search is one type of dichotomizing search.

bionics   A relatively new branch of technology attempting to relate the functions, characteristics, and phenomena of living systems to those of hardware systems.   There would appear to be a remarkable similarity between an electronic gate circuit and the network associated with a neuron.   Little is known about synapses and neurons except for the fact that synapses are capable of at least some logical operations.   If neurons alone are to be considered as logical elements, then the brain represents a computer with 10,000,000,000 logical elements (there are estimated to be 1,000,000,000,000,000 synapses in the brain, up to 100,000 per neuron). The advantage of the computer over the brain is a question of speed: transmission of information in the brain proceeds at the rate of one foot in three milliseconds as compared to one foot in one-thousand-millionth of a second in the computer. Although the concept of bionics is a two-way

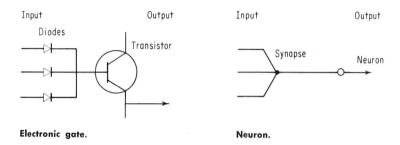

Input	Output	Input	Output
Diodes	Transistor	Synapse	Neuron

Electronic gate.   **Neuron.**

proposition, learning more about machines through the study of the brain, and learning more of the brain through the study of computers, more has been learned of computers than the brain: sonar was improved with the study of echo-location mechanism of the bat, and radar was improved by the study of the frog's eye.

biquinary Pertaining to a number system in which each decimal digit N is represented by the digits ab and such that $N = 5a + b$ where $a = 0$ or 1 and $b = 0, 1, 2, 3,$ or 4. For instance, 6 in the decimal system is represented by 11 in the biquinary system. This system is sometimes called a mixed-radix system with radices 2 and 5. For example:

Decimal	Biquinary	
	(A)	(B)
0	0	0
1	0	1
2	0	2
3	0	3
4	0	4
5	1	0
6	1	1
7	1	2
8	1	3
9	1	4

Thus, the decimal number 185 would be represented as 011310. This system is basic in the abacus, and is also used in computers such as the IBM 650.

bistable Characteristic of a device capable of assuming one of two stable states. A ready example of such a device is the light wall switch, or toggle switch, usually designed to snap to an "ON" or "OFF" position, and which does not remain in an in-between condition by itself. A bistable flip-flop is a device frequently encountered in computers, and which may be considered the electronic analog of the toggle switch. It maintains its position (or condition) until triggered by an input signal, at which time it will assume the opposite state (or condition) and remain in this state until the next input signal, at which time it will revert to its initial state.

bit A binary digit. The term bit is an abbreviation for BInary digiT. In computers, a bit is represented by a pulse (1) or the absence of a pulse (0). In information theory, the bit is the smallest possible unit of information. See CHECK BIT, PARITY BIT.

blank character A character used to produce a character space through an output device. A blank character denotes an empty space on an output medium, or an unpunched column on an input medium (card). It is used to represent a valid character which does not print [some computers upon sensing an invalid character will skip it, i.e., will replace it by a blank (and valid) character]. A blank character should be contrasted with a null character which is no character at all. Replacing a character (including a blank character) by a null character is equivalent to shifting all remaining characters by one position, filling in the space formerly occupied by the nullified character. This results in a shorter string of characters.

bleed See INK BLEED.

block A set of records, words, characters, or digits, handled as a unit. For instance, a magnetic tape written in such a way that each physical tape record contains more than one logical record is called a blocked tape.

A logical record is a block of related items that are to be treated as a whole by a program; a physical tape record is a sequence of adjacent characters on a magnetic tape with an end-of-record (EOR) gap at the beginning and at the end of the sequence. These gaps are blank tape sections of specified size which indicate the ends of physical tape records and which permit the tape driving mechanism to start and stop on sections of tape that contain no data. Because an end-of-record gap occupies as much space as would be required by 500 to 600 tape characters, a tape containing short physical records (for instance, the contents of a standard 80-column card) could consist mainly of blank tape. Blocking such a tape makes the physical records longer and thus allows for more data to be stored on a single reel. Moreover, the number of time-wasting starts and stops will be reduced, resulting in a substantial saving of computer time.

To block is to form blocked records out of individual logical records.

In block diagrams a block is a symbol representing one or more actions to be taken. Its shape is dictated by convention according to the type of action (i.e., I/O decision, unconditional action, etc.), and it is further described by a legend or text that appears within its outline. See BLOCK DIAGRAM.

block diagram A diagram of a system or process in which selected portions are represented by annotated boxes and interconnecting lines. A block diagram is a means of representing graphically the structure or logical organization of something by using blocks representing processes, decisions, or functions connected by lines indicating control, transfer of data, or logical connectedness. Templates are furnished by computer manufacturers, to facilitate drawing the symbols, and such templates may be acquired commercially. The differences between symbols from manufacturer to manufacturer are slight. The symbols shown in the accompanying table are those most frequently encountered in practice.

SYMBOL	DIMENSIONAL RATIO		COMMENT
	WIDTH	HEIGHT	
INPUT/OUTPUT	1	2/3	Represents the input/output function (I/O), i.e., the making available of information for processing (input), or the recording of processed information (output).
PROCESSING	1	2/3	Represents the processing function, i.e., the process of executing a defined operation or group of operations resulting in a change in value, form, or location of information, or in the determination of which of several flow directions are to be followed.
ANNOTATION	1	2/3	Represents the annotation function, i.e., the addition of descriptive comments or explanatory notes as clarification. The broken line may be drawn either on the left as shown or on the right. It is connected to the flowline at a point where the annotation is meaningful by extending the broken line in whatever fashion is appropriate.

SYMBOL	DIMENSIONAL RATIO		COMMENT
	WIDTH	HEIGHT	
FLOW DIRECTION Top to Bottom / Bottom to Top Left to Right Right to Left	Not Applicable	Not Applicable	Represent the flow direction function, i.e., the indication of the sequence of available information and executable operations. Flow direction is represented by lines drawn between symbols. Normal direction flow is from left to right or top to bottom. When the flow direction is not left to right or top to bottom, open arrowheads should be placed on reverse direction flowlines. When increased clarity is desired, open arrowheads can be placed on normal direction flowlines. When flowlines are broken due to page limitation, connector symbols shall be used to indicate the break. When flow is bidirectional, it can be shown by either single or double lines but open arrowheads shall be used to indicate both normal direction flow and reverse direction flow.
PUNCHED CARD	1	1/2	Represents an I/O function in which the medium is punched cards, including mark sense cards, partial cards, stub cards, etc.
MAGNETIC TAPE	1	1	Represents an I/O function in which the medium is magnetic tape.
PUNCHED PAPER TAPE	1	1/2	Represents an I/O function in which the medium is punched tape.
DOCUMENT	1	2/3	Represents an I/O function in which the medium is a document. This symbol can be constructed without a template, although the ratio of width to height of the symbol in the template has been found to be more convenient due to the amount of information usually included within this symbol.
MANUAL INPUT	1	1/2	Represents an I/O function in which the information is entered manually at the time of processing, by means of online keyboards, switch settings, push buttons, card readers, etc.
DISPLAY	1	2/3	Represents an I/O function in which the information is displayed for human use at the time of processing, by means of on-line indicators, video devices, console printers, plotters, etc.
COMMUNICATION LINK	Not Applicable	Not Applicable	Represents an I/O function in which information is transmitted automatically from one location to another.

SYMBOL	DIMENTIONAL RATIO		COMMENT
	WIDTH	HEIGHT	
DECISION	1	2/3	Represents a decision or switching-type operation that determines which of a number of alternate paths is to be followed.
PREDEFINED PROCESS	1	2/3	Represents a named process consisting of one or more operations or program steps that are specified elsewhere, e.g., subroutine or logical unit.
MANUAL OPERATION	1	2/3	Represents any off-line process geared to the speed of a human being.
AUXILIARY OPERATION	1	1	Represents an off-line operation performed on equipment not under direct control of the central processing unit.
CONNECTOR	1	1	Represents a junction in a line of flow. A set of two connectors is used to represent a continued flow direction when the flow is broken by any limitation of the flowchart. A set of two or more connectors is used to represent the junction of several flowlines with one flowline, or the junction of one flowline with one of several alternate flowlines.
TERMINAL	1	3/8	Represents a terminal point in a system or communication network at which data can enter or leave; e.g., start, stop, halt, delay, or interrupt.
ALTERNATE COMMUNICATION LINK	Not Applicable	Not Applicable	Represents an I/O function in which information is transmitted automatically from one location to another. To denote the direction of data flow, the symbol may be drawn with superimposed arrowheads.
ON-LINE STORAGE	1	2/3	Represents an I/O function utilizing auxiliary mass storage of information that can be accessed on-line; e.g., magnetic drums, magnetic disks, magnetic tape strips, automatic magnetic card systems, or automatic microfilm chip or strip systems.
OFF-LINE STORAGE	12	10	Represents any off-line storage of information, regardless of the medium on which the information is recorded.

Courtesy of UNIVAC.

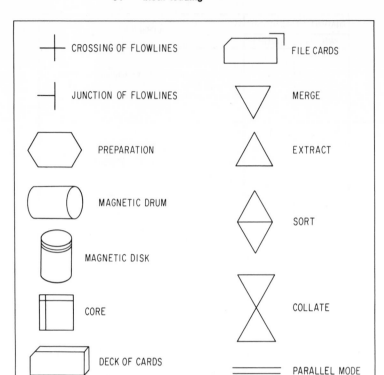

CROSSING OF FLOWLINES

JUNCTION OF FLOWLINES

PREPARATION

MAGNETIC DRUM

MAGNETIC DISK

CORE

DECK OF CARDS

FILE CARDS

MERGE

EXTRACT

SORT

COLLATE

PARALLEL MODE

International considerations.

This table lists the symbols contained in the Second Draft ISO Proposal Flowchart Symbols for Information Processing which are not included in the American Standard Flowchart Symbols for Information Processing, X3.5-1965.

An illustration will show the use of symbols. The following information is contained in an item:

1. Number of days of medical absence
2. Remaining days of medical leave
3. Hourly rate of pay

The problem is to update the medical leave and store the medical pay in a storage location and then continue the solution of the problem in another place. The flowchart might look like the one shown here.

block loading   A program loading technique in which the control sections of a program or program segment are loaded into contiguous positions in main memory.

In simple computers block loading is the only technique available

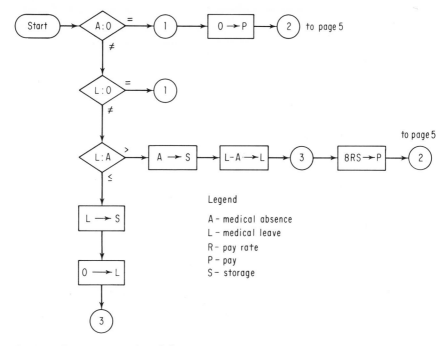

Flowchart illustrating use of symbols.

for positioning programs in memory. With block loading a program segment may be either loaded into a fixed preassigned area in memory (absolute) or moved as a unit to any vacant area large enough to contain it (relocatable). But in no case can a program be broken up and loaded into noncontiguous memory areas in a block loading environment. (Noncontiguous loading is called scatter loading and requires sophisticated hardware and software to be practical.)

In a nonmultiprogramming environment block loading is used for simplicity and confers no disadvantage. A program is designed to occupy a portion of memory and to have data in some of the remainder of memory. The program is merely loaded and run.

In multiprogramming several unrelated programs share available memory. If it is desired to load another program into memory by block loading, then a sufficiently large contiguous area must be available. Suppose that several nonadjacent vacant areas of memory are jointly large enough for the new program. Then the old programs must be moved around, uniting the vacant memory into one continuous piece, before the new program can be added.

Moving a program already loaded can be difficult or impossible, and will be time-consuming. Scatter loading permits adding the new program without moving the old ones, but is itself a complicated undertaking; the designer will have to decide between simplicity with high overhead or complexity with efficiency.

Compare with SCATTER LOADING.

boolean Pertaining to the algebra formulated by George S. Boole (1815–1864), and by extension, to the operations of formal logic. Boolean algebra involves the use of the operators AND, OR, NOT (contrast, loosely, with high school algebra involving the use of ×, +, −). The operators AND, OR inspired the application of Boolean algebra to the design of switching circuits such as are found in control systems. For instance, the statement (A) AND (B) is true if, and only if, both A and B are true. If either A, or B, or both A and B are false, then the statement is false. If one is to accept the convention that a lighted bulb means "true" and an unlighted bulb means "false," then a two-switch series circuit will represent (A) AND (B)

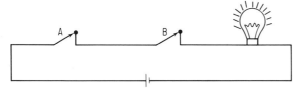

Circuit equivalent of A AND B.

(where a closed switch stands for the corresponding statement to be true). Opening the switch (that is, making its corresponding statement not true) puts the light out; that is, (A) AND (B) becomes false.

Boolean algebra has greatly facilitated the analysis of the intricate switching circuits required for modern computers. As a mathematical tool it has found numerous applications and has been incorporated in higher-level languages. Already in FORTRAN II a set of operators and conventions permitted bit-by-bit logical operations on whole words or parts of words: Boolean operators were indicated by punching a B in column 1 of the FORTRAN statement card.

bootstrap A technique permitting a system to bring itself into an operational state by means of its own action. This technique enables the first few instructions of a routine to bring the rest of the routine into the computer from an input device.

A bootstrap load routine usually consists of a couple of punched cards: the first card is fed into the computer by means of the console and card reader switches, the contents of the card being stored in high-speed storage; the first card calls in the second card automatically, and the two cards together cause the computer to read in the main (or program) deck; the second card of the deck usually causes a transfer to the start of the program where the data read-in and start-execution instructions are to be found. Without a bootstrap load routine it is almost impossible to get the very first program into a newly built computer. A bootstrap card is a card designed to load itself into fixed locations within a computer: it is frequently used for simple actions such as rewinding all tapes.

It is sometimes possible to bootstrap language processors into existence. Suppose that a new computer has been designed, and it is desired to construct a powerful assembler for it. Initially no compiler or assembler exists to assist in writing any program (including the assembler or compiler). Let a very simple assembler be written in actual computer instructions. Using this assembler and the simple language it supports, a more complex assembler (in assembly language) is written, the better assembler using the original assembler. (It should now be possible to have an assembler that can assemble itself, since the newer language usually includes all features of the simpler language.) Now the ultimate assembler is written in this better assembler language. When it is assembled and debugged, the most powerful language is ready to run. This same technique can be used for powerful compilers, providing that the powerful compiler language enables a compiler to be written in it (not all languages do allow this). Then, if a subset of the compiler is implemented by some other technique (e.g., assembly language), the compiler can be bootstrapped up to its final level of sophistication.

A challenging problem is to specify the simplest subset of a language that will enable the next level of language processor to be written. The solution to this problem will specify the simplest processor that has to be obtained by other means such as simulation.

borrow An algebraically negative carry. The standard operation carried out when subtracting one number from another, digit by digit, and subtracting a higher-valued digit from a lower-valued digit, as in $6243 - 5354 = 889$.

BOS. Basic operating system A disk-oriented, more powerful extension of tape BPS.

BOS is the smallest and simplest disk-resident operating system for the IBM 360. BOS requires 8K of memory, a printer, a card reader/punch, and one 2311 disk-pack drive. BOS offers job-to-job transition via control cards, support of a disk-resident library of programs, a linking loader, checkpoint and restart capability, and the ability to refer to I/O devices by symbolic names. Included in BOS are a disk assembler and a disk RPG (decimal feature required), and a disk sort (requiring at least two 2311's), but no tape sort. It is possible to include elements of BPS tape on the systems residence disk (this makes available the tape sort/merge capability).

The disk files of BOS include random, sequential, and indexed sequential organizations. These can be upward compatible with the larger DOS and OS systems. The IOCS permits overlap of I/O with processing and queuing of requests for I/O service. However, requests are queued by channel, not by device, which sometimes limits the simultaneity potential of the multiplexor channel. (The same is true of BPS tape IOCS.)

BOS may be used profitably on 8K and 16K installations. The core occupied by supervisor and IOCS for complex configurations (disk and tape or possibly other peripherals) will exceed half the capacity of an 8K memory. This will leave very little room for problem programs. However, the same core occupancy is smaller than would be required on a 16K similar configuration using DOS. There are very few installations having a great number of peripheral devices with only 8K of memory, thus this limitation is not too binding in practice. BOS may be used up to 65K memory if it is required to have very small system resident routines. On a minimum-configuration computer having only the required peripheral gear, less than 4K of memory will be occupied by BOS resident routines.

TOS and DOS used to be known as BOS tape and BOS disk. This usage has been discontinued and should cause no further confusion. BOS does not support any compilers other than RPG (i.e., no FORTRAN, COBOL, AUTOTEST, PL/1, etc.).

boundary   See BYTE BOUNDARY, CHARACTER BOUNDARY, DOUBLE-WORD BOUNDARY, FULL-WORD BOUNDARY, HALF-WORD BOUNDARY.

box   A hardware element which holds a number that can be added to (or, in some cases, subtracted from) the address portion of a computer instructon to form an effective address. See B BOX.

BPS. Basic programming support   Actually two different systems, BPS card and BPS tape, these are the simplest and smallest operating systems available for the main-line IBM 360 computers.

BPS card was the first 360 software released by IBM. It contained an assembly system, an RPG (decimal feature required), and some utility programs (core dump, etc.). No program-to-program transition or file management was included in card BPS. Every program created by BPS included its own supervisor, loader, and I/O routines, so that programs were not relocatable and no attempts at sophisticated I/O were included. However, card BPS did support 2400 series magnetic tapes and 2311 disk-pack drives. This unexpected feature was included because, for a while, card BPS was the only 360 software, and tapes and disks would have been unusable without this support. Even today, tape or disk utilities independent of any operating system are written in card BPS assembly language. Card BPS is employed today only by users having 8K of memory and neither tapes nor disks.

Tape BPS is the simplest true operating system for the 360. It requires 8K of memory, three magnetic-tape units, a card reader/punch, and a printer. Tape BPS offers an assembly program, an RPG (decimal feature required) and a tape sort/merge utility. With tape BPS, an installation can create a tape-resident library of programs, enjoy job-to-job transition via control cards, use a linking loader to unite independently written routines, and refer to I/O devices by symbolic (not absolute) device addresses. A checkpoint capability is included for restart of long programs. The I/O control routines allow limited overlap of I/O with processing, improving run efficiency. Today's tape BPS is used by installations having only 8K of core, and tapes but no disks.

Neither BPS supports FORTRAN, COBOL, PL1, AUTOTEST, etc., and neither offers much compatibility with larger operating systems.

branch One of the sets of instructions executed between two successive decision instructions.

The ability to branch, i.e., to select certain parts of the program to be executed to the exclusion of others, is one of the computer's most fascinating characteristics. Consider a program capable of checking an income tax report. Depending on his age, a taxpayer may claim one exemption if he is under 65 or two exemptions if he is 65 or over. In checking the exemptions, the program could appear as shown in the accompanying table. This is an example of pro-

Instruction location	Instruction contents
1000	PLACE AGE IN ACCUMULATOR.
1001	SUBTRACT 65.
1002	IF ACCUMULATOR IS POSITIVE, GO TO 1003; IF ACCUMULATOR IS NEGATIVE, GO TO 1005.
1003	NUMBER OF EXEMPTIONS IS 2.
1004	GO TO 1006.
1005	NUMBER OF EXEMPTIONS IS 1.
1006	(PROCEED WITH THE REST OF THE PROGRAM.)

gramming with two branches: after reaching instruction 1002, the computer will have to select branch 1003–1004 or branch 1005. Instruction 1002 is known as a branch point, or conditioned branch instruction, that is, a point in the program where more than one exit is possible (here, exit to 1003, or exit to 1005). Instructions 1003 and 1004 represent one branch leading from the branch point, instruction 1005 represents the second branch from the branch point. Instruction 1004 which causes a jump to instruction 1006 (required here to skip instruction 1005 if the taxpayer's age is 65 or over) is called an unconditional branch since the computer has no choice but to jump from instruction 1004 to instruction 1006. The branch 1002–1003 is, in contrast, called a conditional branch since it depends upon the outcome of the test in instruction 1002.

branch point A point in a program where a branch is selected, that is, a point in a flowchart or program from which more than one exit (continuation of action) is possible. Such points are represented usually by decision-type instructions. See BRANCH.

breakpoint A point in a program where an instruction, instruction digit, or other condition will enable the programmer to interrupt the run by external intervention or by a monitor routine. Breakpoints are normally used to facilitate debugging a program. When a particular instruction is executed, the program flow is interrupted, and either a monitor program or a computer operator may make an inspection of the results thus far achieved by means of a printout or some other test. A breakpoint signal is usually provided by software for a monitor interrupt and by hardware for an operator interrupt. In the latter case, a breakpoint switch is involved, that is, a switch which, when in a specific position, will cause the computer to halt after a preselected instruction is executed. For instance, after the computer stops, the operator may specify the areas to be printed or punched, and starts the dump program if this is required. When the dump program is completed, the operator will then set the computer back to the instruction following the breakpoint.

breakthrough In optical character recognition (OCR), an interruption in the intended character stroke.
  The size of a breakthrough is determined by
  1. The distance obtained at the point where the broken lines come closest to meeting (dimension A), measured parallel to the direction of the line, and
  2. The distance between the closest points on each side of final breakthrough at which the inked area crosses either average edge (dimension B), also measured parallel to the direction of the line.

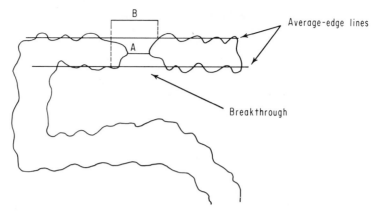

Example of breakthrough.

Breakthroughs may accrue to both printed and handwritten characters owing to imperfections in the paper. More commonly, they are the result of the human element employed in OCR handwriting transcription. Accordingly, OCR information coders are cautioned to join all lines and close all loops.

Breakthroughs of sufficient number and size are cause for character rejection; individual hardware manufacturers will specify what these limitations are.

brightness   In character recognition, the average reflectance of paper measured in relation to a standard surface.

The reference surfaces utilized in the measurement of brightness are usually those consisting of magnesium oxide or magnesium carbonate. Other surfaces that have been utilized, mainly because of their greater durability, include the plastic chip or ceramic tile. However, these latter surfaces should be checked regularly for yellowing or other changes.

Other considerations for measuring brightness include:

1. Standard geometrical features.

2. Opacity. Generally, the test paper should be backed by a small pile of similar sheets since most papers are not completely opaque.

3. Type of lighting. The light used in measuring brightness should be similar to that which will be encountered in an optical scan.

This foremost optical property concerns itself with the future interaction of the paper itself and the images to be inscribed. Contrast with BACKGROUND REFLECTANCE which is reflectance of ink-free areas at the time of input recognition.

buffer   A storage device used to compensate for a difference in data handling rates when transmitting data from one device to another.

As a storage device, a buffer is used to hold data between the time when the data become available and the time when the data are required.   Suppose that an input tape is to be read.   If the program issues a READ command and has to wait for the tape to be read, valuable time is wasted while waiting for tape to pass over the head. However, if the first record of the tape has already been read into a buffer, the READ command simply moves the first record into an active storage area and, as a by-product, initiates a second READ command which reads the second record from tape into the buffer which has been emptied of the previous record.   This permits the computer to operate on the first record while, simultaneously, the tape being in motion, it reads the second record from the tape, before this record is actually needed.   As an isolating circuit to prevent interaction between two given circuits, a buffer is usually a one-transistor amplifier.

The function of the buffer may be performed by a specially constructed hardware device, but it is more commonly carried out by an area of main memory, set aside for that purpose by the current program.

built-in check   An error-detecting mechanism provided by the hardware requiring no program or operator attention until an error is actually discovered.   See AUTOMATIC CHECK.

bus   A conductor used in the transmission of signals or energy.   A single or multiple parallel paths for power or data signals to which several devices may be connected at the same time.   A bus may have one source of supply and several sources of demand, or several sources of supply and one source of demand.   Buses with multiple sources of supply and multiple sources of demand are less frequent.   A memory bus connects a storage element to all devices that require access to core, that is, devices such as the central processing unit (CPU), input/ output (I/O) channels, internal timers, etc.   A large-scale computer may have several memory buses connected to all devices, so that an unoccupied bus can be used for transmission of data even though some other data are flowing between other pairs of devices.   A power bus is a collection of heavy cables making available power supplies (of typically +20 volts, +6 volts, 0 volts or ground return, and −6 volts) to all units of a computer.

business data processing   Loosely, the data processing for business purposes, such as the routine financial transactions of a business.

Also called commercial data processing, and just plain data processing. Data processing can be broadly divided into on-line data processing in which the data processing is carried out in about the same time as the time required by the process being controlled, and off-line data processing in which control of the process may occur after the process has taken place. Airline reservations are an example of on-line data processing: an agent dealing with a customer must have an immediate reply to his inquiry regarding the availability of a seat after specifying date, flight number, and origination-destination cities. The reservation of such a seat updates the memory banks, thus closing the feedback circuit. If the system is fully automatic at all stages of the game, it is known as a closed-loop system. If human actions are required for data gathering or to complete certain control instructions, the system is known as an open-loop system. Oil company credit cards are an example of off-line data processing. The amount of money involved for each customer is small on a daily basis, and gathering the slips from service stations imposes a lag between sales and recording.

byte   A string of binary digits, usually shorter than a word, operated on as a unit. Loosely speaking, a byte is one character of data: it is the smallest division of memory that can be accessed as a unit by the computer, usually a character in length or a portion of a memory word in length. In computers that are not provided with character-accessing instructions, a byte is a subfield within a data word which contains one character of data. A programmer may very well define a byte for some specific purpose in his work.

In the majority of cases, a byte is 8 bits long. A 6-bit byte is commonly called a character, and a 4-bit byte is usually called a digit.

byte boundary   Any core address within the computer in the IBM 360 System.

C

CAL Acronym for Conversational Algebraic Language, a higher-level language, developed by the University of California especially for time-sharing purposes.

Using CAL, a user sits at his remote-console typewriter and is directly connected to the computer. He can work out and solve his mathematical problems on-line with considerable help from the computer. In many cases, CAL will identify errors and provide examples to illustrate the proper format required.

CAL programs consist of a series of steps. The entire set of steps constitute a program, which may be executed once and destroyed or saved for future use at the discretion of the user.

CAL provides for arithmetic operations, conditional expressions, editing capabilities, and manipulation of data files.

Numbers may be expressed as integers, in floating-point form, or in scientific notation, and variables may be subscripted with an unlimited number of levels.

Variables may be assigned values using the SET command. CAL allows individual commands to be executed, acting like a powerful

desk calculator. This is accomplished using the TYPE command.
For example, the sequence

```
> SET A = 3
> SET B = 4
> SET C = A + B
> TYPE A, B, C
```

results in the computer printing out

```
A = 3
B = 4
C = 7
```

To write a program in CAL, each step is numbered, and a beginning
statement is indicated. The following is a small sample program
to calculate the hypotenuse of a right triangle.

```
>2.1   DEMAND A, B
>2.2   SET C = SQRT (A ↑ 2 + B ↑ 2)
>2.3   TYPE A, B, C
>2.4   TO STEP 2.1
> TO STEP  2.1
```

The computer will then ask for values for A and B:

```
A = 3
B = 4
```

The 3 and 4 are supplied by the operator.
The computer then types:

```
A = 3
B = 4
C = 5
```

The computer will continue to execute this program until told
not to.

CAL allows statements to be deleted or added, thus simplifying
program debugging. Saving the program for future use is made easy
by typing LOAD. Thus CAL maly be used to do either relatively
simple one-time calculations or more complex repetitively used programs.

The following is an example of calculating compound interest
using CAL:

PLEASE LOGIN! 1234JKL; JONES Cr	PLEASE LOGIN! is printed by the computer. All underlined words are computer-printed. Nonunderlined words are user-typed-in. User identification is account number, a password, and user's name. Cr is the carriage return key and terminates a line.
READY 5/22 14:20 Cr	This indicates that the computer is ready to communicate. The date and time are printed.
—CAL Cr	This indicates to the computer that the CAL language is desired.
CAL (Version no. Date) Cr	This indicates that CAL is ready to accept program statements.
NUMBER OF STEPS = 20 Cr	CAL asks for the approximate number of program steps. In this case the user enters 20.
TITLE: Cr	CAL asks for the title of the program.
INTEREST CALCULATION Cr (seven lines are skipped)	The title is typed in.
INTEREST CALCULATION P 1 Cr	CAL repeats the title together with a page number.
> 1.1 DEMAND P, R, Y Cr	This statement sets up the three variables P, R, and Y. We will let P = principal, R = yearly rate, and Y = number of years. The command is to ask the user for values for the three variables.

> 1.2 SET V = P * (1 + R/200.000) ↑ (2. 0 * Y) Cr	This sets V for value at the final value of the deposited money. The ↑ symbol means exponentiation. In this example, interest is compounded semiannually.
> 1.3 TYPE P, R, Y, V Cr	This informs CAL to type the three entered factors and the computed value of the money.
> 1.4 TO STEP 1.1 Cr	This is a branch to statement 1.1. This causes the program to execute continuously.
> TO STEP 1.1 Cr	The absence of a statement number indicates that this is a command to CAL rather than a program statement. Execution now begins at statement 1.1.
P = 100.00 Cr R̄ = 6.0 Cr Ȳ = 2.0 Cr	As per the DEMAND statement, the value of P is requested, followed by R and Y.
P = 100.00 Cr R = 6.0 Cr Y = 2.0 Cr V = 112.550881 Cr	The program calculates V, then goes to the TYPE statement and proceeds to type P, R, Y, and V.
P =	After the TYPE command, a go to was encountered which caused execution to begin all over again, demanding a value for P. Execution may be terminated by pressing the ESC Key.
> (ESC) (ESC)	Log out begins by pressing the escape key twice.

—LOGOUT Cr	The user indicates that he wishes to log out by typing LOGOUT followed by carriage return.
TIME USED hours: minutes	The computer then prints the time used in hours and minutes, which completes the log out.

calculator   A device capable of performing arithmetic, with frequent manual intervention, but capable of carrying out logic and arithmetic digital operations of any kind.   In contrast to computers, a calculator is incapable of guiding itself, and must be directed at almost every step by the operator.   Calculators are usually mechanical or electro-mechanical devices.   Electronic and even pneumatic calculators are now becoming current.

call   To transfer control to a specified closed subroutine.   When writing a program it may occur that a certain action may have to be repeated frequently.   For instance, in extracting the square root of a number, the programmer faces two choices: he may establish a sequence of instructions to perform this operation, and insert the instructions in the program every time the square-root extraction is required (this sequence of instructions is called an open subroutine); or he may elect to write this sequence of instructions once and for all, and leave them out of the main program—in this case he has a closed subroutine—.   In the latter case, when the computer executes the program and reaches a point where a square root must be extracted, the program calls the subroutine.   Actually, the subroutine is not called, but control of the computer passes from the main program to the subroutine, and once the instructions in the subroutine are executed, returns to the main program at a specified point.   A closed subroutine may be called from as many points in the program as required.   Schematically, calling a subroutine will appear as illustrated in the accompanying figure.

The subroutine's final action, passing control back to the program that called it, is known as a return.   Almost all modern digital computers have an instruction designed specifically for efficient calling of subroutines.   Usually this instruction transfers control to a designated instruction (the start of the subroutine) and leaves the address of the calling instruction (sometimes: the instruction after the calling instruction) in a known location.   In computers having index registers the address of the calling instruction is usually inserted into a specific index register. This makes it very simple to return or to obtain the addresses of arguments.

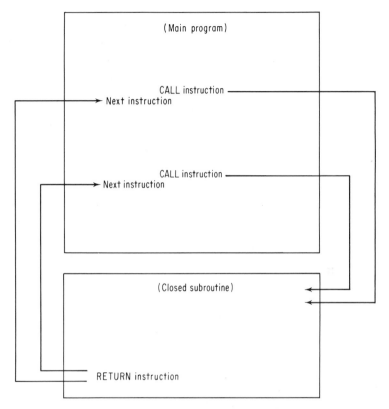

Calling a subroutine.

A subroutine can itself call another subroutine, and this process may be extended to any finite depth. Very great complexity may thus be built with relatively few computer instructions.

See CALLING SEQUENCE.

calling sequence A specific sequence of instructions to set up and call a given subroutine. Besides calling the subroutine and making available the data required by it, the calling sequence tells the computer where to return after the subroutine is executed. Consider, for instance, a program in which a set of pairs of values alpha and beta are repeatedly obtained from raw data, and which are eventually converted in some way by a long sequence of operations. Instead of programming the conversion instructions for every alpha and beta, the programmer writes a conversion subroutine. The calling sequence calls (that is, it causes execution to be transferred to) the subroutine, tells it where to find the current alpha and beta, and at

Main program	
Instruction location	instruction
. . . .	. . . . .
800	STORE ALPHA IN LOCATION 6001.
801	STORE ADDRESS PART OF 800 IN LOCATION 1002.
. . . .	. . . . .
998	STORE BETA IN LOCATION 6002.
999	STORE ADDRESS PART OF 998 IN LOCATION 1003.
1000	LOAD LOCATION 1000 INTO AC.
1001	GO TO 9000.
1002	(ADDRESS OF ALPHA) 6001.
1003	(ADDRESS OF BETA) 6002.
1004	(MAIN PROGRAM SEQUENCE).
. . . .	. . . . .
Subroutine	
9000	ADD 2 TO AC.
9001	STORE ADDRESS PART OF AC IN 9015.
9002	ADD 1 TO AC.
9003	STORE ADDRESS PART OF AC IN 9066.
9004	ADD 1 TO AC.
9005	STORE ADDRESS PART OF AC IN 9100.
. . . .	. . . . .
9015	(OPERATE ON ALPHA) 6001.
. . . .	. . . . .
9066	(OPERATE ON BETA) 6002.
. . . .	. . . . .
9100	GO TO 1004.

A calling sequence. (Instructions 1000 through 1003 are the calling sequence.)

which point to return control to the main program.   This technique is illustrated in the accompanying figure.

Instructions 1000 through 1003 form the calling sequence.   Instruction 1000 loads itself in the AC and enables the addresses of the addresses of alpha and beta to be readily accessible since 1002 and 1003 can be known relative to 1000.   In the same way, location 1004 can be calculated as point of return.   The next time an alpha and beta are calculated, the calling sequence may be as shown in the following table:

Main program	
Instruction location	Instruction
. . . . .	. . . . .
2224	LOAD LOCATION 2224 INTO AC.
2225	GO TO 9000.
2226	(ADDRESS OF ALPHA) 7461.
2227	(ADDRESS OF BETA) 7477.
2228	(MAIN PROGRAM SEQUENCE).
. . . . .	. . . . .

The subroutine will again locate the new pair alpha and beta and after execution return control, this time, to instruction 2228.   It can be assumed, for instance, in this example, that the subroutine stores the converted values alpha and beta where the unconverted values were first placed.   If the unconverted values are to be kept, then the new values could be stored elsewhere, and the addresses of these locations stored in predetermined locations relative to the reentry point.

capacity   See STORAGE CAPACITY.

card   An information-carrying medium, common to practically all computers, for the introduction of data and instructions into the computers either directly or indirectly.   See MAGNETIC CARD, PUNCHED CARD, TAPE TO CARD.

card hopper   A device that holds cards and makes them available to a card-feed mechanism.   Except for one-card-at-a-time devices, all card machines are fed from a hopper.   Synonymous with input magazine.   Contrast with CARD STACKER.

card image   A one-to-one representation of the contents of a punched card, such as a matrix in which a 1 represents a hole and a 0 represents the absence of a hole.   A card image is the representation of the information contained on one punched card in any other data recording medium, for instance, as 80 character records on a magnetic tape or a disk.   A card image may be generated by reading a punch card and used as input to a computer program, or may be generated by a computer and used to punch a card at a later time. For example, powerful computers with limited multiprogramming ability (the faster second-generation machines) would be slowed down considerably if they had to read and punch actual cards.   A significant increase in speed is achieved by reading and writing card images on the powerful computer and using an inexpensive peripheral support computer to punch and read the actual physical cards.

card stacker   An output device that accumulates punched cards in a deck.   As an output queuing device for a card handling machine, a card stacker ensures the correct sequencing of emerging cards. Contrast with CARD HOPPER.

card-to-disk conversion   A straightforward operation which consists in loading the data in a deck of cards onto a disk by means of a utility program.   See CARD IMAGE.

card-to-tape conversion   A straightforward operation which consists in loading the data in a deck of cards onto a magnetic tape by means of a utility program.   See CARD IMAGE.

carriage   A mechanism designed to hold a paper in the active portion of a printing or typing device, as for example, a typewriter carriage.   See AUTOMATIC CARRIAGE.

carriage return   The operation that causes the next character to be printed at the extreme left margin.   This operation usually advances to the next line at the same time.   Carriage return is also the term applied to the button or lever which initiates this operation; it also refers to the non-data control character causing the carriage-return operation to be performed as in computer typing and teletype transmissions.

cascaded carry   A carry process in which the addition of two numerals results in a partial sum numeral and a carry numeral which are in turn added together, this process being repeated until no new carries are generated.   A cascaded carry is best illustrated by an example:

	Decimal			Binary	
	39	Augend		100111	
	+ 18	Addend	+	10010	
1st step	47	Partial sum		110101	1st step
	+ 10	Carry	+	000100	
2nd step	57	Partial sum		110001	2nd step
	00	Carry	+	001000	
		Partial sum		111001	3rd step
		Carry		000000	

This addition process ends when the carry is zero in any base (or radix) arithmetic. A similar process takes place during multiplication (which is repeated addition combined with left shifts). Contrast with HIGH-SPEED CARRY.

catalog

1. All the indexes to data sets or files in a system.
2. (Sometimes) the index to all other indexes, the master index.
3. To add an entry to an index, or to build an entire new index.

A modern data processing center has a very large amount of machine-readable information to keep track of. The computer can assist in this chore by maintaining hierarchies of successively finer (more detailed) indexes in which the location and identification of each data set (data file) can be found. It is usually only the lowest-level index (most detailed) that contains the exact location of an item. This permits updating only one index when an item or data set is moved. Generally, the volume on which the data resides contains this lowest-level index, often in the form of a volume table of contents (VTOC). If the data set has its own index for internal organization, this is the finest level of indexing and also usually resides on the same volume.

In general, a catalog or index is an alphabetic list of names of data sets or files, with a location indicator (next level of index, volume, or location within a volume) and possibly other descriptive information (kind or type of data, creation date, quantity of data, etc.). The catalog is itself a data set, with all of the properties of data sets except one: The catalog is not listed in the catalog. (If you could find the entry you would not need it.)

Other files may also be uncataloged, but these are often temporary, private, and/or secret, or punched-card files unsuitable for cataloging. See INDEXED SEQUENTIAL DATA SET, PARTITIONED DATA SET.

cataloged procedure   A group of control cards (job control language) statements) that has been placed in a cataloged data set.

Job control language is powerful and flexible, offering many options and alternatives to the user. The price of this flexibility is the obligation to specify which options are desired. The result is that many, many specifications must be given to describe even a simple job. To avoid having to submit the same large set of control cards every time a job is run, it is possible to catalog a set of control cards as a cataloged procedure, and invoke the effect of these cards by using a single // EXEC card to call the cataloged procedure. Then all jobs of a similar nature can be submitted, using this condensed form of job description.

An installation can catalog a set of standard procedures for every type of commonly used job, and thus obtain convenience, standardization, and relative freedom from error.

When an EXEC card names a cataloged procedure, the indicated set of control cards is retrieved from a direct-access device and used to control the processing of the next one or more job steps. If a particular run differs in a few details from the general-purpose cataloged procedure, it is possible to override parts of the cataloged procedure by including explicit control cards after the // EXEC card. This overriding changes the execution of this job only, and does not alter the contents of the cataloged procedure as it resides on auxiliary storage.

Reductions in control card volume of 20 to 1 are not uncommon. This is reasonable because short procedures are not worth the bother of cataloging, and procedures longer than 40 to 50 cards are uncommon.

cell Generally, a cell is a storage or memory location capable of containing one character, one byte, or one word. The capacity is defined by the natural storage unit of the computer under consideration. See BINARY CELL, STORAGE CELL.

centerline See STROKE CENTERLINE.

central processing unit The part of a computer containing the circuits required to interpret and execute the instructions. Usually called the CPU.

In general, the CPU performs the following functions:

1. Keep track of the location of the instruction being executed in a location, or program counter.

2. Fetch the instructions from memory and interpret, or decode these instructions.

3. Execute the instructions by using the corresponding arithmetical, logical, testing, and shifting hardware units.

4. Direct the I/O (i.e., the input/output) hardware when I/O instructions are encountered in the program.

The CPU may contain high-speed registers to be used for computation, address modification, or other such purposes. The CPU may contain equally error-detecting circuits to catch certain types of errors.

In general, a computer can execute simultaneously as many programs as there are CPU's available on that computer.

chad   The piece of material removed when forming a hole or notch in a punched tape or punched cards.   The word chad is both singular and plural.

chadded   Pertaining to the punching of tape which results in chad being formed.   Chadded describes a punched paper tape from which the material punched from the holes has been completely removed. Contrast with CHADLESS.

chadless   Characteristic of a paper tape from which chad does not result.   A chadless tape is a tape in which the holes are made by achieving an incomplete circular cut and folding the resulting flap of material under the tape.   Chadless tape eliminates the requirement of chad removal, but the chadless tape is not acceptable by every type of tape reader.   Moreover, the folded-back flaps increase the effective thickness of the tape, reducing the capacity of a given reel or spool by more than 50 percent.

channel   A path along which signals can be sent, such as data channels, output channels, or the portion of a storage medium that is accessible to a given reading station.   In modern computers, a data channel is a hardware device designed to carry out input/output (I/O) operations.   It is considered an integral part of the computer and not part of the attached peripheral equipment.

A basic central processing unit (CPU) normally performs only one of three functions at one time: reading, processing, writing.   Concurrent, or overlapping, operations, that is, handling two or more of these functions at the same time, reduce processing time: modern computers have data channels for reading and writing functions, that is, for input and output controls.   A data channel compensates for differences in speed between I/O and processing speeds.   A programmer dealing with a data-channel computer issues a WRITE instruction: the CPU sets up the proper controls for writing, and while the slow writing operation sequence takes place, the CPU can carry on high-speed processing operations.   A data channel has the following properties: (1) It is started, tested and directed by the CPU under program control.   It will stop itself when finished or may be stopped by the CPU.   (2) It executes its own input/output control and transfer commands, and in this way has the flexibility of stored program devices. (3) It selects, activates, and passes data to or from an attached I/O device or I/O device controller to or from the main memory of the computer. (4) It operates without constant supervision of the main program but simultaneously with it. There are two main types of data channel: the selector channel which operates one I/O device at a time and handles any data required by the I/O device; the multiplexor channel which operates several I/O devices at the same time and executes a separate program for each device. A multiplexor channel replaces a collection of slower selector channels at a lower cost. See DATA CHANNEL.

character   An elementary mark used to represent data. A character is usually in the form of a graphic spatial arrangement of connected or adjacent strokes. These definitions refer mainly to optical character recognition. In computers, a character is a small collection of adjacent bits used to represent a piece of data, addressed and handled as a unit. A character is essentially an elementary division of the main memory. It is often used in the same way as byte.

The most common characters used in EDP are the alphabetic characters, and the numeric digits. Other characters represent selected punctuation marks and special symbols (e.g., $, #, @, /, . . .) or serve as control information (e.g., group mark, carriage return).

See BLANK CHARACTER, BYTE, CHECK CHARACTER, CONTROL CHARACTER, ESCAPE CHARACTER, SPECIAL CHARACTER.

character boundary   In character recognition, a real or imaginary rectangle which serves as the delimiter between consecutive characters and/or successive lines on a source document.

In some cases, as with handwritten data inscription, the boundaries are of constant size and are visible on the coding sheet; in others, the boundaries are of various sizes and are associated with the varying character dimensions on a particular type font.

Manufacturers may use character boundaries for different reasons such as determining the amount of background reflectance required for unique character identification, or defining the extent to which character misregistration will be tolerated.

character emitter   In character recognition, an electromechanical device which conveys a specimen character in the form of a timed pulse or group of pulses.

Physically, a character emitter is a component part of the property detector of a character reader. As such its function is to convert a normalized character, which possesses deterministic qualities, into a form that can be recognized by the decision mechanism.

The emitted character may be a waveform (analog) or a digital representation to be matched for validity against the item read.

character misregistration In character recognition, the improper state of appearance of a character, on site in a character reader, with respect to a real or imaginary horizontal base line.

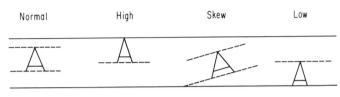

Normal   High   Skew   Low

Character misregistration.

Character misregistration takes the form of character high, character low, or character skew. During the reading process, if character misregistration occurs, then a normalizing routine will be performed to pull down, push up, or "twist" the character in an attempt to remove it to its intended position. Compare with MISREGISTRATION, CHARACTER SKEW.

character outline In character recognition, the graphic pattern formed by the stroke edges of a printed or handwritten character.

Also, that graphic pattern which serves as a replica of any character of a particular type font. In this latter sense, all valid character outlines may reside on a font reticle within those readers which utilize certain mask-matching techniques. In these cases, font reticles are used to determine whether the input character shape conforms to the outline shown on the reticle, and also to ascertain whether the character stroke width falls within the acceptable range.

character reader In character recognition, any device capable of locating, identifying, and translating into machine code handwritten or printed data appearing on a source document.

Character readers serve as a high-speed input device for an electronic data processing (EDP) system, as they have effectively eliminated card keypunching and verifying of input data in many cases. The process of compiling or assembling programs can also bypass the card stage, as some readers are capable of digesting handwritten coding sheets.

Character readers, which may be connected on-line to an EDP system or off-line to various output media, have been conventionally separated into four component parts in order to facilitate discussions of various component techniques. The scanner, normalizer, property detector, and decision mechanism may be termed "black boxes," but in no way do they exist independently.

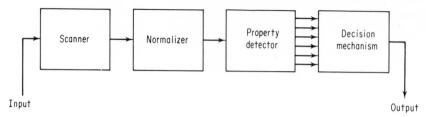

A character reader: component parts.

The scanner converts the presented character into a suitable electrical signal. The normalizer modifies the signal in order to obtain a standardized version, from which the property detector extracts a set of characteristic properties. The decision mechanism then examines the properties and determines the character's most probable identity.

character recognition   The area of computer technology devoted to the automatic handling and conversion of printed or handwritten data into machine language.

Character recognition attempts to achieve the fastest and most reliable method of obtaining a discrete signal for each input character, thereby eliminating costly and time-consuming keypunching operations.

The success of the various character-recognition systems to date has depended on many factors, the foremost of which are the scanning methods employed, the document handling system, and those paper and print qualities which affect the character as laid down.

See OPTICAL CHARACTER RECOGNITION (OCR) and MAGNETIC-INK CHARACTER RECOGNITION (MICR).

character skew   In character recognition, a form of character misregistration, inasmuch as the image to be recognized appears in a "twisted" condition with respect to a real or imaginary horizontal base line.

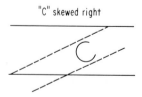
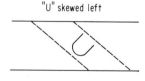

Character skew.

Character skew is tolerated and correctible to a certain degree, primarily insofar as it doesn't begin to resemble another character in its own misregistered state. For example, a handwritten C skewed right at a certain point begins to resemble a U skewed left. Compare with CHARACTER MISREGISTRATION.

character stroke See STROKE.

character style In character recognition, a distinctive construction that is common to all members of a particular character set. Character styles of varying sizes are proportional in all respects.

check Test necessary to detect certain types of mistakes. There are, in the computer field, two types of mistakes: mistakes such as illegal operation codes, I/O instructions for devices not present, which will cause the computer to halt; and mistakes such as wrong data, wrong transfer addresses, which will not cause the computer to halt. Checks are required to detect those mistakes which would otherwise permit the computer to proceed uninterrupted. Some checks, such as the checks required to test for erroneous input data, can become quite complicated. Other checks, such as are required to ensure that the program carries out the needed operation, although at times elaborate, are routine. See AUTOMATIC CHECK, BUILT-IN CHECK, DUPLICATION CHECK, ECHO CHECK, MODULO N CHECK, ODD-EVEN CHECK, PARITY CHECK, PROGRAMMED CHECK, RESIDUE CHECK, SELF-CHECKING CODE, SUMMATION CHECK.

check bit A binary check digit. This binary check digit is an extra bit added to a character so as to verify that the equipment has not gained or dropped a bit. The value of the check bit is 1 or 0, depending on the manufacturer. If the character 5 is represented by 011000, the check bit can have a value of 1, and be called an odd-parity bit (since there will be now an odd value of 1's in this character), or it can have a value of 0 and be called an even-parity bit (since there will now be an even number of 1's in the character), and the character five will appear as 1011000 or 0011000. Bearing in mind that characters appear as successive columns on a tape, longitudinal check bits (or longitudinal parity bits) can appear at the end of the word, thus diminishing the probabilities of undetected errors. The equipment will flag a word whose parity bits do not match the word's bit makeup. For instance, the word "1967" in excess-three code could appear as shown in the table.

Name	1	9	6	7	Longitudinal parity bit
Parity bit channel	0	1	1	1	1
Zone channels	0	0	0	0	0
	1	1	1	1	0
Number channels	0	1	1	1	1
	1	1	0	0	0
	0	0	0	1	1
	0	0	1	0	1

Even-parity check.

or as:

Name	1	9	6	7	Longitudinal parity bit
Parity bit channel	1	0	0	0	0
Zone channels	0	0	0	0	1
	1	1	1	1	1
Number channels	0	1	1	1	0
	1	1	0	0	1
	0	0	0	1	0
	0	0	1	0	0

Odd-parity check.

Check bits reduce the capacity of a circuit. For instance, assume that a circuit has the capacity to accept 35 six-bit characters per second. If the user cannot tolerate errors, check bits are added and the circuit capacity drops to 30 seven-bit characters per second. As a matter of fact, the capacity of the channel will drop below 30 seven-bit characters per second since detected errors will automatically stop, and hence slow down the equipment. See CHECK CHARACTER.

check character A character used to perform a check. This character contains only the information required to verify that the group of preceding characters is correct. For example, a check character could be generated so that the sum of all the characters in a block (including the check character) is equal to zero. In such a sum, carries are ignored. If at a later time in the process the sum of the characters is not zero, an error is then indicated. With this information, recovery of most error conditions is possible.

Check characters are frequently written at the end of tape records and are then sometimes called longitudinal check characters. Economics is the leading consideration in selecting the method of generating check characters.   Consequently, there are a number of ways in which check characters are produced in existing equipment.   See CHECK BIT.

check digit   A digit used to perform a check.   A check digit conveys only the information that the number to which it is attached is correct.   There are a number of ways in which a check digit could be formed.   For instance, a digit could be affixed on a decimal machine so that the augmented number is an exact multiple of 9:   thus, the number 3842 would become 3842 − 1.   The digit 1 is the check digit.   The number 3862 would have 8 as a check digit: 3862 − 8. This procedure would be similar to casting out nines, a check often performed with manual calculations.   The sum of the digits of such a number (which includes the check digit) would then be a multiple of 9, and would thus be reduced to zero were the digit-summing carried out to a one-digit final result.   The above example would not be of much use as it stands since 3862, 3682, 3268, 3286, etc., would have the same check digit.   More elaborate systems are in use, such as multiplying each digit by the corresponding digit of a fixed sequence, and then forming the check digit such that the new number is an even multiple of some fixed number.

checkpoint   A place in a routine where a check is performed, or where data are recorded for restart purposes.

A difference is made in practice between *checkpoint* (one word) and *check point* (two words).

By check point is meant a part of the routine where a test is carried out to verify that the operation is being performed correctly. When malfunctions do occur, it is far more probable that they will take place in input/output operations than in processor operations. In input operations tapes will be reread two or more times if the first reading does not pass the parity test; cards will be read from two stations and the data accepted only if no discrepancy is found. In output operations the tape or cards may be written and immediately reread and echo-checked against memory or buffer where the same information is located.   Such checks are hardware check over which the programmer has no control.   In processor operations the programmer can introduce check points in his program: the test can involve simultaneous identical operations along two paths and a test for equality of results, or it can consist in a repeat of the operation and a comparison of the two results.

By checkpoint is meant a part of the routine at which the entire state of the computer (memory, registers, etc.) is written out on auxiliary storage (tape, disk, cards).   If the program is to be restarted later, the contents of the auxiliary storage are read back into the computer and restarted. The program begins anew at the point following the checkpoint-creating routine. The record so written is called a checkpoint record. If a computer malfunction occurred during a lengthy run and checkpoints had been taken before the malfunction, then only that portion of the run after the last checkpoint would have to be repeated. The saving in time to be expected must be weighed against the cost of writing checkpoints that may not be needed. The computer routine used for writing checkpoints is sometimes called a checkpoint routine.

circuit A means of two-way communication between two points, consisting of "go" and "return" channels.

In computer hardware, a circuit is a small collection of elementary devices (wires, resistors, transistors, etc.) which accomplish a specific function. For instance, a timing circuit, an AND circuit. Contrast with CHANNEL.

circulating register A shift register in which data move out of one end of the register and reenter into the other end as in a closed loop. Such an operation performed on the contents of the register is called a circular shift.

Some memory registers are circulating registers, several words in length. When a particular word is required, the copying of the word begins only when the bits making up the word reach the end of the register and are being sent to the other end of the register. Such a memory device is usually called a delay-line memory.

clause A part of the statement in the COBOL language. A clause may describe the structure of an elementary item, or it may give initial values to items in independent and group work areas, or it may redefine data previously defined by another clause. See COBOL.

clear To place a storage device into a specific state usually consisting of zeros or blanks. Equally, to fill a binary cell with zeros.

Clearing storage devices is part of the production work of a data processing center.

For instance, required areas are filled with blanks before a file is loaded into disk storage (some character will be used to indicate unused locations when a track is read from the disk): the program required for this type of servie is called a utility program. In this specific instance, the program is called a clear disk-storage utility program. Although, as a rule, writing a word in memory erases whatever word was there previously, there may be occasions when a programmer wishes to have an area in core memory cleared. Such a routine is established by the programmer and inserted, where required, in the main program.

clear area   In optical character recognition (OCR), any area designated to be kept free of printing or any other extraneous markings.

clear band   In character recognition, a continuous horizontal strip of blank paper which must be obtained between consecutive code lines on a source document. Individual manufacturers prescribe what should be the minimum width of this strip.

clock   A device that generates periodic signals used for synchronization.

To coordinate a synchronous computer, the clock emits uniformly spaced pulses along special timing signal paths. As a device measuring time, the clock is a register accessible to the programmer and contains time information which is automatically updated by the hardware at regular intervals. The programmer may test (and usually initialize) the internal clock to determine the length of time required by a certain part of his program.

closed shop   A data processing center so organized that only professional programmers and operators have access to the center to meet the needs of the users.

In a closed shop, each client or user must explain his wants and needs to the data processing center analyst or programmer. Consequently, the user must accept the data processing center design and feasibility decisions and can do no more than guide the problem-solving effort.

The closed-shop organization permits professional-caliber people to make efficient use of the hardware facilities, but it occurs at times that incomplete communicaton between client and data processing center personnel results in less-than-optimum solutions (and sometimes, useless results) from the client's point of view.

Closed shops are easily scheduled and controlled because a known and constant group of individuals, professionally trained, are involved and unpredictable situations are minimized. There is no need for the client to acquire computing skills, but the data processing center personnel may have to learn about the client's departmental and professional problems.

Closed-shop organizations are ideally suited for long-term projects and complex programs which must be run and updated continuously. In such an environment, professional and disciplined systems design and implementation will achieve the most efficient use of facilities. There will be time for full communication to be established between data processing department and the various departments involved in the long-term project, high standards of documentation are arrived at and maintained, and jobs of little or no value can be rejected to allow important work to get done.

The advantages of a closed-shop operation can be briefly summarized as:

1. Efficient utilization of resources
2. Efficient control of scheduling, priority, and discipline
3. Accurate budgeting of each task through precise cost allocation
4. No need for clients to acquire computing skills

Such advantages are of necessity acquired at a cost that represents the disadvantages of a closed-shop operation. These disadvantages may be summarized as:

1. Lack of a complete understanding of a user's problem
2. Less-than-optimum solution for some small problems
3. Professional time used to understand departmental problems
4. Uneconomical solution of one-shot programs
5. Resentment of company personnel at being denied free access to facilities and opportunity to learn something about computers
6. Consequent slow growth of acceptance of the data processing center capabilities by the rest of the company.

See OPEN SHOP.

closed subroutine   A subroutine that can be stored outside the main routine and can be connected to it by linkages at one or more locations.

A closed subroutine is compact and unified, and consists of a nearly self-contained set of computer instructions designed to accomplish a specific task such as calculating a transcendental function, extracting a square root, or sorting a set of values. It may be called in by the main program as many times as required, and will return execution to the main program after its purpose is accomplished. In this fashion, the set of required instructions appears in only one location in memory, although it may be called for execution more than once.

Subroutines are usually prepared by expert programmers and maintained in a subroutine library: They may be kept on tape, drum, or disk if they exceed core storage. Consequently, a programmer may reduce his program in certain cases to little more than calling sequences, that is, a series of jump instructions to guide the program from one subroutine to another. A calling sequence in the main program supplies certain facts needed by the subroutine, such as where data to be operated on are located, and where to return execu-

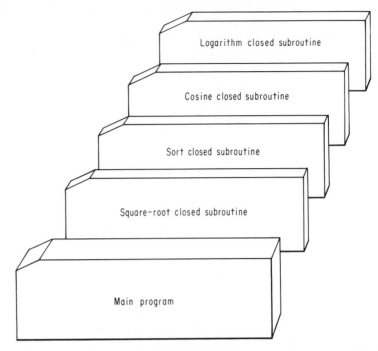

Logarithm closed subroutine

Cosine closed subroutine

Sort closed subroutine

Square-root closed subroutine

Main program

Main program deck and closed-subroutine decks.

tion in the main program: in addition, the contents of some registers may have to be saved for the return. Closed subroutines are
basically independent of the main program, can be stored in any
desired sequence, and need not even be in contiguous locations.

See CALL. Contrast with OPEN SUBROUTINE.

COBOL   A procedure-oriented language used in programming commercial and business problems: COBOL is an acronym for common
business-oriented language.

COBOL was developed by the Conference of Data Systems Lan-
guages (CODASYL) in 1959, and has been maintained and revised
since then. It provides full facilities for describing the program
(IDENTIFICATION DIVISION), the computer it is to be run on
(ENVIRONMENT DIVISION), the data formats and files it will use
(DATA DIVISION), and the operations to be performed on the data
(PROCEDURE DIVISION). These four divisions must be included
in that order in all programs.

COBOL allows for great flexibility in describing data and operations. For instance, a field called STATISTICS may be divided into

subfields called AGE, MARITAL STATUS, BIRTHPLACE; MARI-TAL STATUS can be made to take on the values SINGLE, MAR-RIED, DIVORCED, while AGE will take a numerical value, and BIRTHPLACE receives an alphabetical value. Yet, this complete heterogeneous record can be moved from one area to another storage area by a single MOVE verb referring to the name STATISTICS. If another area, DATA, has subfields called AGE and BIRTHPLACE, it is possible to move like-named items and ignore all others by simply writing a MOVE CORRESPONDING verb. Some versions of COBOL have their flexibility increased even further by the addition of REPORT GENERATOR, SORT, and assembly-language features. Such optional features allow for the generation of multiple reports and summaries, sorting data and resuming the flow of the program, and in writing any possible machine action beyond the scope of the pure COBOL language.

The extreme flexibility of COBOL has a price: A considerable amount of writing is required in setting up a program, and compile time is relatively slow. However, a COBOL program is easily read, even by a nonprofessional programmer on account of its similarity to English. In recent years, COBOL has been used as a bridge to execute programs on successive computers as computer centers replace old equipment by new. This is entirely feasible owing to the machine-independent characteristics of the language. If, for instance, capital growth at compounded interest were to be calculated (see ALGOL, FORTRAN examples) a program in COBOL could be made to appear as shown in the accompanying table.

COBOL program	Explanatory comments
IDENTIFICATION DIVISION.	Identifies the beginning of the identification division of the program.
PROGRAM—ID. 'EXAMPLE'.	Names this particular program.
AUTHOR. JANE—DOE—CODER.	Names the author of this program. Other statements may be included in the identification division, for instance, SECURITY . . . , DATE COMPILED . . . , etc. The identification division does not affect the compiler or the program: it is required solely for identification purposes.

ENVIRONMENT DIVISION.	Start of the environment division of this program.
CONFIGURATION SECTION.	The configuration section identifies the hardware used for compiling and executing the program.
SOURCE – COMPUTER. DESK CALCULATOR.	An implementation-dependent statement to identify the computer configuration used to compile.
OBJECT – COMPUTER. DESK CALCULATOR.	An implementation-dependent statement to identify the computer configuration used to execute the program. Normally, this computer is the same as the one used to compile. This division also assigns names of particular input/output devices used by the program, and otherwise takes care of all hardware-dependent features of the program.
DATA DIVISION.	Start of the data division. This division identifies in great detail the format and composition of all data items, data groups, logical records, and files used by the program. This division permits the program to tailor the object code to the data format used.
WORKING-STORAGE SECTION.	The working-storage section describes the data areas used only by this program. Thus, no input/output can be performed directly on these variables.
77 INCREASE USAGE IS COMPUTATIONAL – 2, VALUE IS ZERO.	Defines a single, isolated, and independent data item called INCREASE. Data names may be up to 30 characters long. INCREASE is declared to be a high-precision, real-valued (internal floating-point notation) number with an ini-

	tial value of zero. The 77 is a data-level number reserved for independent data items (those not part of larger data structures). Normally, more than one item appears in a working-storage section.
LINKAGE SECTION.	The linkage section appears only in subroutines or programs that refer to files with user-specified labels on them. It is used to describe data that are not read or written by a program, or contained within a program, but made available to the program by indirect means at execution time.
01 FIELDSIN	Defines a group item with the name FIELDSIN. The level number 01 indicates that FIELDSIN included all data items up to the next 01 level item as subsets of itself. Thus a group, or subgroup of data items, can be referred to as an entity by referring to an inclusive name for the group or subgroup.
02 VALU PICTURE S9(7)V99, COMPUTATIONAL – 3	A field VALU is defined as the first item within FIELDSIN. The spelling VALUE could not be used because VALUE is a reserved word, that is, a part of the COBOL language. VALU is composed of nine decimal digits and a sign S. As indicated in the PICTURE clause, seven digits (9999999 or 9(7) for short) fall before the decimal point (denoted by V) and two digits (denoted by 99 or 9(2)) fall after the decimal point. COMPUTATIONAL – 3 simply indicates a decimal representation suitable for computation purposes.

02 PRINC PICTURE S9(5)V99, COMPUTA-TIONAL – 3	The name PRINC is given to the next seven digits of storage. The five 9's (or 9(5) for short) each denote one digit position in storage, the V denotes the decimal point, and the 99 denotes the two last digit positions in storage. Note that the figure 9 in this statement does not stand for the value 9, but simply as a symbol for digit: in the same manner, the symbol B in this expression would stand for "blank," the symbol A would stand for an alphabetic character, X would stand for any acceptable character such as $, &, etc. As a matter of fact, a picture clause can describe almost any internal or external display of data.
02 RATE PICTURE IS 9V999, COMPU-TATIONAL – 3	The quantity RATE is defined. Since RATE has no sign(s), it will always be positive. The expression 9V999 indicates that the value of rate can be anything from 0.000 to 9.999. RATE will appear in memory 16 positions after the start of FIELDSIN since a nine-position item and a seven-position item precede it in the description of FIELDSIN. The character V does not represent an actual decimal point in memory at execution time, but it is used by the compiler to generate the required decimal-point alignment instructions.
02 NYEARS PICTURE IS S999, COMPU-TATIONAL – 3	NYEARS is the last subfield of FIELDSIN. It is a signed integer which may receive a value of −999 to +999. A data description in COBOL may contain many

	more descriptive clauses than shown in this example. For instance, PICTURE could be omitted and its information spelled out with adjective clauses such as SIZE IS, USAGE IS, JUS-TIFIED RIGHT, BLANK WHEN ZERO. This variety of data forms provides a great power to COBOL, but demands a great deal of writing for complete de-scriptions, and this leads to slow compile and execution time performance.
PROCEDURE DIVISION.	Start of the PROCEDURE DIVISION. This is the ac-tion part of the program.
ENTER LINKAGE.	Enter is an escape clause provided in COBOL. When a language facility, not pro-vided in COBOL, is needed, ENTER may be used to be-gin a non-COBOL segment of coding. In this instance, "begin program linkage lan-guage" is the meaning of ENTER LINKAGE. It is sometimes possible to insert symbolic machine instruc-tions by means of ENTER AUTOCODER or similar constructions.
ENTRY SUBROUTN USING FIELDSIN.	A program entry point is defined named SUBROUTN. At run time, a set of argu-ments similar to FIELD-SIN will be provided by the calling program.
ENTER COBOL.	Return to COBOL language.
SECTION HEADING	Sections are similar to para-graphs: they are units of thought or action. Sections are defined and named by section headings, as SEC-TION HEADING in this case.

COMPUTE INCREASE = 1.000 + RATE/ 200.000.	The COMPUTE verb results in the evaluation of an arithmetic expression. INCREASE equals the ratio of values at the end and beginning of an interest period. Other computational verbs are ADD, SUBTRACT, MULTIPLY, DIVIDE, ADD CORRESPONDING, etc. The three zeroes written after 1. and 200. are placed there to eliminate the need for decimal-point alignment instructions.
COMPUTE VALU ROUNDED = PRINC * INCREASE ** (2 * NYEARS)	Finally, the value of the sum held at interest compounded semiannually is calculated. As in FORTRAN, * means multiplication, / means division, and ** means exponentiation or repeated multiplication. ROUNDED indicates that VALU will be calculated to an extra place of accuracy, then rounded off.
ENTER LINKAGE.	Escape clause.
RETURN.	Return control to the calling program, end of subroutine action.
ENTER COBOL.	Return to COBOL. No formal end of program is provided: COBOL is one of the very few languages without this feature. For any compiler, end of program must be indicated by some non-COBOL means.

code A set of rules that is used to convert data from one representation to another, or the set of representations themselves.

Since the social, business, and scientific worlds have a long familiarity with the decimal system, people are led to assume that this system is objectively natural. However, anyone remembering the difficulties encountered in memorizing multiplication tables (and the complications involved in subtractions with carries) will realize that the decimal system is not an easy one. Besides which, the decimal system is not the only one in use: one has but to 'think of 12 unit inches to the unit foot, 3 feet to the unit yard, 1760 yards to the unit mile, or simply 60 unit seconds to the unit minute, 60 minutes to the unit hour, 24 hours to the unit day, and so on, not to mention weights, volume, and degrees, to realize that there are many numerical systems in the scheme of things.

In the computer field, business prefers the decimal system because it is familiar with it, computer designers, on the other hand, prefer the binary system because it is easier (and consequently cheaper) to build equipment with components allowing for two stable states rather than 10. To satisfy all involved, two procedures have been adopted: decimal numbers will be used for input and output and either (1) the processor handles the conversion of decimal to binary and binary to decimal or (2) decimal numbers are directly coded by means of four binary digits to a decimal digit (this conversion being simpler than the one in the first solution, but entailing longer numbers since more binary digits are required).

As business applications are characterized by large input and output operations with little in-core calculations in contrast to scientific and engineering work, business-directed computers may be designed with a code such as the binary-coded decimal. This code is easily converted to and from another code for other applications.

See BINARY CODE, CODING, ERROR CORRECTING CODE, EXCESS-THREE CODE, GRAY CODE, INSTRUCTION CODE, MACHINE CODE, MINIMUM DISTANCE CODE, OPERATION CODE, REFLECTED BINARY, SELF-CHECKING CODE, TWO-OUT-OF-FIVE CODE.

coded   A means of representing decimal numbers by means of binary digits. See BINARY-CODED DECIMAL.

code line   In character recognition, the area reserved for inscription of the printed or handwritten characters to be recognized. Also known as encoding strip (MICR).

coding   The process of converting a program design into an accurate, detailed representation of that program in some suitable computer language.

A program design begins as a concept in the mind of the designer (programmer or analyst). It is usually expressed initially as a block diagram, record layouts, prose descriptions, etc. This is suitable for comprehension by human beings but not acceptable to a digital computer. Coding begins by selection of a language suitable for expressing this program and also capable of being understood by the intended computer. An assembly language may be used if very close control of the computer instructions is needed. Otherwise, a procedure-oriented language such as COBOL, FORTRAN, or RPG may be preferred. The computer uses a language processing program (assembler or compiler) to convert the selected language statements into computer instructions. Coding directly in actual computer instructions is possible but very rarely done today.

The coder uses a coding form when writing the program. This form is designed to represent the acceptable statement formats used with the selected language. It represents every column or character space distinctly, permitting accurate keypunching of the written statements.

The coder procedes to describe the data to be manipulated and the actions to be performed according to the conventions established by the computer language. He must also describe actions to be taken under exceptional or erroneous conditions. In addition, the professional coder will distinguish himself by including comments and human-directed descriptions in his coding. Almost every computer language provides for annotations which are ignored by the computer but may be used for making the program more comprehensible to people. Good coding practice requires that the code be comprehensible to another knowledgeable person as well as correctly representing the program to the computer.

See AUTOMATIC CODING, BLOCK DIAGRAM, RELATIVE CODING, SKELETAL CODING, STRAIGHT-LINE CODING, SYMBOLIC CODING.

COGO   A civil-engineering-oriented, higher-level language originally developed by Professor C. L. Miller and his staff at MIT in association with the staff of the Puerto Rico Department of Public Works, Bureau of Highways.

Several versions of COGO have been implemented, one of which is QUICKTRAN/COGO. This is a time-sharing system.

The COGO programming system is designed for civil engineering problems, although it may be used in other application areas. COGO is based on a technical vocabulary familiar to engineers. An engineer merely writes a problem using the special vocabulary, feeds it to the computer, and COGO computes the results. No intermediate programming is required.

The basis of the system is the use of a coordinate table. The engineer expresses his problem in terms of angles given in degrees, minutes, and seconds, and points ($X + Y$ axis intersection). These points are entered into the coordinate table. All subsequent COGO commands make use of the data in the coordinate table. Each point is given an identification number, and is referenced by that number whenever it is needed.

The COGO command is a single word or short phrase followed by the angles, points, distance, etc., needed by COGO to execute the command. For example:

KNOWN
2 / 1 / 125 / 250 / 2 / 300 / 400

means that there are two points being defined here, the ID number of the first point is 1, it is at location 125 on the Y axis and 250 on the X axis, the ID number of the second point is 2, and it is at 300 on the Y axis, and 400 on the X axis.

Some of the other commands request specific output from COGO based on not only what is entered in the command itself, but also data previously entered. For example:

DISTANCE
1 / 2

is a command to COGO to compute the distance between points 1 and 2.

Similarly, COGO may be instructed to do such things as dump all coordinates, locate points a given distance and bearing from a known point, locate a line parallel to a given line, output the distance and bearing between two points, compute an angle at a point between two lines drawn from that point to two other points, etc.

All in all, COGO is a very versatile tool in the hands of an engineer who has spent the small time necessary to learn its techniques.

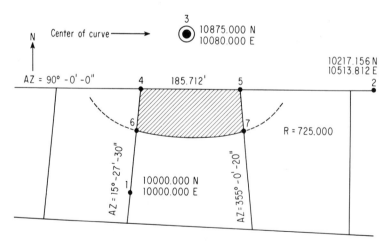

Reference diagram for COGO program.

The following example illustrates COGO.

Consider the following piece of land. Because of new road construction, a curve is going to be cut through the front of the existing property. It is now necessary to calculate the area of land being removed and the new property frontage length.

Assume that the following are among the known information:

1. The coordinates of the center of the curve (point 3) and the radius of the curve

2. The coordinates of point 1 on the westmost boundary and the azimuth of that boundary

3. The present frontage, the azimuth of that frontage, and the coordinates of point 2 on that boundary

4. The azimuth of the eastmost boundary

With this information at hand, what follows is the user input commands and computer responses which would solve the problem. Computer printouts are underlined.

KNOWN 3 / 1 / 10000. / 10000. 2 / 10217.156 / 10513.812 3 / 10875. / 10080.	This is the command to COGO to store point coordinates. Three points are defined, numbered 1, 2, and 3, and their respective Y and X locations are entered.
AZ/ INTERSECT 4 / 1 / 15 / 27 / 30. / 2 / 90 / 0 / 0.	This command instructs COGO to locate and store point 4. It indicates that point 4 is at the intersection of two lines. Each of the two lines is defined by naming a known point and a bearing. The number sequence 1 / 15 / 27 / 30. means the line passing through point 1 and making a 15°27'30" angle with the Y or vertical axis. 2 / 90 / 0 / 0. defines the second line.
PT4 10217.156 N 10060. 053 E	The computer now responds with the coordinates of point 4.
LOC / AZIMUTH 4 / 5 / 185. 712 / 90 / 0 / 0.	This command requests location of point 5 from point 4 a distance of 185.712 feet and on a 90°0'0" angle with the Y axis.

PT5 10217.156N 10245. 765E	The computer again prints out the new point's location.
ARC / AZIMUTH / INTERSECT 6 / 3 / 725. / 1 / 15 / 27 / 30. / 1	This command requests location of point 6 and defines a circle and a line, point 6 being at the intersection. The circle is point 3 as the center with a 725' radius, and the line passes through point 1 and makes a 15°27'30" angle with the Y axis.
PT6 10151. 009 N 10041. 760E	The computer's response.
7 / 3 / 725. / 5 / 355 / 0 / 20. / 1	This requests location of point 7, in the same manner as point 6. The command need not be typed in when repeated.
PT7 10170. 181 N 10249. 870E	The computer's response
AREA 4 / 6 / 4 / 5 / 7	This requests the area in square feet and acres of the area enclosed by the four points 6, 4, 5, and 7, each connected by a straight line.
AREA = 11069.361 SQ FT, 0.254 ACRES	The computer responds with the square footage and acreage.
SEG/ PLUS 6 / 7 / 725.	This command requests that the area of the circle segment, passing through points 6 and 7 and with a 725' radius, be added to the previous area. The exact segment area calculated is the small wedge formed between a straight line drawn between points 6 and 7 and the arc passing between points 6 and 7. The PLUS indicates that this segment area is to be added to all previous areas calculated, thus resulting in the total area being subtracted from the original plot.

CHORD LENGTH = 208.991 ARC LENGTH = 209.721 SEGMENT AREA = 1055.820 SQ FT AREA = 12125.182 SQ FT, 0.278 ACRES	The computer responds by printing out the various results, including arc length which is the new property frontage, and the area of the property being removed.
	End of Program.

collate To compare and merge similarly ordered sets of items into one ordered set.

Collating means performing four operations either simultaneously or individually. These operations are: merging, sequence checking, selection, and matching.

Collating occurs when data required for, say, a printing operation must be obtained from two or more physically separated files. Consider, for instance, a file containing names and addresses and a file containing accumulated earnings. To set up an output file combining name, address, and earnings would require collating the two input files. If the entries of the files are identical in sequence and number, the whole job is then nothing but a simple merge. This state of affairs is, however, rare. Consequently, each entry of a file must be matched with the corresponding entry on the second file. This matching operation ensures that, for instance, no W-2 form will be produced lacking address, or name, or some other income tax information: this could occur without matching since an employee roster is never static, owing to promotions, terminations, changes of address, marital status, etc. If an entry in a file is unmatched in the other file, it must then be set aside for special consideration. This selection operation not only singles out unmatched entries, but can be used equally to set aside, for special reports, earnings over a certain amount. Lastly, one must consider the sequence of entries in files to be merged. If, for some reason, an entry has been moved out of its location, the fact may be detected by means of the sequence checking operation.

Collating and merging are often used interchangeably. Merging, in fact, is a special case of collating. See MERGE.

collating sequence The ordering of a set of items such that sets in that assigned order can be collated.

The assigned ordering of all the unique characters of a character set will result in a before/after relationship between any two characters of the set. The most common collating sequence in use is simply the alphabetic order. A collating sequence is used in the same way as the alphabetic order in assigning an arbitrary precedence relationship between any two items.

For instance, the sets

H,   I,   I,   L,   P,   P
A,   D,   I,   J,   N,   O,   R

can be collated without any further ado:

A,   D,   H,   I,   I,   I,   J,   L,   N,   O,   P,   P,   R.

On the other hand, the sets

A,   E,   C
D,   B,   F

would have to be ordered before collating.

To say that a computer or computer language has a collating sequence is to say that a unique before/after relationship is established for any two different characters acceptable to the computer or language.

Suppose that a listing is printed of different words arranged in collating sequence. If blanks collate before letters and digits, then shorter words appear before longer words having the same initial letters (example: pen before pencil). If digits collate low, numbers would print before alphabetic words (example: 29B before B29). IBM commonly collates blanks before letters and digits after letters. This could result in a listing like

AN
ANY
AN4

collator   A device to collate decks of ordered punched cards into an ordered sequence.

The collator consists basically of two separate feed hoppers, the primary feed hopper and the secondary feed hopper; four card stackers to which the cards from the hoppers can be directed; and sufficient circuitry to be able to test whether two values are equal, one is greater than the other, or one is less than the other. The card stackers receive cards that are matched, or cards from a hopper not matched to a card in the other hopper, or any special cards singled out by means of the collator control panel. See COLLATE.

column   A vertical arrangement of characters or other expressions.

In computer hardware column refers usually to a specific print position on a printer or a vertical area on the card. See CARD, PRINTING, PUNCHED CARD.

column binary   The binary representation of data on punched cards in which adjacent positions in a column correspond to adjacent bits of data.   Thus, each column in a 12-row card may be used to represent 12 bits.

Binary data can be handled either row-wise or column-wise.   For instance, the CDC 3600 computer normally will use four columns for its 48-bit word, whereas the IBM 7094 will normally use a row of 72 bits for two 36-bit words if the information is handled by on-line equipment and three columns per word if the information is handled off-line.

However, hardware considerations are the only ones that the programmer bears in mind when deciding how to have the computer handle the data.   Utility programs will readily convert column binary or row binary, and whichever method is the easiest and most natural to the computer will, in most cases, be the method selected by the programmer.

combinational logic element   A device having at least one output channel and several input channels, each characterized by discrete states.   The state of each output channel is determined by the state of every input channel.

The combinational logic element accepts one or more input signals and after a very short time (the propagation delay time) gives out a uniquely determined output or set of outputs.   The basic function of the combinational logic element is to transform the input signal or signals into an output signal or signals according to some prescribed set of rules.   The output, however, must not depend on previous values of the input, output, or internal state of the device.   A simple example is the inverter: if a signal 1 is fed to the inverter, the output signal will be a 0; if the input signal is a 0, the output signal will be a 1 (see illustration).   If the input signal has a high voltage

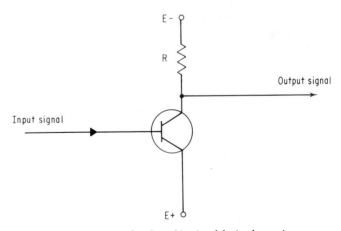

Inverter. (A simple example of combinational logic element.)

($E+$ or higher), the output signal will have a low voltage since there is no current through R and hence no voltage drop across it. On the other hand, if the input signal has a low voltage (smaller than $E+$), the current will flow from $E+$ to $E-$, and due to the voltage drop across R, there will be a high voltage (relative to $E-$) as an output signal. If a high voltage is represented by 0, then for an input signal 1 or 0 there will be an output signal 0 or 1.

For two input channels and two output channels, a combinational two-terminal switching circuit, the accompanying table summarizes the various possible situations.

Input 1	Input 2	Output 1	Output 2
0	0	1	0
0	1	0	1
1	0	0	1
1	1	1	0

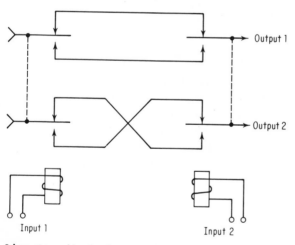

Schematic combinational two-terminal switching circuit.

command   A control signal, or loosely, an instruction in machine language.

As a control signal, the command is usually of the YES (do it) or NO (do not do it) type.

When it is meant as an instruction, a distinction should be made: in some computers, an INSTRUCTION is an instruction given to the central processing unit (CPU), whereas a COMMAND is an instruction to be executed by a data channel, for instance, an input command (READ) or an output command (WRITE).

In some higher-level languages, a command is a verb or action-indication part of the language. This word COMMAND, and other words such as PAUSE, JUMP, DO, ADD, etc., reflect the extension of human beings that computers, as tools, have become. But these words are no more indication or proof of independent thought or will on the computer's part than the expression "My car won't start" confers to an automobile a will or intelligence of its own.

communication link   The physical means of connecting remote locations so as to transmit and receive information. Communication links such as telephone lines, microwave relays, teletype lines, and coaxial cables are acquiring great importance in the data processing field with the advent of time-sharing and real-time systems. Four examples of the many types of linking that involve computers are shown here.

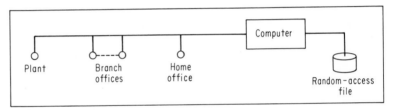

1. Example with one communication line.

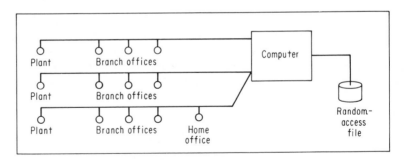

2. Example with several communication lines.

compile   To prepare a machine-language program from a program written in a higher programming language usually generating more than one machine instruction for each symbolic statement.

The preparation, or transformation, is carried out by a specially written computer program called a compiler. A distinction should be made, however, between an assembler and a compiler: both

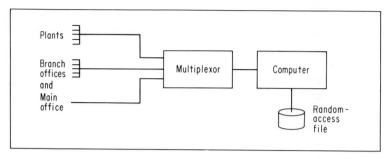

3. Example with a separate line control computer.

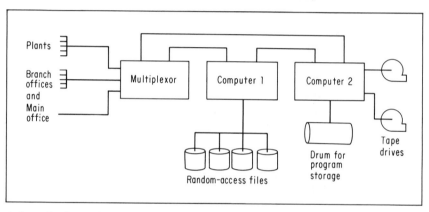

4. Example of a multicomputer system.

transform programs easily read by a programmer into equivalent programs easily read by the computer (and difficult to read by the programmer), but the assembler is used when the original program is a symbolic representation of computer instructions, and the compiler is used when the original program implies (but does not explicitly state) the computer instructions. For instance:

Compiler language	Assembly language	
$X = (P + Q) * R$	CLA	A
	ADD	B
	MPY	C
	STO	D

Both programs here carry out the simple operation of adding P and Q and multiplying the sum by R. In the compiler language there is no explicit statement as to what the parentheses stand for: the compiler will have to translate these into actual instructions. In the assembly language each step is clearly explicit, CLA standing for "Clear accumulator and store in it contents of location A" (A, B, C, and D are the addresses, or locations, where P, Q, R, and X are to be found or to be stored); STO meaning that the result is to be stored in location D.

A program written in a compiler language is relatively computer-independent; that is, it may run on another computer by making minor changes when necessary and submitting it to the compiler for that computer (e.g., FORTRAN, COBOL, ALGOL). An assembly-language program is highly computer-dependent: in general, it could not be used on another computer unless the two computers were compatible, that is, the two computers had essentially the same internal computer language.

compiler A program to translate a higher language into a machine language.

The most important item of support of a computer is the software package (that is, the set of programs established by the manufacturer for that computer) and one of the most important of these programs is the compiler. The compiler is a special program that converts programs written in a procedure-oriented language (that is, in higher-level language) into a form suitable for loading into, and executing on, a computer.

The input to a compiler is a program, or subprogram, written in a relatively computer-independent language such as FORTRAN or COBOL. This input, called a source program (or a source module in the IBM 360 System), describes the data to be handled and the processing to be performed. The compiler allocates portions of memory to the data required by the program; keeps a temporary record of names, locations, and characteristics of each data item in a list called the symbol table; interprets the procedure specifications of the source program; and determines what computer instructions are needed to perform the work. The compiler then generates the determined instructions, allocates storage for these instructions, supplies the correct data addresses and required constants to the program, and thus produces an executable program.

The output from the compiler usually contains a listing of the source program, a memory map showing the names and locations of all data items, and a machine-language deck called the object deck (or the object module in the IBM 360 System), the object deck containing the machine-readable computer instructions. The printed listing will probably contain messages indicating programmer errors discovered by the compiler, and it may contain a description of the instructions generated for the object deck. The object deck may be in absolute format (that is, containing only fixed addresses), or, as is more frequent, the object deck may be in relocatable format. A relocatable deck has its addresses almost specified so that it may be loaded into any area of memory with the final addresses to be determined by the loading program. The programmer has some control over the compiling process through the processor control statements. The programmer may require the output listing, or the information where to place the origin of the program at object time or where to place subroutines in storage, etc. See ASSEMBLER, INTERPRETER.

compiler-level languages Higher-level languages normally supplied by the computer manufacturer. Examples of higher-level or compiler-level languages are ALGOL, COBOL, JOVIAL, NELIAC, SNOBOL.

complement The complement of a number A is another number B such that the sum $A + B$ will produce a specified result. A radix complement added to the number A produces all zeros in the digit places and a 1 digit carried to the next leftmost position (this 1 is usually dropped since it will normally exceed the capacity of the register holding the sum). Thus, for example:

	Binary system	Decimal system
Number A	1011	11
Radix complement	0101	89
Sum	1 0000	1 00

A radix-minus-one complement is one less than the radix complement of the number A. In this case the above example becomes

	Binary system	Decimal system
Number A	1011	11
Radix-minus-one complement	0100	88
Sum	1111	99

The complement of a number A is used, in some computers, to represent the negative of A. Thus, the computer representation of the symbols X and $-X$ could be added to produce a zero sum. In most computers not using this technique the hardware must generate a complement for a subtraction operation. See NINE'S COMPLEMENT, ONE'S COMPLEMENT, RADIX COMPLEMENT, RADIX-MINUS-ONE COMPLEMENT, TEN'S COMPLEMENT, TRUE COMPLEMENT, TWO'S COMPLEMENT.

component   An elementary part used to create a composite structure. The components of computers throughout the ages have been mechanical (Babbage,) electromechanical (relays), electronic (tubes), solid state (transistors), monolithic-integrated circuit element (complete circuits integrated as one unit).   See SOLID-STATE COMPONENT.

computer   A computer is a mechanism capable of manipulating data, but, unlike a desk calculator which must be manually guided step by step, a computer should be capable of guiding most of its own operations.   Some solid-state desk calculators, however, have started to earn the name of computers since certain functions, such as statistical calculation, have been wired in permanently.

From a conceptual point of view, computers have been with us for a long time.   Probably the largest, from a physical point of view, known today can be seen at Stonehenge.   According to the findings of Hawkins and White (using an IBM 7090 for their calculations), Stonehenge should be classified as a special-purpose computer dedicated to the calculation of calendar time as measured from specific moon and sun positions.   Astronomy, apparently, was equally the basis for a computer found near Antikythera, a small island halfway between Crete and the Greek mainland.   This computer, however, was a small portable one, built about 2000 years ago, whose dials probably indicated the motions of stars and planets as calculated by a complex set of gears mounted eccentrically on a turntable in the back, functioning as a sort of an epicyclic, or differential, gear system.

Five hundred years before the Greek computer, however, the Chinese had already introduced the abacus (still in use today in many parts of the world), and it was not until the seventeenth century that a mechanical digital calculator was produced by Pascal.

After Pascal, a number of mechanical devices were created, but they were inefficient, laborious, and time-consuming.   In the early part of the nineteenth century, Babbage developed a mechanical apparatus which could reliably generate an entire numerical sequence; he proceeded to draw the plan for an ambitious machine that would feed back certain answers to form the data required in a complex problem.   This machine was never finished, but conceptually was the forerunner of modern computers.

During the first half of the twentieth century, a host of mechanical calculators made their appearance on the scientific and business market.   At first mechanical, these calculators became electromechanical in the late 1930's, and were hailed as a great step forward in the art of calculations.

With the advent of radio, it became only a question of time before electronic circuits were oriented toward practical applications.

What would be considered today as special-purpose computers were developed, here and there, for radio control operations of plane and ship models. Since such applications were strictly military, little is known about these devices.

R. K. Richards records the development of the Atanasoff-Berry computer between 1938 and 1942 at Iowa State College. Its purpose was to compute algebraic equations, and it contained 300 vacuum tubes.

What may well be the first known computer in the modern sense of the word is probably the ENIAC built for the U.S. Army at the University of Pennsylvania in 1942 to 1945: it contained 18,000 vacuum tubes and was used to compute ballistic trajectories.

The first stored program computer was the EDVAC in 1952, and the first concept of building blocks in computer construction was found in the SEAC of the Bureau of Standards in 1950. The first drum computer, the ERA 1101 appeared equally in 1950, and the first data processing, magnetic-tape-using computer was the UNIVAC in 1951.

The concept of speed became dominant, and MIT'S WHIRLWIND achieved a speed of 20,000 instructions per second. With speed came the concept of power, and the LARC was followed by the STRETCH, then the ATLAS, and today some consider the CDC 6600 the most powerful computer in existence. The word powerful, however, is not defined today in a unique way since not only speed, but also multiprogramming, memory, and simultaneity of operations are to be taken into consideration. For this reason, it is no easy matter to compare the CDC 6600 with, for example, the Burroughs 8500.

Both business and scientific fields have, today, a wide array of computers to choose from.

Basically, today's computers consist of

1. Input devices to bring in information from the outside into the computer (for instance, punch-card readers, or magnetic-tape drives)

2. Memory devices (such as core memory, or thin-film memories) capable of storing the information before, during, and after the processing of that information

3. An arithmetic (or logic) unit which will operate (numerically or logically) on the information

4. A control unit which interprets the instructions given to the computer, transfers the information from unit to unit, and permits the arithmetic unit to perform the required operations

5. Output devices which bring out the information in an acceptable form (such as the printer, or a CRT)

6. A repertory of conditional jump instructions, that is, instructions which will transfer control to certain instructions depending on the outcome of simple tests such as comparing two numbers

7. The ability to store a program internally, that is, to store a sequence of elementary instructions by means of which the computer user can have the computer carry out any information processing required

There are no known fields in which computers cannot be used successfully, and the explosive growth of computers and computer applications have, at regular intervals, given rise to conjectures on the threat of computers to man's independence of thought and will. As though to allay this fear, statements have been often made to the effect that computers do nothing but what they are told to do. Such statements are extremely misleading. Indeed, computers, in the truest sense of the word, are devices capable of carrying out processes involving manipulation and transformation of information. But in order to make computers the versatile tools they are getting to be, techniques have been designed which permit computers to modify their original programs when external conditions (or internal intermediate results) so require it. This ability of modern computers to adapt to changing situation is highly helpful to the user, and highly impressive to the nonuser.

In man's constant strife to achieve supremacy over, and understanding of, his ever-widening surroundings, the computer has thus become the symbol of a mute and faithful servant. And, although there is no more occasion for computers to take over the world than there is for automatic transmissions to take over automobiles, the recently programmed ability of a computer to talk back (when in the conversational mode) to his user has endowed the mute and faithful servant with another lifelike characteristic. It is such characteristics that are often confused with the use made of computers by man.

"Do computers think?" is a common question. Fundamentally, this question cannot be answered since the verb think is conceived in context of human emotions and mysticism. If, to define and reduce the scope of the verb think, think is equated to the ability to predict a logical consequence, then a computer outthinks his creator. Indeed, it would be hopeless to expect a man to visualize correctly the most remote consequences of interface betwen adaptive behavior of computers on the one hand and job environment on the other hand, and this after millions of information processing operations.

It could be argued that only the speed of computers gives computers an edge, and that given enough time and patience, a man could equally foresee all possible consequences of a computer operation: this would certainly be true in terms of brute-force solutions, a brute-force solution being one in which every single alternative is examined for validity. For instance, the problem "How many men, women, and children attend a show if the theater sold 100 tickets for $100 at $5 per man, $2 per woman, and 10 cents per child?" can be solved by examining every one of 5050 logical combinations and finding that the set of 11 men, 19 women, and 70 children satisfy the problem. Brute-force solving is clearly no sign of independent thought.

Brute-force solutions, however, are not always feasible. For instance, were a computer, programmed to play chess, to use a brute-force approach in answering its opponent during the first few moves of a game, it would require 10^{110} years between acknowledging its opponent's move and making its own move. What a computer must possess in such a game is the ability to overlook sterile combinations and examine only paths that could lead to acceptable solutions. If thinking is to be then defined as possessing the ability to carry on a selective search, a computer may be considered as having the basic elements of intelligent behavior.

There exists no proof that a computer and a program for that computer will not exhibit together, eventually, an intelligent behavior beyond man's ability to judge. Unless such a proof is found, it may be assumed that present developments will lead to a man-machine relationship in which no difference can be made between artificial and human intelligence. See ANALOG COMPUTER, ASYNCHRONOUS COMPUTER, AUTOMATIC COMPUTER, DIGITAL COMPUTER, GENERAL-PURPOSE COMPUTER, INCREMENTAL COMPUTER, SPECIAL-PURPOSE COMPUTER, STORED-PROGRAM COMPUTER, SYNCHRONOUS COMPUTER.

computer center   See EDP CENTER.

computer instruction   A machine instruction in a specific computer. A machine instruction would appear as a sequence of digits (or bits) which, when stored in the memory of a computer, can be interpreted by the hardware of the central processing unit (CPU) and which, after interpretation, will cause some specific action to be performed by the computer. For instance, if 01 is interpreted by the computer to mean ADD TO THE ACCUMULATOR REGISTER, then

01   273

will be an instruction causing the computer to add the contents of locations 273 to the contents of the accumulator register. The code 01 is the operation code, and its position in the instruction is known as the operation part of the instruction. The number 273 is the address of the quantity to be processed, and it occupies the address part of the instruction. This instruction, to be used, should be tagged with its own address, that is, the location it would occupy in the memory. The complete instruction would then appear as

114   01   273

with 114 indicating the location of the instruction. Such a computer would be limited by its instruction format to a maximum of 100 distinct operations (00 to 99) and a maximum of 1000 memory locations (000 to 999). See INSTRUCTION.

computer program A systematic plan for solving a problem on a computer.

In the narrowest sense of the word, a computer program consists of a set of computer instructions necessary to accomplish the task that the program was set out to do.

Implicit in the narrow task of preparing machine instructions is the necessity of having to satisfy a wide range of requirements if the computer program per se is to be meaningful. These requirements may be divided in four broad categories:

1. Problem definition: nonrecurring or recurring problem, symptom, or cause

2. Problem analysis: (*a*) input data format, input availability, output format, total answer requirements, output units, and (*b*) computer configuration, capacity, availability, organizational environment, limitations, and restrictions

3. Solution planning: languages available or required, subroutines available, files required, outline of logic or mathematical steps

4. Program implementation: detailed charting, coding, testing, debugging, documentation, and, if the program is to be used regularly, detailed instructions for input data preparation, file maintenance, program maintenance, testing for validity of results, feedback system for error corrections, distribution, and follow-up.

See PROGRAM.

computer system A set of related, but unconnected hardware parts (general sense), or a set of related and connected hardware (specific sense), that is, a computer.

In the general sense, a catalog representing the various central processing units, I/O devices, and other peripheral devices of a brand name such as the RCA SPECTRA 70, or the IBM 360 represents a computer system.

In the specific sense, a computer system consists of one or more central processing units (CPU), I/O and other peripheral devices, all pieces of hardware being related and interconnected, and capable of simultaneous operation: such a computer system is often referred to as a computer. Two adjacent computers, not interconnected form two computer systems.

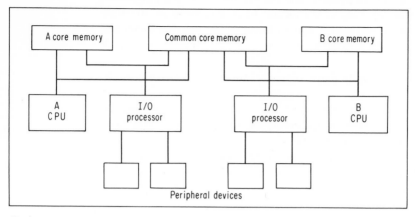

Single-computer system.

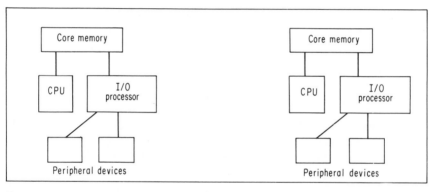

Two-computer systems.

computer word   A set of bits or characters treated as a unit which can be stored in a single computer location.   Synonymous with machine word.   In digital computers a computer word is the smallest number of characters usually accessed as an indivisible whole.

Once determined by the manufacturer, the word length is incorporated in the circuitry.   For instance, a word length could be fixed at 16 bits (DDP 116), 32 bits (IBM 360 System), 36 bits (UNIVAC 1107), 48 bits (CDC 3600), or 60 bits (CDC 6600).   Such word lengths would characterize these computers as fixed-word-length computers. If a data item does not fill in a word, the excess positions can be filled with zeros or blanks.   Fixed-word computers thus may use a great amount of space for relatively few elements of data: data may be packed in words but would then require additional instructions for unpacking and individual processing.

Since business data processing deals often in long and short data elements, that is, in elements of variable lengths, a number of computers (for instance Honeywell 200, RCA 301, IBM 1401) are characterized by variable-length words. In this case the word is identified either by opening and closing characters defining the word, or by identifying the first or last character and the number of characters involved, or by a combination of these methods. The capacity of fixed-word computers is given in number of word storage available (16,000 words, 32,000 words), and variable-word computers have a capacity defined by the number of character (or byte) storage available (20,000 characters). In fixed-word computers, an instruction usually occupies one word of storage.

concatenated data set   A temporary data set formed by uniting the contents of several independent data sets in a specified sequence.

Concatenation makes it possible to treat several independent sequentially organized data sets as though they were one long data set. This convenience applies only to input operations, and the concatenation endures only for a single job step. The power of concatenation is that data from various sources and/or various times may be united into a single input stream for processing. For example, one program requires as input a file consisting of one day's transactions, and another requires as input all the transactions of one week. The five, six, or seven individual data sets required by the first program can be concatenated to form the single input to the second, without requiring the second to know that it is dealing with multiple input files.

Concatenation is indicated by entering // DD cards for each data set in sequence, but leaving the DDNAME blank on all except the first DD card. If the data sets are similar in record size and organization, and all reside on similar recording media (all tape, all disk, etc.), then the program will not know when one data set ends and another begins. It is possible to concatenate dissimilar data sets (differing in one or more essential details). In this case an end-of-data condition will be given at the end of each individual data set, requiring a CLOSE and an OPEN to continue processing. (The CLOSE/OPEN allows adjustment of data control block entries to account for data set differences.)

Automatic concatenation of data sets or files is not possible in simpler machine/operating-system environments. In these cases the processing of consecutive files must be explicitly programmed.

conditional jump   A jump that occurs if specific criteria are met. Probably the single most important instruction in computer code.

This instruction enables the computer to select certain paths at the exclusion of others, thereby permitting the computer to modify its program, recalculate addresses, ignore certain restraints; in other words, letting the computer act as though "deciding" on its own.

Basically, the conditional jump is an operation that causes the computer to go to a specific instruction if a certain condition is met; otherwise to go to another instruction. For instance, the condition to be tested could consist in determining whether the accumulator is negative, zero, or positive. If the accumulator were negative, the computer should go to the next instruction in sequence; if the accumulator were zero, it should go to the second instruction in sequence; and if the accumulator were positive, it should go to the third instruction in sequence. Consider, for example, a program in which, at some point, packaged goods were to be classed as A, B, C, depending upon their weights (12, 6, or 3 ounces), and the totals in each class were to be added up. The section of the program dealing with this problem is illustrated on the accompanying figure.

Instruction location	Instruction
. . . .	. . . .
1001	PLACE WEIGHT X IN ACCUMULATOR.
1002	SUBTRACT 6 FROM ACCUMULATOR.
1003	{ CONDITIONAL JUMP } IF ACCUMULATOR IS NEGATIVE GO TO 1004. IF ACCUMULATOR IS ZERO GO TO 1005. IF ACCUMULATOR IS POSITIVE GO TO 1006.
1004	GO TO 1011.
1005	GO TO 1016.
1006 1007 1008 1009	(INSTRUCTIONS REQUIRED TO ADD 1 TO CLASS A TOTAL).
1010	GO TO 1020.
1011 1012 1013 1014	(INSTRUCTIONS REQUIRED TO ADD 1 TO CLASS C TOTAL)

Instruction location	Instruction
1015	GO TO 1020.
1016 1017 1018 1019	(INSTRUCTIONS REQUIRED TO ADD 1 TO CLASS B TOTAL)
1020	(PROCEED WITH PROGRAM)
. . . .	. . . . .

Program with conditional jump.

Since the computer has no choice (due to the circuitry) but to take the next instructions in sequence, unless specifically instructed to jump to some instructions other than the next one, the sorting of the packaged goods will be properly carried out in this example.

Instructions of the type GO TO as found in locations 1004, 1005, 1010, and 1015 are called unconditional jump instructions. Unconditional jumps, in this example, keep the computer from carrying out two (or more) mutually exclusive operations such as adding 1 to the class C total *and* to the class B total if the weight X were equal to 3 ounces. The computer has no other alternative with a GO TO instruction but to jump where told. The three instructions JUMP, BRANCH, TRANSFER all mean a transfer of control from one part of the program to another part of the program.

connector A flowcharting symbol which represents the convergence of more than one flowline into one, or the divergence of one flowline into more than one. It also stands for a break in a single flowline for continuation in another area. A connector is usually represented by a small circle. The use of connectors is illustrated on the accompanying figure on page 124.

console The interface, or communication device, between the operator and the computer.

A console contains indicator lights, switches and knobs, occasionally a meter or cathode-ray-tube display (CRT), and sometimes a typewriter or keyboard for entering messages. These elements are grouped in a specific location for easy access by the operator.

A remote console permits an operator to use a computer even though the computer may be thousands of miles away. Remote consoles always have keyboard input devices and CRT or teletypewriter output devices. See TIME-SHARING.

content-addressed storage   A memory mechanism by which means a computer memory can be interrogated. With such a mechanism it is sufficient to present a data item, and the computer will return the related data item (or data items) stored in memory.

Normally, a memory is accessed by address, that is, by specifying the memory location where the required piece of data to be processed is stored, or where the data item is to be stored. For instance: PRINT X (which is) IN LOCATION 01242, or FETCH Y (which is) IN LOCATION 05661 are instructions which access memory by means of addresses, which, in this instance, are 01242, 10772, 05661.

When a computer has a content-addressed memory (or associative

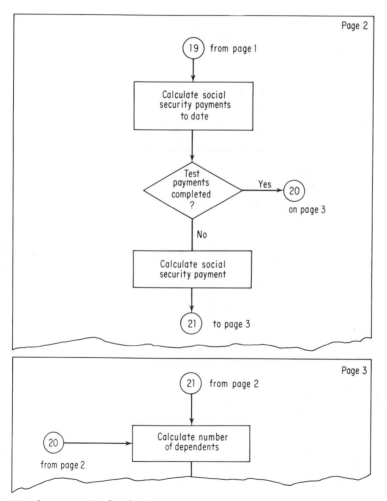

Use of connectors in flowcharting.

memory, or associative storage), the instructions would appear instead in the form PRINT BALANCE OF M. BRODERICK, or FETCH LAST BALANCE OF M. BRODERICK, or STORE NEW DEBIT IN M. BRODERICK, where the data items are represented by BALANCE, LAST BALANCE, NEW DEBITS, and the addresses are represented by the combination of data items and M. BRODERICK.

It seems safe to say that content-addressed storages could greatly alter the customary ways of using computers. It is presently believed that a human memory is organized on content-addressable principles. See ASSOCIATIVE STORAGE.

continuous forms   In character recognition, any batch of source information that exists in reel form, such as tally rolls, or cash-register receipts.

continuous stationery readers   In optical character recognition (OCR), that special class of character readers which only process continuous forms of predefined dimensions.

The most common form of continuous stationery is the tally roll of recorded cash-register receipts. Accordingly, the document transport is tailor-made for paper width and roll size, with the result that the problem of document handling becomes much easier than with the cut-form reader. In addition, the problem of static electricity (as it develops among sheets in cut-form document readers) is virtually eliminated.

The operation of the continuous stationery reader is similar to that of a magnetic-tape unit inasmuch as the roll can be stopped, rewound, and reread under program control. However, reading speeds are usually quite slow, owing to the poorer quality of the paper employed.

Character readers of this class have one obvious limitation, namely, the inability to process varying-sized documents.

contour analysis   In optical character recognition (OCR), a reading technique that employs a roving spot of light which searches out the character's outline by "bouncing" around its outer edges. The result is then compared to a library of the complete character set in an attempt to identify which of the possible characters has just been traced.

Handwriting character-recognition systems utilize contour analysis in lieu of more sophisticated methods as a result of the unstandardized appearance of input, especially with regard to a character's size and shape.

Illustrating contour analysis.

control Means or devices to direct and regulate a process or sequence of events. For instance, a control mechanism that actuates functions in a sequential order, the order being predetermined, such as the time mechanism in an automatic washing machine, or a more elaborate device such as used on machine tools to guide the work on a piece of metal (usually by means of a prepunched paper tape, or magnetic tape, or programmed real-time computer). See NUMERICAL CONTROL.

control block A storage area containing (in condensed, formalized form) the information required for the control of a task, function, operation, or quantity of information.

Control blocks allow the communication of parameters from routine to routine in an operating-system environment. Normally, a service routine operates on one of many similar entities at a time, and governs its operation by the parameters found in the particular control block associated with that entity. To change from one thing to another it merely redirects its attention to the control block of the latter. Typically, the number of entities (jobs, data sets, tasks, etc.) changes from one moment to the next, but since the service routine can examine only one control block at a time, it need not know the detailed dynamics of the entire situation.

example:

A program wishes to perform input from a given data set (external data file). The program establishes a data control block (DCB) containing certain known parameters (input or output, file organization, record format, etc.). By issuing an OPEN macroinstruction for this DCB the program causes the operating system to complete the unfilled portions of the DCB at execution time. The completed DCB now contains correct information concerning the hardware address of the data set, the type of media used to record the data, etc. The operating system can now properly perform input or output for this data set because all the required control information is contained within the DCB. Were the DCB contents expressed in human-readable form, it might appear like this:

data control block:

DATA SET NAME = MASTER
INPUT OR OUTPUT = INPUT ONLY
OPEN OR CLOSED = OPEN
HARDWARE ADDRESS OF I/O DEVICE = 1CO
STARTING ADDRESS WITHIN DISK = 024457
CURRENT RECORD ADDRESS = 030082
RECORD FORMAT = FIXED, BLOCKED

LOGICAL RECORD LENGTH= 200 CHARACTERS
PHYSICAL RECORD LENGTH = 800 CHARACTERS
TYPE OF I/O DEVICE = DISK PACK
ADDRESS OF ERROR RECOVERY ROUTINE = 00284
ADDRESS OF END-OF-INPUT-DATA ROUTINE =' 00340
NUMBER OF BUFFERS = 2
ADDRESS OF CURRENT BUFFER = 08977
ADDRESS OF NEXT LOGICAL RECORD = 09177

In actuality, the DCB is recorded in a compact form, and most of the items in the example occupy only a few bits in a specified area within the formal structure of the control block.

Other control blocks are used to coordinate jobs (JCB), tasks (TCB), events (ECB), etc. Event control blocks establish coordination in time; most other control blocks coordinate allocation of resources, i.e., hardware devices or memory space. In this way complete control of a system can be obtained in an orderly fashion.

control character   A character whose purpose is to initiate, modify, or stop a control operation, as, for example, the character that controls the carriage return. The control character is embedded in the data stream: its purpose is to control an action rather than to convey information. In computer operation, a control character may (as first character in a text) control the line spacing of the printer; or it may control the output hopper selection in a card punch. The control characters in the last two examples are neither printed nor punched: they only direct the electromechanical device they refer to.

Some sets of characters such as ASCII (American Standard Code for Information Interchange) and EBCDIC (Extended Binary Coded Decimal Interchange Code) sometimes include special symbols reserved exclusively for control functions (for instance, delete, line space, carriage return). These characters, not conveying information, are easily detected by the device. However, this detection implies that all characters must be interpreted to determine whether they stand for text or control.

control panel   The part of a computer console containing manual controls. By control panel is sometimes meant plugboard.

A plugboard is an array of jacks or sockets in which wires (or other elements) may be plugged to control the action of an electromechanical device such as a printer.

A manual telephone switchboard is similar in appearance to many plugboards.

control section   The smallest integral subsection of a program, i.e., the smallest unit of code that can be separately relocated during loading. All of a control section must be loaded into contiguous locations in memory, but different control sections can be loaded into noncontiguous areas.

Originally (and today on small computers) programs were written with absolute addresses. The programs had to be executed from the memory locations initially assigned to them. When it became desirable to link together a program and independently written subroutines, relocatable coding was developed. Now each program could be loaded in consecutive memory locations, but the starting address of each program could be adjusted to begin right after the end of the previous program or routine. Thus separately written segments could be united into a compact, contiguous program system.

Still more sophisticated programming techniques give the programmer the opportunity (or the obligation!) to subdivide a program or subroutine into separately relocatable sections called control sections. Originally a control section consisted of a symbolic (named) origin followed by its associated instructions and data. Then an instruction 182 locations after the origin (control section) CSECT1 could always be found 182 locations after the beginning of CSECT1, wherever that happened to be. Now several programs could share a common control section. The origin of the control section would be determined by the first program loaded that contained any references to it. Each additional program which referred to that control section would be adjusted to refer to the established origin address during loading or linkage editing. In this way, data or routines could be shared by several programs, and a control section could be recompiled without having to recompile the other control sections in its original program. Provided that the newer version of a control section was loaded first, the earlier version(s) would automatically be deleted when the loader encountered them.

The control-section concept made practical not only communication and symbolic cross-references between routines and replaceability of portions of programs, but also scatter loading. With scatter loading a program could fit into memory, even if no single vacant memory area could contain it. If a vacant area could be found for each control section, then the program could be loaded into noncontiguous memory locations and successfully executed.

The NAMED COMMON data area in FORTRAN IV is a control section that contains data but no instructions. The unnamed or blank common area in earlier FORTRAN II is not a control section, but a form of absolute addressing used in an otherwise relocatable program to produce predictable (hence shareable) allocation of data storage space.

The hardware base-displacement addressing scheme used in some computers (Spectra 70, IBM 360) almost forces the division of programs into independent sections 4096 bytes or less in length. A general-purpose register then contains the starting address of each active section, and locations within it are distinguished by the displacement contained in the instruction address part.

A dummy control section (DSECT) is a description of the relative internal structure (memory layout) of a control section not actually contained in the current program or routine. At execution time, a real (nondummy) control section of the same name must be present in another subroutine or an error condition will result. The DSECT permits references to be made to the contents of a control section without recompiling the control-section contents into every routine that refers to it. Thus the dummy control section is a virtual or fictitious control section that is realized (made real) at load time or at linkage edit time: for example, a control block is described as a DSECT. When the address of any real control block is provided, the contents of all of that control block become accessible to the program. By changing the pointer to the beginning of the block, another control block may be swiftly substituted for the first control block.

conversational time-sharing The simultaneous utilization of a computer system by multiple users, each user being equipped with a remote terminal.

The conversational mode of time-sharing permits a man and a computer to cooperate as partners in the solution of complex problems. The man contributes experience, guidance, intuition, and insight while the computer performs calculations and stores volume of data. This man/machine combination can at times be more powerful than either partner in certain situations.

The adjective conversational underlines the fact that man and computer communicate in a give-and-take, question-and-answer fashion. If the man makes a coding mistake, the computer makes him aware of it instantly by printing the error out on the terminal printer; if through a logical flow in the program, partial results lead the man to visualize a wrong final result, he may stop the computer, and alter the program.

The man begins by telephoning himself into the computer and identifying himself. The following example, combining various existing techniques, will illustrate the process. The man's communications are underlined:

HELLO
WHAT IS YOUR NUMBER? . .   X27   013
LANGUAGE TO BE USED? . .   FORTRAN
NEW PROBLEM OR OLD? . .   OLD
PROBLEM NAME? . .   BIQUAD
WAIT
READY
RUN
WHAT ARE A, B, C?   −27.06, 172.9, 1.73$
INPUT NOT IN PROPER FORMAT . . RETYPE IT
−27.06, 172.9, 1,734
SOLUTION OF A + BX² + CX⁴ = 0
. . . . .
ETC.

The user, in this example, typed in a dollar sign instead of a 4. The computer singled it out immediately, and allowed the user to correct the error on the spot. Had the user sent his input to a data processing center for execution during the night shift (which is the cheapest), he would have found next morning an error diagnostic and a day lost in getting his solution. Through conversational time-sharing, only a few seconds were required between wrong and corrected input.

What may appear illogical at first sight is that this advantage offered by conversational time-sharing, correcting program errors on the spot, is combined with a drastic reduction of cost in computer utilization. In fact, the same $600 per hour computer which a user may routinely access two or three times a day for a few instants may cost the same user $15 an hour in conversational time-sharing mode. The reason for this apparent paradox is that in using a system in the usual non-time-sharing way, a programmer actually rents time for the whole system, including those parts he is not utilizing at the time. In time-sharing mode, he pays only for the part of the system he uses, and since anywhere, depending on the system used, from 40 to 200 users will be sharing a computer in time-sharing mode, a user's share of the system rental is correspondingly reduced. Although the user only accesses the computer a few milliseconds out of every second, he is not made aware of the interruptions, and indeed feels he has a continuous, uninterrupted service from the computer.

The principal components of a conversational time-sharing system are as follows:

1. A central processor for high-speed computations
2. A large random-access file for storing data and programs
3. An input/output supervisor to coordinate communications
4. Transmission links
5. Terminals with various input/output facilities

Small-scale conversational time-sharing systems will commonly couple two computers together. One computer supervises communications, handles the accounting, allocates time and resolves priorities; the other computer concentrates on problem solving and switching rapidly from program to program as data become available. On large-scale conversational time-sharing systems, one very fast processor may handle both functions, but use of multiple processors is not excluded.

The random-access file is almost always a disk file, but disk, drums, tapes, and other media are being combined in certain systems.

Transmission is achieved by means of telephone or telegraph lines when the distances between users and systems are large. Coaxial cables may be used for short distances and high-volume transmission. Economic considerations usually dictate the choice of the transmission media.

The simplest and most common remote terminals are the teletypewriter units (such as the no. 33 Teletypewriter of AT&T) and the electrical typewriters (such as the IBM 1050). Cathode-ray tubes (CRT) with light pens are more glamorous, but they are getting more common where large amount of graphic work are involved.

The control of a conversational time-sharing system is a complex undertaking: priority schemes must be developed to service all users; users must be protected against all other users; programs and data must be unaccessible to all but the original user; file contents must be organized, and unwanted data purged; lines must be polled to monitor all communication activities; hardware malfunctions must be detected immediately; and, above all, the system must protect itself from all users, be it through ignorance or mischievousness.

When conversational time-sharing activities are low, as for instance during the midnight to 8 A.M. shift, the idle time can be used for batch background programs. These are conventional, non-real-time, long-running programs of low priority which can be profitably run during otherwise idle time. Some systems permit conversational time-sharing users to initiate a background program, and then disconnect themselves from the system. Communications will be reestablished only when the work is completed.

Some nonconversational applications of time-sharing are found in the monitoring of production processes (as in chemical plants) and in the information-inquiry services (such as airline reservations).

Most of the pioneering work in conversational time-sharing was carried out at the Massachusetts Institute of Technology (Project MAC). Commercial conversational time-sharing is presently being offered by a number of hardware manufacturers such as GE, IBM, and SDS.

See TIME-SHARING.

conversion routine A flexible, self-contained, and generalized program which only requires specifications about very few facts in order to be used by a programmer. Conversion routines are used to change the presentation of data from one form to another as, for instance, from binary to decimal, or from card to disk.

convert To transform the representation of data. For instance, to change numerical data from decimal to binary, or from cards to tape.

To convert may equally refer to the act of adapting an existing program (written for a given computer) to another computer which is not compatible with the first. This adaptation (or conversion) may be as simple as changing a few cards and recompiling, to as complex as entirely rewriting the old program. The difference between these two definitions resides in the fact that the first definition covers data conversion only whereas the latter concerns method (or procedure) conversion.

Program conversion has proved sufficiently expensive to warrant a two-pronged attack on the problem: a varying degree of compatibility among computers of the same family, and a set of languages (ALGOL, COBOL, FORTRAN, etc.) acceptable to many computers with only a minimum amount of modifications.

copy To reproduce data without altering the original data. For instance, printing on multipart paper, duplicating a punched-card deck by means of a reproducer, duplicating a magnetic tape. Synonymous with duplicate.

core-array A rectangular grid arrangement of cores. As a rule, a core array of $n \times n$ cores is said to have n words of n bits in an array. For instance, if each core is represented by a square, the following core array would contain eight words, each word 8 bits long:

000								
001								
002								
003								
004								
005	0	1	1	0	1	0	0	1
006								
007								

The numbers 000, 001, 002, etc., to the left of the core array represent the addresses for each one of these words. Thus, in this example,

the content of address (or memory location) 005 is: 011 01001.
See MAGNETIC CORE.

core bank A stack of core arrays and associated electronics, the
stack containing a specific number of core arrays. Thus, a core bank
represents a functional unit of digital computer memory. The core
bank will be found frequently to contain 1024 or 4096 words, but
many other sizes are presently in use. See CORE STACK.

core-image library A collection of computer programs residing on
mass-storage device in ready-to-run form. There exists a method of
finding a particular program in the library and loading into internal
memory. The associated documentation is not considered a part
of the library: in general, only the instructions on the mass-storage
device make up the core-image library.

core stack A number of core arrays, next to one another, and
treated as a unit. See CORE ARRAY.

COS. Compatible operating system Not a true operating system,
COS is a series of programs which allow IBM 1401 programs under
emulation mode to operate intermixed with IBM 360 programs and
BOS and DOS.

An optional emulator feature allows a model 360/30 to process
1401/1440/1460 programs without any program modifications. This is
done via a combination of hardware and software which is quite efficient
(runs faster than a 1401) but is incompatible with every 360 operating
system. To run a 360 program after a 1401 program, the operator must
dismount the emulation software residence volume, replace it with a system 360 operating system residence volume, throw some console switches,
and IPL (initial-program-load) the 360 software. To avoid this operator
intervention, and also increase operating efficiency, a PROGRAM MODE
SWITCH was offered as an option to the emulation option. With this
inexpensive added feature, a 360 program can enter 1401 mode, and a
1401 program can enter 360 mode, by means of program instructions.

Initially, IBM offered no programming support for the program
mode switch. Therefore, software to allow 1401 programs to run
under DOS was developed by an IBM user, and was called COMPAT.
This same software is distributed by (but not supported by) IBM
under the name COS so that all users may have the opportunity to
use it.

COS requires a 360/30 configuration having at least 32K core,
compatibility mode (1401/1440/1460), program mode switch, and one
selector channel. In addition, COS supports emulation of the 1311

disk pack on the 2311 disk pack, and even allows the content of more than one 1311 to be placed on one 2311 (the 2311 holds more data than a 1311, but is physically interchangeable). Using COS, all I/O is performed in overlapped 360 mode, permitting very high speed operation of emulated programs. In many cases it is not necessary to rewrite a 1401 program in 360 language because of the high-efficiency operational convenience of COS.

counter A register or storage location used to represent the number of occurrences of an event.

In certain types of punched-card data processing equipment (such as the IBM 604 electronic calculating punch), the counter plays the role of accumulator and multiplier quotient: the results developed in the counter during calculations can be punched into the card. In other machines (such as the IBM 101 electronic statistical machine), counters are used for counting unit records. When a unit record meets certain requirements, a 1 is added to the unit counter.

In most computers counters are created by the programmer anywhere in memory. Consider, for instance, a program in which data cards must be read and a record kept of the number of cards read in for checking purposes. Such a program could appear as shown in the table. Memory location 2000 acts as a counter in this ex-

Instruction location	Instruction contents
1000	READ CARD.
1001	ADD 1 TO LOCATION 2000.
. . . .	. . . . .
1500	TEST FOR ADDITIONAL CARD. IF YES, GO TO 1000. IF NO, GO TO 1501.
1501	(PROCEED WITH PROGRAM.)

ample. The contents of location 2000 can be printed and will thus serve as an additional check that the proper number of cards were read in during the execution of the program. See INSTRUCTION COUNTER.

crosstalk The unwanted energy transferred from one circuit to another, from the "disturbing" circuit to the "disturbed" circuit.

Usually expressed in decibels, the crosstalk is the measure of the ratio of energy in the disturbing circuit over the energy induced in the disturbed circuit. It is almost always considered undesirable.

cut form   In optical character recognition (OCR), any document form, receipt, etc., of standard dimensions which must be issued a separate read command in order to be recognized.

Cut forms may contain information about a single event or transaction, such as a shipping invoice; or they may contain multiple lines of information, e.g., a coded sheet of daily sales.

Other examples:

1.   In magnetic-ink character recognition (MICR), a personalized check

2.   In OCR, an oil company receipt reflecting a gasoline purchase

Contrast with CONTINUOUS FORMS.

cybernetics   The theory of control and communication common in the machine and in the animal.

The road to cybernetics started with a legend, for since Daedalus, men have been fascinated by the mechanical imitation of living organisms. And as man's automata graduated from bird-man to Golem, from Golem to clockwork music boxes, from clockwork music boxes to steam engines, from steam engines to photocell door openers, and from photocell door openers to computers, man steered away from power engineering to communications engineering for a deeper insight into automation.

Today's automata represent only a branch of communication engineering with the cardinal ideas of message, noise, and quantity of information to be transmitted. This realization crystallized the concept of cybernetics as the discipline looking into the process common to nervous systems and mathematical machines, and the development of the theory of control and communication in machines and living organisms was based on the concept of feedback mechanisms.

A feedback mechanism is well illustrated by the voluntary act of picking up this book: there is here no conscious effort of the will to contract the necessary muscles in sequence, but a feedback mechanism permitting information to travel from the nervous system to muscles to sense organs and back to the nervous system. The analysis of such a mechanism combines physical and biological studies, and it is a characteristic of cybernetics that the development of a generalized theory will require the team-of-scientists approach, each scientist having a sound acquaintance with the fields of his teammates.

cycle   The interval of space or time required by a set of events or phenomena to be completed. By extension, a set of operations repeated regularly in the same sequence, the operations being possibly subject to variations on each repetition.

As a rule, a reference to "cycle" in the EDP field usually is a reference to the memory cycle, that is, to the shortest time elapsed between one store (or fetch) and the next store (or fetch) in the same memory unit.

The memory cycle customarily sets the pace for the entire computer. For example, an instruction cannot be completed in less than one cycle because the computer must wait for the next instruction to be fetched. This bottleneck is avoided in some computers by permitting access to more than one instruction per cycle, or by having multiple independent memories and overlapping cycle times. Since the memory cycle dominates the rate of execution of instructions, it is sometimes called the machine cycle, or major cycle. There may be another cycle in some computers, a much faster cycle which is internal to the hardware and which is called the minor cycle, or clock cycle. The time value of this cycle determines the initiation of each elementary subtask of the execution routine. The minor cycle is characteristic of synchronous computers.

cyclic feeding   In character recognition, a system employed by character readers in which each input document is issued to the document transport in a predetermined and constant period of time.

Thus, machines that operate under cyclic feeding obtain a constant feed rate (number of documents per unit of time) which is timed to accommodate the longest document under consideration.

The disadvantage of cyclic feeding is that it limits the effective document throughput rate in those cases where shorter-length documents are utilized.

Consequently, in order to reduce the gap between documents, and thereby maximize the throughput rate, most manufacturers offer acyclic feeding systems in which the feeding of a document is timed from the trailing edge of the preceding document.

cyclic shift   A shift by means of which the data move out of one end of the storing register and reenter into the other end, as in a closed loop.

The cyclic shift is sometimes called a circular shift since it consists in joining the two ends of a linear sequence to produce a closed loop. This closed loop, or cyclic sequence, is then rotated to produce a cyclic shift, and is broken only at the new locations of the two ends of the shift register when the operation is completed. There are some powerful and very fast computers (such as the CDC 6600) which have only two kinds of shift: a right shift, and a left shift. A right-shift operation causes the word to loose right-hand side bits, and is similar to dividing the word by powers of 2: the bits dropped are generally lost.   The left-hand shift is equal to a cyclic (or circular) shift, for the bits leaving the register on the left reenter the register in sequence from the right: in this fashion, a very fast bit (or character) scanning can be carried out.   It is interesting to note that the existence of only two types of shift instructions in computers can be found at the other end of the scale, that is, in small computers not having a very large set of operation codes.

D

data Any representations of characters or analog quantities to which meaning, if not information, might be assigned.

Data, as the plural form of datum, is loosely employed to convey the meaning of numerical information. It is sometimes (if incorrectly) found being used in the singular sense, as in the expression: "This volume is the data I need."

data channel A bidirectional data path between I/O devices and the main memory of a digital computer. Data channels permit one or more I/O operations to proceed concurrently with computation, thereby enhancing computer performance.

The simplest kind of input/output may be found in computers that have no data channels. For example, the IBM 1401 READ A CARD command consists of a single operation code with no address or modifiers. All computation halts while one card is read into a fixed area of memory. At the conclusion of the read, the program resumes at the instruction following the read command. No problem of timing coordination arises, because the program simply cannot get ahead of the card reader.

Compare this situation with that of a similar computer having a very elementary kind of data channel, the Honeywell H-200. To read a card, the programmer assigns a data channel to the card reader and directs it to begin reading into a specified area of memory. The program is then free to go on calculating and/or initiating more I/O operations on other data channels. When it wishes to use data from the card, the program must first check to see if the READ is completed. If nothing can be done until the read finishes, the program is forced to wait. This may lead to reading cards before they are needed, and holding the data in areas of memory assigned to be input buffers, so that the waiting will be minimized by these anticipatory read operations. The program can use the card image in one buffer while the data channel is filling another buffer simultaneously.

In computers of greater power, the data channels are correspondingly more sophisticated. A typical data channel is capable of executing a sequence of commands when properly initialized by a single instruction from the central processing unit. A common method is for the program to contain one I/O initiating operation, which designates an I/O device, a data channel, and the location of a data-channel command stored in main memory. This command in turn contains the detailed instructions for performing one I/O operation or step, and directions about what to do when the instruction is completed. If a CONTINUE type of command is given, the data channel will fetch the next command from the location following the current command and execute it. In this way, an arbitrary number of individual I/O actions (involved in the same I/O device) can be initiated by a single program instruction, and performed without further attention from the central processor.

A typical data-channel command may include such detailed directions as:

1. When this command is finished, (do, do not) execute the next one.
2. When this command is finished, get the next command, but use only the address and amount of data fields, treating the remaining fields as with this command.
3. Begin I/O transfer at this address.
4. Transfer no more than this many characters, bits, or words.
5. (Do, do not) transfer data into/out of memory (permits skipping).
6. When this command is finished, interrupt the central processor for attention.
7. (Do, do not) test for a particular kind of error condition.
8. Transfer an entire record, or stop when the count (amount) is satisfied and ignore the rest of the record.
9. Read multiple records, if necessary, to satisfy the count.
10. Either conditionally or unconditionally, get the next command from the following (nonsequential) address: (specify location of next command).

There are now two kinds of data channels on some computers (example: IBM 360 System, RCA Spectra 70): the selector channel which executes one command at a time, on a single device, at whatever speed the device itself requires, and the multiplexor channel, which can execute several commands at once, on different devices. Any mix of input/output may occur concurrently, provided only that the maximum data rate of the channel is not exceeded. Multiplex operation is possible only on low data transfer-rate devices (punched cards or tape, typewriter terminals, teletype lines).

A multiplexor channel shares the main memory side of its hardware among all devices, but has one subchannel for each I/O device (sometimes two if the device is bidirectional, as for example: reader/punch, typewriter). The subchannel contains all external interface hardware, channel-command-status storage (for addresses in main memory count, options specified), and data buffers at least one character in size.

The multiplexor/subchannel concept permits cheaper construction than an equivalent design with many selector channels, and increases the amount of simultaneous I/O that an inexpensive computer can sustain.

data-code conversion   The translation of alphanumerical information into a language acceptable by the computer. The conversion of data code is normally handled directly by the computer during the input operation. Some older, pure-binary machines require a programmed computation to translate input decimals into internal binary numbers.

data definition (DD) statement   A control card that describes a data set to be used by a job step in OS/360.

A DD statement is an element of job control language which relates the program's internal description of the data that it wants to the external data set actually provided for this job step. A DD statement contains at least some of the following information:

DDNAME	The name of this DD statement. Used by the program to refer to the data set described by this DD card. Omitted only for concatenated data sets or parts of indexed sequential data sets.
DSNAME	The name of the data set as it might appear in a catalog, independent of any programs.
LABEL	Parameters used in constructing and/or checking data-set labels.
DISP	Disposition: is this a new data set being created; should it be deleted, kept, passed to another job step of this job, cataloged, uncataloged, etc.

DCB	Additional data control block parameters, such as DSORG: data-set organization. BLKSIZE: physical record maximum size.
UNIT	Specific device or type of device on which data set is mounted.
SEP, AFF	Parameters governing assignment of selector channels, allows optimizing I/O simultaneity.

Other options allow specifying that this data set consists of records following this DD statement in the current input device, or contains no records at all, or may contain control card images, or is described in another DD statement subsequent to this DD statement.

Indeed, there are so much optional data that could go on a DD card that IBM has found it necessary to devise elaborate flowcharts to assist people in proper preparation of them.

Information not supplied on DD cards can be supplied by DCB parameters in the program, or else from the data-set label.

data division The section of a program (written in the COBOL language) which describes each data item used for input, output, and storage. The data division corresponds roughly to a dictionary in which the entries (or data names) are related to the data (or data items) to be processed.

For every data item used in a program, the data division describes its name, its length (the amount of storage occupied), its format (numeric or alphanumeric, decimal or binary, etc.), and its location relative to associated data items. The COBOL compiler needs this description to generate the proper instructions whenever a data item is referred to in the procedure division.

See COBOL.

data field An area in the main memory of the computer in which a data record is contained. See DATA RECORD.

data item A unit of information of one kind pertaining to only one thing. Sometimes called a datum. For instance, the age of an employee, the name of a subscriber, the address of City Hall represent three different data items.

data management (DM) A collective term referring to the totality of all OS/360 routines that provide access to data, enforce storage conventions, and regulate the use of I/O devices.

Under data management we lump together all the data-set organizations (sequential, indexed sequential, partitioned, direct, telecommunications), macroinstruction languages, basic and queued access methods, the catalog and its various indexes. The term DM includes all the conventions, languages, utility, and service routines which permit OS/360 programs to read, write, keep, and destroy data.

There are five major kinds of data-set organization:

Sequential	Logically similar to mag tape, paper tape, printer, cards, etc.
Partitioned	Contains sequentially organized "members," each with its own name. Used for program libraries. Resides on direct-access device.
Indexed sequential	A sequential organization with an index permitting both random and sequential access, intermixed. Must reside on direct-access device.
Direct	Typical random-access device organization.
Telecommunications	Used for remote processing, transmissions.

The graphic DS organization is sometimes excluded from data management, though this distinction is artificial.

The data records of a data set can have any of 6 record formats:

F	The simple fixed-length format commonly used for card and print files.
FB	Fixed-length, blocked (multiple logical records per physical record) used on tape, disk, etc.
FBS	Standard fixed-length, blocked, the most efficient record format available for disk. "Standard" means that every block contains the same number of records except possibly the last, which may contain fewer.
V	Variable-length. Each record is preceded by a byte-count (nondata) length indicator. Used to save space.
VB	Variable-length, blocked. Each physical record is preceded by a length indicator, and each logical record is also prefixed with a length indication.
U	Format undefined. Records are considered to be unblocked. They are written to specified length, but reading is terminated by either end of record or specified size limit being reached. The data management is not concerned with the contents or construction of U-format records.

The first character in the logical record of any format may be data, or it may be a (nondata) control character to govern form spacing (printing) or stacker selection (punching). This option is indicated by suffixing A for ASCII control characters, or M for machine-language control characters to the format specification above. Thus: FBSA is standard fixed-length, blocked, with ASCII control characters. If the data set is assigned to other than a printer or punch, control characters are treated as data. Interpretation of control characters is performed by appropriate data management service routines.

The logical record is the data grouping that the program expects to manipulate. A physical record is one or more logical records, together with associated length indicators and control information, and is written or read as a unit. (In some FORTRAN systems, it is possible to construct long logical records that occupy several physical records each, but this is not common.)

It is necessary to describe logical records at compile/assembly time, and physical records must be defined at execution time. However, it is possible to not specify physical record construction at assembly/compile time, and supply the missing information at run time via DD card parameters. This permits the same program module to be used with blocked and unblocked, tape/disk/data cell resident data sets interchangeably. In this way, a run-time system of great flexibility is provided. However, the price of this power is complicated control card conventions.

In addition to providing logical record/buffer supervisory routines and physical record/device supervisory routines, data management also includes numerous other services such as password protection of confidential or sensitive data. Password protection requires the operator to make a current (secret) response at OPEN time, or else the program is not allowed to access the protected data set. The password data set may itself be protected by a password, thus "locking up the keys to the other locks."

Data management also supervises the conversion from one character set or encoding to another. Thus 8-bit bytes can be written on 6-bit (7-track) magnetic tape using the data conversion feature, or EBDIC (8-bit) codes can be written on magnetic tape using 6-bit BCD codes via the translate feature. Similarly, cards can be punched in a Hollerith or EBDIC codes and converted by data management, or paper tape can be read/punched in a variety of widths and character sets.

Data management maintains "generation" data sets. A generation data set is one derived from a similar, earlier data set by a periodically executed program run. For example, a weekly payroll history tape is updated by corrective regeneration every week. This week's tape is the current generation (son), last week's tape is the "father" generation, and a two-week-old tape is of the "grandfather" generation, etc. Data management allows similarly named data sets to be distinguished by absolute or relative generation number. It is also possible to change a generation data set without creating a new generation (e.g., correct an error by an exceptional run) by changing its version number on a constant-generation update. Generation data sets commonly reside on magnetic tape.

Data management is responsible for queuing the requests for activity on particular data channels and devices, assuring the maximum utilization of installed equipment. Naturally special routines must be added to support shared data channels, read-while-write feature, track overflow, extended search, etc., etc. These optional routines are specified at system generation time to allow best matching of the hardware and the data management routines of an installation.

In random-access devices, DM can perform track overflow (with hardware assistance), effectively linking the individual tracks of a cylinder together. In addition, use of track overflow, cylinder overflow, and independent overflow areas allows additions to an existing direct-access data set. DM "marks" a record for deletion by writing all "1" bits in the first few bytes of a record. (For this reason, no mass-storage record should begin with a negative binary integer.)   Marked records are omitted when a DS is being read or reorganized.   As an option, marked records can be deleted when adding new records to an existing direct-access file.

See also: ACCESS METHOD, BASIC ACCESS METHOD.

data media   See CUT FORM, CONTINUOUS FORMS.

data organization (also known as data-set organization)   Any one of the data management conventions for physical and spatial arrangement of the physical records of a data set.

The five data management organizations are:

1. Sequential
2. Partitioned
3. Indexed sequential
4. Direct
5. Telecommunications

These organizations differ in the arrangement of records on storage media, and also in the manner of accessing a particular record.   The choice of organization will influence processing speed and efficiency, and also the density with which data can be packed (storage efficiency).   In particular, the "HIT RATIO" (number of records accessed per run divided by number of records in data set) will often dictate the choice of organization.

Sequential organization is the only permissible organization for punched-card, unit-record, magnetic-tape, or paper-tape data.   In sequential organization the individual records follow one another in serial order.   A header label at the beginning and a trailer label at the end may be used to define the limits of the data extent.   When processing sequential data sets, it is necessary to access every record between the current record and the desired record.   For low hit ratios, much wasted data movement results.   For 100 percent hit ratios, no organization can be more efficient.

Partitioned organization describes a data set composed of one or more sequentially organized members.   A member is a set of records collectively identified by a member name unique to the data set. Partitioned data sets must reside on direct-access devices.   The members may appear in any order and be accessed randomly.   A directory contains the relative address of the beginning of each member.   Normally an entire member is processed if any of its records are accessed.   Program libraries are partitioned data sets.

Indexed sequential contains data records stored in (almost) ascending sequence.   The records are identified by and ordered by keys (defined subfields of data).   An index (or hierarchy of indexes) permits finding any particular record without having to scan the intervening records. Overflow areas are deliberately left vacant at the creation of the indexed sequential data set so that records may be inserted into the data set after its initial creation, without violating sequential order too severely. For example, insertion of a record into an already filled track forces the last record off the track and onto an overflow track. An address pointer permits finding the displaced records. The sequential order can be restored by recreating the indexed sequential data set by copying onto a new volume. Both random order and sequential order processing can be performed on an indexed sequential data set, but random processing is inefficient owing to index searching. Indexed sequential data sets must reside on a direct-access device.

Direct organization is used when records are randomly ordered on a direct-access device. Records are stored and accessed by either relative or absolute hardware addresses. Absolute address prevents moving the DS once it has been created. Relative addresses permit moving the DS but must be converted to absolute addresses by the supervisory routine. Alternatively, a hardware search for a specified key may be requested. The programmer is responsible for associating the address with the desired record, and some complicated schemes may be needed for this purpose. It is usually possible to add records by merely writing them at the end of the currently filled space.

Telecommunications organization differs from the others in being dynamic, not static, and also because it is time-organized, not space-organized, in nature. As such, it is less under the control of data management than the other organizations.

data processing Referring to any operation or combination of operations on data, including everything that happens to data from the time they are observed or collected to the time they are destroyed.

data processor Any device capable of performing operations on data, as, for instance, a desk calculator, an analog computer, a digital computer. Also, a person engaged in processing data. One of the very loose terms that can eventually acquire a very specific meaning in localized areas.

data record A collection of data items related in some fashion, and usually contiguous in location. Thus, for instance, for any employee, the employee number, employee name, employee address, employee hourly rate of pay, employee year-to-date earnings, and employee withholding tax paid, represent a data record consisting of six data items.

data reduction   The transformation of raw data into a more useful form.

Data reduction may take the form of replacing a table of values by the equation from which these values may be calculated, or simply replacing a set of data by the average value of these data. In a loose sense, data reduction reflects the first operations performed on data, whatever these operations might be.

data set   A named collection of similar and related data records recorded upon some computer-readable medium.

The concept of data set is one of the most fundamental concepts in System 360 and data processing. In an inactive condition, a data set contains one or more records, spatially arranged, according to one of the data management data organizations. Each record contains a number of related data items, formatted according to one of the data management record formats, and encoded in some computer-interpretable form. In this static condition a data set is merely some data, waiting to be used.

In an active condition, a data set is a stream of input data to be processed by a program, or a repository for output data generated by a program, or both. At any moment, a program has a distinct set of data sources and data receivers, and each corresponds to a data set. However, from run to run, and sometimes from moment to moment within a run, the identity of the data set serving as a particular input or output may change. The operating system is responsible for linking the proper data sets to the program's inputs and outputs, thereby giving a program a measure of independence, permitting it to process various data sets as the need arises.

The terminology data set describes a concept that used to be (and still is) called data file, or simply file for short. However, confusion arose because file sometimes meant a set of data records and sometimes meant the storage device currently containing the data. For clarity, the term volume now describes the latter and data set the former.

Every data set begins as a computer program's output stream or is prepared in computer-readable form by noncomputer means (keypunch, data gathering system, automatic recording device, etc.). It may begin and end with a label. These labels are standard-format data records, containing such data as data-set name, date of creation, security or privacy code, volume identification. These labels delimit the data set and permit the operating system to assure that the correct DS is being used. A data set may also contain a directory or indexes which serve to help locate a particular record or group of records. A data set may be cataloged, which makes its volume of residence known to the operating system. A DS may be used in an uncataloged state, but the operator is then responsible for using the correct volume or data set.

A data set ends its existence by being uncataloged (if cataloged), deleted (from a random-access storage device), or dismounted (if on a removable recording medium) and discarded. If it was on a random-access device, the space that it had occupied may become available for reuse by another data set.

A dummy data set is a set that contains no data records but has a name. Dummy data sets permit a program to run with a data set for every data control block but supply no input data and record no output data. They are sometimes used for program checkout.

Data set is not to be confused with Dataset, a Bell Telephone device which permits digital data to be transmitted over ATT lines.

data-set control block (DSCB) In a direct-access device, a standard-format control block specifying for one data set the parameters needed to describe and manipulate the data set.

The DSCB serves as the standard data-set label when resident on any direct-access device. Each DSCB contains parameters such as data set name (identification), data organization (relation of records to one another), record format (internal structure of data records), extent (location and amount of space allocated to this data set), date of creation, security or privacy, etc., etc.

On a given direct-access volume, all the DSCB's are grouped together to form the volume table of contents (VTOC). The VTOC is itself a data set (lowest-numbered address) after the volume label and IPL records, and so always begins in a known location. The VTOC DSCB describes the extent of the VTOC, and thus the number of DSCB's in the VTOC and the number of data sets on the volume.

DSCB is not to be confused with DCB. A DSCB describes data resident on a direct-access volume. A DCB (data control block) describes an input and/or output stream of data records for a particular program. Thus a DCB is program-dependent and dynamic; a DSCB is program-independent and static.

data-set label (DSL) A generic term covering DSCB's for direct-access devices and the data-set labels used on sequential access devices.

The DSL serves to identify, describe, and delimit a data set. It identifies by giving the data-set name. It describes by indicating record format, date of creation, extent, security or privacy, etc. It delimits either by marking the beginning and end of a data set (sequential access devices) or by indicating the boundaries of the space allocated for the data set (direct-access device).

The standard label appears in a format particular to the device being used to store the data set. Optional user labels (one or more) may accompany the data set. However, no labels are used on printer-output files and many punched-card (unit-record) files.

On magnetic tape, special one-character delimiting records called tape marks are considered to be part of the labeling convention. In some cases, particularly temporary data sets, tape marks could be the only labels.

DDA   See DIGITAL DIFFERENTIAL ANALYZER.

debug   To test for, locate, and remove mistakes from a program or malfunctions from a computer.

Whereas the detection, location, and removal of malfunctions (or bugs) in a hardware device are carried out by maintenance personnel by means of testing procedures furnished by the manufacturer, the debugging of a program is a programmer's responsibility and involves (1) designing a test or check-out method; (2) detecting the bugs; (3) isolating and identifying the bugs producing the observed errors; (4) correcting the errors; (5) rechecking the revised program; (6) making the required modifications in the documentation.

It is most important to design an economical test which will put to work all segments of the program logic, singly and in combination, and which will include all types of permissible data. The output of this test must be such that it can be easily scanned for errors. If a program must be capable of rejecting, or otherwise recognizing invalid inputs, the test should also include invalid inputs.

Once the test is performed, the output should be carefully examined for any discrepancy with the expected output. Any observed error should be such as to allow for a rapid identification of the segment of logic responsible for the error. If necessary, a more detailed test of the section or sections will be carried out until the source of the error is accurately known. The revised logic is then coded, and the program retested to ensure a correct functioning. The prepared documentation will then be altered if and where necessary, so as to indicate what is in the program, rather than what should have been in the program.

In major programming work, a check-out test design is often performed by programmers not of the program development task force. This ensures adequate recognition of the difficulties of checking a large program system, and may well lead to the discovery of lapses in the planning by the program designers. Debug is synonymous with troubleshoot.

decimal   Pertaining to the numeration system with a base of 10. Also describes a digital computer organized to calculate by decimal arithmetic.   See BINARY-CODED DECIMAL.

decision   The definition of a future action.   Also a test, the outcome of which will determine which of several alternative actions will be performed next.   See CONDITIONAL JUMP.

decision instruction   An instruction that determines the selection of a branch of a program, also called a conditional jump instruction. The decision instruction forces the control to one of alternate successor instructions depending on the outcome of a test.   See CONDITIONAL JUMP.

decision mechanism   In character recognition, that component part of a character reader which accepts the finalized version of the input character and makes an assessment as to its most probable identity.

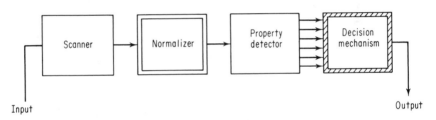

Input   Output

Character reader: component parts.

Making a decision as to the character's most probable identity involves not only a comparison of the given signal (analog or digital) against a library of perfect specimens, but also an assessment of the reliability of the decision.   If the reliability should fall below a prescribed limit, then the character is classified as unrecognizable, and the system is usually left with one of the following courses of action:
1.   Visual display of rejected character with option to make a manual correction (some character readers can remember where this interruption occurred, with the advantage that processing can continue while the correction is being made)
2.   Rejection of the whole document with an indication as to the approximate location of the doubtful character
3.   Rereading the line containing rejected character—perhaps under changed reading conditions

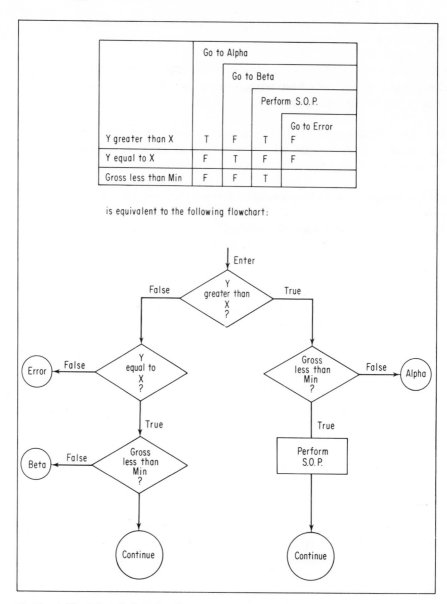

	Go to Alpha	Go to Beta	Perform S.O.P.	Go to Error
Y greater than X	T	F	T	F
Y equal to X	F	T	F	F
Gross less than Min	F	F	T	

is equivalent to the following flowchart:

Decision table and equivalent flowchart.

decision table A table of contingencies to be considered in the definition of a problem, together with the actions to be taken. Decision tables are sometimes used in place of flowcharts for program documentation.

The decision table is a compact method of summarizing the actions to be taken, depending on conditions existing at the time the table is consulted. Usually, a decison table is represented by a rectangular array, the rows representing independent conditions (or tests), and the columns indicating the actions to be taken. Each entry of the array, that is, each intersection of rows and columns, is a symbol: this symbol indicates the column action that will be taken if the corresponding row condition is true (T) or not true (F). If the action is independent of the condition, the entry will be blank.

In the following illustration, if Y is greater than X, and Gross is greater than or equal to Min, control is given to whatever instruction is located at Alpha. When Y is equal to X, and Gross is not less than Min, control is given to Beta. When Gross is less than Min and Y is greater than X, the instructions at location SOP are executed, and then control is returned to the instructions following the decision table. The last column shows that when Y is less than X, control should be passed to the instruction at the location Error, whatever the value of Gross and Min may be. The case where Y equals X and Gross is less than Min is not explicitly considered in the table. This omission is taken to imply that control would, in this case, pass to the next instruction in the program (indicated by Continue in the flowchart).

If the conventions agreed on for the decision table consider a blank entry illegal, the blank-entry column must be replaced by two columns, the first entry marked T, the second entry marked F, and the two corresponding actions being (in the above case): Go to Error.

	Go to Alpha				
		Go to Beta			
			Perform S. O. P.		
				Go to Error	
					Go to Error
Y greater than X	T	F	T	F	F
Y equal to X	F	T	F	F	F
Gross less than Min	F	F	T	T	F

Decision table with no blank entries.

In some applications, no omissions are acceptable. In this case, Y equal to X, and Gross less than Min would have to be included. This would be equivalent to adding the missing columns, with "Continue" for the indicated action.

deck   A collection of punched cards.

A deck of cards is one of the standard means of input to a computer (a roll of paper tape is another). When the deck is prepared on the computer site, the input should be converted to magnetic tape as soon as possible. If the deck is to be shipped to a computer center, a few precautions should be taken: (1) Create in duplicate a listing of the deck; (2) duplicate the deck to cover the contingency of the deck getting lost; (3) ship the listing with the deck; (4) generate a new listing on receipt of the deck, and compare both listings.

decode   To apply a code so as to translate some previous encoding.

Decoding is the basic function of the control unit of a computer. Consider, for instance, a program in which the number 30 must be added to the number 20. Assume the number 20 is already in the accumulator. Assume further that, in this computer, an instruction is made up of a two-digit operation code and a four-digit address. The instruction to add 30 has just entered into the control unit, and could appear in the instruction register as

111500

To decode this instruction, each character must be analyzed in sequence. In this instance, the two first digits 11 are found to represent the operation code for addition: As a consequence, various pulse signals are sent out to activate the circuits controlling addition. The next four digits 1500 are analyzed, and the address or memory location 1500 is determined: more pulse signals are sent out which bring the contents (in this case the number 30) out of location 1500 and into the accumulator through the adding circuits. The end result of this decoding operation will be the substitution of 20 by 50 in the accumulator. See INSTRUCTION.

decoder   A decoding device, and by extension, a matrix of logic elements selecting one or more output channels depending on the combination of input signals present.

The decoder is a device found in the control unit of the computer. Its purpose is to translate the instructions and data items read into the computer into pulse signals required to carry out the required operations. See CONTROL.

deferred entry/deferred exit The passing of control of the central processing unit to a subroutine or to an entry point as the result of an asynchronous event. This transfer causes a deferred exit from the program that did have control.

A normal or ordinary entry (or exit) is the immediate transfer of control to a designated entry point as a result of the execution of a computer instruction. In contrast to this, an asynchronous (unexpected or unpredictable time) entry is made under program control by a statement that means: "When this event occurs transfer to there." The program that set up this waiting-for-a-designated-event condition then continues to process normally. When the event occurs (detected by hardware as a pulse signal), control is transferred to the designated routine, suspending the normal sequence of processing and beginning a new sequence. The routine thus activated may or may not return control to the interrupted program (i.e.: it could have been an end-of-job signal). See INTERRUPT, TRAP.

delay The length of time by which an event is stayed. Delays are generally used to permit synchronization, that is, to allow an event to be carried out to completion before the delayed event is initiated.

delay line A sequential logic element with one input channel and one output channel. The state of the output channel at an instant T is the same as the state of the input channel at the instant $T - N$, where N is a constant interval of time for a specific delay line.

Pulses of information are space-stored in delay lines; that is, a pulse of information enters a delay line at a given time and is issued from the delay line a given time later. See ACOUSTIC DELAY LINE, ELECTROMAGNETIC DELAY LINE, SONIC DELAY LINE.

delay time The amount of time elapsed between one event and the next sequential event. In signal propagation, the delay time is the time that must elapse after an input signal is applied to a combinational logic element and before the output signal, or output signals, become reliably available.

delimiter A character that separates items of data.
A delimiter may be a pulse, a character, a digit, a bit, or even a pause to indicate the end of an item of data and the beginning of the next item of data. For instance, spacings will act as delimiters to define words, periods as delimiters with which to identify sentences, indentations as delimiters with which to identify paragraphs. Several kinds of delimiters may be required in a single string of data (such as spacing, comma, semicolon, period).

Any character not normally needed to represent data may be used as a delimiter, provided the computer is prepared to recognize the delimiter as such. For example, it is possible, within the same program, to enter 2/1/19 and A/B and have the computer recognize the slash in A/B as a "divided by" symbol, whereas 2/1/19 will be treated as an identifying date: this differentiation is achieved by means of context. No computer could recognize data without real or implied delimiters. Synonymous with SEPARATOR.

density   Density generally refers to the number of bits per unit of recording medium. The most common example is that of the magnetic tape: the density is expressed as the number of bits per inch of track. The same units are equally used for disks, drums, or other mobile magnetic media. In certain types of memories, such as photographic, electrostatic, thin films, density is expressed in terms of bits per square inch.

The meaning of density has been expanded with the advent of microelectronic components and refers to the number of components per square inch in monolithic integrated circuit construction, and even to number of components per cubic inch.

Increasing the density reduces the size, cost, access, propagation delay time, and sometimes reliability of a device. In magnetic tapes, a lower density may be used for long-term storage reliability. See PACKING DENSITY.

description   Usually refers to the definition of a problem, the most complex communication link between programmer and computer user. The degree of detail varies and would seem to be a function of the programmer's experience and background, and of the user's understanding of his problem and familiarity in dealing with programmers. See PROBLEM DESCRIPTION.

design   The specification of working relationships among the parts of a system. See FUNCTIONAL DESIGN, LOGIC DESIGN.

destructive read   A read process, beyond programmer's control, that erases the data in the source as it reads the data. In computers having destructive read instructions, it is customary to have the read instruction succeeded by an automatic hardware write-back cycle to prevent loss of data. This is why the core memories of such computers present output in about one-half the time required for a full read cycle. In such memories, all read instructions are actually read-and-write-back, and all write instructions are really read-erase-and-write-new. Some newer core storages have nondestructive read instructions which eliminate the necessity of a separate cycle to re-write what has just been read.

device   A general-purpose term used, often indiscriminately, to refer to a computer component or the computer itself, much as the word gadget could be used in the same way.   See STORAGE DEVICE.

diagnostic   The detection and isolation of a malfunction or mistake. Refers equally to compiler messages containing error information, or to the program used for diagnostic purposes.   In such applications, the word is used as a noun.

diagram   A graphic representation of relationships, usually in an abstract or symbolic form.   See BLOCK DIAGRAM, FUNCTIONAL DIAGRAM, LOGIC DIAGRAM, VENN DIAGRAM.

dichotomizing search   A procedure for searching an item in a set, in which, at each step, the set is divided into two parts, one part being then discarded if it can be logically shown that the item could not be in this part.   The search ends when the retained part of the set contains only one item.   The term dichotomizing search is a generic term which includes binary search but is not equivalent to binary search.   See BINARY SEARCH.

differential analyzer   A mechanical or electromechanical device designed primarily to solve differential equations.

The differential analyzer was built around 1930 by Dr. Vannevar Bush at the Massachusetts Institute of Technology.   The principal component of this device was the wheel-and-disk integrator (see drawing).

The shafts on which wheel and disk are mounted are mutually perpendicular shafts, the wheel being in contact with the disk.   The distance between the rim of the wheel and the center of the disk is equal to y; as the disk turns, the rotation is equal to dx.   By suitable motion of the wheel shaft (longitudinal and rotational) the wheel turn becomes thus equal to the integral of $y\,dx$.   The combination of such components through shafts and gears, prime motion being injected through the independent variable shafts, allowed for the solution of many-term differential equations.

The high-cost, low-speed, and time-consuming problem setup was responsible for the replacement of differential analyzers by electronic analog computers.   See ANALOG COMPUTER.

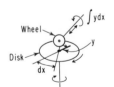

Wheel-and-disk integrator.

differentiator   A device whose output function is proportional to the derivative, or rate of change, of the input function with respect to one or more variables. For instance, a resistance/capacitance network can be made to select the leading and trailing edges of a pulse signal: in this case, the differentiator has an output voltage proportional to the rate of change of the input voltage. A common form of this device (and the simplest) is shown in the margin.

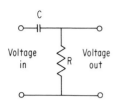

The value of the product *RC* is large compared to the period of the applied waveform. An ordinary transformer produces an output voltage proportional to the rate of change of the input current, but its use as a differentiator is not common.

digit A character used to represent one of the nonnegative integers smaller than the base of the system. For instance, in the decimal system, a digit is any one of the characters 0 to 9. Digit is also used in decimal digital computers to mean an elementary cell or character of memory, that is, the space reserved for the storage of one digit of information, as for instance: "An IBM 1620 computer with 20,000 digits of memory." See BINARY DIGIT, CHECK DIGIT, EQUIVALENT BINARY DIGITS, SIGN DIGIT, SIGNIFICANT DIGIT.

digital Characteristic of data in the form of digits. As applied to representation, storage, manipulation of data in the form of digital quantities: thus, a digital computer, a digital memory device.

Digital refers to discrete, noncontinuous quantities (usually multiples of some elementary unit) as contrasted with continuous quantities. Contrast with ANALOG.

digital computer A computer operating on discrete data by performing arithmetic and logic processes on these data. In general, any device that performs arithmetic, logical, and comparative functions upon information represented in digital form, and operates under the control of an internal program. In this context, "digital" means that the computer uses data in the form of numbers, and "computer" indicates that the device manipulates the data without step-by-step guidance of a human operator.

Customarily, a computer consists of the following elements: (1) an arithmetic unit that multiplies, divides, adds, subtracts, changes signs, and compares numbers; (2) an instruction counter indicating which instruction is currently being executed; (3) a control unit in which the logical circuits will interpret the instructions and direct the remainder of the computer's functions (arithmetic and control units together with the instruction counter form what is generally called the central processing unit, or CPU); (4) a memory that stores numbers and provides them upon request from the CPU (this function is usually performed by magnetic cores); (5) input and output devices that permit communication with the outside world, and also permit economical storage of masses of data too large to be contained in memory; and, (6) in all but the simplest digital computers, input/output channels to enable input/output operations to proceed at the same time as computations and with minimal attention from the CPU.

A digital computer executes instructions. Instructions are digital data items capable of specifying explicitly and unambiguously the operations to be performed. The instructions are arranged into programs, and programs direct the computer to accomplish the desired tasks. In larger computers, a special collection of programs called monitor (operating system, executive) provides services commonly needed in programs, so that the programmer need not write these complex routines whenever he needs them. Contrast with ANALOG COMPUTER.

digital differential analyzer A differential analyzer which uses numbers to represent analog quantities. A digital voltmeter may be considered as an elementary digital differential analyzer.

digitize To display data in a digital form.

direct access The ability to read or write information anywhere within a storage device in an amount of time that is constant regardless of the location of the information accessed and of the location of the information previously accessed.

Every site available for storing data in a direct-access device is identified by a unique, numeric address. The datum stored in that site is called the content of the address. The datum is placed in storage by a write operation which, at the same time, completely erases whatever information was previously stored there. A datum is retrieved from storage by a read operation which usually preserves the stored datum, thus enabling the same datum to be retrieved over and over again.

Since a direct-access storage device usually holds much more information than is involved in one read or write instruction, it is necessary to be selective and access only one distinct location of memory at any time. This is accomplished by using the address to designate which data storage site is under consideration. Thus, an address must be used with every read and write instruction. This procedure is in contrast to the procedure followed in sequential access devices where pieces of information can be accessed only by reading the next piece of information following the current one (as is done with card decks, magnetic tapes, or paper tapes). In sequential access devices, no address can be used, and each piece of information must be examined until the correct piece of information is found. In a sense, direct accessing may be compared to dialing the telephone number of a specific person and having him answer the phone directly, whereas sequential accessing may be compared to dialing the telephone numbers of a directory in sequence and asking repeatedly whether so-and-so is at that number.

In modern computers, main memory is usually a direct-access device. Some small computers use drums or disks for main storage, and have what is called random-access memories. In such a computer, if the information currently read is at location 201, and the next information required is at location 349, the computer has to wait until the drum or disk brings location 349 under the read/write heads. Consequently, efficient programs require careful planning of the location of each instruction and data item so as to minimize the number of revolutions required. Such timing considerations are absent in direct-access devices whether the addresses run consecutively or randomly within memory.

See RANDOM ACCESS, SEQUENTIAL ACCESS.

direct address   Any address specifying the location of an operand. An immediate and explicit indication of the location referred to. It is usually a part of the computer instruction specifying the location of the operand or the location of another instruction. Contrast direct address to INDIRECT ADDRESS which specifies the location at which the real address of the operand may be found. Indirect addressing may be continued to any level (address of address of address . . .), but is a wasteful process of time and memory capacity if carried to extremes. See ONE-LEVEL ADDRESS.

direct insert subroutine   A body of coding or a group of instructions inserted directly into the logic of a program, often in multiple copies, whenever required. In general, only the simplest of functions can be so treated, or else the size of a program becomes too large to be managed efficiently. For instance, assume that a certain sequence S of operations is to be performed five times throughout the program. The programmer need only write this sequence S of operations once, have it reproduced four more times, and insert it where required:

Program

. . . . (Sequence S of operations required) Sequence S of instructions	Original
. . . . . (Sequence S of operations required) Sequence S of instructions	Copy
. . . . . (Sequence S of operations required) Sequence S of instructions	Copy
. . . . . (Sequence S of operations required) Sequence S of instructions	Copy
. . . . . (Sequence S of operations required) Sequence S of instructions	Copy
. . . . .	

See CLOSED SUBROUTINE, MACROINSTRUCTION, OPEN SUBROUTINE.

direction   See FLOW DIRECTION.

disk   An external or auxiliary storage device.   A magnetic disk consists of a thin, circular, rigid plate rotating very rapidly about its center with one or both of its surfaces capable of being magnetized. Information is recorded on the surface by creating at a specific spot a magnetic field by means of a recording head in a way similar to that employed by tape recorders.   Reading is performed by recording heads sensing magnetized areas.   See MAGNETIC DISK.

disk operating system (DOS)   A versatile operating system for 360 installations having direct-access storage devices.   The simplest operating system to support almost every peripheral device available for System 360, and possibly the most commonly used operating system for nonelementary installations, DOS is a more powerful twin of TOS.

DOS consists of a supervisory program, a job control language, data management routines, language translators, and utility programs.

Together these elements give the programmer and operator full control over the computer while relieving them of most nonessential overhead tasks.

The supervisor is permanently resident in the bottom (low-numeric address) of main memory. All absolutely essential services are included here, such as interrupt servicing routines, physical input/output device servicing routines, program loaders, memory protect and interval timer supporting routines. The remainder of the required service routines share occupancy of a transient area (actually two independent 1024-byte areas) next to the permanently occupied memory. When needed, the remaining operating-system service routines are loaded into a transient area and executed.

The job control language is interpreted by the job scheduler (batch processing input stream) and by the operator communications routine. The control cards, or job control language statements in the input stream provide for all preplanned directions to the supervisor. Any unexpected changes can be entered by the computer operator via a console type-in. The console messages have priority over conflicting job-stream statements, so that the operator does have the last word (greatest authority) over processing operations. Together the control cards and console type-ins direct the assignment of I/O devices to jobs, initiate and terminate job steps, and otherwise keep the computer running smoothly with a high percentage of utilization.

In DOS (and also in TOS), programs refer to I/O device using symbolic names, generally 6-character mnemonics beginning with SYS . . . At run time the symbolic names are associated with physical devices by job control language statements (either console or input-stream). This permits using any suitable available device for each I/O function.

When the printer does not work, listings are written on tape or disk. Run-time substitution of I/O devices allows for efficient setup (mounting and dismounting) and also to a degree for configuration independence (can move to another computer).

Run-time device assignment is made possible by dividing IOCS into physical input/output control system (PIOCS) and logical input/output control system (LIOCS). One PIOCS routine (and queue of waiting requests) is resident in the permanent supervisor for each kind of I/O device attached to the system. Thus PIOCS is a kind of extension of the hardware, an interface between the programs and the data channels. The LIOCS routines handle buffering, blocking, label checking, overlap of I/O with processing, etc. LIOCS routines are thus job-dependent, and are edited into each problem program that needs them by linkage editor. Unused LIOCS routines never occupy core memory, and unused PIOCS routines are discarded during system generation (creation of individualized

DOS for an installation), thereby achieving great economy of memory residence.

Some version of every language supported by System 360 is included in DOS. At the 10K design level are an assembler (BAL), compilers for FORTRAN, COBOL, PL/1, an RPG, and the AUTO-TEST system for assembly-language debugging. However, DOS does not support the larger compilers (44K or 200K design level). Routines written separately in the various languages can be integrated by linkage editor into unified, operable program modules.

Linkage editor processes object modules (the output of assembler, compiler, or RPG) and converts them into unified, loadable program modules. Either link-and-execute or link-and-catalog (into core-image library) operation can be obtained, but not both on the same run. As all programs must go through linkage editor before execution, and linkage-editor output must be on a direct-access device, it is not possible to obtain a self-loading or free-standing (operating-system-independent) program using DOS. Linkage editor can create simple or complex overlay structures when directed to do so. This permits running programs that are too large to be accommodated in memory all at once.

The librarian is a service routine that supervises up to three libraries. The core-image library contains ready-to-run programs and DOS service routines. A relocatable library contains object modules, fragments of programs, and the LIOCS routines. If relocatable library is omitted, no programs can be created by DOS, but core-image programs can still be executed. This omission does save disk space, but is rarely used in practice. A truly optional source statement library supports macroinstructions for BAL, external COPY clauses for COBOL, and whatever else the installation wishes to catalog in source-language form. A directory precedes each library, and is used to speed retrieval of members. Every library is organized as one partitioned data set.

Disk-resident tape sort/merge and disk sort/merge are provided in DOS. Other utilities are provided for copying data sets (with reformatting, if required), dumping memory or external storage, etc.

Multiprogramming is available on computers having more than 32K of core and memory protection. This is a fixed-partition system with a background area (minimum size 10K) and one or two foreground areas (minimum size 2K). Background jobs run from job-stream input, but foreground tasks are initiated/terminated via operators' console.

DOS supports teleprocessing in either background or foreground mode. Only BTAM is provided, which means that blocking/unblocking, overlap of I/O with processing, etc., are the user's responsibility.

BTAM cannot run in background and foreground at the same time. 32K of core is required for teleprocessing.

DOS can be run on any 360 having 16K of core, one 2311 disk-pack drive, one card reader/punch, a printer and a console. At the 16K level many facilities of DOS are not available, but on simple-configuration computers most of the universally useful features of DOS can be used. Any DOS facility can be used on 32K of core (if memory protect, decimal and/or floating point or other required features are installed). On the 65K (or greater) configurations, every facility of DOS can be used simultaneously, and the maximum power of DOS becomes available. DOS will support computers up to 1,048,576 bytes of memory, and allow almost any peripheral to be used (exceptions: 2314 disk cluster, optical character readers, film scanners, and the large console option are not supported). However, users can, and have, written their own PIOCS routines if they simply must have those devices. DOS data-set formats are upward-compatible with full OS formats, but the converse is not necessarily true. Because DOS has less core residence and timewise overhead than OS, it is frequently used even on installations where the larger OS could be used. Most users who do not require the ultimate in sophistication or flexibility find that DOS meets their needs very well.

Both DOS and TOS were initially known as BOS, i.e., BOS (disk) and BOS (tape). To avoid confusion, the current names were adopted, and BOS became a distinct, simpler operating system. Family resemblances still exist, however.

See BOS, OS, TOS.

dispatching priority In a multiprogramming or multiasking environment, the priority assigned to an active (non-real-time, non-foreground) task. The DP is used to establish precedence for the use of the central processing unit when the operating system is ready to return control to a problem program.

There are several kinds of priority in a multitasking environment. The jobs entered to the system but not yet initiated await in input queues. Availability of facilities and scheduling priority determines which task is to be initiated next. Once a task has been initiated, it is removed from the input queue. It then competes with other ready tasks for CPU time. All the initiated but not yet finished tasks are either waiting, ready, enqueued, or active (in control of CPU). A waiting task cannot use CPU time until a specified event occurs (usually completion of an I/O operation). An enqueued task has placed itself in a first-come, first-served waiting list for some serially reusable system resource. When the system finishes processing a request for supervisor services, control will be passed to the highest-priority ready task. In this way the priority specified for various jobs will be honored at run time.

display　The visible representation of information, whether in words, numbers, or drawings, on a console screen connected to a computer. By extension, display may also mean the object on which the data are projected, it may also stand for the image of the data, and it may equally mean the total system leading to the representation of information. The word display will be used here as visible representation of data, and the words display system will denote the combination hardware and software required to achieve a display. Although the sundial is the precursor of many a display system, the computerized display system will be the only one considered here.

A display system is a subsystem of an information system rather than of a communication system, since an information system requires data processing for data utilization. The place of a display system within an information system is broadly indicated in the accompanying illustration (Figure 1). It should be noted that feedback is just as important in a display system as it is in an information system if the human intelligence they both serve is to predict and control events by means of its decision-making abilities.

In the early computer days, the on-line printer was the display system. The numerical results were checked by the programmer, the

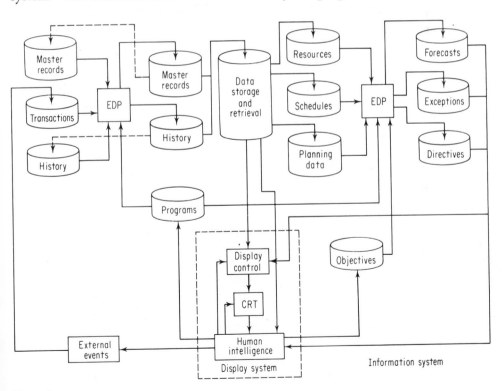

Figure 1.

program was rerun if errors were found, and the computer output was then forwarded to the user. To satisfy engineering and scientific requirements, an X-Y plotter was incorporated in the display system, and a faster (and more accurate) plotting of curves was achieved. With the appearance of business applications, as triggered by linear programming and simulation techniques, the on-line printer became a bottleneck: an obvious modification of a parameter would require days and sometimes weeks for its execution. To reduce the turnaround time, a two-pronged attack was launched on the problem: one attack resulted in time-sharing (where more than one user may use the computer at the same time), and the other attack resulted in a variety of display devices.

Display devices now on the market can be divided into projection-type displays (cathode-ray tube or CRT, smoked glass and scriber with projector, filmed CRT for wall projection through color filters), small-scale displays (electroluminescent, numerical readouts as with Nixie tubes), and long-range xerography-type display which can serve as computer input and output in addition to its usual graphic transmission function.

The most common display device is the cathode-ray tube, or CRT. The information displayed on a CRT is usually called for through a keyboard and modified by a light pen. The display may be had in predetermined format (a fast method) or by means of a format specified through the keyboard (a slow method): a compromise is usually sought between speed and flexibility of presentation. Updating the display can be achieved through real-time computing, periodic modifications, on request, or by exception, and the display may be distributed among users according to priorities, security, or specific requirements.

The programming system required to handle a general display system is best described by considering the programs as divided into functional blocks (see Figure 2), these blocks being generally called input processing, data storage and retrieval, display control, display formatting, display input, CRT, and display request.

The input processing block handles the input of external data into the system. Basically, input data are tested to determine whether the data are standard inputs destined to update the data base and display files, or whether they represent new inputs for which new files must be created in the data base file. The new data are then transmitted to display control and/or data storage and retrieval.

The data storage and retrieval block updates and maintains existing files, defines new files, indexes, chains, links, and retrieves data as requested. Updating and creating new files are triggered by the input processing block; indexing, linking, chaining, and searching are triggered by the display request block.

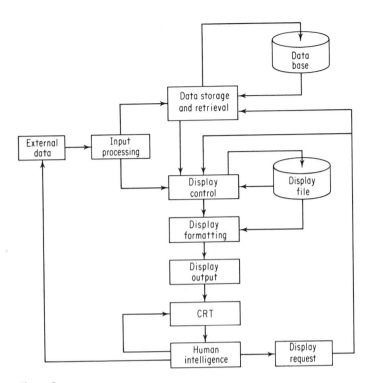

Figure 2.

The function of security and updating displays is carried out by the display control block. This block determines where information is to be sent, allows for updating information while it is being displayed, and determines what information is to be deleted from the display file.

The physical appearance of a display is controlled by the display formatting block. This block generates drawings, graphs, or alphanumeric reports. Scaling is automatically set up, thus permitting blowing up required areas of the display. For instance, if a report consists of too many lines to fit on the CRT, the display formatting block will cause the report to appear in successive pages until all the information has been displayed.

The display output block performs the necessary work to complete the display by generating lines between the points of a graph, generating the proper spacing between characters and words, spacing lines of alphanumeric characters, including dates and identification with each display, orienting symbols and lettering for greater graph legibility, and generally ensuring that all data are channeled to the proper display units.

The information is displayed on a CRT, and may be photographed for a permanent hard copy. For instance, one typical 12 × 12-inch screen can display simultaneously 3848 characters in 52 lines with 74 characters per line. Entries of modified information can be carried out by means of a light pen, the identification being achieved by synchronizing memory and light-pen operations.

The human intelligence which calls for, and receives, the displayed information will tend to modify both, the external data through elaborate decision making, and the displayed data by means of a keyboard or a light pen. It is of interest to note that although the reaction time encountered in altering CRT displays is measured in milliseconds, the reaction time encountered in decision making to affect external data may be measured in days, or even months. The situation is analogous to steering a jet plane with one hand, and a liner with the other.

The request for a display is fed into the display request block, where it is decoded and analyzed. The necessary instructions are then transferred to the data storage and retrieval block (to extract the required data from the data base file if required), and to the display control block (for specifications and to obtain the necessary display rules). The resulting data are then processed by the data formatting block, and control is then given over to the display output block: the required information is then displayed on the face of the CRT.

Before a display system can be put into operation, a considerable amount of work must be carried out to determine true information needs, data availability and identification, specifications on display format, controls, and security, processing functions, interfacing, and methods and procedures. The proper assignment of responsibilities for the work is probably the largest single problem faced by an organization planning a display system: wrong assignments of responsibilities, or abdication of responsibilities will defer important decisions to a level not informed of the system objective, hardware capabilities, or software limitations. A thorough analysis is required, and decisions have to be made as to format flexibility: with increased flexibility the display file will be small, and the input processing programming will be simple, but programming required for data storage and retrieval and display control will become very complex, and the data base file will become very large. On the other hand, little flexibility in display formatting will simplify the programming for data storage and retrieval, and the data base file will become smaller; however, the programming required for input processing becomes highly complicated, and the display file may become unwieldy and large.

The basic purpose of a display system must be to improve the speed and correctness of decision making by providing fast man/ machine communications and reducing reaction time. Furthermore, it is believed that the coordination of different operations will be more efficient with information readily available from one unique source.

The growing interest of business in display systems stems in part from the success achieved by such systems in the military fields (NORAD) and in certain applications such as the SABRE system in information systems should be more properly classified as information retrieval systems since they contain large bodies of relatively static data). Whereas military, educational, medical, and legal requirements are specific, business requirements cover the whole gamut of human activities. For this reason, display systems have not progressed in the business community with the speed that they have progressed in, say, military activities. The development of new ideas in displays, however, offers remarkable features for future applications, and not the least of these new developments is the use of laser holography.

Although the historical development of holography dates back to airline reservations. Educational and medical disciplines are growing increasingly aware of display systems potential (although diagnostic the early 1950's, the demonstration of practical holography dates back only to the early 1960's. By holography is meant the technique of bouncing a laser beam off an object and a mirror so that the reflected rays intersect on a photographic film. After development, if the laser beam is directed against the film, a real image will be formed which will remain in sharp focus at all depths, thus creating a true three-dimensional image. Although at this time it would appear that holography cannot contribute to large-scale projection displays, the history of computers is made up of periodic limitations which a rapidly evolving technology has consistently bypassed. A breakthrough in holography could be of far-reaching significance in medicine, education, advertising, and engineering.

dissector   See IMAGE DISSECTOR.

distance   See HAMMING DISTANCE, SIGNAL DISTANCE.

divided slit scan   In optical character recognition (OCR), a device consisting of a narrow column of photoelectric cells which scans an input character at given intervals for the purpose of obtaining its horizontal and vertical components.

Optical scanners which utilize this scanning method often employ the motion of the document as an integral part of the scan. As the constituent horizontal component of the character to be recognized appears at the luminous source, the individual cells, which comprise the vertical structure, record the presence or absence of reflected light. The resultant binary series is then saved until the remaining character components have been processed, at which time the final results are submitted to the normalizer for further character evaluation.

The number of individual cells used in a divided slit scan depends upon the resolution required in the vertical direction. Resolution requirements vary widely, depending on the size and style of the character set, and also on the allowance desired for character mis-registration.

(Although the divided slit has been employed primarily in OCR systems, it is possible to obtain the vertical structure of magnetic-ink characters in a similar way by utilizing a magnetic head comprised of a stack of narrow tracks, as in multitrack tape recorders.)

The divided slit is an extension on the original slit scan; the original method reduced all vertical components to aggregated amplitudes and therefore lost all vertical detail. As the size of character sets grew larger, it was necessary to preserve this detail in order to produce a more accurate character identification.

Both the slit and divided slit are considered as one-dimensional devices inasmuch as they process only one vertical component at a time. There also exists today other devices which are referred to as two-dimensional devices since all components of the character are processed simultaneously. Some of the more common two-dimensional devices are the mechanical scanner, flying-spot scanner, TV camera, and photocell matrix.

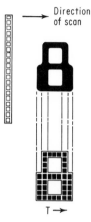

Direction of scan

T →

Divided-slit scan.

division Any one of the four major parts of a program written in the COBOL language. The purpose of the divisions is illustrated as follows:

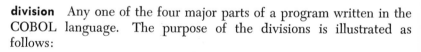

> IDENTIFICATION DIVISION
> > Name of program
> > Name of author
>
> ENVIRONMENT DIVISION
> > Computer configuration to compile
> > Computer configuration to run
> > Input devices required
> > Output devices required
> > File assignments
>
> DATA DIVISION
> > File description
> > Record description
> > Data name description

PROCEDURE DIVISION
   Specification of operations to be performed on files, records, and data names.

Each division thus uniquely identifies the elements (data, I/O devices, etc.) that are required to run the program successfully.   See DATA DIVISION, ENVIRONMENT DIVISION, IDENTIFICATION DIVISION, PROCEDURE DIVISION.

document   Any record, printed or otherwise, that can be read by man or machine.   Equally, to document, that is, to prepare a written text and charts describing the purpose, the nature, the usage, and the operation of a program or a system of programs.   The manual (or document) so produced is called the documentation of a program.

   The importance of clear, detailed, and correct documentation for an existing program can never be overemphasized.   Too often a programmer inherits a program written by a programmer since gone, and the sketchy documentation does not reflect the changes upon changes carried out in this program.   As a consequence, the new programmer will face frustrating hours analyzing a program insufficiently documented, or else, as is most frequently the case, spend many days, or weeks, rewriting the same program.   See EDP CENTER, OPTICAL CHARACTER RECOGNITION.

document alignment   In character recognition, that phase of the reading process in which a transverse or gravitational force is applied to the document in order to identify its reference edge with that of the machine.

   The majority of character-recognition systems perform document alignment during the document transportation phase, at which time the transverse forces are usually quite significant.   This may result in rotating or skewing a form that is nearly square in shape.   For this reason most systems specify a limiting length-to-width ratio for the document.   Skew failure increases as this limit is approached.

   In the remainder of character-recognition systems, the document is

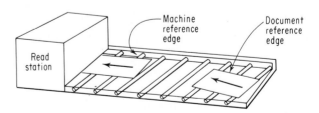

Illustrating document alignment.

transported on edge, rather than in a flat position. In these cases the lining up of reference edges is accomplished in the feed hopper and feed station by using a vibrating base in the feed hopper which joggles the documents so that all reference edges are flush with the hopper base plate. As the document is fed to the read station, care is taken to prevent skewing.

documentation   The collection, organized and stored, of records for the purpose of making information easily accessible to the user. Records that describe the purpose, the use, the structure, details, and the operational requirements of a program are absolutely necessary in order for a program to be used by anyone other than the author of the program. In fact, such documentation is frequently required by the author himself after a short lapse of time.

A normally acceptable documentation for a program should consist of:

1. A user's guide, a brief document containing:
    a. The name of the program
    b. A short description of the purpose of the program
    c. Instructions for running the program, including data preparation
    d. Items of significance of which the user should be aware
    e. Operating environment required by the program (for example: XYZ/200 with a 20K memory and multiprogramming monitor)
2. A precisely annotated and up-to-date listing of the source language of the program

Documentation for multiprogram systems is more exacting than documentation for single programs. It is a tool that must be fully developed before a single program instruction is put down on paper. Since a programmer will have to alter the logic of a planned program as he constructs it, he must make others aware of his modifications if the system is to be successful. The documentation must therefore allow for easy communication among programmers. Such a documentation should contain:

1. The functional description of the system as a whole
2. Specification of the data used and referred to as follows:
    a. Storage requirements for the different types of records
    b. Layout of core-memory requirements
    c. Logical file specifications
    d. File record layout specifications
    e. Program layout specifications
3. Program, common subroutines, and supervisory programs specifications
4. Program documentation

Not all parts of this documentation can be completely spelled out in detail from the start, since the actual programming will tend to modify established requirements. However, if some experience is brought to bear in the development of the documentation, the restraints imposed on the programmers will prove to be no obstacle to their work.

document handling In character recognition, the process of loading, feeding, transporting, and unloading a cut-form document that has been submitted for character recognition.

The term also applies to continuous forms as a matter of convention. However, continuous-forms readers are much simpler, and in fact entail very little document handling.

More generally, by document handling is meant the consideration of all human and machine contacts, traceable from the document's source, insofar as they affect machine readability before the document's final disposition.

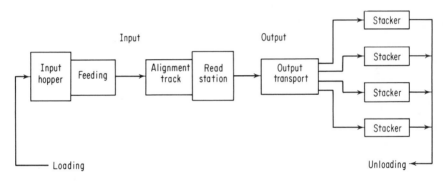

An automatic document-handling system.

document leading edge In character recognition, that edge which is the foremost one encountered during the reading process, and whose relative position defines the document's direction of travel. It is usually perpendicular to the document reference edge.

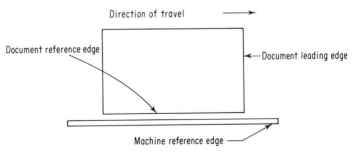

Illustrating document leading edge.

document misregistration   In character recognition, the improper state of appearance of a document, on site in a character reader, with respect to real or imaginary horizontal base lines.

A cut-form document may be misregistered if the document was mutilated in any manner, or if preprinted registration marks were misplaced.

A continuous document does not contain registration marks as such, but may be misregistered if it contains consecutive askewed lines in relation to its reference edge.

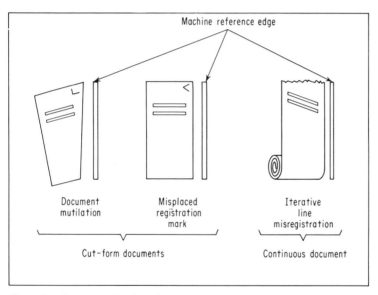

Illustrating document misregistration.

Document misregistration manifests itself through a condition of iterative line misregistration; however, the same term has sometimes erroneously been used to describe a condition due to document misalignment.   More properly, this latter condition is a mechanical defect referred to as skew failure.   This distinction should be recalled when it is desired to determine the cause of document rejects.

document reference edge   In character recognition, that edge of a source document which provides the basis of all subsequent reading processes, insofar as it indicates the relative position of registration marks, and the impending text.

The document reference edge also assists in document transportation and alignment.   It is usually perpendicular to the document leading edge.

Document reference edges play a prominent role in determining the cause of many rejected documents. Reference edges which aren't properly aligned could cause skew failure, whereas mutilated reference edges, along with misplaced document registration marks, may result in document misregistration.

document transportation   In character recognition, that phase of the reading process which is charged with the effective delivery of the source document to the read station. See DOCUMENT ALIGNMENT.

document types   In character recognition, the generic designation of varied printing methods, the category of which is one of the most important considerations of data preparation.

Depending on the printing process employed, there are certain irregularities that accrue to a character as laid down. These include variations with respect to ink density, character-stroke width, extraneous marks, and so forth. Hence the following printing methods are mentioned as having been exploited in an attempt to discover the ones best suited to a particular character-recognition system.

1. Letterpress
2. Lithography
3. Photogravure
4. Typewriting
5. Embossed plate printing
6. Encoding
7. Line printing: From chain
    From drum
    From cathode-ray-tube display (xerography)
8. Phototypesetting

double precision   The use of two computer words to represent a number.

In fixed-word-length digital computers, the numerical accuracy available in one word is fixed by the number of digits in the word size. For example, if the word size were 6 digits long, the computer would show

$$236.128 \times 127.148 = 30023$$

that is, dropping the digits after the decimal. By coupling two words to represent one number, a higher accuracy will be obtained. With the above example, the computer will show

$$236.128000000 \times 127.148000000 = 30023.202944$$

Double precision refers to double-precision numbers themselves, or to the arithmetic operations which use such numbers as operands.

double-word boundary   In the IBM 360 System, any address ending in 000, that is, which is divisible by 8, is a natural boundary for 8-byte double-word items.   Any item in this class must be referenced by an address falling on a boundary of the corresponding type.

downtime   The time interval during which a device is not operating correctly owing to machine malfunction.   The downtime includes the time required to repair the malfunctions, but does not include non-productive time due to lack of work, or due to the absence of the operator.   Downtime will be most probably high after the installation of the computer because of injury to the equipment during shipping, or simply because defective components will break down early.   After the initial shakedown period, the equipment will usually prove quite reliable.

After allowing for the usual maintenance, downtime will be taken care of most of the time if jobs are scheduled on the basis of operating at 80 to 90 percent of capacity.

drive   Usually refers to the mechanism on which a magnetic tape is mounted so that information may be read from, or recorded on, the tape.   It consists of a supply reel and drive motor, a capstan to move the tape, a record-read-back head, and a takeup reel and drive motor.   See TAPE DRIVE.

drum   An external or auxiliary data storage device consisting of a rapidly rotating (usually 3600 or 7200 rpm) cylinder made of a material capable of being magnetized.   Record-read heads are positioned along the cylinder so as to have access to the external surface.   Information is recorded by the head on the drum by creating a magnetic field on a specific area, and information is read by having the head detect the presence or absence of magnetic field over specific areas.   Compare with MAGNETIC DISK.

A drum is considered to be the fastest auxiliary electromechanical storage device available, but it is also the most expensive device on a dollar-per-bit basis.   See MAGNETIC DRUM.

dummy   An artificial piece of information which is inserted solely to fulfill prescribed conditions in a system, and permits the system to function properly without otherwise affecting the system.   Often used as an aid in debugging or developing something which will interact with the real thing that the dummy represents.

dump   To copy the contents of all or part of a storage (usually from an internal storage device into an external storage device).

Whenever an error occurs in a program, usually during the development stage of the program, there exists a real need to find out what the program looked like in the computer, when the trouble arose. This is achieved by printing, or dumping, the contents of memory on paper. Dumping is highly selective: it may print all of memory, or specific parts of memory, as required by the programmer. A dump may be called for at any time, but it is usually reserved for critical spots in the program. Dumps may reveal a great deal about the process under investigation.

Although dumping is rarely used during the running of an established program, it may occur that a program with crash priority is to be run immediately. If another program is already on the machine, dumping will permit the removal of a running program, and after the crash program is through, returning the previous program to the computer at the point of operation it had reached before it was removed. See DYNAMIC DUMP, POSTMORTEM DUMP, SELECTIVE DUMP, SNAPSHOT DUMP, STATIC DUMP.

duodecimal Pertaining to the numeration system with a base of 12.

The duodecimal system is still in partial use (12 inches to the foot, watch dial). It is considered a convenient system because many common fractions result in a single-digit expansion. For example, if the duodecimal system were represented by

0, 1, 2, 3, 4, 5, 6, 7, 8, 9, A, B,

the decimal and duodecimal numbers corresponding to certain common fractions would appear as shown in the table.

Fraction	Decimal	Duodecimal
1/6	0.16666. . .	0.2
1/4	0.25	0.3
1/3	0.33333. . .	0.4
1/2	0.5	0.6
2/3	0.66666. . .	0.8
3/4	0.75	0.9
5/6	0.83333. . .	.A

duplex In communications, a simultaneous two-way independent transmission in both directions.

Sometimes used as a synonym for "dual," meaning complete duplication of a facility. Contrast with HALF DUPLEX; see FULL DUPLEX.

duplicate To create a record containing the same information as the original data record. Same as COPY.

duplication check   A check based on the identity in results of two independent performances of the same task.

For example, the well-known method of summing first across and then down, and then squaring to get the same result:

	1st sales	2nd sales	Total sales
Item 1	10	20	30
Item 2	30	50	80
Total sales	40	70	110

The total 110 is obtained by

40 + 70
and
30 + 80,

a duplication check known as squaring.

dyadic operation   An operation on two operands. For instance, division (A/B), but not necessarily addition (A + B + C).

dynamic dump   A dump performed during the execution of a program.   A printout of all or some area of memory which is performed following a programmed interruption of the program.   As soon as the dump is completed, the program is automatically resumed.   Dynamic dumps are used while debugging programs under development.

dynamic program loading   A process of loading a program module or routine into main memory when a currently loaded and executing program makes a reference to it.

The normal or customary method of loading a program involves locating and loading every routine that could be referred to during a run prior to execution.   This is static program loading, for all the required programs have been found and united into an integrated package.   At run time the program content of memory does not change.

Suppose that a routine will call any one of a great many possible subroutines, the selection being made as a result of factors computed during a run.   With static program loading, attempting to load every possible routine will be wasteful of load time and memory capacity.   Dynamic loading of programs will conserve both time and space.   One must use caution in deallocating (releasing the memory occupied by) a dynamically loaded program if it might be used again soon.

Dynamic loading offers another possible flexibility. Suppose that the name of a program to be used is read as input by another program. It is impossible to execute such an initially unspecified program without dynamic program loading. Yet this method of selecting a program module offers very great versatility and permits extension of a system of programs at any time.

dynamic program relocation   The act of moving a partially executed program to another location in main memory, without hindering its ability to finish processing normally.

It is generally true that a program loaded into memory has lost its relocatability. The information required to load the program into an arbitrary memory area is not retained when the load process is completed. If dynamic program relocation is desired, this information must be saved (in main or auxiliary storage) for possible use, but may be eliminated after completion of program execution.

Suppose that five programs reside in main memory. Programs 2 and 4 have finished, and it is desired to load program 6 into the space thus made available. If program 6 is bigger than either 2 or 4, but smaller than both combined, program 6 can be loaded by using dynamic program relocation: Move program 3 up against program 1, and then the new program can be moved into the (expanded) interval between programs 2 and 5. The ability to move partially executed programs therefore gives an operating system increased flexibility, but at the expense of storing relocatability information.

If the program in relocatable form was loaded from a program library (on line program storage), the desired relocation data can be found, undisturbed, in that library without having to be explicitly saved.

dynamic storage allocation   The process of making memory capacity available to a program on the basis of actual, momentary need.

The usual procedure, static memory allocation, attempts to find enough storage space (before loading) to satisfy the anticipated, predicted, or maximum requirement of a routine. Static allocation is simpler for the operating system to manage, but dynamic allocation is more flexible. Dynamic storage allocation allows programs whose total maximum requirement exceeds available memory to be run together, provided that both do not have peak memory demands at the same time.

When memory conflicts arise, the lower-priority program is inactivated until enough memory becomes available.

Dynamic allocation is used for three principal purposes:

1.   To allow adjustment of I/O buffer usage to meet current I/O traffic demands.

2.   To allow construction of temporary, large tables of data.

3.   To allow dynamic program loading.

See DYNAMIC PROGRAM LOADING.

E

EAM. Electrical accounting machine Data processing equipment that is predominantly electromechanical in nature, such as keypunches and mechanical sorters.

All automatic data processing was done on EAM equipment before the advent of electronic computers, and some of it is still carried out on EAM. Only recently have some small computers been competitive, pricewise, with EAM for small installations.

EAM equipment consists of devices such as card sorters, tabulators (card-to-paper printers), card duplicators, card interpreters (card contents printed on card), card punches, etc. Such devices are mostly programmed by plugboard wiring. They are also known as TAB equipment (short for tabulating), as in "a tabshop operation."

echo check A method of checking the accuracy of transmission of data in which the transmitted data are returned to the sending end for comparison with the original data.

Echo checking is thus a reading test to guard against malfunctions during output operations. The station will read the contents of the

card or tape just written, compare them with the contents in storage
or buffer for identity, and if a mismatch is found, operations will be
halted. This is a time-consuming but highly reliable system for
detection of errors in transmission.

edit   To modify the form or format of an output, or input, by inserting or deleting characters such as page numbers or decimal points;
edit is also a computer instruction directing that the above be performed.

When editing a single data word, the most common method uses
a sending, or source, word and a receiving word called an edit mask.
The sending field contains variable data (usually numeric), while the
edit mask contains format-directing and size-specifying information.
Suppose, for example, that the source word at location S contained
+001206 and that the receiving word R contains the edit mask
ZZZ,ZZ9.99. In this mask Z stands for INSERT CHARACTER WITH
LEADING ZERO SUPPRESSION, 9 represents INSERT ONE
SOURCE CHARACTER HERE, and the dot and comma stand for
INSERT A DOT and A COMMA IN THE INDICATED LOCA-
TIONS. An instruction EDIT S to R results in S being unchanged,
but R will contains [] [] [] [] [] 12.06 (where each [] represents a
blank). The comma was replaced by a blank because it is em-
bedded in a zero suppression area. If the edit mask had been
$$,$99.99 the result would have been [] [] $ 12.06. The $ symbol
stands for zero suppress with floating dollar sign. The $ floats
rightward through every suppressed leading zero.

An edit mask of **, *99.99– would give **** 12.06 [] because **
means check protection symbol in deleted leading zero positions, and
the – means PRINT – IF SENDING WORD IS NEGATIVE, BLANK
IF POSITIVE. Editing our source word into 9999.99+ would print
0012.06+. The + symbol means SHOW THE CORRECT SIGN
HERE, UNCONDITIONALLY.

Observe that the edit mask determines the size of the edited item.
The edit mask itself is destroyed by the edit instruction. To over-
come this problem, edit masks are saved in an area remote from the
receiving field. Each edit operation then requires two instructions:

1. MOVE edit mask TO receiving field.
2. EDIT sending field TO receiving field.

In an editing operation, any symbol other than Z, +, –, 9, B, $, *,
decimal point, CR, and comma in the edit mask will be preserved in
place in the edited result. Thus the mask PRICE: ZZ,ZZ9.99– would
be edited into PRICE: [] [] [] [] 12.06 [], but $,$$9.99–BILLION
would edit into [] [] [] 12.06 [] [] ILLION. In this last example
B was replaced by blank according to the rules of editing.

The notation used here for edit-mask characters is essentially that of COBOL. Similar usages exist in the instruction sets of many computers.

Editing also refers to formatting an entire line of print by arranging fields therein.

EDP. Electronic data processing Data processing equipment that is predominantly electronic in nature, such as electronic digital computer. The heart of the electronic data processing equipment is the electronic data processor, an internally stored program computer. The program is a sequence of explicit instructions which are stored in the same way and place as the data to be processed. The main characteristic of the computer, however, is its ability to alter its program as the processing takes place. This ability to modify instructions allows the computer to adapt itself to a variety of situations.

The number of instructions accepted by a computer varies with the type of computer and the manufacturer: it may reach into the hundreds with a large computer. The execution speed of the instructions equally depends on the computer and manufacturer: a rate of millions of executed instructions per second is not uncommon. See COMPUTER.

EDP center Electronic data processing center, the complex formed by the computer, its peripheral equipment, the personnel related to the operation of the center and control functions, and, usually, the office space housing hardware and personnel.

A common EDP center organization is indicated on the organization chart, Figure 1; the functional flow between these elements is outlined in Figure 2; and the following text outlines a standard or composite picture of EDP centers in various branches of industry (automotive, banking, food, petroleum, and textiles). Although there are many variations of this organization structure between companies, the intent here is to portray average major functions and their interrelationships.

The first computer centers basically consisted of tabulating equipment; and the EDP center, because of heavy financial processing, traditionally reported to the controller, or the financial vice-president. In the last two years, however, there appears to be a trend to have the EDP center director report to the administrative vice-president, or to the executive vice-president. This move is due mainly to the growing utilization of computers in fields other than accounting, namely, in manufacturing, research, distribution, and, more recently, in marketing. Since the EDP center is essentially a service center, the philosophy underlying the reporting line is to ensure a proper

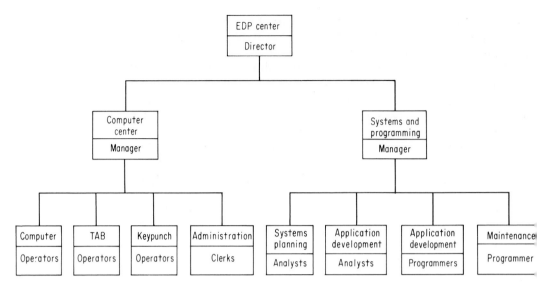

Figure 1. EDP center-functional organization.

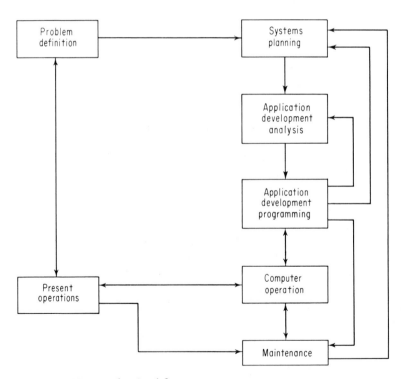

Figure 2. EDP center-functional flow.

balance of service and support to all functions of the company. Whatever area will provide the best objective overall, as well as unbiased scheduling and equipment selection, should direct the EDP effort.

The director of the EDP center has extensive experience with the company; is fully familiar with its organization, systems, procedures, and objectives; and is able to devote himself fully to the management of the EDP center. Moreover, he has had a number of years of experience in using computer systems, should be familiar with EDP design concepts and programming techniques (often through a higher-level language such as COBOL or FORTRAN), and is fully familiar with the equipment on the premises. In addition to attending seminars on system utilization on a periodic basis, he updates himself on equipment and techniques through trade magazines and by first-hand contacts with selected competitive hardware manufacturers' representatives.

Reporting to the EDP center director are at least two department heads:

1. The manager of systems and programming
2. The manager of the computer center

The area of systems planning is the nerve center of the EDP center, and the continued success or failure of the EDP center will rest largely on the effectiveness of systems planning. Its major function is to single out in proper sequence the areas of the company that can profitably use the computer services, to carry out this operation with a minimum of friction and a maximum of speed, and to develop a complete integrated management information system with a minimum of remodeling of finished jobs.

The combining of data elements from various runs to form an integrated information system will take advantage of the capabilities of the new generation of data processing equipment. The development of this type of plan often takes concerted informed effort and is best accomplished by a forward-planning systems group in conjunction with various departments of the company, as well as other elements of the EDP function.

The manager of systems planning is an experienced programmer with either a commercial systems design, programming, operations research, or an industrial engineering background, who should be fully familiar with all operations of the company. His staff is composed of systems analysts, usually professional data processing people who are equally at ease in business and scientific branches of the business enterprise and data processing disciplines and techniques.

Systems analysts usually master two or more higher-level languages, and the assembly language required for the company EDP installation. Moreover, systems analysts are completely familiar with one or more of the design aspects applications to be computerized, and with the objective of the application. As a rule, a large percentage of the system planning staff should come from within the organization, but it is good policy to bring in experienced analysts from outside the company. Their lack of knowledge of the organization can be compensated by their knowledge of more sophisticated equipment or software techniques. Such outsiders may well serve for a time as consultants to the other systems analysts and to the programmers, and also learn in this process. Very often, the systems planning area is supplemented by a manual systems expertise that is dedicated to the study of the flow of work or forms design. This balance supplements the pure data processing point of view to develop a sound business approach for achieving superior design results.

Performance standards for the systems planning department are difficult to establish. As a rule, the effectiveness of the departmental staff is measured by the efficiency, speed, and smoothness with which they achieve computerization of the various divisions of the company. However, after an initial period, definite guidelines based on service and economic justification can be measured against systems effort and the potential for savings on an increased service pattern basis.

Application development is the nerve center of the near-term operating environment, and supplements the systems planning activity that concentrates on future planning. The main concern of this function is to bring into fruition those specific applications that fall into the developed systems plan, or to satisfy current improvements in all areas of the business. Although this function, as it is placed in this structure, closely interacts with both the systems planning and programming activities, it is not unusual to find companies having combined the systems and programming functions. In those situations the logic and flow and even the machine coding can be done by one person or group. Detail or routine coding is often done by trainees or individuals who prefer the strict machine orientation.

The programming department is concerned mainly with two activities: developing programs initiated and outlined by the systems planning department or application development analysts, and maintaining operational existing programs (since businesses are dynamic, few programs are ever written which require no modification with time). In addition, there is usually in this department a technical standards activity that serves to support the entire programming group by establishing programming standards and modifying software.

The programming manager is a professional programmer able to guide and follow every job under his supervision. One of his functions, a most important one, is to establish guides for the performance of his staff. Such guides, to be established, demand from him a keen ability to estimate accurately the time required for the completion of an operational program (depending upon the programming language estimates usually run from 10 to over 50 instructions a day, including debugging and documentation time). The programming manager's staff is made up of program logic designers and program coders (under the generic term of programmers).

Programmers are usually divided into senior and junior programmers and trainees. Senior programmers normally have five or more years of experience and master one or more assembly languages, and one or more higher-level languages. They are capable of writing a complex program based on the statement of problems, and also outlining flow diagrams for instructions to juniors and trainees. Junior programmers usually have less than three years of experience, and are familiar with a higher-level language. Junior programmers will often work under the direction of a senior programmer on a problem subset, thereby acquiring the additional experience which will lead them into senior status. Trainees or coders are normally beginning programmers with less than a year of on-the-job experience after programming education.

The program maintenance is usually left to the less experienced programmers, since these tasks, although extremely vital, are more routine than is the creation of new applications.

A necessary function of programmers and coders is to maintain complete and detailed documentation on all programs established and modified. It is often easier to rewrite a program requiring modification than to modify it, particularly if the author of the program is not available and no documentation exists. Consequently, a job that could have been done in a matter of days, had it been properly documented, may require weeks or months. Thus, the importance of establishing and adhering to standards becomes even more apparent. Also, the necessary interaction among seniors, juniors, and maintenance programmers on a formal project-by-project basis vital to successful programming demands a well-planned, formalized documentation system.

Programmers and coders should attend advanced programming courses periodically to become familiar with the more sophisticated techniques constantly developed by computer manufacturers. These courses can be conducted by computer manufacturers, or developed by the systems planners or senior analysts or programmers.

The computer center is the hardware and processing area. This center may be run as a closed shop or as an open shop (the terms as used here have nothing to do with union membership). When it is run as an open shop (usually in an engineering or scientific environment), the programming function is not limited to the data center programmers. Personnel from other areas of the business that have developed programming skills can outline, develop, code, and run their own problems without relying on close assistance from the programming department. When the center is run as a closed shop, all problems are directed to the EDP center for solution with no other departments having access to the hardware. There is equally some combination of open- and closed-shop activities with different time periods established to handle both. As a rule, the open shop often can handle scientific problems better because it eliminates the time spent in problem definition between analysts and an operating department; the closed shop often operates more effectively in a commercial environment.

The computer center manager has considerable EDP experience, and is proficient in scheduling and analyzing machine utilization. He has a sound ability to predict capacity requirements for the near future (up to three years). He is responsible for the equipment (computer, peripheral equipment, and auxiliary equipment; that is, tabulating equipment, and keypunching or mark-sensing equipment); the supplies (such as paper and tapes); and the personnel required to run the computer center. His staff consists of supervisors, operators, and control personnel. The last are responsible for the control of input, flow or work, and the report distribution functions. Tape librarians and machines schedulers are often part of the control activity.

Computer operators are usually trained by classes run by the hardware manufacturers and also have an understanding of basic logic of the jobs they operate. Depending on their background and abilities, they form a natural pool from which programmers may be trained and transferred to the programming department. In many companies these operators are familiar with specific jobs because they had run them on tabulating equipment.

The current trend is to have the operators become machine experts rather than have an operator, say, who is familiar with accounts receivables and processes just that job. By the creation of machine console specialists the computers tend to be utilized more efficiently.

The bulk of auxiliary equipment operators is made up of keypunchers, requiring the skills usually found in typists, and tabulating equipment operators who prepare data input for computers, or manipulate output data that are not economical or efficient for a computer to accomplish.

Standards are often relatively difficult to establish for the computer center, even though each operation can be accurately timed: the input volume is often an unpredictable variable. However, operating standards must be established, evaluated, and adhered to continually.

Maintenance of the equipment is generally handled by the manufacturer leasing the equipment. When the equipment is purchased, it is customary to contract for maintenance service with the same manufacturer.

The physical area provided for the EDP center should permit adequate, properly laid-out space. Both systems planning and programming should be located nearby, not only for the savings in time offered by the close proximity of the computer proper, but to allow for meetings among the various individuals working on common projects. Also, many other functional areas (such as keypunching) should be located with an eye to efficient flow of input and output. The anticipated trend of low-cost, remote-input terminals may alter this requirement.

The computer center itself may occupy anywhere from 3000 to 5000 square feet. The console should occupy a central position, permitting the operator in charge to keep an eye on the peripheral equipment directly connected to the central processing unit. There should be enough space around tape units, disks, drums, printers, and power units not only for normal working accessibility, but equally for maintenance purposes. As a rule, 3 to 4 feet of clearance around each piece of equipment is considered adequate.

An area should be reserved for magnetic-tape reels, with its corresponding control and identification system controlled by a tape librarian. Other areas must be earmarked for maintenance personnel and equipment, supplies, power, and office space for the computer center manager, and at least one office room with desks for the operators.

Refrigeration is specified by the manufacturers, but as a rule it can be estimated at one ton for every 3.6 kilovolt-amperes. Although floor loading requirements are provided by the manufacturer, sound-proofing is often left to the user. Modern equipment demands nominal soundproofing, and except for high-speed printers, requires little beyond the acoustic-tile ceiling found in secretarial pool areas.

The selection, installation, and manning of an EDP center are a unique problem. Planning such a center can be, and often is, a major expense item. Neglecting this phase, or skimping on it, however, has often led to an inefficient center, resulting in a most costly operation.

See OPEN SHOP, CLOSED SHOP.

EDP system An electronic data processing system is the aggregation of men, machines, and methods to perform data processing operations with a minimum of manual help. An EDP system consists of the following:

1. An internally stored program computer
2. Peripheral equipment such as input/output devices and auxiliary storage
3. Instruction routines, or programs
4. Personnel such as analysts, programmers, operators, keypunchers
5. Plans and procedures for the most efficient utilization of men and equipment

An EDP system may have to handle two distinct types of processing:

1. Business and financial data processing, usually characterized by large input and output volumes, and relatively few internal computations
2. Scientific and engineering data processing, usually characterized by relatively small amounts of input and output data, but with massive internal calculation

To obviate the need of more than one computer in most cases where both types of processing are required, general-purpose computers attempt to offer high-speed input/output devices and high-speed internal operations. Selection of equipment, personnel, and methods is often correctly left to specialists in the field. See EDP CENTER.

effective address The address that is obtained by applying any specified indexing or indirect addressing rules to the specified address; the effective address is then used to identify the current operand.

It should be noted that the effective address of an operand is the actual address of the operand when all indirect addressing, index registers, and hardware relocations have been resolved.

Indirect addressing means that the location indicated contains not the desired data but the address of the desired data. See ADDRESS OF ADDRESS.

The index register is a hardware register containing an increment which is added to, or subtracted from, the address part of an instruction to modify this address. While the address is modified, the instruction itself is unchanged. The purpose of this address modification is to refer to a different location every time the content of the index is altered. See INDEX REGISTER.

Hardware relocation is a feature found in some of the newer computers. This feature permits a program to be written as though the first instruction were written in location zero regardless of where it will be loaded in memory.

Consider a program in which two instructions are located at A and B positions in memory. Instruction at A contains the number B in its address part. An index register will transform B into $B + 1$, $B + 2$, $B + 3$, etc., every time the index register is altered. In location B, the instruction contains the operand Q in its address part; in location $B + 1$, the instruction contains $Q1$ in its address part, and so on. When the program is executed, locations A, B become A', B' after hardware relocation. If the index register has been altered once, it is then said that $B' + 1$ is the effective address of the operand of the instruction now located at A'. However, the instruction at A' still contains the original value B in its address part.

electrical accounting machine   A data processing machine in which the processing is done electromechanically, that is, by means of relays and similar devices. Electrical accounting machines (EAM) include card sorters, tabulators, reproducers, interpreters, and punches. Almost all EAM equipment operates on punched cards. See EAM.

electromagnetic delay line   An electromagnetic delay line is a device used to introduce specific time delays as needed for digital computation and for controlling the shape of pulses. In general, this device will have the form of either a distributed line or a lumped constant line.

The transmission time of electrical waves propagating in an ordinary transmission line with an air dielectric is equal to the propagation time of light (0.001 microsecond per foot). For dielectrics other than air, the transmission time is longer, depending on the dielectric constant of the material separating the line elements. In general, the transmission time T per unit length is equal to the square root of LC, where L is the series inductance per unit length and C is the shunt capacity per unit length. For a coaxial cable (such as the RG-64 U) for example, a delay of 0.04 microsecond per foot is typical. By winding a spiral transmission line, delays of 0.1 to 1 microsecond per foot are possible. Beyond this, lumped constant lines constructed of series coils and shunt capacitors are normally used and can be built to give delays of 1 to 10 microseconds per foot. In general, as the delay time is increased, the range of frequencies that will be transmitted without distortion is decreased. A lumped line of 10 microseconds per foot typically has a passband of 5 megahertz (5,000,000 cycles per second).

In addition to the line itself, input and output signal-conditioning amplifiers are required, along with the usual gates, to control the read-in, readout, and erase functions in the case of a line used for cyclic storage.   See SYNCHRONOUS COMPUTER.

electronic data processing   Refers to data manipulations performed by equipment that is mainly electronic in nature and requires little human intervention.   See EDP.

electrostatic storage   A storage device that stores data as electro-statically charged areas on a dielectric surface.

Electrostatic storage was usually represented by a device similar in construction to a CRT (cathode-ray tube), but provided with a viewing screen which preserved electromagnetic charges.   These spots were written on the screen by means of an electron beam, and could be read from the screen by the same electronic beam.   This method of storage is no longer common because of the high cost per bit capacity and the nonpermanence of the data in event of power failure.

element   A circuit or device performing some specific, elementary data processing function.   In general, an element transforms an input signal into an output signal according to some prescribed law.   See COMBINATIONAL LOGIC ELEMENT, LOGIC ELEMENT, SEQUENTIAL LOGIC ELEMENT.

elimination factor   In information retrieval (IR), the ratio obtained in dividing the number of documents that have not been retrieved by the total number of documents in the file.   Ideally, if it is assumed that all relevant documents have been retrieved, this factor should be high, that is, very close to one.   If the system is assumed to be effi-cient, the elimination factor is a measure of the heterogeneity of the file.   Contrast with RESOLUTION FACTOR.

embossed plate printer   In character recognition, a data preparation device which accomplishes printing through the paper medium by allowing only the raised character to contact the printing ribbon.

encode   To transform according to the rules of a code.

There are two types of encoding encountered in data processing:

1.   The encoding required to represent a set of data in a form suitable for input to the computer (see CODE)

2.   The encoding required to distinguish each item from all other items

In the latter case, a great deal of study and research are required before selecting a code that will eliminate problems of duplication, overlapping, and cost. The necessity of a code must be clearly established, as must be its purpose: for instance, security, ease in sorting, and frequency of conversion. When properly selected, the code should allow for

1. Possible expansion within categories, such as insertion of new items between existing items
2. Representation of interrelationships, such as division, department, section, individual
3. Ease of interpretation by the user
4. Ease of manipulation by the user
5. Unique identification of any one item
6. Restrictions imposed by the computer on hand

encoder   In character recognition, that class of printer which is usually designed for the specific purpose of printing a particular type font in predetermined positions on certain size forms.

Encoders were initially developed for the preparation of MICR (magnetic-ink character recognition) bank checks, but their use has now expanded into other areas of MICR and OCR (optical character recognition) in those applicatons where the printing standards are very exact.

encoding strip   In character recognition, the area reserved for the inscription of magnetic-ink characters, as in bank checks.

end-around carry   A carry from the most significant digit place to the least significant digit place.

End-around carry is an alternative method of using the nine's complement in subtraction. The method is as follows:

$$\begin{array}{r} 42 \\ -24 \\ \hline \end{array}$$

is replaced by

$$\begin{array}{r} 42 \\ +75 \\ \hline \end{array}$$

where 75 is obtained by subtracting each digit of 24 from 9. The addition is then carried out:

$$\begin{array}{r} 42 \\ +75 \\ \hline 117 \end{array}$$

and the leftmost 1 is taken out and added to the rightmost digit of 117:

$$17$$
$$+1$$
$$\overline{18}$$

This method is sometimes used for subtraction purposes in computers, since it is simpler (and cheaper) to form a digit-by-digit complement than to build borrow circuits.

endorser   A special feature available on most magnetic-ink character-recognition (MICR) readers that imprints a bank's endorsement on successful document reading. The endorsement is usually accomplished without a reduction in the effective throughput rate.

entry point   The location to which control can be passed in a routine. A program may have several entry points, each point corresponding to a different function to be performed. This type of program structure differs from a structure having several single-entry-point subroutines since common coding and constants may be shared in the several-entry-point program.

environment division   The section of a program (written in the COBOL language) which contains the following information:
1. The specific hardware configuration required to compile the COBOL program, and the specific hardware configuration to run the compiled program
2. The specific devices required to read in the program and data (card reader, magnetic tape, or magnetic disk)
3. The specific devices involved in the output (card punch, magnetic tape, magnetic drive, or printer)
4. The assignment of files
See COBOL.

equivalence   A logic operator having the property that if P, Q, R, etc., are statements, then the equivalence of P, Q, R, etc., is true if and only if all statements are true or all statements are false. In Boolean algebra, propositional functions are said to be equivalent if and only if these propositional functions are either all true or all false.

In FORTRAN, EQUIVALENCE is a statement that specifies that several variables are to occupy the same location in memory. The purpose of this statement is to save space by using the same area for different functions at different times. For instance,

EQUIVALENCE (A (2), C), (D, E, F(10))

means that C occupies (or begins at) the second word of the array A, and that D and E and the tenth word of the array F are to occupy the same location.

Equivalence is also used either to ensure that different arrays are located continuously or to permit performing integer and floating-point operations on the same word of data.

equivalent binary digits   The number of binary positions required to enumerate the elements of a given set.

For example, if a set has five elements, three equivalent binary digits will be required to enumerate the five members of the set: 1, 10, 11, 100, 101. If a computer word is made up of three decimal digits and a sign (+ or −), there are 2000 different combinations possible; that is, the set would contain 2000 elements. Such a set would require 11 equivalent binary digits to enumerate all its elements.

The number n of equivalent binary digits required to enumerate the m elements of a set is the smallest value of n such that 2^n is at least equal to m. Thus, if there are 1000 elements in a set, 10 equivalent binary digits would be required since $2^{10} = 1024$, but $2^9 = 512$.

error   Any discrepancy between a computed, observed, or measured quantity and the true, specified, or theoretically correct value of that quantity. An error is only one of the three factors (the other two being malfunction and mistake) giving incorrect results.

The difference between the given quantity and its calculated approximation is due to the numerical method used. A frequent cause of errors is the automatic rounding of short numbers during repeated operations. For instance, if a result is to be expressed in whole numbers, then 3/2 will give 2 as an answer. More sophisticated rules are required for this type of rounding, or else rounding should not be carried out before all operations have been completed.

A common method of reducing errors is to carry more digits in calculations than will be needed in the final answer. Where great accuracy is required, programmers will use double-precision arithmetic; where machine language is used, the sequence of arithmetic operations is important: multiplications should be performed before division, when possible, to retain precision.

Since scientific calculations give rise to longer numbers than do accounting and business calculations, the programmer should check the degree of precision necessary in the result before deciding how

many digits to use for a data item. See ABSOLUTE ERROR, DOUBLE PRE-
CISION, INHERITED ERROR, MALFUNCTION, MISTAKE.

error-correcting code   An error-correcting code is a data representation that allows for error detection and error correction if the error
is of a specific kind.

Consider, for example, a code of seven-binary-digit form. A correctly
coded character will have a unique representation, but changing any one
bit will produce an unacceptable character. There will thus be seven unacceptable coded characters related to the correctly coded character. If,
during transmission, any one bit is lost, it will be possible to detect the
error instantly on reception, and through the family relationship, recover
the correct character. However, the number of different characters represented will be $2^7/8 = 16$: thus, only 57 percent of the transmission
will be reserved for information, 43 percent being utilized for error detection and correcting purposes. If a 15-bit code were used, the number
of characters available would be 2048, and the information efficiency
would be equal to 73 percent.

The cost of using error-correcting codes is high, and the losses attributed to errors should be weighed against such costs before deciding on the use of error-correcting codes.

error range   The difference between the highest and lowest error
values. The error range is a measure of the uncertainty associated
with a number.

escape character   A character used to indicate that the succeeding
character or characters are expressed in a code different from the
code currently in use. An escape character is simply a means of escape from the limitations imposed by the code being used.

For example, the shift key on a typewriter will permit mixing
upper- and lowercase characters while still using the same code
(keys): as long as the escape character (shift key) is used, all code
characters (keys) will have a meaning different from the one they
had before the use of the escape character (shift key).

The escape character Δ (delta) is used on some magnetic tapes
(IBM 7070) to change from numeric to alphanumeric, or from alphabetic to numeric characters.

event   The moment of time at which a specified change of state occurs. Usually an event marks the completion of an asynchronous
I/O operation.

There are millions of events occurring inside a computer every second. Of these, the only significant events are the ones that some program is waiting for. These significant happenings are the events referred to in our definition. In OS/360, a program or task indicates to the system that it cannot continue until a specific event has happened. The task activates an event control block which identifies the particular event. This activation is caused by issuing a wait macroinstruction, and until the event occurs, the task is placed in an inactive, waiting state. In multiprogramming environment, other programs can be executed while this time elapses. In a nonmultiprogramming environment, no program is processed, but the system executes a tight "loop" until the desired signal arrives. The event must announce itself to the system by a hardware interrupt or other signal. At that time the event control block is marked completed, and the task(s) waiting for that event are marked ready and removed from the waiting state. The system then returns control of the CPU to that ready task having the highest dispatching priority.

It is possible for a task to wait for more than one event, and it is also possible for several tasks to await the same event. The system must be adaptable to all combinations of these two possibilities.

event control block   A control block, or formalized unit of storage, used to control the status of tasks waiting for an event to occur.

It may happen that a program finds that it cannot continue processing until one or more events (specified changes of state) occur. In OS/360, the program (or task) issued a WAIT macroinstruction that activates one or more ECB's. (For example, it is possible to specify that the program must wait until any n out of m possible events have occurred. Normally, a program waits on a single event, usually completion of an I/O operation.) The ECB's designated by the WAIT are initialized to a waiting status, and processing of the task is suspended. At the completion of each event, the ECB(s) waiting on that event are marked complete. When the required number of "complete" are marked, a waiting task is returned to ready status. (This may produce an incomplete but not waiting state in another ECB of the task if the event of that other ECB has not yet been recognized but is no longer essential for the program to continue processing.)

The ECB is itself one 32-bit word. The leftmost bit contains the waiting (on/off) indicator. The next bit contains the completed (yes/no) indication. The remaining 30 bits are used by the system while the incomplete indication exists. (These bits point to the next ECB in the list, if any, or mark the end of the ECB chain.) At completion time, a post code of up to 30 bits may be placed in this area to return information to the waiting task. For example, a POST macroinstruction can be used by one task to complete and fill the ECB of another task (to facilitate task-to-task coordination in a multiprogramming situation).

excess-three code   A binary-coded decimal representation in which each decimal digit N is represented by the binary equivalent of N plus 3.   For example:

Decimal	Binary	Excess-three code
0	0	0011
1	1	0100
2	10	0101
3	11	0110
4	100	0111
5	101	1000
6	110	1001
7	111	1010
8	1000	**1011**
9	1001	1100

The excess-three code (usually shortened to XS3) has two important characteristics:

1.   Whenever a carry is generated in decimal addition, a corresponding carry is generated in the binary addition of the XS3 representation.

2.   The nine's complement of any decimal digit corresponds to the one's complement of the corresponding XS3 code.

These two characteristics offer distinct advantages in carrying out decimal arithmetic in a binary arithmetic machine.   These advantages are best brought out by analyzing addition and subtraction in the XS3 code.

Consider the addition of two decimal digits M and N.   The XS3 codes for M and N are the 4-bit binary numerals with a value of $M + 3$ and $N + 3$.   Suppose $M + N \leq 9$ (that is, requiring no carry).   In the XS3 code, $(M + 3) + (N + 3)$ would result in $M + N + 6$: consequently, a 3 (that is, a binary 11) must be subtracted from the result then to get $M + N + 3$.   There will be no overflow since a 4-bit configuration allows for all values from 0 to 15 and since $M + N$ was defined as not exceeding 9, $M + N + 6$ will not exceed 15.

If, on the other hand, $M + N > 9$ (that is, involving a carry in decimal arithmetic), the XS3 coded numerals will also generate a carry, or a binary overflow digit.   For example, let $M + N = 10 + Y$, where $Y \leq 8$.   Consequently, in XS3 code:

$$M + 3 + N + 3 = 10 + Y + 6 = 16 + Y$$

The quantity 16 is, in binary, equal to 10000 and as such will be the overflow bit, the true value of Y remaining in the 4-bit adder. The XS3 code requires then a 3 to be added this time to Y.   In other words:

Decimal	XS3	Decimal	XS3
7	0011 1010	7	0011 1010
+2	+0011 0101	+4	+0011 0111
9	0110 1111	11	0111 0001
	−11 −11		−11 +11
	0011 1100		0100 0100
	(no carry)		(with carry)

Thus, to decimally add on binary arithmetic hardware, the procedure routinely adds binary digits and records the presence (or absence) of a carry across a 4-bit "decimal digit" boundary. If no carry crosses the boundary, a 3 is subtracted from the resulting digit to the right of the boundary; if a carry does cross the boundary, a 3 is added to the right of the boundary. This procedure permits not only serial addition but equally parallel addition with the consequent increase in speed of operation.

In the case of subtraction, it is usually cheaper to form a complement numeral and use addition circuits than it would be to build separate subtraction hardware.

In using ten's complement, a subtraction is replaced by addition if the nine's complement replaces every digit of the subtrahend except its rightmost digit which is replaced by its ten's complement, any carry beyond the leftmost digit being ignored. For instance:

$$\begin{matrix} 9326 \\ -8768 \\ \hline 0558 \end{matrix} \quad \text{is replaced by} \quad \begin{matrix} 9326 \\ +1232 \\ \hline 0558 \end{matrix}$$

In using nine's complement, the same procedure is followed with the sole exception that a 1 is added to the rightmost digit of the result. For example:

$$\begin{matrix} 9326 \\ -8768 \\ \hline 0558 \end{matrix} \quad \text{is replaced by} \quad \begin{matrix} 9326 \\ +1231 \\ \hline 0557 \\ +\quad 1 \\ \hline 558 \end{matrix}$$

Whereas the nine's complement (in a sense) would require a table to indicate that 1 becomes 8, 2 becomes 7, 3 becomes 6, and so on, the one's complement in binary simply means replacing 1 by 0 and 0 by 1. Thus:

Decimal		XS3	
Straight	9's complement	Straight	1's complement
0	9	0011	1100
1	8	0100	1011
2	7	0101	1010
3	6	0110	1001
4	5	0111	1000
5	4	1000	0111
6	3	1001	0110
7	2	1010	0101
8	1	1011	0100
9	0	1100	0011

The carrying out of the above example in XS3 code would thus appear as follows:

```
 9326      1100  0110  0101  1001
-8768     -1011  1010  1001  1011
```

which are replaced by 9's and 1's complements:

```
 9326      1100  0110  0101  1001
+1231     +0100  0101  0110  0100
 ────      ────  ────  ────  ────
 0557      0000  1011  1011  1101
+   1     +                     1
 ────      ────  ────  ────  ────
 0558      0000  1011  1011  1110
         + 11  - 11  - 11  - 11
           ────  ────  ────  ────
           0011  1000  1000  1011
```

Note that a binary 3 was added to the leftmost digit since a carry crossed the 4-bit decimal digit boundary, and a binary 3 was subtracted from each other digit as no carry crossed the boundary.

exchange buffering   An input/output buffering technique that avoids the internal moving of data.

Simultaneous I/O and processing are made possible by allocating areas of main memory to serve as buffers.   A buffer is either FILLED (waiting for processing, if input; or waiting for writing, if output), EMPTY (waiting for input from an input device, or waiting for output data from the program), or ACTIVELY IN USE (currently being used by an I/O device).   The program manipulates the data either in the buffer area itself (while no I/O uses that area) or more commonly in a work area outside the buffer.

Exchange buffering begins with distinct areas set aside for work and for buffering.   Consider an input file with fixed-length logical records blocked four logical records per physical record. Initially, four adjacent 100-character areas (beginning at locations 2300, 2400, 2500, 2600) form the input buffer and are filled with data. A work area (location 1100) is provided by the program, and three empty areas (2700, 2800, 2900) are reserved for additional buffers by the system. Each of the eight areas is equal in size to one logical record. When the program requests input data, the program's area, 1100, is exchanged with a filled buffer area, 2300. The data are not moved, but the addresses of 1100 and 2300 are traded between the program and the data management routine. 2300 becomes the program's work area, and 1100 becomes the fourth empty buffer. Now there are four empty buffers, and so the next physical record is read into 2700, 2800, 2900, 1100 using the data chaining facility of the data channel to read into disjoint areas. At the next request for data, 2300 is traded with 2400. The work area address now points to 2400, and an empty buffer address points to 2300. The 100-character data records have not moved, but their three-character addresses are interchanged. (Programs refer to items within a record via relative addressing, such as by index register or base register and displacement.)

Consider an application in which an entire file is read, updated, and written out in one run (for example, payroll file). Let the logical records be 150 characters long, three logical records per block. Initially, the input and output files are opened, the first physical block is read in, but no data have been manipulated. Parts of core look like this:

1200	1350	1500	3800	2000	2150	2300
Filled input buffer #1	Filled input buffer #2	Filled input buffer #3	Program's work area unused	---Empty output buffers--- #1	#2	#3

The program issues a GET to obtain the first logical record. Memory now looks like this:

1200	1350	1500	3800	2000	2150	2300
Work area in use	Input #2 filled	Filled input #3	Input empty #1	Output empty #1	Output empty #2	Output empty #3

After processing, a PUT releases the data for output:

1200	1350	1500	3800	2000	2150	2300
Filled output buffer #1	Input #2 filled	Filled input #3	Input empty #1	Work area empty	Output empty #2	Output empty #3

Next, a GET to obtain the second record:

1200	1350	1500	3800	2000	2150	2300
Filled output buffer #1	Work area in use	Filled input #3	Input empty #1	Input empty #2	Output empty #2	Output empty #3

Then PUT:

1200	1350	1500	3800	2000	2150	2300
Filled output buffer #1	Filled output buffer #2	Filled input #3	Input empty #1	Input empty #2	Work empty	Output empty #3

Then GET:

1200	1350	1500	3800	2000	2150	2300
Filled output buffer #1	Filled output buffer #2	Work in use	Input empty #1	Input empty #2	Input buffer empty #3	Output empty #3

A new read operation begins to fill 3800, 2000, 2150 before and while processing resumes. The program gives its next PUT:

1200	1350	1500	3800	2000	2150	2300
Filled output buffer #1	Filled output buffer #2	Filled output buffer #3	Input active here	Input empty #2	Input buffer empty #3	Work empty

Now three output buffers are filled, and so a write operation begins for areas 1200, 1350, 1500. *Note:* These originally were the *input* buffers. Meanwhile, running simultaneously, the program has issued another GET:

1200	1350	1500	3800	2000	2150	2300
Output channel active here	Filled output buffer #2	Filled output buffer #3	Work filled in use	Input channel active here	Input buffer empty #3	Input buffer empty #4

At this point, all former input buffers are output buffers, all former output buffers are input buffers, the program's original work area is again a work area, and two data channels and the program are running concurrently. No data have been moved except those actually manipulated by the program.

For blocked records, data channels capable of writing or reading discontinuous areas of memory under their own control must be used. If hardware does not permit this for a particular device/CPU, then data management must substitute a different buffering technique. OS automatically reverts to a move-mode conventional buffering technique in these cases, leaving address pointers intact. Thus the same program can be run with or without data chaining channels, without having to be adjusted (i.e., machine independence is achieved).

If the record format of a file or data set is unblocked, data chaining is not needed. If two buffers are attached to each data set, one for use by the program and the other by the data channel, then a simple form of dual buffering results. This simpler "flip-flop" buffer allocation is common on many elementary systems. Many programmers using this technique do not realize that they are practicing exchange buffering.

EXCLUSIVE OR A logic operator which has the property that if P is a statement and Q is a statement, then P EXCLUSIVE OR Q is true if either but not both statements are true, false if both are true or both are false. P EXCLUSIVE OR Q is often represented by P V Q, P $\oplus$ Q. If P and Q are statements, and T stands for true and F stands for false, the EXCLUSIVE OR truth table is as follows:

P	Q	P v Q
T	T	F
T	F	T
F	T	T
F	F	F

For example, "He was born in Paris, or in New York" is an instance of EXCLUSIVE OR, whereas the statement "milk or sugar?" is an example of the logic operator OR which allows for "milk or sugar" to be true even if both statements are true.

EXCLUSIVE OR equally refers to a computer instruction which performs the EXCLUSIVE OR operation on a bit-by-bit basis for its two operand words, usually storing the result in one of the operand locations. Thus, EXCLUSIVE OR A, B means that if a bit of A is 1, the corresponding bit of B is changed to its opposite value (for a zero bit in A, the corresponding bit in B is unchanged). A does not change in this instruction:

Initial   A = 01001110
Initial   B = 00001111

Resulting   A = 01001110
Resulting   B = 01000001
Contrast with OR.

exclusive segments Parts of an overlay program structure that cannot be resident in main memory simultaneously.

No matter how much central memory is provided for a computer, it will always be possible to write a program too large to fit. The most common way to handle this situation is to segment the program into overlays. An overlay (or overlay segment) is called into memory from auxiliary storage; executed, possibly written out for temporary saving, and destroyed by the loading of the next overlay. In this way memory capacity is extended at the cost of running time.

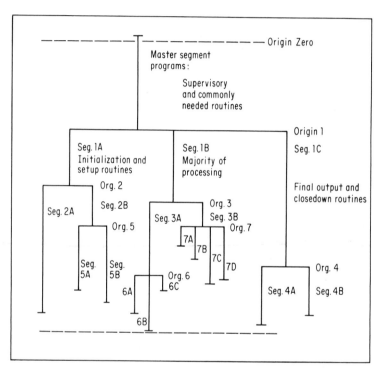

Overlay structure—exclusive segments.

An overlay structure must be planned in order to minimize load/search time and still obey memory limits. Usually a main segment remains in memory and calls in the first-level overlays. Any overlay segment may call in additional lower-level segments, but cannot call a segment in a level equal to or greater than its own. (To do so would be to destroy itself, preventing proper return after the called routine finished.) The mutually exclusive segments are called exclusive segments. Passage of control from one exclusive segment to another must be regulated by the resident (or root) segment.

Overlay structures often are diagrammed in a treelike fashion (see illustration). The vertical lines are segments, and the horizontal bars are origins (the initial address of all overlay segments extending down from the horizontal bar). A segment in a higher or lower position is then inclusive to a given segment. All segments crossed by any horizontal line (not shown) are mutually exclusive.

Control may pass freely up and down (Example: 1B can call routine in 7B; 6A can call routine in 3A); but sideways transfers are prohibited (4A cannot call 2B).

executive routine   The routine that controls the execution of other routines. An executive routine simplifies the operator's work so that the computer can run more efficiently.

A basic executive routine will load the program in the computer, handle input and output operations, and take corrective action, or halt operations, when certain kinds of errors are encountered.

A more advanced executive routine carries out the complex functions required by multiprogramming. If many programs are fed into a computer simultaneously from remote input/output units, the executive routine places the programs in nonconflicting storage locations. Each program is examined in turn for instructions to be performed. Since instructions from various programs may require the same units, the executive routine will seek programs having instructions not requiring the same units. Programs are thus advanced by groups of instructions until, as they are completed, they can be replaced, one by one, by a new program.

A less sophisticated type of executive routine can handle a sequence of programs. The programs are prestored on tape, and the executive routine calls them one after the other, calls in the assembler or compiler as required, loads the machine-language program in the computer, and starts the processing. Such a routine is called a compile-and-run executive routine.

The developments in executive routines provide powerful, efficient capabilities for increased computer usage. See SUPERVISORY ROUTINE.

extent   The physical locations in a mass-storage device or volume allocated for use by a particular data set.

The recordable part of a storage device (disk, drum, tape, etc.) always has a definite capacity for holding data. Each data set written onto the volume occupies a certain amount of space known as its *ex-*

tent. When a volume is mostly empty, the extent is usually allocated as a single contiguous area of storage. On a volume that is largely occupied and has seen extensive use, there may be no single area large enough for the entire data set. In this case the required space is allocated from the available disjoint areas, largest area first until either a limiting number of areas is allocated or enough space has been provided. Whether one or more areas are needed, all are referred to as the extent of the data set (singular).

external reference   A reference to a variable, or item, that is not defined in the program module (subroutine, segment).

Programs written in assembly or compiler languages refer to the locations of data and/or instructions by associating programmer-defined symbols with the desired locations. A large program system may contain many independently written routines which are united and integrated before execution by a linkage editor or a linking loader. In this case, a program can refer to a datum or instruction outside of itself (i.e., in another subroutine) by referring to the external symbol associated with the desired location. This appearance of an as-yet-undefined symbolic location constitutes an external reference.

The assembler (if assembly language is used) must be told explicitly that a symbol is external, or it will detect an error condition. The EXTERN pseudoinstruction found in several assembly languages is provided for this declaration. Many compilers require similar explicit declarations, but usually can identify EXTERN symbols by their context. Example: In FORTRAN, an EXTERNAL statement identifies subroutines whose names will be passed to other subroutines via calling sequences.

Naturally, the program that defines and contains the desired location must use the same external name for it. If interprogram coordination fails, the linking program (which is no mindreader) cannot complete the reference, and the programs will not be allowed to execute. See EXTERNAL SYMBOL.

external storage   Usually synonymous with auxiliary storage or secondary storage, and therefore meaning large-capacity, relatively slow access data storage attached to a digital computer, and used to store information that exceeds the capacity of main storage.

In some cases, external storage, secondary storage, and auxiliary storage may be distinguished from one another. For example:

Secondary storage includes all dynamic (moving) storage mechanisms attached to a computer, typically composed of magnetic tapes, drums, and disks.

Auxiliary storage is part of secondary storage used by the operating system for temporary or permanent retention of programs (data) outside of main memory.

External storage is the remainder of secondary storage and available for use by programmers to hold programs and data. External storage contains both temporary (working storage) and long-term collections of data and programs.

external symbol   A symbolic location name appearing in an external symbol dictionary (or equivalent) of a program that permits the named location to be referred to by other programs.

In all but the simplest of modern digital computers, programs are composed of separately written routines which function together to accomplish the desired processing. Even when the programmer thinks he has written a unified and complete program, his input and output are probably handled by systems-provided utility routines (IOCS, data management, etc.). The separately written programs must be integrated and united before execution to permit them to function together. This integration is performed by a linkage editor or a linking loader.

The linking is performed by relocating the programs so that they occupy adjacent, nonoverlapping regions of memory and then resolving the interprogram references. Each program may refer to a data item or instruction defined in some other program (external reference), and each program may supply (or define) locations referred to by other programs (external symbols). Each instruction or datum defined in a program that may be needed by other routines can be made known to the other routines by being entered into an external symbol dictionary (ESD). This makes the name and (relocatable) address of the symbolic location known to the linkage editor. While the linkage editor relocates all the programs, it converts the addresses in the ESD's to absolute addresses and prepares a unified external symbol list. This unified list permits the linkage editor to substitute the correct resolved address for each external reference. Completion of this process results in the several programs being unified into a single coherent program module.

If an external reference cannot be resolved (that is, if a program refers to an undefined external symbol), the program module is incomplete and cannot be executed. But if an external symbol is never referred to, no harm is done: a wasted entry was made in the unified symbol list and then discarded when the linking process was completed. There must be agreement between the names used in the defining and the referring programs, or else the correct connection cannot be made.

external symbol dictionary (ESD)   A list of external symbols and their relocatable addresses which allows the linkage editor to resolve interprogram references. An ESD is associated with every object module and every load module except those having the "not editable" attribute.

Both external symbols and external references appear in an ESD. An ESD appears at the beginning of every object module and at the beginning of every load module *except* those that are "not editable." (A "not editable" module occupies less storage space on disk precisely because it lacks an ESD, but must be fully re-created if any change, however slight, is to be made in it.)

The entries in an ESD are either external names or external references. An external name is defined within the module. It can be a control-section name, and entry name, or a blank or named COMMON area for FORTRAN programs. A special kind of external name is the so-called private code. This is a control section whose length and starting locations are defined, but whose name contains only blank characters. A private code control section cannot be referred to from outside the module. An external reference is the symbolic name of a location referred to but not defined within this module. The symbol and the location of every reference to this symbol appear in the ESD.

Every record of an ESD begins with a code identifying it as containing ESD information. Every symbol appears with a code identifying its type (what kind of external name or external reference) and one or more addresses denoting its appearances within the module. Control-section names are also described by length and starting location information.

extract instruction   An instruction that requests the formation of a new expression from selected parts of given expressions.

Consider the existence of three registers in the arithmetic unit: the accumulator register, the filter (or extractor) register, and the memory (or edit) register.

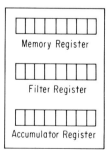

Memory Register

Filter Register

Accumulator Register

The number 21306 is to be transformed into \$213.06 for output purposes. The number 21306 is unpacked, that is, shifted right and left until it appears as 00213006 in the accumulator. The number 11000100 is placed in the filter register, and the number "\$." is placed in the memory register:

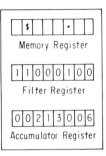

Upon executing the extract instruction, every character in the memory register will replace the corresponding character in the accumulator register if, and only if, the corresponding character in the filter register is a one. If the corresponding character in the filter register is a zero, the character in the accumulator register remains unchanged. Upon execution, the three registers will appear as follows:

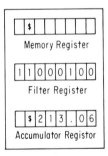

The function of an extract instruction is thus to remove from a word all the characters that meet a specific criterion (as dictated by the extractor) and replace them by other characters (as dictated by the edit word in the memory register).

F

face A particular or characteristic style in which characters or letters are formed. See TYPEFACE.

factor A number by which another number (or numbers) is multiplied so as to transform the magnitude of the latter in a known way.

Also, one of the two or more numbers that are multiplied (or divided) by one another to form a product (or a quotient). In additive relationships such an element is called a term.

Also, a number that is an integral divisor of another number: 2, 3, 6 are factors of 12. See SCALE FACTOR.

fan-in The number of signal sources that can be connected to an input terminal of a circuit without impairing its functioning, that is, the number of simultaneous 1 or 0 pulses that may be safely applied to an input of a circuit.

The flexibility of a circuit or logical component depends in part on the number of devices that can be connected to its inputs (fan-in) or outputs (fan-out). For instance, consider the testing of a 32-bit word for an all-zero-bits condition. It is possible to OR together the 32 bits (OR is 1 if any, or some, or all bits are 1) and test the OR result for zero, or to NOR (not-OR) the 32 bits, which will give a 1 output only if all 32 bits are 0. Suppose that the OR gates (or NOR gates) had a maximum fan-in of 16: three OR gates would be needed instead of one. For instance:

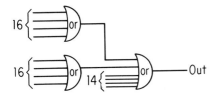

If the fan-in were to be increased to 17, two gates could be used:

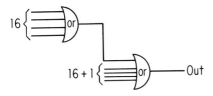

And if fan-in of 32 or more were achieved, one gate would suffice.

The number of driving signals must be limited, however, for the power delivered by too many simultaneous pulses or signals could destroy the input device. See FAN-OUT.

fan-out The number of circuits that can be supplied with input signals from an output terminal of a circuit or device.

The versatility of a digital circuit depends in part on the number of devices that can drive or be driven by one circuit of the type under consideration. The number of elements that one ouput can drive depends on the power available from the output and the power required by each input. The problem is analogous to the number of light bulbs that can be lit by a given battery or household circuit.

Suppose that it is required to construct a high-speed left-shifting device for a 32-bit word computer. There are a source-data register and five receiving registers. The paths from source to receivers are shifted 1, 2, 4, 8, and 16 bits, respectively, but nonshifted paths are provided for returning the contents of the receiving registers to the sending registers. In this way, with a maximum of 10 register-to-register transfers, one can shift the word from 1 to 31 bits to the left (this same arrangement could be part of a high-speed binary multiplication scheme).

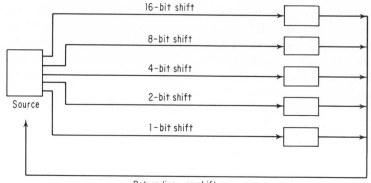

Suppose that each bit position of the sending register could drive only three output lines. It would be required to provide buffer amplifiers in the data path, which would increase both cost and signal delay time.

Modern FET (field-effect transistor) and IGFET (insulated-gate field-effect transistor) circuits have very high input impedances (each absorbs very little power) which makes possible very large values of fan-out. However, fan-in is still limited in these devices. See FAN-IN.

fault Any physical condition that causes a component to fail in its performance. See PATTERN-SENSITIVE FAULT, PROGRAM-SENSITIVE FAULT.

feeding See CYCLIC FEEDING, ACYCLIC FEEDING.

fetch To locate and load into main memory a requested load module, relocating it as necessary, and leaving it in a ready-to-execute condition.

Fetch is also a service routine that accomplishes the above, or a macroinstruction requesting that the above be performed.

More generally, to fetch is to obtain data from a memory or storage device. Contrast with STORE.

F-format In data management, a fixed-length logical record format.

The size of the logical record is of concern to data management, and its contents are the sole concern of the processing programs.

A data set has F-format logical records if every logical record (except possibly label records) has identical length. Unblocked F-format records are exactly as long as their physical records. The physical records of a blocked F-format (FB) data set are all some multiple of the size of the logical record, except possibly for a few truncated blocks. A truncated block contains a smaller integral number of fixed-length logical records. A standard blocked F-format (FBS) data set has at most one truncated block, and that one must be the last one in the DS. All other FBS physical records are of equal, maximum length. F-format is required for unit record data (card readers, printers, card punches, etc.) and may be used with any data medium if the job requires it. FBS is the most efficient form of storing sequential data on random-access devices.

An F-format logical record may contain an ASCII control character or a machine-control character in its first byte of information. This is indicated by suffixing A or M (not both) to one of the formats above, as for example, FBM (blocked, machine character) or FBSA (standard blocked, ASCII control character). The control character is treated as nondata, and used to control form skipping (printer) or stacker pocket selection (punch). If neither printer nor punch is used, the control character is treated as data.

In FORTRAN, the F-format is an input/output specification directing that fixed-point numeric data be read or written, with conversion to/from internal floating-point form being automatically supplied.

An F-format item is a floating-point number whose external representation contains a fixed decimal-point location. This is specified as FORMAT (Fw.d)—where w and d are unsigned integers: w specifies the total width of the area allocated to this item, and d specifies the number of digits to appear after the decimal point. Thus F8.0 specifies eight integral places and no fractional digits, and F20.5 specifies a 20-column field containing a number right-justified, displaying five fraction-part digits. On input, if a decimal point appears, it overrides the d specification. If no decimal point appears, d places are assumed. On output d places always appear, with right-trailing zeros supplied if necessary.

Negative numbers are indicated by a minus sign appearing just left of the leading digit. Positive numbers have no sign for output, but may have a leading plus for input. Therefore, the w specification must be wide enough to allow all wanted digits, plus decimal point, plus sign.

In PL/1 an F format is an input/output format specification similar to FORTRAN usage, and a similar F format usage is permitted in edit-directed transmission. In a format list, the specification may appear as F(w), F(w, d), or F(w, d, p). When d and p are omitted, they are assumed to be zero. The specifications w and d are as in FORTRAN, but the p specification directs that data be scaled by a power of 10 during conversion. Negative p specifications are allowed.

The most common use of the p-specification option is to permit printing percentages, but calculating in actual ratios. Thus 52 percent can be the external form of the internal number 0.52, and the I/O format routine will make all necessary adjustments.

On output, F(w) will cause an integral value of up to w digits (or w − 1 digits + sign) to be printed, with no decimal point. This is similar to the I format of FORTRAN in appearance.

field   A specified area used for a particular category of data. For instance, a group of card columns used to represent a salary, or a set of bit locations in a computer word representing the address of the operand.

When a field length is constant, programmers speak of fixed field. Fixed fields are common in scientific work where results are generally expected with a known number of significant digits expressed as

$$2.3567 \times 10^2$$
$$1.1967 \times 10^{-8}$$
$$4.1160 \times 10^9$$

rather than expressed as

235.67
.000000011967
4,116,000,000

Fixed fields are employed less in business data processing since the variations in number sizes would cause a considerable amount of wasted space in the storage devices. Variable-length fields are used in this case. Such a method requires a special symbol to indicate the end of each field.

file   A collection of related records treated as a unit. Thus in inventory control, a line of an invoice will form an item, a complete invoice will form a record, and the complete set of records will form a file.

Files represent accumulated input available for processing. Efficient file systems ensure that the required data will be available on demand: however, too many items in a file will result in excessive running time on the computer. In designing an efficient file system, the following information should be gathered and analyzed:
1. Specification of processing requirements
2. Specification of output requirements
3. Form required for input data
4. Classification of the various data items for consolidation purposes
5. Frequency of updating
As a rule, it will be found that a slight excess of raw data is preferable to insufficient data. The guiding principle is to concentrate in any one file all information bearing on any one company operation.

A file is called a data set in the IBM 360 System terminology.

file maintenance   The activities involved in keeping a file up-to-date by adding, changing, or deleting data.

The input to many data processing operations consists of master data (permanent information records kept from one reporting cycle to the next) and transaction data (reflecting variations in business during any one cycle). The collection of master data forms the master file, and the collection of transaction data forms the transaction file. Updating a master file by means of a transaction file at periodic intervals is called file maintenance.

Updating a master file involves sorting the transaction file, detecting the errors introduced when recording the transaction data, validating the correctness of the transaction data, documenting changes carried out on the master file, and gradually removing relatively inactive items to be placed on an inactive master file. File maintenance can come to represent a substantial part of data processing activities in business data processing. File maintenance is the only economic way to maintain an up-to-date historical record since the alternative consists in building a new file from scratch whenever updating is required.

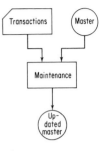

File maintenance.

film   Photographic film used for graphical data processing, input and output, or read-only data storage.

Also, a hardware component obtained by depositing a thin layer of special material on an inert substratum. Film commonly refers to a high-speed memory constructed by thin-film techniques. See MAGNETIC THIN FILM, THIN FILM.

filter   A device or program that separates data or signals in accordance with specified criteria.

A filter is a means of extracting a particular field of information from a longer field containing irrelevant information. This is done by means of a word, or bit pattern, operated on by a bit-by-bit logical AND instruction, or extract instruction.

A digital filter is an arithmetic process that operates on a digitized data stream in much the same way as an electric filter operates on continuous (electrical) data. Its purpose is to eliminate irrelevant data (noise). See EXTRACT INSTRUCTION, MASK.

fixed-cycle operation   An operation completed in a specified number of regularly timed execution cycles.

A fixed-cycle operation is independent of the data being processed, or of the state of the machine. For example, a register-to-memory store instruction is always executed in one cycle: hence this type of instruction is called a fixed-cycle operation.

Note that a multiply operation is faster with a one-significant-digit multiplier than with multidigit numbers and thus is not always completed in the same time. Consequently, a multiply instruction is not a fixed-cycle operation.

See VARIABLE-CYCLE OPERATION.

fixed point A numeration system in which the position of the point is fixed with respect to one end of the numerals, according to some convention.

In integer arithmetic, the decimal point is always to the right of the rightmost digit of each number. There are no fractions possible in integer arithmetic.

In business data processing, dollar and cent calculations automatically consider the decimal point as placed between the second and third digits starting from the rightmost end of the number.

In FORTRAN, fixed point refers to an integer-valued number and integer-valued arithmetic.

fixed storage A storage device in which stored data may not be altered by computer instructions. A magnetic-core storage with a lockout feature and a punched paper tape are examples of fixed storage.

Fixed storage is used in some computers to hold commonly used subroutines (square root, sine, etc.). In other computers, fixed storage allows for the economical obtention of a large instruction set. Each instruction is, in fact, a subroutine in an elementary language, and these subroutines are incorporated in the fixed storage provided for the purpose. See MICROPROGRAM, NONERASABLE STORAGE, PERMANENT STORAGE, READ-ONLY STORAGE.

flag Any of various types of indicators used for identification, such as a word mark, or a character that signals the occurrence of some condition, such as the end of a word.

A flag is also a character (or characters) printed by an assembler or a compiler to indicate that a particular kind of error was detected in a program: in the leftmost column, a U is printed to indicate "unknown address," an O is printed to indicate "invalid operation code." The absence of a flag signifies that no error was detected.

A flag can equally be a portion of a computer instruction. For instance, in the IBM 7090, a flag field containing two 1-bits indicates the use of indirect addressing.

A flag is also a data character, or bit, used by a programmer to record and test the occurrence of an event. For example, a digit will be set equal to zero before searching a string of characters; this digit will be altered to one whenever a blank space is found in the string of characters. If after the search the programmer finds the flag equal to one, he will know that at least one blank space exists in the string of characters. See MARK, TAG.

flip-flop A circuit capable of assuming only one of two stable states at a given time.

In general, a flip-flop circuit maintains a steady output of either one or zero, either state being transformed into the other state by the application of an input pulse. This device is sometimes called a trigger.

A flip-flop is also a programming technique used to alternate input-output devices during processing.

floating point A numeration system in which the position of the point does not remain fixed with respect to one end of the numerals.

By point is meant the character, or the location of an implied character, separating the integral part of a numerical expression from its fractional part.

Floating point usually refers to both a representation of numbers and a method of performing arithmetic. In each instance the point (decimal point in the decimal system, binary point in the binary system) is at a location defined by the number itself.

In general, a floating-point number is composed of two distinct parts:

1. The exponent, normally a two-digit number, which when positive indicates how many digits (and zeros) are located to the left of the point, or when negative how many zeros are found between the point and the leftmost digit.

2. The mantissa, a number composed of the most significant digits of the given number. The sign of the number usually precedes the mantissa.

For example:

Number	Floating-point representation	
	Exponent	Mantissa
234.72	03	23472
−2059.69	04	−205969
.00004314	−04	4314
−.00000002	−07	−2
.72	00	72
3000	04	3

In some instances, the exponent part is found on the right:

234.72 = .23472   03

Floating-point arithmetic is carried out by means of subroutines, although hardware is used to that effect in many computers.   Multiplication is achieved by multiplying mantissa by mantissa, and adding
the exponents together.   For example:

65.0 × 2.5 = 162.5

is carried out as

(02   65) × (01   25) = (03   1625)

Addition requires shifting the mantissa of the smallest of the two
numbers prior to addition.   This addition procedure requirement has
a peculiar result in some computers such as the IBM 7094:   floating-
point addition is more time-consuming than floating-point multiplication.

flow   See FLOW DIRECTION, NORMAL DIRECTION FLOW, REVERSE DIREC-
TION FLOW.

flowchart   A graphical representation for the definition, analysis, or
solution of a problem, in which symbols are used to represent operations, data, flow, and equipment.   To be meaningful, flowcharts are
established at various levels of detail, from "PREPARE-RUN-
DISTRIBUTE" to the step-by-step procedure of extracting a square
root.

In the general design of a system, flowcharts should not give details of single operations.   The level of detail should be uniform in
flowcharts.   For instance:

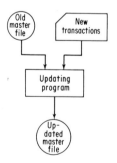

At this level of detail, also called system flowchart, process diagram,
or run diagram, relatively few symbols are needed for flowcharting

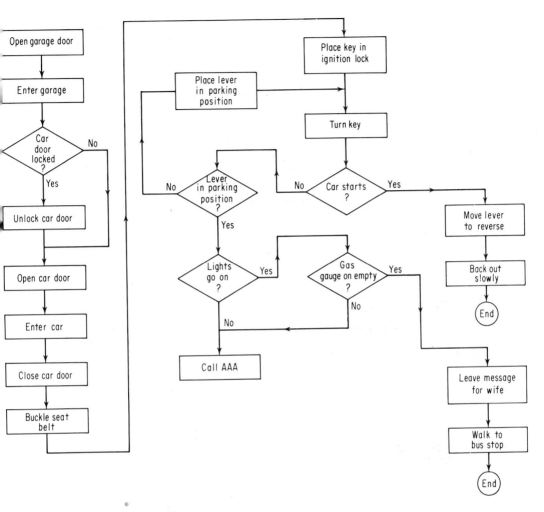

Flowchart of a common domestic problem.

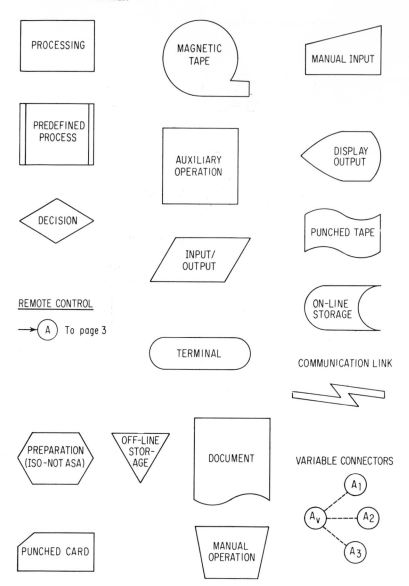

Flowchart symbols.

since a few key words will suffice to expand the meaning of a symbol. For instance:

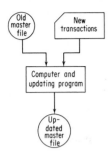

The main flowpath of action is represented by arrows entering and leaving the symbol. The illustration on page 217 uses some of the symbols in common use (see FLOWCHART SYMBOL) and represents the basic principles of flowcharting.

Flowcharts, as adjuncts to program documentation, are important. They will enable a programmer to follow with ease another programmer's job. Each symbol should indicate the number of instructions it refers to. The time saved in program modification, when flowcharts properly made are available, will more than compensate for the time used in flowcharting.

Although block diagram and flowchart are terms used interchangeably, block diagram often carries an implied static representation of events whereas flowchart implies a representation of changing events. See BLOCK DIAGRAM.

flowchart symbol   Any of the existing symbols normally used to represent operations, data flow, or equipment in a problem description.

The most usual symbols encountered in practice are shown in the illustration on the facing page.

flow direction   The antecedent-to-successor relation, indicated by arrows or other conventions, between operations on a flowchart. See FLOWCHART.

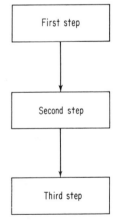

Flow direction.

flowline   The connecting line, or arrow, between symbols on a flowchart or block diagram.   See BLOCK DIAGRAM.

flying head   A read/write head used on magnetic disks and drums, so designed that it "flies" a microscopic distance off the moving magnetic surface supported by a film of air.

The read/write heads on magnetic tape (and similar-type devices, for example, CRAM) touch and actually deform the moving-magnetic materials. Because the total life of a tape is usually measured in terms of tens of thousands of read/write operations, such wear is tolerable. But on a magnetic drum spinning at several thousand revolutions per minute, a wear life of several hundred minutes would be intolerable. To minimize wear, the surfaces of modern disks and drums are polished mirror-smooth. A head is shaped according to aerodynamic principles and is supported by springs in position very near the rapidly moving surface. The force of the air in narrow gap keeps the head at a constant distance above the surface. Because no contact is involved, wear and friction are essentially zero, and long life results.

The penalty for a flying head is less-than-ultimate packing density (bits per inch). The separation from the surface reduces the resolving power of the head, requiring coarser spacing of bits.

flying-spot scanner In optical character recognition (OCR), a device that determines the form of an image by projecting a small point

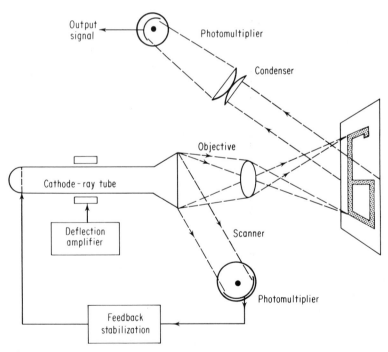

A flying-spot scanner.

of light rapidly moving in a rectangular scanning pattern onto that image and measuring the variations in reflected light intensity. The result of this operation is an analog waveform which is the basis for the subsequent decision as to the character's most probable identity.

The flying-spot scanner is second to the mechanical scanner in terms of actual usage in the OCR field to date. The main reason for this seems to be a practical one, inasmuch as the character under study is illuminated from the scanning-light source, and therefore all ambient illumination on the character must be controlled in order to achieve optimum performance.

However, when this lighttightness has been successfully attained, the flying spot has an effective scanning rate of up to several thousand characters per second. This rate is limited only by the time required for the light emitted from the CRT phosphor to decay after the scanning spot has moved on.

font   See TYPE FONT.

font reticle   In character recognition, a system of lines forming various character outlines which is placed on the image of an input character to determine whether that character conforms to the prescribed shape and range of dimensions.

There are also other miscellaneous outlines on the font reticle which check for such things as the minimum space between lines and characters, and the maximum size of punctuation marks.

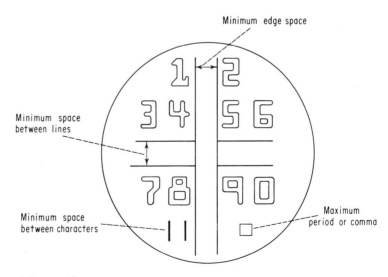

A font recticle.

foreground A program or process of high priority that utilizes machine facilities when and as needed but allows less critical background work to be performed in otherwise unused time.

One of the earliest, and simplest, schemes of multiprogramming is known today as foreground/background processing. Foreground/background involves a small, fast program (the foreground) which resides permanently (or nearly so) in part of a digital computer memory. This program is activated by external interrupts which suspend the routine processing of the background program and give control to the foreground program. This program saves the state of the machine to permit later resumption of the background, and then executes a brief routine in response to the interrupt signal. When it finishes, it restores the machine state to the saved condition, and the background program continues, unaware that the interrupt has occurred. In effect, the foreground program steals moments of time from the background to process high-priority work.

Foreground/background is the only multiprogramming scheme that is practical on computers of modest capacity (medium-small second-generation machines). It is the simplest, best understood, and least overhead-cost system for running two (sometimes three) programs at once with minimum interference or degradation.

Foreground/background is used in two principal areas: in inquiry processing (real-time conversational information retrieval as in airline reservations or stock quotations), and to permit utilization of slow peripheral gear (paper tape read or punch, card punch, slow printer typewriter) on a pseudo-off-line basis (IBM spool or IBM simultaneous peripheral operation on line), that is, with minimum attention from the CPU (central processor unit).

formal logic The study of the permissible relationships between propositions, study that concerns itself with the form rather than the content. See BOOLEAN.

format The specific arrangement of data on a printed page, punched card, etc., to meet established presentation requirements.

Equally refers to the division of an instruction into its component parts as OPERATION CODE, ADDRESS, INDEX REGISTER DESIGNATOR, etc.

In FORTRAN, the format is a statement that defines the arrangement of data in an output (or input) record. For example:

710 FORMAT (10X,F8.2,I3)

stands for the following:

1. The format number is 710.
2. Ten characters are to be skipped (or filled with blanks): 10X.
3. A field eight characters wide contains (or will be filled by) a floating-point number having two digits after the decimal point: F8.2.
4. An integer is contained (or will be placed) in an adjacent field three columns wide: I3.

FORTRAN An acronym for formula translation, this is a family of procedure-oriented languages used mostly for scientific or algebraic applications. FORTRAN was the first language to permit a non-programmer to communicate effectively with a computer. For this reason FORTRAN was responsible for starting the explosive spread of computing beyond the first few special-purpose applications.

The original (unnumbered) FORTRAN language persists today on a few small computers. The principal dialects today are FORTRAN II (now obsolescent) and FORTRAN IV. The latter has been codified as ASA Standard FORTRAN, and a simpler subset has been designated ASA Basic FORTRAN.

All FORTRAN languages treat arithmetic operations by means of a statement which commands evaluation of an expression and substitution of the result for the current value of a variable. A variable is a named location in which data are stored and replaced. Normally, variables with names that begin with I, J, K, L, M, or N have integer values only, and all other variables are floating point (may take on any value; large, small or fractional).

The basic logical decision is an IF statement; this causes an expression to be evaluated and control transferred to one of three statements, depending on the result being less than, equal to, or greater than zero.

FORTRAN II and IV permit writing and calling subroutines. Both permit ordinary subroutines (defined by SUBROUTINE heading statements and called by CALL statements) and FUNCTION subroutines (return one arithmetic value, defined by FUNCTION header statements and called by being named in arithmetic expressions). Some FORTRAN's on larger computers permit use of logical (TRUE/FALSE) variables, or complex arithmetic, or double-precision (extended accuracy) arithmetic.

To illustrate the use of FORTRAN in problem solving, consider a FORTRAN subroutine which calculates the final amount VALUE of a sum PRIN placed at compounded interest RATE during NYEAR years:

Program	Comments
FUNCTION VALUE (PRIN, RATE, NYEAR)	This is a subroutine which will be called by writing VALUE in an arithmetic expression. The computed answer will be used in the arithmetic expression.
REAL PRIN, RATE, INCR	REAL declares P R I N, RATE, and INCR to be floating-point numbers: they may assume a fractional form.
C EVALUATE RATIO OF INCREASE	Comment cards begin with a C in column 1. They should be freely interspersed in a program to aid in documentation.
INCR = 1.0 + RATE/100. T = PRIN	The expressions are calculated and the value substituted for INCR, and PRIN for T.
DO 10 I = 1, NYEAR	The statements from this point until statement number 10 are evaluated. Then I is increased by 1, and the statements are reevaluated, until I = NYEAR.
10 T = T * INCR	The expression T * INCR is evaluated, and the numerical result substituted in T on the left-hand sign of the = sign. This is not an equation. The next time around, the present value of T on the left will become the value of T on the right, and the product formed will then become the value of T on the left.
VALUE = T	Since VALUE is the name of the function, the evaluated expression T is returned to the calling program.

Program	Comments
RETURN	End of the subroutine logic. Control is now returned to the calling program. Note that there may be several returns in one subroutine, controlled for instance by an IF statement.
END	End of the program or sub-program. The compiler directing statement must have one END for each program, that is, the last card in the deck.

The following table illustrates some of the differences between FORTRAN II and FORTRAN IV:

Feature	FORTRAN II	FORTRAN IV
Names of function subroutines	Must end with F Ex: SINF	Any Ex: SIN
Reading BCD tape	READ INPUT TAPE 5, 7	READ (5, 7)
Writing BCD tape	WRITE OUTPUT TAPE 6, 91	WRITE (6, 91)
Logical IF	None	IF (A. EQ. B + 4.) Z = A + B $*$ Z
Declare variable REAL (override first-character convention).	None	REAL IX, ANY, ALL
Declare variable integer (override name convention).	None	INTEGER SOME, MOST
Define initial value of variable	None	DATA INIT, OUT/12, 18.5/
Double-precision arithmetic	Punch D in column 1 of card.	Define some variables by double-precision statements.
Complex arithmetic	Punch I in column 1 of card.	Define variables in complex statement.

four-plus-one address An instruction that contains four operand addresses and a control address. See INSTRUCTION.

full duplex Equivalent to two data paths (one in each direction) but usually treated as a unit. Most commonly used in data transmission, but has also come to mean complete duplication of any data processing facility. In this latter case, one of the two systems is often a "spare," to be used if the other fails and thus provide uninterrupted service. See DUPLEX.

full-word boundary In the IBM 360 System, any address ending in 00, that is, divisible by binary 4, is a natural boundary for a 4-byte machine word. A word in this class must be referenced by an address falling on a boundary of the corresponding type.

function The specific purpose of an entity, or its characteristic action.

The useful purpose served by a thing, thus its reason for being. For example: "The function of the multiplexor is to provide overlapped servicing of the memory banks."

The way or manner in which a device performs its duties. For example: "The interval timer functions as an endless-loop detector by alerting the monitor every 3 seconds."

The mathematical relationship between a set of variables, the value or values being determined by the values assigned to quantities called independent variables or arguments.

In FORTRAN, a subroutine of a particular kind which returns a computational value whenever it is called. A FORTRAN function is defined and named by a subroutine which begins with a function statement and ends with return(s) and an end statement. Within the subroutine the function name is assigned an arithmetic value by a computational statement. The function is called by writing its name in an arithmetic expression in some other program. At execution time, the evaluation of the arithmetic expression is interrupted by a call to the subroutine. The subroutine then evaluates the function. When the subroutine returns control to the calling program, it also returns its arithmetic value, which is used like any other number as the evaluation of the arithmetic expression resumes. As an example:

Main program calls for function ALPHA	Program
	. . . . $Y = 76. * ALPHA (1.0, B) + G (12, K)$ IF (Y) 21, 30, 42 . . . .

Subroutine defining and evaluating ALPHA	FUNCTION ALPHA (C, D) R = 12. * C/ (D + 12.) DO 18 I = 1, 10 . . . . 18 CONTINUE ALPHA = R + T RETURN END

Note that when ALPHA is evaluated in this example, C has the value 1.0, and D has the value of B.   See ARGUMENT.

functional design   A level of the design process in which subtasks are specified and the relationships among them defined, so that the total collection of subsystems performs the entire task of the system.

Functional design is concerned with operations, actions, and interactions, but not with hardware or software details.   If an element of a total system were replaced by another of similar performance but different construction, the functional design of the system would be unchanged, but the detailed design (implementation level) could be profoundly altered.

functional diagram   A diagram that indicates the functions of the principal parts of a total system, and also shows the important relationships and interactions among these parts.

Used to quickly illustrate the important features of the organization and design of a system.

G

gap An area devoid of information content, used to mark the end of an area containing information. Usually a uniformly magnetized area in a magnetic storage device (tape, disk).

A record gap denotes the end of a record (a single continuous grouping of information). A file gap is a longer gap denoting the end of a file (a group of related records). See RECORD GAP.

gate An element of hardware which presents an output determined only by the current state of the input signals according to some rule.

AND gate: A device such that an output is 1 if and only if all the inputs are 1.

OR gate: A device such that an output is 1 if and only if at least one input is 1.

NAND gate: (Not and) a device such that an output is 0 if and only if all the inputs are 1.

NOR gate: (Not or) a device such that an output is 0 if and only if at least one input is 1.

ANALOG gate: A device such that the continuously varying output is the same as one of the inputs if the second digital input is 1. When the digital input is zero, the output is zero (turned off).

gather write An operation that creates a single output record from data items gathered from nonconsecutive locations in main memory.

On some digital computers, input/output is handled by data channels which are programmable processors specialized for this work. Simple data channels can take a specified number of characters or words and read or write them in one operation. Sophisticated data channels can do this, but they can also collect information to be written from a specified sequence of independent memory areas. This capability allows a programmer to create output records of any length without having to set aside a memory area of the same length and copy data into it in the correct sequence.

This is accomplished by data-chaining the commands to be executed by the data channel. The first command describes the size and location of the first sending data area and specifies that data-chaining is being used. When the first command is finished executing, the channel immediately begins to process the second command as a continuation of the current output record. If the second command also specifies data-chaining, the third command will be similarly used, and so on until chaining is no longer specified. The data channel may begin to output another physical record without further attention from the central processor, or it may stop and indicate that it is ready for further assignments.

The inverse operation is called SCATTER READ.

general-purpose computer A device that manipulates data without detailed step-by-step control by human hand, and designed to be used for many different types of problems.

A general-purpose computer contains a number of functional elements which are organized by a program to perform a given task. By simply changing the program, a different organization is achieved to perform a different task.

Because of its very nature, a number of computer parts are not used by a specific problem at a given moment in time, or at best, are not fully used by the problem. At worst, some problems may not be solvable on the general-purpose computer, and will require large-scale computers.

The purpose of a general-purpose computer is to eliminate the need for two or more computers, such as a business computer and a scientific computer. See THIRD GENERATION, TIME-SHARING.

generate   To create a particular program by selecting parts of a general program skeleton (or outline) and specializing these parts into a cohesive entity.   For example, a sort generator may contain elementary outlines of codes that extract a key field from a data record, codes that read a data record, codes that write a data record, and codes that embody sort/merge logic.   When directed by parameters to create a particular sort program, the generator selects the appropriate code skeletons, modifies them for correct record length, key location, etc., and then links the modified fragments together to form a special-purpose sort program.   See GENERATOR.

generation data group (GDG)   A family of similar data sets, related to one another in that each is a modification of the next most recent data set.

The members of a generation data group all have the same name. They may be distinguished from one another by their generation numbers and their successive dates of creation.   No two data sets in a GDG have the same creation date, so that the earlier/later relationship always has a valid meaning.   The earlier (older) data set always has a lower numerical generation number.   The very oldest data set has generation number 0001.

Normally, a generation data group arises when a set of data is updated at periodic intervals.   For example, any file containing year-to-date information, every item valid as of the same date, is an obvious candidate for a generation data group.   Payroll history files are usually in this category.   The payroll program calculates current pay and deductions based on historical data (old GDG data set) and current information, and writes a new payroll history file as a by-product (new GDG data set).   The output data set is said to belong to the "son" generation; the input (last week's) data set thus becomes the "father" data set.   In the same way the next most recent data set is the "grandfather."

Suppose that it is required to update a member of a GDG without increasing its generation number.   (Example: an employee is terminated between payroll periods, or else an error was discovered.) This can be accomplished by increasing the version number of the data set within the same generation (creating a new data set in the process).

The data sets in a GDG have a common name but different generation and version numbers.   The qualified name of a data set in the GDG is written: SETNAME.G0023V00.   The first generation is G0001, and the 4-digit number is incremented by one with each generation.   The first version is V00 within any generation number, and is likewise incremented by one when it changes.   The 4-digit generation number is the absolute generation number. For convenience, relative generation numbers may also be used. Thus SETNAME (0) is the most recent complete data set (whatever its G*xxxx*V*yy* might be), SETNAME (−1) is the one next older, and (+1) denotes the data set currently being created. Data management, through its cataloging facility, converts relative numbers into absolute generation numbers, to assure that the correct data sets will be used. (SETNAME is used here for the fully qualified name shared by all data sets in a GDG.)

generator   A program that produces specific programs as directed by some input parameters.

A generator contains embryonic segments of code, called skeletons, which contain models of program logic in a nonspecialized form. The generator selects the correct segments, adjusts them to the needs of the desired program, links the segments together (by resolving addresses and intersegment references), and thus produces a particular program.

For instance, a report generator contains models of code for counting lines of print on a page, writing page headings and footings and paragraph headings and footings, reading input records, extracting data from input records, and adding items to form cumulative sums. Each segment of code may be used once, several times, or not at all in a particular report program. The selected segments are particularized and united to form the desired program.

It is possible to write a general-purpose report writer (for example), but it would be too big and too slow for any one individual application. By writing the general routine as a program generator, small and efficient programs can be used for production running. See GENERATE.

GIGO   An acronym for garbage in, garbage out.

This statement is often stressed during introductory courses in computer utilization as a reminder that, regardless of the correctness of the logic built into the program, no answer can be valid if the input is erroneous.

grain direction   In character recognition, the arrangement of paper fibers in relation to a document's travel through a character reader. See LONG GRAIN.

gray code   A code in which sequential numbers are represented by binary expressions, each expression differing from the preceding one in one place only.

For example, a gray code could be as follows:

Decimal	Binary	Gray
0	0000	0000
1	0001	0001
2	0010	0011
3	0011	0010
4	0100	0110
5	0101	0111
6	0110	0101
7	0111	0100
8	1000	1100
9	1001	1101

Gray codes are very commonly used in digital pickoff devices to measure quantities at remote locations and transmit data to a central processor, but they are not used for computer internal representation or for calculation. Conversion from gray code to binary code is sometimes a problem. See REFLECTED BINARY.

half-add A computer instruction that performs bit-by-bit half additions (i.e., logical EXCLUSIVE OR without carry) up on its operands. See HALF ADDER.

half adder A combination logic device having two inputs and two outputs related as follows:

Input		Output	
A	B	C	S
0	0	0	0
0	1	0	1
1	0	0	1
1	1	1	0

where S denotes the sum of A and B without carry, and C denotes the carry.

The results of S are A EXCLUSIVE OR B, and the results of C are A LOGICAL AND B.

half duplex In data transmission, a data path capable of transmitting in either direction, but only in one direction at any one time. For example, the original telegraph could transmit or receive on a wire, but could not do both at once.

half-word boundary   In the IBM 360 System, any address ending in 0, that is, divisible by binary 2, denotes a natural boundary for an item of 2 bytes in length. An item of this class must be referenced by an address falling on a boundary of the corresponding type.

hamming distance   Same as SIGNAL DISTANCE.

hardware   The physical, tangible, and permanent components of a computer or data processing system.

Software, by contrast, is provided to the computer after it is built. Software is read into a device, and may be completely changed by reading in new software. Hardware is more permanent, and usually can be modified only by trained technicians or engineers.

Hardware is what a computer maker sells or rents, but software is what the user uses. This last fact has caused some people to define "computer" as an environment in which software can be activated. Contrast with SOFTWARE.

hash total   A safety device that ensures that the correct number of data have been read by the computer.

A hash total is a meaningless sum obtained by adding together numbers having different meanings (e.g., adding hours and dollars). This total is calculated during preparation of input data, and is included as the last item of input. As the data are read, a corresponding total is calculated, and compared to the hash total supplied as input. A difference indicates that an error has been made, but does not permit finding or correcting the mistake. An item count is also used for error detecting, but is less reliable than the hash total.

See ACCUMULATED TOTAL PUNCHING.

head   A device that reads, records, or erases data on a storage medium such as a drum or tape. Usually, a head is a small electromagnet, but the word head may be also used for the sensing devices that read perforated tapes or punched cards, or the devices used to punch cards or paper tape. Head is sometimes used to indicate the beginning, or initial part, of data records, files, data sets, etc.

heuristic   A method used when several approaches to a solution are known, but no method is known that always works, that is, when no algorithm is known for consistently solving the problem. A heuristic method examines the problem, and tries each of its approaches or methods on any part of the problem for which it may seem appropriate.

The heuristic program should be able to judge whether the problem is closer to solution after each attempt. When no more approaches are applicable, the program reports failure on this particular problem. For example, a heuristic program called Student attempts to perform formal integration. It examines the integrand and tries any technique which seems to fit. It keeps testing for parts of the problem which may appear in a form that has a known solution. These parts are then integrated, printed, and eliminated from consideration. The program stops when a nonintegrable remainder appears after every transformation. Contrast with ALGORITHM.

hexadecimal A number system using the base 16.

Each hexadecimal digit may be represented by 4 binary bits as follows:

Binary	Decimal	Hexadecimal
0000	0	0
0001	1	1
0010	2	2
0011	3	3
0100	4	4
0101	5	5
0110	6	6
0111	7	7
1000	8	8
1001	9	9
1010	10	A
1011	11	B
1100	12	C
1101	13	D
1110	14	E
1111	15	F

An example of hexadecimal addition is:

Hexadecimal	Operation	Decimal
1 A 9	$1 \cdot 256 + 10 \cdot 16 + 9$	425
$=$	$=$	
+B 1 7	$11 \cdot 256 + 1 \cdot 16 + 7$	+2839
C C O	$12 \cdot 256 + 11 \cdot 16 + 1 \cdot 16$	3264
	or	
	$12 \cdot 256 + 12 \cdot 16 + 0$	

Note the carry from the rightmost column to the middle column. See SEXADECIMAL.

high-speed carry Technique in parallel addition to speed up the propagation of carries. See STANDING-ON-NINES CARRY, and contrast with CASCADED CARRY.

holistic masks   In character recognition, that set of characters residing within a character reader, which theoretically represents the exact replicas of all possible input characters.

When holistic masks are employed, an input character will be accepted only when it is a perfect specimen, that is, only when it exactly matches one of the residing replicas. All direct matching systems of this sort are critically dependent upon the quality of print and the position of the character as presented. For these reasons holistic masks to date have seldom been employed in fully operational systems.

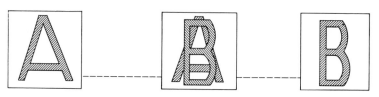

Holistic-mask matching.

Hollerith, Herman (1860–1929)   Although Charles Babbage had already suggested the use of punched cards for storing numbers in his Analytic Engine, and even used them to control the sequence of operations in the arithmetic unit, Herman Hollerith, American statistician, combined the idea with electromagnetic inventions developed since Babbage's work. In Hollerith's system a perforated card was placed over a mercury-filled tray of cups; metal pins descended, and when a hole was encountered, the pin was able to touch the mercury below and complete an electric circuit. Using punched cards in this manner, Hollerith was able to classify and count the data from the United States Census of 1890 in one-third of the time it had taken to process the data from the previous census of 1880 by means of handwritten tally sheets drawn up by government clerks. Hollerith directed census takers to punch holes representing the various characteristics of the population in predetermined locations on the cards, and the holes were then counted by machine through completion of electric circuits. In addition to saving time, this system helped reduce error by mechanically controlling counting, and also increased flexibility by enabling several characteristics to be counted in each handling of the cards.

In 1911, Hollerith formed, with two other companies, the Computing Tabulating Recording Company, whose name was later changed to International Business Machines (IBM).

hopper   See CARD HOPPER.

identification division The section of a program (written in the COBOL language) which contains the name of the program and the name of the programmer. See COBOL.

identifier A symbol whose purpose is to identify a body of data. Its usage is similar to the one in ordinary English.

image A copy of the information contained in a punched card (or other data record) recorded on a different data medium. Most commonly: an 80-character magnetic-tape record containing a one-for-one copy of punched-card columns. See CARD IMAGE.

image dissector In optical character recognition (OCR), a device that optically examines an input character for the purpose of breaking down the character into its prescribed elements. An example of the use of image dissection may be found under STROKE ANALYSIS.

immediate address The information contained in the address part of an immediate address instruction.

Normally, a digital computer instruction contains the address(es) of its operand(s). However, when operands are small in size, both time and storage may be saved by including the operand in the address part of the instruction.

> **example:** instead of using ADD (address of one) to (address of number) to increment a field, the faster instruction ADD IMMEDIATE (1) to (address of number). The first instruction requires at least four memory cycles for execution, while the second needs only three cycles of time.

See IMMEDIATE ADDRESS INSTRUCTION.

immediate address instruction   An instruction that contains the value of the operand in its address part rather than the address of the operand.

Thus, a DIVIDE Y instruction causes some number to be divided by the number stored in location Y. But, the DIVIDE IMMEDIATE Y instruction causes some number to be divided by the number Y itself.

The immediate address instruction is used frequently for incrementing a count by a fixed amount, masking a partial-word field of data, testing whether a specific character (or byte) is identical with the immediate character (or byte) in the instruction, or inserting a fixed character (or byte) into a fixed or variable location.

For instance, a loop may be programmed to process every fifth location in some memory area. The index counter would be incremented by using an ADD IMMEDIATE 5 instruction, and the index counter would be immediately tested for a value exceeding its upper bound. The loop would then be repeated as long as the upper bound were not exceeded. See ZERO-LEVEL ADDRESS.

inclusive or   A logical operation (usually indicated by OR), the result of which is false (or zero) if both operands are false, and true (or one) otherwise. If P, Q are the operands:

P	Q	P OR Q
F	F	F
T	F	T
F	T	T
T	T	T

P	Q	P OR Q
0	0	0
1	0	1
0	1	1
1	1	1

The INCLUSIVE OR is also a computer instruction which results in two binary strings being connected by the logical operation OR bit by bit to create a new string ensuring that particular bits be equal to 1. As a rule, one of the original binary strings is replaced by the resultant string.

For instance:

STRING P	0 1 1 0 1 0 0 1 1 1 0 1 1 0 1 1 1 1
STRING Q	1 0 0 0 1 1 0 1 1 0 1 0 1 0 1 0 0 0
STRING (P or Q)	1 1 1 0 1 1 0 1 1 1 1 1 1 0 1 1 1 1

Contrast with EXCLUSIVE OR.

inclusive segment   Two or more different segments in a program overlay structure that can be in main memory simultaneously.

Normally, all inclusive segments lie on a single path from the root segment to the lowest segment. See EXCLUSIVE SEGMENTS.

incremental computer   A special-purpose computer that processes changes in the variables or the absolute value of the variables themselves. A digital differential analyzer is an incremental computer.

An electric clock may be considered a very elementary incremental computer: it does not require a feeding of 6 digits per second (two for the hours, two for the minutes, two for the seconds), but rather a single pulse, the local "computer" providing the correct time for display.

Since only change (or incremental) information is transmitted, the initial value must be correctly established by some outside means.

All incremental computers display the same two properties:
1. Conservation of I/O activity (e.g., display)
2. Requirement of initialization (e.g., setting the time initially)

index   The portion of a computer instruction which indicates what index register (if any) is to be used to modify the address of an instruction.

In the IBM 360 System, a table of keys and hardware addresses used to locate the records in an indexed sequential data set, or a table used by data management to locate data sets (part of the catalog system of OS/360).

The operating system locates a data set that has been cataloged by searching one or more indexes. The data set to be found has a name which consists of one or more simple names connected by periods. A simple name cannot exceed eight nonblank characters in length, and the fully qualified name cannot exceed 44 characters in length. (Each simple name before the last is a qualifier, and represents an index that must be searched in order to find the data set.) A maximum of 22 levels of qualification is thereby permitted.   (Requires 22 periods and 23 simple names one character long, although one simple name could be two characters long.)   Normally no more than three or four qualifiers are used.

The very first index is the volume table of contents (VTOC) (which see) on the system residence volume.   This has an address pointer to the beginning of the catalog proper, which is the index in which the first simple name will be found.   If only one simple name is used, the data set is then located.   Usually it will be necessary to search one or more additional indexes.

An entry in an index will contain an eight-character simple name, address associated with that name, and some control information which describes the nature of the entity named (i.e., index or data set, on this volume or another, etc.).

If the index pointed to by the first index entry is on the current volume

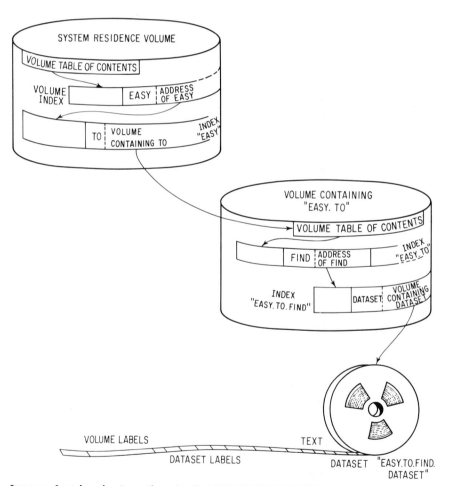

Structure of catalog, showing path used to find EASY TO FIND DATASET.

'the volume now being searched), then the address of the beginning of that ndex is indicated in the current index entry. When the next index resides on another volume, that volume's identification is contained in the current index entry. The actual hardware address of the beginning of the next index will have to be determined by searching the VTOC of the volume on which it resides. The lowest-level index points to the volume(s) in which the data set resides. If there is more than one volume, all will be indicated. The hardware address or starting location will have to be determined by searching the VTOC of the volume of data-set residence.

Even if the data set resides in the same volume as the last index, it must still be located via the VTOC. (A multiple-data-set tape will have to be searched to find the data set's header label. The position of a data set on a tape can be represented by a sequence number—such as first, second, third—but this can be used only for error checking.)

In OS/360 (also DOS, TSS) the elements of every index must reside on a direct-access device. The most important collection of indexes is the catalog used to locate data sets. Other indexes are used to locate records in indexed sequential data sets, and the directory is used to locate members in a partitioned data set.

See INDEXED SEQUENTIAL DATA SET, INDEX REGISTER.

indexed sequential data set   Indexed sequential is a data-set organization combining the efficiency of sequential organization with the ability to rapidly access records out of sequence. It must be used only on direct-access devices.

Data records are initially written in sequence in an area called the prime area. The sequence is ascending by keys, where the key is the identification of the data record and distinguishes it from other records in the data set. Within the prime area, a key and a record gap precede each data record. (For blocked records, the key of the last logical record identifies the physical record; for unblocked records, the key data precede each record: key data are reproduced within each logical record if blocked, and also sometimes on unblocked records. Usually unblocked records do not duplicate key data within the logical record in order to conserve storage space.) In DOS, only fixed-length (F format) records are allowed, and the prime area must be one contiguous extent. In OS, variable-format records are also allowed, and the prime area may occupy several disjoint extents of storage.

A track index must be present for every cylinder of storage allocated to the prime area. It is written at the beginning of the storage space in that cylinder and identifies, for every track in the cylinder, the home address of the track and the key of the highest logical record on the track. An optional cylinder overflow control record may be the first entry in a track index. This allows addition of records in sequence to overflow the capacity of this cylinder without the need to reorganize every cylinder following this one.

One cylinder index must be present for every indexed sequential data set. The entries in this index contain, for every cylinder, the highest key stored in that cylinder and the home address of the track index for the cylinder. If a cylinder contains no data, a special configuration indicates an inactive cylinder in that entry of the cylinder index.

If the cylinder index becomes too long, a master index may be created to index it. Typically a master index is justified if the cylinder index exceeds four full tracks. In DOS, one master index is permitted and appears just before the cylinder index (i.e., at the beginning of the area allocated to the ISDS). OS permits up to three levels of master indexes, and these may reside anywhere in direct-access storage (even on different devices).

Each master index describes the next lower index and is logically constructed exactly like the cylinder index. (A master master index is appropriate if the master index exceeds four tracks; similarly a master master master index may be constructed if the master master index exceeds four tracks. If a master master master index is constructed, it is probable that the data set has exceeded the capacity of a single disk pack, i.e., 2000 tracks.)

It is possible to specify that a cylinder overflow area be included when the data set is created. Then some number of entire tracks are reserved within each cylinder for growth room. If records added in sequence cause the data to overflow the original prime tracks, the surplus will be written in the overflow tracks. Suitable adjustments to the cylinder overflow control record of the original tracks are used to point to the displaced records. No additional access-arm movements are needed to access overflow records because they are still in the original cylinder.

It is also (independently of the cylinder overflow areas) possible to request an independent overflow area at data-set creation time. The independent area need not be adjacent to the prime area, and consists of a number of entire cylinders. This area holds records overflowed from the original prime cylinders. (The independent area must reside on the same type of direct-access device, but need not be on the same volume.) All overflow records are chained together via appended address information (which the programmer never knows about) so that they may still be processed in sequence even though not physically in sequence.

Any record of an ISDS may be accessed by key to achieve true random-access operation in a straightforward manner. It is also possible (and faster) to access records sequentially. The same data set may be accessed both ways by different parts of the same job, or by different jobs. The ISDS is of real advantage when some randomly selected group of consecutive records must be processed. Then one obtains the start-anywhere ease of direct organization, together with the processing speed of sequential organization, for example, a complex payroll with monthly, semimonthly, and hourly (weekly), etc., employees grouped together. One can process all semimonthly on the 15th of the month without having to access every record, and yet whenever every record must be read (year-end W-2 time), this is efficiently accomplished.

index register   A hardware element which holds a number that can be added to (or, in some cases, subtracted from) the address portion of a computer instruction to form an effective address.

The address modification is performed only at the discretion of the programmer, and never modifies the instruction itself; only the location of the operand is affected.

A computer may have no, one, a few, or a great many index registers. For instance, the IBM 1620 usually has none, the SDS Sigma 2 has two, the IBM 7090 has three, the Honeywell 200 has six, the UNIVAC 1108 has fifteen, and the IBM 7070 has ninety-nine. The IBM 360 System, on the other hand, has 0 to 15 index registers depending on usage.

The index registers may be separate hardware (accessible only by special index-register instructions as in the IBM 7090 and IBM 7040), or they may be selected arithmetic registers (accessible also by ordinary arithmetic instructions as in the IBM 360 System), or they may be preassigned locations in main (or core) memory (accessible by STORE or FETCH instructions as in the Honeywell 200 and the IBM 7070).

The in-core index registers cost less to build than arithmetic index registers, but they are slower at execution time, since they require additional memory cycles. Synonymous with B BOX.

indirect address   The address of the location containing the address of the data, that is, an address not contained in the instruction that needs it, but residing in another location in memory.

A digital computer instruction not only specifies an action to be performed, but also indicates the location where the data to be manipulated are to be found. Normally, the instruction contains one or more address parts, each of which designates the location of a data item within the computer. When the address (or location) of a datum is completely specified within the instruction itself, direct addressing is said to be used.

However, to provide for greater flexibility and convenience in coding, today's computers allow for address modification. Address modification permits the effective address of the data to be changed without altering the instruction itself. And to increase the power of address modification, indirect addressing is used.

An immediate analogy of indirect addressing is the cross-reference procedure found in book indexes as, for instance:

ADDRESS, INDIRECT: See INDIRECT ADDRESS.

where the "See" entry indicates not the page number containing the required information, but the index location that contains the page number (or address) where the required information will be found. In the same manner, indirect addressing permits a computer to look up the address of a datum.

Upon examining the current instruction, the computer hardware recognizes the bit configuration signaling indirect addressing: it then obtains from memory the contents of the location designated in the address part of the current instruction. It then interprets this new information as an address, exactly as though it had appeared in the address part of the original instruction itself.

Since many different instructions may refer to the same indirect addressing location, a single modification in the indirect addressing location will have the same effect as modifying all the referring instruction simultaneously, a considerable increase in programming power.

The complexity (and power) of address modification can be further increased by directing the contents of an index register to be added to an indirect (or direct) address in such a way as to change the effective address of the datum. This change will not alter the instruction, the indirect address contents, or the index register contents. Some computers (such as the IBM 7094) permit both—index registers and indirect addressing—to apply to the same address; other computers (such as the Honeywell 200) allow for index-register modification, or indirect addressing (or neither) but not both; the IBM 360 System does not allow indirect addressing.

Consider, for instance, a routine that has to analyze the contents of several tables stored in memory. By using indirect addressing, the program will point to the current table, and an index register will step through the successive entries of each table. The principal logic could look like this:

Instruction location	Instruction
. . .	. . . . .
0600	MOVE TABLE ADDRESS TO POINTER
0610	MOVE ZERO TO INDEX 1
0620	ANALYZE (INDIRECT ADDRESS POINTER) USING INDEX 1
. . .	. . . . .
0700	ADD 1 TO INDEX 1
0710	GO TO INSTRUCTION 0620
. . .	. . . . .
0880	MOVE NEXT TABLE ADDRESS TO POINTER
0890	GO TO 0610

Suppose that transactions applying to several different accounts had been read and stored consecutively in memory, space for an address having been left next to each entry. It is required to link together all transactions referring to the same account number. This can be accomplished by examining every transaction in sequence, scanning backward until the first earlier transaction with the same account number is found, or until the beginning of the list is reached. If a matching account number is found, its address (with an indirect addressing indication) is placed next to the examined transaction. When no match is found, the adjacent address is set to point to the item itself without indirect addressing. Upon completion, all transactions will have been linked in backward sequence: an instruction that refers indirectly to the last address field will fetch the first transaction with the same account number. The hardware will follow the chain of indirect addresses until the direct address of a transaction is found.

Note that if two address fields had been associated with each transaction, both forward and backward chaining (or linking) would be allowed. Each item could then point to its predecessor and successor, allowing hardware and software to search in either direction. This kind of noncontiguous item linking is called list processing, and is a very powerful tool in modern programming practice.

See ADDRESS OF ADDRESS.

industrial data processing Data processing for industrial purposes. In other words, all data processing except for abstract, scientific, or mathematical research, and some government data processing activity.

information The meaning assigned to data by some conventions.

By data is meant the text or content of a message, especially that property of a message which is not changed or altered by transforming the message into another physical (electronic or magnetic) equivalent form.

In information theory, information is that which reduces the amount of uncertainty (or ambiguity) that would exist were information not supplied. As such, information is "negative uncertainty."

In information theory an endlessly repeated message conveys no information after the first transmission (it can be predicted by the receiver, and therefore does not dispel any ambiguity). In the definition of data given above, an endlessly repeated message carries the exact same information over and over.

information processing The manipulation of data so that new data (implicit in the original) appear in a useful form. For instance, finding the sum and average of a set of numbers, or arranging the numbers in descending sequence. In each case new information is made available based on the supplied information, but this information is implicit in the original data.

information retrieval (IR)   The technique and process of accumulating, classifying, cataloging, storing, and searching large amounts of data, and reproducing (or displaying) the required information contained within the data.

Although information retrieval (or IR) is not new in concept (book index, library catalog, and indexing systems are examples of IR techniques), there was a flurry of activity in computerized information retrieval in the late 1950s and the appearance of numerous research papers which coincided with the appearance of the first large-scale computers. A more formal approach was attempted in laying down the rules by means of which a workable information retrieval system could be conceived and established. As of 1967, no real system had been developed although partial success was achieved in a few highly specialized fields. However, it is difficult, if not impossible, to categorize the various methods presently underway since security precautions cover most efforts in this field.

The problems confronted in building an information retrieval system can be divided into three classes:

1. Problems involved in the selection of data which will make up a request

2. Problems defined by relevancy, that is, the determination of the order of importance of key words in an index which will clearly identify the indexed document

3. Problems of economics with regards to response time, since a short response time exponentially increases the cost of the information retrieval system, and a long response time severely impairs the value of the system.

The essential basis for an efficient information retrieval system appears to be a self-organizing system, capable of updating itself since an a priori system would be too confining in any operational environment. It need only be recalled how technological information requests shifted from steam engines to internal-combustion engines to fission reactors to fusion reactors to visualize how dynamic retrieval problems get to be with scientific advances. For such a self-induced reorganization to operate smoothly and continuously, the requests themselves have to become part of the system to assist in the regrouping and the corresponding changes in the scanning sequences. Just as the problems involved in developing more powerful computers have added impetus to the new field of bionics, the beginning assaults on the complexities involved in information retrieval systems would appear to underline a close relationship between self-organizing files and human beings.

The growing awareness of both government and business of the needs of a workable and generalized information retrieval system will in time, undoubtedly, increase the efforts and monies required to achieve a breakthrough in this important field.

inherited error The error existing in the data supplied at the beginning of a step in a step-by-step calculation as executed by a program.

initialize To set counters, switches, and addresses to zero or other starting values at the beginning of, or at prescribed points in, a computer routine; to begin an operation, and more specifically, to adjust the environment to the required starting configuration. For example, when calculating a sum on an adding machine, one begins by setting the running-total register to zero, or, when opening a savings account at a bank, one initializes the amount to the amount of the first deposit.

Initialization covers the initial steps of any data processing operation (large or small, simple or complex), provided that the operation can be resolved meaningfully into smaller parts. In programming, for instance, when beginning a repetitive data processing operation (called a loop), all the parts of the program that will be modified must first be set to the correct starting values. Inclusion of the initialization steps in the program permits the same loop to be reused many times during a run. See LOOP.

initial program loading (IPL) The process of bringing a program or operating system into a computer for the first time, and the data records that participate in the above process, or the console button that initiates it.

One of the trickiest (yet elementary and common) problems in the computing field is the art of loading a complete program into a computer when the memory of that computer contains no cooperative program. Once a program loading routine is established in memory, it is obviously possible to load and execute any other desired program. Usually a console button is provided which reads one record into memory and transfers control to the beginning of the data thus stored. That first record must load the second record, and the two of them must load all successor records, etc. This process is known variously as bootstrap or as IPL, and the associated records or instructions are known as bootstrap cards, IPL records, etc.

Various manufacturers split the IPL task in various ways between hardware and software, i.e., between circuitry and programming of IPL records. Example: CDC 6400 has a 12 × 12 matrix of toggle switches by which the first 12 instructions of a load routine may be entered into memory and executed. Many computers have simply a card-load button which reads one punched card and transfers control of it. Other variations exist also. At least one powerful computer is noted for its lack of a convenient IPL provision, a design weakness that limits its otherwise fine design.

In System 360, every disk pack begins with an IPL record in track 0, cylinder 0. If the disk contains an operating system, this record loads the resident nucleus of that system. Otherwise the IPL record loads itself, prints a warning message, and stops. This is not a show-off trick, but a necessity, for if an improper record were used for IPL by accident, it could leave the computer in a state in which a correct IPL could not be performed easily. The dummy IPL records prevent this from happening. See BOOTSTRAP.

initiator/terminator   The routine or program that makes a job step ready to run in a computer, and that also performs cleanup housekeeping after the job step has terminated.

In an operating system, a job or job step waiting to be executed (in the input work queue) is selected by a job scheduler as the next step to be run. Before it can be executed, the job step must be made ready in a variety of ways. The memory space that it will use must be allocated and cleared of extraneous data. The various control blocks used by the operating system to keep track of the job's progress must be created and assigned. From available memory space, buffers for the input/output files must be allocated and formatted. When all setup work is completed, the initiator/terminator turns control over to program fetch for actual program loading.

At the termination of a job step, the terminator ensures that all output buffers are properly written out, that control blocks are removed from the supervisors control block lists, and that all memory and I/O devices are deallocated. This places the computer in a condition suitable for accepting the next job.

In some IBM 360 operating systems, and some others, the initiator/terminator occupies the memory space allocated to the job step before and after the job step is resident there. This means that the smallest memory allocation must be big enough to contain the initiator/terminator. For example, suppose that the initiator/terminator occupies 10,000 locations, 16,000 locations are available, and a 9,000 location job and a 4,000 location job await. If the 4,000-location job is started first, 12,000 locations remain, and so the initiator/terminator can fit in that space to start the

9,000 location job.   However, if the large job is initiated first, only 7,000 locations remain, and the smaller job cannot be initiated, even though it needs less than the available amount of space.   When both jobs are running, if the small job finishes first, it cannot be deallocated until the larger job is also terminated.   Thus the size of the initiator/terminator strongly influences the flexibility of the operating system.

ink   See MAGNETIC INK.

ink bleed   In character recognition, the capillary extension of ink beyond the original edges of a printed or handwritten character.

ink smudge   In character recognition, the overflow of ink beyond the original edges of a printed or handwritten character.

ink squeezeout   In character recogniton, the overflow of ink from the stroke centerline to the edges of a printed or handwritten character.

in-line procedures   A short body of coding (or instructions) which accomplishes some purpose.   This coding is inserted in the program each and every time this purpose or function is required.   In this instance, in-line procedure is synonymous with open subroutine.

In the higher-language COBOL, in-line procedures are the procedural instructions that form part of the main sequential and controlling flow of the program.

See COBOL, OPEN SUBROUTINE.

input   The information that is delivered to a data processing device from the external world, the process of delivering this data, or the equipment that performs this process.

Usually, input is provided at the request of the computer since feeding data in a system is not a simple proposition.   The importance of input is evidenced by the common use of the term GIGO, "garbage in, garbage out."   Input normally appears in the form of punched cards or punched paper tape.   Recent developments in optical character recognition permit written or printed numbers to be read directly onto magnetic tapes, and from there into the computer.

It is sometimes said that a computer program is defined by its input and output.   See OUTPUT.

input job stream   The principal source of input to an operating system, most commonly in the form of punched cards or card images.

The input job stream contains beginning-of-job indications, directions for processing this job, optional programs and/or input data, and end-of-job indications. The operating system will initiate jobs according to some scheduling method, and direct or assist the operator in mounting/dismounting particular input/output volumes. When ready, each job is run, and either normal or abnormal end-of-job actions are taken. Most output will appear on the regular system output stream, which is normally a printer or print-image file. By having one principal input stream and one regular output stream, the majority of jobs flow smoothly through the computer with a minimum of operator intervention.

To the supervisory parts of the operating system, the important parts of the IJS are the control cards or job control statements. For a language processor, the input stream consists of source language statements. To a problem program the input job stream is the main source of input. Thus each reader of the input has a particular emphasis or interest. Each reader must be capable of recognizing the end of its particular input, returning control of the input stream to the supervisor. This will prevent accidental overreading causing destruction of the following job.

input magazine   A part of a card handling device which supplies the cards to the processing portion(s) of the machine: the place where the operator stacks the input cards or blank card supply.

An input magazine usually has the capacity of 800 to 3000 cards, depending upon the device in question (the faster the device, the larger the capacity of the input magazine). See CARD HOPPER.

input/output control system (IOCS)   A set of flexible routines that supervise the input and output operations of a computer at the detailed machine-language level.

In the simplest digital computers, input or output operations cause processing to be suspended while I/O is in progress. In this case no questions of synchronization or overlap of I/O with computing need concern the programmer. There is no way to conduct more than one I/O operation at a time on these elementary machines. Programming is very simple: READ, TEST FOR ERROR, are all that are required.

Most modern computers are much more sophisticated and powerful. They have data channels that allow one or more I/O operations to proceed simultaneously with computing. Simple data channels can be directed to start transmission at location x and transmit until condition y is met. Sophisticated data channels are versatile, powerful processors with complex internal logic, capable of performing whole sequences of instructions (commands) without detailed supervision from the central processing unit (CPU).

The complexity of I/O programming introduced merely by having versatile data channels was not too great, but to get high efficiency out of the hardware a sophisticated programming logic was required. This logic had to be present in every program (how many programs have no input or output?) and lay beyond the skill of the average programmer. A natural solution to this problem was the development of IOCS routines. One or more very good programmers would write an all-purpose input/output control system which would reside permanently in the computer and be used by every program. Alternatively, the IOCS instructions could be copied into every program that needed them, a practice common on new small-scale computers. The majority of programmers could then be relieved of detailed I/O considerations.

A typical IOCS package sets aside two or more memory areas for each I/O device used by the program. Whenever possible, these areas (called buffers) will be used to read input data before the program needs it, and to store output data until the device is ready to accept it. These buffers therefore provide a degree of timing flexibility as well as simultaneous input/output with processing.

Consider the steps in processing an input file: The program requests (by an OPEN statement) that the file be readied for processing. IOCS then readies the device, checks input labels if any, and fills all the input buffers with data. A READ request is executed by making available the already-read contents of an input buffer and directing the device to refill a processed input buffer if any are available. Control is returned to the program before very much I/O activity has occurred, and so the program was delayed for an interval much shorter than the time required to read a record. It is precisely this saving that justifies complex IOCS logic. Depending on total systems complexity, program running time can be reduced to one-half or one-third of its non-IOCS-overlapped running time.

Simple IOCS logic uses two buffers per device and attaches them alternately to the I/O device. A more sophisticated IOCS will maintain a pool of like-sized buffers, and attach buffers to input or output files as required by the moment-to-moment demands of the program.

Consider, for example, a pool of seven buffers: Initially two are filled with input, two are reserved for output, and three are spares. The program begins with high input activity, resulting in five input and two output buffers. There follows a period of balanced activity (four output and three input buffers). The program ends with a burst of output activity after the input is exhausted (giving zero input and seven output buffers). Clearly this IOCS gains hardware efficiency at the cost of complex logic.

Other IOCS duties include end-of-input sensing, error detection and correction, blocking and unblocking, and label checking. If multiple devices share a data channel, the IOCS may schedule I/O activity to maximize joint throughput. However simple or complex it may be, IOCS makes computers more efficient and programming simpler for everybody. Today, no operating system is complete without a built-in IOCS facility.

input work queue   The jobs submitted for processing but not yet begun: In a first-come, first-served operating system, the input work queue consists of programs, data, and control cards waiting in the input job stream but not yet read; in this case the work queue and job stream are almost synonymous.

In an operating system that schedules jobs according to any other principle, the input work queue consists of programs, data, and control cards read in, hence known to the system, but not yet initiated or selected for processing. With this kind of operating system the programs and data are kept in auxiliary storage, while the control cards are examined to determine the nature of the jobs, and a condensed abstract of each job's requirements is maintained in a separate list. This condensed list of job descriptions may also be called the input work queue. In every case, the computer decides what job to begin next by examining the input work queue.

inscribing   In character recognition, the act of preparing a source document for automatic reading.   Inscription includes both handwriting and printing processes.

instruction   A pattern of digits which signifies to a computer that a particular operation is to be performed and which may also indicate the operands (or the locations of operands) to be operated on.

An operand is a data item that participates in a data manipulation. An instruction may have 0, 1, 2, 3, or more operands depending on the computer type. For instance:

Instruction	Operands
STOP OR PAUSE	0
SET SIGN (OF X) POSITIVE	1
MOVE (X) TO (Y)	2
ADD (X) TO (Y) AND STORE IN (Z)	3
TEST (X) AND BRANCH TO: (A) IF X IS POSITIVE (B) IF X IS ZERO (C) IF X IS NEGATIVE	4

The word instruction is preferable to the words command and order, sometimes used synonymously. Command should be reserved for electronic signals, and order should be reserved for sequence, interpolation, and related usage.

In some IBM computers, the following distinction is made:

1. An instruction is to be executed by the CPU.
   For instance: MULTIPLY BY . . .
2. A command is to be executed by a data channel.
   For instance: READ RECORD FROM . . .
3. An order is to be executed by a peripheral device.
   For instance: REWIND TAPE No. . . .

See COMPUTER INSTRUCTION, DECISION INSTRUCTION, EXTRACT INSTRUCTION, LOGIC INSTRUCTION, MACHINE INSTRUCTION, MACROINSTRUCTION, REPETITION INSTRUCTION.

instruction code That part of an instruction which distinguishes it from all other instructions, and specifies the action to be performed.

It is customary for the instruction code to be the first (leftmost) digits in the entire instruction pattern, the remainder of the instruction consisting of modifiers, operands, and sometimes meaningless or (wasted) digits. Digits may be binary or decimal. See OPERATION CODE.

instruction counter A hardware register used by a computer to remember the location of the next instruction to be performed in normal sequence.

However, an instruction indicated by the instruction counter will not be executed if any one of the three following conditions is present:

1. An INTERRUPT which causes a different routine to be given control
2. A BRANCH (or TRANSFER, or JUMP) which is to be executed
3. An EXECUTE instruction which is to be carried out

At all other times, the contents of the instruction counter are used to select the next instruction.

An EXECUTE instruction is an instruction that causes another instruction (not in the normal sequence) to be executed. Control usually passes to the instruction following the EXECUTE unless the remote instruction effects a TRANSFER (or BRANCH).

EXECUTE is usually employed for three principal reasons:

1. Because the proper instruction is not known or may often change
2. To permit address modification of the subject instruction
3. To test a program by means of another by executing the first one step by step, and printing the result after each step

The term instruction counter is synonymous with location counter, program counter, sequence counter. See BRANCH, INTERRUPT, JUMP.

instruction register   A hardware element that receives and holds an instruction as it is extracted from memory. The register either contains, or is connected to circuits that interpret the instruction (or discover its meaning).

In a computer organized around character or byte memory, the instruction often extends across several memory locations. In this case the instruction register holds the first characters (or bytes) while the remaining ones are being fetched, and the interpretation of the instruction begins while the fetch process continues.

instruction repertory   The set of all the operations (instructions) that a particular computer can perform.

The fewer the instructions in this set, the less expensive (and sometimes the faster) the hardware can be. The more instructions there are, the simpler the programming task could become. From the programmer's point of view, the instruction repertory defines the power of the computer.

integrator   In digital computers, a device that can perform many high-speed multiplication operations and keep a running total of the product terms. It is sometimes called a convolver.

This special-purpose accessory is attached to an I/O channel, and acts as a magnetic-tape unit. It is supplied with pairs of numbers by a WRITE operation of the channel and returns the sum of the products via a READ operation.

In analog computers, the integrator is a device that performs the calculus operation of integration (repeated summing of infinitesimal quantities). This device operates in an analog manner, and may operate on mechanical, electronic, hydraulic, or other principles.

The resistor/capacitor network

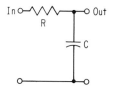

is the simplest known form of integrator, and also the most common. The product RC should be large compared to any time period or interval in the input. The output voltage is the time integral of the input current,

$$V_{out} = \int I_{in} \, dt$$

provided that very little or no current is drawn from the network by the voltage-measuring device attached to the output terminals.

intelligence A characteristic of behavior exhibited by human beings but not yet observed in the behavior of any electronic device.

Intelligent behavior is characterized by learning, adaptation to changes of environment, initiative and originality, and anticipation of the probable consequences of an action.

Some computer programs have shown limited forms of one or two kinds of the above behavior, but no program has yet exhibited them all. See ARTIFICIAL INTELLIGENCE.

interface The place (or places) at which two different systems (or subsystems) meet and interact with each other.

Considerable attention is presently paid to man/machine interface and the problem of achieving a good (or efficient) interaction between human beings and computers. The results to date consist of a number of items such as cathode-ray-tube display devices, keyboard and light-pen input devices, and graphical and "Englishlike" communication languages. By teaming the nonoverlapping capabilities of men and machines so that each performs what it is best at, it is possible to accomplish what neither could achieve alone.

Some computer systems (RCA S/70, IBM 360, H-200) offer a standard peripheral interface. This means in effect that all I/O devices and control units connect to the same kind of multiple-pin socket at the back of the computer and operate on standard patterns of electric control and data signals. The inference is that one device can be substituted for another by merely plugging it in, thereby eliminating the necessity of reprogramming. Such advantages are often not so simple to achieve as they are made to sound.

interleave To alternate parts of one sequence with parts of one or more other sequences in a cyclic fashion such that each sequence retains its identity.

Consider for instance the three sequences:

(1) $A_1A_2A_3A_4A_5A_6-A_p$
(2) $B_1B_2B_3B_4B_5B_6-B_q$
(3) $C_1C_2C_3C_4C_5C_6-C_r$

where each item A_1, A_2, . . . is an item of information.

The sequence:

$$A_1B_1C_1A_2B_2C_2A_3B_3C_3 \quad \cdot \quad \cdot \quad \cdot$$

is obtained from the orginal sequences by selecting consecutive items in the cyclical order:

(1) (2) (3) (1) (2) (3) . . .

The more complicated sequence:

$$A_1B_1A_2B_2A_3B_3C_1A_4B_4A_5B_5A_6B_6C_2 \quad \cdot \quad \cdot \quad \cdot$$

is achieved by interleaving the original sequence in the cyclic fashion:

(1) (2) (1) (2) (1) (2) (3) (1) (2) (1) (2) (1) (2) (3)

It is possible for many processes to appear to occur simultaneously in the same unit by interleaving the operations from the several processes. Suppose that, in the above example, each sequence was a program, and each item an instruction of that program. All three programs would appear to be executed simultaneously, although on the average each would be executed at one-third the speed of the processor.

Interleaving is used in large digital computers to achieve increased speed at the cost of hardware complexity. Two principal kinds of interleaving should be mentioned.

Memory Interleaving: Consider two equal banks of memory, each capable of supplying one memory reference every x microseconds. If one memory bank is operated 1/2 cycle later than the other, then a reference to memory can be accomplished every $x/2$ microseconds. When all even memory addresses are in the first bank, and all odd addresses are in the second bank, interleaving of memory accesses can be accomplished 80 percent of the time. The effective memory cycle time is thus reduced by about 20 percent. In a similar manner, many banks of memory may be operated a fraction of a cycle apart, significantly improving memory speed. For example, the IBM 7094 II (two 36 bits interleaved) is faster than the IBM 7094 (72 bits per cycle noninterleaved). It might be mentioned that the CDC 6600 has a 10-way interleaving of 60-bit memory banks and also a 10-way interleaving of 12-bit memory banks which permit it to run at extremely high speed.

Functional Interleaving: An example of functional interleaving is the Honeywell H-200 with only one of its data channels working. It has a memory capable of being accessed every 2 microseconds, and a data channel that can deliver information at 6-microsecond intervals. Then, in every 6-microsecond interval the central processing unit can be given two accesses to memory and the channel can be given one access. If there is no information on the channel, the CPU proceeds at the faster 3 accesses per 6-microsecond rate. I/O and computing proceed independently, but memory access is interleaved. See OVERLAP.

interpreter A program that translates and executes each source program statement before proceeding to the next one.

There are three principal uses for an interpreter:

1. It enables a programmer to have a computer execute the machine-language instructions of another computer. The first computer is then said to simulate the second. This eliminates, to a degree, the necessity of rewriting programs when the user moves from one computer to a more powerful one.

2. It permits a programmer to use a conversational language and write his program on line. Any programming error (or result) is immediately reported by the computer, thus helping the programmer in planning his next step.

3. It allows a programmer to use string-manipulating languages in which a given character may alternately be an instruction or part of a text to be manipulated. This self-modification of programs at the source-language level prevents assembly or compilation of such programs.

An interpreter is also a device that prints onto a punched card the data already punched in the card in straight 80-80 card-image printing.

interrupt To stop a running program in such a way that it can be resumed at a later time, and in the meanwhile permit some other action to be performed.

Interrupt equally may refer to the action performed when the above interrupt is taken. See INTERRUPT ROUTINE.

interrupt routine The program that performs the interrupt action.

In computers that have data channels, I/O activity is started by the CPU, and then proceeds independently. To coordinate I/O with processing, a series of interrupts are used.

When an I/O operation is finished, the computer saves the state of the running program, stops it, and begins an I/O interrupt routine. This routine determines which operation just ended, checks for detected errors, determines what I/O operation is to be performed next, and initiates that action.

Control is then returned to the running program, which never knows that it had been interrupted. Without this system of interrupts, the program would have to keep checking for I/O device status, and branch to an I/O routine whenever the not busy condition was found.

Some interrupts are initiated by the computer operator when he wants to give a command, or by a remote user who wishes to request service.

I/O Usual abbreviation for input or output, or both.

Pertaining to all equipment and activity that transfers information into or out of a computer. I/O is the interface between the real world outside a computer and the abstract mathematical and logical internal environment of a computer.

IPL-V The fifth of a series of list-processing languages developed principally by Newell, Simon, and Shaw, IPL-V is the acronym for information processing language–V. It is a good language for manipulating tree structures.

IPL-V instructions consist of four parts: the name, the prefixes, the symbol, and the link.

The name may be the name or label of the routine, or it may be the label point for an internal transfer of control.

The prefixes (called P and Q) indicate the meaning of the symbol part and the level of indirect addressing. P and Q are 3-bit numbers, or blanks.

The symbol represents the element of the list qualified by the prefixes P and Q: it may be a list, a datum, or any type of information qualified by the prefixes.

The link contains the address of the next statement to be processed.

A string of empty lists is increased by adding erased lists no longer required by the program.

Suppose, for example, that when a raw material is ordered from a supplier, it is placed on a list that keeps a record of orders for that material. If it is desired to find the last order placed for a particular material, a routine, which will be called S1, could be coded in the following manner:

Name	PQ	SYMB	LINK	Comment
S1		J60	9-1	Find the next order.
9-1	70	9-2	S1	Repeat if more exist.
9-2	52	HO	O	Store last order in HO.

The first statement indicates the following:

(1) S1	Routine name
(2) P = blank or zero	Routine to be executed
(3) Q = blank or zero	Routine to be executed is J60.
(4) J60	An IPL-V routine to locate the next cell.
(5) 9-1	The next statement to be processed.
(6) Find the next order.	Comment on function.

The second statement indicates the following:

(1) 9-1	The name of this instruction
(2) P = 7	A test to see if next cell is empty
(3) Q = 0	Indicates that 9-2 is a branch possibility.
(4) 9-2	If next cell is empty, this branch is taken.
(5) S1	If next cell is not empty, this branch is taken.
(6) Repeat if more exist.	Comment on function.

The third statement indicates the following:

(1) 9-2	The name of this instruction
(2) P = 5	Replace contents of the designated cell (in this case HO) by the contents of the last nonempty cell.
(3) Q = 2	Designates the type of list specified in SYMB (in this case HO).
(4) HO	Location information is to be stored in.
(5) 0	End of routine
(6) Store last order in HO	Comment on function.

item A set of adjacent digits, bits, or characters which is treated as a unit and conveys a single unit of information. This meaning is similar to the English usage for word or number. Consider the following hierarchy of data structures:

> A data set (or file)

is composed of

> records

which are composed of

> items (or words, or fields)

which are composed of

> characters (or digits)

which are composed of

> bits

An item contains a name, an amount, a yes or no indication, or a similar amount of information. Contrast with FILE.

iteration   The process of repeating a sequence of instructions with minor modifications between successive repetitions. One single cycle of a repetitive process is called an iteration.

The power to repeat a sequence of operations, stopping on a predetermined or dynamically varying condition, is one of the strongest advantages of stored-program computers. If one iteration (a single case) requires N instructions, then M iterations can be performed by coding $N + 3$ or $N + 5$ instructions, or thereabouts, instead of the $N \times M$ instructions that would be required by noniterative coding. A small penalty is paid in time for this convenience, as $M \times (N + 5)$ instructions must be executed instead of $M \times N$. But only in very few cases is $M \times N$ small enough to fit into a computer.

example: To calculate the interest and new balance on every savings account in a bank on interest-due day one can code

```
FOR ALL ACCOUNTS
INTEREST = BALANCE × RATE
NEW BALANCE = BALANCE + INTEREST
```

instead of

```
FIRST INTEREST = FIRST BALANCE × RATE
FIRST NEW BALANCE = FIRST BALANCE + FIRST INTEREST
SECOND INTEREST = SECOND BALANCE × RATE
SECOND NEW BALANCE = SECOND BALANCE +
    SECOND INTEREST
THIRD  .   .   .   .   .   .
.   .   .   .   .   .   .   .   .   .
2074th INTEREST = 2074th BALANCE × RATE
```

Greater power is obtained by nesting one iterative loop inside another. For instance:

```
FOR ALL BRANCHES:
FOR ALL ACCOUNTS:
    INTEREST =
    NEW BALANCE =
```

And still deeper nesting is possible. The innermost loop should be carefully coded for speed.

See LOOP.

J

jam   In punched-card equipment, a feed malfunction causing blockage of passages with crumpled cards.

There are various kinds of card-feed malfunctions. Failure to pick a card and picking two cards at once are examples of malfunction. When a malfunction, such as picking two cards or bending one card, causes the card passages to become obstructed, a jam condition exists. (To pick is to select the next card from an input stack for feeding into a card machine. Picking may be accomplished by picker knives (narrow edges on moving part) or by friction wheel against bottom of stack. Normally an entrance slot too narrow for two cards prevents multiple picking.)

The sight of cards feeding normally into a machine but no cards emerging from the machine will alarm any operator. Stopping the machine and opening it will reveal dozens or hundreds of crumpled cards, sometimes neatly folded into accordion pleats, jamming every available space inside the machine. The usually favorable design criterion of positive card feeding causes many cards to be fed after there is no more room for them. Extracting the cards can be painful enough, but recapturing lost data could be impossible.

261

Many jams are caused by overly flexible cards bending, but some are caused by out-of-alignment parts or other causes. Overdry air increases static electricity charges on moving cards, and may cause them not to drop into hoppers fast enough to get out of the way of succeeding cards.

jitter Short-term or high-frequency displacement of a signal in time and/or space.

On a CRT (cathode-ray-tube) display, jitter causes figures to seem to jump or shake in vertical or horizontal position. In data transmission, jitter is small irregularity in (otherwise regularly repeating) time of arrival of pulses.

For viewing by human beings, jitter must be reduced to prevent fatigue and avoid appearance of blur. This may conflict with the requirement to avoid flicker because rapid rewriting of the screen, but not in the exact same place, kills flicker but aggravates jitter.

For reading by machines, jitter must be reduced to avoid misrecognition, or loss of synchronization of receiver with sender.

job A unit of work to be done by the computer. A job is a single entity from the standpoint of computer installation management, but may consist of one or more job steps.

Strictly speaking, a job is defined by the person who submits it to the computer, and consists of everything between the beginning-of-job and end-of-job signals. Thus a job is whatever a job is defined to be. The administration of the computer center uses the job as the basis of charging the cost of operating the system to various users.

A job normally begins with a job card, containing the name of the submitter and the charge numbers to be used. There follow control statements directing the operating system to perform the various job steps. Programs and data may be interspersed with control cards in the input job stream. A job ends with a delimiter, marking the end of job, or else with the appearance of a new job statement.

See JOB STEP, TASK.

job control statement Any of the statements used to direct an operating system in its functioning, as compared to data, programs, or other information needed to process a job but not intended directly for the operating system itself.

In the days before operating systems, the computer operator was responsible for the correct loading and execution of all programs. Today operating systems relieve the operator of much of this work, and also greatly increase the throughput of a computer.

Early operating systems were directed by control cards to perform or omit various actions. The control cards, with the programs and data, defined the job in enough detail to permit it to function. As operating systems became more flexible, control cards became more complex, for every new option presented a choice that had to be made on some control cards. Today's operating systems for the 360 have evolved a so-called job control language. This is nothing more than the old control cards, but with increased flexibility and complexity, and generalized so that input media other than punched cards can be used. The elements of job control language are called, appropriately, job control statements.

In OS/360, the most commonly used job control statements are:

//	JOB	Used to introduce and identify a new job, its submitter, accounting information, etc.
//	EXEC	Used to introduce and identify a job step, and indicates the program or procedure to be executed.
//	DD	Used to link data sets to the programs that are to use them.
/*		Delimiter, marks end of data in input stream.
//		Null statement, marks end of input stream, no more work to be done follows.

job library A partitioned data set, or a concatenation of partitioned data sets, used as the primary source of object programs (load modules) for a particular job, and, more generally, a source of runnable programs from which all or most of the programs for a given job will be selected.

If a user keeps most of his runnable programs on a volume of storage that can be mounted and dismounted as required, he gains three advantages: his programs are protected and private, searching for his programs is faster because other user's programs do not have to be skipped, and he may use his own private, modified versions of standard programs without danger of accidentally having the standard program found and loaded instead of his own. The disadvantages are associated with the cost and effort of maintaining and mounting his own particular library when common libraries are already mounted, free of additional effort.

job scheduler The control program that examines the input work queue and selects the next job to be processed.

There are various systems used to schedule jobs. In some operating systems it is possible to select a job scheduler whose method of operation best meets the needs of the particular computer installation. A small computer user would normally select the simple first-come, first-served discipline. This would result in a small and fast job scheduling program. On more complex systems one might want a priority scheduler. High-priority programs would be run as soon as possible, and low-priority programs would be run when nothing more urgent remained undone. Another job scheduler distinguishes nonsetup jobs from other jobs. A nonsetup job requires no action by the computer operator other than loading it into the input job stream. For example, suppose that six tape drives were available: A nonsetup job using no tapes could be run while the operator dismounts six reels (old job) and mounts six new reels (next job). Thus the nonsetup job is run in time otherwise wasted between two jobs requiring a lot of operator setup time.

job step   A unit of work from the viewpoint of the user.

One or more job steps constitute a job. A job step begins by allocating computer resources (hardware and software facilities of the computer), loading the first program, and transferring control to the program. A job step ends when a program terminates its operation (either normally, or abnormally through a fault) and the operating system deallocates the resources that have been used. The program that terminates need not be the same as the one that began the job step. A job step is composed of one or more tasks, each of which is a unit of processing.

A job step is defined by a control card marking beginning of job step. This control statement is often called EXECUTE, or EXEC for short. Other control statements describe the resources required by the job step for its operation. Programs and data may be interspersed with these control cards. End of step is defined by another EXECUTE card or by an end-of-step delimiter statement.

When the job step can be run, the resources that it requires are readied and made available to it. Then the program named in the EXEC statement is loaded and begins its operation. This marks the beginning of a task, or sequential set of elementary operations. A program may cause other programs to be located, loaded, and executed.

The new programs (dynamically) called may form part of the same task, or may be new tasks, competing with the first task for computer time. Thus the amount of memory, number of programs, and number of tasks may vary from moment to moment. However they change, all components of a job step may use only the I/O devices allocated at the beginning of the job step. It is this property, commonality of input/output devices, that unifies the tasks of a job step. As step follows step, the I/O devices used by a job may increase, change, or decrease. Normally the job steps within a job will have some I/O files (data sets) in common, but they need not be related at all. The hierarchy of job/step/task allows both programmer and operating system great flexibility in the utilization of a computer. See JOB, TASK.

JOSS A language developed by the Rand Corporation originally to make quick calculations of a nature too involved for a calculator. The original implementation was on a Johnniac computer, and consequently, JOSS is the acronym for Johnniac open-shop system. JOSS has since been implemented on a PDP-6 computer, and is capable of serving well over 100 consoles.

JOSS is a time-sharing language, designed for concurrent use by a number of people, each at his own console typewriter. The user is completely oblivious to any other person using the computer, and feels, in effect, that he has a powerful computer all to himself.

JOSS was not designed for certain functions, such as large data-file handling, extremely large programs, long running programs, but rather to be able to perform moderate programs, and to be easily used in an interactive environment. For this reason, JOSS does not support many general-purpose features.

The JOSS language is simple and relatively easy to learn. It is similar to other algebraic languages, and it contains some powerful features of its own. Wherever possible, things are defined and told to JOSS implicitly. For example, wanting to store an expression rather than execute it immediately is indicated by writing a step number with an expression. JOSS allows certain powerful functions. For example, SUM indicates the sum of a range of numbers, PROD the product, MIN and MAX the minimum and maximum values over a defined range of values.

All JOSS arithmetic is performed on numbers carried in scientific notation, an integer magnitude and a decimal exponent. However, input and output on the typewriter are in integer or decimal form as the case may be.

JOSS permits a user to save his program for subsequent recall, and it provides the verbs FILE, RECALL, and DISCARD for this purpose.

JOSS responds to user errors with specific error messages when it is possible to be specific, and with "EH?" when it is not possible.

The following example of calculating interest on capital illustrates many of the features of JOSS.

1.1 DEMAND P, R, Y.	The three variables, P for principal, R for rate, and Y for years, are defined here. The demand verb instructs JOSS to have the user type in values once program execution begins. The step number indicates indirectly that this statement is to be stored, rather than executed immediately.

1.2 SET V = P · (1 + R/200.000) *(2.0·Y).	This expression, once executed, will calculate the value of the money P held for Y years at R% interest compounded semiannually. Note in this language that multiplication is indicated by a center dot, and exponentiation by an asterisk. After calculating the value of the expression, a variable named V will be set equal to it. V will be value of money.
1.3 TYPE P, R, Y, V, IN FORM 1.	This output command tells JOSS to type out at execution time the current values of the variables P, R, Y, and V.
1.4 GO TO STEP 1.1.	This is an unconditional branch, and indicates that after typing the results, the program is to be repeated.
FORM 1: P = ____ · ____ R = ____ · ____ Y = ____ · ____ V = ____ · ____	This is an output format statement, which the TYPE command referred to. It indicates that constants should be printed out, and where and in what form the variable values should be printed. In this case, the entire printout will be contained on one line.
DO PART 1.	This statement tells JOSS to execute all statements beginning with a step number of 1 point something.
P = 100.00 R = 6.0 Y = 2.0	The computer demands values for P, R, and Y, which are typed in as 100.00, 6.0, 2.0.
P = 100.00 R = 6.0 Y = 2.0 V = 112.55	The computer now calculates the value of the money, and prints out the various values per the TYPE and FORM commands.
P =	Since the final statement (step 1.4) was GO to 1.1, the program repeats.

DELETE STEP 1.4 1.4 STOP.	If we wanted to replace the GO TO 1.1, we could first delete it, and then type in the new command.
DELETE ALL	If we were all through, we could cause all our work to be destroyed by typing DE-LETE ALL.
TYPE ALL.	If we wanted then to check that all our work had actually been deleted, we could type TYPE ALL.

JOVIAL JOVIAL is an acronym for Jules' (Schwartz) own version of the international algorithmic language. It is a procedure-oriented language derived from ALGOL and is commonly used in programming command and control procedures. The major deviation from ALGOL is in the types of data that can be described and manipulated. In JOVIAL, data can be controlled on the "byte" and even "bit" level if desired. This added capability extends the power of the language to the extent that software such as compilers have been written in the JOVIAL language. Hence, although JOVIAL was created specifically for command and control applications (primarily used by government agencies and the military), it has found use in many other types of applications: real-time programs; software; some commercial applications.

The program written in the JOVIAL language is translated or compiled by a program called a compiler, which interprets the program statements and outputs, an object code on which the particular computer can operate.

Although the rules of the language are extensive, the basic structure of a program is simple. A program consists of PROCEDURE CALLS (INVOCATION) and DEFINITIONS. A procedure definition consists of other PROCEDURE CALLS and LANGUAGE STATEMENTS. There are language statements that define and initialize data, and others that manipulate and test the data.

To illustrate a JOVIAL program, the example calculates the final value (VALUE) of an amount (PRIN) at a rate (RATE) percent compounded quarterly during NYRS years.

JOVIAL program	Commentaries
PROC VALUE (PRIN, RATE, NYRS) $	Actual values of PRIN, RATE, NYRS will be supplied from outside this program. The answer, VALUE, will be returned.
ITEM PRIN F $ ITEM RATE F $ ITEM NYRS F $	Defines the items as floating point.
"THIS PROCEDURE EVALUATES THE WORTH OF A SUM 'PRIN' INVESTED AT 'RATE' PERCENT INTEREST, COMPOUNDED QUARTERLY FOR 'NYRS' YEARS."	Comments are freely interspersed outside of, as well as within, statements to improve readability and self-documentation.
BEGIN ITEM INC F $ ITEM INCL F $ ITEM NN I $	The values INC and INCL are floating, and NN is integer.
INC = NYRS $ INCL = (1 + RATE/400) $**$ 4 $ NN = NYRS $	INC is given the value NYRS, INCL is the ratio of value at end of 1 year per value at start of 1 year. NN is given the value of the integer part of NYRS.
IF NYRS LS 1 $ GO TO FINISH $	Skip to FINISH if no whole number of years are available.
FOR M = 1, 1, NN $ BEGIN	Repeat the following NN times.
PRIN = PRIN $*$ INCL $ INCL = $+$ 1 $ END	Calculate increase for each year. INC measures amount of increase not yet calculated.
FINISH. IFEITH INC GR 0 $ M = 4 $*$ INC $ ORIF INC EQ 0 $ M = 0 $	Set M depending on whether INC was zero or not.
VALUE = PRIN $*$ (1 + RATE/400) $**$ M $ END VALUE	Evaluate VALUE to be returned to the calling program.

jump A transfer of control which terminates one sequence of consecutive instructions and begins another sequence at a different location. Equally refers to a computer instruction which causes the above action to be taken.

Consider a portion of a program logic in which a single action is followed by one of several alternative actions (which one is chosen depending on conditions that exist at the time), all actions eventually uniting or converging into a single final action. After the first action, one or more conditional jump instructions cause a transfer of control to the correct alternative action routine, depending on conditions existing in the machine, which conditions are capable of being tested.

Each of the alternative action routines ends with an unconditional jump instruction which force the computer to bypass all other actons and begin the common final action routine (see diagram).

Synonymous with BRANCH, TRANSFER. See CONDITIONAL JUMP.

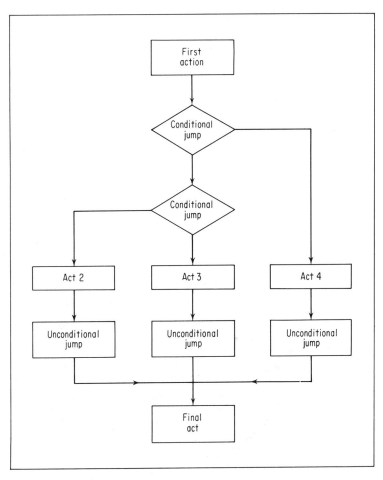

Jumps.

K

key A data item that serves to uniquely identify a data record.

The key may be embedded within the record, or it may immediately precede the record, or it may be separated from the record and contain the address of the rest of the record.

When sorting a collection of records, a key within each record is examined to determine the correct ordering of the records. In some magnetic-disk memories, a key field is recorded before each record and identifies the record. The keys and records are separated from each other by gaps of unrecorded surface. Sometimes it is possible to search the disk by asking the hardware to find the key that matches a key supplied by the program. This feature saves time, but is expensive.

When sorting or rearranging records within main memory, it is possible to swap entire records until the final order is obtained. It is faster to extract the identifying keys and attach the address of the record to each key. Then the keys (which are shorter than the records) may be reordered at high speed. A final move relocates the records in the order given by the new arrangement of the keys.

When move time depends on record length, this roundabout way is often faster.

keypunch   A keyboard-actuated device that punches holes in a card. Keypunches range in size and complexity from portable, manually operated one-hole-at-a-time devices to semiautomatic IBM 029 keypunch machines.   The latter device can automatically skip columns, duplicate fields, and right-justify a number within a predefined card field under the control of a program punched on a drum card.   Some keypunches will print the punched information at the same time that the holes are punched.

kludge   A sometimes humorous, sometimes deprecating term denoting a poorly designed system composed of ill-fitting, mismatched components. For example: "This kludge shouldn't work but, somehow, it does."

L

label A data item that serves to identify a data record (much in the same way as a key is used), or a symbolic name used in a program to mark the location of a particular instruction or routine.

The label is treated by the computer as equivalent to a memory address. It is sometimes used to mark a data area, as well as an instruction, particularly in assembly languages.

The use of labels makes it easier to write programs, for mnemonic names may be used for labels (making their meaning easier to remember), and the programmer is relieved of the detail of maintaining the layout of locations assigned in the computer memory.

lag The amount of time by which one event falls behind (is later than) another event. Similar to the ordinary English usage.

language A set of words and rules for constructing sentences that can be used for communicating.

Historically, languages were used principally for human-to-human communication. With the advent of computers, artificial languages have been devised for man-to-computer communications (computer-to-computer communication is still handled by codes, the formalism of which is too rudimentary to deserve the name language).

The study of language has been divided into two principal parts: semantics, the study of meaning, and syntax, the study of grammar, rules of formation, and word relationships. Workers in modern man/computer language design have invested much effort in formalizing syntax so that compilers can be taught (that is, programmed) to analyze sentences. Less attention seems to have been given to semantics.

Computer languages have restricted vocabularies and constraining rules of construction compared to human languages, but they have precisely defined meaning. In fact, the final and absolute definition of a computer language resides in the compiler or assembler which accepts the language and translates it. The translating program either produces a unique and determinate output from its input or rejects the input as having no meaning (by contrast, human beings may accept meaningless inputs and still act according to some personal logic).

When communicating with computers, a number of levels of languages must be distinguished:

1. Problem-oriented languages which are used to describe a problem to be solved (for instance, structural analysis problems are expressed in STRESS, an engineering language). These languages are made similar to the specialized language of workers in a field. Users of these languages need not know much about computers, and indeed need not know how to solve the problem themselves. Since the problem-oriented languages cannot be used to describe the method of solution, the solution method is an inherent part of the program.

2. Procedure-oriented languages which are used to describe the input, output, and logical functioning of a program. The problem to be solved must be described (implicitly or explicitly) by the input to the language-translating program (compiler), and the method of solving the problem must be known beforehand to the programmer. FORTRAN is an example of such a language.

3. Assembly languages (symbolic machine languages) which are mechanical aids in writing actual computer instructions. In contrast to the higher-level languages above, assembly languages are very highly computer-dependent. An example of such a language is the EASYCODER for the Honeywell 1200.

4. Macroassembly languages which are very sophisticated assembly languages in which the programmer still has complete control over the generated instructions, but with which the trickiest parts of the program can be performed by the computer. An example of such a

language is the basic assembly language for the 360 system (equally known as BAL).

In all the above languages, a computer programmer writes his program in a source language (a program readable by human beings), and a translating program (compiler or assembler) produces the program in an object language, which is the computer code corresponding to the source.

A machine language or absolute language is not a language at all, but the actual computer instructions themselves. These have semantics (meaning) but may have no syntax since there is no sentence structure involved inside a computer. See ALGORITHMIC LANGUAGE, ARTIFICIAL LANGUAGE, MACHINE LANGUAGE, NATURAL LANGUAGE, OBJECT LANGUAGE, PROBLEM-ORIENTED LANGUAGE, PROCEDURE-ORIENTED LANGUAGE, PROGRAMMING LANGUAGE, SOURCE LANGUAGE, TARGET LANGUAGE.

language translator   A generic term with a number of specific meanings:

1. Any assembler or compiler that accepts human-readable statements and produces equivalent outputs in a form closer to machine language (such a language translator is used daily at almost any computer installation and is now indispensable in program creation).

2. A program designed to convert one computer language to equivalent statements in another computer language, perhaps to be executed on a different computer (such a program is rarely used, and if so, then by individuals involved in conversion from one computer to another).

3. A routine that performs or assists in the performance of natural language translations, such as Russian to English, or Chinese to Russian. (This type of language translator has not been completely successful yet.)

latency   The waiting time between the order to read/write some information from/to a specified place and the beginning of the data-read/write operation. A term normally used when reading input from (or writing output onto) magnetic storage devices of the rotating type (disk, drum, tape loops).

When the read/write head has to move to the desired track, this head movement is sometimes called seek time. Then the term latency is reserved for the rotational delay time to bring the specified part of the track under the head.

The latency time is often stated to average about one-half the time for one rotation: it depends, however, on the application. The average latency could in fact be much smaller than, or nearly twice as great as, the time for half a rotation.

The corresponding delay from static (nonmoving) memory devices (core, thin film) is called ACCESS TIME.

leader The unrecorded length of tape that enables the operator to thread the tape through the drive and onto the take-up reel without losing data. Similar in function to leader on a movie film.

The end of the leader (and the beginning of data recording) is indicated by a reflective (or sometimes, transparent) spot on the tape.

Similar arrangements exist at the other end of the tape, i.e., a distinguishing spot and a trailer length of tape.

learning A process by which a computer modifies its program (or other internally variable states) and thus its behavior, according to its experience (or history).

Two important classes of machine learning exist:

1. In a digital computer, paths of logic may be activated or deactivated, and parameter values may be changed by discrete amounts: these steps take place in a sequential order since most digital computers can do only one "thinking" thing at a time. An example of digital computer learning is given by the chess-playing program.

2. An analog or continuous computer can adjust its parameters in a continuous manner, and even can adjust several parameters simultaneously. This permits, on occasion, an entirely new kind of interactive phenomenon to occur. Examples of application of this adaptive behavior are found in the Perceptron learning device, and adaptive autopilots for aircraft.

A sequential learner can explore several paths, remember the results, and select one for further processing; however, an analog simultanous device cannot backtrack so easily.

See HEURISTIC, MACHINE LEARNING.

Leibnitz, Gottfried Wilhelm Von (1646–1716) Leibnitz, the Austrian historian, philosopher, and mathematician, invented in 1671 (and completed in 1694) a more advanced adding machine than Pascal's arithmetic machine of 1642. Whereas Pascal's machine could only count (that is, add by units), add, and subtract, Leibnitz's stepped reckoner could also multiply, divide, and take square roots. His contribution to computers is not, however, his stepped reckoner, but his realization of the advantage of the binary over the decimal system.

length Usually associated with the terms record and word.

By record length is meant the number of characters, digits, or words that comprise a data record in a particular file (or data set). Fixed-length records are easy to handle, being of known format and predictable size.   Variable-length records are more difficult to process, as their size must be determined every time, but they usually make for more efficient use of storage media space.

By word length is meant the number of bits or digits (or characters) that comprise a word in a specific type of digital computer.   Most types of digital computers are organized around fixed-length words. The whole word is addressed as a unit, and calculations are usually done in registers, not in memory.

However, most digital computers in number, not in type, are organized with variable-length words.   In such computers each character is individually addressable, and words are defined by punctuation or other indications.   (Some computers such as the IBM 360, the RCA Spectra 70, the SDS Sigma 7 combine both organizations.)

letter   An alphabetic character used to form words in a written language.   The character may be a printed or written symbol (a graphic) or a computer internal representation having the same meaning.   This usage is similar to ordinary English usage.

letterpress   In character recognition, a printing method employed in the preparation of source documents in which the paper is impressed on an inked raised surface.

library   A computerized facility containing a collection of organized information used for reference.

In most instances, the term library refers more specifically to an organized collection of computer programs, together with the associated program listings, documentation, user's direction, decks, and tapes.

library routine   A computer program that is part of some program library.

A library routine may be an entire (self-contained) program or a subroutine which will be used by many other programs.

light reflectance   See BRIGHTNESS, REFLECTANCE, BACKGROUND REFLECTANCE.

light stability   In optical character recognition (OCR), the ability of an image to retain its spectral appearance when exposed to radiant energy.

limit priority   An upper bound to the dispatching priority that a task can assign to itself or any of its subtasks.

In a multitasking operating system, the computer normally contains several partially completed tasks. These tasks are either active (capable of being executed further right now) or waiting for some change of status. The inactive tasks allow the active tasks to run during the time when the inactive tasks themselves could not run.

Suppose that a task is to be executed by the computer. Which task should be chosen by the operating system task dispatcher? The ready tasks compete with one another on the basis of dispatching priority (momentary relative importance). A task may change its own priority, or attach a new task with a priority different from its own. The limit priority prevents any task from unfairly monopolizing computer time by setting an upper limit to the dispatching priority that can be created by a task. Limit priority is established at the time when the job step is begun. A task may attach a new task with a limit priority lower than its own limit priority, but never higher. Thus limit priority and dispatching priority may both change dynamically, but cannot exceed the initial limit priority of the job step.

If no multitasking is taking place, both dispatching and limit priorities become meaningless. However, scheduling of jobs can still be performed on a job priority basis.

linear program An algorithmic program used to handle a class of problems satisfied by a set of solutions, the requirements being to select the least costly (or the most profitable) solution belonging to the set. This class of problem is characterized by linear relationships between the variables, and by the existence of a linear function (the cost, or profit function) which is to be optimized. The solution of such problems finds its application, for instance, in the determination of least costly transportation patterns, in the elaboration of most profitable product mixes, or even in the most efficient use of tactical weapons.

Linear programming by computer is widely used today, not only because it is so broadly applicable and can handle the thousands of variables that real problems often deal with, but also because it can be applied without an understanding of the underlying mathematics, much as a car can be driven without an understanding of mechanical engineering. It permits the building of a mathematical model, with the linear program and the computer operating on the model to obtain the desired solution. By suitable change of constants, it is possible to simulate a variety of conditions and obtain the optimal solution for each. Building the model has thus, in many instances, become the crucial engineering art, with the linear program and the computer doing the rest.

By contrast, nonlinear programming—in which some of the variables have exponents different from 1—is still a largely unknown and unexplored field. Some nonlinear programs do exist, but with such severe restrictions imposed on the number of variables and the restraints acceptable to the programs as to make these more an object of mathematical curiosity than a working tool for business and industry.

line misregistration In character recognition, the improper appearance of a line of characters, on site in a character reader, with respect to a real or imaginary horizontal baseline.

Normal	High	Skew	Low	Irregular

Line misregistration.

Line misregistration takes the form of line high, line low, line skew, or line irregular. During the reading process, if line misregistration occurs, then a normalizing routine will be performed to pull down, push up, or "twist" the line in an attempt to remove it to its intended position.

If a line is misregistered irregularly, that is, if some characters are high, others low, etc., then line registration is bypassed in favor of character registration. Compare with MISREGISTRATION, LINE SKEW.

line printer A device that prints an entire print line in a single operation, without necessarily printing one character at a time.

line printing The printing of an entire line of characters as a unit.

Line printing is the fastest mechanical method of computer-directed printing used for the great majority of all digital computer output today. In this method, a continuous strip of paper (in roll or fanfold form) is fed through the printing mechanism, one or more line spaces per step. The entire set of printable characters is rapidly exposed to each print position.

In a chain printer, the type pieces reside on a horizontally moving continuous chain. In a drum printer, the type is embossed on a drum, which rotates on a horizontal axis, so that each character moves vertically past the paper. As the correct character passes each print position, an electrically actuated hammer strikes the paper from behind, pressing the front of the paper against an inked ribbon which has the typeface behind it. In this way the character is imprinted on the paper. After all columns have printed, the paper may be advanced to the next line.

The examination of a page of computer printout will reveal the printing process used: if the top edges of a character are less sharp than the side edges, a drum printer was used; if horizontal parts of a printed character are sharp but sides are fuzzy, a chain printer was used. If all parts of the characters are equally sharp, a typewriterlike mechanism was used, or possibly an electronic display/photographic process. Although the last named is the fastest computer output device today, it is also the most expensive and least common.

line skew   In character recognition, a form of line misregistration, inasmuch as the string of characters to be recognized appears in a uniformly "slanted" condition with respect to a real or imaginary baseline.

Line skew manifests itself as iterative character misregistrations beginning at one end of the line; it is correctible if the individual elements possess regularity between one another.

Regular

Irregular

Line skewness.

If irregular line skewness is present, then the process of character registration prevails in lieu of line registration. Compare with LINE MISREGISTRATION.

link   To unite two or more separately written and compiled (or assembled) programs (and/or subroutines) into a single, unified operational entity. The process that accomplishes this action is called linkage.

In the IBM 360 terminology linking is accomplished by a special program called linkage editor. This program acts to resolve interprograms symbolic references by substituting the correct address components for the symbols. It also performs relocation, so that programs do not overlap one another.

In OS/360 a LINK macroinstruction will cause the named program module to be located in an external library and loaded into an available portion of memory. Control will then pass to the named module exactly as though a CALL macroinstruction had been given. If a usable copy of the named program module is already in memory (as from a previous LOAD macroinstruction), the finding and loading are bypassed, and an ordinary CALL is performed. When no program having the designated name is found, the job that issued the LINK request is terminated by the operating system. This facility to find and call programs during a run is a valuable feature. It permits seldom-used routines (not needed for every job) to be called when needed without tying up main memory space during the times when they are not needed. Also, if many alternative routines exist but only one or two will be used depending on decisions made while running, only the routines actually needed will be loaded while the others remain in external storage.

In a number of systems, a link is a program residing on a chain tape which may be called into the computer under program control. A chain tape is a core-image library. It contains an actual image of the contents of main memory in a ready-to-execute condition for each of several programs. A chain is composed of links, which are the individual members of the core-image library.

A link is called by specifying its identifying number and the tape on which it resides. A chain program (or subroutine) searches the tape and loads the indicated program, if found. Each link completely destroys the program that called it, but may preserve some of the data in the FORTRAN common area.

See COMMUNICATION LINK, LINKAGE EDITOR.

linkage A group of instructions included partly in a calling program and partly in a called program according to some linkage convention, which permit the two routines to communicate effectively and exchange control.

Since, for a given computer, several methods of passing control are possible, many different linkage conventions exist. Both programs, however, must use the same convention if they are to communicate. For instance, in the IBM 709, it is customary to provide a return address in index register 4 although using index registers 1 or 2 would be equally valid.

A linkage is also a process that unites different program routines into a unified entity. This process may be performed by the programs themselves, by an operating system service routine, by the program loader, or by a separate and special program (as, for instance, by the linkage editor in the IBM 360 System). In this way, programs written by different individuals can be made to work efficiently together. This possibility allows for the farming out of various segments of a program to different programmers.

linkage editor A service routine that converts the output of assemblers and compilers into a form that can be loaded and executed.
In the process of this conversion the linkage editor can:

1. Combine separately produced object modules (compiler output).

2. Incorporate all or parts of previously processed load modules
(linkage editor output) into their new load module.

3. Resolve symbolic cross-references between the various input
modules.

4. Replace, delete, or insert entire control sections.

5. Create overlay facilities in the load module if so requested.

In OS/360 and also DOS and TOS, a linkage editor run is required before any program appears in loadable format. In TSS/360, linkage editing
is optional, for compiler outputs are directly executable. Lesser operating
systems do not provide linkage editor facilities, and so it is difficult to unite
separately produced program segments on the simpler 360 operating systems.

The output of a compiler (or assembler) is an object module—similar in
content to a load module but not acceptable to the program loading FETCH
routine: it begins with an external symbol dictionary. This names and
identifies every externally accessible symbol defined within this object
module, and also names every symbol defined elsewhere but needed by
this module. Then follows the text of the program: It is in final form
except for relocatable and external symbolic addresses; after the text is
the relocation dictionary. The RLD (relocation dictionary) gives FETCH
instructions for initializing every relocatable address constant within the
module.

Normally a load module has the same three parts as an object module.
This permits it to be input to either FETCH or linkage editor. It is
possible to omit the ESD from a load module (to save storage space), but
this prevents a link edit run from modifying the module. An object module
can be punched onto cards, but a load module has records much too long
for an 80-column card.

When programs to be united must interact at run time, they must communicate somehow. Programs are compiled (assembled) with symbolic
references to externally defined symbols. Another object module defines
the symbol by having it appear as an external symbol in its ESD. Linkage
editor matches the external reference of the first module with the external
symbol in the second module. The relocatable address of the external
symbol entry point is inserted into the first module's text at every point
where it is required. Thus the external reference has been resolved, by
replacing it with the correct known and defined address.

If all external references can be resolved and eliminated, the output
load module can be marked loadable, for it is complete and self-contained.
If any unresolved symbolic references remain after link editing, the module
is unloadable because it refers to unknown locations.

An object module is composed of one or more control sections, whose names and locations are given in the ESD. A control section is the smallest unit of program that can be separately relocated, deleted, added or replaced. As modules enter the linkage editor, their control section names are noted. If a duplicate section name appears in a subsequent module, the duplicated control section is eliminated. Thus only the first control section having any particular name is retained unless otherwise specified. Control sections may contain data or instructions, or both. In FORTRAN, the named common sections are control sections. Any reference to a location within a control section is to whichever section of that name is retained in the load module.

Overlay is a means of executing large programs on small computers. It divides a program into links, only some of which can be found inside the computer at any particular moment. Linkage editor assembles the links from object modules and control sections according to an externally specified plan. If an overlay structured module is input to link edit, its original overlay structure is ignored. The output load module will not be an overlay structure unless explicit directions are provided to link edit for this purpose.

It can be seen that link editing gives very flexible control over the final form of a load module. It is possible to write parts of systems in different languages and unite the object modules into a coherent whole. Overlay structures can be created out of existing nonoverlay modules to permit running on a new, smaller computer. Likewise overlay structure can be removed from a program to permit faster execution on larger machines. Individual control sections can be rewritten and replaced without having to reassemble the entire program or object module.

Actually, services similar to these were offered on earlier operating systems which employed linking loaders. The difference is that linkage editor output can be saved in a program library, thus avoiding the overhead operations associated with linking at every program loading.

In OS/360 and TSS/360 it is possible to minimize link editing by dynamically loading and linking during program execution. This facility is very flexible, but slow.

LISP LISP is an interpretive language developed for manipulation of symbolic strings of recursive data. LISP is an acronym for list processing. While the language has been developed to aid in the handling of symbolic lists, it can be and has been used successfully in the manipulation of mathematical and arithmetic logic.

The LISP and the techniques incorporated into it are the tools that have become popular in the development of higher-level languages. LISP lends itself quite readily as a language in which languages including itself may be written.

The LISP expressions are evaluated within an interpretative routine and return the value of the expression. This interpreter accepts the first argument as the function to be applied, while the second argu-

nent is the value or list of values to which the function is to be ap-
·lied and the interpreted value returned.

The functions acceptable to the interpretation routine are numerous
nd are listed as an object list. Examples of the types of function
vould be PLUS, MINUS, TIMES, QUOTIENT, GO. Included in
he list are functions, such as DEFINE, which enable the user, by
nanipulation of existing functions, to define functions usable within
·is problem. The function names on the OBJECT LIST are reserved
·s function names unless the user desires to destroy the LISP inter-
·retation of that name. LISP also contains condition indicators such
·s Boolean, magnitude, and absolute.

The LISP expressions are enclosed in parentheses and the variables
·isted for a given function are enclosed within their own delimited
·arenthesis. The elements within a variable list are delimited with
·ither a space or a comma.

The following problem, dealing with the calculation of the amount
·esulting from a sum invested at compound interest, will illustrate
·he principles of LISP:

CSET(INT 0. 05)	The value 5% is interpreted to be the floating-point number available when the label INT is referenced.
CSET(YRS 5)	The value 5 is interpreted to be the fixed-point number available when the label YRS is referenced.
CSET(PRIN 150.00)	The value 150.00 is interpreted to be the floating-point number available when the label PRIN is referenced.
DEFINE	The interpreter is being instructed to DEFINE THE EXPRESSION that will follow.
(COMINT(LAMBDA(ADD1 INT)))	Define the value of COMINT to be any value in INT plus 1. In this example, the interest is being set to 105%.
(TOTINT(LAMBDA(EXPT COMINT YRS)))	Define the value of TOTINT to be any value of COMINT raised to any power whose value is expressed in the label area YRS. In this example TOTINT is equal to $(1.05)^5$.

(TOTPRIN(LAMBDA(TIMES PRIN TOTINT)))	Define the value of TOTPRIN to be any value of the product of the values in label area TOTINT and PRIN. In this example, TOTPRIN is equal to 150.00 times 1.05^5.
))	The interpretative routine has been informed that the DEFINE list has been terminated
TOTPRIN(INT YRS PRIN)	The interpretative routine has been given a function, TOTPRIN, and its argument list (INT, YRS, and PRIN) for execution to obtain a value.
(PRINT TOTPRIN)	The input/output routine within LISP will execute the printing of the computed value of TOTPRIN.
STOP))	The interpreter is informed of the completion of the executable program.

list A last-in, first-out storage organization, usually implemented by software, but (as in the SDS SIGMA 7) sometimes implemented by hardware. This is essential in writing recursive routines (programs that use themselves as subroutines).

In FORTRAN, a list is a set of data items to be read or written. In an output statement, the variables named in the list are output in succession until the list is exhausted. For input, items are read and stored until the list is satisfied.

For example, in the FORTRAN statements:

    PRINT 10, AOK, JOHN, GLENN
    10 FORMAT (5X, A5, I6, F10.4)

the list consists of AOK, JOHN, GLENN.

See PUSHDOWN LIST, PUSHUP LIST.

list processing A programming technique in which list structures are used to organize memory.

In list processing, computer memory is organized into several lists, or structures of data items. Each list has a symbolic name, a header or starting record, and some number of entries. The header contains (among other things) the address of the first data entry in that list. Each data entry contains one or more related data items and the address of the next data entry in this list. The last entry cannot contain a successor address, so it may have either an end-of-list signal or the address of the header record. The header is in a known location and serves to give the list processor a fixed starting location when searching or operating on that list.

Initially, all memory is organized into an empty-space list. The lists are created in space removed from this master list, and may be destroyed by returning memory addresses to the empty-space list.

See LIST STRUCTURE, LISP, IPL-V.

list structure   A set of data items, connected together because each element contains the address of a successor element (and sometimes a predecessor element).

This structure permits a fixed storage capacity to be allocated to several lists, and as long as the total capacity is not exceeded, each list may grow to any size. A list structure may be contrasted with a fixed-size table which saves space by not storing addresses, but limits the size of each table, and possibly causes wasted space in unfilled tables.

It is easy to insert or delete data items anywhere in a list structure. Suppose that an entry located at address ALPHA is to be inserted in a list between the Nth and (N + 1)th entries. Remove the address of the (N + 1)th entry from the Nth entry's address field and copy it into the address part of the new entry. Then insert the address ALPHA into the address field of the Nth entry. The insertion is now complete, unless a two-way list is being used. In that case, ALPHA would be inserted into the predecessor address of the (N + 1)th entry, and the address of the Nth entry into the predecessor address of the new entry.

In a similar manner any insertion or deletion can be accomplished by changing two (or four) address fields without actually having to move the data records at all.

See INDIRECT ADDRESS.

lithography   In character recognition, the process of preparing source documents whereby printing is accomplished from a virtually flat surface on which the character image has been made ink-receptive and blank areas have been made ink-repellent.

load   To place data into an internal register under program control (placing data from a register into main memory under program control is usually called store).

To load is equally to place a program from external storage into central memory under operator (or program) control, particularly when loading the first program into an otherwise empty computer.

Load does not usually refer to the input of data (as contrasted with problems) in main memory.

By load is also meant an instruction, or operator control button, which causes the computer to initiate the load action. A tape-load button loads from a tape; a card-load button loads from cards. Some computers can load from any attached input device (for example, the IBM 360, Honeywell 200, or Spectra 70).

In OS/360 and DOS/360, a program may issue a LOAD macroinstruction to cause a named program module to be located in an external library and brought into main memory in a ready-to-run condition. If the designated program is already in memory, no action is taken. When the named program module cannot be found, the job issuing the LOAD will be terminated by the operating system. The loaded program does *not* begin execution when loaded, but only when a proper starting macroinstruction (LINK, CALL, XCTL) is given. A program brought into memory by LOAD remains there until a DELETE macroinstruction removes it or the job ends. This facility allows program loading to occur only when it is established that a routine will be needed, and thus avoids loading initially every routine that might be needed.

load-and-go An operating technique with no stops between the loading and execution phases of a program. It may include assembling or compiling.

By not stopping, more rapid response and simpler operation are achieved. On simpler computers, operator intervention is required to execute a just-compiled (or assembled) program. Compile (or assemble) load and go is frequently abbreviated as compile and go (or assemble and go). This technique usually requires an operating system (supervisor, monitor, executive) to perform the step-to-step transition.

load module A program in a form suitable for loading into memory and being executed. The output of a linkage editor run.

A load module usually contains three principal subdivisions: an external symbol dictionary (ESD), a text section (TXT), and a relocation dictionary (RLD) in that order.

The ESD contains the names and locations within the module of all entry points (specific locations accessible by name from outside of the module). Entry points usually are the first instruction of subroutines or programs, but they can equally be data-item locations. External symbols also include control section names. A control section is the smallest unit of program that can be separately loaded, replaced, or deleted. Finally, the ESD contains external references, or the names of symbols not defined within this load module. For each external reference at least one resolvable (symbolically defined) address must exist within the body of the load module. If any unresolved external references appear in the ESD, the load module cannot be loaded. The ESD contains resolved external references that permit the linkage editor to re-resolve the affected addresses in the event that a control section, containing the definition of a symbol, is replaced by a newer control section.

The TXT portion of a load module contains computer instructions in final form, and also data defined with specified initial values. In addition, room is reserved for data areas that have unspecified initial values. The addresses embedded within TXT that are external references or relocatable address constants are not in final form, but are subject to modification by fetch or by linkage editor.

The RLD contains directions which enable program fetch to properly initialize all relocatable address constants within TXT. Relocation is accomplished by accounting for the actual starting address of the load module in memory, and also the incremental difference between the desired address and the initial address of the module. Thus an address constant intended to be the address of the 218th instruction within the module will be initialized to the correct value, no matter where the module is loaded in memory.

A load module is described by its name (actually its member name within a partitioned data set) and also by its attributes. Some possible attributes and their usage are:

Scatter load (SCTR): the module is in a form which can be loaded into disjoint areas of memory, one or more control sections per individual memory area. When SCTR is not specified, the module must be block-loaded into one contiguous area of memory. SCTR modules can also be block-loaded, of course.

Overlay (OVLY): the load module is organized into an overlay structure. Normally only selected portions of the entire program will reside in memory at any one time. The program will load portions of itself, as needed, into memory already allocated to the module, without further attention from the program fetch routine. SCTR and OVLY are mutually exclusive attributes—an overlay cannot be scatter-loaded because it does not use fetch.

Reenterable (RENT): after loading into memory, this module can be used by more than one task at a time. Thus, if the module is being used by a task, and the currently executing task also wants to use the module, both tasks may use the module without interfering with each other. Each task must provide its own copy of a working-storage control section to the RENT module, to allow all the data and modifiable addresses of the task to be preserved when the other tasks are using the reenterable module. RENT is meaningless in a nonmultitasking environment.

Serially reusable (REUS): after having been loaded into memory and executed to completion by one task, this module may be reused by the same or any other task without having to fetch a fresh copy of the program from auxiliary storage. In practical terms this means that the module initializes itself as it runs, so that it can be reused any number of times. Both RENT and REUS are uncommon attributes; both require unusual planning by programmers. RENT and REUS are mutually exclusive attributes, but a RENT module can obviously be reused serially if desired. If neither of these two attributes is specified, a fresh copy of this program must be loaded each time it is to be executed.

Not editable (NE): the load module has no ESD and cannot be reprocessed by the linkage editor. Used only to conserve direct-access storage space.

Only loadable (OL): can only be brought into main memory by a LOAD macroinstruction given from another module. Some control programs use smaller control blocks when a module is loaded than when LINK, ATTACH, or XCTL is used. This saves memory and reduces the effective size of the module at run time.

TEST: the load module contains symbol tables for use by the test translator during program check-out. Omission of this attribute saves memory space for debugged programs. TEST can be used only with assembler-generated modules, and cannot be used in RENT or REUS load modules.

locate mode   A method of communicating with an input/output control system (IOCS), a method in which the address of the data involved, but not the data themselves, is transferred between the IOCS routine and the program.

IOCS routines were developed to spare the programmer from having to incorporate detailed, machine-level input/output logic in every one of his programs. Instead, IOCS resides in memory and communicates with the running program, and performs input/output as directed by the program. When operating in move mode, IOCS causes the input data to be delivered to an agreed-on memory area, and also copies output data from a predetermined area into its own output buffers before writing them out. In the locate mode, the data remain in an input buffer area, or are built up in an output buffer area, and only the address of the data need be passed to or from the IOCS routines. This avoids moving the data (time-consuming and nonproductive), but requires the programs to operate on data in areas whose locations are not known a priori.

In practical terms, locate-mode operation requires that the computer hardware be equipped with index registers or base registers which enable run-time address computation to proceed while the individual computer instructions are being interpreted. This makes it possible for the program to proceed as though it knew where the data were, and let the hardware registers account for the constantly changing actual locations. Usually the address of the first character of an input or output logical record is placed in the hardware register. When the program wishes to access the 19th character of the record, it uses an instruction address of 18 modified by the contents f the appropriate index or base register. The hardware adds 18 ɔ the contents of the register and so produces the correct address f the desired character. The 19th character will always be found 8 characters after wherever the 1st character happens to be. Neither he instruction nor the contents of the hardware register are altered ɪy this process. If address-modifying hardware is not available, lo- ate mode is a very inefficient process and is omitted from the IOCS lesigns.

ocation   Any place in which data may be stored. Location is simi- ar to address, a unique identification of the site at which data are ɔ be placed or retrieved. It is usually expressed as a number.

In any conventional (nonassociative) memory or random-access torage device, each character, word, etc., resides in a physical space listinct from all the other parts of the device. To refer to this space, he address or location is used to specify the one particular space lesired.

A location, or address, is comparable to a post office box number, ɔrovided that the post office box could hold only one letter at a time, ɪnd could be emptied repeatedly without depleting it. By using a Zip Code (equivalent to core bank number or sector address), one ɔarticular post office out of all in the country could be designated. The box number within the post office could be used to specify the lestination of a letter, or the source from which the letter is to be ːetrieved.

See PROTECTED LOCATION.

logic   The science of reasoning, being particularly concerned with ɪalid means of deduction, demonstration, or proof. Usually deals ɪwith propositions which must be either true or false, but not both. See FORMAL LOGIC, SYMBOLIC LOGIC.

logical expression   In FORTRAN IV, two arithmetic expressions connected by the relational operators

Operator	Meaning
.EQ.	Equal
.NE.	Not equal
.GT.	Greater than
.GE.	Greater or equal
.LT.	Less than
.LE.	Less or equal

or a logical variable, or a logical constant (true or false) or som
logical expressions connected by logical operators.

In some other procedure-oriented languages, similarly constructe
logical expressions are allowed, perhaps with different notation b
always with similar meaning. A logical expression when evaluate
must have the value TRUE or the value FALSE, but not both.

logical IF   In FORTRAN IV, a statement of the form IF (logic
expression) executable statement. When the logical expression
"true," the statement is executed; otherwise the executable statemen
is bypassed. See LOGICAL EXPRESSION.

logical operator   In FORTRAN IV, an operation that acts on on
or two logical variables or logical expressions.

These consist of AND. (logical product), .OR. (logical sum), an
NOT. (logical complement). See LOGICAL EXPRESSION.

logical record   A group of adjacent, logically related data items.

A logical record is defined as a unit for purposes of usage or i
terms of content as opposed to a physical record, which is a group o
related, adjacent data items defined as a unit by its hardware charac
teristics, or physical format. A logical record is what a programme
would like to treat as a unit, while a physical record is what th
hardware must treat as a unit. A logical record may be defined b
its initial location address and its length, but a physical record i
defined by its physical beginning and ending.

A physical record may contain one logical record (unblocked) o
many logical records (blocked). Blocking is used to reduce the
storage volume of physical records, or the time required to perform
input/output, or both. Large logical records are frequently recorded
unblocked, to conserve buffer space in main memory. Each physical
record on a magnetic storage medium is delimited by record gaps, or
intervals of unrecorded space. By putting n logical records in one
physical record, the number of gaps required is reduced by a factor
of n. This reduction in unrecorded space accounts for the time and
space savings of blocked records.

logical variable   In FORTRAN IV, a variable that may have only the
value true or false.

In other procedure-oriented languages these may be called Boolean
variables.

logic design   The design of a computer at the level which considers
the operation of each functional block and the relationships between
the functional blocks.

Logical design is concerned with connectivity, control, and sequential ordering. The designer must account for all exceptional circumstances as well as the routine conditions. Hardware considerations are secondary at this stage. See FUNCTIONAL DESIGN.

logic diagram   A graphical representation of the logic design, or a portion thereof. The logic diagram displays the existence of functional elements and the paths by which they interact with one another. Hardware implementation is sometimes taken into consideration in a logic diagram.

logic element   A hardware circuit that performs a simple, predefined transformation on its input or inputs, and presents the resulting signal at its output. In modern integrated-circuit technology this may be less than one entire silicon chip (of a multifunction array), but this piece of silicon chip acts as though it were several discrete components: it is to be considered an entity by itself for purposes of logic design.

A combination logic element has no memory: its output is determined only by the present state of its inputs.

A sequential logic element has an output determined by present and past input signals: it has some degree of retention, or memory.

logic instruction   A digital computer instruction which forms a logical combination (on a bit-by-bit basis) of its operands and leaves the result in a known location. Typical functions are AND, INCLUSIVE OR, EXCLUSIVE OR (or HALF-ADD), and NOT. The result is usually in the location of one of its operands.

For instance, to ensure that the second bit of location 376 is a 1, the instruction OR could be used:

Instruction	Location 492	Location 376	
OR 492, 376	0100000	0001101	Before
		0101101	After

If, at a later time, it were necessary to ensure that the second bit of location were 0, the instruction AND could be used:

Instruction	Location 492	Location 376	
AND 492, 376	1011111	0101101	Before
		0001101	After

If, at a still later time, it were necessary to fill location 376 with zeros, the instruction EXCLUSIVE OR (or HALF-ADD) could be used:

Instruction	Location 376	Location 376	
HALF-ADD 376, 376	0001101	0001101	Before
		0000000	After

See AND, EXCLUSIVE OR, OR.

logic shift A shift operation that treats the operand as a set of bits, not as a signed numeric value or character representation. This contrasts with arithmetic shift, in which a number changes in magnitude but preserves its sign. A logic shift may be linear (bits shifted beyond one end are lost) or circular (bits shifted beyond one end appear at the other end).

The use of a logic shift is best illustrated by an example. Assume that a programmer wishes to pack two half words LEFT, RIGHT into the field WORD, the computer having 18-bit words. The sequence of instructions could read as follows:

LOAD LEFT into register 2.
LOGIC SHIFT LEFT 9 register 2.
OR RIGHT into register 2.
STORE register 2 into WORD.

logic symbol A symbol used to represent logic elements or elementary logical functions in a logic diagram.

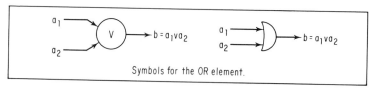

Symbols for the OR element.

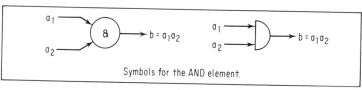

Symbols for the AND element.

$$A \oplus B = A\bar{B} \lor \bar{A}B$$

A EXCLUSIVE OR B defined by (A AND NOT B) OR (NOT A AND B)

Symbols for the definition of the EXCLUSIVE OR function.

Logic symbols.

long grain   In character recognition, a favorable machine-paper arrangement which is achieved:

1. When the grain obtained during the formation of the paper runs in the direction of its longest dimension, and

2. When such paper, as a cut-form document, travels through a character reader in the direction of its longest dimension.

Long grain has several advantages in character-recognition systems. It has been shown that damaged leading edges and reference edges are usually less noticeable under this arrangement.

The long-grain arrangement also allows for a greater output stacking rate owing to the extra longitudinal strength that is needed to withstand the deceleration forces. Some manufacturers have even utilized this arrangement to induce a lengthwise bow which provides additional rigidity to the document as it enters the output stacker.

Although long grain is most desirable, other system requirements (such as those encountered in dealing with turnaround documents) may dictate the use of another combination of paper grain, and document direction of travel.

look-up   An operation or process in which a table of stored values is scanned (or searched) until a value equal to (or sometimes, greater than) a specified value is found.

The result of the look-up is the location of the matching table entry, associated information stored in the table, or both. The look-up operation may be performed by hardware (as in the IBM 650 with its drum look-up instruction) or by means of a subroutine.

See TABLE LOOK-UP.

loop   A sequence of computer instructions which are executed repeatedly, but usually with address modification changing the operands of each iteration, until a terminating condition is satisfied.

The ability to loop, and thus reuse instructions without duplicating them and wasting memory, is probably the single most important advantage gained by stored-program computers. This one feature alone set modern computers apart from their externally programmed predecessors (EAM equipment) and made possible the computer revolution of today.

The use of a loop is illustrated by the following problem: a list of numbers is stored in locations 750 through 875. In location 518 is stored a count of the number of items from the list which are to be added together. This count is variable, and it has been determined by previous program steps (and is unknown to the programmer). Moreover, the computer for this example has at least three registers (R1, R2, R3).

The following coding adds the required number of numbers and goes to location 608 when the sum is formed in register 1 (R1).

	Instruction location	Instructions		Working storage
Initialization	741	ZERO R1	176	(Constant) 1
	742	LOAD 518 into R2	290	(Dummy instruction)
	743	LOAD 290 into R3		Add 750 to R1

	Instruction location	Instructions		Working storage
Loop	744	STORE R3 into 746		
	745	BRANCH to 608 if R2 zero	518	Number of items to be added
	746	((space for add instruction))		

	Instruction location	Instructions		Working storage
	747	SUBTRACT 176 from R2		
	748	ADD 176 to R3		
	749	BRANCH to 744		

The first three instructions initialize the loop; that is, they prepare the computer for executing the loop. A zero sum is in working register 1, the count of items is in register 2, and a dummy instruction is in register 3.

The instruction at 744 stores the correct ADD instruction into location 746. The address of the operand changes during the loop, and so it must be stored before each execution of the loop.

The instruction at 745 is the conditional test that terminates the loop. It tests for zero because we are counting down during the loop. It is placed here to permit returning a zero sum if no items are to be added.

The terminating condition test is usually the last instruction of the loop, but it may be anywhere.

An ADD instruction placed into location 746 adds the next number to register 1. This is the only instruction that actually contributes to forming the sum. The other eight instructions serve to execute 746 the correct number of times.

In 747 the count of the number of remaining items is reduced by one. Note that 176 is the address of the constant 1. In most computers the operand cannot be part of the instruction, but the address of the operand must be in the instruction.

In 748 the address part of the ADD instruction (originally 750) modified to point to the next number to be added. In modern computers this function is performed in an index register (specially esigned hardware for rapid address modification).

The unconditional transfer in 749 closes the loop by returning 744.

Observe that this function could have been performed by 126 con-cutive ADD instructions without looping. Additional instructions ould have been needed, however, to zero register 1 and to begin at ie correct ADD instruction (depending on the contents of 518), and go to 608 when finished. It may be seen that looping provided saving of more than 100 instructions in this example.

M

machine   In the context of data processing there are two types of machines: physical devices that are real and tangible (such as computers, tabulators, sorters, and collators), and mathematical, abstract machines (the Turing machine and its descendants).

Among the real machines are all the mechanical, electrical, and electronic devices that one can see, touch, and buy.

The mathematical machines, on the other hand, are simplified abstract models of internally programmed computers. They are used to understand real computer performance better, and equally to determine whether mathematical problems are solvable.   (A solvable problem is one that can be answered or solved by a mathematical machine in a finite number of steps: not all problems, indeed, not even all simple problems are solvable.)

The Turing machine is the basis of all abstract machines.   It is to be conceived as having one tape, which is considered to be a linear sequence of squares.   Each square contains a letter from an alphabet, although usually a zero or a one is used.   The tape may be finite or infinite.

The Turing machine can read or write one square at a time, and can advance the tape one space left or right after each operation. The machine has a finite number of internal states. For each internal state and current tape digit there exists a rule that specifies the action of the machine. An action consists of writing a character, advancing left or right, or not advancing. There is a unique successor internal state, and a unique state known as STOPPED. A solvable problem is one that stops the machine in a finite number of steps.

Other mathematical machines generalize the Turing machine by having more than one tape, more general alphabets, or more general (and complicated) rules for changing their internal state.

See TURING MACHINE.

machine address   The actual and unique internal designation of the location at which an instruction or datum is to be stored or from which it is to be retrieved.

The address is almost always expressed as a number, and distinguishes a particular storage or memory location from all other such locations.

The locations in central memory (core or thin film) are addressed by their number. Magnetic-drum memories are addressed by track number and word number within the track. Magnetic-disk storage is addressed by cylinder number, track number, and word within the track.

In multiregister computers, the high-speed registers are designated by fields within the instructions, but these fields are generally not called addresses, although they serve the same function. As a rule, the larger the capacity of storage, the more complicated the address must be. Same as ABSOLUTE ADDRESS.

machine code   Usually, any one of the following definitions:

1. A computer representation of a character, digit, or action command in internal form

2. A computer instruction in internal format, or that part of the instruction which identifies the action to be performed

3. The set of all instruction types that a particular computer can execute

The term machine code is somewhat ambiguous because of its many possible meanings. It is best understood from context. See ASCII, BINARY-CODED DECIMAL, and OPERATION CODE.

machine instruction   A computer instruction, that is, a set of digits, binary bits, or characters that a computer can recognize and act upon.

The instruction, when interpreted or decoded, indicates the action to be performed and which operand is to be involved in the action

The instruction is composed of one or more of the natural or basic information units of the particular computer (for example binary words, alphanumeric characters, bytes, or digits). Instructions are of either fixed or variable length (1 to 12 digits, bytes, or characters of a nonword computer). In some variable-length computers instructions are delimited by nondata punctuation bits or word marks. In other variable-length computers the instruction size is included in the operation code.

Machine instruction may also mean a computer-assisted instruction (CAI), a process of training people with the assistance of mechanical or electronic devices. These aids to education range in complexity from programmed learning texts (ordinary books) to time-shared, on-line computers.

In this context, machine instruction appears best suited for rote learning of a specified set of information. It usually allows each pupil to advance at his own pace. The opportunity to preserve and reuse the best presentations offers a real advantage. The main disadvantage, however, resides in its inability to follow the student's interests or ideas, or to answer unexpected questions, thus requiring supplemental human teaching.

machine language   The set of instructions available to a particular digital computer, and by extension the format of a computer program in its final form, capable of being executed by a computer. This term, however, is a misnomer, because it is not a language since it has neither grammar nor sentence structure.

In general, machine language is comprehensible only to computers, but some programmers and operators are able to interpret the machine-language instructions of computers with which they are familiar.

machine learning   The process or technique by which a device modifies its own behavior as the result of its past experience and performance.

The usual process is as follows: The device is given a goal or criterion of performance and a means of evaluating its own performance. Periodically the device modifies its behavior in some way. It evaluates the resulting performance for a specific length of time. When an improvement is noted, an additional change in the same direction is indicated: a change in the opposite direction is tried if degradation of performance is observed.

Another machine-training scheme is commonly used with pattern-recognition circuits and other devices. These devices are provided with reward circuits. The training scheme is similar to the above, but an external agent (human) evaluates the performance. A stimulus is presented, and the device makes a possibly random response. The reward circuit reinforces the existing machine state, while punishment, or no reward, causes some possibly random modification of the behavior-determining elements.

Note that this description is not limited to computerlike devices. Any mechanism can be self-improving provided that suitable means exist for changing its behavior (or structure) and that the required feedback is provided. Aircraft autopilots are sometimes made this way.

A possibility exists for using trainable machines to find optimal design parameters, and consequently mass-producing cheaper fixed-performance devices using the discovered values.

machine word   The fundamental unit of internal information in a word-organized digital computer.

Depending on the design, a word consists of a fixed number of binary bits, decimal digits, characters, or bytes. The word is usually the size of the computer instructions and the high-speed registers, if present.

In a variable-length or non-word organized computer, a unit of information may also be called a word. In one common organization, the leftmost end of a word is indicated by a nondata punctuation bit called a word mark (as for instance in the Honeywell 200, and the IBM 1401). The rightmost end of a word is then specified by the computer instructions, or else is one position to the left of the next rightmost word mark. Note that constants with identical leftmost characters but different lengths may occupy the same memory position in this organization, so that uniqueness in some sense is lost.

In the IBM 360 System and in similar machines, a word is equal to four 8-bit bytes. These computers can also access 2-byte (16-bit) half words and 8-byte (64-bit) double words. Half words, words (or full words), and double words can all be manipulated in a word-like manner, as can single bytes, so that these computers could be considered to have four different word organizations simultaneously. Although this complex structure cannot be learned as easily as simpler organizations, it does provide powerful data manipulating facility.

Synonymous with COMPUTER WORD.

macroinstruction   An instruction in a higher-level language which is equivalent to a specific set of one or more ordinary instructions in the same language.

The language processor, when compiling or assembling the macroinstruction, expands or converts the macro into a predefined set of fundamental instructions and then processes the expanded instructions

The macroinstruction concept is a very important part of modern computing sophistication. It permits programmers to retain complete control over the program they are writing, but yet permits programming languages to be extended and redefined by the programmer.

A macroskeleton (or model) defines the macro in a precise but content-free way. When the processor encounters a macroinstruction, it finds the corresponding model and particularizes it as directed by macroinstruction parameters. The expanded instructions replace the macroinstruction in the program as though the macroinstruction itself had never existed.

A programmer conceives and codes a macrodefinition to extend the existing language to meet a recurring need. Once the macro has been defined, he and others may use it in their programs. This permits concise and accurate specification of ideas in a program. Macro's are now commonly used in assembly-level languages (symbolic computer instructions), but the concept is also being applied to higher languages. In principle, a macro preprocessor could be written to perform macroexpansion in any computer language before the compiler ever processed the text.

For instance, let a macrodefinition be given by the following:

1		MACRO	
2	$LOC	SOME	$A, $B, $C
3	$LOC	CLA	$A
4		MPY	RATE
5		ADD	$B
6		STA	$C.ER
7		ENDMACRO	

In this example (from a hypothetical computer assembly language) line 1 defines the following text as a macrodefinition. Line 7 indicates the end of the definition. Line 2 is the macro header line. It defines the name of the macro as SOME with one parameter ($LOC) in the leftmost field and three substitutable parameters in the rightmost field. When the macroinstruction SOME is identified in the program, any parameters it contains will be substituted for $LOC, $A, $B, and $C. In this language $ is reserved for names of substitutable parameters.

The macroinstruction:

KIM SOME MINE, 37, ANSW

will be expanded to read as follows:

8	KIM	CLA	MINE
9		MPY	RATE
10		ADD	37
11		STO	ANSWER

Note that KIM = $LOC, MINE = $A, 37 = $B, and ANSW = $C. On line 4, RATE is not a substitutable parameter, and so it appears unchanged on line 9. On line 6, $C.ER means "take the third substitutable parameter on the right and concatenate it with the letters ER." Thus ANSW in the macro appears as ANSWER on line 11.

Macrocapability can extend greatly beyond the simple example shown here. In some cases a parameter or parameters may be omitted and replaced by default options. Conditional assembly instructions cause some code to be generated or omitted depending upon some test being passed or failed at assembly time. Assembly-directing instructions cause the assembler to repeat, include, or skip to some other part of the code.

Some macrofacilities can test the number of substitutable parameters actually provided, instead of being confined to a fixed number. Some can accept parameters in any order, with identifying tags or labels. Some macrofacilities can test the attributes of the arguments used in the macroinstruction, or count the number of times a macrodefinition was used in this program. And finally, in some systems, a macro can be used to create other macrodefinitions which can be used by the programmer.

In this manner the macro concept has made possible the concept of this self-extending language, which each programmer can define to meet his own individual needs or desires.

macrolibrary A collection of prewritten, specialized but unparticularized routines (or sets of statements) which reside in mass storage.

These routines may be selectively found by an assembler which reads them, particularizes them (by replacing general parameters by specific parameters), and incorporates them into programs. The form is symbolic, not at the instruction level.

See MACROINSTRUCTION.

magazine That part of a punched-card-using device in which the cards are stacked before processing, in other words, the input hopper

This term is also used to describe holders of microfilm or magnetic recording media strips.

See INPUT MAGAZINE.

magnetic card A card with a magnetic surface on which data can be stored by selective magnetization.

The card is usually made of durable but flexible plastic material and coated on one side with a mixture of magnetic oxide particles in a suitable binder. The entire construction thus resembles a piece of an uncommonly wide (and thick) magnetic recording tape.

Information is recorded on the card in tracks (longitudinal narrow strips) each of which contains many hundreds of bits of information. Along each track the magnetic material is fully magnetized (saturated) in one direction or the opposite direction. The location and existence of each magnetic flux reversal serve to encode information on the surface. Information is read from or written on the card by mechanically moving the card past fixed read/write heads similar to those used in conventional tape recorders.

In some computer random-access memories, the cards are physically identified by notches cut in one end of the card. These are so designed that a particular card may be selected by mechanically gripping all the slots of the unwanted cards, thus releasing the selected card. In another design the cards have protruding index tabs (like a loose-leaf index insert). Mechanical fingers push aside the tabs on either side of the selected card, allowing the selected card to be easily picked. No matter how selection is accomplished, the card is temporarily attached to a revolving drum (usually by vacuum pressure) and moved repeatedly past the read/write heads before being returned to the magnetic-card bin.

By using multiple (individually removable) magnetic-card bins a random-access storage of almost any total capacity can be constructed. These devices are characterized by large capacity, low cost, and slow speed.

magnetic core A configuration of magnetic material that is placed in a spatial relationship to current-carrying conductors and whose magnetic properties are essential to its use. It may be used to retain a magnetic polarization for the purpose of storing data, or for its nonlinear properties as in a logic element. It may be made of such material as iron, iron oxide, or ferrite, and in such shapes as wires, tapes, toroids, or thin film. It is the most important method of internal storage of data in digital computers today.

Core memories range in size from a few hundred to several million bits, with cycle times ranging from about ½ to at most 20 microseconds. The reasonably large capacity, high speed, and plausible cost of today's core memories have made the modern computer attractive in cost per performance terms to an increasingly large worldwide market.

A magnetic core usually consists of a mixture of iron oxide or ferrite particles mixed with a suitable binding agent, formed into a tiny doughnutlike (toroidal) shape and fired in an oven to obtain final strength and hardness. The individual magnetic cores are strung on fine insulated wires and assembled into flat planes (or arrays) containing 16 to 10,000 cores apiece. In these arrays all the cores are accurately aligned and have two, three, or four wires passing through the hole in each. The individual planes are placed against one another like pages in a book, forming stacks containing 8 to 72 arrays. A stack, together with its associated selecting and read/write electronics, forms a core bank or module of memory. An entire memory is composed of one or more banks, the ultimate size being limited only by economic considerations.

In use, the core is fully magnetized in one of two directions (clockwise or counterclockwise around the hole). Information is written onto the core by sending pulses of electricity through the wires threaded through it. When the additive simultaneous strength of these pulses exceeds a certain threshold, the core is switched to the desired magnetized state. The same wires that pass through the selected core also pass through many other cores of the array. Each nonselected core sees only one pulse, or about half the energy required for switching. In this way the nonselected cores retain (or remember) their original states.

Normally a core is read by applying pulses of electricity of sufficient strength to cause it to change state. If it was already in the zero state, no energy is absorbed from the writing wires or delivered to the sense output wire because a change of state does not occur. If the core does change state, a one is indicated as output. Observe that this reading action destroys the original contents of the memory. The memory is restored by writing back the information that has just been read. The complete read/rewrite process is called one memory cycle. It defines the time that must elapse before another memory reference can be accepted. But information read can be made available for computing halfway through the memory cycle. For this reason an access time of about one-half the cycle time is sometimes quoted as a memory speed rating.

Magnetic cores ranging in size from 100 to 10 mils (thousandths of an inch) have been made and used. The most common sizes today are 50, 30, and 20 mils. A 15-mil core is too small to be readily seen with unaided normal human vision. Yet two to four wires are threaded through each, normally by hand! The smaller cores are faster but harder to wire. This problem (wiring planes by hand) is probably the greatest obstacle to cheaper, faster, and larger memories today. To overcome this obstacle, manufacturers have been seeking new kinds of memory elements that could be batch-fabricated by printing-press techniques.

Magnetic cores are also used in power and signal transformers, and in transformerlike logical elements. The logical elements are much cheaper than electronic circuit logic, but operate in milliseconds, not microseconds.

magnetic disk A flat, circular plate with one or two magnetizable surfaces, on which data can be read or written by magnetic recording techniques.

The disk is made to rotate about its center at high speed (like a very fast phonograph record). Data are recorded in circular data areas called tracks. Data are read or written by moving a read/write head to the track position while the disk is spinning.

The recording technology is similar to that of ordinary tape recording, with one important difference: the heads do not touch the surfaces, but float or fly about one-thousandth of an inch away. This flying-head construction reduces the attainable data density somewhat, but provides essentially zero wear of the record surfaces or heads, with a consequent very high data reliability.

In one disk drive (mechanism auxiliary to the disk itself) there may be one or more disks rotating on a common shaft, with 2 to 100 data recording surfaces. Modern practice is tending toward a removable module of six disks with 10 recording surfaces per disk pack. There may be only one read/write head for the whole stack (as in the IBM 1301) which has to be moved from disk to disk as well as from track to track. In modern usage, there is usually one head per recording surface, mounted on a comblike access mechanism. Indeed, in some disk drives there are four or more heads per surface. Each additional read/write head adds to the cost, but reduces access time and optimizes other design parameters.

In the designs that have one or more heads per surface, the recordable area is viewed logically as being divided into cylinders. A cylinder is all the area that can be used in one position of the access arm. This results in a series of concentric magnetic drums rather than parallel plane surfaces. This view is adopted because track-to-track transition is accomplished electronically within a cylinder, but mechanically and therefore slowly between cylinders.

For users with low budgets and reasonable patience, a small, cheap, slow computer connected to an adequate magnetic disk has properties very similar to those of a computer with unlimited internal memory. The disk looks very fast to a slow computer, and the low cost makes waiting economically feasible.

magnetic drum A cylinder with a magnetizable external surface on which data can be read or written by magnetic recording techniques.

Drums are made to revolve at high speed about their axes while many read/write heads float a few millionths of an inch off their external surfaces. These surfaces are usually plated with magnetic alloy and very highly polished.

The surface of a drum is divided into circular tracks, each as wide as a read/write head. In most devices the heads remain fixed, and each defines a track. There exist some movable-head drums with a behavior similar to that of magnetic disks.

Data are addressed on a drum by specifying the track number and word number within the drum. Often, one or more (non-data-storing) clock tracks serve to index the drum by providing current word-number indications (as in the IBM 650).

Drums offer large-capacity data storage with the fastest access of any mechanical (moving) storage, but at relatively high cost per digit because of the need for many costly read/write heads and for precision machining of surfaces.

magnetic ink A printer's ink that contains iron oxide particles. Magnetized characters of the same size and style can be directly sensed through automatic means.

magnetic-ink character recognition (MICR) That branch of character recognition which involves the sensing of magnetic-ink characters for the purpose of determining the character's most probable identity. Contrast with optical character recognition (OCR).

magnetic storage A storage device utilizing magnetic properties of materials to store data. May be roughly divided into two categories: moving (drum, disk, tape) and static (core, thin film).

Moving-storage devices operate by moving the recorded surface past a read/write head. The surface is magnetized alternately in one direction and the opposite direction. The existence and location of the flux reversals serve to record the data. In the technique called NRZI (nonreturn to zero, change on ones), a magnetic flux reversal indicates a one bit, the absence of a reversal being a zero bit. In phase encoding, the timing of the reversals indicates 0 or 1, and a reversal is guaranteed for each bit. Many other coding schemes exist.

Static memory devices operate at higher speeds, limited only by logical switching circuits and electrical propagation delays, but cost more per bit of information. Magnetic cores are the most common static storage today. Magnetic thin films are coming into use in very high speed applications. NCR has developed a magnetic-rod static storage, and General Precision has developed a woven-wire static memory. Bell Telephone Laboratories has a twistor memory element (spirals of hard and soft magnetic materials wrapped around a thick wire), RCA has a printed-circuit flat ferrite wafer, ITT (England) has a similar waffle-shaped ferrite sheet, and UNIVAC uses a plated-wire memory in its 9300 computer. All operate by magnetizing discrete cores or parts of continuous magnetic media.

magnetic tape   A tape with a magnetic surface on which data can be stored by selective magnetization.

The tape is a long ribbon of polyester plastic, coated on one side with a suspension of magnetic oxide or ferrite particles in a suitable binder. The most usual tape size is ½ inch wide, 1½ mils (0.0015 inch) thick, and 2400 feet long. Tape widths of ¼, ¾, and 1 inch and lengths of 200, 300, 600, 1200, and 3600 feet are also used in the digital computer field.

Data are recorded on the tape by magnetizing narrow lengthwise stripes (called tracks) in alternating directions. The data are encoded by the existence and location of the magnetic flux reversals. The density of recorded information is commonly 200, 556, or 800 bits per linear inch, but 1100- and 1600-bit-per-inch (BPI) tape is also used. The capacity of a common seven-track 2400-foot tape is about 5 million to 20 million characters, depending upon density (compared to 7 million for an IBM 2311 disk pack). Magnetic tape is the least expensive vehicle for storage at this time. Its shortcoming is that it has to be read serially, and consequently may be time-consuming if the required information is randomly distributed throughout the tape.

It took over 70 years to develop O. Smith's 1880 invention, a cotton thread impregnated with steel dust, into the up to 1600-bit-per-inch tape available today. Smith's work was improved by Poulsen who developed the necessary technique to record with steel wire. By 1927, a high-quality reproduction was available, and Pfleumer started experimenting with paper and plastic tapes coated with powdered magnetic materials. The first commercially successful voice recorder was probably the Lorentz machine, a wire recorder, and the first magnetic-tape machine was the Magnetophone. The main impulse to magnetic tape was given by the advent of computers on the commercial scene, and new magnetic-film carriers are constantly being developed.

Almost every computer can be adapted to use IBM-compatible tapes. IBM standard formats for ½ inch tape are seven-track, even parity (200, 556, and 800 BPI) and nine-track, odd parity (800 and 1600 BPI). Other computer manufacturers have noncompatible tape formats which they believe offer advantages over the IBM standards. Honeywell prefers to use odd parity as standard (as it is easier to detect blank characters or dropped bits), and UNIVAC has a Uniservo format (a clocking or synchronizing feature to compensate for tape speed discrepancies).

A magnetic tape may also be a ribbon of uniformly magnetic material, with one or two electrically insulated surfaces, used to make some kinds of magnetic cores. When this ribbon is formed into a tight roll, a toroidal core of magnetic material results. These cores are commonly used to make transformers for low-power signal circuits. Magnetic-memory cores are not usually constructed this way, however, because the technique cannot be used for the very small sizes encountered in memory applications.

magnetic thin film　A layer of magnetic material, usually less than one micron thick, used for logic or storage elements.

Strictly speaking, a thin film is a film whose physical properties are determined mostly by the surface effects (most of the atoms or molecules in the film lie on or near a surface). A thick film is one whose physical properties are determined by the bulk properties of the material (most atoms are surrounded by other atoms).

Thin film has sometimes been loosely used to refer to both types of film.

Magnetic thin-film devices offer very high speed and small size, but costs are high because of the great difficulty encountered in maintaining consistent results and achieving the desired quality in the production process.

main storage　A digital computer's principal working storage, from which instructions can be executed or operands fetched for data manipulation.

A modern computer has a variety of types of memory, or storage. Each type has its own characteristic speed and cost per bit. The computer designer attempts to balance the quantity of each kind of memory to achieve maximum processing capability at minimum cost. In order of decreasing speed and decreasing cost per bit, the memories are as follows:

1. Active registers such as transistors and integrated circuits
2. Scratch-pad memory: thin film or very high-speed core
3. Main memory: usually magnetic core, sometimes thin film or drum
4. Magnetic drum and disk
5. Other storage: magnetic tape, punched card, perforated tape

Scratch-pad-type memories and magnetic drums or disks may be omitted in some designs, but active registers, cores, or thin films, and magnetic tapes, punched cards, or perforated tapes are always present. Active registers are embedded in the computing circuitry itself, and magnetic tapes, punched cards, or perforated tapes are generally the usual means of input and output.

All computer programs must be located in main memory when they are being executed. Computer instructions can only be executed from locations in main memory (occasionally from drum, but this is rare). Most of the data to be operated on must also be in main memory, or execution time for a program will be very long. From these considerations it can be seen that the capacity of main memory directly affects the complexity of problems that can be economically solved on a given computer. By using lower-level memory, it is possible to solve problems of great complexity, but at substantial cost in running time.

The cycle time of main memory determines the rhythm or allowable operating speed of the electronic components. For this reason the speed of the main memory is just as important as its capacity.

maintenance Any activity intended to keep equipment or programs in satisfactory working condition.

Preventive maintenance is a routine procedure performed once, twice, or three times daily, designed to keep a computer running in optimum physical condition and prevent any preventable malfunctions. Typical functions include cleaning read/write heads, running diagnostic (error-detecting) programs, checking voltages, and emptying chaff baskets. By sacrificing 15 minutes out of every 8 hours of operation, the reliability of the operation during the other 7¾ hours is greatly increased.

File maintenance is any procedure designed to keep a data file or data bank current. This usually involves the routinely scheduled running of a program which adds new information to the file and deletes obsolete or out-of-date information. The operation is often performed by copying (with additions and deletions) from an old file to a new one. The old file may be saved as backup data in case the new file develops mechanical data reliability problems. This is called the grandfather data-file concept.

Program maintenance is the correction of detected errors in a program that has been declared operational. It should be emphasized that (except in the case of very simple programs) no program is ever fully debugged or infallible. All computing centers have procedures for correcting their programs as errors or shortcoming are discovered. Ideally, a record of all program errors and corrections should be included in the documentation of the program.

Software maintenance is a form of program maintenance, but on a larger scale. A computer manufacturer supplies with his computers a set of programs called software, for example, assemblers, compilers, operating systems, and sorting routines. There should be established procedures for reporting detected errors to the manufacturer. He in turn warns all users of the error condition and then releases a revised program with the error correction incorporated. The users should have personnel assigned to keeping the software in use at each computer center up-to-date on the latest revisions by the manufacturer.

majority A logic operator having the property that if P, Q, R are statements, then the function (P, Q, R . . .) is true if more than half the statements are true, false if half or less are true. This concept finds an application in the majority voting logic.

Majority voting logic is a form of hardware organization used where utmost reliability is required. It involves duplicating all functional elements an odd number of times, supplying each duplicate element with identical inputs, and comparing the outputs. An output must be generated in identical form by an absolute majority of the redundant units in order to be considered valid. Naturally, the majority-comparison circuits must be duplicated too. This duplication of components has been made feasible by modern integrated-circuit technology, which permits constructing numerous circuits in a very small volume and at low cost.

The failure of one adder to function properly does not prevent the correct sum from being provided to the next stage. In addition, the majority logic elements can function as error/failure detectors. As two out of three adders would have to fail in order to stop the operation, reliability is much higher than for each individual adder. Naturally, cost, power consumption, and time delay (voting logic) are sacrificed for reliability. See accompanying illustration.

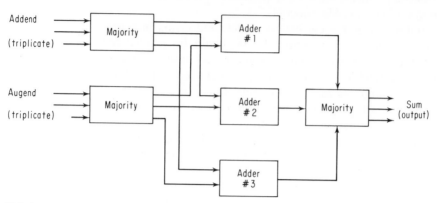

Majority.

malfunction Similar to ordinary English. For example: the failure of a card reader to read every card in a deck.

manual input The entry of data by hand into a device at the time of processing.

If in computing, a request for an item of information is issued to the operator by the computer, the computer halts (or does some other task) until the operator answers by entering the required information through a keyboard or other device. Both action and information are called manual input. This practice is particularly wasteful of the time of large, fast computers, but is conservative of memory in small, slow machines.

Manual input is more commonly used in data processing devices less powerful than computers.

map An output produced by an assembler, compiler, linkage editor, or relocatable loader which indicates the (absolute or relocatable) locations of such elements as programs, subroutines, variables, or arrays.

This type of map helps a programmer find his program parameters inside the computer at execution time or in a dump of memory.

By extension, map is an index of the storage allocation on a magnetic disk or drum.

MAP is also an acronym for macrossembly program, a set of assembly (symbolic machine) languages for the IBM 7090 and 7040 series of computers, and the assemblers for these languages. The

MAP assemblers operate under the IBSYS operating systems and prepare relocatable or absolute binary output in computer language.

The MAP language, as its name indicates, includes a powerful macroexpansion facility. Certain macros (SAVE, RETURN) associated with program linkage are built in the assembler, but any others can be defined by the programmer.

A noteworthy feature of MAP is its ability to handle relatively complex addresses, leaving them in a form that the relocating loader can resolve just before execution time. In this way an address relative to an undefined symbolic location can be assembled into an instruction.

marginal check A preventive maintenance procedure in which certain operating conditions are varied about their nominal values in order to test for incipient defective parts.

For instance, suppose that a circuit is to operate from a normal dc supply voltage of 22 volts, but is rated for correct operation at 20 to 25 volts. A marginal check would be conducted at 20 or 25 volts, using a test program or other procedure.

Naturally, the supply would be adjusted to 22 volts for normal operation. It is expected that a device that operates correctly under marginal conditions will function properly at its correct operating condition.

mark A distinguishing feature used to signal some particular location or condition. See FLAG.

mark detection That class of character-recognition systems which employs coded documents, in the form of "boxes" or "windows," in order to convey intended information.

EXAMINATION QUESTIONS

1. Mark Detection is a method of character recognition
   Answer: Only one
   A. True
   B. False

2. The most common form of Mark Detection is:
   Answer: Only one
   A. Mark Sensing
   B. Toe-the-Mark
   C. Mark Reading

3. Other method(s) of character recognition include:
   Answer: One or more
   A. Mechanical Character Recognition
   B. Optical Character Recognition
   C. Character Guidance
   D. Magnetic Ink Character Recognition

EXAMINATION ANSWERS

An example of mark detection: examination answers.

Mark detection is often thought of in terms of its most common form, mark reading (the two terms have been used interchangeably). Mark-reading systems employ optical character-recognition (OCR) techniques; whereas mark-sensing systems seek out the presence and/or absence of graphite particles.

The detection of coded marks has found many applications in data capture such as census returns, meter readings, and examination answer sheets.

Information is recorded by making a distinct mark in the desired windows. In the event that a mark is made in error, it may be deleted by erasure. The degree to which erasure is accomplished determines whether it will be recognized as a mark, no mark, or a doubtful mark. Doubtful marks, which may also result from extraneous pencil marks, thumb marks, etc., may be a cause for document rejection in some machines.

mark reading   In character recognition, that form of mark detection which employs a photoelectric device for the purpose of locating and conveying intended information. The information to be conveyed appears as special marks on special sites ("windows") within the document coding area.

The scanner utilized for mark reading is usually a row of photoelectric cells which measure the reflected light from the document. Each cell is usually assigned to one column of windows and detects the presence of a mark when the reflectance falls. If the reflectance falls quickly enough and far enough, then a mark has been detected. If the change in reflectance is slow or too small, then the mark is considered doubtful. Contrast with MARK SENSING. See also MARK DETECTION.

mark sense   A means of supplying information to data processing machines. It involves electrically or optically sensing black marks made in designated places on a form or card by a dark pencil. A common example is the electronically graded questions and a preprinted answer form:

	T	F		A	B	C	D
13	″	″	39	″	″	″	″
14	″	″	40	″	″	″	″
15	″	″	41	″	″	″	″

The advantage of mark sense is that no special skill or equipment is needed to prepare the data; the disadvantage is that marks are easily misplaced.

mark sensing In character recognition, that form of mark detection which depends on the conductivity of graphite pencil marks in order to locate and convey intended information. The information to be conveyed appears as special marks on special sites ("windows") within the document coding area.

This form of detection presupposes the use of graphite pencils and is not applicable to printed outputs or pens. The reject rate is generally higher than that of mark reading. Contrast with MARK READING. See also MARK DETECTION.

mask A pattern of characters used to control the retention or elimination of portions of another pattern of characters.

A mask is usually a word or string of characters containing all 1-bits in positions where data of another string are to be preserved, and containing 0-bits in all positions where data of the second string are to be ignored (or deleted). The mask is usually combined with its target data in a logical AND operation (sometimes called extract).

example

Mask before and after	Target before	Target after
000111000	010011100	000011000

This action kept the middle 3 bits out of a field of 9 bits.

To mask an interrupt is to prevent a particular condition or signal from interrupting the computer at this time. An interrupt that has been masked off is either ignored or held waiting until the mask is removed. See FILTER, INTERRUPT.

mask matching In character recognition, a method employed in character property detection in which a correlation or match is attempted between a specimen character and each of a set of masks representing the characters to be recognized.

Mask-matching techniques are based on the condition that the characters are deliberately registered on the reference masks. Therefore there is an inherent disadvantage in this method primarily insofar as no allowance is made for character misregistration.

The masks presently being utilized in direct matching procedures include:

Holistic masks: which require an exact match

Peep-hole masks: which provide more lenient character appearances but still act on go–no go basis

Weighted area masks: which assign a most probable identity to the input specimen

matched filter   In character recognition, a method employed in character property detection in which a vertical projection of the input character produces an analog waveform which is then compared to a set of stored waveforms for the purpose of determining the character's identity.   See PROPERTY DETECTOR.

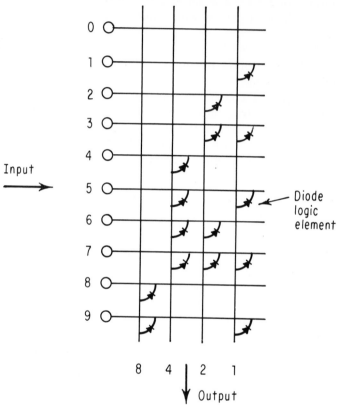

Input

Diode
logic
element

8   4   2   1

Output

Diode matrix.

mathematical model   A mathematical representation of a process, device, or concept by means of a number of variables which are defined to represent the inputs, outputs, and internal states of the device or process, and a set of equations and inequalities describing the interaction of these variables.

The model is used by specifying the inputs and solving the equations (subject to the constraining inequalities).   The resulting output variables should predict the output of the thing being modeled.

A model usually does not attempt to describe something in complete detail, but is generally simplified to be of manageable complexity. A model should include all pertinent effects, however, so that the desired information is correctly predicted.

matrix A latticework of input and output leads with logic elements connected at some of their intersections.

A common example is the diode matrix which is used to additively combine a number of inputs into outputs without interaction among the inputs.

Such a diode matrix will encode decimal into binary. For instance, a positive pulse on input line 5 will be admitted on output lines 4 and 1. The output terminals (in this case) will have the configuration 0101 (where 1 indicates a pulse status), which is the binary equivalent of decimal 5. The blocking property of diodes prevents any output signal from influencing the output lines (in this case, input lines 1, 3, 4, 6, 7, 9).

mechanical scanner In optical character recognition (OCR), a device that projects an input character onto a rotating disk, around the periphery of which is a series of small uniformly spaced apertures. As the disk rotates, a photocell collects the light passing through the apertures. The result of this operation is an analog waveform which is the basis for the subsequent decision as to the character's most probable identity.

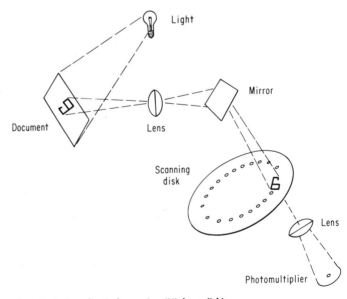

A method of mechanical scanning (Nipkow disk).

In the mechanical scanner the area to be scanned is brightly illuminated by some convenient light source. The illuminated area is then projected, through a lens, onto the rotating disk, the aperture of which may be of varying shapes and relative positions.

One disk, known as the Nipkow disk, has circular apertures located at varying radial distances, and arranged in such a way that in the course of a complete revolution a two-dimensional area is exhaustively scanned.

Another disk employs square apertures cut at equal radial distances about the periphery. The horizontal-scan component is then given by the document motion.

Mechanical scanning has been the most-used method of OCR to date, in spite of its relatively low scanning rate. Some of its most obvious advantages are its simplicity of operation and maintenance, low cost, and less stringent requirements, especially with regard to ambient illumination.

media   See CUT FORM, CONTINUOUS FORMS.

medium   The material, or configuration thereof, on which data are recorded, usually not applied to disk, drum, core, but rather to storable, removable media such as paper tape, cards, and magnetic tape.

memory   Any apparatus in which data may be stored, and from which the same data may be retrieved.

Most high-speed memories today use magnetic principles for storage. Electrostatic memories use specially constructed vacuum tubes or capacitors. Acoustic memories use sound waves on mercury puddles or in glass blocks. Electronic memories use transistors (discrete or integrated) or vacuum tubes in flip-flop configurations.

Central memory is the internal high-speed large-capacity working storage of a digital computer. All instructions executed by a computer are fetched from central memory. Auxiliary or external memory devices (tapes, disks, drums, etc.) are usually called storage to distingiush them from central memory. (The IBM 7080, however, has both memory and storage internal.)

See STORAGE.

mercury storage   A storage device utilizing the acoustic properties of mercury to store data.

Basically, it consists of a long, narrow, and shallow puddle of mercury with a piezoelectric element at each end. The first element converts electricity to sound waves which travel on the surface of the liquid to the far end. The other element, acting like a microphone, converts the sound back to electricity. The electric signal is amplified manyfold (to account for losses) and reinserted at the original piezoelectric element. Thus each signal travels in a closed circuit, with time delay provided by the acoustic wave. A signal is read out by waiting for it to emerge at the microphone end, and copying it out.

The signal is inserted by actuating the sending transducer at the correct time. Because of the delay-line nature of the device, mercury storage is somewhat slow in access time. Other disadvantages of mercury are susceptibility to shock or jarring, high cost, poisonous fumes, tendency to oxidize, and nonpermanence of data in event of electrical failure. Mercury storage is not used much at the present time.

merge To create an ordered set of data by combining properly the contents of two or more sets of data, each originally ordered in the same manner as the output data set (combining sets of data by uniting them one behind the other is called concatenation).

For example, reports from several branch offices can be merged into one unified file:

Files to be merged			Merged file
Item #	Item #	Item #	Item #
1004	2560	1501	1004
2198	3675	2732	1501
2407	3741	4950	2198
3952		6800	2407
			2560
			2732
			3675
			3741
			3952
			4950
			6800

message An arbitrary amount of information with beginning and end defined or implied: usually, this quantity of information originates in one place and is intended to be transmitted to another place. The information content of a message is called its text. On a transmission medium with only two ends (or terminals), a message could consist entirely of text. In a message switching system a message usually consists of the header (start of message, destinations), the text, and the trailer (end of message, and sometimes, origin of message). This is best illustrated by means of a letter:

Heading ⎫
Salutation ⎰   Header
Body of letter   Text
Signature   Trailer

Message can be contrasted with record, a quantity of related information that is physically contiguous and is treated as a unit. A record does not imply transmission but usually storage; a message implies transmission.

mickey mouse   A verb frequently used in computer centers whenever new equipment or systems are introduced.

To mickey mouse is to play with something new, hardware, software, or system, until a feel is gotten for it and the proper operating procedure is discovered, understood, and mastered.

microprogram   The sequence of elementary steps which permits the computer hardware to carry out a computer instruction.

A microprogram may be considered as the last act in the series of operations involved in solving a problem on a computer. These operations can be illustrated as follows:

1. The problem to be solved is transformed by the analyst into one or more formulae or procedures.

2. Each formula or procedure is transformed by the programmer into a set of higher-level programming language instructions.

3. Each higher-level programming language instruction is transformed by the compiler into a set of computer instructions.

4. Each computer instruction is transformed by a microprogram into a set of microinstructions, and it is these millions of microinstructions which, collectively, perform the formal logic or procedures originally set forth by the analyst.

A microinstruction is thus the smallest unit of action that a computer can perform.   Each microinstruction is coded as several bits, one bit for each functional unit or data path in the computer hardware. The one-for-one correspondence between bit positions and functional units allows for very simple interpretation of each microinstruction. The size of a microinstruction (that is, its number of bits) depends directly upon the complexity of the hardware of the computer: small computers use small microinstructions but may correspondingly require a larger number of microinstructions than larger computers with larger (that is, a greater number of bits) microinstructions.

A microinstruction word contains the address of the next micro-instruction to be executed. Either a separate "decision" microinstruction or a decision capability built into each microinstruction word available allows for testing, looping, branching, and subroutine structures to be implemented at the microprogram level. This permits similar computer instructions to share microprogram steps, thereby increasing efficiency and reducing costs.

A simple microprogram can serve as an illustration. Consider a LOAD INTO ACCUMULATOR REGISTER instruction for a computer having one address per computer instruction, indirect addressing, and index register. The microprogram might appear as follows:

A. Transfer address field from current-instruction register to address-modification circuit.

B. Transfer contents of designated index register to address-modification circuit; signal address addition to be performed.

C. Transfer address from address-modification circuit to address register of memory control; signal read operation to be performed.

D. If the indirect address to be performed is not specified in the current-instruction register, go to microstep F, otherwise go to microstep E.

E. Transfer index register designator, address field, and indirect address designator from memory-data register to the current-instruction register; go to microstep A.

F. Clear accumulator to zeros; transfer the entire memory-data register to the accumulator register; go to the read-next-instruction microprogram.

Microprogramming came of age with the third-generation computers. The operation code (which identifies the computer instruction) was interpreted by wired-in logic elements in all first-generation computers. Most second-generation computers also had wired-in logic elements to interpret codes, but practically all third-generation computers carry out this op code interpretation by means of microprogramming. Wired-in interpretation is fast but expensive, thereby limiting the number of op codes that can be interpreted. It is cheaper to establish a microprogram memory which can hold many microprograms and thus allow for a large set of computer instructions which can be interpreted and implemented on simple and inexpensive computer hardware. In such computers, sometimes called microprogrammed computers, each computer instruction operation code defines the beginning of the corresponding microprogram stored in the microprogram memory. Although microprograms are usually fixed permanently in memory, alterable microprogram memories have been developed to allow for many sets of different instructions to be implemented on the same computer hardware.

The development of faster and more efficient microroutines is the responsibility of a special breed of programmers called microprogrammers.

minimum distance code   A binary code in which the signal distance does not fall below a specified minimum value.

A minimum distance code has the property of being interpretable under specific noise conditions.

> **example:**   A code of minimum distance 3 is constructed so that at least 3 binary digits (bits) must be changed to convert one valid code to another.   A great many invalid codes will thus be unusable for data transmission, but will be recognized as errors when received. Suppose that only one bit has been incorrectly received.   The resulting invalid code is at a signal distance of 1 from the correct code (i.e.:   it differs by only one bit) but is at a distance of 2, 4, or more from every other valid code.   Thus most errors, and all 1-bit-per-code errors, can be corrected at the receiving station.
>
> A 6-bit code of distance 3 can accommodate 27 distinct valid characters, compared to 32 characters for a distance-2 (error-detecting but not self-correcting) code of 6 bits, and 64 characters for a maximum-density 6-bit code.

misregistration   In character recognition, the improper state of appearance of a character, line, or document, on site in a character reader, with respect to a real or imaginary horizontal baseline.

If registration marks are employed, witness a handwriting coding sheet, then the horizontal baseline is real.   Otherwise the baseline is imaginary as in the case of tally rolls.

Misregistration occurs when the character reader cannot locate the desired element in relation to its horizontal baseline.   Consequently, a corrective routine is performed hopefully to normalize the element, and present it to the reader in its intended position.   Contrast with REGISTRATION.   See DOCUMENT MISREGISTRATION, LINE MISREGISTRATION, CHARACTER MISREGISTRATION.

mistake   A human action producing an unintended result.

It is becoming the usual practice to differentiate mistakes, errors, and noise in the following way:

1.   Mistakes occur in human actions.
2.   Errors occur in computer operations.
3.   Noise occurs in transmission systems.

mixed radix   Pertaining to a numeration system using more than one radix, such as the biquinary system.

Immediate examples of mixed-radix systems are the English currency (pounds, shillings, pence) and time (hours, minutes, seconds).

In ordinary positional numerals (decimal, octal, binary), each position indicates a power of a fixed base or radix. Thus:

$$204.5_{10} \text{ means: } \quad 2 \times 10^2 + 0 \times 10^1 + 4 \times 10^0 + 5 \times 10^{-1}$$
$$\text{or: } \quad 200 \quad + \quad 0 \quad + \quad 4 \quad + \quad .5 \quad = 204.5$$

In mixed-radix numerals, each position indicates a different interpretation of the digit, but the base or radix changes. In biquinary, successive digits are alternately to base 2 and base 5. Thus every numeral is represented by digits with the following weights:

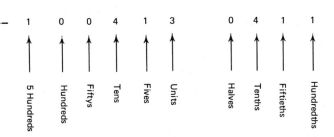

Each digit position thus increases (or decreases) in value by alternately 2 or 5. The first digit of each pair (binary) is 0 or 1; the second (quinary) digit is 0, 1, 2, 3, or 4. *Any* decimal numeral of *N* digits can be written in 2*N* biquinary digits.

Biquinary was used for decimal representation in the IBM 650, but mixed-radix numerals are rare nowadays.

mode   One of several alternative conditions or methods of operation of a device.

For instance:

1. An input/output device such as magnetic tape operated in transmitting mode is actually reading or writing; in nontransmitting mode it is only skipping tape (rewinding).

2. A magnetic tape written in BCD mode has even parity and a particular encoding of data: a tape written in binary mode has core-image representation of data and odd parity.

3. A computer operating in emulation mode actually executes the instructions of a different (simpler) computer; in normal mode it executes its own instructions.

4. A computer operating in supervisor mode can execute all its own instructions, including the privileged instructions not normally allowed to the programmer; in the problem mode, the privileged in-

structions cannot be executed:this prevents a program from upsetting the supervisor program or any other program.

See ACCESS MODE.

model A thing that is used to represent or describe another thing (the latter sometimes called the prototype). This model may be similar in form (a model boat) or entirely dissimilar in form (a mathematical model) from the prototype.

The purpose of a model in data processing is to enable one to learn about the thing or process being modeled. See ANALOG, MATHEMATICAL MODEL.

Modem An acronym for modulator-demodulator. A hardware device that converts data from one form (or code) to another, usually for purposes of transmission. Thus a *modem* is commonly the interface between a data-sending (or receiving) device and common carrier lines. By more sophisticated coding techniques a *modem* may permit faster transmission over a given channel than a competitive *modem*.

module A generic term which may stand for a distinct and identifiable unit of program for such purposes as compiling, loading, and linkage editing; a functional entity of program in some language and some format; a functional element of hardware, having considerable internal complexity; more frequently nowadays, one memory bank and associated electronics.

In all cases, a module is a functional unit having known properties. In general, a system of interacting components is modular if it is possible to add, remove, or interchange modules, to convert from one organization to another operable organization having different or similar functional properties. An example is a high-fidelity system consisting of separate but interconnected radio tuner, record player, preamplifier, power amplifier, and speakers. It is possible to exchange the tuner for a newer and more sensitive tuner, thereby upgrading the quality of radio reception. This is an example of interchanging similar-function modules. It is also possible to add a tape recorder, thereby adding new capability to the system. Finally, it is possible to replace any malfunctioning unit with an identical, operable unit. This interchangeability improves the ease of repair.

Much as in the above example, many computer designs permit adding or replacing hardware modules to vary the capability of the system. Memory modules may be added, additional I/O devices and data channels, and even multiple processing units (CPU's). The larger IBM 360 systems, the SDS Sigma 7 series, the Burroughs 5500 series, and the UNIVAC 9000 series computers are examples of modular computer designs.

A program module could be a source module (as written by the programmer, or transcribed into computer-readable form), an object module (output of an assembler, compiler, or generator), or a load module (a program in a loadable form, essentially ready to be executed). Modern complex operating systems are composed of modules or interchangeable instruction routines. An installation may choose the modules that best meet its needs, including or omitting any optional modules, and so construct an operating system specialized for its own particular needs.

modulo N check A procedure for verification of the accuracy of a computation by repeating the steps in modulo N arithmetic and comparing the result with the original result (modulo N).

In modulo N arithmetic, no number is allowed to get larger than $N - 1$ in magnitude. All numbers are cyclic; thus: 0, 1, 2, ..., $N - 1$, 0, 1, . . . , $N - 2$, $N - 1$, 0, 1, ... A number is *congruent* to another number, modulo N, if the remainder after dividing each number by N is the same. Thus 5 and 23 are congruent modulo 9.

Repeating an operation in modulo N arithmetic usually involves much less computation than repeating it in full-precision (ordinary) arithmetic. If the answer is congruent to the original answer modulo N, then the answer is probably right.

For instance, the checking process called casting out nines is really a modulo 9 check. This may be seen as follows:

$$
\begin{array}{ll}
52 \quad 7 & 52 = 10 \times 5 + 2 = 9 \times 5 + 5 + 2 \quad 7 \\
21 \quad 3 & 21 = 10 \times 2 + 1 = 9 \times 2 + 2 + 1 \quad 3 \\
\quad\quad\quad \text{since} & \\
9 \quad 0 & 9 \quad\quad\quad\quad\quad\quad 9 \times 1 + 0 \quad\quad\quad 0 \\
\overline{82} \quad \overline{1} & 82 = 10 \times 8 + 2 = 9 \times 8 + 8 + 2 \quad \overline{10} \\
& \quad\quad\quad \text{and} \quad 10 = 9 + 1 \quad 1
\end{array}
$$

Same as RESIDUE CHECK.

monadic operation An operation on one operand, as for instance, a negation.

monostable Referring to a device that has only one stable state. A monostable device (or circuit) may have several states, but it will spontaneously leave every state except its one stable state (for instance, a child's knockdown, self-erecting toys).

A common electronic example is the monostable flip-flop, a circuit that has two output states. It is normally in one state, but may be switched to the other state by an input signal. After a fixed time delay, the flip-flop spontaneously reverts to the stable configuration. A flip-flop is used to generate pulses of fixed duration but of variable frequencies.

move mode   A method of communicating between an operating program and an input/output control system (IOCS) in which the data records to be read or written are actually moved into and out of program-designated memory areas. This method may be contrasted with LOCATE MODE in which the data records remain in place but the addresses of the data areas are communicated.

Input/output operations of modern digital computers (in all but the very simplest designs) are handled by standardized, all-purpose input/output routines called IOCS (or by some similar names). The problem-solving programs direct the I/O operations by passing parameters and data records to or from the IOCS routines. In almost every case, move mode operation is offered by the I/O routines. A program requests an input operation by writing something like

READ   Filename, Location.

Filename designates the input file, data set, device, or input stream to be read, and Location is the address of the first character (leftmost position) of the area of memory to receive the input data. The I/O routine reads the data and moves the next logical record into the designated area.

In the same way, an output operation is requested by

WRITE   Filename, Location.

Here Filename designates the destination of the data, and Location is the address of the beginning of the data to be written out. IOCS copies the data into an available output buffer, schedules the hardware operation, and returns control to the problem program for further processing. Naturally the exact details of the operation depend on the computer and operating system being used.

The I/O routines normally handle label writing and checking, blocking, unblocking, padding, and overlap of I/O with computing. Parameters to control these operations are provided in a manner that is usually independent of move mode or locate mode operation.

On computers having no index registers, base registers, or other address-modifying hardware, move mode operation must be used.

multiaddress   Referring to an instruction that has more than one address part.

The number of operands involved in an operation depends on the nature of the operation. For instance:

Operation	Number of operands
Halt	0
Change sign	1
Move A to B	2
Add A to B giving C	3

It is clear that efficiency is increased by allowing each instruction to have the number of operands it needs, but no more than that number. If the instructions of a computer are of fixed format (constant number of address parts), then a compromise is reached on the number of operands that must be used. This number will vary with the computer. For instance:

(1) IBM 7090.
   Single-address add: Add A-address (to current contents of accumulator; leave sum in accumulator)
(2) Honeywell 200.
   Double-address add: Add A-address to B-address (leave sum in B-address)
(3) CDC 6600.
   Triple-address add: Add address 1 to address 2 with result in address 3 (no implied information)

It can be seen that multiaddress (multiple operand) instructions add power and flexibility compared to a single-address instruction.

multijob operation   The concurrent or interleaved execution of job steps from more than one job.

Multijob operation is a kind of multiprogramming (running multiple programs on an interleaved, or simultaneous, basis). While any job step is waiting for some external event to occur before it can continue processing, another program is running. In this way all parts of the computer attain high productivity.

In multijob operation, each program, job step, or task within the system has its own instruction and data areas. There may be sharing of I/O devices between tasks (this, however, is rare, and occurs only if multiple tasks are within the same job step). To simplify the control of the system, there is no attempt to share an internal copy of a routine among several tasks. In effect, a multijob operation fragments the computer into many noninteracting individual sections. The various jobs divide the I/O devices among themselves, with no sharing (except possibly for the operating system resident device). The several job steps take turns using CPU time. Scheduling is concerned principally with what it is possible to run, and which job has priority.

A more complex form of multiprogramming is called multitask operation. See MULTITASK OPERATION.

multiplex   To interleave or simultaneously transmit two or more messages on a single channel.

Two principal forms of multiplex operation should be noted.

1.   In communications, many analog and digital signals can be transmitted on one broadband channel by modulating each signal on a carrier of different frequency. This type of multiplexing is known as frequency multiplexing. (A very similar principle is used to transmit FM stereo).

2.   In some communications applications, time-division multiplexing is used. Conceptually, the time of transmission is divided into frames of equal duration. During each frame, every signal would be sampled and the samples transmitted in a known sequence. This may be visualized as a circular switch of many contacts (called a commutator) which successively connects each input in turn to the output line. The time of one revolution of the switch defines the duration of a frame. If one signal needed twice the transmission bandwidth of the others, it could be connected to two contacts on the rotary switch (that is, it is sampled twice per frame), a technique called supercommutation. If two signals each need only half the typical bandwidth of other signals, they may be connected alternately to one contact (each sampled once per two frames). This is equal to a commutator feeding a commutator, and is consequently called subcommutation.

In digital computers, a multiplex input/output channel operates in a manner similar to communications time-division multiplexing. Instead of operating on a fixed schedule, the various devices attached to the multiplex channel function in a demand-feeding mode. The multiplexor interrogates each device in turn at high speed, and tests whether it is ready to transmit or receive a character. This operation is called polling. If the device is ready, the character is sent and delivered to the correct destination within the computer.

The multiplexor must keep track of the current status of each subchannel (including transmit/receive/idle activity state) and of the current internal location of data in main memory.

multiprocessor   A computer capable of multiprocessing. Literally any device capable of performing more than one process at a time.

An everyday example is the V-8 automotive engine, with eight identical four-stroke thermodynamic processes occurring simultaneously, these processes being synchronized but out of phase with one another by a fixed amount. The engine has common outputs (shaft power, gases) and inputs (fuel, air), but parallel processing chambers (cylinders).

An exact parallel analogy in computers is offered by the 10 peripheral processors of the CDC 6600. This computer is equipped with 10 (identical, synchronized, but out-of-phase by a fixed amount) small computing units specialized in performing input, output, and overhead (housekeeping) duties for the central computing system. At any one instant, 10 independent programs (which may be similar or dissimilar) are in process, but each at a different degree of completion. There is a common input to all 10 processors (the central processor's memory) and common outputs (the peripheral I/O equipment) for the 10 processes. The structure is thus very much like a "V-10 data processing engine."

The central processor of a 6600 is a different type of multiprocessor. It executes only one program at any instant, but has many multiply, add, shift, and test functional units operating at the same time to improve processing speed.

The Honeywell 800 was an early powerful multiprocessing computer. It was equivalent to 8 conventional computers sharing a common memory. A hardware/software executive coordinated the eight processes to ensure efficient operation.

No other digital computers with extensive multiprocessing have been mass-produced to date, although one-of-a-kind examples do exist.

All analog computers multiprocess since simultaneity is the very basis of analog processing.

multiprogramming The interleaved execution of two or more programs by a computer.

Multiprogramming is a technique by means of which a digital computer can appear to process several programs at once, and yet still operate in a strictly sequential (nonparallel) manner. This is accomplished in the following way: If two or more different programs reside in main memory at the same time, the computer performs a number of instructions of the first program, then switches to the second program, performs a set of its instructions, then switches to the next program, and eventually comes back to the first program again, performs a few more instructions, and so on, until all the programs are completed.

There are three different but important reasons for multiprogramming:

1. To share a powerful processor among many users requiring its services, incidentally giving to each user the impression that he alone has the attention of the computer

2. To keep all the hardware of a powerful computer busy, thus increasing the productivity of the device by eliminating idle time

3. To permit real time on demand response from a computer without devoting it entirely to one task

In the first place, advantage is taken of the thousandfold speed superiority of electronics over neurons. The computer switches from task to task in a fixed-time interval, fixed-schedule, round-robin mode of operation, servicing every user for a few milliseconds out of each second. Each user then seems to have continuous, undivided attention of the computer.

In the second place, each program is executed until some event causes an interrupt, and a new program gains control. For example, a disk drive has moved its access arm, waited for the correct sector of the disk to come under the read/write head, and transferred a record while program 2 is operating. Completion of the event causes a return to program 1 (which issued the disk I/O request). Thus program 2 runs in the time that program 1 is waiting for any external event. This is an example of foreground/background organization, practical for medium-to-large computers. By properly mixing several concurrent programs, all of a large computer can be kept busy. Naturally the cost in memory space and overhead time must not be too high, or multiprogramming will not be warranted.

In the third place, an intermittent external event requires immediate service. A fast computer is required, but cannot be allowed to stand idle while waiting for important service requests. Therefore, the remainder of the computer's time and memory is devoted to conventional processing tasks. This last instance is similar in some aspects to the first two instances, and would find application in an information retrieval system (small scale) where requests for information would occur only a small fraction of the time.

multitask operation   A sophisticated method of multijobbing (that is, multiprogramming), or operating many programs on a simultaneous or interleaved basis. Multitask operation extends beyond ordinary multiprogramming in that it allows a single copy of a program module to be used by more than one task.

By job is meant a unit of work that is submitted by one person and that will have its costs charged to one account. A job consists of one or more job steps, each requiring a certain amount of the hardware facilities of the computer system. The operating system governs the usage of the computer and assists the programs by performing certain routine services for them. The job scheduler within the operating system may initiate new job steps until not enough machine facilities remain free to satisfy the requirements of any unstarted job steps. A job step may be divided into one or more tasks, each of which share the hardware allocated to the job step. All active tasks compete for processing time, and are served on the basis of their dispatching priority. Inactive tasks allow other work to be done while they are waiting for some event to occur. A task contains one or more program modules, or units of computer instruction routines. Only one program module can be in use by a task at any one time. Multijob operation allows a computer to attain a very high rate of productivity by falling back to a lower-priority task whenever the current task cannot be processed further. Multitask operation increases efficiency further by allowing several tasks to use one and the same program module to fill their processing needs.

A reenterable program module can be used by several tasks almost simultaneously, i.e., in an interleaved fashion. The module contains only the instructions and the constants that it needs, while all variable data, instructions, working storage, etc., are grouped together in a control section (unit of physically contiguous memory). The reenterable program module specifies the size and organization of this working-storage control section by means of a prototype control section. A prototype is a pattern or model of the working-storage area that must be provided by any task that uses the module for processing.

A serially reusable program can also be used by several tasks, but only by one task at a time. As soon as a task finishes using a reusable program module, another task can begin using this program module. In practical terms, this means that the reusable program reinitializes itself as it is used. This kind of module cannot be simultaneously shared in real time without loading a copy of the program for each task that must use it.

Programmers create reenterable or reusable modules by means of coding with the appropriate conventions and disciplines for each class of usage. The sharing of program modules among tasks conserves main memory space and saves program loading time, but complicates the scheduling and organizational chores of the operating system. The accompanying illustration summarizes the multitasking operation concept.

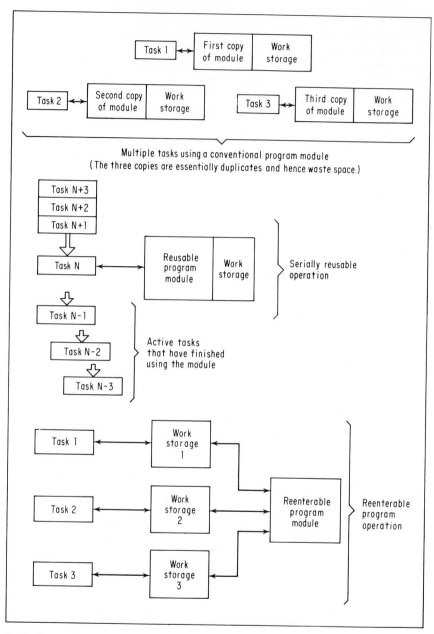

Multiple tasks using a conventional program module
(The three copies are essentially duplicates and hence waste space.)

Multitask-operation concepts.

N

NAND A logic operator having the characteristic that if P, Q, R, . . . are statements, then the NAND of P, Q, R, . . . is true if at least one statement is false, false if all statements are true.

The name and the operation itself is a combination of NOT and AND. AND is true if and only if all inputs are true, and the logical negation of this is false if and only if all inputs are true.

NAND has assumed inordinate importance in recent years because of a combination of technology and economics. Certain methods of constructing logical elements can produce NAND and NOR gates inexpensively and with simplicity. For this reason, designers of digital computers have sometimes been obliged to synthesize all desired logic from NAND and NOR circuits. Improvements in competitive circuit technology will undoubtedly eliminate this artificial situation.

natural language A language whose rules reflect and describe current rather than prescribed usage.

A natural language is often loose and ambiguous in interpretation, meaning different things to different hearers. This characteristic makes poetry and other verbal arts interesting and meaningful, but useless for computer application. This has led to the creation of artificial languages, usually much more precise and logical.

The precision of artificial languages renders them efficient for programming computers.

negate To convert an initially true value to false, or an initially false value to true as in logic, or to change the sign of an arithmetic quantity, as from +5 to −5, or to nullify or cancel, especially the effects of an earlier event.

NELIAC An acronym for Navy Electronics Laboratory International Algol Compilers, NELIAC is an early dialect of ALGOL.

Unlike ALGOL, NELIAC is not primarily concerned with being used for complex scientific and engineering calculations. NELIAC, in fact, was developed for a specific data processing application. For that reason, arithmetic is fixed point, only one dimensional arrays are allowed, etc.

One of the significant features of NELIAC is that it is written in its own language. This means that a listing of the system is its own description and can never be out of date.

The only reserved NELIAC words are FOR, IF, IF NOT, GO TO, DO, and COMMENTS. If for no other reason than this, NELIAC is a relatively easy language to learn.

A NELIAC program is divided into two parts. The first part of the program is a noun list. This symbolically defines all areas, sets initial values, and defines arrays and lists. The noun list ends with the first semicolon.

The second part of the program specifies the logical procedures to be followed. This is done in algorithm-type notation.

NELIAC's I/O ability is limited in some versions, and entirely missing in others, in which case use is made of subroutines, or complete I/O packages.

To illustrate the NELIAC language, the following program calculates the final amount represented by $10,000 invested at 6 percent compounded semiannually for 15 years.

YEARLY RATE = 6.0 × 0,	This sets up a field called YEARLY RATE which has an initial value of 6.0 times 10 to the 0 power. The 10 need not be written; it is implied.
NUMBER OF YEARS = 15,	This sets NUMBER OF YEARS at an arbitrary 15. If the initial value is a whole number, a power of 10 is not needed. The number may be written directly.
INCREASE = 0 × 0,	Here a zero floating-point field is set up.
PRINCIPAL = 1.0 × 4,	The initial value is arbitrarily set at 10,000.00 dollars.
VALUE = 0 × 0,	A field is set up at zeros to hold the final value after interest computation.
INTEREST PERIODS = 0 × 0;	This field will hold the product of 2 times the number of years, which is the number of 6-month interest periods. The semicolon ends the noun list.
COMPUTE INCREASE:	This is similar to a paragraph name.
1 + YEARLY RATE / 200 → INCREASE,	This calculates the factor which when multiplied by the amount, gives the amount plus interest. This is one time calculation.
2 × NUMBER OF YEARS → INTEREST PERIODS,	This multiplies two 6-month periods per year times the number of years which equals the number of times interest is to be calculated.
GO TO FIND TOTAL VALUE. FIND TOTAL VALUE:	An unconditional GO TO.
PRINCIPAL × INCREASE → PRINCIPAL,	This is a computation of principal times the 6-month interest rate (1.03). This must be executed once for each 6 months of deposit.

IF INTEREST PERIODS = 1: PRINT RESULTS.	This is a test to determine when the loop has been executed as many times as there are interest periods. If the condition is met, execution proceeds from beyond the colon up to the first period, then jumps to beyond the second period. Otherwise, the statements between the first and second periods are executed. Where the equal comparison is made, any of the following could be used: $\neq, <, >, \leq,$ or $\geq$.
IF NOT, INTEREST PERIODS − 1 → INTEREST PERIODS,	This is the alternative statement for the above comparison. One is subtracted from the remaining interest periods.

GO TO FIND TOTAL VALUE.
PRINT RESULT:
    , PRINT HEADING
        { <<COMPUTED VALUE>> }
	This is a heading line output statement, and is rather crude. The words COMPUTED VALUE will be printed on the systems printer.

, PRINT VALUE { <PRINCIPAL> } . .	This format prints numerical output data. The double periods indicate end of program.

network analyzer   A device or program for analyzing networks: essentially, a special-purpose analog computer.

Typical applications for network analyzers cover such fields as the following:

1. Electricity: power distribution over long transmission lines (power grids), dc circuit analysis, etc.

2. Electronics: analysis of performance of passive and active component networks (circuits), particularly frequency response and pulse response.

3. Hydrodynamics (hydraulics): flow through network of pipes, as in sewers or water supplies. Usually similar to electricity programs (above) because of strong electrical/hydraulic analog similarity.

4. Management and control techniques: PERT (program evaluation review technique) and CPM (critical path method) are means for

optimizing and controlling the elapsed time and/or cost of a project involving many separate operations.

5. Psychology (neurology): simulations of neuron networks, simple models of brain behavior.

Neumann, John Von (1903–1957)   Although primarily a pure mathematician, Von Neumann studied extensively the mathematical logic of the computer. In 1947, he devised a method for converting ENIAC, the computer built during World War II, from an externally programmed to a stored-program machine. Previously a problem had to be entered by making hand adjustments of the connections from one unit to another; Von Neumann first permanently wired a selection of operations for groups of units, and then placed these under central control. He suggested that numerals be treated as instruction codes, which could be stored electronically just as data numerals were stored, thus eliminating special instruction wiring. This stored-program concept led naturally to the development of self-modifying computers since machine commands could now be manipulated by arithmetic operations. Shortly before his death, Von Neumann began development of the theory of a machine capable of reproducing itself; this work, like much of Charles Babbage's work, remains unfinished but suggestive of future developments.

nine's complement   The radix-minus-one complement of a numeral whose radix is 10.

In decimal numeration, the nine's complement is a number which is constructed in such a way that, when added to an original number, a numeral of all nines results.

For example:

Number:	529130
Nine's complement:	470869
Sum:	999999

Nine's complement is used for representing negative numbers in some computers and, more commonly, in desk calculators.

N-level address   A multilevel address specifying N levels of addressing.

N-level addressing is an example of deeply nested (chained) indirect addressing. Let the N-level address designate a location ALPHA. ALPHA contains an indirect address of $N - 1$ level which points to BETA. BETA is an $N - 2$ level address which points to

GAMMA, and so on. Eventually, after N address fetches, an $N - N$ or zero-level address (direct address) is obtained. This address refers to the desired operand (data or instruction).

Multilevel addressing in this manner can lead to considerable ease in programming (especially in list processing), but it is an expensive (in time and memory requirements) method of programming.

noise The random variations in one or more characteristics of any entity (such as voltage, current, or data), or any disturbance tending to interfere with the normal operation of a device or system, or, more specifically, an error in the transmission of data.

The real world contains certain irreducible amounts of noise: such permanent noises arise from cosmic rays, thermal agitation of atoms, and the quantum nature of the microscopic-scale world. Removable noises are caused by vibration and shock, pulsating electric and magnetic fields, etc.: they may be reduced by proper shielding and isolation techniques. Solvable noises are those that can be detected by validity checking and corrected by self-correcting coding techniques.

noise factor In information retrieval (IR), the ratio obtained in dividing the difference between the number of documents retrieved and the number of relevant documents retrieved by the number of documents retrieved:

$$\text{Noise factor} = \frac{\text{documents retrieved} - \text{relevant documents retrieved}}{\text{documents retrieved}}$$

The noise factor is a measure of the efficiency of the information retrieval system, and ideally should be close to zero in value. Contrast with PERTINENCY FACTOR.

nondestructive read A reading process that does not erase the data in memory. Nondestructive read sometimes includes a destructive read immediately followed by a restorative write-back.

A read operation normally destroys the data in core memory since static memories must absorb electric power to produce an output, and this power is the cause of data loss.

A nondestructive read is important to a read-only memory: the read-only memory cannot be written into, and is used to hold microprograms in microprogrammed computers. A nondestructive read may also refer to a special kind of memory where the magnetic cores are no longer doughnut-shaped, but have two holes, this characteristic permitting the data to be read without being destroyed.

Magnetic tapes, disks, drums, and cards are usually read nondestructively since in these moving devices mechanical energy provides the output signal power.

Photoelectrical reading is equally a nondestructive read process.

nonerasable storage A device that permits a nondestructive read.

Punched cards, electrically conductive sheets, or paper tape can be sensed without destroying the medium. This equally holds true for black or clear spots on photographic records which are optically sensed, and for devices based on the existence or nonexistence of electric connections, either of the fixed-type (soldered) or of the programmable type (plugboards, switches). Certain kinds of magnetic-core memories can also be considered nonerasable storage.

Nonerasable storage is almost always used to hold decision rules, constant data items, and programs such as microprograms.

Microprogramming is a technique in which each of the instructions used by a program is executed as a short program with a much more elementary instruction set separately stored in a computer. A typical microinstruction contains one bit to activate or deactivate each functional unit in the CPU hardware, a test or branching condition, and the address of the next microinstruction. This language is so elementary that the hardware executes it without further interpretation or logic. Since it defines the normal programmer's operation repertoire, it may be considered part of the hardware. Microprogramming is an ideal application of high-speed nondestructive read storage.

Because of its very nature, nonerasable storage is seldom if ever used for variable or temporary data storage.

Synonymous with FIXED STORAGE and READ-ONLY STORAGE. See MICROPROGRAM.

NO OP An instruction telling the computer to do nothing, except to proceed to the next instruction in sequence.

The commonly used mnemonic (or abbreviation) is NOP. This is a do-nothing instruction for a digital computer and usually consumes only the time required to extract it from memory. Some uses for NOP include the following:

1. Filling space to make the next useful instruction begin at a particular location, such as an even-numbered location.

2. Consuming time in precisely figured time-delay loops. Such waste of time could be used to synchronize I/O or other simultaneous process. Usually an interval of some microseconds is involved.

3. To overlay an instruction, so as to cause it not to be executed. For example, a one-time routine begins by NO-OPing the branch

instruction which caused the one-time routine to be entered. Sub-sequent executions of what used to be the branch do not transfer control.

4. Reserving space for an instruction not yet present.

NOR A logic operator having the property that if P, Q, R, . . . are statements, then the NOR of P, Q, R, . . . is true if all statements are false, false if at least one statement is true.

NOR is a contraction of NOT-OR which correctly describes the operation. An OR is true if any variable is true, false only if all are false. The NOT inverts the value of the ouput or result.

It should be noted that interchanging the electrical levels interpreted as true and false converts a NOR element into a NAND element. The very simplest logic that can be implemented with transistors and diodes is NAND, NOR, and NOT (one transistor per function). The natural result is a tendency of computer designers to prefer these three logic functions to others as a basic set. See NAND.

normal direction flow The direction from left to right or top to bottom in flowcharting.

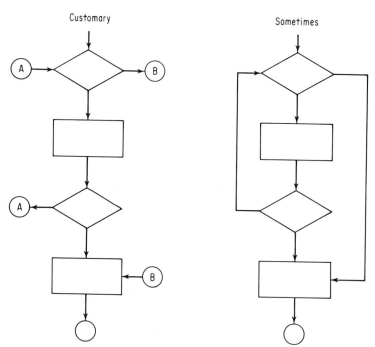

Examples

Customary

Sometimes

Normal direction flow (with arrows).

This tradition is derived from the customary ways of reading Hindu-European-written texts.

In some flowcharting conventions a transfer to an earlier location exits to the left, proceeds upward, and enters the left side of the destination symbol. A transfer to a later location exits right, flows down, and turns left to enter the symbol. This results in all on-one-page arrows flowing in a clockwise direction, and the main-line logic flowing downward.

Note that the normal flow conventions permit eliminating the arrowheads (where not contrary to convention) without loss of clarity. See accompanying illustrations.

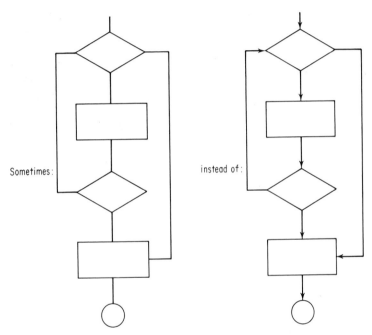

Sometimes: instead of:

Normal direction flow (with no arrowheads).

normalize   To adjust the representation of a set of numbers so that the representation lies within a prescribed range.

To normalize in floating-point numbers is to shift the mantissa and simultaneously adjust the exponent until the first mantissa digit (or leftmost digit) is a significant digit. This operation does not change the value of the number, but does represent it in a standard form:

$.6428 \times 10^3$ instead of 642.8

$.5248 \times 10^{-3}$ instead of $.0005248$

More generally, to normalize is to uniformly scale each of several sets of data (by means of a different factor for each) so as to permit comparison on a nondimensional or normalized scale. For example, to express class rankings as a percent in order to avoid the effect of class size (ranking tenth in one's class will mean one thing if it is a class of 100, and quite another if the class is of 10).

normalizer   In character recognition, that electronic component of a character reader which modifies the signal from the scanner to obtain a processed version of the input character more suitable for detailed analysis.

Normalizing is essentially a quality-improving operation and should not alter the fundamental shape of the character. Optical character readers employ a normalizer to standardize the amplitude and position of the character signal, improve the contrast and quality of character, and transform it into a binary or analog signal.

Magnetic-ink character normalizers essentially perform the same function by filling in any voids and eliminating extraneous additions which have invaded the encoding strip as a result of erasures or document mishandling. Similarly normalizers employed by mark-reading and mark-sensing systems complement voids and subtend breakthroughs.

Ideally the normalizer would convert a distorted input pattern into its intended "perfect" form. The degree to which this is achieved offers a basis for comparing normalizing techniques.

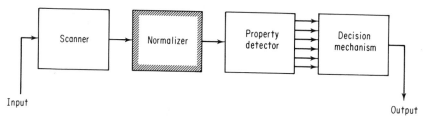

A character reader: component parts.

normal orientation   In optical character recognition (OCR), that determinate position which indicates that the line elements of an inputted source document appear in parallel with the document's leading edge.

Most optical readers are designed to be free-form to the extent that they can be programmed to accept a wide variety of character styles, type fonts, field lengths, and other parameters that affect the reading operation. Normal orientation is that parameter which directs the optical reader to perform its scan across the width (in relation to the leading edge) of the source document.

Contrast with PLUS-90 ORIENTATION.

See also OPTICAL SCANNING.

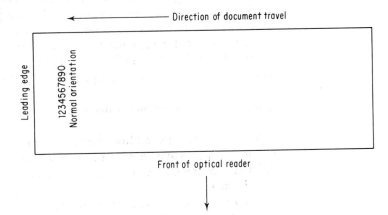

Normal orientation.

NOT A logic operator having the property that if P is a statement, then the NOT of P is true if P is false, false if P is true. The NOT of P is often represented by -P.

NOT is a unary operation since it has only one argument, and it is one of the most fundamental logic operators.

A	−A
True	False
False	True

or

A	−A
1	0
0	1

notation Usually refers to any one of several systems in which the value of a digit is defined not only by its numeric value but equally by its position within the number. See POSITIONAL NOTATION.

nucleus The portion of an operating system or control program which must reside in main memory, and by extension, the volume of main memory so occupied.

Normally, a sophisticated operating system (OS) is so large and complex that little or none of the computer would remain unoccupied if the entire system were loaded into main memory. For this reason control routines essential to ordinary operation are grouped together in the resident nucleus while the remainder of the operating system is kept in auxiliary storage (magnetic tape, disk, or drum). The nucleus loads portions of the nonresident routines into memory as their services are required. During a job, small routines may be loaded into a transient area reserved for this purpose. Between jobs, larger sections of code may be placed in memory ordinarily occupied by problem programs, that is, in memory outside the nucleus area itself. This transient area is considered to be part of the nucleus by problem programs. It is possible to trade memory capacity for operating speed by increasing the size of the nucleus and including frequently used, but normally nonresident routines, in the extra space. This avoids frequent loading operations, but ties up extra memory.

number   An abstract mathematical notion which should not be confused with numeral.

A numeral can be written down, manipulated, and interpreted accurately only when the radix is specified. Thus 120 will have different meanings whether it is expressed in octal, decimal, and hexadecimal.

A number can be expressed by many different numerals, but it cannot be pinned down and examined. See BINARY NUMBER.

number system   Loosely, a defined set of numbers, not to be confused with systems of numeration.

Mathematically, some well-known number systems are:

Whole numbers: 1, 2, 3, 4, . . . (positive integers)
Integers: . . . , −3, −2, −1, 0, 1, 2, . . .
Rational numbers: 2/2, 2/8, 3/16, 4/49, . . . , 19/14, . . .
  (fractions, including improper)
Irrational numbers: $\sqrt{2}$ (1.414213562373 . . .), π (3.14159265358 . . .), e (2.718281828459), etc. . . .
Complex numbers: A number of the form $2 + 3i$ where $i = \sqrt{-1}$

Not all number systems are infinite: for example, a digital computer with a 10- (decimal) digit word could represent 10,000,000,000 different numbers at the maximum, and if floating-point numbers were allowed, this set could almost double in size (there would be some duplication: 2.00 = 2). The size of such a system is large, but the number of items is known and finite.

numeral   The tangible or realizable representation of an abstraction called number.

For example:

365¼   VII 18×10^{-4} 110110100010110

are numerals.

A numeral may have many meanings unless its system is defined. Thus, the numeral 10 means

Two in binary
Eight in octal
Ten in decimal
Sixteen in hexadecimal
Nothing at all in Roman numerals.

Numerals permit pencil and paper, desk calculators, digital computers, taximeters, and clocks to function.   See BINARY NUMERAL.

numeral system   An orderly and mutually understood system of encoding numbers into numerals and numerals into numbers.

Numerals such as

XIV
8½
1967

are clear through familiarity with the numeral systems involved. However, the numerals

8.27×10^{49}	(Scientific)
$4.07 + 16.59i$	(Complex)
$\doteq$	(Babylonian)

are not as simple to visualize.

A numeral system should be compact, easy to understand, and easy to manipulate.

Synonymous with NUMERATION SYSTEM.

numeration system   A method of representing numbers by numerals which permits each numeral to have a unique numerical value.

Each numeral (or representation) has a number (or concept) associated with it, but indefinitely many numbers have no finite (hence, realizable or practical) numeral representation.

Thus 5 2/3 has the value of five and two-thirds, but the number x which satisfies $x^2 = 2$ has no exact numeral representation. Instead we write $\sqrt{2}$ or $2^{1/2}$ or 1.414213562373 . . . for x.

The best-known numeration system is the decimal system using arabic numerals.   In this system the admissible digits are 0, 1, 2, 3, 4, 5, 6, 7, 8, 9, qualified by the three symbols +, −, (.).   The value assigned to any digit depends on its distance from the (real or implied) decimal point.   Thus:

$$1234. = 1 \cdot 1000 + 2 \cdot 100 + 3 \cdot 10 + 4 \cdot 1 = 1 \cdot 10^3 + 2 \cdot 10^2 + 3 \cdot 10^1 + 4 \cdot 10^0$$

A positional numeration system can similarly be constructed to any radix, say x $(x \geq 2)$. The numeral whose digits are a_3 a_2 a_1 a_0. a_{-1} . . . in the base x system has numeric value $a_3x^3 + a_2x^2 + a_1x + a_0 + a_{-1}/x$ . . The most commonly used numeration systems are as follows:

Base	System
2	Binary
8	Octal
10	Decimal
12	Duodecimal
16	Hexadecimal
60	Sexadecimal

A trivial system to base $x = 1$ could be devised: such a system would use equally weighted counters, the number of which would match the number being represented.

example:

2 = II
5 = IIIII
7 = IIIIIII

This trivial system was possibly the first system used by human beings.

numerical analysis The study and application of the methods of finding numerical answers to practical problems in science, engineering, and business.

Numerical analysis is concerned with the methods and techniques of solving equations and other problems. The practitioners of this art soon found that error and accuracy considerations were an inseparable part of the analysis.

No equation, however sophisticated, is enough by itself to build a bridge. An answer or solution being required, the equation must be solved: the actual dimensions of the bridge members can then be determined. Since a bridge will be built with a factor of safety, answers accurate to 1 percent are often sufficient, requiring calculations with three or four significant digits. Designing an airplane, with more critical weight penalties, requires more sophisticated analysis and a higher precision answer. Four to six significant digits may be required. In design of quality photographic optics, the very high precision desired dictates calculations using 7, 11, or 15 digits. One method of synthesizing electrical filter networks fails if less than 30 digits of precision are used.

The classical problems of numerical analysis include:
Simultaneous linear equations
Matrix inversion
Solution of differential equations
Numerical quadrature (integration)
Approximation of functions
Zeros of polynomials
Some of these problems were old in the time of Newton, and were studied by such mathematicians as Gauss and Jacobi; others are as new as the space age.

Matrix inversion is most commonly used in solving simultaneous linear equations, but other applications exist. Simultaneous linear equations are used in such areas as structural analysis, electric circuits, and least-squares approximations.

Solution of differential equations is required in ballistics, trajectory analysis, and heat-flow problems.

Numerical quadrature is used to find areas and volumes bounded by curves and surfaces. Many of the required techniques can be obtained by specializing the methods of solving differential equations.

Approximations are used to reduce computational burdens and find coefficients from experimentally measured data.

numerical control   In today's terminology, numerical control refers to the control of machine tools, drafting machines, and the like, by punched paper or magnetic tapes suitably encoded with directive information.

As most numerically controlled devices have very limited logical or arithmetic capability (to keep costs low), they rely on their input tapes for detailed and explicit guidance. This may mean 8 bits for every .001 of motion, or a great amount of data on the tape. It is common for a computer to prepare the control tapes, using information presented in a more manageable and concise form. An example is the APT (automatically programmed tools) system, developed by an aerospace industry combine and currently supported by IITRI.

Using APT, the designer describes his tool and the desired part in a high-level, geometrically oriented language. A preprocessor program accepts the high-level language and digests it into a simpler, formalized internal representation. The central program (tool independent) converts the material, tool, and geometrical information into tool motion commands. A postprocessor program prepares the tool motion information in a format suitable for the particular control mechanism being used. If desired, a simultaneous output for a numerical control drafting machine permits preparation of detail blueprints while the robot tool is making the part.

Although numerical control tools (and the computer processing) are expensive, their very high productivity and accuracy actually reduce the cost (and time required) of producing few-of-a-kind parts. Numerical control in devices with five or six simultaneous degrees of freedom is a must since a human operator cannot perform five or six operations simultaneously and efficiently.

Numerical control devices include:

All kinds of machine tools (milling, drilling, grinding, etc.)

Phototypesetting and other typesetting

Point-to-point electrical wiring

Drafting, plotting, and drawing devices

Steel plate, bar and tube mills

O

object language When translating or converting information from one language to another, the original language is the source language and the intended and desired output language is the object language.

In mechanical translation of natural languages, the object language is a language spoken by human beings. At this time the output of mechanical translators needs touching up by a human editor to improve readability.

In assembly or compilation of computer languages, the object language is considered to be internal computer representation of the information supplied in the source language. This is in the form of binary or decimal digits, or characters, recorded on some suitable medium.

In fact, the output of an assembly or compilation is often not identical with the internal computer representation. It is generally intermixed with control characters and other (nonstored) information which designates the location or address of the text information, the symbolic name of unresolved addresses, etc. Thus, the object language must be interpreted by a loading program before the internal representation is actually attained.

See TARGET LANGUAGE.

object module An output of a compiler or assembler, containing a computer program in instruction form and also control information to guide the linkage editor.

In most cases (IBM, TOS, DOS, and OS/360) the object module is in relocatable, but not loadable or executable format. In TSS/360 an object module may be directly loaded and executed, but in all other instances it must be operated on by the linkage editor before it becomes operable.

An object module begins with an external symbol dictionary, or ESD. This contains symbolic information to allow separately written programs to be united into a coordinated load module, and also contains the names and locations of control sections within the text of the object module. A control section is the smallest unit of code that can be added, deleted, or replaced by the linkage editor.

The instructions and data of the object module are contained in the text (TXT) or body of the module. The TXT is the part actually loaded into memory for execution, whereas the ESD and RLD (relocation dictionary) do not appear in a computer at run time. The RLD is the last section of an object module. This section contains instructions to the loader for properly initializing the address constants within the module. While the ESD makes it possible to edit modules together before loading, the RLD makes it possible to load the edited module into any sufficiently large available area in main memory. This latter property is called relocatability, and it accounts for much of the flexibility of modern digital computers.

The last record of an object module contains the identification END, and may also contain the address of the first instruction to be executed when the program is initiated.

object program The computer language program prepared by an assembler or a compiler after acting on a programmer-written source program.

The source program is a description of the method of accomplishing some task written in a source language that is comprehensible to the programmer and interpretable by a compiling or assembling program. The object program is the same description expressed in object language that can be interpreted by the computer hardware.

object (program) library A collection of computer programs in the form of relocatable instructions, which reside on, and may be read from, a mass storage device.

The object program library differs from a core-image library by being relocatable, whereas the core-image library is absolute.

octal Pertaining to a numeration system with a base of 8. Octal and hexadecimal are widely used in computing as a shorthand way of expressing binary quantities: for instance, 1370_8 is much easier to express than 001011111000. The eight permissible octal digits and their binary representations are:

0 000
1 001
2 010
3 011
4 100
5 101
6 110
7 111

Upon viewing a display of on and off lights, a trained person can mentally group the lights by threes and read off the octal digits. It would be much more tedious and error-provoking to read the binary number directly.

It is easy to add in octals if one bears in mind that 8 is 0 and carry 1 ($8 = 10_8$). Thus:

Decimal	Octal
186	272
+	+
396	614
582	1106

odd-even check A means of detecting certain kinds of errors which uses an extra bit that is set to zero or one so as to make the total number of 1-bits even or odd. Also called PARITY CHECK.

If 1, 3, 5, etc., bits are accidentally changed, the parity of the data bits will be changed. When two errors occur at once, no parity error can be detected. In effect, one declares half of the possible bit configurations to be illegal. In return for the sacrifice in data-form availability, the great majority of 1-bit errors are immediately detectable.

The use of odd parity makes no bits an illegal condition, and prevents misinterpretation or miscounting of all-zero characters. Even parity is used where hardware considerations or compatibility dictate its need.

By arranging data bits in a rectangular array and using both row and column parity bits, any one-bit error can be detected, located, and thus corrected.

off-line Describes equipment not connected to a computer, or temporarily disconnected from one. Off-line equipment is either idle, undergoing repair, or performing a task under its own (possibly operator-assisted) direction.

For example, a device that reads paper tape and records the information on magnetic tape is called an off-line tape-to-tape converter. Most devices of this type cannot interact directly with a computer, and not being computers themselves, are permanently off-line. In this sense off-line means an independent, asynchronous, and parallel operation compared to that of the principal computer.

Another example (UNIVAC 1004) is a device that can print, read punched cards, and punch blank cards. This device can operate off-line under its own (plugboard programmed) control, or can be connected to a computer to perform on-line input/output. For this device off-line means logically or functionally disconnected from the computer, even though electric (power) connections may remain intact.

offset In optical character recognition (OCR), an unintentional transfer of ink which adversely affects a document's readability.

Offset may appear at any interval during the life of a document, but it occurs most commonly among two freshly printed sheets in a document delivery stack, at which time the back of the succeeding document displaces some of the ink from the face of the preceding document.

Offset manifests its adverse effects in two ways:

1. Mostly, it affects the character, as laid down, with regard to its gloss and evenness of ink density.

2. More remotely, it may result in extraneous marks that appear on the face of a succeeding document which isn't completely opaque.

The degree to which offset occurs is a function of the absorbency of paper and the properties of the printing ink employed. In any event there exists an antisetoff powder which reduces, if not completely eliminates, the occurrence of ink transfer.

Whereas offset redistributes the density of ink of a character laid down, INK SMUDGE extends the ink beyond a character's boundary.

offset lithography See LITHOGRAPHY.

omission factor In information retrieval (IR), the ratio obtained in dividing the number of nonretrieved relevant documents by the total number of relevant documents in the file.   Ideally, the omission factor should be close to zero, as it is a measure of the efficiency of the system.   Contrast with RECALL FACTOR.

one-level address   In digital computers, an address that directly indicates the location of an instruction or some data.

Each memory or storage location that can be used by a program is distinguished from all other such locations by its unique address. Reference is made to these locations and their contents by including an address part in the computer instructions.

one-plus-one address   Describes a digital computer instruction format which contains two address parts.   One address designates the operand to be involved in the operation; the other indicates the location of the next instruction to be executed.

This type of instruction is used when the location of the next instruction affects the speed of operation of the computer, as is the case when the instructions are stored on a revolving magnetic drum (IBM 650).

The one-plus-one address instruction has only the power (or flexibility) of a one-address instruction, because only one operand reference is included.   The function of the additional address part is to allow the programmer to optimize the (nonsequential) location of consecutively executed instructions when access latency must be taken into account.

In random-access main-memory computers (core, thin film, etc. or any static storage), the function of the second address is performed by an instruction counter (program counter, sequence counter, or location counter) which increments, after each instruction fetch, to point to the next instruction.   Sequentially executed instructions are sequentially located, and *the instruction after this one* is understood to be the normal successor instruction, the additional address required by drum computers becoming unnecessary.

one's complement   A numeral in binary notation, derived from another binary number by simply changing the sense of every digit. The sum of a number and its one's complement is a number of all 1-bits and no 0-bits.

For example:

001	010	011	100	Number
110	101	100	011	One's complement
111	111	111	111	Sum

By contrast, the sum of a number with its two's complement is a number of all zeros with an (ignored) carry out of the high-order position. For this reason a two's complement is a one's complement with 1 added to the units position. See TWO'S COMPLEMENT.

on-line Generally refers to equipment capable of interacting with a computer. This equipment may be under control of the CPU (center processing unit), or it may provide data input to be accepted by the computer.

On-line equipment operates at the same time as the computer, or in cooperation with the computer, in accomplishing a task. Examples of on-line devices are the following:

1. A drawing or plotting device attached to, and controlled by, a computer to prepare graphical output displaying calculated information.

2. A CRT-keyboard console on-line to a computer to permit a human being to interact conversationally with a computer.

3. A card reader attached to a computer to avoid the need for an off-line card-to-tape converter.

4. An analog-to-digital converter to permit a real-time process control computer to monitor an industrial process.

Contrast with OFF-LINE.

open-ended Said of techniques designed to facilitate or permit expansion, extension, or increase in capability; the opposite of closed in and artificially constrained.

An example would be a self-extending translator permitting users to add new language features by defining them in terms of already defined language features. This kind of program allows each user to create a programming language to meet his own needs and wants. The only limitation of the process is dictated by the imagination of the user, and by the translator processing time (which increases with increasing language power).

A library of subroutines that can be expanded until one runs out of storage medium is an open-ended system. The STRESS structural problem-solving system and the APT numerically controlled tool programming system are systems designed to permit extension of capability by the user.

The program design and documentation make such extension practical, although not trivial.

open-ended system In character recognition, a system in which the input data to be read are derived from sources other than the computer with which the character reader is associated. See DOCUMENT TYPES for the various kinds of open-ended data preparation.

open shop   A data processing center organization in which individuals from outside the data processing community are permitted to implement their own solutions to problems.

In an open shop, the data processing center makes available computing facilities and assistance to each individual having a valid reason for using those facilities.   The emphasis is on accessibility and flexibility, ease of programming and debugging, and service to the user.   This should be contrasted with closed shop, in which only professional programmers and operators are allowed to use the data processing center.

Much programming is done by nonprofessional programmers (who may be highly skilled in non-EDP fields) in an open shop.   This results in inefficient coding practices and poor or nonexistent documentation. In some circumstances, particularly in scientific or engineering jobs that are run only once or twice when debugged, this condition of inefficiency is less objectionable than the longer elapsed-time-to-solution condition that would result from closed-shop operation.   Open-shop centers must provide higher-level languages (problem-oriented languages, procedure-oriented languages) and easy-to-use utilities for their clients.

Briefly, the advantages of open-shop operation are the following:

1.   Programs and operations are well matched to the needs (real or psychological) of the user.

2.   The user gets a feeling of accomplishment that only direct involvement can provide.

3.   Small or simple problems are rapidly solved.

4.   There is no communication gap between client and programmer.

On the other hand, the disadvantages of open-shop operation are as follows:

1.   Difficulty in allocating costs, encouraging waste of money.

2.   Discipline and order are hard to enforce.

3.   The educational burden will be high, and the need to learn will be resented by some users.

4.   Scheduling will be very difficult, and many short runs and nonpredictable events will occur.

5.   Less than fully efficient utilization of facilities is achieved.

open subroutine   A set of computer instructions that collectively perform some particular function and are inserted directly into the program each and every time that particular function is required.

An open subroutine should be tight (that is, it must contain only a small number of instructions) because many copies of it could exist in a program.   Typically, an open subroutine will convert floating-point numbers to fixed-point numbers or fixed-point to floating-point (four to six instructions), find the next larger integer value, or find the absolute magnitude. The advantages of open subroutine consist of simple usage (no calling sequences), faster execution, and if used sparingly, conservation of memory.

By contrast, a closed subroutine appears at most once in each program. It too is a set of instructions that performs a defined function, but control is transferred to the one common routine every time this function is needed. The closed subroutine and the calling program must jointly arrange to communicate data and return control to the original program when the subroutine finishes. This program/subroutine interface is called a linkage convention. The advantages of closed subroutines consist of conservation of memory, if used often, and no limitation on subroutine size or complexity.

operand   A data or information item that participates, or is involved, in an operation.

For example, in the mathematical operation of division, the dividend and divisor are two operands. The quotient and the remainder are not usually considered to be operands.

Most digital computer instructions have one or more operands, each indicated by a field within the instruction. In second-generation computers, all operands usually reside in core memory, and are designated by address parts of the instruction. In third-generation computers, many operands reside in high-speed registers, and are designated by 3- to 5-bit register fields within the instruction. This change in residence shortens the instructions (since it requires fewer digits for addressing) and speeds up execution (since fewer memory cycles are required).

In some instructions, an immediate operand is located within the instruction (usually in the field otherwise reserved for an address).

In some cases the location of the operand is implied by the instruction; that is, a specific register or core location is always used in the specified operation.

operating system   A set of programs and routines which guide a computer in the performance of its tasks, assist the programs (and programmers) with certain supporting functions, and increase the usefulness of the computer's hardware.

A typical operating system:

1. Interprets operator commands and/or control cards which describe to it the work to be done.

2. Gives control of the computer to the job programs in the proper sequence, and handles job-to-job transition.

3. Schedules and performs input/output and related functions for the job programs, relieving the programmer of hardware-oriented considerations and optimizing I/O device utilization.

4. Governs the operation of compilers, assemblers, and other manufacturer-provided software.

5. Protects the various programs from one another; that is, keeps one program from altering the work of another program.

6. Provides debugging and error diagnostic services including traces, dumps, snapshots, and error messages.

7. Assigns various physical I/O devices to the logical files referred to by the programs: this permits run-time substitution of alternate devices or accommodated changes in equipment configuration without reprogramming.

8. Handles those program-to-program transitions that involve loading additional instructions into the computer from an external storage within a single job.

9. Provides dynamic allocation of storage and other resources in a multiprogramming environment.

10. Enforces the discipline required to run many programs at once in a time-sharing environment.

11. Allocates tasks to processors (or vice versa) in a multiprocessing environment.

Perhaps the simplest current operating system is the Mod 1 operating system on the Honeywell 200. This system consists of a program loader which resides in memory and loads selected programs (or segments of programs) into memory from tape, drum, or cards. Mod 1 handles only functions 1, 2, and 8 of the above list.

The most complex of the currently planned operating systems is probably the time-sharing system (TSS) for the IBM 360/67. TSS will handle all the listed functions (except possibly the multiprocessing function). The complexity of this system is so great that it could not function unless the hardware were specifically designed to assist it. Indeed, the hardware and software of TSS/360 are so closely intertwined that it is sometimes difficult to distinguish one from the other. Naturally, TSS/360 permanently occupies a rather large portion of computer memory, denying that part to problem program.

In economic terms, an operating system makes the computer easier to program and keeps the hardware busy (reducing wasted rental and lowering the cost of computing), but reduces the amount of computer space and time available for problem solving. Therefore, a balance must be struck. The more powerful (and expensive) a computer is, the more memory is available for a resident operating system. The larger computer can spare the overhead required for a complex operating system, but the smaller computer may be economically operated, somewhat less efficiently (timewise), but with reduced overhead with no operating system, or a very simple one.

It thus appears that each level of computer hardware power can be matched with an optimum level of operating-system sophistication. This idea led IBM to the BPS/BOS/TOS/DOS/OS/TSS sequence and other makers to offer stand-alone/batch processing/multiprocessing/universal monitors for their various lines of hardware.

OPERATING SYSTEM 360 (OS/360) A very flexible operating system designed to be used with the largest and most powerful configurations of IBM 360 computers. OS/360 spans a range from the medium-power computers using sequential scheduling up to the very largest computers operating with multiprogramming and variable number of task multijobbing.

Originally, OS/360 had been planned to service the entire range of IBM 360 computers from the smallest to the largest. In one unified concept it would have offered interchangeability of programs among all computers in this computer family, and allowed each installation to tailor OS capabilities to suit its own machine and operating needs. It soon developed, however, that the range of computers was too great to be adequately served by a single operating system concept, and so simpler systems were developed for the smaller machines while OS was specialized for large-computer operations.

The principal features of OS/360 include:

1. A modular organization that allows each component of the system to be implemented in several versions with varying degrees of sophistication and flexibility, the installation thus choosing one module for each component, and assembling a particularized OS for the system in question

2. A job control language, which allows the computer operators and programmers the greatest possible control over the operation of the machine and the utilization of data and programs

3. A data management, which gives a very flexible allocation of data and input/output devices to programs, and offers a very high degree of device independence for the OS programs

4. A support of almost all hardware components in the system 360 family

The modular organization of OS allows it to meet the needs of many and diverse users. Each distinct function that an operating system must perform (such as program scheduling, input/output, and interrupt handling) is usually handled by one module, and several levels of interchangeable modules are offered for each function. An installation may choose one module for each function, and by performing a system generation can thus create an operating system tailored to its hardware and operational needs.

By system generation (which see) is meant a process that creates an operating system specifically configured for the individual installation. By judiciously selecting from available options, the systems programmer can thus tailor the operating system to meet the individual hardware and operational requirements of his users.

For example, a 64K (that is, 64,000 bytes of core memory) computer typically has a simple monoprogramming job scheduler, a small linkage editor, and small compilers; a 128K or 256K computer will use a faster and larger linkage editor, more powerful and larger compilers, a priority scheduler, and/or simple multiprogramming; a computer of 512K, or more, will use the most powerful modules available, employing a variable number of task multiprogramming and multitask operations.

The memory required for the system routines alone in a large-scale computer can exceed 128K, making it a physical impossibility to offer maximum OS capability on the smaller computers. In addition to operational options, the system generation will specialize the operating system for the hardware configuration, that is, for the number of data channels, type of I/O devices, memory protect, optional instruction sets, and data channel switches that are available on this particular computer.

Job control language gives the job scheduler information needed for selecting jobs and job steps to be processed. In addition, it gives full specifications for the structure and location of the data sets to be used by a program. Because the detailed nature of I/O is specified only as each job is submitted (and not when programs are written), a large degree of I/O flexibility is obtained at the cost of complicated control card preparation. Thus, a single program may be run with card input and printer output, or tape input and disk output, or data cell input and no output, without any program modification being required.

Data management includes the routines required to realize this I/O flexibility. It also has a complex cataloging facility which can be used to relieve the operators and programmers from having to remember where and how data are stored. Data sets instead may be cataloged and referred to by name. Data management supports basic and queued access methods (which see), allowing greater flexibility and/or efficiency in I/O scheduling.

The largest and most powerful compilers available for system 360 can be used only with OS. These include H-level FORTRAN IV, and G- and H-level compilers of the future. Powerful compilers support the most flexible language sets, and include code-optimizing routines to permit creation of compact, efficient object code (at the expense of compile time) if desired. Larger linkage editor and initiator/terminator options allow extra-fast program loading and/or larger programs.

Operating system 360 can fully support any IBM 360 computer having more than 32K of memory (except models 44 and 67, which have noncompatible instruction sets). Many commercial installations with 128K or less of memory prefer to run DOS (which see) for simplicity and efficiency. The large requirement in memory space and instruction execution time that is a consequence of the versatility of OS makes it attractive only for the 360 models 50, 65, and 75, having 256K or more of memory.

operation A process or procedure that obtains a unique result from any permissible combination of operands, or the sequence of actions resulting from the execution of one digital computer instruction. In general, an operation is a single irreducible step in the performance of a computer program.

Examples of operations in computer programs are:

Shift the contents of a register left three positions.
Multiply the contents of a register by a designated number.
Rewind the tape on a particular drive.
Change the internal state (operating mode) of the CPU.

In some higher-level languages, an operation is a single higher-level step (such as finding a square root). This is strictly justified if the meaning is defined by context, or the hardware has an instruction for finding square roots (as in the ATLAS computer).

See OPERAND, OPERATION CODE.

operation code A field or portion of a digital computer instruction that indicates which action is to be performed by the computer.

The operation code is almost always located at the left end (high-order positions) of the computer instruction, and has a constant (or specified) length. The operation code is composed of one or more bits, digits, characters, or bytes and can be uniquely interpreted as specifying a particular action or state.

Upon fetching an instruction, a computer performs the following tasks (serially or in parallel):

1. Interprets the operation code and checks for invalid instruction (if applicable).

2. Resolves operand address(es) by indexing, memory map, indirect addressing, etc.

3. Fetches the operands (if located in memory) or gets them from registers.

4. Performs indicated actions, thus developing results.

5. Stores resulting data (if they are to be located in memory) or places them in registers.

6. Fetches the next instruction and repeats the above tasks.

The shorter operation codes (5 or 6 bits) result in simpler, faster instruction-decoding hardware and conserve memory space, but provide smaller sets of distinct instruction. Longer operation codes (7 or 8 bits) provide more different instruction types (resulting in greater power), but they cannot be decoded as rapidly by the hardware. The use of read-only storage (microprogramming) reduces the latter difficulty and has promoted a trend toward longer operation codes.

In some short-operation-code computers, all the operations involving no operands (addresses) are grouped together, using one or two escape operation codes. When these escape codes are detected, the address part of the instruction is interpreted as an extended operation code instead of an operand designation. Shift instructions are the most common examples of this type.

For example:

Enter floating-point trap mode.
Exchange AC and MQ contents.

In variable-word-length computers (such as the RCA 501 and Honeywell 200) the operation code is distinguished by a word mark and is usually one character long. If further qualification of the operation code is desired, variant or modifier characters appear in the instruction after the address part.

operation part That portion of a digital computer instruction which is reserved for the operation code.

The operation part is usually at the left end of the instruction, and is of fixed length.

In word-oriented computers, the sign of the word may or may not count toward the interpretation of the operation code, and so may or may not be included in the operation part. See OPERATION CODE.

operator In mathematics, a symbol designating an operation to be performed, such as: ÷ (division), − (subtraction), + (addition), · (multiplication), Σ (summation), ∫ (integration), ‖ (concatenation). By extension, anything that designates an action to be performed, especially the operation code of a computer instruction.

In general, the following are commonly recognized operators:

Arithmetic:

> $+$ (addition); $-$ (subtraction); $\times$ (multiplication); $\div$ or $/$ (division)

Logical:

> $\ulcorner$ (not); $\wedge$ (and); $\vee$ (or); $\Rightarrow$ (implies); $\Leftrightarrow$ (equivalence)

Calculus:

> $\int$ (integration); d/d (differential); ∂/∂ (partial differential)

Algebraic:

> Σ (repeated sum); Π (repeated product)

String manipulation:

> $\|$ (concatenation)

Miscellaneous:

> $|\;\;|$ (absolute magnitude); $\lim(\;)$ (limit of); $\max(\;)$ (maximum of); $\min(\;)$ (minimum of); $[\;\;]$ (integer part of)

Relational:

> $>$ (greater than); $<$ (less than); $=$ (equal to); $\geqq$ (greater than or equal to) $\leqq$ (less than or equal to); $\neq$ (not equal to)

Matrix Operators (as superscripts):

> T (transpose); -1 (inverse)·

Geometrical:

> $\sim$ (similar to); $\cong$ or $\equiv$ (congruent) $/\!/$ (parallel); $\perp$ (orthogonal perpendicular)

Algol Notation:

> $:=$ (substitution); $\uparrow$ (exponentiation)

optical character recognition (OCR)   That branch of character recognition which concerns itself with the automatic identification of handwritten or printed characters by any of various photoelectric methods. Contrast with MAGNETIC-INK CHARACTER RECOGNITION (MICR).

optical scanning   In character recognition, a process that involves projecting a character's image by reflected light through a lens system onto a particular target from which an attempt will be made to identify the character. See SCANNER.

optical type font In optical character recognition (OCR), a somewhat unconventional type font constructed in similar size and style, but designed in such a way that its individual members obtain a particular uniqueness. Optical type fonts are considered unconventional inasmuch as their machine readability takes preference over their human readability.

Historically, optical type fonts were constructed from limited character sets which contained only numbers. Later, special symbols were incorporated; and more recently, some character sets were expanded to include alphabetic symbols.

OR A logical operation which produces a false result only if every one of its operands is false, and a true result if any operand is true. The effect of OR is summarized in the following truth table:

P	Q	P or Q
T	F	T
T	T	T
F	T	T
F	F	F

As a digital computer instruction (and its associated operation), OR compares corresponding bits of its two operands and stores 0's in the result if both bits are 0, and stores 1's in the result if either or both corresponding operand bits are 1. This digital computer instruction is frequently used to ensure that specified bits are set to 1, while preserving all other bits. Thus an assembler could insert an operation code into an instruction that it is generating.

OR is also an element in some higher-level languages which commands that the operation OR be performed on two operands.

order A command interpreted and executed by a device controller.

In general, an instruction is executed by the CPU (central processing unit), a command is executed by a data channel, and an order is executed by a device or device controller. The difference between instruction, command, and order is best illustrated by examples:

Instruction	Clear and add from location 129.
Command	Input 1 record starting at location 3048.
Order	Seek track 016 on access arm 2.

The verb order is similar to the verb sort. It means to rearrange without altering the individual items.

The noun is frequently qualified by ascending (in ascending orders, successive items are equal or greater) or descending (successive items are less or equal).

OR gate   A circuit element or functional block having multiple inputs and a single output. The output has value 0 if all inputs have value 0, and value 1 if any or all inputs have value 1.

If 1 means current and 0 is no current, then OR can be implemented by connecting the inputs directly to the output (this is called the wired-OR function). If the inputs must be isolated from one another, a set of diodes is used to admit signals but prevent interaction of the input lines:

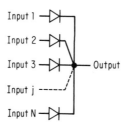

Further isolation and power gain can be achieved by including transistors or other active elements in the circuit.

output   A generic term for a number of things:
The data produced by a data processing operation, or the information that it is desired to obtain and which is the objective or goal in data processing. Without revealing this information, a computer would be a useless secret-keeping device.

The data actively transmitted from within the device to an external device, or onto a permanent recording medium (paper, microfilm).

The activity of transmitting the generated information, constituting a process or action.

The signal line which carries away the information developed within a logic element or gate. For a simple circuit, one or a few data lines suffice. In a sophisticated application, different effluent lines are required.

The readable storage medium upon which generated data are written, as in hard copy output. While output is actually information, the paper, film, etc., containing these data are often called output.

The simplest kind of output is probably a steady voltage level, such as a flip-flop or a remote thermometer might generate.

The most complex output (not yet invented) could probably be a dynamic, multicolor, three-dimensional display.

Compare INPUT.

output work queue   The data generated as output by various programs, data that are temporarily saved on auxiliary storage until they can be printed or punched in final form. Output work queue, by extension, is also the control information describing the location and intended disposition of the above data.

As various programs are processed (either sequentially or concurrently), output data are generated at uneven rates. At times, print output is created at a faster rate than the printer can handle, whereas at other times print output is not generated at all. These data can be either sent directly to the printer (a simple but inefficient use of both printer and computer), or absorbed in an external storage area to be printed later at an efficient, uniform rate. The use of output data queues not only provides full use of hardware capability and higher computing speeds, but it also allows the use of multiple, virtual output devices.

Suppose that a program prepares three separate output reports and directs each report to a different printer. This program can be run on a computer with only one or two printers by directing one or more reports to an external storage area (virtual printer) for later printing. In this way a certain amount of hardware independence can be obtained.

All references to printer in the above paragraph apply equally as well to card punch, paper-tape punch, teletypewriter, or any slow-output device. Note that no amount of output queueing will allow a computer to continuously create more output than its output devices can handle, for the output delay will simply grow longer and longer until all the external storage is filled. An installation must still have enough output devices to handle its normal work load.

See OUTPUT WRITER.

output writer   A service routine that moves data from the OUTPUT WORK QUEUE (which see) to an output device.

Output writers are provided by the operating system in order to keep the computer's output devices efficiently busy. The processed data are stored temporarily in external storage as an output queue, and are transferred to the actual output device by an output writer at a speed determined by the natural rate of the output device.

The computer operator directs the operating system to initiate an output writer via a console command. He designates the output device to be used; and the system selects, loads, and initiates a suitable writer program. The output writer becomes a task (or foreground program) that operates when needed and is synchronized to the output device by hardware interrupts. Other programs are running while the writer is waiting for I/O to finish.

An operator may start as many output writers as he chooses, but each output device may be used by only one writer at a time. A large computer with three printers could thus have 0, 1, 2, or 3 print-output writers active at any time. Each writer remains active until stopped by a hardware malfunction, the computer operator, or a lack of processed data waiting to be printed out.

overflow   Usually that part of the result of an arithmetic operation which exceeds the storage capacity of the indicated result-holding storage. The most significant digit(s) are considered to be overflow.

If two M-digit numbers are added, an $M + 1$ digit number may result by generating a carry from the leftmost position. In a word-organized computer the results are held in registers of fixed length, or in a variable-word-length (or character-organized) computer the results are stored in a destination area of prespecified size. In either case an overflow condition can occur. Digital computers can detect the generation of an overflow condition in order to warn the programmer of incorrect results. Often an overflow indicator is turned on, and may be tested by a branch-on-overflow instruction. At other times, an overflow interrupt occurs, stopping the current program and activating an error-handling program.

Overflow may be caused by addition or multiplication, or division by zero, or too small a number. True subtraction (addition with unlike signs) never causes overflow.

Those records (or parts of records) that cannot be accommodated in the normally allocated area in a random-access storage device are called overflow. Also, the additional area allocated in storage to hold overflow records is called overflow. A file stored on a random-access device (magnetic disk) is allocated a storage area large enough to hold the expected number of records. If more records (or larger records) are added to the file, a lack of space condition can result. One way to handle this condition is to assign an overflow area for the surplus information. The original area and/or the file index is modified to point to an area in the overflow space, and the excess data are written in the indicated area. One overflow space can serve every file on the device, thus conserving capacity. At intervals the storage device may be cleaned up by copying its information onto another device, reassigning areas to the files to reflect their current sizes, and moving the files back onto the storage device in an orderly manner. In this way all overflow can be moved back to the parent files.

To generate a too-large result by performing an arithmetic operation is called to overflow.

overlap To perform some or all of an operation concurrently with one or more additional operations.

In the development of increasingly faster computers, progress was achieved by going from mechanical devices to relays to vacuum tubes to transistors to monolithic integrated circuits. Today's fastest computers are limited by physical law: no signal can travel faster than light. (Indeed, the fundamental unit of time in today's ultra-fast computers is the time it takes an electrical pulse to travel only 8½ inches!) Thus, increased speed can be obtained only by making computers physically smaller, thereby reducing travel time.

If still greater computer power is desired while devices in use are presently going as fast as they can, design modifications or different approaches are required. Unable to perform operation X in time less than T, one can only try to perform two independent operations X with some degree of simultaneity—so that both operations will be finished in less than $2T$ time units: the effective time for one operation X would then last less than T units. This method, known as overlapping one operation with another, requires not only duplicate processing units, but equally additional supervisory logic to coordinate the various processors.

It is in fact possible to overlap some parts of the operation of a digital computer and let the remainder operate in a strictly sequential, nonsimultaneous fashion.

In a typical computer, input/output, being at least partly mechanical. in every instance is the slowest activity (with time measured in milliseconds); main memory operates at intermediate speeds (with time measured in microseconds); and the electronic logic operates at nearly the speed of light (with time measured in nanoseconds or picoseconds): In other words, the arithmetic unit has to wait for memory, and memory has to wait for input/output. The very slow computers operate in strictly sequential fashion, and thus all processing halts until a single I/O operation is completed.

The majority of today's computers, however, have data channels allowing data input and output to proceed simultaneously with arithmetic/logic operations: this operation is called overlapping I/O with processing. I/O overlap is a great improvement over strictly sequential operations, but it still leaves the electronics waiting for the slower main memory.

Suppose that memory is divided into two equal, independent units:

one-half of the memory (or bank) storing all even-addressed words or bytes, the other half of the memory holding all odd addresses. If each memory bank consists of fast magnetic cores with 1-microsecond cycle time, every location can be accessed in 1 microsecond. But if it is required to access a location in each module, each module can be cycled independently of the other module. In the long run, this permits up to 2 cycles per microsecond allowing a single access performance comparable to ½-microsecond cycle time (complete overlap is rarely possible, because two successive requests for attention can sometimes require the same memory module).

Normally, core memories are manufactured in banks of about 4096 words each. A medium or larger-scale computer contains four or more such modules. If the designer wishes to pay for proper memory-coordinating logic, each bank can be overlapped with all the others, giving four-way or higher multiplicity of overlap. For example, the central memory of the CDC 6600 has 8, 16, or 32 modules, and a synchronizer capable of handling 10 transactions per microsecond. With 8 modules, only eight actions per 1-microsecond cycle are possible, so some interference is expected. With 16 banks interference is rare, and an effective cycle time of 1/10 microsecond is attained. With the larger 32-bank memory, the degree of overlap is constrained by the synchronizer, and the fullest potential performance is not obtained.

The following tables graphically illustrate the operation of overlap as compared with interleaving.

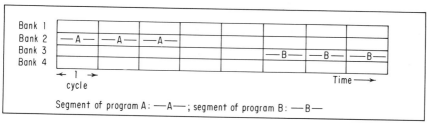

Segment of program A: —A—; segment of program B: —B—

No overlap, no interleaving.

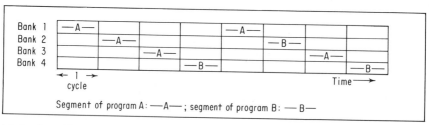

Segment of program A: —A—; segment of program B: —B—

Interleaving without overlap.

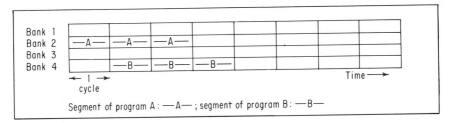

Overlap without interleaving.

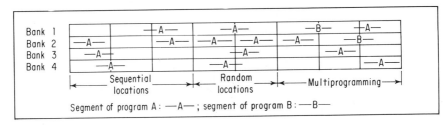

Interleaving with overlap.

Different degrees of simultaneity must be distinguished:

1. Interleaving operations of several programs on one processor creates the impression of several programs running at once: but when time-sharing (or multiprogramming) in this way, however, only one program is actually running in any particular picosecond.

2. Operating several independent processors at once (multiprocessing) is not considered a true instance of overlap, but rather of complete duplication of facilities.

Overlap is the preferred term when some simultaneity is obtained in various parts of one process or program, that is, when overlapped operations have a common goal or objective.

overlay The technique of writing new data over old data, a technique that allows for repeated use of the same blocks of internal storage during the different stages of a problem. Thus, when a routine is no longer needed in memory, another routine can replace all or part of it.

All computers have a fixed internal storage capacity which limits the size of the programs written for a particular computer. When a program and its data are too large for the computer, the program must be divided into segments and so constructed that only the active segments (or overlays) need be in core. By active segment is meant that part of the program required at that moment in time. In this manner, by repeatedly changing the contents of memory (one could say space-sharing as opposed to time-sharing), any size program can be accommodated in the computer. However, this technique is achieved at the expense of increased execution time. When the additional time penalty becomes too large, faster I/O devices or a larger memory will be warranted.

One of two conditions will exist with respect to the data being overwritten by a new overlay (1) if it has been altered and will be needed again, it must be written out and saved before the new overlay destroys it or, (2) if it will not be needed again, or if a valid image of it already exists in auxiliary storage, it need not be saved.

It is common to structure initialization routines as overlays, because they are used once and then discarded. Similarly, an end-of-job routine is a logical candidate for overlay status. Savings in time can be achieved by keeping the most-often-used routines in the computer at all times. By careful planning (or keeping an accounting record by an operating system) the execution time of an overlay-organized program can be optimized.

By overlay is meant also transparent film with permanent markings upon it, which is laid over a cathode-ray tube or other display to superimpose additional fixed information and/or to divide the display into predefined subareas. This device conserves the capacity of the display or display-generating devices.

P

pack   To reduce the amount of storage required to hold information by changing the method of encoding the data.

A common method of packing squeezes the wasted blanks out of a text image.   Let two binary numbers (typically 6 bits each) indicate the total width of a field, and the number of characters following the two binary numbers.   The two control numbers are followed by the indicated number of text characters.   When unpacking, enough blanks are added to the right to restore the entire field to its indicated width, and the control numbers are deleted.   Observe that if fewer than three blanks are supplied in unpacking, then no saving of storage has occurred.   This method is used to reduce source-language punched cards (FORTRAN language, assembly language, etc) to a compact form for convenient storage and handling.

To pack is also to place two or more data items into a single word by using part (a contiguous subfield) of the word for each data item. In fixed-word-length computers, a large set of small-size items may be compactly stored by dividing each word into several parts: for instance, a 24-bit word could be packed as four 6-bit characters, three

8-bit bytes, two 12-bit half words, twelve 2-bit fields, or one 24-bit word. The fields need not be of equal size. In list processing, each word could contain two 1-bit indicators, a 10-bit next-item address, and a 12-bit data field. These related items should logically share the same word.

To pack also means to store two decimal digits per 8-bit byte of storage by using two 4-bit subfields for the two digits. In computers with 8-bit bytes (characters), the space required by a decimal number may be reduced by half by representing each digit by a 4-bit field. As 16 possible 4-bit combinations exist, every decimal digit 0 to 9 can be represented with six codes left over for signs, decimal points, or similar qualifying information. Usually only sign information is allowed, and that must be in half of the byte holding the low-order digit. In the IBM 360 System and related computers, all decimal arithmetic is done in packed-decimal form. Computer instructions convert to and from packed-decimal form for programming convenience.

packing density Describes the amount of information per unit of storage medium, as characters per inch on tape, bits per inch on drum, or bits per square inch in photographic storage.

In magnetic tape, two factors determine the rate of data transfer in bits per second (bps): the number of bits per inch (packing density) multiplied by inches per second (tape speed). The tape density is usually fixed at 200, 556, 800, 1100, or 1600 bits per inch for compatibility with other computers. The tape speed can be anything within the mechanical capability of the equipment. As speed increases, cost and power requirements mount, and tape writing becomes more difficult owing to the higher bit-per-second rate. On the other hand, tape reading becomes easier because higher voltages are induced in the read heads. Similar considerations apply to all moving magnetic media.

In photographic and electrostatic tube storage, increasing bits per square inch increases capacity and possibly reduces the cost per bit, but makes selecting a particular bit more difficult. The limit is established by the resolution of the optics or the grain of the medium.

page A standard quantity of main-memory capacity, usually 512 to 4096 bytes or words in size, used for purposes of memory allocation and for partitioning programs into control sections. A page is also a standard quantity of source program coding, usually 8 to 64 lines in size, used for purposes of displaying the coding on a cathode-ray tube.

For purposes of memory mapping, each program address is translated by the hardware into an actual hardware address. This is accomplished by considering the program address (virtual address, or logical address) to be divided into two parts: a page address (leading bits) and a byte, or a word address within the page (last 9 to 12 bits of the virtual address). The hardware address conversion replaces the virtual page address with the actual page address, leaving the location within the page unchanged. This kind of memory mapping allows every program to be coded as though it began in location zero and had all the memory to itself. Each program, however, will actually occupy and refer to unique, nonconflicting addresses within the main memory.

It would be possible to express for each program its extent and beginning location in exact terms (14 to 24 bits) for memory allocation, but it is simpler to consider program sizes and memory capacity in terms of pages. A computer may contain 32 to 128 pages of memory (typically), and so only 5 to 8 bits would be required to designate a page belonging to a program. This represents a saving of up to 2048 bits in the memory allocation address tables. When memory mapping is being used, this form of allocation is required. In any case, allocating memory in terms of entire pages makes it very easy to move programs to and from auxiliary storage in page-sized records or blocks. The disadvantage of allocating by pages is the possibility of wasting some memory in a partially filled final page for each program.

In conversational time-sharing using cathode-ray tube displays, a single page of program may be displayed at one time for the users inspection or modification. The capacity of a page in this sense is determined mainly by the capacity of the CRT. This size page bears no relation to the memory page discussed above.

See OVERLAY.

page boundary The address of the first (lowest) word or byte within a page of memory.

Every page boundary is a hardware memory address expressed as a number having 9 to 12 low-order zeros. The exact number of trailing zeros depends on the size of the page used by a particular computer. Nine zeros apply to 512 word pages, while twelve are needed for 4096-byte (or word) pages. The highest address within a page has the same number of low-order binary 1's in its numerical representation. All programs in a paged-memory environment should begin on a page-boundary address.

See PAGE.

page reader   In character recognition, a character reader capable of processing cut-form documents of varying sizes. Some page readers are also capable of reading information in reel forms. Contrast with CONTINUOUS STATIONARY READERS.

page turning   The process of moving entire pages of information between main memory and auxiliary storage. This is usually done to allow several concurrently executing programs to share a main memory of inadequate capacity. The expression page turning is also used in conversational time-sharing systems to mean moving programs in and out of memory on a round-robin, cyclic schedule so that each program may use its allotted share of computer time.

When both main memory and all computer programs are divided into pages of equal size, it is possible to run concurrently more programs than the memory can hold at one time in their entirety. Several pages of each program reside in main memory, and control of the computer passes from program to program. When the momentarily active program needs a reference to one of its own pages that is not then in memory, the supervisor takes over. It deactivates the interrupted program, decides where in memory to place the required program page, initiates suitable I/O activity to accomplish the page changing, and finally gives control to another active program. When the page is loaded into main memory from auxiliary storage, the inactivated program is returned to active status.

In principle, other programs utilize the time wasted by page turning, so that only the supervisor overhead time is lost to productivity. The efficiency of the whole process is markedly affected by the method used to select the memory area to receive the requested page. This area must not contain a page liable to be requested soon by an active program, or else a very high page-swapping activity will result. Clearly, the more programs are crowded together in inadequate main memory, the more inefficient the whole process becomes. An optimum point is reached when adding one additional program would cause swapping time to exceed the average duration of a run segment. If the average program needs a missing page in less time than it takes to load a page, then most program run segments include some time waiting for I/O while no program can actively run. By keeping the population of concurrent programs below this critical level, the supervisor assures high productivity from the computer. Page turning is also known as paging.

See CONVERSATIONAL TIME-SHARING, DYNAMIC PROGRAM RELOCATION.

panel   Usually the face of the console, which is normally equipped with lights, switches, and buttons to:

1. Control the machine.
2. Correct errors.
3. Determine the status of the various CPU parts.
4. Determine the contents of various locations.
5. Revise the contents of various locations.

Panel sizes are much smaller in new computers than in older models.

parallel Pertaining to the simultaneous performance of multiple operations by multiple and related facilities.

When one read/write head writes 8 bits in sequence on one magnetic track, this operation is called serial-write and takes eight 1-bit write time units. If eight read/write heads write 1 bit each on eight magnetic tracks, this operation is called parallel-write and takes only 1-bit write time unit. In all transmission or read/write operations, parallel execution of n operations increases the cost by a factor of n, and reduces time by a factor of n.

In modern technology, the steady decrease in cost of multiple similar-function integrated circuits makes parallel operation cheaper. Because computer logic speed is already limited by the speed of light (the limit to signal propagation velocity), parallel execution offers the best hope for the faster computers of the future.

See MULTIPROCESSOR.

parallel search storage A device for very rapid search of a volume of stored data to permit finding a specific item.

Instead of directing storage to READ OUT CONTENTS OF CELL #27041 (contaning BLOOM), a parallel search storage is directed to FIND THE LOCATION OF THE NAME BLOOM and possibly to read out related information. By searching all (or very many) cells in parallel, the time of the operation is greatly reduced.

As an example of how this could be accomplished, consider each bit to be represented by the output state of a bistable flip-flop. Let the first bit of the desired keyword be applied to the first-bit flip-flop of every storage word, the second key bit to the second bits of storage words, etc. If a one-bit exists in the search pattern, the corresponding bit of each storage word will change state; where zero bits exist in the search pattern, the corresponding stored bits are preserved. The contents of each word is then the EXCLUSIVE OR of the original contents and the search key. By INCLUSIVE OR-ing together all the bits of each storage word, the existence of zero words can be rapidly detected. Since zero words result only from perfectly matching bit patterns, matching words can be found at once.

Of course, the entire memory has been altered by the look-up operation, but it can be restored by repeating the operation with the identical search key. (Performing EXCLUSIVE OR twice nullifies its effect, since this operation is its own inverse.)

The matches detected by the restorative look-up are words that were initially zero. This information can be used to find empty space in the memory, if zero words are to be interpreted as empty.

See ASSOCIATIVE STORAGE.

parallel storage A storage device in which words (or characters, or digits) can be read in or out simultaneously.

parameter A quantity that is assigned a temporarily constant value in order to modify control or influence a process or procedure.

Usually a parameter is similar to an input argument or an internal quantity, but sometimes parameters are output arguments.

Parameters are often used as upper or lower limits, or in other ways as test quantities (decision levels), rather than as computational values. (Computational usage is usually reserved for arguments.) For instance, an input parameter to a subroutine could be 0 or 1 to indicate that some branch of logic is to be skipped or executed, another parameter could indicate how many times a loop is to be performed, parameters here serving as control quantities.

The value of a parameter is constant unless it is changed, but a parameter is not a constant (a quantity whose value never changes) nor is it a variable (a quantity whose value frequently changes). It preserves its value until it is changed for some reason.

In mathematics, a parameter is considered to be of lesser rank (or importance) than other arguments. Thus, in formal integration, the integrand is an argument, but the limits of integration are parameters. They influence the result without being as intimately involved.

parity bit An additional nondata bit that is attached to a set of data bits to check their validity.

If the parity bit is set so that the sum of 1-bits in the augmented set is odd, odd parity is being used. If the sum of 1-bits should be an even number, even parity is used. The parity of the entire set of bits is checked by hardware or by programming. If the expected parity is not found, an error is indicated.

It should be noted that 1 parity bit can only detect the occurrence of an odd number of single-bit errors. No indication of how to correct the errors is given, and an even number of errors cannot be detected.

If data bits are arranged in a rectangular array and a parity bit is appended to each row and column, then:

1. Any 1-bit error can be found and corrected.
2. Any 2-bit errors can be detected but not corrected.
3. Almost all 3-bit errors can be detected.

parity check A check that is performed on the data bits and parity bits of an array to determine whether the number of 1-bits is odd (or even). Usually an odd (or even) condition is expected, and the occurrence of the wrong parity indicates the existence of an error.

Because zero is an even number, a no 1-bits condition correctly represents zero under even parity. However, this condition may be indistinguishable from no data or complete absence of information. With odd parity at least one 1-bit must be on to indicate that data are all zero bits.

Parity check is synonymous with ODD-EVEN CHECK.

part As applied to digital computer instructions, parts are those subfields within the instruction format that are reserved for particular functions. Instructions may be divided into an operation part (what is to be done) and an address part (what it is to be done to or with). Other instruction parts may indicate address modification by indirect addressing or index registers.

partial carry A word composed of the carries generated at each position when adding many digits in parallel.

The partial carry may be shifted left one place and added back in, effecting many carry operations at once. Of course, a new partial carry may be generated by the add-back. The process must terminate after a number of add-backs at most equal to the original number of digits.

partitioned data set A single data set, divided internally into a directory and one or more sequentially organized subsections called members, residing on a direct access for each device, and commonly used for storage or program libraries.

Every partitioned data set begins with a directory recorded in the standard format. This directory contains the name and location of each member of the partitioned data set. If a member has more than one name, the additional names are called aliases. An alias appears in an additional directory entry, with a signal bit set to indicate that this is an alias, or secondary name entry. Any information in the partitioned data set that is not pointed to by some entry in the directory cannot be accessed. Therefore, data in the partitioned data set can be deleted merely by removing its directory entries.

Every member of any individual partitioned data set has the same record format and organization, but this internal structure may differ from one partitioned data set to another. A member is much like a sequentially organized data set in appearance, but it is not a data set. The data records in a member of a partitioned data set are usually fixed length, blocked or unblocked, and follow one another in sequentially ascending locations in the direct-access storage device. In normal processing of a partitioned data set, one or more members are accessed, and each selected member is processed in its entirety.

Like any data set recorded on a direct-access storage control, a partitioned data set is identified and described by a data-set control block recorded on the same device. This data-set control block names the data set, names its location in terms of hardware addresses, indicates that its organization is partitioned, and describes the record format of the members of the data set. Other information in the data-set control block includes date of creation, security password, retention period or expiration date. Much of the value of a partitioned data set lies in the fact that it needs only one data-set control block, no matter how many members it contains.

A partitioned data set may be compared to a low-level index together with a number of sequential data sets. For a fair comparison to be possible, it is required that the sequentially organized data sets have similar internal structures and all be recorded on the same direct-access storage device. The partitioned data set has only one data-set control block and as many directory entries as there are members. The multiple sequential data sets have multiple data-set control blocks, resulting in the redundant recording of a great deal of duplicate descriptive information.

A single DD (data definition) control card and a single open macroinstruction suffice to establish program linkage to any and all members of a partitioned data set. To access several sequential data sets requires a DD card and an open macroinstruction for each. In this way the partitioned data set saves storage space, time, and effort. The penalty for this convenience is that all members of any one partitioned data set must obey the same internal structure.

Partitioned data sets are ideally suited for storing libraries of programs. Typically, the members of the partitioned data set are related programs, but this is not necessarily true. Because all members of the partitioned data set have the same format, it may be required that one partitioned data set hold source programs and a different partitioned data set hold the corresponding object modules or load modules. For example, a partitioned data set named SOURCE could contain the members MAIN, SUB1, and CASE2 as source programs. The result of compiling or assembling these programs would appear in the object module library, OBJECT, with either the same member names or new member names. Usually a member contains one entire program, although several programs or a program fragment could constitute a member.

In time, the space allocated to a partitioned data set may become full. Members are erased by removing their directory entries, but the storage area that they occupied does not become immediately available. This may be remedied by copying the partitioned data set onto another storage device, and then copying it back into the space it formerly occupied. In the copy process deleted members are lost, and additional storage area can be allocated, if required.

Pascal, Blaise (1623–1662)   Blaise Pascal, French mathematician and essayist, in 1642 built a successful digital calculating machine to aid him in computations for his father's business accounts. This *machine arithmétique* was the first adding machine to clearly resemble the modern desk calculator. The apparatus used a mechanical gear system to add and subtract numbers with as many as eight columns of digits. The digits 0 to 9 were engraved on a series of eight wheels, the right-most wheel being the units dial, the second—the tens, the third—hundreds, and so on, in direct analogy to a number hand-written in decimal notation. During addition, when a dial exceeded the digit 9, carrying occurred by means of a series of gears so arranged that they turned the next-left wheel one unit.

patch   To modify a program or routine by inserting a machine language correction in an object deck, or directly into the computer through the console.

In the present era programmers rarely deal with computer language as such. Programs are written in assembly language or a higher-level compiler language (procedure-oriented language). As a program is being developed, it undergoes many changes in the source language, each change requiring another pass through the translating processor. When the program is debugged and accepted for production, it sometimes reveals unsuspected faults. At such times and under production deadline pressures, the fastest possible fix is desired. To this end, a programmer localizes the difficulty and invents a hasty solution. It is possible to avoid the language translation process by working in the computer's own internal language. It may be practical to change the object deck (machine language cards) or add to the object deck. Alternatively, the changes can be made directly through the console.

Computers with internal representation in the form of decimal numbers (such as the IBM 650 and 7070) are easiest to patch. Computers with 6-bit characters (such as the Honeywell 200 and IBM 1401) are next most easy to correct. Binary word computers (CDC 3200, IBM 7090) are more difficult to change. Possibly the hardest computers to patch are of the RCA Spectra 70 and IBM 360 type, because they have 256 possible characters and lack a true object deck. (Hardware relocation and base registers add to the difficulty: the 360 system is deliberately unpatchable, according to IBM.)

The principal disadvantage of patching is that the changes are not indicated in the program documentation or listings. As computers and programs become more complicated, documentation becomes more and more important, and uncontrolled patching becomes of less and less value. The alert program manager limits patching to emergency conditions only, and insists upon after-the-fact source language changes equivalent to the patches.

In some cases, particularly on small computers, patching is a practical aid to normal debugging. On a slow computer a lengthy assembly or two can be avoided by console intervention. The indicated changes must be included in the source language because the program is still under development or check-out. It should be noted that much computer time can be wasted while the man thinks, so that only inexpensive computers permit this approach. On expensive computers, compilations being much faster, console patching is made unnecessary.

The program modification is itself called a patch.

A patch is also the term used for temporary and removable electric connection.

pattern recognition   The automatic identification of figures, characters, shapes, forms, and patterns without active human participation in the decision process.

There are two essentially different ways of performing pattern recognition:

1.   Through specially built devices that can recognize a prespecified set of patterns under particular conditions.

2.   By means of a general-purpose digital computer through a suitable input device, the recognition being performed by programmed logic.

The former method can be cheaper or faster; the latter method is more flexible and adaptable.

A common example of the first approach is called optical character recognition, a method in which devices read documents to prepare a computer input. Generally, a page of text is mechanically moved to a reading position under a lens. A spot of light scans the page until a loss of reflectance indicates that a dark spot (that is, a character) has been encountered. A quick scan locates the top, bottom, and sides of the character. The optics can be adjusted to move the image to a standard viewing area, or frame. In rapid succession a series of positive and negative masks are superimposed on the projected image, and the net transmission of each is measured. A correctly matching negative mask blocks almost all light transmission, and a correct positive mask will confirm the identity of the unmasked character by causing almost no additional loss of light. Proper level sensing and comparison circuits choose the most probable character and generate suitable output signals.

By proper programming a digital computer can be used to perform such functions as recognize patterns, extract signals from noise, or sharpen slightly fuzzy images. Computers can be programmed to find tanks or missiles in jungle or other photographs as an aid to surveillance photograph interpretation, match symptoms to diseases, and interpret EEG or electrocardiogram curves.

pattern-sensitive fault A fault that appears only in response to one or certain patterns or sequences of data.

For example, a program testing for positive, negative, or zero in that order could respond improperly to minus zero, but would respond correctly to all other numbers (on computers that use sign-magnitude representation such as the IBM 650, 1620, 7070, 7094, or 1401, a minus sign can be attached to a zero number; on some binary word machines using two's complement representation of negatives, minus zero cannot be represented and does not exist).

Similar faults can exist with hardware. For example, in a partially defective register which normally behaves well, but has poor tolerance of heat, a certain pattern of activity or data could cause excessive heat dissipation and bring on failure, which would be a pattern-sensitive fault.

PCM Acronym for pulse-code modulation.

A means of transmitting digital or analog information encoded by a string of pulses. The amplitude of the pulses remains constant, but the duration of the pulse (or the interval between pulses) varies according to the data being represented.

This system has much of the noise immunity of FM (frequency modulation), making it attractive in many applications. In addition, the square wave shape of the generated signal dissipates less power in the equipment and uses a simpler technology than that required by the sine wave shape of ordinary FM.

See PULSE-CODE MODULATION.

peephole masks In character recognition, a set of characters (each character residing in the character reader in the form of strategically placed points) which theoretically render all input characters as being unique regardless of their style.

Peephole masks that are invoked during the property-detection phase of character recognition are constructed in such a way that for any given character there is one set of points which represents the coincidence that should obtain between the various strokes of the character and another set of points which represent what should be a clear area.

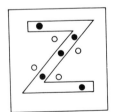

Peephole mask.

permanent storage A means of storing data for rapid retrieval by a computer, and which does not permit changing the stored data.

Permanent storage can be implemented in several ways: by perforated paper tape or cards, which are permanent unless a punch is used, and by developed and fixed photographic images which can be read photoelectrically but not altered; moreover, certain kinds of static magnetic memories (or core) can be very rapidly accessed without being erased.

Permanent storage can be more compact, convenient, and economical than other storage for holding nonchanging data and instructions. For example, a telephone electronic exchange could use permanent storage to associate area codes with outgoing long-line circuits and further, a computer can use permanent storage to store square-root routines, and an off-line device to store a conversion table from seven-level paper tape code to EBCDIC. See FIXED STORAGE, MICROPROGRAM, NONERASABLE STORAGE, READ-ONLY STORAGE.

pertinency factor In information retrieval (IR), the ratio obtained in dividing the total number of relevant documents retrieved by the total number of documents retrieved. The retrieval of nonrelevant documents is due either to the user's loose definition in formulating his query, or to the system's inability to recognize the query, or both. Ideally, the pertinency factor should be close to one, being then a measure of the user's understanding of the system, and of the system's ability to cope with its users. Contrast with NOISE FACTOR.

photocell matrix In optical character recognition (OCR), a device that projects an input onto a fixed two-dimensional array of photocells for the purposes of simultaneously achieving the character's horizontal and vertical components.

Since the reflectance at every point in the input character is measured in parallel rather than sequentially (see divided slit scan), the amount of time required to scan the character is limited only by the response time of the photocells. This time interval has been reduced to fractions of a microsecond.

The biggest shortcoming of the photocell matrix has been its relative inability to allow for and correct character misregistration. Consequently, various mechanisms are being employed that sense the position of individual characters before projection onto the matrix. Attempts to correct the position of the character include re-presentation of the document and adjustment of the angles of mirrors used in the lens projection system.

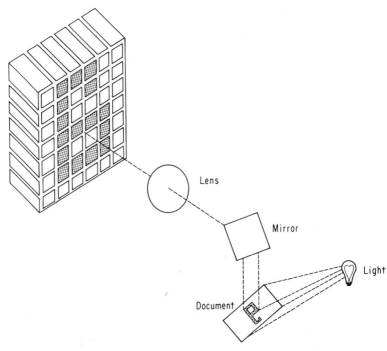

Photocell matrix.

photogravure In character recognition, a method of document preparation in which printing is accomplished from a recessed surface, the character being comprised of small cells which contain the ink.

phototypesetting In optical character recognition (OCR), a process of reproducing type matter, for example computer outputs, on photographic film or paper, for the purpose of improving its quality.

Optical character readers will tolerate character irregularities up to a certain degree, beyond which a high document reject rate will result. Consequently, in order to push through such documents, phototypesetting is available as a form of off-line normalizing.

However, it should be noted that the feasibility of such a technique is questionable in most cases except perhaps for the situations that entail the one-time processing of extraordinary source documents. In applications where optical processing will be done on a periodic basis, it would be more efficient to revert to a different form of data media.

Computer-controlled phototypesetting is also used for computer-generated output when appearance is very important or the output exceeds the capability of ordinary computer output devices. For example, a computer-prepared telephone directory can use upper and lowercase letters, boldface, italics, and variable spacing between characters, all very difficult to obtain on ordinary computer printers. A computer-generated output of mathematical text could use various type faces and sizes, special characters and symbols, subscripts and superscripts, etc. The output of phototypesetting processes is usually of the highest standard of appearance, equal in quality to most printed material.

physical record   A set of adjacent data characters recorded on some storage medium, physically separated from other physical records that may be on the same medium by means of some indication that can be recognized by a simple hardware test.

Each punched card contains a physical record, for it is physically separated from all other punched cards in the deck. On magnetic tape and disks, a physical record is bounded at its beginning and end by interrecord gaps, or IRG's. Magnetic drums and punched paper tape often have no record-delimiting (and space-wasting) gaps, so that records must be distinguished by some other means. For punched cards and magnetic-tape devices, each physical record represents a mechanical start/stop operation of the transporting mechanism. On magnetic disks which rotate continuously, only the data transmission is started and stopped for each physical record being processed.

Normally an entire physical record is transmitted by each hardware input or output operation. However, the programmer may be concerned with a quantity of data larger or smaller than those contained on a physical record. For example, a punched-card file containing logical records (program-usage defined groups of data items) 300 characters long would require four punched cards per logical record. Similarly logical records 25 characters long can be punched one, two, or three per card. If one physical record contains N logical records, the logical records are said to be blocked N, or that a blocking factor of N is being used. A blocking factor may be used to reduce the number of interrecord gaps, the number of mechanical start/stop operations, or both. There does not seem to be a corresponding terminology for the case of multiple physical records per logical record.

See BLOCK, LOGICAL RECORD.

pinboard   A board or panel containing an array of uniform holes into which pins may be inserted to control the operation of equipment.

A typical pinboard contains a square matrix of holes. Each hole is connected to one and only one wire running vertically, and similarly to one wire running horizontally. Each wire is insulated from every other wire until a conductive pin is inserted into a hole, thus connecting a vertical and a horizontal wire.

For example, a 10 × 10 pinboard with 100 holes can connect any of 10 incoming signals (horizontal) to any of 10 outgoing paths (vertical). Two horizontal paths can be connected to each other by connecting each to the same vertical path. A maximum of 19 pins will thus connect all 20 wires together on one circuit, so that no more than 19 pins are needed for any possible configuration: one way of connecting all the wires together would be to use 10 diagonal pins, and 9 pins in any one row or column.

Occasionally, special pins in the form of two-part jacks containing diodes, resistors, etc., are used. Diodes permit several inputs to feed one output without connecting the inputs together. Such a board can be used to convert from decimal to binary. See MATRIX. Compare with PLUGBOARD.

pitch The distance between the centerlines of adjacent rows of hole positions in punched paper tape.

This distance is normally equal to one-tenth of an inch. See ROW PITCH.

PL/1 A multipurpose programming language, developed by IBM for the model 360 Systems, which can be used for both commercial and scientific applications.

PL/1 can be a very simple language to use, or it can be employed to handle extremely complex computing problems. One of its most important characteristics is its modularity, that is, the presence of different subsets of the language for different applications at different levels of complexity. The same also holds true for input/output.

The programmer may control the operations at whatever degree of simplicity or complexity he desires. PL/1 provides for many options in statements, data, and file description. Whenever there are alternatives and no choice has been made by the programmer, the compiler makes an assumption. This assumption is the alternative that would be required in most situations. This aspect of PL/1 is characteristic of its simplicity.

Mixed expressions are permitted throughout the program. This adds to the flexibility and simplicity of the language. If A is declared to be a fixed-point number, B a floating-point number, and C a character string that is 10 characters long, the expression C = A + B would be evaluated as follows: A would be converted to floating point; floating-point addition would provide a result which would then be converted to a character string of 10 characters and assigned as a value to C.

Two or more programs or tasks can be handled simultaneously with PL/1. This feature is extremely important in real-time operations or in the use of a computer with multiprocessing capabilities. During execution of a program, another program or portion of a program may be called (invoked) and executed. This attached task may in turn invoke another, and all three can continue concurrently, the originating task retaining control of the subordinate tasks.

PL/1 has the greatest debugging capability of any existing language. However, since the PL/1 compiler will accept any PL/1-like statement, an incorrectly coded statement can be compiled successfully, and the program not do what the programmer had in mind. This possibility of misunderstanding is PL/1's greatest hazard. It is not inconceivable that PL/1 will become one of the four generally accepted languages in the EDP world, the other three languages being BASIC, COBOL, and FORTRAN.

The following is an example of a compound interest calculation: what is the amount VALUE of a sum PRINCIPAL invested at RATE percent compounded semiyearly for YEARS years.

INTEREST: PROCEDURE;	Program begins with a procedure statement which must have a label. Labels must be followed by a colon; statements must be terminated by a semicolon.
DECLARE PRINCIPAL DECIMAL FIXED (7, 2), RATE DECIMAL FIXED (3, 3), YEARS DECIMAL FIXED (2), INCREASE DECIMAL FIXED (4, 3), VALUE DECIMAL FIXED (7, 2), MASTER FILE INPUT, NEWMASTER FILE OUTPUT;	The DECLARE statement is used to reserve storage areas and describe the data and the nature of each file. In this example PRINCIPAL is a maximum of seven digits, with a two-place decimal fraction. Coding is completely free form—it is not necessary to indent or to write each statement or expression on a separate line.
GETRECORD: GET FILE (MASTER) LIST (PRINCIPAL, RATE, YEARS);	Read input record. The first three fields of input are moved to the storage areas specified.

/ * COMPUTE VALUE. * /	Comments may be inserted in the program wherever blanks are allowed. Any characters, except the combinations of / * and * /, may be used in a comment.
INCREASE = 1 + RATE/200; VALUE = PRINCIPAL * INCREASE * * (2 * YEARS);	Arithmetic expressions are evaluated in the following order: an expression enclosed in parentheses is evaluated before any other part of the expression, exponentiation (* *), multiplication (*) and division (/), addition (+) and subtraction (−). If operators with equal priority appear in an expression, they are evaluated from left to right.
PUT FILE (NEWMASTER) LIST (PRINCIPAL, RATE, YEARS, VALUE);	Write output record. The four fields indicated are moved to the first four output fields.
GO TO GETRECORD;	GO TO statement transfers control to beginning of routine where next input record will be read.
END:	Each procedure is terminated by an END statement. Since this program has only one procedure, the END statement also indicates the end of the program. If there were more than one procedure, each procedure would have to be invoked separately (using a CALL statement) since control is not automatically transferred from one procedure to the next.

plugboard   A board or panel containing an array of uniform holes into which plugs may be inserted to control the operation of equipment.

Usually, a plugboard is a rectangular array of holes, with one contact per hole. Wires of various lengths, with a plug at each end, are connected from hole to hole to form circuits. Thus, most positions on the boards can be identified as sending (active positions) or as receiving (passive positions). Special two-, three-, or multiple-contact connectors are often available for connecting together wires without utilizing plugboard positions for the connections. Two-circuit jacks with shielded cables are used for high-frequency circuits, very high frequencies, or high-fidelity audio applications.

When decisions have to be made, the coils and contacts of specific relays can be connected by means of certain holes in the plugboard: this allows for some data-alterable logic to be wired in. When fixed alternate modes of action are needed, the contacts of manually operated switches can be provided.

Plugboards may be built into the equipment they control (as, for instance, in analog computers), but they are more commonly made removable. Multiple plugboards, each with a fixed setup attached,

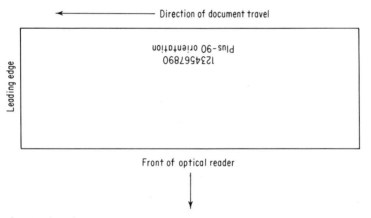

Plus-90 orientation.

permit rapid change of wired-in programs. Most EAM equipment have removable plugboards to regulate their operation.

Contrast with PINBOARD.

plus-90 orientation   In optical character recognition (OCR), that determinate position which indicates that the line elements of an inputted source document appear perpendicular with the leading edge of the optical reader.

Most optical readers are programmable to the extent that they can accept various parameters concerning the form of a source document. A parameter designation of plus-90 orientation directs the optical reader to perform its scan across the length (in relation to the leading edge) of the source document.

Contrast with NORMAL ORIENTATION. See also OPTICAL SCANNING.

point In position systems of numeration, the implied (or explicit) delimiter which separates the integral from the fractional parts of a numeral, e.g., decimal point.

Also: a data item that contains the address or location of another data item is said to point to the latter item.

Polish notation A technique for treating algebraic statements, this technique being attributed to the Polish logician J. Lukasieqicz.

The Polish notation permits mathematical notation without parenthetical expressions: the absence of embedded parentheses permits simpler compiler interpretation, translation, and execution of results. This notation appears in two forms: with prefix operators, and with suffix operators. For example:

(1)	$X = A/(B + C) + D * (E\text{-}F)$	Usual notation, internal operators
(2)	$+/A + BC * + - FED = X$	Polish notation: prefix operators
(3)	$BC + A/DEF - + * + X =$	Polish notation: suffix operators

For instance, the above prefix operator notation stands for:
ADD (QUOTIENT OF A ÷ BY (SUM OF B + C)) TO (PRODUCT OF D AND (SUM OF (−F) AND E)) AND STORE IN (ADDRESS OF X).

The absence of parenthesis results in fast compilation: for instance, the above suffix-operator notation is the form expressing the order in which a computer (scanning left to right) executes the operations, that is:

GET VALUE OF B
GET VALUE OF C
ADD LAST TWO NUMBERS: $(B + C)$
GET VALUE OF A
DIVIDE LAST TWO NUMBERS: $(A ÷ (B + C))$
GET VALUE D
GET VALUE E
GET VALUE F
NEGATE LAST NUMBER: $-F$ (this is a unary operation).
ADD LAST TWO NUMBERS: $(E + (-F))$
MULTIPLY LAST TWO NUMBERS: $(D * (E - F))$
ADD THE TWO (remaining) VALUES:
$(A/ (B + C) + D * (E - F))$
GET ADDRESS OF X
STORE VALUE INTO X

One computer, the Burroughs 5500, actually structures its machine language in Polish suffix notation, with addresses and operation (OP) codes following one another as needed, without any fixed ratio of addresses to the operations.

The operands are kept in a stack or pushdown list. The top two items of the list are in hardware registers, the remainder of the list being in core memory, in inverse order. The appearance of an address syllable causes data to be added to the list, while an operation syllable usually causes the top two numbers to interact to form one new value, shortening the list by one number (exceptions are unary operations (negate), transfers (jumps), and store operations).

polling A process that involves interrogating in succession every terminal on a shared communications line to determine which of the terminals are in need of servicing.

Before communication can occur on a transmission path, the sender must be prepared to send and the receiver must be prepared to receive. Consider a party-line situation in which economics dictates the sharing of a common transmission line by many remote terminals, all of which intermittently communicate with a common central station. If each terminal could demand attention from the central station by means of some signal, it would be possible to establish communication whenever necessary. However, if the terminals are independent and uncoordinated, there will be no way to prevent two terminals from demanding servicing at the same time, a situation which would result in garbled transmissions. This conflict can be resolved by giving the initiative and control duties to a single, central station.

A terminal wishing to transmit continuously emits a signal. The central station interrogates each terminal in turn, and sends a proceed signal to the first requesting terminal that it encounters. When that transaction is finished, polling resumes at the next terminal in the list, and continues until another transmission ready signal is encountered. Polling prevents multiple transmissions by giving complete authority to the central station. If the transmission line is idle, no terminal will have to wait longer than the polling cycle time before the beginning of transmission. When the line is busy, the remaining terminals are obliged to wait.

If two-way transmission is possible, the terminals can be directed to receive whenever the central station wishes to send, provided they are in working order. Reception has a higher or lower priority than transmission, depending on message priority and/or system design.

Some simple computers must program polling activity into their normal operating schedules, a requirement that results in either inefficient processing or long polling cycle times.   Sophisticated computers have transmission controls with automatic polling circuitry, these controls resulting in higher efficiency but higher hardware costs.

positional notation   Any of several systems of numeration characterized by the common property of valuing each digit both by its numeric value and by its position with respect to the units position.

Such systems are the decimal, octal, binary, biquinary, hexadecimal, etc.

Let a numeral be written in the form

$$\ldots\ a_3a_2a_1a_0 \ \cdot \ a_{-1}a_{-2}a_{-3} \ \ldots$$

where the a's are any admissible digits for the particular system.

We may denote the value of the units position by $b_0 \ (= 1)$ and the value of the other positions by:

$$\ldots\ b_3b_2b_1 \ \ldots \ b_{-1}b_{-2}b_{-3} \ \ldots$$

Then the value of the numeral is:

$$\ldots\ a_3 \cdot b_3 + a_2 \cdot b_2 + a_1 \cdot b_1 + a_0 \cdot b_0 + a_{-1} \cdot b_{-1} + \ \ldots$$

In the systems cited above the b's will appear (in decimal) as:

Position	Binary	Biquinary	Octal	Decimal	Hexadecimal
b_3	8	50	512	1000	4096
b_2	4	10	64	100	256
b_1	2	5	8	10	16
b_0	1	1	1	1	1
b_{-1}	1/2	1/2	1/8	1/10	1/16
b_{-2}	1/4	1/10	1/64	1/100	1/256
b_{-3}	1/8	1/20	1/512	1/1000	1/4096

By knowing the system (the b's) and the numerals (the a's) any numeral may be interpreted to its correct numeric value.

postmortem   Any action taken after an operation is completed which helps to analyze that operation.

Usually, when an unexpected or inexplicable difficulty is encountered, a postmortem dump is taken to record all available information about the failed state of a program: then a postmortem analysis is made to discover the cause of the difficulty.

Sometimes the cause is obvious (as when due to bad data still intact), but at times the cause cannot be determined (as when an indirect transfer of control to a random location may cause any number of erroneous actions to be taken before halting: such a malfunction can often hide its own causes).

Most corrective actions taken after this analysis are not considered to be postmortem actions.

postmortem dump   The printout showing the state of all registers and the contents of main memory taken after a computer run terminates normally or terminates owing to fault, and the program which generates the printout mentioned above.

Suppose that a computer program gets into some difficulty and halts, or is stopped by the operator.   As much information as possible must be recovered to facilitate correction, and yet computer time must be conserved.   The operator either loads or transfers control to a (resident) postmortem dump routine which prints out (or writes on a print tape) the contents of all registers, as much of the console as it can read, and the contents of main memory.   The location of the last instruction to be executed is noted by either the operator, the dump routine, or both.   Armed with this information, a programmer may perform a postmortem analysis to discover the cause of the trouble.

In some computers (as in the IBM 7070) it is possible to tell whether a particular item is alphanumeric or numeric (computational): in this case each item can be printed in correct format.   However, in most computers such identification is impossible: in this case, each item must be printed in a manner that reveals every digit (octal, decimal, hexadecimal).   If only two interpretations of each location are possible, both may be printed (as in the case of the Honeywell 200:   octal and alphanumeric).

precision   The accuracy to which a quantity is correctly represented or expressed: normally, precision is measured as *so many digits of accuracy.*

The assumption made here is that an error is being committed. For example, a 10-decimal digit word or a 32-bit binary word can represent exactly the number 29, but precision is normally mentioned when one attempts to represent a number beyond the capacity of the computer.   Thus, one says that a 27-bit binary number has approximately the precision of an 8-decimal digit number.   This expresses the fact that $2^{27} \approx 10^8$, or equivalently, an error of 1 part in 2^{27} is about the same accuracy as an error of 1 part in 10^8.

For instance:

$$2^{10} = 1024 \approx 1000 = 10^3$$

Thus, a 10-bit binary number has 2.4 percent more possible values than a three-digit decimal number: consequently, 10 bits is slightly more precise than three digits. In fact, each decimal digit requires approximately 3.32 binary bits ($3.32 = \log_2 10$) to match its precision.

If q is the smallest integer such that $2^q > 10^m$, it does not follow that any m-digit floating-point decimal number can be converted to a q-bit binary floating-point number and recovered unchanged by the inverse conversion. It has been shown that $q + 1$ bits are sufficient for arbitrary decimal-point locations, but q bits are enough for integers.

predefined process   In the documentation of programs, a process, procedure, or routine that is named in one place but described in another place.

When writing a flowchart it is sometimes desirable to condense an entire routine into a single box on the chart. A special shape, elongated hexagon, has been reserved for this use. The process can be a subroutine, a macroinstruction, or simply a block of logic explained elsewhere. Whatever the predefined process is, it must have a single entry and a single exit.

preset   As an adjective, preset describes a variable whose value is established before the first time it is used, and as a verb, to preset is to initialize a value of a variable before the value of the variable is used or tested.

For a simple example, consider numbering the pages of a report to be printed. The first page is always page 1, so that the page counter is preset to 1 before the program prints anything. After each page is printed, the counter is incremented before printing the next page. When page 2 is printed, the preset value has been destroyed (1 replaced by 2).

A preset value may be initialized by the assembler or compiler, by the computer operator (rarely), or by the program itself during start-of-run logic. Sometimes a preset value is not changed during the run. It then behaves as a predefined constant.

A value initialized by the language translator saves core and execution time. Initializing via programming permits a program to run stacked problems by reinitializing itself.

previewing   In character recognition, a process of attempting to gain prior information about the characters that appear on an incoming source document. This information, which may include the range of ink density, relative positions, and so forth, is used as an aid in the normalization phase of character recognition.

printing Usually refers to the process of printing an entire line at a time.

Modern computers can print 600 to 1100 lines per minute on one to six copies per pass through the printer. Alternatively, lithograph masters can be machine-produced, permitting volume production of computer generated output.

Printers of up to 30,000 lines per minute exist, but 1100 lines per minute is the fastest common speed. Higher speeds are obtained by CRT microfilm devices.

print line A set of printed characters and spaces, arranged in a horizontal row and considered as a unit.

problem A situation or state that results when some unknown information (the solution) is to be discovered, and some known information is available to assist in finding the solution.

problem description A written explanation of a problem, which must describe the known and the unknown (or desired) information, and which may also describe the method of solution, or the solution itself.

If one assumes that data processing is done in order to solve problems, it follows that data processing begins with a problem description. Experience has shown that the clearer the problem definition becomes, the more efficient the problem solution will be. Indeed, the more that an analyst or programmer knows about the problem, data, time requirements, etc., the more efficient the final program will be.

problem-oriented language A language·designed to facilitate the accurate expression of problems belonging to specific sets of problem types. Problem-oriented languages should not be confused with procedure-oriented languages (which see). A classical example of problem-oriented language is given by STRESS, a language similar to a civil engineer's shop talk. STRESS is tolerant of spacing, spelling errors (to some extent), and arbitrary punctuation, and yet is both clear and complete.

A problem-oriented language may contain no features capable of specifying the method to be used to solve the stated problem. Usually the method of solution is built into the computer program that interprets problem-oriented language statements. This enables some users to obtain computer solutions to problems that they could not solve themselves.

See COGO, SIMSCRIPT, STRESS.

procedure   A sequence of actions (or computer instructions) which collectively accomplish some desired task.

Traditionally the steps of a procedure are to be performed in some (not necessarily consecutive) sequence. Some work is being done today, however, with procedures in which some steps are performed simultaneously. In fact, some recent COBOL and PL/1 implementations have language features to support asynchronous processing of simultaneous tasks.

A procedure to be performed by human beings can tolerate some looseness of definition; a procedure for a computer must be precise and explicit.

Every procedure must describe
1. What is being manipulated: the data.
2. What is done with the data.
3. Where to begin.
4. When to stop.
See ALGORITHM.

procedure division   The section of a program (written in the COBOL language) in which a programmer specifies the operations to be performed with the data names appearing in the program. For example, if three data names, UNIT-PRICE, TOTAL-ORDERS, GROSS-AMOUNT, have been defined, then the procedure statement: MULTIPLY UNIT-PRICE BY TOTAL-ORDER GIVING GROSS-AMOUNT will be correctly interpreted by the computer to mean:
$$GROSS\text{-}AMOUNT = UNIT\text{-}PRICE \times TOTAL\text{-}ORDER$$

procedure-oriented language   A language designed to facilitate the accurate description of procedures, algorithms, or routines belonging to a certain set of procedures.

A procedure-oriented language is normally relatively computer-independent. For instance, although ALGOL is implemented on comparatively few computers in the United States, it is a widely used procedure-oriented language.

Any procedure-oriented language must provide for descriptions of
1. What is to be manipulated.
2. Which manipulations and tests are to be performed.
3. Where to begin.
4. When to stop.
COBOL, for instance, provides explicitly for describing WHY and WHO by means of its identification division. Other procedure-oriented languages are represented by: FORTRAN, PL/1, LISP, IPL-V, SIMSCRIPT, SNOBOL, SLIP.

APT III (automatic programmed tools, a numerical control language) falls into both procedure- and problem-oriented language classifications. Its vocabulary includes purely geometric (problem-oriented) terms as well as tool motion descriptors (procedure-oriented terms).

process   An operation having inputs, internal functions, and outputs. Unlike a procedure, a process need not (but may) have a beginning and an end.

processing   See AUTOMATIC DATA PROCESSING, BUSINESS DATA PROCESSING, DATA PROCESSING, ELECTRONIC DATA PROCESSING, INDUSTRIAL DATA PROCESSING, INFORMATION PROCESSING, MULTIPROCESSOR.

processor   From a hardware point of view, a device that performs one or many functions. Usually means a central processing unit, often abbreviated to CPU.

From a software point of view, a processor is a program that transforms some input into some output: usually called an assembler or a compiler.

Since a processor performs processes, it has inputs, internal workings, and outputs. Normally, a (hardware) processor is a central processing unit, capable of executing program instructions. Thus a processor does arithmetic, makes comparisons, tests for conditions, and supervises input/output. Some computers can accept more than one CPU, thus permitting multiprocessing of programs. There are also input/output processors.

A program that accepts an assembly (symbolic computer) language program, or a procedure-oriented language program and produces a machine-usable output program is called a processor.

Other processors are *not* language translators (such as the linkage editor).

The programs that interpret problem-oriented languages and the programs that interpretively run procedure-oriented language programs are also called processors.   See DATA CHANNEL.

program   A detailed and explicit set of directions for accomplishing some purpose, the set being expressed in some language suitable for input to a computer, or in machine language.

A program is usually considered to be self-contained, and it may be divided into a main routine and subroutines for the convenience of the programmer. The subroutines themselves are sometimes considered to be programs.

It is possible to divide or partition a program in two distinct ways: in routines, or independently written sections of the program, or in segments or overlays which may be in residence in the computer at different times. Each routine or subroutine may be written by a separate programmer, and, possibly, each routine may be written in a language different from that of the other routines. The boundaries of the segments or overlays may or may not coincide with the boundaries of the routines. An overlay segment is loaded into the computer as a unit and as required. Thus, program segments are run-time entities, but the boundaries between subroutines disappear before run time (at loader prepass or linkage editor time).

Programming is an activity that begins with the understanding of the problem, proceeds through several levels of detail logic design, and may end with coding (writing in keypunchable form). The debugging activity that reduces the program to a reliably running form may or may not be considered part of the programming activity. (The head of the EDP center will not observe this distinction, but the programmer and his supervisor will.) The programmer's job ends with the final documentation, generally not considered a programming activity (it contributes nothing to the computer code), but nevertheless indispensable. See DOCUMENTATION.

program library   An organized set of computer routines and programs which may consist of the following:

1. A catalog of program titles and abstracts, together with directions for obtaining the programs in computer and/or human-readable form, or

2. A reel of magnetic tape or a cabinet of punched cards or perforated tape with various programs contained therein (which may or may not have an index or catalog), or

3. A source program library, containing machine-readable programs in assembly or compiler language form, or

4. An object program library, with programs in relocatable machine-language form (usually not loadable, incomplete and/or not yet relocated), or

5. A core-image library, containing programs in executable and loadable computer-language form.

The last three types of libraries are usually distinct (not intermixed) and equipped with computer-readable indexes. There is provision for a user to obtain a listing of the contents of the library and to call for a member of it. There may, or may not, be facilities for the average user to add or to remove programs from the library.

Most operating systems (OS) for complex third-generation computers maintain types 3, 4, and 5 of the above libraries, and moreover, may contain many individual libraries of each kind.   The latter type can be classified as:

1.   System-provided, to be used by anyone and changed by none
2.   User-private, provided by, and reserved for, a particular user
3.   User-shared or public, provided by a user for use by several or all users

In general, several levels of indexes may be needed to keep track of all the catalogued library materials.

The operating systems control libraries on magnetic disk (and occasionally drum), but magnetic tape is also used.

programmed check   An error-detecting operation programmed by instructions rather than built into the hardware.

Consider, for example, the test to avoid division by zero before dividing.   Most hardware will detect this illegal operation, but the computer's error response may not be the response that the programmer desires.   By checking with instructions, the programmer can choose his own course of error action.   Only the program knows when some condition is improper.   Thus, in payroll, no computer knows that it is improper to deduct FICA for more than $6600 of salary (1967), and consequently, only programmed checking can enforce this rule.

See AUTOMATIC CHECK.

programming   See AUTOMATIC PROGRAMMING, LINEAR PROGRAM, MULTIPROGRAMMING, PROGRAM.

programming language   A language, other than machine language, used for expressing computer programs.   Material written in a programming language may (but need not be) provided as input to a language processing program for conversion into computer instructions.   The same material may (but need not be) provided to an interpretive processor for step-by-step execution without overall translation into computer instructions.   Finally, programming language text may be (but need not be) published for dissemination among the programming community without ever going near a computer.

The major kinds of programming languages are as follows:

1.   Assembly, or symbolic machine languages: one-to-one equivalence with computer instructions, but with symbols and mnemonics as an aid to programming
2.   Macroassembly languages, which are the same as assembly or symbolic machine languages, but permitting macroinstructions (which see) for coding convenience

3. Procedure-oriented languages for expressing methods in the same way as expressed by algorithmic languages (which see)

4. Problem-oriented languages for expressing problems (which see)

Procedure-oriented languages (which see) may be further divided into:

a. Algebraic languages (numerical computation)

b. String-manipulating languages (text manipulation)

c. Simulation languages (such as GPSS, DYNAMO)

d. Multipurpose languages (such as PL/1)

See ASSEMBLER, COMPILER.

program-sensitive fault A hardware malfunction that appears only in response to a particular sequence (or kind of sequence) of program instructions.

An example may be found in computers with instruction look-ahead features. These very fast computers fetch and interpret the next instruction while the current instruction is being executed. A hardware flaw could result in the improper execution of some sequence of two instructions, for example, the second beginning before the first was fully finished.

Even on simple computers without program look-ahead it is possible for a fault to cause some particular unit to operate more slowly than intended, with effects that only appear in particular sequences of action. Thus, if the output of some element is still changing at the time when it is sampled by the next circuit, an ambiguous value is delivered. One transistor in 10,000 while passing speed tests when the hardware is built and delivered could slow down (that is, deteriorate) enough in use for this to occur.

This fault only manifests itself when the instruction sequence causes the output from the slow element to be applied to an early-sampling circuit input.

property detector In character recognition, that electronic component of a character reader which processes the normalized signal for the purpose of extracting from it a set of characteristic properties on the basis of which the character can be subsequently identified.

The purpose of the property detection unit is to extract from the normalized inputted character a set of corresponding statements or measures which provides a basis for a decision as to its most probable identity. The type and sophistication of properties detected depend on two factors: the quality of the signal to be processed, and the size of the character set to be recognized.

Historically, this second factor has proved to be one of the foremost considerations in the evolution of character recognition. It is remembered that initially only numbers could be automatically recognized, eventually certain symbols were included, and most recently certain character sets were expanded to include alphabetic characters.

Property-detection units presently utilize various techniques, the most commonly used being mask matching, matched filters, and stroke analysis.

By way of illustration it is noteworthy to mention the methods employed in the property detection of the E13B and CMC7 magnetic-ink character-recognition fonts.

In the case of E13B property detection, a normalized character is converted by means of a vertical projection which reduces the signal to an analog waveform. (This is accomplished by a slit scan utilizing the matched-filter technique.) Subsequently this waveform will be submitted to the decision mechanism for final disposition.

CMC7 property detection also performs a vertical projection in order to convert all elements to a standard base and to ensure that the heights of the resultant elements conform to the hardware specifications. However, it is not the resultant waveform that is submitted for final disposition, but rather it is a digital series (binary) which represents the condition of long and short intervals that exist between the individual elements of the character.

Ideally, the property-detector response would be invariant under conditions of varying quality, style, or position; thus the degree of tolerance that accrues to the various detection techniques provides a useful basis for comparison.

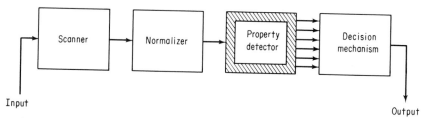

A character reader: component parts.

protected location   A storage cell arranged so that access to its contents is denied under certain circumstances.

The following kinds of protection for memory locations are common:
1. Full protection: cannot be written into or read from
2. Write protection: can be read but not altered (that is, cannot be written into)
3. Operand only: data may be fetched, but instructions cannot be executed from this location
4. Open, or no protection: free accessibility

Normally, protection applies to programs and to storage locations jointly. The program has a certain status or access key, and the storage cell has a protection key. If the program's access key matches the protection key, then access is granted. A supervisory program may have a master key giving it access to all locations.

A foreground/background organization is used on simpler computers. Programs in a supervisor or interrupt state can access all of memory. Programs not in the special state can only access non-protected locations.

The basic purpose of protection is to prevent programming accidents from destroying essential (or anyone else's) programs and data.

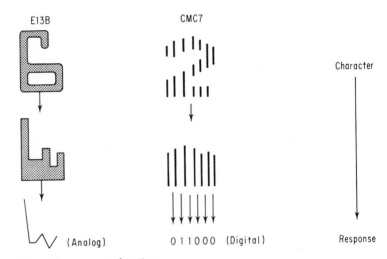

Illustrating property detection.

protection key   An indicator, usually 1 to 6 bits in length, associated with a program, this indicator being intended to grant the program access to those sections of memory which the program can use, and to deny the program access to all other parts of memory.

Each program in some kind of memory-protection environment has a protection key associated with it. When this program is running, a special portion of the computer remembers this key. Each location in memory (or block of locations) has associated with it a storage key which determines whether access is to be allowed to the running program. Any attempt by the program to reference a memory area whose storage key differs from the program's protection key will result in the program being interrupted and a supervisory program being activated to handle the situation.

There must be a master protection key (usually all zeros) for the supervisor to have access to all of memory. There may also be a master storage key (also usually zeros), permitting some section of memory to be accessible to all programs. In some computers, one bit of the storage key can be set to allow READ ONLY or to allow READ OR WRITE; such a capability further extends the memory-protection concept.

Note that protection keys and storage keys are only needed in multiprogramming environments when programs are running from scattered locations in memory. If each program occupies a single contiguous memory area, a simpler memory-protection scheme is available. The hardware provides a relocation register and an upper-bound register, which hold the beginning and ending addresses of a program's allowable memory space. The contents of the relocation register are added to each program address reference, thus giving the actual location referred to. If the sum exceeds the contents of the upper-bound register, no reference to memory is allowed. This scheme combines memory protection and dynamic relocation within the same mechanism.

pulse-amplitude modulation (PAM)   Encoding a continuous (analog) signal onto a uniformly spaced sequence of constant-width pulses by amplitude-modulating the intensity (amplitude) of each pulse.

This system is similar to ordinary AM broadcasts, except that the carrier is a pulse and not a sine wave. It thus suffers from all the noise susceptibility of AM.

The advantages of pulse-amplitude modulation lies in an easy-to-design transmission/reception gear, in the simplicity of encoding, and if the pulse length is much less than pulse-to-pulse interval, in the possibility of multiplexing (which see).

For example, a phone company could transmit eight independent signals (bandwidth of 4,000 hertz each) on one 37,000-hertz channel. Every 1/8 millisecond is divided into nine equal slices. One PAM pulse from each channel is transmitted in the first eight intervals (one pulse per interval), and a zero-level synchronizing pulse is given in the ninth interval. At the receiver end, each signal is applied to the proper sample-and-hold output by a commutator. This gives 8000 dc voltage levels per second on the output lines, which become smoothed to the original 4,000-hertz waveform by the low-frequency response of the outgoing terminal lines. Pulse-amplitude modulation needs no amplitude-quantizing of signal.

The disadvantages of pulse-amplitude modulation are that PAM is subject to noise, to loss of information via distortion or poor frequency response, and the need for wideband low-noise channels (high-fidelity transmission).

pulse-code modulation (PCM)   The sampling and quantization of signals in the transmission of continuous (analog) data, the value of the quantized sample being transmitted as a unique pattern of pulses. For example, the value can be expressed as a binary number and transmitted as a sequence of pulses (1's) and spaces (0's).

With this modulation technique, some means of marking the beginning of a pattern is needed.   A synchronizing pulse (of distinctive amplitude or duration) or nondata synchronizing pattern (seven consecutive pulses, for example) must be sent at intervals.   The pulses and spaces are of uniform duration, repetition rate, and amplitude. Therefore, most of the pulse-duration interval is available for the receiver to discriminate between pulse and space.   The exact time of voltage change need not be detected, for the voltage transition time does not carry signal information.

The advantages of PCM are the ability to receive under noisy conditions because averaging of noise during pulse-duration time can occur; if error-detecting or error-correcting coding is used, data rate is sacrificed but precise reception is assured (unless total loss of signal occurs).

The disadvantages of PCM are its need for synchronization and the requirement to transmit many pulses to report accurately a single analog quantity.

pulse-position modulation (PPM)   The transmission of continuous analog data by pulses of uniform width and amplitude, in which the departure of the time of the pulse from its uniform time indicates the amplitude of the data.

Time is divided into a number of consecutive equal-sized intervals: if a zero signal is indicated by a pulse in the center of the interval, then a negative datum could be represented by an early pulse and a positive datum by a late pulse.   Digital and analog signals may be PPM encoded.

The advantages are that PPM needs no quantizing of signal; uniform size and approximate, uniform spacing of pulses minimize distortion and frequency requirements.

The disadvantages of PPM lie in the need for accurate timing at both receiver and transmitter ends, the transmission of a periodic synchronizing signal in order to define accurately expected time of pulse, and the need for accurate detection of time of pulse.

punched card   A medium by means of which data is fed into the computer in the form of rectangular holes punched in the card.

A punched card measures 7⅜ by 3¼ inches and is 0.007 inch thick. It is divided into 80 columns numbered 1 through 80 from left to right, and into 12 rows numbered 12, 11, 0, 1, 2, 3 ,4, 5, 6, 7, 8, 9 from top to bottom. (The 90-column round-hole card was dropped by UNIVAC at the end of 1966.) Rows 12 and 11 are sometimes called the Y and X rows, the top and bottom edge being called the 12 edge and 9 edge. The upper left corner of the card is usually cut although cards with uncut corners, or a cut upper right corner, may be found. Cards will be fed, depending upon the computer, face up, face down, 12 edge first, or 9 edge first.

A number is represented by punching a hole in the corresponding row position, one digit per column, and letters or special characters are represented by punching specific combinations of holes in the same column. As the card passes through the reader, metallic contacts normally separated by the cards will be closed where a hole appears. The position of the hole in the card indicates to the computer what digit is there.

Groups of columns may be reserved for certain types of data: such groups are called fields. A field may consist of from one to 80 columns. For instance, if each field is 10 columns wide, a card is said to be divided into eight fields. Although punched cards still represent the most common method of introducing data and programs into a computer, other means are equally available such as magnetic cards, punched paper tape, magnetic tape, MICR (magnetic ink character recognition), and OCR (optical character recognition).

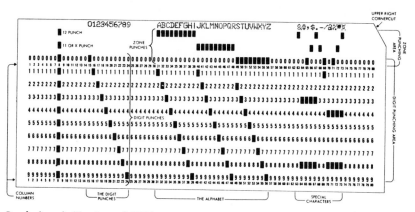

Punched card. (Courtesy of IBM.)

Perforated cards originated with J. M. Jacquard at the end of the eighteenth century; Jacquard devised his cards to control the lifting of warp threads according to a desired pattern. The use of punched cards for computers was first imagined by Charles Babbage in the middle of the nineteenth century as he developed the concepts of his analytical engines, and punched cards to actually handle numbers were devised by H. Hollerith some years later. This idea of Hollerith was realized when the results of the 1890 U.S. Census were tallied by means of these cards.

With the development of tabulating machines in the twentieth century, punched cards became an astonishing engineering achievement as can be realized by considering some of the many specifications established for the general-purpose paper card for information processing:

Outer: height, 3.257 inches; base length, 7.380 inches.
Inner: height, 3.247 inches; base length, 7.370 inches.
Thickness: 0.0070 inch ± .0004 inch.
Angles: 90 degrees ± 5 minutes.
Corner cut: 60 degrees to the long edge of the card and removing 0.250 inch ± 0.016 inch from the long edge and .433 inch ± 0.016 inch from the short edge.
Basis weight: 99 pounds ± 5 percent per ream of 500 sheets, 24 × 36 inch.

not to mention rigid specifications for such characteristics as composition, grain, stiffness, friction, hydrogen-ion concentration, expansion and contraction, and so on.

The two main advantages of punched cards are permanency of records and easy grouping of records. Since the environment conditions for cards are found in all computer installations, cards may be retained for long periods of time, thereby eliminating the necessity for rekeypunching the same data every time they are needed.

As every card is a record in itself, all the necessary information required for one transaction can be contained in the fields of one card, permitting all similar transactions to be readily grouped. This is commonly referred to as the unit record principle.

punched tape   A paper or plastic ribbon having one longitudinal row of small sprocket feed holes and five, seven, or eight rows of larger data-representing holes.

The advantages of paper tape are low cost of tape and equipment, reduced storage volume, easy identification by simply writing on the tape, and permanence of recorded data (nonerasable).

The disadvantages consist of no reuse possibility, slower speed than offered by magnetic tape or punched cards, the possibility of reading backward accidentally, lower reliability in reading.

The early use of paper tape was in repeating stations in teletype (Western Union) systems: tape punched from incoming lines was accumulated, torn off, and threaded onto readers for proper outgoing lines. It was also used as a storage medium to buffer time usage on outgoing lines.

Nowadays, paper tape is used by numerous adding machines, teletypewriters, computers, and cash registers. It is used mostly for transmission of data, and as computer input medium.

There are many types of punched tape on the market today:

Oiled Paper Tape: paper tape lightly and uniformly impregnated with oil for lubrication and easy punching.

Nonoiled (Dry) Paper Tape: a nonoiled, more common, less messy paper tape (some tape punches require oiled paper, some tape readers require nonoiled paper tape).

Mylar Tape: a tape with a plastic base for durability, uniformity, and strength. It may be blackened, aluminized, or both.

Chadless Paper Tape: a paper tape in which data are represented by partially cut holes, leaving flaps attached to paper ribbon and folded back. This paper tape is easy to punch, and needs no chip basket. However, it cannot be read by some tape readers.

Chadded Paper Tape: in this tape holes are fully punched out, requiring collection of chips (chad); it can be stored in less space, owing to reduced thickness (no folded-back flaps).

5-, 7-, or 8-level Tape: there are many encoding schemes; parity-type error-detecting codes may or may not be used; channel 8 may be reserved for an end-of-record signal or not so reserved.

The physical form of punched tape may be any of the following, depending on length:

Strips: usually 2 to 4 feet long.

Fan-folded: usually longer than strips, but shorter than rolls or reels.

Rolls: up to 700 feet long, usually read from center of roll, not outside end first. This saves rewinding when reading data in the same sequence as when punched.

Reels: up to 1000 feet long, usually read from the outside end.

Two principal hole-punching formats are now recognized:

Center-feed: the sprocket holes are centered on the same centerline as each character of data (10 per inch).

Advance-feed: the sprocket holes are not in line with the data, but somewhat ahead. This tape cannot be read on some readers. Advance-feed allows visual identification of the beginning end of the paper tape. (See accompanying illustration.)

pushdown list   An ordered set of data items so constructed that the next item to be retrieved is the item most recently stored, in other words, last-in, first-out.

The most common (but not the only) use of pushdown list is the saving of information to permit recursive use of program routines.

Consider a compiler that is interpreting algebraic expressions. A typical expression involves adding, multiplying, subtracting, and dividing terms and parenthesized expressions. One can handle parentheses correctly by writing an expression evaluator that can treat everything except parentheses. Let this evaluator scan from right to

Center feed.   Advance feed.

left, replacing parenthesized expressions by the single term that results from valuating the expression in parentheses. Note that the parenthesized quantity is itself an algebraic expression. Then the same routine that evaluated the outer expression can be used to evaluate the inner expression. Whenever a left parenthesis is encountered, the routine stores its current status in a pushdown stack and begins anew on the enclosed expression; when a right parenthesis is encountered, the expression so evaluated is reduced to a single term, and the routine picks up what it was doing before by getting the top item off the pushdown list. In this way, nested parentheses to any depth can be handled in a simple way.

Most recursive routines can be programmed in nonrecursive fashion if desired. Thus the expression evaluator could scan for the first right parenthesis, back up to the first left parenthesis to be now encountered, and evaluate the resulting nonparenthesized expression. Continuing in this way, it evaluates every expression in a nonparenthesized order. Recursive logic is sometimes simpler or more compact than the equivalent nonrecursive logic.

An interrupt routine saves (or pushdowns) the state of the interrupted program for later resumption. If this is, in turn, interrupted by a higher-priority interrupt, a pushdown list of interrupted programs results.

A magnetic tape that writes forward and reads backward is a good (but not the only) implementation of this procedure.

Synonymous with pushdown stack.

pushup list An ordered set of data items so constructed that the next item to be retrieved will be the item that was inserted earliest in the list, resulting in a first-in, first-out structure like a waiting line outside a box office.

This structure is used more than any other in data processing. Punched tape, card files, magnetic tape (except magnetic tape read backward) are read in the same order as they were created, that is from the earliest character first to the last.

The pushup-list concept is used whenever there is a queue of approximately equal-priority requests that are waiting to be serviced, such as job queues in a simple batch-processing environment, and output queues on disk waiting for attention of a printing routine.

Simple-priority schedulers maintain several pushup lists of nearly equal priority. The first item in the last list moves up to the last item in its proper place in line.

It is possible to organize lists with neither LIFO nor FIFO. In fact, the very idea of list processing permits items to be inserted into the middle of lists without moving any of the other items in the list: hence, the use of stack for list to avoid confusion.

Synonymous with pushup stack.

Q

qualified name A name that is further identified by associating it with additional names, usually the names of things that contain the thing being named.

In COBOL, it is possible to have different items similarly named provided that they can be distinguished by using qualification. For example, in a record called MASTER there can be a field called DATE which is itself divided into subfields called MONTH and DAY and YEAR. In this same program, there can be a record called UPDATE which contains a field called DATE-1 which also is divided into three subfields called MONTH, DAY, and YEAR.

If a programmer were to write

MOVE DAY TO DAY.

the ambiguity of the instruction would result in no computer action. The meaning of the instruction is clarified by using qualified names to refer to the subfield:

MOVE DAY OF DATE-1 TO DAY IN MASTER.

Now the computer knows that it is to move one subfield from the record UPDATE to the similarly named subfield in MASTER. In this example the words OF and IN denote name qualification, and DAY IN MASTER is a qualified name. In COBOL, any higher-level name may be used to qualify a lower-level name (provided ambiguity does not result), even if the names do not apply to adjacent levels of data structure.

Data sets in some operating systems may also have qualified names to assure uniqueness. However, in this case, qualification may be needed to assure successful index lookup even when every name is unique (that is, not duplicated). Qualification is designated by periods separating the individual names. Example: LIBE1. FOGARTY. FRIDAY means: Look in the index called LIBE1 to find the address of the index FOGARTY; look up FRIDAY in the index FOGARTY: this is the required data set. Even if no other index were named FOGARTY, and no other data set or index were named FRIDAY, it would not be possible to find FRIDAY without using its qualified name. FRIDAY would not be listed in the master (un-qualified name) index. Note that in this use of name qualification, every level of qualification must be included, or the search procedure will fail.

See COBOL, INDEX.

qualifier   A name used to qualify another name.

Like an adjective, a qualifier is used to give additional information about a name (noun), but, moreover, a qualifier is used to distinguish the named thing from other things having the same name.

See QUALIFIED NAME.

quantification   The act of quantifying, that is, of giving a numerical value of measurement to something.

One of the main problems in some computer applications is the problem of quantification, that is, of giving a numerical value to vary-ing quantities such as like, dislike, want, hope, etc.

Certain attempts have been made to give discrete values to human behavior characteristics by means of statistical techniques such as discriminant analysis. Other methods, such as used in market re-search or certain psychological tests, consist in giving a numerical value to a sequence of attitudes such as like very much (2), like some (1), indifferent to (0), dislike some (−1), dislike very much (−2), the subject then being asked to circle the number best corresponding to his attitude.

quantization   The subdivision of a continuous range into a finite number of distinct elements, and a process similar to analog-to-digital conversion: the approximation of a real (or infinite-precision) value by a number of prespecified resolution. For example, the conversion of a 1- to 100-volt signal to a 12-bit number.

A digital computer deals not with numbers but with numerals of finite length. Thus some approximation must be made except in the case of those particular numbers that can be represented exactly. For instance, a computer with a 32-bit word can represent 4,294,-967,296 fixed-point numbers exactly, or almost the same number of floating-point numbers (with some duplication of values occurring for nonnormalized floating-point numbers). But since there are an infinity of numbers between 0. and 1.0, approximations are very common in computer work.

Quantization assures loss of accuracy, but on the other hand, it may also ensure against total loss of data in transmission: it is possible to transmit binary digits much more reliably (that is, with less noise) than it is possible to transmit continuous quantities.

See PULSE-CODE MODULATION.

QUIKTRAN   A time-sharing language developed by IBM for use on an IBM 1050 terminal connected to an IBM 7044 computer. As a programming system it provides concurrent computer access to a maximum of 50 remotely located terminals from a centralized data processing system having tape, drum, and disk storage.

The programming language itself is compatible with most FORTRAN processors and is augmented by a set of operating commands and a set of terminal commands.

Some of the ways in which the user's requirements are met are as follows:

1. Output data are as problem-oriented as the source language.
2. Diagnostic messages are definite enough to allow program debugging to take place as the program is being constructed.
3. The user has immediate and continued access to the computer.

QUIKTRAN, therefore, combines an old technique of interpretive execution with the relatively new one of time-sharing.

QUIKTRAN is comprised of program statements which are similar to FORTRAN statements, operating statements which allow the user to regulate the systems, and terminal commands which allow the user to regulate operations at the terminal.

Execution of a QUIKTRAN program can be done in program mode or command mode.

Program mode is that mode of operation which allows the user to construct his program, statement by statement, and retain it in temporary storage at the computer center. This type of program is executed only at the request of the user, most likely on completion of the coding. The user may also enter single statements, which are executed immediately, while in program mode. However, these statements are not retained as part of his active program.

Command mode is that mode of operation which requires each statement to be processed immediately, and statements cannot be retained.

Examples of QUIKTRAN operating statements are: COMMAND which places the terminal in command mode; LOAD which places the terminal in program mode; SAVE which places the currently active program into the user's library; START which starts execution on the currently active program.

Examples of QUIKTRAN terminal statements are: ;USER (ID code) which identifies the user to the system, ;CONSOLE which sets up the terminal for transmission, ;FINISH which deactivates the user for billing purposes, ;ECHO (test pattern) which tests for machine-transmission malfunction.

The following example indicates the general appearance of a QUIKTRAN program: if capital growth at compound interest were to be calculated, a program in QUIKTRAN could be made to appear as follows:

Program	Comments
Terminal Statements	
; USER (BA0001)	Identifies the user with ID code BA0001 to the system.
; CONSOLE	Sets up the terminal for conversational operations.
Program Statements	
PROGRAM EXAMPL PRINC = 00000.00 RATE = 0.000 YEARS = 000.0	Names the program. Assigns the value zero to the real variables PRINC, RATE, YEARS.
1 FORMAT (F7.2, F4.3, F3.0)	Specifies the type of data conversion to be performed on the input data. F signifies real variables without exponents: F5.2 corresponds to PRINC, F4.3 to RATE, and F3.0 to YEARS.
2 READ (7,1) PRINC, RATE, YEARS	This inputs PRINC, RATE, and YEARS, using the format statement labeled 1 from the input device labeled 7.

3 C = PRINC * (1 + RATE/200.000) * * (2.0 * YEARS)	The value of the sum held at interest compounded semi-annually is calculated.
END	This signifies the end of the program. Each statement was compiled as it was received by the computer. Diagnostic errors that were not detected as the program was coded are now displayed.
Operating Statement	
START (O)	Execution of the program is begun at the first statement.
ALTER (2,3) READ (6,1) PRINC, RATE, YEARS C = PRINC * (1 + RATE/400.000) * * (4.0 * YEARS) ALTERX	This command will cause program statements to be replaced or additional statements to be inserted. Suppose that we wish to change the input unit from 7 to 6, and change the calculation to quarterly. The sequence at the left will do this. ALTERX terminates the alter sequence. (2,3) signifies that statements begun with label 2 through label 3 will be deleted.
SAVE	The currently active program is placed in the user's library.
; FINISH	Indicates to the system that the user wishes to terminate operations.

quinary   A positional numeration system to the base (radix) 5.

Quinary numbers are composed of the digits 0, 1, 2, 3, 4.   Thus 10_5 is 5, 100_5 is 25_{10}, 1000_5 is 125_{10}, 111_5 is 155_{10}.

This system is not very much in use, for it has no special advantages.

A form of quinary system is used by people who tally in the following way:

$$\text{HH   HH   II} = 12$$
$$\text{IIII} \qquad\quad = 4$$
$$\text{HH   HH   HH   III} = 18$$

R

radix In positional numeration systems, the ratio of the value assigned to a digit position to the value assigned to the next rightmost digit position. It is also the number of distinct digits required by a positional system.

In any positional system of numeration, 1 means one, 10 has the value of the radix, and 100 has the value of the radix multiplied by itself (or squared). Thus, if B denotes the radix, and a_0, a_1, . . . denote digits chosen from the B admissible integers (values of 0, 1, . . . , $B - 1$), then a number $a_2 a_1 a_0 \cdot a_{-1} a_{-2}$ . . . has the value $a_2 \cdot B^2 + a_1 \cdot B + a_0 + a_{-1} \cdot B^{-1} + a_{-2} \cdot B^{-2}$. The radix of any system plays the same role as ten does in the decimal system.

Synonymous with BASE.

radix complement A numeral in positional notation that can be derived from another by subtracting the original numeral from the numeral of highest value with the same number of digits, and adding 1 to the difference. If a number is added to its radix complement, the result is a 1 followed by a 0 for every position in the

Radix number	Unary (1)	Binary (2)	Ternary (3)	Octal (8)	Decimal (10)	Hexadecimal (16)
1	I	1	1	1	1	1
2	II	10	2	2	2	2
3	III	11	10	3	3	3
4	IIII	100	11	4	4	4
5	IIIII	110	12	5	5	5
6	IIIIII	101	20	6	6	6
7	IIIIIII	111	21	7	7	7
8	IIIIIIII	1000	22	10	8	8
9	IIIIIIIII	1001	30	11	9	9

original number. Radix complement is used in some computers (CDC, SDS, IBM 360) and desk calculators for representing negative numbers.

Thus, in the decimal system:

Radix = 10   2043 = number
           + 7957 = ten's complement
           ―――――
             10000

In the octal system:

Radix = 8   2043 = number
          + 5735 = eight's complement
          ―――――
            10000

An N-digit number added to its N-digit radix complement results in a word of N zeros and a high-order overflow which is ignored. Thus, with N digit numbers to base B, a negative quantity $-X$ is represented by $B^N - X$.

In addition: $Y + (B^N - X) = B^N$ (implied overflow) $+ Y - X$ = answer.

In subtraction: $Y + (B^N - (B^N - X)) = Y + X$ = answer.

For instance, subtracting in the decimal system would appear as follows:

Without complementing

$$
\begin{array}{r}
4096 \\
- 1024 \\
\hline
3072
\end{array}
$$

With complementing

$$
\begin{array}{r}
4096 \\
+ 8976 \\
\hline
1|3072
\end{array}
$$

       ↖overflow ignored

See RADIX-MINUS-ONE COMPLEMENT.

radix-minus-one complement   A numeral in positional notation of base (or radix) B derived from a given numeral by subtracting the latter from the highest numeral with the same number of digits. The radix-minus-one complement is one less than the radix complement. The principal use of radix-minus-one complement may be found in forming RADIX COMPLEMENTS (which see).

In base B notation, the highest-valued single digit has value $B - 1$ (9 in decimal, 7 in octal, etc.).

To construct a radix minus-one complement, each digit of the original numeral must be subtracted from $B - 1$.

The complement of the complement is the original number. For instance:

$$Y = (B^N - 1) - X$$
$$X = ((B^N - 1) - (B^N - 1) - X) = (B^N - 1) - Y$$

where N is the number of digits in both X and Y.

The radix-minus-one complement is easier to construct than the radix complement because no carry digits are ever created.

In the binary system, the radix-minus-one complement is simply a bit-by-bit inversion of a number, with no arithmetic required.

random access   A data storage device having the property that the time required to access (read or write) a randomly selected datum does not depend on the time of the last access or the location of the most recently accessed datum. Random access also describes a process in which data are accessed in nonsequential order and possibly at irregular intervals of time.

The true random-access devices are static memories: core, thin film, electrostatic cathode-ray tubes, electronic.

Most of the so-called random-access devices—drum, disk, tape loop, magnetic card file (or data cell)—are really cyclic access devices.

Thus in a drum rotating at M revolutions per second, each data item becomes accessible every $1/M$th of a second. In a memory equipped with a head-positioning mechanism (mostly disks and some drums), or a card-selecting mechanism, the activity could best be described as partitioned cyclic or nonconsecutive cyclic. The true meaning of random access in such cases is nonconsecutive access.

Random-access processes arise in three principal kinds of applications:

1. When a large file of records is maintained and only a small percentage of the records is required at any one time.

2. When demand for access to records is being generated by a process not under control of the program, as in a real-time system such as a question-answering service

3. When several programs are running at once (as in time-sharing or multiprocessing), even if each program is accessed consecutively, the resulting effect being similar to random access

Contrast with SEQUENTIAL ACCESS.

raster In optical character recognition (OCR), a system of intersecting scanning lines covering the complete area of the projected image.

read-around ratio The number of times that a particular bit in electrostatic storage may be read without seriously affecting nearby bits.

In electrostatic storage, reading, writing, and erasing are all performed by electron beams. Consequently, a certain amount of writing occurs when a read is performed. This causes noise to accumulate on the storage surface. Periodically the store must be cleaned and refreshed if loss of data is to be prevented.

This is accomplished by copying the data to another store, erasing the electrostatic storage, and copying the data back to its original site. A high read-around ratio means greater reliability and reduced data-refreshing overhead cost.

reader/interpreter A service routine that reads an input stream, stores programs and data on random-access storage for later processing, identifies the control information contained in the input stream, and stores this control information separately in the appropriate control lists. A reader/interpreter may be considered very nearly as the opposite of an OUTPUT WRITER (which see).

The principal input stream for a computer is often in the form of punched cards, although magnetic tape, communication lines, and other devices may be used. Usually the input device cannot deliver the data as fast as they can be processed. A small-scale computer ignores this limitation and reads data when and as needed, the simplicity of the system in a sense compensating for the increase in computing time. A sophisticated computer with a multiprogramming operating system is able to read ahead by using a reader/interpreter as one of the several, simultaneously operating programs. The input data are stored in large-capacity fast-access files from which they are read, when needed, with a very small loss of time.

After having been read, the input stream is located as follows: various programs and data sets reside temporarily in available mass storage; the control information is stored separately, partially digested or reduced to condensed form; and the addresses of the associated programs and data are stored with the control information. This control information constitutes the INPUT WORK QUEUE (which see). The work queue is read by the JOB SCHEDULER (which see) and is used to determine which waiting job will be started next. Thus, this scheme allows high-priority jobs to be processed sooner than lower-priority jobs that were entered earlier.

One reader/interpreter must be started when the computer begins its operation. If multiple input streams exist, the operator may initiate additional reader/interpreters. The operating system notes the input device to be used, and locates and loads a suitable routine. Each reader operates until stopped by the operator, or by an end-of-input-stream control message.

read-only storage A medium for storing data in permanent, or non-erasable form. Usually a high-speed static storage mechanism is indicated, for punched paper tape and other such memories are not generally referred to as read-only storage.

Read-only storage is used for rapid access to information of a permanent nature. Thus, common routines like exponential and square root could be wired in a computer for high-speed execution. The result is indistinguishable from a computer instruction from the programmer's point of view. This concept leads in a natural way to microprogramming, in which every instruction is a permanent subroutine in a read-only storage. This microprogramming concept has lead to economical realization of complex instruction sets in simple computers.

If a telephone directory were to be encoded and stored in a random-access read-only storage, an electronic switching center could connect telephone calls by name if the correct number were unknown. PARALLEL SEARCH (which see) or ASSOCIATIVE STORAGE (which see) would enhance this operation. If in a digital computer every instruction is a wired-in subroutine in a read-only storage, then by changing the read-only storage, a different set of computer instructions may be obtained. This notion leads to emulation, that is, running the instructions of one computer on the hardware of another computer.

Read-only stores are not to be confused with nondestructive read-out memories, memories that may be altered but can be repeatedly read without loss of data. Although expensive, nondestructive read-out memories combine the best features of both static memory types. The majority of internal storage systems erase their contents when read, and data must be rewritten if they are not to be lost.

read screen In optical character recognition (OCR), that transparent component part of most character readers through which appears the input document to be recognized.

Read screens are primarily a mechanical device employed as an aid in the positioning of a document. They also assist in holding down a document which might otherwise appear mutilated.

ready   The status or condition of being ready to run. A program, task, or hardware device that is in ready condition needs only a start signal in order to begin operation.

In a multiprogramming computer, several programs usually reside in main memory at any one time, but only one can be active or actually processing. All other programs, or tasks, are waiting to be served. Some of these other tasks are in a waiting state, and as such could not begin processing even if the computer had nothing else to do. A task is said to be in a waiting state if it requires an input or output operation to be finished before it can resume, or if it is enqueued in a waiting line for service by some computer facility.

The programs that can continue but are not now running are said to be in ready status. The currently active task will be interrupted when it enters a waiting state or commits an error or exhausts its allotted time. The operating system will then process its overhead or supervisory duties for a short time, and then will transfer control to one of the ready tasks. Thus the several ready programs compete with one another for use of the computer, and the task dispatcher will choose one according to some rule or priority system.

real time   A term used to describe a system that controls an ongoing process and delivers its outputs (or control inputs) not later than the time when these are needed for effective control. For instance, airline reservations booking and chemical processes control are real-time systems.

Real time usually denotes the rate of time during which an event transpires. Thus, to simulate in real time is to simulate at exactly the real-world time rate. Most simulations, however, must be faster than real time to be useful.

Real time usually evokes images of systems that respond in seconds or milliseconds. This very fast response time is not essential to the concept of real time. An inventory control system determining a factory output is an example of a real-time information system with a response time measured in days. Controlling a hot steel rolling strip mill is a different story: a one-second delay could be disastrous. Guiding a space vehicle during launch or docking imposes even more severe time constraints with reaction and control times measured in milliseconds.

The most common real-time system is the input/output control system (IOCS) found in all medium- and large-scale computers. It responds to an interrupt whenever a peripheral device finishes some task. Thus, IOCS controls an ongoing process (input/output) and must deliver inputs before computation can continue. IOCS, however, has the power to delay the request for service until it can be filled. Most real-time systems do not have this capability, and so must always have excess capacity built in to enable them to meet unexpected peak work loads.

recall factor   In information retrieval (IR), the ratio obtained in dividing the number of retrieved relevant documents by the total number of relevant documents in the file. The recall factor is a measure of the efficiency of the information retrieval system and ideally should be close to one. Contrast with OMISSION FACTOR.

recognition   The act or process of identifying (or associating) an input with one of a set of known possible alternatives.

There must exist a set of patterns or specifications which represent the things to be recognized in the input. There could be one or more members of the set of patterns. These patterns represent the subjects under investigation, and explain them to the recognizing device.

An input must be presented in a form suitable for interpretation. It could be an optical image, entire or digitized. It could be a set of switch closures or a sequence of pulses arriving on a wire.

The process of recognition usually consists of three steps:
1.   Localizing the image in the input,
2.   Comparing against all patterns, and
3.   Choosing the best fit.

Localization may mean scanning a light field for the first dark mark, as in optical character recognition, or selecting each group of n adjacent bits (overlapping or nonoverlapping groups) in an input stream, or systematically examining every part of the input. Rotations, reflections, or other permutations may be needed to exhaust all possibilities.

Comparing is usually either pattern matching or a sequence of logical tests, according to the representation of the pattern.

The decision may be a simple yes/no as when scanning for a synchronizing signal in an input stream. More often it involves choosing the most probable of several alternatives, based on a goodness-of-fit scale.

record   A group of adjacent data items, manipulated as a unit.

A logical record is the collection of related data items that the program logic treats as a unit. A physical record is a set of adjacent data characters terminating with an end-of-record indication. A physical record is also the unit of transmission to input/output devices.

If physical and logical records are of equal length, then the physical record is described as unblocked. If several physical records comprise one logical record (a procedure wasting storage space and transmission time) some means of indicating end-of-logical record is required. If several logical records comprise one physical record, the physical record is described as blocked. Blocking records becomes possible when enough room is available for large input/output areas (or buffers). Blocking conserves storage space and transmission time. This saving occurs because each I/O operation requires a start/stop, or access time, independent of the number of characters transmitted. By blocking for longer physical records, fewer start and stop or access intervals are needed, and fewer record gaps appear on the storage medium.

The logical record size is dictated by the application, and can be any size from 1 to any number of characters. The logical record size is dictated largely by the device and buffer space available.

Punched cards usually appear only in 80-character length. Magnetic and paper tape admit any size records (within reason), whereas drums and disks have tracks of fixed length. The data, control characters, and gaps should be chosen to nearly fill the tracks on rotating magnetic storage devices.

For example, consider a disk with a 3600-character track: physical records 289 characters long can be packed 12 records per track, and so waste 24 characters (0.6 percent); records 302 characters long can only fit 11 records per track, and thus waste 278 characters (7 percent); records 1199 characters long waste 3 characters per track; records 1201 characters long waste 1198 characters per track; the choice of record size thus requires considerable attention if efficient use of computing time is to be made.

record gap (interrecord gap, or IRG)   In a storage medium, a record gap is an area devoid of information. The record gap is used to indicate the end of a physical record (and the beginning of a new one).

On a magnetic tape, a record gap is 0.4 to 0.75 inch long; 0.75 inch is the old standard, and 0.6 inch is the newer standard. On a magnetic disk, the record gap is 0.125 inch or more, but less than 0.75 inch.

On tape, the IRG serves two purposes: it delimits records, and it allows the tape to stop and start between records in area free of data. This prevents loss of data while tape accelerates. Shorter gaps are used on disks and drums, for these rotate uniformly and do not need to be stopped within the gap.

Data sometimes are collected by incremental recorders. Incremental recorders write on magnetic tape one character at a time. If not used carefully, they will result in an absence of interrecord gaps which will create records much longer than what a computer can read. An IRG can be created by inserting 250 to 450 no-bit characters at suitable intervals in such instances.

recursion   A technique in which an apparently circular process is used to perform an iterative process.

An example of recursion can be found in Robert's *Rules of Order Revised* where Section 20 refers the reader to Section 14 which in turn refers the reader back to Section 20 and to Section 31 which in its turn refers the reader back to Section 20.

Recursion often occurs, if unwittingly, in programming. For instance, the expression:

LOG (A + B + C * LOG(D))

where A, B, C, and D are correctly defined beforehand is a clear case of recursion. To take the logarithm of an expression is equivalent to calling the logarithm subroutine, and while operating within the subroutine, the subexpression LOG(D) in turn calls for the logarithm subroutine. In other words, the subroutine calls itself.

By recursion is basically meant a method of calculation in which the value of a function is derived from a more elementary value of the same function.

Suppose it is required to find S(N), the sum of the first N positive integers. The calculation could be performed iteratively as follows:

Algorithm 1

    1.1 Set S = 0, Set I = 1.
    1.2 Set S = S + I, Set I = I + 1.
    1.3 If I is not greater than N go to 1.2.
    1.4 End

or the sum could be evaluated recursively as follows: *Algorithm 2*

    2.1 Function S(N)
    2.2 If N = 1 then set S = 1,
    2.3 otherwise set S = N + S(N − 1).
    2.4 End

or the sum could be evaluated directly as follows:

Algorithm 3

    3.1 Set S = N × (N − 1)/2.
    3.2 End

Algorithm 1 may be said to calculate S "from the bottom up": it keeps forming successively higher sums until the desired S(N) is reached. By contrast Algorithm 2 calculates S "from the top down": S(N) is made to depend upon the evaluation of S(N − 1), which depends upon S(N − 2), etc., until the directly calculable S(1) = 1 is reached. Calculation of any S cannot be completed until all simpler values of S have been found by recursion. Some simple form of the function must be directly calculable or an unending chain of simplifications will be generated.   Observe that Algorithm 2 looks simpler than Algorithm 1 but is more complicated for the computer and its compiler, which are required to keep track of an initially unknown number of incomplete evaluations of S.

The direct approach of Algorithm 3 can only be used in those cases where a closed-form solution can be found by analysis.   If available, direct methods are usually faster than recursive or iterative procedures; iterative procedures are generally faster than the equivalent recursive techniques.

Recursion may be compared to the mathematical method of proof by induction.   In an inductive proof, a theorem is shown to be valid for its first few (simple) instances, and then it is proven that the theorem must be true for any given case if it is true for the preceding case; the first cases have been shown to be true, so it follows by induction that all subsequent cases must be true too, and the proof is thus complete for all cases.

Recursion is explicitly outlawed in most systems with the exception of certain powerful systems for languages such as ALGOL and for certain list-processing languages such as LISP.

Recursion can be avoided by replacing, for instance, the expression LOG (LOG(A)) by:

$$Y = LOG(A)$$
$$Y = LOG(Y)$$

It should be noted that the notation LOG (LOG (X)) in FORTRAN is not regarded as a recursion.   The FORTRAN compiler, when faced with nested parentheses, operates first on the innermost parenthesis. Consequently, LOG (X) is first calculated by calling the subroutine, and then the logarithm of the result is calculated by calling the subroutine a second time.   See RECURSIVE PROCEDURE.

recursive procedure   Any procedure A which, while being executed, either calls itself or calls a procedure B which in turn calls procedure A.

Consider a program requiring the computation of many factorials (the factorial of a number, say 5, is equal to $5 \times 4 \times 3 \times 2 \times 1$, that is, is equal to 120).   Let us assume that a subroutine FACTORIAL(N) is written and is called simply by writing the statement:

FACTORIAL(P)

where P then replaces N.   The subroutine could be made to appear as:

(100) SUBROUTINE FACTORIAL(N)
(101) IF N IS 1 THEN FACTORIAL IS 1
(102) IF N IS NOT 1 THEN FACTORIAL = N * FACTORIAL (N − 1)

Say that the execution of the program reaches the statement:

(55) Y = FACTORIAL(3)

The subroutine FACTORIAL(N) is called, and N is given the value 3. Since the statement (101) is not met, the statement (102) is executed:

FACTORIAL = 3 * FACTORIAL(2)

The subroutine FACTORIAL(N) calls itself, N is now assigned the value 2, and statement (102) is again followed:

FACTORIAL = 2 * FACTORIAL(1)

Upon calling itself for the third time, and statement (101) being met, the subroutine so-to-speak "unwinds" itself, and FACTORIAL(3) is now calculated to be $3 \times 2 \times 1$ or 6.

A recursive procedure is thus a procedure which reduces a complex problem to a succession of progressively simpler problems until an explicitly solvable problem is formed, and then reaches the solution of the original problem by retracing its path and restoring the original complexity.

Suppose the following subroutine had been written to calculate the value of a sum invested at 4 percent interest compounded annually:

1 Function Value (Principal, Years)
2 If Years < 2 then Value = Principal
3 Otherwise Value = 1.04 * Value (Principal, Years − 1)
4 Return
5 End

The calling program provides the values of Principal and Years, and the location of the instruction where control should be returned when the subroutine has finished.   If this procedure is compiled in a system that does not allow recursion, then the call to Value on line 3 will cause the original return location to be overwritten with the address of line 4 of the subroutine.   The original return address is lost because only one save area is provided to hold it.   When line 4 is executed it returns to itself, then keeps returning to itself endlessly.

A system accepting recursive procedures avoids this problem by providing separate save areas and working storage locations each time the procedure is called, so that no data are inadvertently overwritten and lost.   A push-down stack is used to provide a new memory allocation at each call, and releases the newest allocation of memory every time a return is executed. In this way control returns correctly to the calling program after one return has been executed for each call that was required.   The push-down stack may be implemented in the main memory of the computer, or it may be on a magnetic tape if the expected number of calls is high.

Because recursive procedures (when acceptable to the system) can be cumbersome, requiring as they do many subroutine (or procedure) calls, an effort is usually made to reduce recursive procedures to iterative processes.   Thus, the above factorial computation could be made to appear as

(10) Y = 1
(20) I = 1
(30) Y = Y * I
(40) IF I IS 3 GO TO 70
(50) IF I IS NOT 3 ADD 1 TO I
(60) GO TO 30
(70) Proceed with program

and result in assigning the value 6 to Y.   As a subroutine, this program would be called only once for each factorial computation and consequently would require less computing time than its equivalent recursive procedure.   See RECURSION.

reduction   A process by which data are condensed.

Reduction can take several forms: changing the encoding to eliminate redundancy, or extracting significant details from the data and eliminating the rest, or choosing every second or third out of the totality of available points.

The most common usage of data reduction is represented by the extraction of means, standard deviations, trend lines, Fourier coefficients, or polynomial coefficients.   Vast amounts of data can be expressed in terms of a few significant numbers, thus reducing storage and aiding in the interpretation of the data.

For example, 2000 observations of an orbiting satellite can be reduced to six orbital parameters; these six orbital parameters will then permit the next observation to be accurately predicted.   An accurate prediction is not possible with the original 2000 observations as such.   Furthermore, suppose that the 2000 observations were collected at five different sites, at the rate of 400 observations per site. If each site reduced its data to polynomial or trigonometric coefficients (with their standard deviations), each site could transmit 9 to 18 numbers instead of 400 pairs of numbers.   This reduction would result in some increase in local computing time, but would save transmission time and central computing time.

reenterable   The attribute that describes a program or routine which can be shared by several tasks concurrently.

A digital computer can normally process only one program at a time, and similarly a program can serve only one task at a time.   A multiprogramming computer appears to run several programs concurrently by switching from one to another at high speed.   Similarly, a reenterable program can service several tasks concurrently by switching from one task to another task at high speed.   Just as a digital computer should incorporate certain design features to allow it to multiprogram efficiently, a reenterable program must incorporate certain design features.

A reenterable program must be divided into two logically and physically distinct parts: a constant part and a variable part.   The constant part is loaded into memory once and services tasks until it is overwritten by another program.   One copy of the variable part belongs to eack task that is being serviced.   This copy is usually created (that is, it is allocated memory space) when the task begins to use the services of the reenterable program.   This creation of the variable section is controlled by a prototype control section which resides on auxiliary storage. Within this area are stored all data manipulated by the constant part, and address and control information relating to the task that is being served. There also must be a task control block reserved for holding the instruction counter (or program status word) and hardware registers associated with this task. When the task is not active, the machine state data are stored in this area, and allow the computer to resume processing correctly when this task is reactivated by the operating system. The task control block, the fixed or constant part of the reenterable program, and the variable section combine to allow the reenterable program to be shared by various tasks concurrently.

reentry system   In character recognition, a system in which the input data to be read are printed by the computer with which the reader is associated. See TURNAROUND SYSTEM.

reflectance   In optical character recognition, the relative brightness of the inked area that forms the printed or handwritten character.

We wish to make the distinction between reflectance, background reflectance, and brightness, as oftentimes reflectance has been used to connote the other two. Each one of these concepts is an important consideration of any document that has been prepared for OCR. Brightness of paper is measured in relation to a standard surface; after data inscription, the paper obtains reflectance of inked areas and background reflectance of ink-free areas.

Reflectance accrues to inscribed characters as the result of the interaction between various properties of the paper and ink. The acceptable range of reflectance is usually specified as a percentage of the background reflectance.

reflected binary   A code using the binary 0 and 1, and so constructed that each successive code is derived from its predecessor by inverting only one bit. Reflected binary is a particular form of gray code.

Decimal	Gray code	Binary code
0	000	000
1	001	001
2	011	010
3	010	011
4	110	100
5	111	101
6	101	110
7	100	111

It will be noted that the binary and gray codes use the same symbols, but in different orders. The code is called reflected because of the systematic rule used in its construction. Let the first 2^N reflected code patterns be given, for any N greater than 1. The next 2^N code patterns are derived by changing the $(N + 1)$th bit from the right from 0 to 1 and repeating the original 2^N patterns in reverse order in the N rightmost positions. There are now $2^{N + 1}$ patterns, and the rule may be used again to derive the next $2^{N + 1}$ codes. By starting with $N = 1$, codes $= 0, 1$, the entire sequence is derived from this add one and reflect the rest rule.

It will be noticed that, were a line drawn between rows 3 and 4, the entries in the lower half of the gray-code column are the mirror image of the upper half. Hence its name, reflected binary.

registration Pertaining to the alignment of positions relative to a specified reference or coordinate. The term registration is taken from the printer's use of "register": in book work, a correct register denotes maintaining the same margins from page to page, and in color printing, a close register of impressions will create neither overlap nor white space where two colored areas meet.

In EDP, registration refers to such problems as hole alignments within specified tolerance in punched cards, positioning of preprinted form in the printer, and positioning of images in optical character-recognition devices.

In character recognition, the act of positioning a character, line, or document in such a manner that the scanning operation can be performed according to certain predefined standards.

When an input document is transported to the read station, the individual characters to be recognized may be irregular or misregistered insofar as they are not in the same relative position to which the scanner is accustomed. Consequently, registrations are performed in order to normalize the appearance of the various elements.

The registration processes for a cut-form document are performed as often as necessary, and are accomplished according to the following hierarchy:

1. Document registration
2. Line registration
3. Character registration

Continuous forms, by their nature, require only one document registration, the act of which is referred to as tape registration.

Also, the condition that results from the proper positioning of a character, line, or document. Contrast with MISREGISTRATION.

registration mark   In character recognition, a preprinted indication of the relative position and direction of various elements of the source document to be recognized.

Registration marks appear and are recognized as
1. Document registration marks
2. Line registration marks
3. Character registration marks

A cut-form source document may contain any combination of registration marks, and each combination serves its own purpose by indicating to the character reader the orientation or horizontal/vertical baselines.

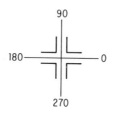

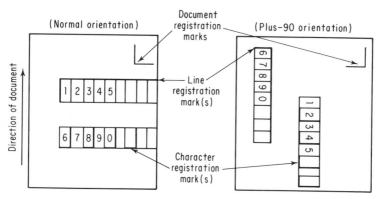

Registration mark.

Registration marks usually appear in the form of an L, the position of which, in relation to the document's direction of travel, indicates information concerning data organization.

As a special by-product, registration marks take on the form of spacing guides when used in conjunction with handwriting applications.

relative address   The numerical difference between a desired address and a known reference address.

Relative addressing is used in two principal ways:

1. In ASSEMBLY LANGUAGE (which see), to denote locations a number of positions before or after other specified locations. These are resolved by the assembler before the program is run. For example:

Relative address	Explanation
BRANCH * + 2	Branch to an address two locations after this instruction. * is the address of the current instruction for any instruction.
ADD M + 2, Z − 4	Add contents of the location 2 beyond M to the location 4 before Z.

2. At run time, certain computers with short word length permit addressing relative to the current instruction. Thus, a 7-bit relative address could access 63 locations before and 64 locations after the current one.

Relative addressing can give an odd appearance to a program. Assume that a number in location 1058 is to be doubled. The program, using relative addressing, could be written as follows:

Location	Instruction	Explanation
1000	CLA + 58	Clear and add the word 58 locations beyond this instruction into the accumulator (arithmetic register).
1001	ADD + 57	Add from location 57 beyond this instruction to current contents of the accumulator.
1002	STO + 56	Store accumulator contents into the word 56 locations beyond this instruction.

The constant absolute address 1058 was referred to as relative address +58, +57, and +56 in these instructions. A hardware element in the computer adds the base addresses 1000, 1001, and 1002 to the relative addresses as each instruction is executed.

See RELATIVE CODING.

relative coding A form of computer programming that uses instructions employing relative addressing. In other words, the address part of an instruction indicates not the desired address but the difference between the location of the instruction and the desired address.

For example, the CDC 160 A computer has a 12-bit binary word in memory modules of 4096 words. Obviously the actual 12-bit address cannot be contained in a 12-bit instruction. The computer, consequently, has the following address modes:

Immediate: the 12-bit address is stored in the next word after this instruction, giving 24-bit instruction format.

Absolute: the 6-bit address refers to one of 64 first locations in the core bank.

Indirect: the 6-bit address points to one of the first 64 locations in a bank, the contents of that word being the desired 12-bit address.

Relative: the 6-bit address is relative to the current instruction location.

In each case the operation code of the instruction indicates the desired type of addressing.

When using relative addressing, the operands must be located near the instructions that refer to them.

A technique called desectorizing has been developed to relieve the programmer of addressing considerations. The programmer codes in assembly language as though all of memory were directly addressable. The assembler then devises the optimum locations of instructions and operands, and chooses addressing modes as needed. This is another "Let the computer do the work" concept to aid the work of the programmer.

Many small-word computers use addressing schemes similar to the above. However, as words become longer, relative coding becomes less necessary. Thus, most 12-bit computers use it, some 16-bit computers do, but few 24-bit or longer instructions utilize relative addressing.

Relative coding is not to be confused with base register–displacement addressing as practiced by the system 360 and similar computers. This latter scheme allows up to 16 arbitrary blocks of 4096 locations to be directly accessed, and does not permit indirect addressing at all.

reliability The quality of freedom from failure, usually expressed as the probability that a failure will not occur in a given amount of usage.

Reliability depends on the definition of failure. Thus, any amount of reliability can be obtained by proper choice of definitions and levels of confidence. (The level of confidence is, in a way, a measure of the reliability of our measure of reliability.)

For a given computer, reliability may be expressed as a 92 percent probability that it will not miscalculate even 1 bit in three days, a 98 percent probability that it will not cease functioning within a week, and a 99.9999 percent probability that it will not break down completely within 10 years.

relocate   To establish or change the location of a program routine while adjusting or modifying the address references within the instructions to correctly indicate the new locations.

There are two principal ways of relocating a program, and two principal reasons for wanting to do so.

Consider a program as a collection of semi-independent routines which have to be linked together before execution. If the routines are to function correctly, they must not overlap or occupy the same space at the same time, and space is wasted if gaps are left between routines. The solution is to establish the first routine and relocate each additional routine so that it comes immediately after the one before. This is most easily accomplished by final specialization of relocatable machine-language programs by a relocating program loader. Alternatively, when running several unrelated programs at once, each must fit into areas not used by the other programs: relocation makes it possible to insert programs wherever they fit.

Relocation of instruction addresses can be accomplished by either software (programming) or hardware (the moving of programs must be done by software loaders). A relocatable machine-language program has each address requiring modification identified, and the correct modification rules (if more than one rule exists) indicated. One to six extra bits or characters are used to carry this information for each address part of an instruction. The relocating loader interprets these extra bits, performs the indicated address modification, and then the design of the computer includes one or more registers whose contents are automatically added to each instruction address part at execution time.

For example, both the Honeywell 1200, and the CDC 6600 have lower-bound registers which define where location zero is for the currently active program. The contents of this register are added to every load, store, or branch address. Both computers have upper-bound registers which define the upper limit of permitted memory accesses for the currently active program. Together these registers perform relocation and memory protection.

On the IBM 360 and the RCA Spectra 70, each instruction address part designates a register whose contents are added to the instruction part. In this way only a few words need be changed to relocate the addresses of a whole program. (These words load the registers with the proper values of relocation factors.) Multiple registers permit a program to be loaded in disjoint fragments, or modules, and yet still to be executed as though it were stored in a single continuous area within the computer.

reperforator   The receiving terminal in a system for transmitting information encoded in paper tapes.   It punches a new tape according to signals transmitted from the paper-tape reading transmitter.

Also a device that duplicates a paper tape, consisting of a reader and a punch coupled together, and two independent paper-tape transports.

When electronic amplifiers were in their early stages, repeater stations containing a reperforator and transmitter sets permitted transmission of teletype signals across the continent.   Each repeater station was sufficiently close to the others so that no intolerable degradation of the signal occurred.   A message was sent with a sequence of headers indicating the repeater stations along its route.   Thus at each site a message emerged from the reperforator with the label in front identifying the current site.   This first header was torn off, and the next header indicated the next station destined to receive the message.   The paper-tape strip was fed through the proper transmitter, and destroyed after receipt was acknowledged.   Each sending set generated new electric signals afresh, ready for another few hundred miles of wire.

Modern message switching circuits and amplifiers have obsoleted paper-tape repeaters for long-distance transmission, but they are still useful for low-cost digital transmission of data over short ranges.

repetition instruction   An instruction that causes one or more other instructions to be repeated a specified number of times, usually with systematic address modification occurring between repetitions.

One of the most powerful capabilities of stored program computers is the ability to reuse instructions to perform similar operations on a sequence of data items.   This may be accomplished by program logic which returns to an earlier instruction if the loop is not yet finished, or by a repetition instruction.

Normally a repetition instruction operates on instructions immediately following it.   The general repetition-instruction format may be written as

REPEAT n, m, i

which means: repeat the next n instructions m times, incrementing the effective address of each instruction by i after each repetition.

When the repetition instruction is finished, the $(n + 1)$th instruction following it is executed, and the n repeated instructions are in their original form (that is, they need not be reinitialized).   Depending on the computer involved, n may be fixed equal to 1, and i may be fixed at 1 or 0. Naturally, m must be variable or the power of the repetition instruction is lost.

Some assemblers provide pseudoinstructions which generate m copies of the next n instructions with or without modifying addresses. Such assemblers may include the ability to repeat a repeat, but hardware repetition instruction cannot repeat a repeat. The software repetition instruction is a poor substitute for hardware repetition instructions. It is convenient, but it occupies a lot of memory.

rerun point   A location in a program from which the program may be started anew after an interruption of the computer run.

In general, it is not possible to start a program from just any arbitrary instruction. A program must be started from its first statement. If an error occurs near the end of the program, causing a stop of the program, the computer time up to this point may be wasted although the results up to that point were correct. In very short programs this situation is of little concern to the programmer since running times are extremely short compared to setup times. However, in longer programs, this situation would be unbearable.

To avoid a costly duplication of computer time rerunning the portion of a program successfully completed the first time out, the programmer includes rerun points in his program. As each restart point is reached, restart information is written out in machine-readable form. The time required for this write operation must be balanced against the cost of a repeated run and the probability of not completing the computer run correctly the first time.

See CHECKPOINT.

residue check   An error-detecting check that is performed by dividing a number by some quantity n and comparing the remainder with the originally calculated remainder. Also called a modulo n check.

When a number to be checked is originally introduced into a system, the residue modulo n must be calculated and recorded alongside the number. At any later time the number may be checked by recalculating the residue and comparing it against the originally recorded residue. Agreement indicates probably correct rereading of the recorded number. If a matching residue is not found, then the reread number, the reread residue, or one of the two residue calculations must be incorrect.

A well-known example in decimal arithmetic is casting out nines, or modulo 9 check. Note that in the binary system, the parity bit is not a modulo 2 check.

resolution factor In information retrieval (IR), the ratio obtained in dividing the total number of documents retrieved (whether relevant or not to the user's needs) by the total number of documents available in the file. As a general rule, the magnitude of this factor will be a function of the degree of specification of the user's query. Ideally, the resolution factor should be low, that is, close to zero; it then becomes (assuming an efficient system) a measure of the heterogeneity of the file. Contrast with ELIMINATION FACTOR.

resolver A device that translates an angular rotation position input into a digital output.

An angular resolver is widely used in servomechanisms to report the angular orientation of a controlled object. Two principal types of angular resolvers are used: contact resolvers, using stationary electrical brushes contacting rotating conductive patterns; and photoelectric resolvers using shadow masks affixed to their input shafts, and photocells for sensing. The latter offer a higher-frequency response, and less friction and noise, but are more expensive.

A synchro, or servomotor which reports angular position, but does so with polyphase analog outputs that are easily interpreted only by a matching motor, is another type of angular resolver.

A resolver is also a device that accepts a single vector-valued analog input and produces for output analog or digital signals proportional to two or three orthogonal components of the vector: such a resolver is called a vector resolver.

The required mechanism of the joy stick in a plane is an example of vector resolver. The pilot moves the control in any manner, and the craft must faithfully follow his signal. By using separate (concentric) pivots for forward-backward, left-right, and torsion (twisting), it is possible to separate the motion into separate coordinates. A separate pickoff on each pivot reports the magnitude of each component of the control's position.

retina In optical character recognition (OCR), a scanning device. See PHOTOCELL MATRIX.

return To return control from a subroutine to the calling program.

The return usually involves the setting of output argument values, the restoring of saved index registers, and giving control of the computer to the proper instruction of the calling routine.

RETURN is also a statement in FORTRAN, and other languages, that causes the above actions to occur. A RETURN marks the logical end (end of execution, as distinct from the physical end) of a subroutine.

Return also stands for carriage return, a command signal which causes the printing mechanism of a typewriterlike device to return to the left margin of the page. It is not to be confused with line feed, an action that usually accompanies a carriage return.

See CALL, LINKAGE, SUBROUTINE.

reusable An attribute that describes a program which can be used by several tasks without having to be reloaded. Reusable is a generic term that includes REENTERABLE and SERIALLY REUSABLE (which see).

A reusable program or routine does not have to be reloaded into the computer each time it is to be used, provided a copy of the routine is already in memory. A serially reusable program can be restarted (reentered) as soon as the current user has finished with it. If several users or programs wish to use the routine, they must enqueue (form a waiting line) because only one user may utilize the program at any one time. A reenterable program is still more versatile, for many users may be served at once. As each new user requests the services of a reenterable routine, he need not wait for others to finish using it. Actually, the routine serves only one task at a time, but it can switch rapidly from one partially completed job to another.

The concept of reusable programs arose when it was observed that in some computer installations a majority of the programs were written in FORTRAN, therefore using the same input/output routines (specifically, the input/output routines required by FORTRAN programs). Normally, with every program loading, a fresh copy of these I/O routines was loaded into memory and linked to the newly loaded programs. It was observed that some time could be gained by reusing the already resident input/output routines: consequently, the loader was modified to carry out such an operation.

Creating programs with a reusable attribute is an exacting work, requiring a scrupulous observance of the proper rules. The justification for this work may be found in MULTITASK OPERATION (which see), a sophisticated multiprogramming scheme in which reusable programs need not be reloaded if already in memory.

In a multitask operation, both load time and memory capacity are conserved by taking advantage of reusable program modules. Any frequently used subroutine that is small and fast can be made serially reusable (such as sine/cosine subroutines, and random-number generators). A frequently used service routine or subroutine, relatively slow in execution (such as input/output routines, debugging aids), can be made reenterable, and can thus be shared by several tasks as required.

Normally, only operating systems or other manufacturer-supplied software routines are made reusable. However, some current compilers can produce reenterable programs for use by many users simultaneously in a time-sharing environment.

reverse-direction flow   A logical path that runs upward or to the left on a flowchart.

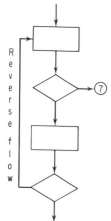

Reverse-direction flow.

In a modern digital computer, instructions are normally executed sequentially, one after the other. The normal flow of logic may be broken by conditional or unconditional jumps, branches, or transfer instructions. When a section of code is to be repeated, as in a loop, or the next problem is to begin, the logic may revert to an earlier instruction instead of a later one.

This situation is represented on a flowchart as a reverse (counter to normal) flow of logic. By custom (from western reading habits) flowchart logic normally flows left to right or top to bottom. It follows that reverse logic arrows run bottom to top or right to left.

On some flowcharts arrowheads are omitted for normal directions of flow. Reverse flow must be indicated with arrowheads on this or other type of flowchart. See accompanying illustration.

roll in   To restore to main memory a section of program or data that had previously been rolled out. See ROLL OUT.

roll out   To make available additional main memory for one task by copying another task onto auxiliary storage.

The space formerly occupied by the second task becomes available memory. The program that was rolled out can be resumed when its memory area becomes free again by copying it back into the same (or a new) area of memory.

When running one program at a time, essentially all of main memory can always be used, but computers with multiprogramming operation normally devote only a fraction of main memory to each resident task. A program can request additional memory by properly signaling the operating system. This DYNAMIC STORAGE ALLOCATION (which see) allows a program to use memory as needed, otherwise releasing it to other programs when not needed, instead of tying up its maximum amount of memory for the entire duration of its run.

A problem arises when the requested increment of memory cannot be supplied from available memory. The operating system has a choice: suspend operation of the requesting task until enough memory becomes available, or suspend operation of some other task, roll it out to be saved for later resumption, and make the space thus freed available for the requesting task. This decision will be resolved by considering the priority of the tasks involved.

When main memory is released by any program, or a task terminates and its space becomes available, a task that had been rolled out can be rolled in and restarted. Either the original memory locations must be reused or the restored program can be loaded into another area using DYNAMIC PROGRAM RELOCATION (which see).

root segment The master of controlling segment of an overlay structure which always resides in main memory. Usually this is the first segment within the program, and it is always the first to be loaded at program initiation time. The root segment contains the logic required to bring the other segments into memory when needed.

See OVERLAY.

round-off To truncate the least significant digit or digits of a numeral, and adjust the remaining numeral to be as close as possible to the original number.

Also: the error committed in this process, round-off error.

In decimal arithmetic, the normal rule is to add 5 to the rightmost digit to be dropped, perform any carries, and then truncate. Difficulties may arise when the digits to be dropped represent exactly one-half unit of the last digit retained, or when the number is negative.

A common problem in financial, accounting computing is to round off according to some rule such that the sum of rounded numbers is equal to the rounded sum. For example:

Original column	Original rounded to integers
17.50	18.
4.10	4.
7.50	8.
11.50	12.
2.70	3.
43. (30)	45.

In the first column, the rounded sum of the original numbers is very nearly equal to the original sum (43 versus 43.30). If the initial rounding has been carried out on each number, an error of nearly two digits would have appeared (45 versus 43.30). This error would not be discovered if the sum of the original numbers were not known.

In any job where much adding and rounding are used, precautions must be taken to guard against errors of this type.

routine A set of digital computer instructions designed and constructed so as to accomplish a specified function.

A routine may contain from two to many thousands of instructions, but most routines number in the high tens or low hundreds (40 to 300 instructions). Routines may be specific in function, mildly general, or very general. For instance, a specific routine could approximate a sine function in the range of 0 to 30 degrees; a mildly general routine could calculate bank or bond interests for various terms and amounts, interest rates and maturity schedules; a very general routine could handle input and output, buffering and overlapping, blocking and padding for every program run on a machine (such a routine is called an input/output control system, or IOCS, routine).

A routine may be self-contained and independent, but it is more commonly used in interaction with other routines.

Two routines may appear in master-slave relationship (calling and called routines), an equality relationship (two routines independently called by the same monitor), or in complete independence of each other.

row binary   A method of encoding binary information onto punched cards in which successive bits are punched row-wise onto the card.

When punching and reading equipment reads 1 row at a time, row binary is the logical method of punching binary cards. Normally a hole encodes a 1-bit and no hole encodes a 0-bit in the corresponding position.

Equipment that punches and reads one column at a time favors column binary cards. It is possible to read either encoding on any type of equipment, but programmed rotation of the information is required.

Most cards have 12 rows of 80 columns, giving 80-bit words. Very few binary computers have a word size that is a divisor of 80. It has thus become common to use the first 72 columns only, which permits twelve 6-bit, nine 8-bit, six 12-bit, three 24-bit, or two 36-bit words to be punched in each row.

The earliest generations of card machines read row-wise; today a strong preference for column-wise reading is evidenced. Row-wise reading is faster for slow-moving cards, but column-wise reading requires fewer sensor and buffer-memory elements, and so is cheaper. Column-wise readers with speeds as high as 2400 cards per minute can be had nowadays. Similarly, row-wise and column-wise card-punching equipment exists.

Contrast with COLUMN BINARY.

row pitch   The distance between the centerlines of adjacent rows of holes in punched cards and paper tapes.

A large pitch is easier to read, cheaper to make, and stronger, whereas a small pitch reduces bulk, reading time, and the cost of raw material.   In common usage standard, industry-wide dimensions are observed.

run   A single, complete execution of a computer program, or one continuous segment of computer processing, used to complete one or more tasks for a single customer or application.

A computer run can be defined by the actions of the computer operator.   He begins and ends the run, and whatever is accomplished depends on the programs and the input.   When a means of automatic job-to-job transition is used (with no operator intervention required), the definition of a run becomes obscure; a run could get very long and complex.

To a programmer, a run is a single access to a computer.   He prepares a program and its input, and submits a run (a unit of computer-scheduling demand).   When he gets the results, he is able to prepare the next submission for running.   Thus, a run is what connects a programmer's input to the resulting output.

In a time-sharing environment, the concept changes slightly.   A run begins with log-on (recognition and acceptance of the user by the system) and ends with sign-off (termination of interaction with the user).   Input and output are usually intermixed during this process, and beginnings and endings are hard to define.   The dominant concept is that of a single, continuous, distinct, uninterrupted computer processing interval completely accomplishing some specific task.

S

sampling Obtaining the instantaneous value of a continuously time-varying variable, at one or more regular or irregular time intervals; or obtaining measured values of some quality of a set of items, using the measurements of a randomly chosen subset of items to represent the entire group.

Sampling is used when it is impossible, impractical, expensive, or undesirable to obtain all measurements of some kind. A suitable subset, or sample, of values is chosen and used to represent the whole set. Thus, polls may indicate a TV program's popularity without testing every TV set owner, opening and closing prices of stocks may represent the activity of a stock without detailing every different price paid during the day.

In measuring a time-varying quantity, the sampling interval required (or number of samples per unit time, that is, the sampling rate) can be deduced from an estimate of the highest frequency expected in the behavior of the variable (frequency in the Fourier sine-wave sense). For example, if 10 cycles per second represents the highest frequency expected to be of significance, then no more than 20 to 30 samples per second are required.

The amount of sampling required of a set (spacewise) may be deduced from statistical considerations, such as the level of confidence desired. A small sample yields less confidence in the result than a larger sample, but is easier to obtain. If no initial information is known, a trial sample may be taken and used to estimate the item-to-item variability of the set. Then another sample (excluding the already measured items) may be used to finish the sample size required. Elaborate randomizing schemes may also be used to ensure the fairness of a sample.

scale   To change the magnitude of a variable in a uniform way, as by multiplying or dividing by a constant factor, or the ratio of a real thing's magnitude to the magnitude of the model, or analog of the real thing.

The problem in both cases is that something will not fit into something else. Thus a graph of a quantity which varies from 1 to 100 inches will not fit on a 10-inch graph unless a scale of 10 to 1 (or greater) is used. On a digital computer with an 8-decimal digit word, the budget of the federal government could not be represented, unless it were scaled down a thousandfold (that is, expressed in thousand-dollar units).

Enlarging scales are also used to bring out detail and improve resolution. Thus an analog computer may be adjusted to compress hours into minutes (to save time) or to expand milliseconds into minutes (to display the detailed behavior of a fast transient, for example).

Scaling may or may not change the dimensions or units involved. Thus 100 miles = 1 inch is a length-to-length scale, the distinction between miles and inches being artificial. An oscilloscope display is frequently calibrated in a scale of x volts per centimeter vertically, and y milliseconds per centimeter horizontally; yet neither volts nor milliseconds are measurements of length.

Scaling may not be a linear or uniform transformation, but it will always be one-for-one mapping. Thus a logarithmic scale is used to reduce the dynamic range of a signal (floating-point numbers are quasi-logarithmic) or to agree with human perception (our senses operate logarithmically for the above reason, the enormous range of illumination or sound level that we perceive being thus made manageable).

See SCALE FACTOR.

scale factor   That quantity by which a representation or analog of something must be multiplied to obtain the true magnitude of the original thing.

The most familiar examples are maps and hobby models of all

kinds. In these common analog representations, scale factors ranging from 2 to 1 to 1,000,000 to 1 are used. These scales map distance into distance, and geometric similarity is preserved. Scale factors need not preserve the nature of the thing being modeled, and geometry need not be involved. Thus a thermocouple is used to measure temperature remotely, and is calibrated using a scale factor of x degrees centigrade per millivolt.

In digital computer applications, by their very nature, all scale factors are ratios of numbers. Scale factors are used to make the size or range of numeric values more convenient to work with. Sometimes scale factors are absolutely necessary for correct operation. Thus a scale factor of 100 to 1 is used to convert percentage (a human concept) to ratio (a computational quantity).

In analog computer work, most ratios are something per volt, excepting the scaling of time. A trivial case is volts per volt. Thus, a particular 1-volt signal could represent microinches of deflection, pounds per square inch of pressure, degrees of temperature, or whatever the particular problem required. It is also possible to scale time up or down, for various purposes.

Scale factors are confined exclusively to linear multiplicative transformations, a uniform expansion or contraction.

scan To examine part by part in a continuous, systematic fashion.
Scanning is performed for two principal reasons:
1. To find a feature of interest in a large collection
2. To convert a simultaneous set of values (two- or three-dimensional field) into a linear or sequential set.

Scanning in sense 1 is used in pattern recognition to locate the boundaries of the object to be recognized, and in sense 2 to convert the pattern to a computer-manageable form.

When the original data are sequentially organized, a scan for purpose 1 is called a search.

The digital computer is, at this time with very few exceptions, a sequential, one-thing-at-a-time processor. As such it cannot handle photographs (still or movies) or three-dimensional fields of values, for instance, until they are converted to linear sequential form. Scanning converts such unmanageable entities into a form suitable for transmission over data links (TV broadcasts) or for input to digital computers. (An analog computer can and does examine many parts of an entity at once, and analog pattern-recognition devices exist which do not scan.) Devices exist that copy still photographs into memory, quantized but in image form, but since memory is then addressed sequentially, scanning is still required.

scanner In character recognition, the transducer. A magnetic (MICR) or photoelectric (OCR) device which converts the inputted character into corresponding electric signals for processing by electronic apparatus.

The scanner so defined is only a component part of an optical character reader which also includes the electronic components of normalizer, property detector, and decision mechanism. Loosely interpreted, the term optical scanning has oftentimes referred to the total process of optical reading.

The purpose of the scanner is to convert the two-dimensional characters into an electrical form which is then in suitable form for normalizing, and the subsequent property-detection and decision processes.

Normally, scanning involves linear vertical and horizontal examination of a rectangular field, as in a TV set. However, radial (polar coordinate) scanning patterns exist as on radar displays; in addition, spiral scanners are used (phonograph records, a search in ever-widening circles about a presumed center).

Some scanners operate by moving the sensor over a relatively stationary field (TV camera); others by moving the specimen past a relatively stationary sensor (phonograph). Optical character recognition falls into the first category; Magnetic-ink character recognition into the second.

The scanning method employed depends jointly on the property-detection system and the document-handling mechanism employed. In many scanning systems the document motion itself forms an integral part of the scan.

To date, the most commonly used property-detection systems employ the slit scan, mechanical scanner, flying-spot scanner, TV camera, or photocell matrix.

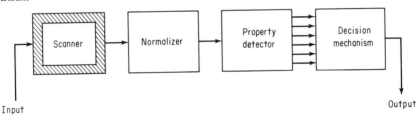

Input   Output

A character reader: component parts.

scanning In character recognition, any process that attempts to seek out and focus on an input character for the purpose of determining its vertical and/or horizontal structure.

scatter loading The process of loading a program into main memory such that each section or segment of the program occupies a single, connected memory area but the several sections of the program need not be adjacent to each other. Only programs having the scatter-loadable attribute may be so loaded, for splitting an ordinary program into discontinuous segments would prevent it from operating correctly.

In a multiprogramming environment, main memory is occupied by several programs or tasks. When space becomes available in memory, it usually appears as disjoint fragments throughout memory. Suppose that enough total memory were available to permit loading an additional program, no single space being large enough to hold the entire program. The remaining programs can be moved about to unite the free memory areas (see DYNAMIC PROGRAM RELOCATION), or the new program can be fragmented and loaded into the available areas wherever they may be. Scatter loading thus avoids the nonproductive overhead involved in moving the other programs around.

A scatter-loadable program must be divided into distinct segments, usually called control sections. There must be some provision for informing the running program where each segment is located. Alternatively, memory mapping can be used to make every program scatter-loadable, by making discontinuous areas appear connected to the program.

scatter read   An input operation that places various segments of an input record into noncontiguous areas in central memory.

A normal read operation on any digital computer takes a data record and deposits it in one single continuous area of main memory. If a sophisticated data channel is available, it is possible to deposit selected portions of the input data into several distinct and unrelated areas of memory. This facility usually includes the ability to ignore or bypass certain undesired sections of the input data record.

Scatter reading conserves time and memory by making it possible to read an input record into areas collectively smaller than itself (ignoring selected subfields of the record) and by avoiding the necessity of moving the data out in sections after they have been read.

For example, a tape record containing much information about a customer is being read by a program which merely prints address labels for a mailing. The channel can be instructed to deposit the first 12 characters (customer identification number) in a computational area and the customer address in a label-image area for later output, and to ignore the remainder of the input record. This may be accomplished by giving the data channel one command for each input area to be stored and one command for each section of data to be bypassed, and indicating by data chaining indications that all these commands are to apply to a single input record.

A complementary output operation is called GATHER WRITE.

search   To seek a desired item or condition in a set of related or similar items or conditions.

Normally, search is applied to sequentially organized sets or non-organized (no precedence) sets, and scan is used for multidimensional sets (tables, matrices, etc.).

The simplest method of searching involves testing items in sequential order, starting at the beginning and stopping when the desired item is found or proved to be missing. This is a serial search, and the average time for finding an item in a set of n items is $n/2$.

For larger tables or faster searching, a binary search is used. At each step approximately half of the remaining possibilities are discarded. Search time is proportional to $\log_2 n$, but the search logic is somewhat more complicated.

In still larger collections, an indexed search may be used. An index is used to divide a large set into smaller subsets. First the index and then the subset are searched by one of the above techniques. In very large sets hierarchies of indexes may be useful.

secondary storage   Any means of storing and retrieving data external to the main computer itself but accessible to the program.

Internal or primary memory consists of registers (usually transistor), scratch-pad memory (thin film or fast core), and main memory (core, sometimes thin film, or drum). Secondary storage consists of magnetic tape, drums, and disks attached to the computer and operated by it.

A printer or card punch may not be considered secondary storage since its function is strictly for output purposes.

seek   To position the access mechanism of a random-access storage device at a designated location or position, and by extension, the command directing the positioning to take place.

A dynamic auxiliary storage device consists of some means of moving a magnetic surface past a read/write head. Disks, drums, tapes, and magnetic cards are common examples of this principle. Because read/write heads are expensive, designers often try to reduce the cost by sacrificing speed, and using less than one head per track. In order to do this, an access mechanism must be provided to move the head or heads from track to track. The computer program must remember where the access mechanism is at any time, and direct it to seek whenever it has to access a different track. This concept also applies when the access mechanism carries multiple read/write heads.

The time required to seek must be added to the latency time (time required to bring the desired portion of the track beneath the head) when calculating the access time of the device.

segment   A single section of an overlay program structure, which can be loaded into main memory when and as needed.

A segment is also, in some direct-access storage devices, a hardware-defined portion of a track having fixed data capacity.

selective dump   An edited or nonedited listing of the contents of selected areas of memory or auxiliary storage.

In the early days of computers, memories were small, programs occupied the entire computer capacity (there was no sharing with other systems), and a printout of all of memory was both manageable and necessary.   For example, the entire 2000-word drum of the IBM 650 could be neatly displayed on 8 pages of 11 × 16-inch printout.   In this environment the complexity of a selective dump program was unjustified.

As computers became larger and faster, operating systems developed (filling memory with program structures unfamiliar to a programmer), and multiprogramming appeared (sharing memory with unrelated programs and data).   Today, a full dump of a large computer contains unmanageably much information (131,072 words of eight hexadecimal digits each) of which little is of interest to a particular programmer.   In addition, a particular area of memory contains binary bits, a character string, a packed-decimal number, a floating-point or fixed-point binary (or hexadecimal) number, or computer instructions.

Fortunately, more powerful computers can support sophisticated dump routines.   These are able to dump each required area in the proper format and to ignore irrelevant data.   It becomes the programmer's responsibility (sometimes shared with the operating system) to indicate what is to be dumped, when, and in what format.

self-adapting   Describes the ability of a system to modify itself in response to changes in its environment.

A familiar example is the traffic light in a vehicle-detecting adaptive traffic-control system.   When traffic in one direction exceeds its cross-traffic density, that direction is favored.   The ratio of red to green times adjusts to maximize throughput and minimize delay time. Observe that the hardware remains the same, but its performance (decision levels, operational policy) adjusts automatically to changes in environment.

A less familiar example is a computer-controlled elevator installation.   It operates under several different (adaptive) programs—peak up load (morning), normal day load, peak down load (evening), night load (most elevators idle).   Each program modifies dispatching and stopping behavior in response to demand (button pushing) and elevator-car load (weight sensors). The programs differ in objective (what is to be optimized), but all are optimizing. Switching from program to program occurs manually, in response to a time-of-day clock, or automatically in response to demands.

In operating systems, several interchangeable but equivalent modules may be available for particular purposes. For example: job schedulers, first-in, first-out; priority; multiprogramming or batch processing.

Usually a choice of alternatives is made and fixed at system generation time, a human being picking one out in response to anticipated need.

If a giant computer operating system were capable of choosing among alternatives on a dynamic basis, it could use a complex priority multiprogramming scheduler for a many-small-programs environment and a simple FIFO queue batch processing scheduler for a few-large-slow-programs work load. Such an adaptive system (which does not exist today but should be found on giant computers of the near future) would need to monitor the statistical properties of its evolving work load, and exercise a self-modification routine when a transition was indicated. The stored program concept would thus enable adaptive systems to change their structure as well as their performance.

self-checking code   An encoding of data so designed and constructed that an invalid code can be rapidly detected. This permits the detection, but not the correction, of almost all errors.

For example, suppose 1 bit in 10,000 were in error over some channel. If 6-bit characters are transmitted, 6 characters in 10,000 will be in error, with no means of detecting the errors. Suppose that a seventh parity bit were added, and so constructed that every 7-bit character would have an odd number of ones and an even number of zeros. Then 7 in 10,000 of the characters would be in error, but only 21 in 100,000,000 of the characters would have undetected errors. The problem of correcting the errors remains, but only 3 errors in 10,000 errors would remain undetected.

self-organizing   Describes the capability of a system to arrange its own internal structure.

Living systems are self-organizing, and inanimate systems are sometimes self-organizing to a lesser degree.

One class of self-organizing systems are the trainable devices, for example, perceptrons: these devices modify themselves and ask the human trainer whether the resulting behavior is better or worse than before. After sufficient trials the new behavior achieves sufficient accuracy to be left alone.

The important point is that the final organization is inherent in the initial, man-designed structure. The final state might not be predictable, but a device cannot transcend its creator by more than what the designer enables it to do at design time.

See SELF-ADAPTING.

separator   A datum or character that denotes the beginning and/or ending of an entity of data.

In English, common separators are quotation marks, commas, colons, semicolons, parentheses, and periods. In COBOL the important separators are spaces and periods.

Normally data exist with a hierarchy of successively finer structures and subdetails. This book (delimited by hard covers) consists of entries (delimited by headings) composed of paragraphs (denoted by spacing or indenting) which contain sentences (limited by periods), composed of words (delimited by spaces), which in turn consist of letters (bounded by narrower spaces). We use parentheses and commas to divide the sentences into other subdivisions, thus creating intermediate levels of structures.

In computers, other forms of separators exist. In magnetic tape, interrecord gaps and tape marks denote records and files; in memory, delimiters are word boundaries, position in memory, special characters, and/or special-purpose bits (word marks).

The use of separators is analogous to the use of index tabs in a looseleaf binder. Synonymous with DELIMITER.

sequence   To rearrange the members of a set into correct precedence order.

It is often important to assure that precedence relationships are observed. If a given order is once established, it can be preserved by assigning ascending numbers to the items; and then preserving the order (or restoring the order) can be performed by referring to the sequence numbers.

sequence check   To verify that correct precedence relationships are obeyed, usually by checking for ascending sequence numbers.

It is common for programmers to sequence-number their program statements to indicate the intended order of instructions. The program that processes the program statements may be asked to sort the statements into a sequence based on the numbers. This allows a programmer to insert forgotten instructions between already written ones by assigning them intervening sequence numbers.

The usual form of sequence check consists of comparing each two adjacent sequence numbers, and testing for the later number being higher than the earlier.

Sequence check is also the name given to the fault found when an out-of-sequence condition is discovered.

sequence number   A number assigned to an item to indicate its relative position in a series of related items.

Sequence numbers are often assigned with intervals between them (commonly, 10 apart) to permit later insertion of intermediate values. In contrast, serial numbers are assigned in strict numerical sequence (serial numbers are assigned in order at time of creation, making it impossible to later insert an intervening value).

sequential access   A process that involves reading or writing data serially, and by extension, a data recording medium that must be read serially, as a magnetic tape.

Before the development of modern random-access storage, all large-scale data collections were organized and processed sequentially. The magnetic tape is the most common example of a sequential device, and data on a magnetic tape are the most common example of sequentially organized data files. Once written, a sequential file has to be read in the same order (or sometimes in the inverse order) in which it has been written. Skipping records is possible, but an

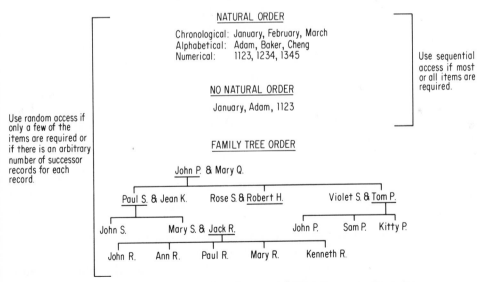

Illustrating the use of sequential access and random access depending upon the order structure and accessing requirements.

arbitrary selection of the next record to be read is not possible. The order of records may be rearranged, but this entails sorting the data in main memory, and rewriting the records in their new order on the tape.

Sequential access is normally used when most of the data must be processed during a computer run. It is most efficiently used when the data have a natural order, such as a chronological, alphabetical, or numerical order, or conversely, when the data have no natural order, such as unrelated items. For family-tree order, however (an order such that any record may have an arbitrary number of successor records), RANDOM ACCESS (which see) is to be favored. See accompanying illustration.

An important difference between sequential access and random access is that sequential-access devices usually have no addresses to distinguish different data whereas random-access devices always have such addresses. In sequential-access operation it is necessary to refer to "first record," "next record," "previous record." If an address structure must be recorded on a sequential-access device, it is then necessary to record a program-defined, synthetic address as part of the data record itself.

sequential logic element A circuit element having at least one input channel, at least one output channel, and at least one internal state variable, so designed and constructed that the output signals depend on the past and present states of the inputs.

A sequential logic element is a device with memory, in that in some way it remembers or retains what has already transpired. For example, a ring counter is such a device. Initially set to 0, it accepts input pulses and increments itself by 1 with each pulse. Upon counting to 9 (or some other predefined number), the next pulse restores it to 0 and causes the generation of an output pulse. Thus three ring counters in sequence can count pulses to a limit of 999 and then recycle. Two ring counters permit selection of every hundredth pulse in an endless sequence of randomly spaced pulses. Another example is the bistable flip-flop, whose output is 0 or 1, and which inverts with every input pulse. Thus a flip-flop is a binary (base 2) ring counter. Compare with COMBINATION LOGIC ELEMENT.

sequential operation Describes the consecutive or serial execution of operations without any simultaneity or overlap.

This is the normal mode of operation of digital computer central processors, data channels, and peripheral equipment. It is *not* the normal mode of analog computer operation.

An elementary digital computer performs only one operation at a time.   There may be pauses or intervals between successive steps, but there are no overlapped or simultaneous operations for programming simplicity and hardware economy (shared logic).

Faster computers perform more than one operation at a time. Data channels permit I/O while computing, instruction/memory overlap allows parts of several instructions to proceed at once, and finally multiprocessors execute several programs at once. This hastens the computing process but makes it difficult for hardware and programmers to synchronize operations.

Since programs are written in sequential order, i.e., as consecutive steps, it is important for any nonsequential processor to ensure that results equivalent to sequential operation are obtained; for example, the IBM 7094 could fetch instructions 3760 and 3761 in the same memory cycle. Executing 3760, it prepares to execute 3761 at the same time. It must always check to see that instruction 3760 does not alter memory location 3761, for if it did, then the incorrect instruction might be executed.

sequential scheduling system   A first-come, first-served method of selecting jobs to be run.

The simplest method of handling job-to-job transition, sequential scheduling is used by all elementary operating systems. The chief advantages of a sequential scheduling system are:

1.   It occupies a minimum of memory and executes rapidly.

2.   Since it needs no direct-access storage capacity, the input stream may be stacked up in the card reader until it is actually read and used.

3.   It gives full control of job sequencing to the computer operator.

serial   Describes the sequential execution of several consecutive similar operations.

The word serial implies timewise adjacency, whereas the term sequential is used for spatial or logical adjacency. Serial execution permits simpler hardware, therefore reducing cost, but the penalty must be paid in time. For example, consider recording 7-bit signals on a magnetic tape. If a single read/write head and associated electronics are used, the signals must be written 1 bit at a time down the length of the tape: It takes seven fundamental intervals to accomplish this. Writing all 7 bits at once (parallel) requires only one interval of time, but equally more complex hardware.

Serial transmission is used for all long-distance, low-speed data transmission because of the economy thus obtained.

In character-oriented memory computers, serial addition permits forming sums with inexpensive hardware. Addition occurs from right to left. In faster, word-organized computers, parallel addition is used.

In disk files with serial recording (lengthwise down a single track), transmission rates of up to 200,000 six-bit characters per second are obtained (1,200,000 bits per second). The more expensive disks with multiple active read/write heads, writing all bits in parallel, attain up to 30 times as fast a data transfer rate.

Contrast with PARALLEL.

serial access   Describes memory devices having structures such that data storage sites become accessible for read/write in time-sequential order: circulating memories and magnetic tapes are examples of serial-access memories.

Serial access also describes a particular process or program that accesses data items sequentially, without regard to the capability of the memory hardware, but as a rule serial access describes the principal mode of operation of small tape-oriented computers.

Serial access is also descriptive of character-by-character transmission from an on-line real-time keyboard.

Contrast with RANDOM ACCESS.

serially reusable   An attribute possessed by a program that can be used for several tasks in sequence without having to be reloaded into main memory for each additional use.

If a program modifies itself during execution, it cannot be restarted from the beginning without first being restored to its initial condition. Serial reusability can be obtained by programming an initialization routine into the beginning of a program, or by programming a restoration routine after a modified section has been used to completion.

The advantage of a reusable program is that time is saved by not having to reload it before each additional usage, not having to locate the program in auxiliary storage, and not having to relocate it again. A reusable subroutine can be reentered again within a job, many existing programs having this property (for example, a SINE subroutine in FORTRAN). In a multitasking environment, a reusable subroutine can be shared between concurrent or successive tasks which may belong to the same or to different jobs.

See MULTITASK OPERATION, REENTERABLE, REUSABLE.

service routine   A section of computer code that is used in so many different jobs that it cannot belong to any one job.

A service routine is written in a manner independent of any one user's needs, so that it can be applied to many or all user's needs.

It must, therefore, be flexible (modified or controlled at run time by user-supplied parameters); yet it must be very fast and occupy a minimum amount of storage. Service routines should be written by highly qualified programmers after a careful analysis of alternative program structures.

The service routines are often supplied by (or are a part of) the operating system, if one exists. To the programmer the service routines should seem part of the hardware; that is, they should be supplied by the manufacturer and available when called without having to be individually written by the user.

The most common service routines are the input/output programs. On all but the simplest computers, I/O operations are complicated by such requirements as timing, simultaneity, overlap, variable format, error detecting and correcting, multiple buffering, and label checking. The use of common I/O routines permits the average programmer to treat I/O as a very simple process, and permits him to concentrate his efforts on the individual or unique aspects of his programs.

Other service routines perform such services as program loading, common calculations (sine, logarithm), tracing, memory dumps, tape dumps, and the like.

servomechanism Any closed-loop, feedback type of control system.

A servomechanism consists of the following elements (which may be distinct or combined-function elements of hardware):

1. An input signal or command line, to indicate the desired state

2. An output sensor, capable of monitoring the actual output state

3. A comparator which determines the deviation from the desired state, based on the above two signals

4. An effector, which has the power to modify the output state or condition

It is not necessary for an explicit input signal to be provided, but an implicit signal must exist in those cases where an explicit signal is missing (for instance, as in the fixed-setting thermostats, or automatic level-seeking devices).

The important feature of a servomechanism is its four-part closed-loop organization as outlined above. Its actual physical implementation or field of application is immaterial.

set To fix the state of a multistate device, usually in a specified condition other than that denoting zero or blank, or to initialize or position a switch to one of its permissible states.

A switch is either an electromechanical device commonly found on control panels (pushbutton, slide, toggle, rotary, rocker, etc.) or a program element used to direct program logic to one of a multiplicity of possible destination locations. The usage set applies to either.

Also, a mathematical term meaning a defined collection of things. A set is defined if it is possible to test anything at all and determine whether the anything is, or is not, a member of the set. This usage has been extended to data set, a collection of data records.

sexadecimal   Describes a system, or property having a multiplicity of 16 mutually exclusive alternatives, or simply, a positional numeration to the base (radix) 16. Both uses are rare; they are usually superceded by the equivalent hexadecimal (not to be confused with sexagesimal, describing multiplicity or radix 60).

Base 16 has become very popular recently, because it fully utilizes the 4-binary bit capabilities of new hardware. Indeed, the recent prevalence of 8-bit bytes (two 4-bit groups, therefore, two sexadecimal digits per byte) has prompted many programmers to learn sexadecimal arithmetic. The former universality of octal (base 8, 3 binary bit groups) is apparently being questioned.

sexagesimal   Describes a multiplicity of 60 distinct alternative states or conditions, or, simply, a positional numeration system to radix (or base) 60.

The sexagesimal system was first used by the Babylonians, to whom we owe the 60-second minutes and the 60-minute hours; and the 360-degree circles of degrees, minutes, and seconds of angular measure. The base 60 has many advantages: a compact representation of large numbers ($323_{60} = 10923_{10}$), and exact representation of 1/2, 1/3, 1/4, 1/5, 1/6, 1/10, 1/12, 1/15, 1/20, 1/30 as 1-position sexagesimal fractions, to name a few.

The sexagesimal is an old, well-established, and forgotten system.

shift   A movement of data to the right or left, usually with the loss of characters shifted beyond a boundary.

The following table illustrates standard shift operations:
A shift instruction must specify
1. The type of shift (acceptable to hardware)
2. The location of data to be shifted (if not hardware-specified)
3. The number of positions to be shifted (called the   count field)
The hardware copies the count field into a register (the count register). After each 1-position shift the count register is decremented by 1. The operation stops when the count reaches 0.

Some hardware permits shifts of 8, 6, or 4 bits as an elementary micro-operation, thus speeding the shift process.

Type	Before	After	Comments
Arithmetic: left shift 2 places	$\frac{1}{\text{sign}}$ $\frac{00110001111}{\text{fraction}}$	$\frac{1}{\text{sign}}$ $\frac{1100011100}{\text{fraction}}$	($\times$ 4)
Arithmetic: right shift 2 places	$\frac{1}{\text{sign}}$ $\frac{00110001111}{\text{fraction}}$	$\frac{1}{\text{sign}}$ $\frac{00001100011}{\text{fraction}}$	($\div$ 4)
Logical: left shift 2 places	$\frac{100110001111}{\text{word}}$	$\frac{011000111100}{\text{word}}$	(Change sign bit.)
Logical: right shift 2 places	$\frac{100110001111}{\text{word}}$	$\frac{001001100011}{\text{word}}$	(Change sign bit.)
Circular: left shift 2 places	$\frac{100110001111}{\text{word}}$	$\frac{011000111110}{\text{word}}$	(2 positions from left to right end.)
Circular: right shift 2 places	$\frac{100110001111}{\text{word}}$	$\frac{111001100011}{\text{word}}$	
Long left shift: (2 places)	$\frac{100110001111}{1 \text{ word}}$ $\frac{000011111100}{1 \text{ word}}$	01100011100 00111110000 bits shifted from word 2 to word 1.	

Examples of shifts.

shift register A hardware element constructed so as to perform the shifting of its contained data.

This usage is usually reserved for hardware designed exclusively for shifting. Thus on the CDC 6600 a separate register is reserved for shift operations. Data to be shifted are moved to this register, and then the shifted data are moved to their final destination. Most fast computers are constructed in this manner though the programmer is not made aware of the fact.

Slower computers tend to use all-purpose registers to perform arithmetic, shifting, and logical operations. This is designed to save hardware, but results in complexity of design and loss of speed.

See SHIFT.

signal An event or occurrence that transmits information from one location to another.

Early signals were visible signs and sounds (heliograph, semaphore, whistles, etc.). Today signal is used in the technical sense for electrical or wireless transmission of information. In the near future, optical (modulated laser) signals may reappear as important communication media.

The simplest signal is a yes/no indication of a remote status or event (for example, the doorbell). More complex signals include digital transmission of quantized information (telephone dialing), and encoded analog transmissions of continuous variables (for example, gas gauges in automobiles, FM stereo broadcasts).

In information theory, the information content of a signal is measured by its unpredictability. Thus a completely predictable signal conveys no new information. However, a timing signal, completely predictable and uninformative, is the fundamental pacesetter for all synchronous computers.

Note the fundamental reliance on transmission: a stationary data representation should be called an indicator.

signal distance The number of bits that are *not* the same in two binary words of equal length. Thus, a signal distance of 0 implies identity, and only n possible codes have a signal distance of 1 from an arbitrary n-bit code character.

To measure the signal distance, the EXCLUSIVE OR of two words is taken, and the number of 1-bits produced is the signal distance. The successive codes of a gray code for instance are 1 signal distance apart.

A minimum distance code is constructed so that at least a specified number of bits would have to be changed to convert one valid code configuration into another valid code. That is, the signal distance between any two valid codes is not less than some minimum. For example, assume that a parity checking code scheme ensures a minimum signal distance of 2 (that is at least 2 bits must be changed to preserve parity). If 1 bit of a parity code is changed, the wrong pattern is at a signal distance of 1 from several valid characters, and, therefore, no correction is possible. If, however, a code has a minimum signal distance of 3 (nonparity), then any 1-bit errors can be recovered (since the wrong code will have a signal distance of 1 from only one valid code).

sign digit A digit containing one to four binary bits, associated with a data item and used to denote an algebraic sign.

Most binary, word-organized computers use a 1-bit sign, with $0 = +$ and $1 = -$.

Most character-oriented computers (6-bit character variable field length) use the two high-order (or zone) bits of the units-position character to denote the sign of a number. In general, if xxxx is a number, then:

10 xxxx = normally a negative number
01 xxxx = normally a positive number
00 xxxx = accepted as positive number
11 xxxx = accepted as positive number

The IBM 1620 uses a nondata punctuation bit (word mark) for sign control. In the units position the word mark indicates a negative sign; no word mark indicates a positive sign. Another word mark in the high-order position delimits the field size. Thus a minimum of two digits is needed for any number.

The IBM 7070 has a 3-bit sign associated with each word. Two out of three must be 1-bits, giving three possible configurations: positive, negative, and alpha. The alpha sign means that the word contains alphanumeric information (letters or symbols), not computational numbers. This three-way sign was a very useful feature.

In 8-bit byte computers using packed-decimal arithmetic, a 4-bit sign resides in the upper positions of the units character (a remnant of the zone bits), and only two acceptable sign configurations exist (of the 16 possible 4-bit values), denoting positive and negative. Both signs have a numeric value (hexadecimal) greater than 9.

significant digit A digit in a (positional numeration system) numeral that contributes to defining the magnitude of a number. A nonsignificant digit is not accurately known and serves only to mark the place of the decimal point (separatrix).

For instance, if the federal budget is exactly $101,035,276,390.48 for some year, then 14 significant digits appear. However, when a member of Congress speaks of $101,000,000,000, he is using three significant digits and nine place-holding zeros. Actually the member of Congress is correct to four significant figures, for the first four digits (rounded) are 1010.... Thus the second 0 is a significant digit (it is exact), whereas the next eight 0's are fillers.

To solve the problem of distinguishing significant digits from place-holders, scientists use exponent notation: 2.50×10^2 instead of 250. Thus, the following values:

$$2.5 \times 10^4$$
$$2.50 \times 10^4$$
$$2.500 \times 10^4$$

have three different levels of significance.

The utmost accuracy is expressed in the form

$$2.50 \pm .02 \times 10^4$$

sign position   That position, always at or near the left or right end of a numeral, in which the algebraic sign of the number is represented.

In word-oriented computers using binary arithmetic with complement representation of negatives, the sign position is always the leftmost bit. In character-oriented computers using serial adders, the sign is always in the rightmost character (byte). In other digital computers, either left or right positioning (rarely both) is used.

simple buffering   A technique for obtaining simultaneous performance of input/output operations and computing. Simple buffering methods involve associating a buffer with only one input or output file (or data set) for the entire duration of the activity on that file (or data set).

A digital computer is usually equipped with DATA CHANNELS (which see) which give the hardware the ability to conduct input and output while the central processing unit is executing internal program activity. Some technique of buffering must be used by the program if this potential for simultaneity is to be realized. With an input file, a memory area called a buffer is set aside, and the channel is directed to read into the buffer area before the data are needed. At the time when the program needs the data, they are moved out of the buffer into a work area, and the next read operation is begun. In this way the input is kept one step ahead of the program, and a high rate of productivity is achieved. For output, the program moves the data to an output buffer, and directs a channel to write them out. The buffer is considered full until the write finishes, and then it is considered empty. If multiple buffers are provided, ouptut data can be moved into the first available empty output buffer, providing greater timing flexibility and simultaneity.

The operations described above constitute simple buffering if the buffer areas remain permanently associated with one file. More complex buffering schemes are used by more sophisticated operating systems to provide increased speed, flexibility, and/or economical utilization of main memory.

See BUFFER, EXCHANGE BUFFERING.

SIMSCRIPT A simulation programming language written for the Air Force by the Rand Corporation.

By computer simulation is meant a system simulation of the behavior through time of such things as transportation and manufacturing systems.

For example, using SIMSCRIPT, a program could be developed to simulate a machine shop. The programmer would define to the SIMSCRIPT system such things as the types of machines used, how many of each, the number of men working, etc. To simulate the shop, the program would be executed, feeding to it in proper chronological sequence information about various work orders. The program would step each order through its various work stations, waiting when machines were busy. At various random points in time, the program could be requested to supply printed information on machine utilization, average order processing time, individual machine backlogs, etc. Certain of the ground rules could be changed, and the program rerun, thus helping uncover the best, or a better, way of doing things. Computer simulation can be a much cheaper way of determining an optimum than experimenting with a real shop.

In writing a SIMSCRIPT program, the programmer must define physical things, called entities, and events.

Example of entities are trucks, men, machines, etc. Entities have attributes that must also be defined. Entities are described on a special coding form.

Events are not described, but rather written as subprograms. Examples of events are the receipt of an order in a machine shop, the shipment of material from one depot to another.

In addition to entities and events, the SIMSCRIPT programmer can set up "sets" of data, allowing future events to be saved until conditions permit them to be processed. For example, when in a machine shop a given order is ready to be processed on a certain machine, if that machine is busy and has several orders to go first, the order is put into the queue for that machine. When the machine frees up, the next order is removed from the queue and is then processed on the machine.

SIMSCRIPT, in addition to being a program generator, has its own language. For example, CREAT ORDER means to establish a record in storage for an order. CAUSE ARRVL AT TIME & TRANT means to schedule execution of the ARRVL event routine at current simulated time plus transit time.

In addition, the SIMSCRIPT programmer may intersperse FORTRAN statements at will among the SIMSCRIPT statements. This is possible since the output of a SIMSCRIPT compilation is a FORTRAN source program, which then gets compiled using a FORTRAN compiler.

To show some of the features of the language, the following program will calculate interest on a bank deposit. Instead of having the program merely execute a standard formula, it simulates the presence of an account from date of deposit to date of withdrawal. As each X number of months of simulated time goes by (X months is the interest compounding period), the program calculates current interest and adds to the prior balance.

Thus it is possible, on any given date that the deposit is in effect, to obtain on a printed report the then current balance, as well as date of deposit, initial balance, rate of interest, and so on.

The following information must be punched into a control card for this sample program.

| 1   30   12 | Time in a SIMSCRIPT program is in terms of days, hours, and minutes and is stored as decimal days. Any dates (day, hour, minute) read in are automatically converted to decimal days, using two SIMSCRIPT functions: MINS, which equals 60, and HOURS which equals 24. Since in this example, we want the date to be year, month, and day, we can produce this effect by modifying HOURS to equal 12 for 12 months per year, and MINS to equal 30 for 30 days per month. This card will change those values before program execution begins. Thereafter, all dates may be considered as year, month, and day, and all conversion from that format to decimal years will be performed accordingly. |

This form describes entities and attributes, and event notices. DEPST describes to the system a temporary entity (able to be created and destroyed). The system is told that an 8-word record is needed to describe a deposit. This record will be set up by a sub program by executing the command "CREAT DEPST". The fields under "attributes" describe the name, format (integer or floating point), and word of the entity record of the various facts about a deposit. The attributes in order are deposit, date, withdrawal date, initial balance, interest period in months, yearly interest rate, interest rate for the interest period, and accumulated balance (initial balance and interest).

This entry describes to the system the storage area to be set up when scheduling the future event "PAYIN" (pay interest). It is a 4-word record with the attribute IDEP. IDEP will hold the deposit identification number, so that when this event is executed, reference can be made to the corresponding deposit entity record. (As set up, many deposits could be made and earning interest concurrently.)

Temporary and event notice entities | **Attributes**

Name (1–8)	Record Size (9–16)	Name (17–24)	Word (25–29)	Mode (30–31)
+ T D E P S T	8	T D D A T E	1	F
		T W D A T E	2	F
		T A M N T	3	—
		T I N T P R	4	F
		T R A T E P	6	F
		T A C C U M	7	—
+ N P A Y I N	4	N I D E P	3	—

EVENTS	This is the heading line of the events list. This is a list of all possible type of events, broken down into events that can be caused externally (from an input tape) and internally (by a subprogram executing the CAUSE command). The events list is used to develop a timing routine.
2 EXOGENOUS	Means that two types of events can be caused externally.
DEPOST (1)	The name of one of the events is DEPOST, and a tape record that causes a deposit event to be executed has an identification number of 1.
ENDSIM (2)	The other event type is ENDSIM and will be used to end the program. A tape record used to cause this event has the ID 2.
1 ENDOGENOUS	Means 1 type of event that is caused internally.
PAYIN	The internally caused event has the name PAYIN. This event is scheduled by executing a command CAUSE PAYIN AT TIME + something. Time + something means current simulated time + some factor, such as 3 months.
END	This signals physical end of the events list.
EXOGENOUS EVENT DEPOST	This is the heading line of the subprogram DEPOST.
SAVE EVENT CARD	This routine will be entered when a deposit tape record is read, and when simulated time equals the deposit date on the tape record. This entry means to save the information on the tape record, because additional optional information is present which will be used to establish some of the deposits' attributes.
CREAT DEPST	This tells the system to create a record called DEPST, using the ID # from the tape record.

READ DDATE(DEPST), WDATE(DEPST), AMNT(DEPST), INTRP(DEPST), RATEY(DEPST)	This instructs the system to read the information just saved from the tape record into the attribute fields of the deposit record, thus helping build a complete deposit record.
FORMAT (M2.2.2, M2.2.2, I6, M2.2.2, D2.3)	This defines the format of the tape. The fields are 6 integers for deposit date (2 each year, month, and day), 6 for withdrawal date, 6 for initial balance, 6 for interest period (also year, month, and day), 2 integers and 3 decimal places for yearly interest rate. All fields in year-month-day format will automatically be converted and stored in decimal years format.
LET RATE P(DEPST) = RATEY(DEPST) * INTRP(DEPST)	The interest rate per interest period is calculated by multiplying the yearly rate times the number of months in an interest period, expressed as decimal years (i.e., 6 months = 0.5 decimal years). This interest rate for the interest period is calculated in this routine when the record is initially created for deposit and stored as one of the deposits attributes, so that interest may easily be calculated in the pay interest routine.
LET ACCUM(DEPST) = AMNT(DEPST)	The accumulated amount attribute of the deposit record is initially set the same as the initial balance value. The deposit entity record is now complete.
IF (TIME & INTRP(DEPST))GR WDATE(DEPST), GO TO 10	Before scheduling the first pay interest routine, we check that the money is not withdrawn before the first interest period has passed. If so, we go to 10. This statement says, "If current simulated time (also equal to deposit date) + one interest period is greater than (beyond) the withdrawal date, go to 10." The program continues if the money is still deposited at deposit date + 1 interest period.
CREAT PAYIN	This tells the system to schedule the pay interest event by setting up a temporary event notice record as defined on the definition sheet.

461

STORE DEPST IN INDEP (PAYIN)	This stores the ID # of the deposit just created in the ID # attribute field of the PAYIN event notice record. This is done so that when the payin routine is executed for this deposit, the routine will have a reference back to the appropriate deposit entity record.
CAUSE PAYIN AT TIME + INTPR(DEPST)	Now that the event notice record has been created, the system is told *when* to schedule that event. The event is scheduled at current simulated time (still equal to the deposit date) + the interest period (stored as an attribute field of the deposit record).
RETURN	This causes control to be returned to the main timing routine.
10 CALL PRINT	10 is the statement number, and was branched to when a deposit was withdrawn before passage of 1 complete interest period. Here, the report generation routine PRINT is called and executed. This routine prints deposit and withdrawal dates, initial balance, and accumulated balance.
DESTROY DEPST	The deposit entity record is destroyed, freeing up core storage for subsequent assignment as a new deposit.
RETURN	Transfers control back to main timing routine.
END	Indicates physical end of event DEPOST routine.
ENDOGENOUS EVENT PAYIN	This is the heading line for the PAYIN routine.
STORE IDEP (PAYIN) IN DEPST	This takes the identification number of the deposit about to be compounded, and puts it in a local field called DEPST. This is the same name as the deposit entity record as a convenience. This field will be used as a subscript to refer to the appropriate deposit record and its attributes.

DESTROY PAYIN	This removes the event notice PAYIN, since it has done its job of getting us here. Core is freed up for subsequent use in this or another routine.
LET ACCUM (DEPST) = ACCUM (DEPST) + ACCUM (DEPST) * RATEP (DEPST)	The accumulated amount is set equal to itself plus (itself times the interest rate for this interest period). In other words, the current interest is calculated and added to the prior accumulated balance.
IF (TIME + INTRP(DEPST))GR WDATE (DEPST), GO TO 20	This statement again checks to see whether the money will still be deposited at current time plus one interest period, which is when interest is to be paid again.
CREAT PAYIN	Create event notice record.
STORE DEPST IN IDEP(PAYIN)	Save deposit identification number.
CAUSE PAYIN AT TIME + INTPR(DEPST)	Schedule the next pay interest routine at current time + interest period.
RETURN	Return control to the timing routine.
20 CALL PRINT	This statement will be executed when money will be withdrawn before next interest payment date. It executes the report generator routine.
DESTROY DEPST	This destroys the deposit record for subsequent core usage by another routine.
RETURN	Return to timing routine.
END	Physical end of the pay interest routine.
EXOGENOUS EVENT ENDSIM	End of simulation routine heading line.
STOP	Stop the program.
END	Physical end of endsim routine.
REPORT PRINT	Report routine heading
SIMULATION OF DEPOSIT OF MONEY	Line heading lines just as you want them to print.

DEPOSIT DATE WITHDRAWAL DATE **/**/** **/**/** INITIAL BAL ACCUM BAL ****** ******	Each set of asterisks specifies printing of some internal stored or accumulated information.
HPART(DDATE(DEPST)), MPART(DDATE(DEPST)), DPART(DDATE(DEPST)), HPART(WDATE(DEPST)), MPART(WDATE(DEPST)), DPART(WDATE(DEPST)), AMNT(DEPST), ACCUM(DEPST)	These lines describe in the same order as the asterisks, which fields are to be printed. HPART, MPART, and DPART all request a part of the date. These must be converted, since all dates are stored as decimal years. These names are all permanently assigned, and SIMSCRIPT automatically does the conversion.
END	This signals physical end of the report routine.

simulate   To mimic some or all of the behavior of one system with a different, dissimilar system.   Thus a computer programmed to behave like a different computer, or like some entirely noncomputational system, can be used to learn about the simulated system.

Simulation is used when direct experimentation is impossible (new system not yet constructed), impractical (simulated wars, for example), uneconomical (a process requiring large quantities of platinum but not known to be profitable), immoral (dealing with human death), or simply too slow (forestry, ecology).

All analog computer applications are simulations by the very nature of the device.   So are wind-tunnel tests, towing tanks, structural models of all kinds.

For simple systems (such as a check-out line at a supermarket), a complete simulation is practical.   For complex systems, approximations, simplifications, and selective omission of unimportant detail are required (such as the U.S. Weather Bureau simulation of atmosphere of entire Earth on the CDC 6600).

Certain systems have been designed to assist simulation on digital computers.   Examples of such systems are languages (SIMSCRIPT, MILITRAN), transactional model systems (GPSS), and analog computer simulators (DYNAMO).

The simulator must decide what he wishes to investigate, and design his model to correctly describe those particular aspects of the total behavior of his studied system.   A molecule-by-molecule simulation is possible only with very small systems.

simulator   A computer program or hardware device that performs (or materially assists in the performance of) simulation.

Normally a simulator is a full-size mock-up or model of a control situation (ship's bridge, plane cockpit, air traffic control center, computer console, radar screen, automobile controls, locomotive, etc.) used to train or experiment on human operators.   It has provision for feeding simulated signals (dial readings, projected scenery, recorded headphone voices) to the operators and reacting to the operator's control responses (throttle, switch settings, etc.).   Usually there are one or more human instructors (or experimenters) outside the simulated environment, but directing in detail the functioning of the simulator. There may be a computer interacting with the system, or simpler simulators of the do-it-alone type.

Simulator is also used for other, less precise, simulating devices. These depart in scale, form, time-lapse-rate, or even number of physical dimensions from the prototype being simulated.   For example, aeroengineers use a voltage measured in a bath of conducting liquid with immersed nonconductive (or very conductive) models: the electric potential simulates velocity potential, yielding streamlines of an inviscid fluid. Curiously enough, electronic engineers sometimes reverse this procedure by using hydrodynamic models of electric potential. Both analogs are analog computers of a highly special type.

single reference   See RANDOM ACCESS.

single step   A mode of digital computer operation, in which pressing a button on the control panel causes one instruction to be executed.

Normally, a digital computer operates under its own timing control —several thousand to several million instructions per second. Naturally a human being cannot follow events occurring at this rate. On nearly every computer, an operator's control can switch from normal to single-step mode of operation. This switch disables the computer's own timing mechanism, and substitutes pulses from the run button on the control panel. This permits an operator to observe the state of the computer after each instruction, and to write down instruction addresses and other data. This is a wasteful use of computer time, and as such, it is favored for small, inexpensive computers only. Indeed, the very fastest computers do not offer this option to the user, but they do reserve it for the maintenance engineer.

On occasion, the execution of an instruction is divided into two or more distinct phases (the IBM 650 has an I instruction cycle followed by an O operation cycle, and the CDC 6600 has a major cycle of 1 microsecond and a minor cycle of 0.1 microsecond). It is then sometimes possible to execute less than one instruction per button push.

The normal use of single step is in program debugging: if an endless loop is observed, the single-step mode is entered, two or more instructions are traced, and then a dump is taken.

If an address stop capability is provided, single step becomes a much better debugging aid. A pause occurs when a specified section of logic is entered, and it can then be followed using single step.

skeletal coding   A set of incomplete instructions in symbolic form, intended to be completed and specialized by a processing program written for that purpose.

A skeleton is written once, by a skilled programmer, and it is intended to be incorporated one or more times into programs of other people. Unlike a subroutine, the skeleton may assume different forms in each appearance; indeed no two occurrences may be alike. The skeleton and its processor constitute a do-it-yourself computer routine kit.

The skeleton contains:

1. Symbolic (assembly-language) computer instructions.

2. Replaceable parameters embedded in the code, recognizable by their construction, which will be replaced by user-supplied symbols or blanks.

3. Conditional-assembly pseudoinstructions: these direct the processor to include, or omit, or modify sections of skeletal code according to tests performed by the processor (normally testing user-supplied parameters).

The processed skeleton is not a set of computer instructions: it is a higher-level language and must be further processed into relocatable or absolute instruction form.   Thus, in an extreme case, the steps shown in the diagram will be required.

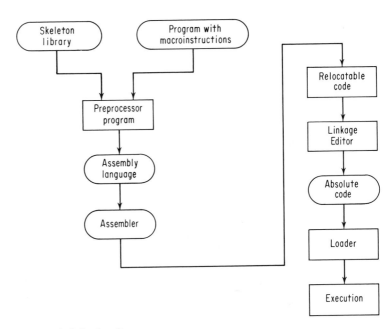

Usage of skeletal coding.

Some special skeleton codes are written which handle COBOL, FORTRAN, or other higher-level languages.   In principle, this idea could be applied by a preprocessor program to any coding language.

skew   In character recognition, a condition arising at the read station whereby a character or line of characters appears in a "twisted" manner in relation to a real or imaginary horizontal baseline.   See CHARACTER SKEW, LINE SKEW.

Location	Operation	Address	Comments	Meaning
$0	EDDY	$1, $2, $3		This defines a macroskeleton with the name EDDY, capable of accepting four different parameters. Whatever values are supplied will replace $0, $1, $2, $3.
$0	ZAD	1, $1	Initialize	If $0 was not blank, it is location of 1st instruction. Whatever is 1st operand parameter is loaded into accumulator 1.
	ADD	1, $2		Second argument is added to first argument.
	IFF	$3.EQ. Blank		Following instruction will be included only if test condition $3 IS EQUAL BLANK is false. If $3 is blank, the next instruction will not appear in generated code.
	ADD	1, $3		Add 3d parameter, if any, to sum.
	IFT	$3.EQ. Blank		If 2 operands, divide by 2.
	DIV	1, = 2		
	IFT	$3. NE. Blank		If 3 operands, divide by 3.
	DIV	1, = 3		
	STO	1, $1	Store Avg.	
	END	EDDY		End of skeleton EDDY.

skew failure   In character recognition, the condition that exists during document alignment whereby the document reference edge is not parallel to that of the read station.

The read station will usually tolerate some skew, but beyond certain limits, skew failure will yield reading failure, the nature of which is not always readily discernible. In this instance, careful examination is required as too often the evidence is of a transient nature. See DOCUMENT ALIGNMENT.

skip   In fixed-instruction-length digital computers, to bypass or ignore one or more instructions in an otherwise sequential process.

An unconditional skip is a computer instruction demanding that the next *n* instructions be ignored. This instruction is very rarely implemented, because the more versatile unconditional branch (transfer, jump) is almost universally available.

A conditional skip is taken if a specified test condition is passed or failed (otherwise the next instruction in sequence is executed).

For instance, in the IBM 709, the following skip instructions are available:

1. LBT: Low-order bit test. If the rightmost bit of the accumulator is 1, the computer skips one instruction and proceeds; if the bit is 0, the next sequential instruction is executed.

2. CAS: Compare accumulator with storage. If the contents of the accumulator are algebraically greater than the contents of the designated memory location, no skip occurs; if they are equal, one instruction is skipped; if the accumulator is algebraically smaller, two instructions are skipped.

In the majority of instances, the instructions skipped are unconditional transfers. The result is as though a single instruction, of double the normal instruction length, having a two-address format, were coded. That is, the transfer may be considered part of the conditional skip instruction. Skip instructions are less common on computers with multiple-address part instruction formats for this reason.

slit scan   In character recognition, a magnetic or photoelectric device that obtains the horizontal structure of an inputted character by vertically projecting its component elements at given intervals.

Slit scans have been employed in optical character recognition (OCR) and in magnetic-ink character recognition, and in both cases the document transport plays an integral part in the scanning process. As the character is passed under the slit, a vertical projection is taken in order to measure the unreflected areas of that horizontal component. The total unreflected area is then reduced to a base amplitude. Thus, when all the horizontal components have been measured, their combined amplitudes will generate a waveform (analog) representation of the character just processed.

It is this waveform, or a modified form in those cases requiring normalization, from which a determination will be made as to the character's most probable identity.

Since the number of unique waveforms is limited, especially after allowances are made for character misregistration, a desire to increase the size of the character set will dictate that another scanning method be substituted in order to achieve the greater detail required. One alternative would be the divided slit scan, which although still a one-dimensional device (that which operates on only one character component at a time), is capable of preserving vertical detail.

The other alternatives are classified as two-dimensional devices since they can recognize all character components simultaneously; among these devices, the most commonly employed are the mechanical scanner, flying-spot scanner, TV camera, and photocell matrix.

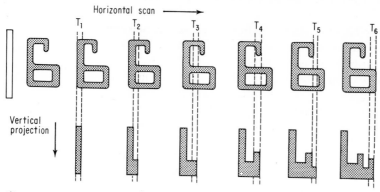

Slit scan.

smooth   To modify a sequential set of numerical data items in a manner designed to reduce the differences in value between adjacent items.

If the original data and the modified data were to be plotted on a single graph, the modified curve would be a smoother (less jagged) curve centered on the original data curve.   Hence, the term smoothing.

Fourier showed that a curve (or data sequence) could be regarded as a summation of harmonically related sinusoidal curves of various frequencies and amplitudes.   Smoothing is a process that reduces the amplitude of the high-frequency components, leaving relative phase and all else unchanged.   Hence the synonymous terms data filtering or digital filtering.

The principle reasons for smoothing are reduction of noise and clarification of general trends (tendencies) and occasionally, data compression (reduction of storage or bandwidth requirements).

Two examples of smoothing are tabulated as follows:

| Observed data : X_i |
| Smoothed data : Z_i |

Moving average	Exponential smoothing
$X_i = \frac{1}{4}Z_{i-1} + \frac{1}{2}Z_i + \frac{1}{4}Z_{i+1}$	$X_i = (1 - \epsilon)Z_i + \epsilon\, Z_{i-1}$ where $0 < \epsilon < 1$

snapshot dump   An edited printout of selected parts of the contents of main memory, performed at one or more times during the execution of a program without materially affecting the operation of the program.

A useful aid to debugging programs. A routine capable of printing parts of memory without disturbing the computer (or else restoring the memory to its state at the beginning of the dump) resides permanently in some part of the computer. At selected points within his program, the programmer inserts instructions which call or activate this routine. After the dump is finished, control is returned to the program at the first instruction following the dump request.

This practice is impossible on small computers (or with very large programs which fill memory) that have no room for a resident snapshot routine. On larger computers, operating systems provide snapshot utility routines.

See DYNAMIC DUMP, compare CHECKPOINT.

SNOBOL   Acronym for string-oriented-symbolic language, SNOBOL is a programming language developed at the Bell Telephone Laboratories by D. J. Farber, R. E. Griswold, and I. P. Polonsky, and has significant applications in program compilation and generation of symbolic equations.

A statement in SNOBOL consists of a rule that operates on symbolically named strings. The basic operations are string formation, pattern matching, and replacement. Facilities for integer arithmetic, indirect referencing, and input/output are included.

The basic concepts of SNOBOL begin with strings and string names. String names may be numbers and/or letters, while strings may be any symbols. The following represents a name, a string, and a statement to create the string.

STRING 1 = 'THIS IS A STRING'

A string may also be created using both literals and other strings.

STRING 2 = STRING 1 'CREATED USING ANOTHER
STRING'

The next concept is pattern matching, which is the process of examining a string for a given substring. To test for the word IS in string 1:

STRING 1 'IS'

The condition may then be tested by /S (YES) F (NO) which is a conditional go to statement: go to YES on success, go to NO on failure.

Pattern matching may be done using several substrings:

STRING 2 STRING 1 *ANY* 'USING'

This statement means—search string 2 for the occurrence of the contents of string 1, followed by anything (given the label ANY), followed by the word USING. A by-product of this statement is the creation of a new string called ANY, containing whatever data was between the first and second substrings. In this case, ANY = CREATED, and the generation of this string is automatic.

The next concept is replacement. A replacement statement takes the form

STRING 2 'CREATED' = 'FORMED BY'

This statement says: search string 2 for the word CREATED, and replace it with the words FORMED BY. String 2 now equals: "THIS IS A STRING FORMED BY USING ANOTHER STRING."

Similarly, it is possible to replace several substrings with a single statement, and substrings may be deleted if desired. Simple integer arithmetic is permitted—a given string may have an element operated on individually, but more complicated expressions such as A + B + C are not permitted.

The following example demonstrates SNOBOL's ability for manipulating data strings. The problem is to sort a set (or string) of words, and rearrange them in alphabetical order.

SNOBOL	
* ALPHABETIZATION USING A RADIX SORT TECHNIQUE	Comments may be interspersed.
FIRST THE SIZE OF THE LONGEST STRING, AND THEN THE LIST OF WORDS IS READ INTO STRINGS OF CORRESPONDING NAMES. AFTER PRINTING THE LIST THE WORDS ON "LIST" ARE EXAMINED USING THE FIXED-LENGTH STRING VARIABLE FEATURE. IF THE WORD IS TOO SHORT, THE WORD IS ADDED TO THE SPECIAL BIN (NAMED "BIN"). OTHERWISE THE LETTER CONTAINED IN "PIT" IS THE NAME OF THE BIN INTO WHICH THE WORD IS FILED USING THE INDIRECT FEATURE. AFTER ALL WORDS HAVE BEEN FILED, THE LIST IS REASSEMBLED AT STATEMENT L5 AND FOLLOWING STATEMENTS. NOTE THAT L5 PLACES THE CONTENTS OF "BIN" IN "LIST" AND AT THE SAME TIME VOIDS "BIN" FOR THE NEXT PASS. NEXT EACH	

OF THE BINS IS ADDED TO "LIST" IN ALPHABETIC ORDER, AND THEN VOIDED. THE NEXT PASS IS THEN MADE. WHEN "SIZE" BECOMES NEGATIVE, THE LAST PASS HAS BEEN MADE AND THE ALPHABETIZED LIST IS PRINTED OUT.

BEGIN SYS .READ *SIZE* ' '	This statement causes the first data card to be read. This card contains the size of the largest word, beginning in column 1. After reading, a search is made for a blank. Anything preceding a blank is set up as a string whose name is SIZE.
START SYS .READ *WORDS* ' ' /F(L0)	The next card is read. This contains a word to be alphabetized followed by a comma and a blank. A search is made for a blank, and anything preceding it (the word plus the comma) is set up as a string with the name WORDS. If a failure to read (last card), control is transferred to L0.
LIST = LIST WORDS /(START)	This creates a list of words equal to the prior list plus the contents of WORDS which is the word just read. Control is unconditionally given to START.
L0 SYS .PRINT 'THE LIST TO BE ALPHABETIZED IS: 'LIST	This statement is executed at last data card. It prints out the literal followed by the contents of LIST, which is the total of all words read in. This logs the input.
SYS PRINT VOID	This prints a blank line.
L1 ALPHABET = 'ABCDEFGHIJKLMNO PQRSTUVWXYZ'	This sets up the alphabet as a data string with the name ALPHABET.
L2 SIZE = SIZE − '1'	This subtracts 1 from the size of the longest word.
SIZE '−' /S(FIN)	This tests size for negative. When size is negative, the sort is complete and control goes to FIN.

L3 LIST *WORD* (,) = /F(L5)	This examines LIST for a comma. If no comma is found, control goes to L5. If a comma is found, the comma and the word are deleted from the list, and the word is set up as a string with the name WORD. Each execution of this statement will cause the next word in the list to be accessed and put into the string WORD.
WORD *HEAD/SIZE* *PIT/'1' * /F(L4)	This statement tests the current word to see whether it has as many letters as the letter position we are sorting on. For example, if we are sorting on the 6th letter position, we test to see whether the current word is at least six letters long. If the word is not long enough, control is transferred to L4. The word is analyzed by breaking it up into two pieces, or by finding two matches to substrings. The first substring can be anything, but must be of length SIZE, and will be named HEAD. This is a case of a fixed-length string variable. The second part of the word can be anything but must be a length 1 and will be called PIT. Thus, when we wish to sort on (when size = 5) the sixth letter, the following word would be analyzed as follows: ANYWO R D HEAD PIT A failure occurs if a word is not long enough to break up into the two lengths SIZE, and 1. In addition to testing the length of the current word, we are also extracting the particular letter by which we want to sort this word. The letter is in PIT.

$PIT = $PIT WORD ',' /(L3)	This is an example of the indirectness feature. This statement creates a string called $PIT containing the previous contents of itself plus the current word and a comma. The word PIT was previously defined and contains the letter of the current word we wish to sort on. $PIT as a label is the equivalent of using the contents of PIT as a label. In other words, $PIT will create a new string for each possible content of PIT. Looking at it another way, $PIT is equivalant to creating a label such as BUCKET and using PIT as a subscript. Each different value of PIT actually refers to a different location. This is more flexible, however, as it is self-defining, and may be any symbol. Core is dynamically assigned when and if needed. So, in effect, this statement is dumping the current word into a unique string depending on the current value of PIT, which is one of the letters of the current word. Control is given to L3.
L4 BIN = BIN WORD ',' /(L3)	When a word was too small to be alphabetized during the current sort cycle, a branch was taken to here. This statement creates a string called BIN to hold all words too short to be alphabetized on any given sort cycle. Control is given to L3. At this point, a loop has been established which obtains a word at a time from LIST, and dumps it into the proper bin by the letter position being sorted, or into a special BIN if the word is too short. When all words in LIST have been so processed, control goes to L5.

L5 BIN *LIST* =	This creates a new string called LIST containing the contents of BIN, which are all words too short for the just completed sort. In addition, BIN is blanked out.
L6 ALPHABET *PIT/'1'* = /F(L1)	This examines ALPHABET for a 1-position "anything," creates a string called PIT containing that anything, and deletes that letter from the string ALPHABET. Each execution of this statement sets PIT equal to the next letter. PIT will now be used as a "subscript" to reference the various bins previously set up. On failure (end of alphabet), control is given to L1. At this time, the current letter position sort is completed.
LIST = LIST $PIT	This sets LIST equal to the prior contents of LIST plus the contents of the bin called $PIT. [Similar to BUCKET (PIT).]
$PIT = /(L6)	This deletes $PIT so that it may be used on the next sort if any. Control is then transferred to L6. At this point, all the words previously dumped into the various bins by letter have been recombined alphabetically by the letter position of the current sort cycle into LIST. On failure at L6, control goes back to L1 to begin the next sort cycle on the next higher-order letter position.
FIN SYS .PRINT 'THE ALPHABETIZED LIST IS: ' LIST	This prints out the completed list. This statement gained control when SIZE became negative, indicating that all the required sort cycles had been made.
END BEGIN	This is the end statement.

The following is the output received when the program is run, using a small number of words: The list to be alphabetized is: ZONE, SOFTWARE, HEURISTIC, SENTINEL, BINARY, NAND, ACCESS, SEQUENCE, LATENCY, FLOW, RECURSIVE, ADDER, CODE, OVERLAY, SYSIN, TAPE, EDIT, WORD, DEBUG, MEMORY, PROCESS.   The alphabetized list is: ACCESS, ADDER, BINARY, CODE, DEBUG, EDIT, FLOW, HEURISTIC, LATENCY, MEMORY, NAND, OVERLAY, PROCESS, RECURSIVE, SENTINEL, SEQUENCE, SOFTWARE, SYSIN, TAPE, WORD, ZONE.

software   The totality of programs and routines usable on a particular kind of computer, although usually only those routines supplied by the computer manufacturer, are included in the term.   Equally the documentation associated with a computer or program, such as manuals, diagrams, operating instructions, forms part of the software.

If a human being were born fully grown physically, he would be analogous to a computer without software: all potential, but no performance.   Education (formal or otherwise) enables man to function; software enables computers to function.

The earlier electronic computers were programmed only by their builders (with a soldering iron, in one case!).   As computers became more numerous, the number of programmers increased, but the level of competence of the average programmer declined.   Software was developed to permit less qualified programmers to produce efficient codes easily and rapidly.   First came assemblers, program loaders, and then IOCS.   In time compilers, operating systems, application-oriented programs, and entire libraries of programs became available from computer makers.   Today manufacturers vie with one another in developing efficient and flexible software packages.   The cost of this software is included in the price of the hardware; in fact, software accounts for more of the cost of IMB 360 than the hardware does.   Hardware can be designed and produced by automation, but software is still largely human-made.   Fortunately, software can be reproduced (mass-produced) at very low cost once it is written.

The owner of a computer has three principal sources of runnable programs:

1.   The manufacturer
2.   Users' group library
3.   Proprietary, written by his own company

solid-state component   A device whose operation depends on the bulk properties of the solid materials of which it is made.

Solid-state components usually refer to transistors, diodes, monolithic integrated circuits, but also may apply to ferrite cores, and some cryogenic components (semiconductor devices).

Strictly speaking, the resistor is the most common solid-state device: its action depends on the volumetric resistivity of its composition.

Devices that are solid, but not solid state are:

1. Inductors, transformers (geometry, number of windings)
2. Capacitors (geometry)

Lesser-known solid-state devices are photoconductors, thermistors, Hall-effect devices, ruby laser, junction laser, tunnel diodes, SCR's, etc.

In computers, solid state simply means no vacuum tubes, and either transistors, monolithic integrated circuits, or both. (In physics, solid state means the study of physical phenomena occurring in solids, especially from a quantum-mechanical point of view.)

The principal advantages of solid-state devices are represented by their small size and low power consumption, which permit a close crowding of components. Today's fastest computers are limited by the time it takes signals to travel from component to component (about 1 nanosecond per 8 inches) so that the closer the crowding, the faster is the hardware. Today the apparent limit is approached by so called LSI (large-scale integrated) circuits involving hundreds of logic elements on a wafer less than 1 inch square: complete computers could be assembled on a card 8 inches square (less memory and peripheral devices only). A by-product of this technology is a declining computer cost.

sonic delay line   An element that repeats at its output the information of its input, but with a fixed time lapse intervening.

The construction of a sonic delay line consists of an input amplifier (optional), an electric-to-sonic transducer (usually piezoelectric, but sometimes electrodynamic), a sound-propagating medium (puddle of mercury, glass block, spring, torsion wire), a microphone, and an output amplifier (optional).

If the output is reconnected to input, a circulating memory results: a fixed amount of data is held, each bit accessible at periodic intervals of time. Closed-loop operation, however, is not required for every application.

sort   To rearrange a set of data items into a new sequence, governed by specific rules of precedence, and by extension, the program designed to perform the above activity.

We must distinguish between in-memory sorts and peripheral-file sorts. In-memory sorts are faster, and are included as a portion of the logic of peripheral sorts. Peripheral sorts (disk, drum, tape) can handle much larger sets of data.

A tape sort begins by distributing the data into strings on work tapes (first pass). It then merges the tapes onto new work tapes, forming fewer, longer partial sequences (merge phase). The final merge (last pass) creates a single and sorted output sequence.

In memory, various kinds of techniques are used, called by such colorful names as exchange sort, radix sort, sieving, etc. The techniques vary in applicability depending on the nature of the input data. Some methods benefit by some preordering in the input data. Other methods are insensitive to preordering, and are not affected by reverse-sequenced data.

The typical manufacturer-supplied sort package has the following properties:

1. It reads control cards describing the data and the configuration of the computer and the sequencing rules.

2. It requires at least 3 tapes (or disk work areas) but cannot handle more than 8 or 16 tapes drives (or work areas).

3. It allows for own code exits, user-supplied routines which modify, inspect, add, delete, or replace data items during the first and/or last pass; these enable the user to convert a general-purpose sort routine into any variety of special results such as the last-pass exit printing an edited report and suppressing all output tape writing.

4. The various phases of coding do not reside simultaneously in memory, saving space but requiring a program input file.

5. It prints periodic messages to the operator, advising him of its progress.

sorter A device with a single input feed and multiple output stacks which can be used by an operator to sort items.

A punched-card sorter usually examines one column at a time in a stack of punched cards. It has 13 card output hoppers; one for each of the 12 rows of holes and a 13th for cards with no holes in the particular column.

The operator runs all the cards through the machine, separating them into distinct groups according to punches in a selected column. This operation is not sorting since no new sequence has been created. The operator then places the output stacks one behind another, forming a new sequence in ascending or descending order, and this is the sorting operation proper: the human being determines the sequence with the assistance of the machine. Card sorters operating at several hundred to several thousand cards per minute are in common use. Banks use check sorters which operate upon MICR (magnetic-ink character recognition) encoded checks which function in an analogous manner.

The card sorters often have controls which disable the sensing of particular rows. The sorter selects on the first hole sensed; sorting multiply-punched columns requires disabling the sensing of already sorted rows.

Most jobs require sorting on more than one column, thus requiring multiple passes. If the operator makes a mistake in picking up the outputs in order, the sort must be repeated from that point onward to correct his error.

source language   The language in which a program (or other text) is originally expressed.

Today, most programs for computers are not written in computer language but in a higher-level language designed to make coding easier. This source-language version of the program forms the input to an assembler or a compiler which processes it to (or closer to) computer instructions.

In machine translation, a source language is any natural language that must be translated to another object language.

source module   An organized set of statements in any source language recorded in machine-readable form and suitable for input to an assembler or compiler.

A source module commonly contains one entire program, but may contain more than one program (if the compiler allows batch processing) or only a portion of a program (if it is to be catalogued in a source statement library instead of being compiled).

A source module must have a name, which is usually invented by the programmer: it will then usually have a mnemonic significance for the programmer.

After having been processed by the language translator (or compiler, or assembler), the source module is transformed into an object module with the same name. The OBJECT MODULE (which see) contains the program expressed in machine-language (or computer-instruction) form.

When a source module consists of punched cards, it may sometimes be referred to as a source deck.

source program   The form of a program just as the programmer has written it, often on coding forms or machine-readable media, and equally a program expressed in a source-language form.

Today, programmers using all but the simplest computers can use the computer itself to make programming easier. (On a very simple computer no programming simplification is possible, for no complicated programs can exist.) This is achieved by using specially written programs to perform the more mechanical tasks of program generation.

Suppose that a small computer is being programmed. The coder writes in assembly language, producing a source program consisting of symbolic machine instructions. The assembler allocates space, converts symbols to machine addresses, converts symbolic operation codes to actual operation codes, and produces an object program and an assembly listing.

On large computers, programming is more commonly done in one or more higher-level languages, problem-oriented or procedure-oriented. Compilers convert source programs written in these languages into object programs, ready (or almost ready) for execution.

Source programs commonly contain three essential elements:
1. Data descriptions, defining the manipulated data
2. Procedure descriptions, defining actions to be performed
3. Comments and notes, allowing another human being to follow the coder's logic more easily

Object programs contain only data and procedure descriptions, but in a radically changed form.

source (program) library A collection of computer programs in compiler language and/or assembler language.

These programs are recorded on, and may be extracted from, a mass-storage device. A common practice is to hold large source decks on tape, and revise and assemble (or compile) these in one pass. This produces a new source-library entry and also an object (or core-image) program suitable for inclusion in the corresponding library.

space A generic term which may mean:
1. A capacity for storing recorded data, as on a disk or a tape or in core, especially applied to not-yet-written memory capacity
2. One or more blank (nonprinting, space-holding) characters such as the spaces between words and sentences
3. The arrangement of output data in a prescribed format, often used for line skipping in a printer

When internal memory is filled and can accommodate no more data, a programmer will say that it has run out of memory space. A more accurate statement could be expressed in terms of so many words, bits, or characters. Space on a disk or drum is measured in cylinders, tracks, words, or characters, or (sometimes) sectors.

Usually, a single character configuration is used to represent internally a column of punched cards containing no holes. This blank character prints as an uninked area on the printer (sometimes several characters have no printer representation, but only one is a true blank). A blank character should not be confused with a null character (absence of a character).

As on a typewriter, single space, double space, etc., denote vertical placement of lines on a written page, and less commonly, horizontal separations, as in spacing out or spacing apart columns on a page.

On some printers, vertical spacing may also be controlled by a carriage tape containing holes in various channels to designate particular lines on a form. This kind of vertical spacing is commonly called skipping, as in SKIP TO CHANNEL 4.

special character   A computer-representable character that is not alphabetic, numeric, or blank.

Such characters include punctuation (comma, period, quote ...); algebraic symbols (+, −, decimal point, 1, ÷); special signs ($, #, @, %); parentheses and brackets; subscripts and superscripts; ½, ¼, c/o, c_r; and many, many others.

Other special characters are not printable or text characters: for instance, line feed, escape, change, shift, delete, synchronize, idle, acknowledge.

In the 7- and 8-bit codes, some character configurations remain unassigned; they may be used for any purpose whatever.

Most computers in the United States recognize 26 alphabetic characters: A to Z. Some also recognize lowercase a to z. However, the IBM 360 System (BAL) has 29 alphabetical characters: A to Z, #, $, @.

special-purpose computer   A digital or analog computer designed to be especially efficient in a certain class of applications.

For example, a message-switching computer (G.E. Datanet, ITT 7300 ADX) designed to economically transmit messages on a store-and-forward basis, reducing cost and increasing the flexibility of communications. A message-switching computer must be able to synchronize many different kinds of transmission lines, codes, levels, and rates. Its design features comprise many overlapped I/O channels, including sophisticated multiplexors, small word size (to permit flexible allocation of data-string space), limited arithmetic capability, table look-up instruction, a variety of data-moving instructions, high-speed disks and/or drums, and interrupt features for responding to on-demand signal service.

Another example of a special-purpose computer is the process control computer (such as the IBM 1800, CDC 1700) designed to control on-line a batch or continuous manufacturing plant. As a built-in cybernetic control center, it must adapt to many situations, but probably will not require extremely high speed. Process control computer design features include environmental ruggedness, flexibility in memory size and processor speed, large number of input/output terminals (but probably limited total I/O capability in terms of rate and simultaneity), fast arithmetic, sophisticated interrupt features for responding to alarms, ability to sense on/off (open/close contacts), and analog/digital and other nonconventional input media.   It may include an ability to batch-process background programs in its idle time.   One type (the IBM 1800) has the ability to simulate itself under monitor control, permitting check-out of new programs when the current (real time) foreground program is idle.

stacked-job processing   A technique of automatic job-to-job transition, with little or no operator intervention.

An operating system that allows for stacked jobs has provision for recognizing and acting on end-of-job/start-of-next-job indications in the input.   Many processing programs also process stacked jobs—but here we have one program (a job to the operating system) processing many unrelated sets of input in succession (each a job to the processing program).

Stacked processing is often confused with BATCH PROCESSING (which see).   In a stacked environment each job is processed to completion before the next job is begun; in a batched environment all jobs are processed by the first program phase, then all jobs are processed by the second program phase, and so on until the last phase completes all jobs.   If only one program phase exists, stacking and batching are identical.   Suppose that n jobs are submitted to an m-phase process. With batch processing, n processing times and m phase-loading times are required.   With stacked processing n processing times are still required but $n \times m$ phase-loading operations are needed.   Batch processing usually requires more careful programming in exchange for its higher speed; stacked processing is simpler.

All operating systems allow for some form of stacked-job processing. The more advanced systems can process in an order different from the order of submission of the jobs.   This permits either priorities to be recognized or an increased hardware utilization to be achieved.

stacker   That part (or parts) of a punched-card handling device which arranges the processed cards into an orderly stack and holds them until they are removed by the operator.

Normally a stacker contains a passage slightly wider than a card, a movable card stack support, and a stacker-full switch to stop the machine when overflow threatens. Other features may joggle cards to align them accurately, dissipate static electricity, and include conveyor belts.

standing-on-nines carry   In high-speed parallel addition of decimal numbers, an arrangement that causes carry digits to pass through one or more 9 digits, while signaling that the skipped nines are to be reset to zero.

For example:

	Normal addition	*Standing-on-nines*
Addend	000050127	000050127
Working sum	099349976	099349976
Carry word	00000101x	00010010x
Working sum	0993999093	099399093
Carry	0000101xx	0000000xx
Sum	099390003	099400103
Carry	000100xxx	
Sum	099300103	
Carry	00000xxxx	
Sum	099400103	

The cause of repeated cycling in normal addition is the long strings of successive carrys, each creating a next string. By adding circuits to specifically check for this, all strings can be made of unit length. One add and one carry-add are all that are then needed. Of course, the time and circuitry for checking for nines with carry must be included in every add cycle, thus incurring a possible time penalty if no carry results.

statement   An elementary specification of action or process, complete and not divisible into smaller meaningful units: a statement is analogous to the simple sentence of a natural language.

In general, a statement is a simple command (unconditional statement) for an action to be performed, or a command that a test be performed and an action be performed based on the outcome of the test (conditional statement). Every statement must have (explicit or implied) a verb (action) and an object (operand data); it may also have a conditional relation or test part.

Note that a statement has meaning, but if any part of it is omitted, it has no meaning. Thus, it is elementary in the sense of being fundamental or indivisible.

For example, in the COBOL statement:

IF QUANTITY IS GREATER THAN LIMIT GO TO EXCESS-ROUTINE.

The words IS, THAN, and TO may be omitted, but every other symbol is essential for the meaning of the statement.

IF QUANTITY IS GREATER THAN LIMIT.

cannot be a statement, since it has no complete meaning. However,

GO TO EXCESS-ROUTINE

is a perfectly correct unconditional statement.

Syntax rules express this by defining a conditional statement as a condition test followed by an unconditional statement.

static dump An edited printout of the contents of main memory and/or of the auxilliary storage, performed in a fixed way: it is usually taken at the end of a program run, either automatically, or by operator intervention.

A static dump is a relatively inflexible procedure, rarely adaptable as to limits of storage dumped, and usually not taken or omitted under program control but rather on fixed schedule. Some static-dump routines permit run-time selection of alternative output formats, though most do not provide this to conserve dump-routine size.

Like all other dumps, the static dump is used principally as a debugging device, providing information otherwise unavailable to a programmer.

Usually, small amounts of information can be obtained from the console. Because of speed limitations, it is not possible to examine the entire machine in this way, and a dump program (resident or self-loading) must be employed for volume data gathering.

Some externally loaded dumps destroy a small part of memory as they load themselves. In such cases, it is possible to read this data via console before loading the dump program.

Contrast with DYNAMIC DUMP.

staticize To capture transient data in stable form, thus converting fleeting events into examinable information, and equally to extract an instruction from main memory and store the various component parts of it in the appropriate registers, preparatory to interpreting and executing it.

Suppose that a person at a remote console is entering information into a system. Each character is an event, over in a few milliseconds, and then lost forever. However, the characters are captured as they arrive, and they are stored in main memory in sequential locations.

In this form they wait until transmission stops to be examined and interpreted as a whole. Thus temporal succession is converted to spacial succession, and transience is converted to stability. (Stable memory may be permanent or erasable, but not volatile.)

The very first steps in executing any instruction are always the same: the bits are extracted from memory, the operation code is stored in the operation-code register, the address part or parts are placed in their respective registers, indirect addressing and index-register modifications are resolved, and the location of the next instruction is placed in the program-sequence (instruction) register. Each hardware element requires a very small amount of time to settle into its new state. The process just described is called staticizing the instruction. The next phases involve fetching the various operands, activating the proper data paths and hardware elements, and so executing the instruction.

Because staticizing is similar for (almost) all instructions, a common hardware or microprogram section is employed to initiate every instruction cycle in most digital computers.

station   One of a series of essentially similar positions or facilities. Thus:

A *tape station* is a tape drive.

A *data station* is a remote input/output device.

A *teller's* or *cashier's station* is a site at which the teller's or cashier's duties are performed, usually with data processing device included.

step   A single instruction or operation.

A step is a distinct and recognizable change in the (internal) environment of a computer. It may be an instruction, or (sometimes) one phase of an instruction that is executed in separate, distinct phases of the operation.

Following a computer routine by permitting only one instruction at a time to be executed, and noting the changes produced by each step, is called stepping through or single stepping.

Most computers have a switch that can be used to place them in single-step mode of operation. The digital computer then executes only one instruction every time a run or start button is pressed.

Suppose that the computer seems to have entered a tight unending loop (this is error condition: the computer repeats a few instructions cyclically without breaking out of the cycle—hence it is locked up and useless). The operator, seeing the console lights assume a stationary pattern (actually repetitive blinking faster than eye can follow), places the computer into single-step mode. If the loop is more than one instruction, the light pattern changes and is steadied. The operator notes the address (and possibly other information) of instruction, and then steps to the next instruction. In a few steps he probably returns to the original instruction: he then takes a postmortem dump to save the information, and releases the computer for further use, thus ending this job and beginning the next program.

On large computers with high cost, operator reflexes are too slow. Thus other arrangements must be made such as tracing, dynamic dumps, and debugging systems of all kinds provided by sophisticated large-computer operating systems.

storage Any device that can accept, retain, and read back data one or more times.

Storage is usually synonymous with memory, but a trend has developed for calling internal (main, central, static, core or thin film) storage memory, and external (auxiliary, on-line, dynamic) devices storage.

Some devices (electrostatic or sonic delay lines, transistor flip-flops) loose their contents if the power is removed or if time elapses: these are called volatile storage. Nonvolatile storages are usually based on magnetic principles, but photographic techniques and holes punched in cards are also to be considered as nonvolatile.

A storage device has one or more electric input lines, and a means of changing its internal state in response to signals on those lines. Upon demand, it interrogates its internal state, and outputs on one or more output lines the data that were most recently stored therein. The terms write and read are used to describe initializing and interrogating operations for dynamic (moving) storage systems such as magnetic tapes; store and fetch are favored for nonmoving storage systems such as core memories.

A seesaw in a playground is a most elementary mechanical memory: it remembers which end was most recently low, unless forcibly disturbed. All static nonvolatile memory is similarly bistable, but usually very small, fast, and magnetic.

Dynamic memories (magnetic) usually operate on principles similar to that of the ordinary tape recorder. Various cyclic (disk, drum) and noncyclic (tape, strip, card) dynamic devices are used, but all are essentially similar in principle.

The use of storage for programs, permitting modification of programs, is probably the most important single principle that has given modern computers the power they have. It should be noted that the word storage implies the concept of a device that can be modified, and as such of being reusable. This concept does not apply to paper tape and punched cards which cannot be modified back and forth, and which do not, for that reason, properly deserve the name storage.

storage allocation The process of assigning storage locations to data and/or instructions in a digital computer.

A cell of storage can hold at most one data item at a time; thus simultaneous storage of several items requires giving each item a different location, or address. A means of assigning nonconflicting addresses is thus required.

A computer instruction cannot manipulate data unless it knows where the data are stored. Therefore, after instructions and data have been allocated storage locations, the proper addresses must be inserted into the address parts of the instructions.

Allocation used to be performed by the coder in designing his program: assemblers today assist in storage allocation, but can be firmly directed in this chore by the programmer, if he so desires. Compilers usually perform allocation automatically and autonomously, and the programmer has difficulty in forcing (in detail) the storage assignments into a particular pattern.

There are two kinds of allocation: relative and absolute.

Relative addresses (and allocation) have exact locations fixed only at the time of loading into memory, but adjacency relationships are specified by relative allocation.

Absolute allocation is final, and is performed initially if the relocatable phase is bypassed.

When relocatable coding is loaded into memory, some supervisor must allocate core in gross blocks to programs (compare with the detailed, character-by-character allocation described above). This process, really a memory-space management, is only somewhat similar to detail allocation since programs vary widely in size and do not intercommunicate as much as program steps do.

storage capacity The quantity of data that can be retained simultaneously in a storage device.

Storage capacity is usually measured in bits, digits, characters, bytes, or words. Today, capacities from a few bits to a few billion bits exist in devices of various kinds, types, sizes, and speeds. The organization of storage into bytes, words, digits, etc., depends on the organization of the computer using the storage.

Typical capacities are as follows:
1. Solid-state flip-flops: a dozen or so bits
2. Thin-film memories: hundreds to a few thousands bits
3. Core memories: thousands to a few millions bits
4. Drums, disks, magnetic tape: tens of millions to hundreds of millions bits
5. Cards, paper tape: unlimited

The density of storage determines the capacity attained in a given size. Densities range from 100 bits per square inch (paper tape) to about 1000 bits per square inch (core, thin film) to nearly a billion bits per square inch (laser-optical methods).

storage cell   An elementary (logically indivisible) unit of storage: the storage cell can contain one bit, character, byte, digit (or sometimes word) of data.

A cell is distinguished from all other cells by its unique address. Therefore, the address structure of a storage device determines its resolution, or the size of the fundamental cell.

An analogy would be a post office box or pigeonhole, with rule limiting occupancy to only one letter at a time. This letter can be withdrawn any number of times without being lost, but is destroyed by inserting another letter in its place.

storage device   A mechanism for performing the function of data storage: accepting, retaining, and emitting (unchanged) data items.

The presently existing storage devices may be tabulated as follows:

Static	Random access.
Dynamic	Serial or cyclic access.
Volatile	Must be refreshed or constantly renewed.
Nonvolatile	May be kept without special attention.
Magnetic	Plated wire, core, tape, drum, disk, card, MICR.
Nonmagnetic	Optical, sonic, delay, electrostatic, mechanical.
Removable	Tape, cards, magazines, disk packs.
Fixed	Drums, core, thin film, some disks.

storage key   A special set of bits associated with every word or character in some block of storage, which allows tasks having a matching set of protection key bits to use that block of storage.

Storage keys and protection keys are one kind of memory-protection system that can be found on digital computers. The memory is divided into equal blocks, and a storage-key area is associated with each block. An operating system allocates blocks of memory to programs or tasks. It then uses special computer instructions to associate matching bit configurations with the program's protection key and the storage blocks' storage keys. Should the program attempt to read or write in a memory area not assigned to it, the hardware detects mismatching keys and stops the program. A master key is assigned to the operating system, which gives it access to all of memory.

See PROTECTION KEY.

store   To record information into a (static) data storage device, or to preserve information in a storage device.

Normally, the internal, main memory of a digital computer is a static, fast storage (such as core, thin film, plated wire). Every action of the CPU (central processing unit) which changes the contents of memory is some kind of a store operation. However, memory contents may also change by an input operation or operator intervention (CLEAR MEMORY button).

Recording on dynamic media (tapes, disk, etc.) is called WRITE in distinction to STORE, while obtaining a specified datum from main memory is called FETCH or LOAD, or CLEAR AND ADD.

Data may be retained for long periods in any nonvolatile storage medium. Short-term storage is usually in internal memory, inter-mediate-duration storage is often in on-line rapid-access devices (drum, disk), but long-term storage is only economical on removable media (disk pack; tape, cards).

stored program computer   A digital computer which executes in-structions that are stored in main memory as patterns of data.

The storing of instructions in the principal data memory device (core, thin films, drums) permits stored programmed computers to modify or even to write their own programs. Earlier programming techniques (plugboard, pinboard, soldering iron, external paper-tape loop) allowed for program modification in only the simplest ways (usually permitting a choice from among a few prespecified actions).

The ability to loop, or repeatedly execute the same instructions with various data stopping upon a program-specified condition, permits the economical execution of programs. Large amounts of nonmodifiable programming would be required to do the same job.

The stored program concept is the most important single idea in digital computing today. It makes possible operating systems (which govern the job-to-job performance of the computer, and provide intra-job services), program libraries (executable or relocatable programs and routines residing in external storage, thus large amounts of very rapidly accessible programming), compilers and assemblers (which make the computer assist the coder in writing programs), interpretive routines (which execute programs not written in machine language, or in a noncompatible machine language), and ultimately all of today's computer concepts.

straight-line coding   A digital computer program or routine (section of program) in which instructions are executed sequentially, without branching, looping, or testing.

A computer program leaves a sequential operation in one of two ways: through an unconditional branch (jump, transfer, analogous to *continued on page 4* in a newspaper) or through a conditional branch (a test or decision). Therefore, straight-line coding must do without the facilities of these two types of instruction. An unconditional branch is logically the same as no break at all, except that several different branches may have the same destination, or the destination could be an earlier instruction.

Conditional branches embody all the tests and decisions that a computer can perform. This means that straight-line coding cannot test anything, but must plow doggedly ahead.

Straight-line coding differs from a program recorded on a unidirectional tape in that it can modify itself. It can initialize future instructions before executing them.

Straight-line coding is not commonly used today, because of the disadvantages outlined above. However, its advantage in execution speed (small though it may be) encourages its use in certain very fast response programs.

STRESS   An acronym for structural engineering system solver, STRESS is designed to solve structural engineering problems using a problem-oriented input language. Thus, a structural engineer could use STRESS after only a minimal study of the manual, and without prior programming experience.

STRESS can analyze structures with prismatic members in two or three dimensions, with either pinned or rigid joints, and subjected to concentrated or distributed loads, support motions, or temperature effects.

The user describes his problem by writing a number of statements specifying the type and size of the structure, the physical dimensions, the loads, and the results desired. The solution provides such information as member forces at the member ends, reactions joint displacements, and support displacements. STRESS employs the recently developed techniques in structural analysis, such as matrix and network formulations.

In order to describe all the members and joints of a three-dimensional structure, it is necessary to have a common reference system. STRESS uses a right-handed, orthogonal cartesian coordinate system.

The origin of the system can be located at any arbitrary point in the structure, for example, one of the support joints. All joint data are described in terms of joint coordinates with respect to the origin of the coordinate system; and all computed joint displacements and reactions are similarly given in the same system.

All data are punched into cards in free format using, for the most

part, words rather than formulas. There are various header statements followed by detailed specification cards. For example:

Joint coordinates

1	0. 0. SUPPORT
2	192. 0. SUPPORT
3	576. 240.

Only those statements that are required for a given problem need
be included, with a few exceptions.

To illustrate STRESS, the following example was chosen. It is a
plane frame with four members, and four joints. A diagram of the
structure, the program, and the output are presented.

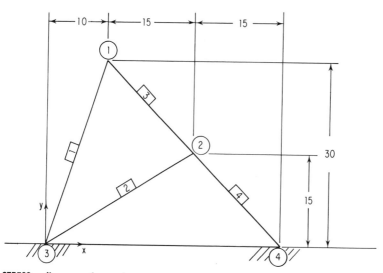

STRESS: diagram of sample structure.

STRESS	
STRUCTURE UNEVEN BRACE	This is similar to a "title" or "job" statement. The description following the word "structure" is printed on every output page.
NUMBER OF JOINTS 4	This specifies that our structure has four joints.
NUMBER OF SUPPORTS 2	Structure has two supports.
NUMBER OF MEMBERS 4	Structure has four members.
NUMBER OF LOADINGS 1	Indicates number of different loadings on structure.

TYPE PLANE FRAME	This identifies to STRESS the type of the structure. Five different types of structures are allowed: plane truss, frame, and grid, and space truss, and frame.
TABULATE FORCES, REACTIONS	The tabulate statement indicates which type of results to include in the output. Here, we desire member forces at the ends of each member, and support reactions and joint loads.
JOINT COORDINATES	This is a heading statement indicating that the coordinates of all joints are contained in the following cards.
1 X 100. Y 300.	The location of joint 1 is at the intersection of point 100 on the X axis (horizontal), and point 300 on the Y axis (vertical).
2 X 250. Y 150. 3 X 0. Y 0. S 4 X 700. Y 0. S	These describe the remaining three joints. The S designates a support.
MEMBER INCIDENCES	This is a heading card indicating that the following cards describe the makeup of the various members.
1　3　1 2　3　2 3　1　3 4　2　4	Member 1 starts at joint 3 and ends at joint 1. The other three members are similarly described.
MEMBER PROPERTIES, PRISMATIC	This is a heading card indicating that the following cards contain member properties. The word "prismatic" applies to all members if it is located in the heading line, thus avoiding repetitious writing.
1 AX 10. IZ 300.	This states that the normal cross-sectional area (AX) of member 1 is 10, and that the moment of inertia about the Z axis is 300 (IZ).
2 AX 10. IZ 300. 3 AX 10. IZ 300. 4 AX 10. IZ 300.	Similarly members 2, 3, and 4 are described.

STRESS (cont.)	
CONSTANTS E, 30Q00., ALL	This allows specification of modulus of elasticity of material. E means Young's modulus, and G means shear modulus. The ALL means that Young's modulus = 30000 for all members.
LOADING 1 CONCENTRATED AT TWO	This is a heading card used to separate two or more loadings. Everything after the word "loading" is printed on the output.
JOINT LOADS	This is a header card indicating what loads are applied at what joints.
2 FORCE Y — 100.0	This specifies a force of —100.0 along the Y axis at joint 2. Moments may also be entered in this statement.
TABULATE DISPLACEMENTS	This specifies that displacements are to be calculated and printed.
SOLVE THIS PART	This is a signal to STRESS that all data have been read in and STRESS should begin computation.
STOP	This terminates processing, and is placed after the last problem.

In this specific instance, the output would appear as follows:

STRUCTURE   UNEVEN   BRACE

LOADING 1 CONCENTRATED AT TWO

MEMBER FORCES

MEMBER	JOINT	AXIAL FORCE	SHEAR FORCE	BENDING MOMENT
1	3	0.5204174	—0.0904696	2.8482141
1	1	—0.5204174	0.0904696	—31.4572101
2	3	71.1795673	0.3030136	46.6196966
2	2	—71.1795673	—0.3030136	41.7231941
3	1	—0.1518223	0.5059337	31.4574213
3	2	0.1518233	—0.5059337	75.8673248
4	2	87.5284729	—1.0769296	—117.5904303
4	4	—87.5284729	1.0769296	—110.8608294

JOINT	X FORCE	Y FORCE	BENDING MOMENT
	SUPPORT REACTIONS		
3	61.1304731	37.3465190	49.4679108
4	—61.1304712	62.6534801	—110.8608294
	APPLIED JOINT LOADS		
1	—0.0000029	0.0000015	0.0002112
2	0.0000014	—100.0000000	0.0000887

JOINT	X DISPLACEMENT	Y DISPLACEMENT	ROTATION
	FREE JOINT DISPLACEMENTS		
1	0.0650988	—0.0222778	—0.0006027
2	—0.0175957	—0.1051242	—0.0000793

PART   1 OF PROBLEM COMPLETED.

string   A set of consecutive, adjacent items of similar type.   Normally a bit string, or a character string.

In general, string means a sequence of variable or arbitrary length, composed of bits, digits, or characters. The beginning and end, or beginning and length of the string, are usually made known to the computer. Characters arriving from a remote console, statements input to a compiler, messages of various kinds, and records on tape are strings.

String-manipulating operations include concatenation (joining two strings to form one new longer one), comparison (testing for equality), scanning (to find the first of a specified character, all of a specified character, or the number of appearances of specified characters).

stroke   A key-depressing operation in keypunching and a straight or curved portion of a letter, such as is commonly made with one smooth motion of a pen in optical character recognition (thus U has one stroke, D has two, H has three, W has four strokes).

Keypunch operators are rated at so many strokes per hour, for instance, 5,000 to 10,000 strokes per hour being rates for good commercial operators (this corresponds to about 100 characters per minute).

In character recognition, a stroke is also that segment of a printed or handwritten character which has been arbitrarily isolated from other segments for the purpose of analyzing it, particularly with regard to its dimensions and relative reflectance. The penlike motion of a focused electron beam in cathode-ray-tube (CRT) displays is also called a stroke.

stroke analysis   In character recognition, a method employed in character property detection in which an input specimen is dissected into certain prescribed elements. The sequence, relative positions, and number of detected elements are then used to identify the characters.

Stroke analysis is limited in application to specific character styles as traditionally all elements were classified as either horizontal or

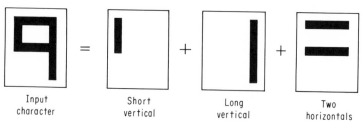

| Input character | Short vertical | Long vertical | Two horizontals |

Illustrating stroke analysis.

vertical. This fact has also limited the size of the character set so that if any future use of stroke analysis is to be made, then the detection devices will have to be able to isolate diagonals as well.

stroke centerline   In character recognition, a line midway between the two average-edge lines. The centerline describes the stroke's direction of travel.

stroke edge   In character recognition, a continuous line, straight or otherwise, which traces the outermost part of a stroke along the two sides of its greatest dimension.

stroke width   In character recognition, the distance that obtains, at a given location, between the points of intersection of the stroke edges and a line drawn perpendicular to the stroke centerline.

The average stroke width is the distance between average-edge lines, also measured perpendicularly to the stroke centerline at a given point.

Stroke width and average stroke width are important considerations in character-recognition systems insofar as they allow manufacturers to define various hardware limitations. Some of the most common specifications include:

1. Minimum stroke width
2. Maximum stroke width
3. Average stroke width (minimum-maximum)
4. Minimum depth of valleys less than average edge
5. Maximum height of peaks in excess of average edge
6. Minimum distance between actual edges of different strokes

subroutine   A body of computer instructions (and their associated constants and working-storage areas, if any) designed to be used by other routines to accomplish some particular purpose, and specifically, a statement in FORTRAN used to define the beginning of a closed subroutine.

Normally a subroutine differs from other subsections of programs by being used more than once. However, a distinct, recognizable-as-an-entity subsection of coding is sometimes called a subroutine.

Subroutines are divided into open and closed types. A closed subroutine appears only once inside a computer, and is called whenever (or wherever) it is needed by transferring control to it via a formalized set of instructions called a calling sequence. An open subroutine appears in-line in the coding whenever it is needed. Thus, short subroutines may be open or closed, but long subroutines should always be closed.

Closed subroutines may be compiled (assembled) separately, and united with their calling programs, before execution, by a linking loader.   Closed subroutines may also be assembled into their calling program (resulting in shared constants, thus saving memory), but open subroutines must be assembled (compiled) into their calling programs.

Closed subroutines save space; open subroutines save time (and space *only* if shorter in length than conventional calling sequences).

All modern digital computers have an instruction designed to simplify calling a closed subroutine.   These instructions transfer control to the designated location (branch, jump), and also save the location of the next instruction in the original sequence (sometimes the location of the transfer instruction itself) in a register of the computer.   The subroutine may store the saved address to permit it to return to the calling program, and must save and restore the contents of any computer register that it uses or modifies.   This saving and restoring make the subroutine transparent to the calling program, so that no unexpected side effects occur as a consequence of the call.

A subroutine may itself call any number of lower-level subroutines, thus becoming itself a calling program.   However, neither the subroutine nor any subroutine that it may call, may call the original subroutine, or else an unending loop may occur (resulting from loosing the original saved return address).   A programming technique called recursion involves the use of subroutines which call themselves, using pushdown stacks to avoid endless loops by saving successive levels of calling information.

substitute mode   One method of exchange buffering, in which segments of storage function alternately as buffer and as program work area.

In substitute mode the address of a buffer segment is interchanged with the address of a program work area.   This interchanges the roles of the two memory areas without actually moving any data from area to area.   Substitute mode allows for high-speed execution of I/O on computers that have good hardware address modification capability.

See EXCHANGE BUFFERING.

summation check   An error-detecting procedure involving adding together all the digits of some number and comparing this sum to a previously computed value of the same sum.

One weakness of the summation check is its inability to detect transposed digits.   Transposing any two different digits will not change the digit sum, but it will change the value of the number (72 and 27 each add up to 9, but they are not equal).

One way to avoid this possibility is to change the radix of the numeral from 2 to 3 or from 10 to 11 before calculating the digit sum. This operation is tedious on slow computers, but will reveal every transposition of the digits of the original numeral.   In addition, smaller values of digit sums may be produced because of the economy of digits obtained from high radices.

If digit summing is repeated until a single digit sum remains, a casting-out-nines check is obtained (decimal arithmetic), but a one always remains (binary arithmetic).   In either case the single check digit is less reliable than the original digit sum, although it is more compact.

supervisory routine   A program or routine that initiates and guides the execution of several (or all) other routines and programs: it usually forms part of (or is) the operating system.

The supervisory routine determines which program is to be executed next, and then initiates that program.

In its decision logic the supervisory routine may use a simple first-come, first-served algorithm, a priority scheme, a scheduled-in-advance or real-time response design, or a combination of any of the above. If multiple programs share the memory (multiprocessing or multi-programming), the supervisory routine may have to consider allocation of resources, current residence requirements, etc.

The supervisory routine may also assist the problem or subordinate programs by offering supervisory services.   These may include:

1.   The conditional or unconditional initiation of another program in response to a programmed directive

2.   The handling of hardware interrupts of various kinds

3.   The supplementing of the hardware by offering data manipulation services not implemented with hardware in this particular computer (for instance, in the case of optional instruction sets not implemented)

In some instances IOCS is considered part of supervisory routine.

The supervisory routine has much the same role as that of a human supervisor of workers: it tells programs what to do and when to do it, and helps them when they get into trouble.   A program (possibly not debugged) that gets into unrecoverable trouble (endless loop, missing input data) is removed from the computer to make way for operable programs.   In other words, the supervisor has the responsibility of seeing that the computer's work gets done.

suppression   Removal or deletion usually of insignificant digits in a number, especially zero suppression.

When a computer is manipulating a number, it allows a certain number of digits for the representation of that number.   Often, not all digits are actually used (example: a sum or total area with provision for seven digits, and a calculation in which a five-digit sum is developed). Failure to provide enough digits may result in overflow and loss of accuracy. Programmers thus try always to ensure that at least one unused digit is available as a safety margin.

When a number is printed out, the human reader does not want to see unnecessary leading zeros, since they clutter the printout, confuse, and make it hard to judge magnitudes. Zero suppression is a process of converting leading, unneeded zeros to blanks (occupying space but not printing). Whereas leading zeros are acceptable to a computer internally, they are to be deleted once the number is outside the computer:

Internal	After suppression, external
000317	317
010024	10024
000099	99
010440	10440

Somehow the computer must scan left to right, replacing leading zeros with blanks until either the end of the numeral is reached or a nonzero digit is encountered.

Less commonly, a number is developed with nonsignificant low-order digits, and these are to be suppressed so as not to seem more accurate than is justified. (A common example is found in radix conversion—for instance, the binary number 1100000000 converts to 768_{10}, but if only one decimal digit may be justified, 800_{10} would be a more accurate conversion.)

In multiplication with three-digit accuracy factors

$$\begin{array}{r} 4.02 \\ \times\ 51.7 \\ \hline 207.834 \end{array}$$

the digits 834 after the decimal point have no meaning, but this kind of suppression is not usually provided by hardware, and so must be program-supplied (however, unnormalized floating-point arithmetic does provide a measure of protection in this case).

Occasionally, whole lines of print or other actions are suppressed (omitted) by program action. Thus, if no detail lines appear on a report, the (zero) total line may be omitted also.

switch A hardware or programmed device for indicating that one of several alternative states or conditions have been chosen, or to interchange or exchange two data items.

On the operator's control panel, indicators (usually lights, and sometimes a CRT) tell the operator about the machine status, and switches tell the machine about the operator's decisions (control actions, commands, etc.).

Hardware switch types include:

1. Pushbutton and rocker types for binary (twofold) decisions, including momentary and steady types; these are the only types commonly available with illuminated indications.

2. Slide and toggle switches for binary and/or trinary indications (center-off, etc.).

3. Rotary switches for higher multiplicity (2- to 40-pole configurations exist, but only 3-, 4-, 8-, 10-, 16-pole configurations are common on computers).

4. Thumbwheel switches, which are really rotary switches mounted edgewise, usually have 11 positions (0 to 9 and blank), and are arranged to display a single digit to indicate their current setting. Multiple thumbwheel switches in a gang (close mounted, parallel) permit entering decimal numbers in convenient fashion (4 gang permits 9999 combinations in only 1½-inch panel space).

Programmed switches usually consist of 1 or 2 bits of storage in some program-testable location for low-multiplicity indications. Frequently a branch operation code is changed to a no-operation operation code to disable the transfer and cause control to pass to the next sequential instruction. This type of switch (operation code) is actually executed rather than tested.

For higher-multiplicity switches, an address area is reserved (either part of a jump instruction or as a data item out of the instruction sequence) and changed to indicate the location of a successor routine. This scheme permits any number of switch settings, up to the addressing capability of the computer.

Some computers having multiple registers include instructions for exchanging the contents of two registers. The normal reason for switching numbers around is to order a string of number into an ascending or descending sequence.

symbol A graphic set of letters, or a sign used to represent or stand for something else, according to convention.

Normally, symbols do not include alphabetic or numeric characters, although these too are symbols for abstract concepts.

Conventionally, symbols stand for logical, mathematical, and relational operators, delimiters, and control characters, and other concepts.

For example:

$ stands for dollars
÷ stands for division
♀ Venus
∠ angle

In programming, symbols are used in higher-level languages to represent data items, locations, computer instructions, etc.   For example:

Assembly language instruction	Symbol translation
TAG SUB TAX, PAY	TAG = location of this instruction SUB = subtraction operation code TAX = A address data item PAY = B address data field

and this instruction results in subtracting the contents of the field TAX from the field PAY.

In the case of a higher-level language:

FORTRAN instruction	Symbol translation
PAY = PAY − TAX	PAY = A address data item TAX = B address data item − = subtract = = replace left-hand side by evaluated results of right-hand-side expression.

This instruction results in the original quantity contained in location PAY being replaced by the original quantity less the quantity contained in location TAX.

These symbols are converted into meaningful instructions by programs called assemblers or compilers.

symbolic address   In coding, a programmer-defined symbol that represents the location of a particular data item, instruction, or routine.

Assemblers and compilers assist the programmer in creating code by handling routine clerical tasks of storage allocation and address assignment.

The programmer is allowed to construct (within the rules) any symbols that are meaningful to him and use these symbols instead of addresses in his program.

For example, a payroll in COBOL would contain in the data division:

02 PAY   PICTURE IS 999999V99 VALUE IS ZERO.
02 TAX   PICTURE IS 99999V99 VALUE IS ZERO.

thus defining PAY to be an eight-digit unsigned decimal item, with six integer places and two fractional places; TAX is similarly defined, but has only five integer places; both are initially zero until changed by the program.   In the procedure division, the statement:

SUBTRACT TAX FROM PAY.

produces instructions in relocatable form, referring to the data fields defined above.

In the first compilation, PAY may be located 1207 positions after the start of the routine, and TAX located 8 positions further on. In a subsequent compilation new variables may be added before PAY, therefore, changing PAY's location to 1376 locations after the start of the program. Because symbolic and not actual addresses were used, the instructions of the procedure division are automatically adjusted to refer to the new location of PAY and TAX.

When the relocatable instructions are finally loaded, the program may begin at location 4276. Then, relocatable location 1376 becomes actual location 5652. The subtraction is again modified to refer to the final addresses of the data, but this last adjustment is independent of symbolic addressing. Indeed it must be so, since the symbols were used up by the compiler and do not appear in the relocatable instruction format.

symbolic coding   Instruction written in an assembly language, using symbols for operations and addresses.

A binary computer instruction normally appears as follows:

001011011000101101101101

whereas a character-oriented computer instruction might appear as

K%AU1P9

To avoid having to write instructions in these ungainly forms, difficult to interpret when an old program is to be modified, programmers write in symbolic coding (assembly) language. The two above instructions might then appear to the programmer as

ADD BENFIT

and

EDIT SUM, MASK 1

which are much easier to remember, read, or write. Assemblers (special computer programs) convert symbolic coding to relocatable or absolute machine instruction form.

In this system, symbolic names are given by the programmer to the locations (addresses) of data and significant instructions. The assembler figures out where each item falls in memory, and replaces the symbolic addresses with actual hardware addresses. In addition, it converts mnemonic operation codes (ADD, SUB, B, MPY, EDIT, etc.) to actual operation codes.

See CODING, SYMBOLIC ADDRESS.

symbolic logic A method of formalizing the operations of logic (the science of truth, falsity, and valid deduction rules) by means of symbols and mathematical representation.

The idea is to condense representations and avoid the ambiguity of natural languages.

synchronous computer A digital computer designed to operate in sequential elementary steps, each step requiring a constant amount of time to complete, and each step initiated by a timing pulse from a uniformly running clock.

Normally, the rhythm of a digital computer is dominated by the cycle time of its memory. The cycle time governs the accessibility of instructions and data.

Electronic circuits operating faster than memory run from a clock that subdivides each cycle into uniform subintervals.

See ASYNCHRONOUS COMPUTER.

syntax The set of rules needed to construct valid expressions or sentences in a language.

Any true language, natural or artificial, must have rules showing how to build and analyze (or interpret) the statements in that language. Without these rules, only ambiguity and confusion are possible. In most languages, occasional ambiguity may exist, but this ambiguity is made tolerable by the *you know what I mean* adaptability of the human brain. For example, the statement "Time flies like an arrow" has three different possible meanings. As a human being, we reject two as nonsense. Computers, however, being literal-minded, absolutely logical, and lacking the *you know what I mean* adaptability, cannot distinguish sense from nonsense. Artificial languages designed for communication with computers must, therefore, be precise and free from ambiguity.

The notion that an artificial language can be almost entirely described by its syntax (semantics, or meaning as largely defined by the program) has led to the idea of a syntax-table compiler. This type of compiler is written to convert high-level languages to machine-code instructions. In a table-driven compiler, the source language is described by a table of syntax rules, while the compiling algorithm and the object language are embedded in the compiler instruction themselves.

Three main advantages may be claimed for such a compiler organization:

1. It is easy to write, and is largely independent of the source language.

2. Once written, it is easily adapted to another language by changing the table (though possibly with some code modification).

3. It allows the programmer to refine the language by giving him the ability to expand the syntax table.

SYSIN A contraction of system input, and commonly used to refer to the principal input stream of an operating system. There can be only one SYSIN at a time, but many devices can be assigned SYSIN functions in succession.

system A plan, design, or method of organization that is intended to accomplish some purpose. By extension, a collection of men, machines, environments, etc., organized according to a plan in order to accomplish some stated purpose.

There are three principal concepts conveyed by system in a combined form in the EDP field: computer system, numeration system, and operating system.

A computer system is usually a set of related hardware, and may represent two different meanings depending on whether it is a general system or a specific system. In the general sense, a computer system consists of the related hardware offerings of a computer manufacturer, that is, the related and compatible devices of a product line as seen in a catalog: the IBM 360 System with its many central processor units and innumerable peripheral devices is a case in point. A computer system, in the specific sense, is a computer: a set of hardware units contiguously installed, operating simultaneously, and logically connected together to act as a unit. Multiple processors may form part of a single system, if connected together. But two adjacent computers, unconnected, represent two different systems.

A numeration system is a method of representing numbers (which in themselves are abstract mathematical concepts) by numerals (which are observable symbols capable of being manipulated). This system provides rules for encoding (that is, for creating or constructing numerals) and decoding (finding the number represented by these symbols). The most common numeration systems are the positional numeration systems as represented by the binary and the decimal systems.

An operating system is an interrelated series of programs and routines designed to make a computer system operate more efficiently and easier to program. In general, an operating system supervises all I/O (its own, and problem programs); performs job-to-job and step-to-step transitions; provides assemblers, compilers, program loaders, utility routines, file and volume management; etc. Normally, the complexity and comprehensiveness of an operating system increase in direct proportion to the complexity and capacity of the hardware. The permanently resident part of the operating system occupies 1 to 25 percent of the main-memory capacity (10 percent is a useful average figure to remember).

A program system is a set of separate but functionally interrelated programs: an operating system is a program system.

system generation   A process that creates a particular and uniquely specified operating system.   System generation combines user-specified options and parameters with manufacturer-supplied general-purpose or nonspecialized program subsections to produce an operating system (or other complex software) of the desired form and capacity.

Suppose that a program or operating system is to be run on many computers, all similar but not identical.   If the program is written at one installation, and copies of it are sent to the other computer users, a conflict arises.   If the program is written so that it can run without change on any computer of a related series of computers, it must run on the least powerful computer of the set.   This means that it will not utilize more powerful computers effectively, and inefficiency will result in almost every instance.   Should the program be written to take advantage of the features of the larger computers, the smaller computers will not be able to use it.   Clearly some means of adjusting the program to each computer should be provided.   (This logic does not apply to programs designed to be run on only one or several particular computers, i.e., user-written proprietary programs.)

When this problem was first recognized, programs intended for distribution were designed to be self-adaptive.   For example, it is common for 1401 programs to accept a control card that specifies the size of the main memory of the computer being used.   The program would store the computer configuration data in memory, and check it before taking any computer-dependent action.   This strategy results in relatively high efficiency on most computers, but extracts a penalty in program complexity and execution speed.

With the development of the macro concept it became possible to distribute programs in the form of macroskeletons, or macrodefinitions. Each installation could specify the computer-configuration parameters and optional operational features that it wanted.   The macroexpansion process would produce a particular program from the general-purpose distributed version.   For example, much Honeywell 200 software is distributed in the form of macro's which have to be expanded and assembled at each individual installation.   This scheme works very well, provided that the total complexity of the programs to be distributed is not too great.   Highly efficient particularized programs are produced which have all the optional parameters or hardware considerations built in. Unneeded instructions, as for example to check memory size, are never created or executed.

Modern operating systems are very complex, containing many programs and program segments. The computer time required to process the entire operating system through the macroexpansion and assembly process would be very great. A sensible approach indicated the development of special system-generation programs, designed expressly for the specialization of very complex general-purpose software. The system-generation program itself would be self-adaptive (in the earlier sense outlined above) while the operating system would be built from a macroskeleton of computer instructions. A user would prepare cards containing a detailed description of the local computer configuration. This information would be used self-adaptively during generation and would also be built into the created operating system. In this way the resulting software would be specialized to run on a configuration having a model "X" CPU, "N" data channels, "M" tape drives, "Y" disk packs, a model "Z" printer with hardware address "QQQ." In addition to hardware configuration, system generation is used to choose from among functional or operational alternatives offered by the operating system design. For example, a priority job scheduler may be used instead of a simpler first-in, first-out scheduler. Similarly, multiprogramming or multitasking capability may be selected or omitted, as can real-time capability. Computer time is saved by performing the specialization upon computer instructions rather than assembly or compiler language. Each selected module of instructions is relocated and united in a fashion similar to the operation of a linkage editor. The time required for a complete assembly or compilation is avoided.

As a result of system generation, each installation can have one or more particular operating systems to suit its individual needs. These operating systems may each be unique; yet they all have a close family resemblance to one another. All will be efficient, each in its own way as circumstances dictate.

T

table A set of contiguous, related items, each uniquely identified either by its relative position in the set, or by some label.

For instance, in a multiplication table, items are identified by their row and column location; on the other hand, in a tax-rate table, an item is identified by its row or income bracket.

A decision table is a compact form of displaying the action or actions to be taken when specified combinations of test results are obtained. The table is normally a matrix, with rows for the possible test outcomes and columns for the resulting actions. In use, the table is scanned by columns from left to right, stopping when the actual test results match the content at the intersection of row and column. The action indicated by the column heading may then be taken.

A truth table is a compact, explicit display of all possible results of an indicated logical operation (formal or symbolic logic). For instance:

A \ B	T	F
T	T	T
F	T	F

is a truth table showing that the logical operation A or B is true if either A or B or both A and B are true, but false if both A and B are false.

Retrieving an item in a relative-position table simply involves calculating the address of the item from a known algorithm. Retrieving an item in a table with identifying labels (such labels are called search keys or arguments) requires repeated label comparisons until either a matching condition is established or a not-in-the-table condition is proved. For short tables sequential testing is acceptable, but for lengthy tables more sophisticated techniques are required. See TABLE LOOK-UP.

table-driven compiler   A compiler in which the source language is described by a set of syntax rules. See SYNTAX.

table look-up   A procedure for searching identifying labels in a table so as to find the location of a desired item. By extension, a digital computer instruction which directs that the above operation be performed.

For instance, let a table consist of adjacent items of fixed length stored in a contiguous manner. Moreover, let each item have as part of itself an argument (equally called label or search key), and let us call value the remainder of the item:

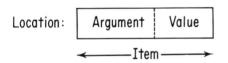

It is required to find the value associated with some given argument, the location of the item being unknown. The method, therefore, consists in matching the arguments in the table with the specified argument until the desired matching condition is found. At this point, the required value can be read. Such a look-up may terminate with equality or with a not-found condition. More rarely, the look-up may end with a greater-than or smaller-than condition.

The simplest and only universally valid search is the sequential scan. Every argument in the table is examined in sequence, starting with the first and ending with the last (or with the matching argument) and compared with the specified argument. Searching a table of N arguments thus requires $N/2$ comparisons on the average. Sequential scan is the only method implemented by means of hardware on digital computers. The earliest such application was probably made available on the IBM 650, a drum-memory machine: its vacuum-tube electronics operated faster than the magnetic drum. A programmed look-up would have required at least one drum revolution per comparison, that is, at most 12,750 comparisons per minute. The TLU instruction available with the machine examined every argument as it appeared beneath the read/write heads, thus allowing for the operation to be completed in a few milliseconds. This TLU instruction was later implemented on other computers such as the Honeywell 2200 and the IBM 7070 and 1410.

When extensive tables (that is, tables containing more than 100 items) are to be searched, and if it is possible to arrange the items in ascending sequence by arguments, a dichotomizing search method, for instance a binary search, may be used. This search method divides the total list in half, and compares the specified argument with the central item argument. If the specified argument is larger than the central item argument, the lower half of the list is ignored, and the upper half of the list divided in two. This method is repeated until a match is found. The maximum number of comparisons required is given by P where P is the lowest number such that 2^P is greater or equal to N, N being the number of items in the list. For instance, if the list contained 1,000,000 items, the following number of comparisons would be required on the average:

By sequential look-up: 500,000
By binary search: 20

tabulate   To order a set of data into a table form, or to print a set of data as a table, usually indicating differences and totals, or just totals.

Normally, to tabulate means to print as a table with various levels shown for subtotals, group totals, intermediate totals, major totals, and grand totals. This operation may be performed on a tabulator, an EAM device capable of reading punched cards, keeping running totals, printing, sensing the need for a subtotal or grand total, and printing total lines. Consequently, to tabulate may also mean to operate a tabulator.

Let an input card image be defined as consisting of one or more of the following: control fields, amount fields, and descriptive fields. Each control field is examined for a break (that is, a control break) or change in value between the current card and the card immediately preceding it. A break in a minor control field causes the printing of a minor subtotal line, the adding of the subtotals to intermediate total accumulators, and the zeroing out of the printed minor subtotals. An intermediate break causes the minor break action to be performed, followed by the printing of an intermediate subtotal line, the adding of the intermediate totals to major total accumulators, and the zeroing out of intermediate total accumulators.   In the same fashion, a major control break produces minor, intermediate, and major break activities in that order.   An end of input condition produces grand totals, the ultimate in breaks.

After each break activity (except the grand total break), each card is edited and printed, and all amount fields are added to the corresponding subtotal areas (an amount that is not to be added is called a descriptive field).   This process builds the body of the table detail line by detail line.

As computers started replacing TAB (short for tabulating) equipment, the tabulation function had to be carried by computers, and the programs required for this operation had to be written at each installation.   To reduce the amount of work involved, manufacturers devised utility programs (such as report generators) which greatly facilitated the writing of tabulating programs.

tag   The symbol written in the location field of an assembly-language coding form, and used to define the symbolic address of the data or instruction written on that line.

The TOPLUP (see illustration) instruction may be arrived at in normal sequence during the execution of the program, or through transfer by using the tag TOPLUP in the address part of a transfer instruction.

A tag can also be used in a reserved portion of a data field (one or more bits in length) to indicate the status of the data item.   For instance:

1.   To mark a data record as processed
2.   To indicate a hardware address modification
3.   To indicate an error detection while gathering data

A tag is also a physical marker, such as a colored punched card to denote a block of cards in a card deck.

tally rolls   See CONTINUOUS FORMS.

tape   A ribbonlike material used to store data in lengthwise sequential position.   See MAGNETIC TAPE, PUNCHED TAPE.

tape drive   A device, including some associated electronics, which moves the tape past a fixed head.   In general, the term tape drive is used in the sense of magnetic-tape drive.

A typical drive includes a tape transport (mechanical), electronics, a cabinet with the related hardware, and the controls for the operator. Moreover, it has associated to it a physical number to distinguish it from other drives on the computer system, and a logical drive number which represents the programmer's tape-drive address. The physical and logical numbers need not be the same.

Tape drives can be unplugged and physically removed to another location by wheeling them away in a short moment of time. This possibility permits changing drives quickly and easily.

The most common pictures of a computer system usually show an array of adjacent tape drives, often creating the impression that tape drives are the computer. Tape drives are just peripheral equipment, often the only moving part of the computer system, and hence, easily the most visually interesting, or eye-catching, part of the computer system.

tape station   A tape reading and/or writing device consisting of a tape transport, electronics, and controls. The terms tape drive and tape station are almost interchangeable but for the fact that tape drive usually refers to magnetic tape exclusively, whereas tape station may refer to both magnetic tape and paper tape.

It is possible for two or more tape stations to share the same cabinet

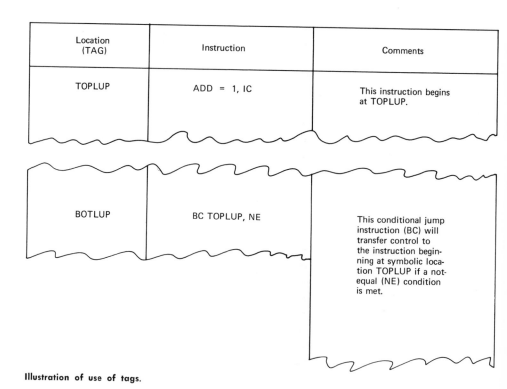

Location (TAG)	Instruction	Comments
TOPLUP	ADD = 1, IC	This instruction begins at TOPLUP.
BOTLUP	BC TOPLUP, NE	This conditional jump instruction (BC) will transfer control to the instruction beginning at symbolic location TOPLUP if a not-equal (NE) condition is met.

Illustration of use of tags.

and power supply.   Nevertheless, each station is logically independent
of the others in the same cabinet.

Tape drives always appear as single units.

tape to card   The operation, or job step, required to transfer data
from magnetic or paper tape to punched card.

This operation is generally performed for storage cost reasons since
the tape, containing the same information as punched on cards, is
easier and faster to handle than the corresponding card deck.

In large computer systems, card-to-tape operations are performed
on off-line equipment: card punching is a slow operation which,
if performed on-line, would be wasteful of computer time.

Modern large-scale computers are their own satellites with regard
to this type of operation, since they can go tape to card (or disk to
card) concurrently with other processing activities after the card-
producing program ends.

The converse operation, card to tape, is more common today.

tape transport   The mechanism that physically moves the tape past
a stationary head.

The transport consists of a capstan (a uniformly rotating cylinder
which drives the tape at its characteristic speed), sometimes a pinch
roller (which presses the tape against the capstan so that friction
effects the driving action), tape guides (which assure the proper
alignment of the tape), vacuum columns (which are reservoirs of
free tape between reels and capstans), buffers (in this instance, a
reservoir of unreeled tape), tape cleaners (usually vacuum-operated),
tape brakes (to bring the tape to a stop), and usually tape reels and
the associated motors.   Besides these mechanical and electromechanical components, the electronic components are represented by the
sensors which detect beginning of tape, end of tape, broken tape,
low tape supply remaining on reels, quantity of tape in vacuum
columns, etc.

The more recent magnetic-tape transports are designed to use
a single capstan, and are so built that nothing except the read/write
head (and possibly the tape cleaners) touches the oxide-coated surface
of the tape.   Any other friction is· minimized by air-bearing surfaces,
that is, surfaces where the air pressure floats the tape away from the
surface itself.   Pinch rollers are eliminated by using vacuum or air
pressure to adhere or slide the tape over porous capstans.

Special, low-inertia motors can provide up to 300 start or stop operations per second, and tape speed can be held constant to within
±1 percent.   It is feasible to start a tape from rest and have it reach
a speed of 112 inches per second over a tape distance of less than

0.6 inch. Some transports will rewind magnetic tape at speeds of up to 400 inches per second (22.7 miles per hour).

Incremental transports will accelerate, move, decelerate, and stop a tape, all within an interval of 1/200 of an inch of tape, several hundred times per second.

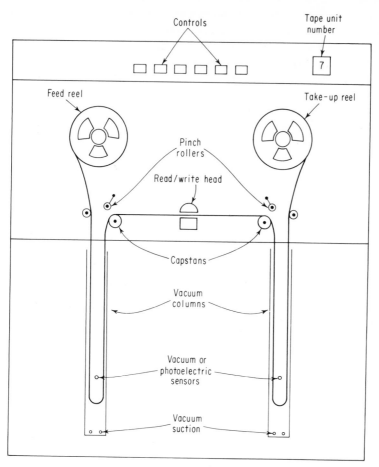

Basic tape unit.

tape unit A tape reading and/or writing device consisting of a tape transport, electronics, controls, and possibly a cabinet.

The cabinet may contain one or more magnetic-tape stations: though single units are quite common, double units are offered by several manufacturers (such as IBM and RCA), and quadruple units are equally available (for instance, the Burroughs tape cluster).

Each tape unit gives the computer access to one or more extra files (or collection of related data records). The design of a program system is often strongly influenced by the number of files available simultaneously, and an extra tape unit can often save additional program steps. Indeed, the difference between feasibility and impracticality of a program often lies with the presence or absence of one or two more tape drives.

Although no actual census is available, it appears reasonable to assume that as of this time, tape units are the most numerous peripheral devices in use today. Multiple printers and card readers are rare, but computers having anywhere from 4 to 10 tapes are quite common.

With the advent of large third-generation systems, the use of multiple disk packs has been increasing. But costs may be a limiting factor in disk packs replacing tapes.

target language   The language into which a program (or text) is to be converted.

In assembly and compilation operations, a programmer-oriented language is converted to a target language for execution on the computer. This target language is made up of absolute or relocatable format computer instructions, in a form acceptable to a program linkage editor (or loader). It should be mentioned that some compilers actually generate an assembly language (that is, symbolic computer instructions) as their output target language, but this practice has been abandoned because of the resulting inefficiency in compile and assembly time requirements. This method, however, did have the advantages of permitting simpler compilers and allowing programmers to modify instructions at the assembly-language level without recompiling. Such a compiler converted FORTRAN II into 7070 Autocoder, and similarly the FORTRAN IV compiler for the IBM 7090 computer in its initial IBSYS versions.

In program conversion, a team of human beings, assisted by computer programs especially designed for the task, translate programs written in machine language, assembly language, compiler language, etc., into equivalent programs in some suitable target languages acceptable to a computer not compatible with the original languages in which these programs were written. The two possible approaches are emulation (which is almost mandatory at machine- and assembly-language levels), and translation of intent (meaning, or function) which is practical at the compiler language level which is more computer-independent.

In computer-assisted translation of natural languages (for instance,

Russian into English), English is the target language. Computers can, and do, assist in parsing and dictionary look-up, but as of today all final editing must be done by human beings.

Synonymous with OBJECT LANGUAGE.

target program The form of program that results from a program translation, compilation, or assembly process: the output of a translating program.

An assembly process converts a program from a machine-dependent symbolic instruction form into a format more suitable for execution on a computer (for example, an absolute or relocatable machine-instruction format); a compilation process similarly converts a program either problem- or procedure-oriented and in machine-independent language into a format more suitable for execution on a computer. In either case, the process begins with a source-language program (or source module in the IBM 360 System terminology) and ends with a target program. The target program is equivalent to the source program in a way defined by the processing program, but the physical or bit representation similarity between source and target programs is usually very slight.

In converting programs for use on one computer to programs for use on another computer, the level of the program language (that is, the closeness to machine language) is preserved. This is in contrast to the process described in the preceding paragraph which always reduces the program-language level. In program conversion, the translation is from the language of one computer to the language of another computer, this latter one resulting in the target program. Program conversion is supposed to preserve the performance of the program while changing the environment to which it was originally adapted. The original computer is called the source computer; the new computer is called the target computer.

In a sense, conversion may be equated to translating a book (program) from English into Russian (for instance, from a SDS Sigma 7 to an IBM 360/67), whereas compiling (or assembling) may be equated to translating shorthand English (symbolic instructions) into everyday English (machine language).

task A set of instructions, data, and control information capable of being executed by a central processing unit of a digital computer in order to accomplish some purpose. In a multiprogramming environment, tasks compete with one another for control of the CPU, but in a nonmultiprogramming environment a task is simply the current work to be done.

A task may be identified as something that has:

1. A definition, or some means of determining what belongs to the task and what does not (an identity)

2. A set of computer instructions, organized into one or more programs

3. Memory locations allocated to it, and containing both instructions and data

4. Some indication as to which instruction belonging to the task is the next to be executed by the central processing unit

In ordinary monoprogramming, a task is simply a job or a job step. Tasks are processed one after another, and collectively they accomplish all the work to be done on the computer. Because task in ordinary operation simply means the currently active program, it is not a useful concept. The true value of the task concept emerges only in a multiprogramming situation.

Consider a multiprogramming computer which contains several partially processed jobs in its main memory. One of these jobs is currently in control of the CPU (arithmetic and program logic processor). This job executes until some temporary condition prevents it from usefully continuing. For example, it has begun a card-reading operation and cannot process further until the data from the card become available. To avoid wasted CPU time, a supervisory routine within the operating system of the computer should give control of the CPU to some other task that is currently ready to process further. A task is therefore operationally defined as a unit of CPU work capable of competing with other similar units for control of the CPU.

In multiprogramming, the central processing unit switches rapidly from task to task under the control of an operating system. There is usually a task waiting to be processed whenever the current task cannot continue, so that the computer is kept busy and productive. To coordinate this action, the task dispatcher associates a task control block (TCB) with each task currently resident in main memory. The task control block may or may not be located near the task it refers to; indeed, the task itself may be situated in fragments all over memory. The task control block contains in part:

1. The dispatching priority of the task

2. The limit priority of the task

3. The location of the next instruction to be executed

4. Other saved machine registers to allow normal resumption of execution

5. The ready/waiting status of the task, and if waiting, an indication of the event, or events waited upon

6.   The address of the next task control block in the list of task control blocks

The information in the TCB's permits the operating system to coordinate the various tasks within the computer.   Since the task dispatcher examines only task control blocks and nothing else, then for an operating system, a task is defined as something that has a task control block.

When the dispatcher must choose the next task to become active, it selects the ready task having the highest current dispatching priority. Dispatching priority is used to resolve the conflict between computing demands for CPU time.   A task may modify its own dispatching priority, but it cannot raise that priority higher than its own (fixed) limit priority.

A task is said to be in ready status when it is capable of being resumed immediately (the computer is stalled only if no task is in ready status, normally a highly improbable situation).   If a task cannot continue until some external event occurs, it is said to be in waiting status (or wait state).   It will be removed from waiting status as soon as the required event (or events) are completed.   Normally, a task waits only for input/output activity, but it may also enqueue itself in a waiting line to use any system-provided serially reusable facility.

A program may call another program as a subroutine.   When this happens, the second program runs while the first program does not. There exists a sequential, nonsimultaneous relationship between a program and its subroutines.   Within one task only one program, or subprogram, may be active at any one time.   However, a program may also activate another program by attaching the new program as another, separate task.   Then the two programs, or tasks, will be executed together on a nearly simultaneous, asynchronously interleaved basis.   Either task may terminate independently of the other, or attach new tasks.

The attached tasks have their own task control blocks (TCB's) and their own limit and dispatching priorities.   Newly created tasks compete with other tasks for the attention of the CPU, and it may happen that a task takes control of the CPU away from its parent task.

See JOB, JOB STEP, MULTIPROGRAMMING, MULTITASK OPERATION.

TELCOMP   TELCOMP is a language developed by Bolt, Beranek, and Newman, Inc., expressly as a time-sharing language.

A company rents a teletype terminal from the telephone company, and connects it with the computer by following the simple procedure of getting it hooked to a telephone line.

Once the computer is connected to the user's terminal, the user has, in effect, a computer all to himself, together with a special programming language. This language, TELCOMP, allows him to use the computer. In that sense, an entire program may be entered, debugged, executed, saved, reloaded, and reexecuted whenever needed.

The language is a highly interactive one, participating throughout the development of a program, indicating errors, and helping in the debugging stages.

TELCOMP handles numbers in ordinary decimal notation, accurate to eight significant digits. Variables may be defined with a one- to three-letter name using the SET command.

In addition to the normal arithmetic operations of addition, subtraction, multiplication, division, and exponentiation, TELCOMP includes a number of common functions, such as square root, logarithm sine, etc. In addition, the system has certain predefined constants such as π.

TELCOMP statements commonly consist of the SET, TYPE, and DO commands. The DO command can execute repetitively a step stored elsewhere, modifying a variable by a given amount until the variable reaches a predetermined value.

TELCOMP allows the use of comparison operators ($=$, $<$, $>$) and combinations of these (for instance, $<>$ means less than or greater than). The IF command is used to control execution based on the results of the comparison. To help control execution, unconditional GO TO's are also provided.

At the end of a program, a STOP or DONE command is executed. TELCOMP allows individual steps to be replaced and deleted easily. A step is replaced merely by typing a new step with the same step number. A delete is accomplished by using the DELETE command.

For input and output, TELCOMP provides first the DEMAND verb which instructs the computer to request a value for a variable on the typewriter. The FORM and PLOT commands allow the user much flexibility in the typed output. In addition, a user may have a paper-tape reader and punch connected to his terminal. Saving and reloading a program are accomplished by using the DUMP, LOAD, and READ commands.

In addition, it is possible to punch TELCOMP program off-line using the paper-tape punch and the teletype, and later entering the tape using the LOAD command. Data may be prepared on paper tape off-line and read into the system with a READ command. Thus, TELCOMP'S I/O facilities are fairly comprehensive and flexible.

The following is an example of calculating compound interest using TELCOMP.

Dial computer center, ask to be connected to TELCOMP, press ORIG key, RETURN key.	This procedure gets you "on-line" with TELCOMP.
	All underlined words are printed by the computer.
DELETE ALL	This clears any other stray programs.
1.1 DEMAND PRN, RAT, YRS	This defines three variables. These stand for principal, rate of interest per year, and years. The command DE-MAND is an input verb and instructs TELCOMP to request the user at execution time, to supply values.
1.2 SET VAL = PRN*(1 + RAT/ 200.000) ↑ (2.0 * YRS)	This statement actually calculates the value of the deposited money. It first defines a variable called VAL, then sets it equal to the principal times the quantity one plus the rate divided by 200 to the two times number-of-years power. The ↑ symbol means exponentiation.
1.3 TYPE PRN, RAT, YRS, VAL	This is an output command and causes the values of the named variables to be typed out at execution time on the typewriter. Any numbers greater than 9999 are typed out in exponential notation.
1.4 TO STEP 1.1	This is an unconditional go to, and causes this program to execute repetitively.
DO PART 1	The DO command may be used within a program to cause a given section of program to be executed. However, it is also used to begin execution of a newly entered program.

Execution begins and the following is printed: PRN = 100.00 RAT = 6.0 YRS = 2.0	The values for principal, rate, and years are requested. The user types in values.
PRN = 100.00 RAT = 6.0 YRS = 2.0 VAL = 112.550881	The computer now calculates the value and executes the TYPE command.
PRN =	Because of the TO command, program execution begins again.
1.4 STOP	Assume that the program is to be executed only once. The TO command (step 1.4) may be replaced by typing a new command and using the same step number. The STOP command will cause execution of the program to stop. The user is, however, still connected to TELCOMP.
Push CLR button	The CLR button disconnects the terminal from TELCOMP.

teleprocessing A term used by IBM to mean the use of telecommunications equipment and systems by a computer. Teleprocessing is used more generally to refer to computer service involving I/O at locations remote from the computer itself.

The following categories may be distinguished (although they do not cover all applications of teleprocessing):

1. Data acquisition: the gathering of information, usually in real time, about the current state of an ongoing process. For example, monitoring production in a factory without necessarily governing the production

2. Message switching: analogous to private superswitchboards, leading to lower cost of communication by store-and-forward routing of message and line concentration

3. Conversational time-sharing: many human users at remote terminals, each seeming to have the entire computer to himself

4. Process control: closed-loop monitoring and regulation of an ongoing process

5. Inquiry servicing: for instance, airline reservation systems, stock market quotation, offered remotely

6. Computer-to-computer communications: network of computer power, analogous to today's electric power grids

temporary storage   The storage capacity reserved or used for retention of temporary or transient data.

Usually, the temporary storage is used for various kinds of data as the program execution proceeds, for instance, when the input files are opened at the beginning of a program and the labels are read into temporary storage for checking purposes. Since these labels will not be referred to again, the storage may then be used for counters, accumulation areas, etc. Indeed, the label checking instructions, not to be used again during the remainder of the program execution, may even be overlaid with data. Temporary storage, in this sense, remains attached to the program, but its layout and contents may be radically altered.

Temporary storage may sometimes not be needed for the total duration of a program run, as for example, when a routine builds up a large table of data from which it prepares certain sums, measures, and statistics. If the remainder of the tabular data are not needed, the table is just so much wasted space at the end of the routine.

A fixed allocation of storage capacity may also be used to hold only a certain specified temporary datum (that is, a data item that will be useless after being created and, nevertheless, is saved). While this is equally considered temporary storage, it is a wasteful practice seldom encountered in professional programming.

Today's more complex computer systems permit dynamic allocation of temporary storage. With dynamic allocation of temporary storage, another program in the system may take over the temporary storage area not required at the moment by a program partially executed.

ten's complement   In decimal arithmetic, the unique numeral that can be added to a given N-digit numeral to form a sum equal to 10^N (i.e., a one followed by N zeros). The addition of the ten's complement to the original number replaces every one of the original N digits by zero and generates a high-order carry. The addition need not be performed in order to define a ten's complement.

On a computer that performs N-digit decimal arithmetic, subtraction may be accomplished by taking the complement of the subtrahend and adding it to the minuend. If a high-order overflow occurs, the sign of the remainder is the same as that of the minuend; otherwise the sign is to be reversed.

For example:

1967		1967
−	becomes	+
1145		8855
822		(1)0822

1967		1967
−	becomes	+
2036		7964
− 69		9931 no overflow: hence
		− 69 change sign and complement

If ten's complement numbers are to be used for negatives, the answer is correct. If sign-magnitude numerals are used, the magnitude must be complemented when no overflow results.

The ten's complement may be generated as follows: in each digit position write down the difference between the original digit and 9; then add 1 to the units position of the resulting numeral. (Without this 1, the nine's complement which adds to 99999 . . . 9 would be obtained.)

Observe that the ten's complement of a ten's complement is the original number. The operation of forming the ten's complement is its own inverse.

See RADIX COMPLEMENT, NINE'S COMPLEMENT.

terminal   A site or location at which data can leave or enter a system. Terminal is a term used in connection with data transmission, and, consequently, a terminal usually refers to a device for entering or receiving data at the end of a transmission path.

A terminal must consist of at least one input or output device (often both) and electronics for interfacing with the rest of the system. A terminal may also contain additional input/output devices, a data buffer for retaining data to permit devices with different bit rates to work together, and timing mechanisms.

An increasing number of terminals which are appearing on the market consist of: a cathode-ray-tube display with alphanumeric capability only, a keyboard for entering data, a few control buttons, and possibly a buffer memory. The device, modern in styling, quiet, and slightly larger than an office typewriter, is used in conversational environments, that is, for question-and-answer operations. This type of terminal has been developed for bank tellers, ticket sellers, and airline seat reservations.

Functionally, teletypewriter terminals are probably the most common type of terminal in use today. They are somewhat slow and noisy, but inexpensive and reliable.

See DUPLEX, HALF DUPLEX.

ternary   A numeration system to the base 3; a descriptor of a quantity that must assume one of three permitted states.

Ternary numerals are composed only of the digits 0, 1, 2. The positions have value

$$. . . \quad 3^3 3^2 3^1 3^0 \cdot 3^{-1} \quad . . .$$

so that $201.2_3 = 2 \times 9 + 0 \times 3 + 1 \times 1 + 2/3 = 19.6666 \quad . \quad ._{10}.$

When ternary quantities are used in data manipulation, they are usually assigned the values -1, 0, $+1$. This is due to the fact that ternary states are usually constructed of two opposite states and a neutral central state: for instance, a magnetic core that can be magnetized clockwise or counterclockwise, or simply unmagnetized.

Ternary data coding is used on some data transmission systems to increase the throughput rate without increasing the frequency response. Data signals consist of positive, negative, and zero magnitude (or quiet) pulses.

Two ternary digits allow nine combinations while three binary bits (conventional transmission) allow only eight states. Thus a 50 percent increase in data rate can be obtained with a slight decrease of pulse transmission rate.

thin film   A method of constructing electronic components, devices, and circuits by depositing films of material on an inert, insulating substratum in specially designed patterns. By extension, a device made by using this technique.

Strictly speaking, workers in this field distinguish thick film from thin film, while nonspecialists tend to call all such devices thin film. A thick-film device behaves according to the bulk properties of its composition atoms (a thick film acts like a flat, but otherwise ordinary, component). A thin-film device, on the other hand, behaves in a manner governed by the surface properties of its materials. Atomic and electronic properties of surfaces (or boundaries) differ markedly from bulk properties of materials.

The most important single class of thin-film device today is the magnetic thin-film memory. A magnetic thin-film memory offers a substantial speed increase over magnetic core (it is 5 to 10 times faster). It may eventually even cost less than core since it can be produced in large arrays in a single operation; core requires expensive stringing and assembly into planes before it can be used. The price of thin-film memory has been very high until recently because of quality-control difficulties. These obstacles are said to be partially overcome, and may be completely eliminated in the future. The Burroughs 8500 is supposed to be given a large thin-film memory, but up to now, only small scratch-pad thin-film memories have been incorporated into commercial computers.

Some success has been reported with active semiconductor devices (transistors, diodes, tunnel diodes, etc.) deposited from vapor in vacuum by thin-film techniques. This makes possible the creation of large, complex circuits (transistors, diodes, resistors, capacitors, thermistors, photoresistors, but not inductors or transformers) in one unified technology. Such devices would be slower since they are larger, but would have higher power capability than monolithic integrated circuits.

thin magnetic film   A storage device consisting of a thin magnetic film of Permalloy deposited by vacuum evaporation or electrochemical deposition.

A thin magnetic film offers certain advantages over magnetic cores: it allows for very fast switching, it offers the possibility of fabricating many cells at a single time, input and output wires do not have to be threaded, and the amount of magnetic material is a thousand times smaller than that of cores, hence allowing for fast power dissipation at very high speeds.

The disadvantage of a thin magnetic film over core resides in the difficulty of obtaining spot-to-spot uniformity. Spots have a diameter of about an eighth of an inch, and a thickness ranging from 500 to 3000 angstroms.

third generation   A term used, somewhat loosely, to describe the general-purpose digital computers introduced in the late 1960's. (This usage may be compared to hi-fi as a description of better-grade radio/phonograph consoles in the mass-produced home entertainment market.)

Although three different generations may be distinguished, it is possible for a particular computer to possess characteristics of several different generations simultaneously. There are three generations of electronic hardware components, three generations of logical organization, and also three generations of software, or programming techniques. A true third-generation computer must belong to the third generation in each category.

Electronic Hardware Generations. Generations of hardware are most easily distinguished by the type of electronic components used.

FIRST GENERATION   The vacuum-tube computers, which reached

their peak of popularity in the late 1950's and early 1960's. Most vacuum-tube computers have now been retired, but a small number are still in use. First-generation computers of this type are characterized by relatively slow operation, high electrical consumption, and heavy air-conditioning requirements. The use of hundreds or thousands of vacuum tubes in one computer meant that at least one tube failure could be expected each week, resulting in frequent malfunctions and high maintenance costs. The most widely used vacuum-tube computer was probably the IBM 650.

SECOND GENERATION Computers with transistors replacing vacuum tubes. Transistorized construction brought great improvements in reliability, smaller size, and reduced electric power consumption and air-conditioning requirements. Second-generation computers are also characterized by magnetic-core memories of high speed and moderate capacity. Improved design principles, smaller size, and core memories made possible higher operating speeds. It was the second-generation computers that fostered the explosive growth of computing during the early-to-middle 1960's. The most common computer constructed with second-generation technology was the IBM 1401.

THIRD GENERATION Characterized by integrated circuits, the third-generation hardware is much smaller, faster, cheaper, and more reliable than first- or second-generation machines. A typical integrated circuit contains 50 to 100 components (transistors, resistors, and capacitors) in a chip only 1/20 of an inch square. An extreme example of the revolution caused by integrated circuits is the Control Data 449 computer: designed for aerospace applications, this device packs an entire medium-scale general-purpose computer (memory, logic, power supply, and input/output devices) into a box of only 4 × 4 × 9 inches. Third-generation computers are also characterized by larger, faster main memories and a great variety of auxiliary storage devices. Typical third-generation hardware is represented by RCA Spectra 70, SDS Sigma 7, and Burroughs 6500.

It must be observed that many computers have mixed second-and-third-generation construction. For example, the Honeywell 1250 has transistors and integrated circuits intermixed. The most common contemporary computer, IBM 360/ (30, 40, 50, 65), is constructed from solid logic technology (SLT) components. SLT represents an intermediate step between transistors and integrated circuits, since transistors and similar components are constructed on a ceramic chip, thus creating a miniature printed circuit board. Consequently, System 360 should not be considered as having true third-generation construction.

Logical Organization Generations

FIRST GENERATION First-generation computers performed one operation at a time, in strictly sequential fashion. An input or output operation would suspend all computation until the data transfer was completed. The complete lack of simultaneous operations made programming conceptually simpler and reduced the cost of hardware by allowing input/output to share hardware with the processor. This organization persists in the smallest computers of second-and-third-generation hardware, for it is the simplest method of constructing a digital computer.

SECOND GENERATION Computers with second-generation organization permitted substantial improvements in speed and productivity by allowing Input/Output operations to proceed simultaneously with calculations. This was accomplished by providing data channels to execute input/output operations with minimal attention from the processor. In order to synchronize simultaneous operations and react to unpredictable, asynchronous events, the ability to interrupt the processor was provided. Any attention signal or event would cause the central processing unit (CPU) to suspend its current operation and begin a special routine to handle the interruption. Second-generation computers were therefore able to increase their productivity by performing several operations (related or unrelated) at one time.

THIRD GENERATION Third-generation organization added special features to the design of computers in order to improve the ability to handle many programs at the same time. Such features include memory-protection circuits (to prevent programs from disturbing one another) and hardware address modification (to enable each program to operate from any actual location in main memory). Third-generation organization also includes a hierarchy of data storage devices, fast but expensive integrated-circuit registers, main memory of core or thin-film construction, auxiliary storage on disk, drum, or both, and magnetic-tape or magnetic-card device storage for exceptionally large files of data. The hierarchy of memory levels can be tailored to adapt the storage facilities of the computer to the needs of the installation at reasonable cost.

Third-generation organization is usually modular. Units (or modules) of computing power (CPU's), main memory, data channels, and auxiliary storage can be added or removed to adjust the power of any computer to meet changing circumstances.

Finally, third-generation organization permits some or all input/output operations to occur at sites remote from the main processor. By means of telecommunications, a third-generation computer can communicate with men or machines located at many different sites, permitting them to use computing power simultaneously for various different purposes. A good example of third-generation organization is Scientific Data System's Sigma 7 computer.

Not every computer organization can be classified as first, second, or third generation. For example, the CDC 6600 has some second-and-third generation design features, but it also has some significant organization principles found on no other computer. (See MULTI-PROCESSING.) Other computers with design features departing significantly from the mainstream outlined above are the Honeywell 1800 (multiprocessing) and Burroughs 5500 (see POLISH NOTATION). It is thus hard at times to assign a generation number to any particular computer.

Software Generations

FIRST GENERATION   First-generation software usually included a program loader, simple utility routines, and an assembler or compiler to assist in program writing. This elementary programming support was dictated by the limited capability of early computers and by the lack of sophistication of the programming community.

SECOND GENERATION   Second-generation software appeared with the introduction of operating systems, which assisted both operators and programmers in their daily work. The operating system provided a uniform environment for writing and running programs. Within the system, an input/output control system (IOCS) relieved the programmer of having to repeat complex input/output logic in every program. The ability to link together independently written pieces of program permitted the construction of program libraries of commonly used routines. The operating system provided job-to-job transition, creating faster and smoother execution of a stack of jobs. Of course all the features of first-generation software remained, but these were extended and improved.

THIRD GENERATION   Third-generation software makes the operating system indispensable to the normal functioning of the computer. Functions are divided between wired-in (hardware) and programmed (software) logic so as to maximize joint efficiency at minimum cost. The operating system (OS) coordinates the complex (and ever-changing) hardware configuration, and handles all interrupts and requests for special attention.

Multiprogramming is commonplace in third-generation operations. This permits a mix of programs to run at any one time, to ensure that all the input/output devices and all of main memory are utilized. Multiprogramming keeps all of the computer busy, avoiding the waste of computer resources by programs that cannot utilize all the available machinery at once.

The third-generation software is also characterized by the availability of conversational programming techniques, permitting human beings and computers to form a partnership that accomplishes what neither could do alone.   Typically this involves many users communicating at once with the machine, using remote typewriters or cathode-ray-tube terminals.   Third-generation operating systems support these conversational applications by providing real-time input/output control systems.

It should be noted that software is continually evolving, being modified and added to as the size and sophistication of the programming community increase.   Thus an existing second-generation system can still be upgraded with many third-generation software features.   It is very easy to switch from one operating system to another, thus allowing third-generation conversational programs to be run during the day, and second-generation stacked jobs to be run at night on the same computer.   For these reasons it is difficult to describe rigid boundaries between the software generations.

Some features of the fourth generation of computers are being predicted with assurance today.   In the fourth generation of hardware, integrated circuits will be replaced with large-scale integration (LSI) devices.   LSI creates thousands of electronic components on a single surface, perhaps half an inch square.   By reducing the cost of performing any function in hardware, LSI promises to shift the balance of hardware/software toward more complex hardware.   This will make programming simpler.   In the fourth-generation organization, there will be continued emphasis on modular design, and on symbiotic relationships between operating systems and hardware.   Fourth-generation computers will employ very large capacity data storage files, possibly using photochromic and/or laser techniques.   In fourth-generation software, the expected trends show more graphical processing, involving two- and three-dimensional displays.   Emphasis will be placed on making computers easier to use, so that operating systems will offer helpful guidance to those whose mistakes now produce only cryptic error messages.

three-plus-one address   An instruction format containing an operation code, three operand address parts, and a control address.

In a certain sense the power or versatility of a digital computer instruction set depends on the number of operands that each instruction can reference.   For example, many arithmetic and data-manipulating instructions really require three operand addresses:

MULTIPLY A BY B GIVING C
TRANSLATE A INTO B USING TRANSLATION TABLE C
EDIT A INTO B VIA EDIT MASK C.

In a computer with only one operand address per instruction, either three separate instructions would be required for any of the above operations to be carried out, or certain operand locations would have to be hardware-specified.

The fourth address refers simply to the location of the instruction to be interpreted next in sequence. In most computers, the address of the next instruction is hardware-implicit; it is the next instruction following this one in memory. Thus, the fourth address does not contribute to the power or flexibility of the instruction set. For this reason, the fourth address is referred to as plus-one, and three-plus-one address structure is thus distinguished from four-address structure.

threshold　A logic operator such that, if P, Q, R, S, . . . are statements, then the threshold will be true if at least N statements are true, false otherwise.

This logic operator is a generalization of AND and OR. AND is threshold with a value of N equal to the number of arguments whereas OR is threshold with a value of N equal to one.

Threshold also refers to the level of marginal detectability of a device. A sharply defined threshold is a valuable noise-immunity feature of digital circuit elements. The threshold allows a 0 or 1 decision to be made with precision, preventing stray voltages of less than a critical size from introducing error. For example, a tape drive, while reading, will accept pulses greater than threshold size as 1, otherwise as 0. Hence, a tape with too weak a signal might not reach threshold level, and so be adjudged blank, or 0, by the hardware. Most tape drives allow for adjustment of threshold voltage to permit reading weak signal while rejecting noise and tape print-through. Misadjustment of this control has been known to render computers incompatible with different magnetic tapes.

See MAJORITY.

throughput　A term used to refer to the productivity of a system, as expressed in computing work per minute or hour. Throughput, however, cannot be readily measured, and indeed its very definition is somewhat imprecise. For example, it is difficult to ascertain whether an operating system overhead contributed to, or detracted from, throughput. In either case, drawing the line between operating overhead and productive work is no simple matter.

The terms throughput and turnaround time often are used together, although they have different meaning. Turnaround time is the average interval between submission of a job and its completion. A computer that does five jobs at a time may increase its throughput by going to six jobs at once, but this may in turn increase its turnaround time since each job is executed more slowly. Only on small monoprogramming computers do the two concepts bear a direct relationship to each other.

time-share   To perform several independent processes almost simultaneously by interleaving the operations of the processes on a single high-speed processor.

Almost simultaneously means that the independent processes seem to be all happening at once, when not examined too closely. In fact, no more than one process at a time can occur, because a single processing agency is involved. Just as the separate frames of a motion picture blend in the human eye to form a continuous moving image, so the intermittently performed elementary operations of each individual process appear to blend together in a continuous action.

Interleaving means that small segments of each process are performed in cyclic order in such a way that after one cycle the first process is again active and all processes have been partially processed. A strictly cyclic operation is called round robin and is rarely completely achieved. Individual processes (if different) must occasionally wait or otherwise vary in momentary processing work load. These variations, if accounted for by scheduling processor time, can improve efficiency by not wasting power on dormant processes.

Time-sharing permits a powerful computer to be devoted to many tasks at once. This results in a twofold benefit:

1. It is cheaper to build one powerful computer than to build N computers each $1/N$th as fast. (According to Grosh's law, processing power is proportional to the square of the cost; that is, we get four times as many jobs done in a computer twice as expensive; therefore, each job costs half as much: $2 \times cost/4 \times jobs = half$ the cost per job.)

2. By proper management, jobs are allocated to idle computer resources, keeping all the computer busy. Thus, the given computer gets more work per hour done by minimizing idleness.

Of course, overhead must be kept within bounds or both benefits will be lost.

On a medium-to-small computer, time-sharing usually involves two processes at once. The smaller (foreground) program steals a few moments at a time from the background or larger program. Normally the foreground program occupies a small part of the total capacity of the machine but must react very quickly to some stimulus.

On a very large computer many programs may be time-shared. High-priority conversational programs interact in a real-time, or on-demand, basis with human beings at terminals in many locations. Symbiont programs perform tape-to-disk and disk-to-print utility routines on an interrupt basis. In the remaining processor time, conventional programs of low priority are run. The large and varied work load ensures that very little of the hardware will remain unused for very long.

An everyday example of time-sharing is a telephone party line: it appears to be almost continuously available to each user, but can serve only one party at a time. Viewed from a span of months, however, it serves all telephones equally and *almost* simultaneously. See INTERLEAVE, TIME-SHARING.

time-sharing The simultaneous utilization of a computer system from multiple terminals.

The purpose of time-sharing is to reduce the turn-around time previously needed from problem definition to computer solution; and with optimum utilization of the computer system, to provide economies through cost-sharing.

The system has two major tasks to perform: to handle the communications with the multiple users, and to execute the users' programs. The processing portion of the system that handles communications provides simultaneous service to the multiple users by use of buffers; the processing portion of the system that handles program execution can handle only one user at a time. It is therefore the latter portion that is time-shared, and a queueing algorithm is used for process scheduling.

The number of terminals is limited to the number that can be served by the communications controller and by the central processing speed. The demands on the system require high-speed random-access devices for external storage.

To use a time-sharing system a user must electronically tie his terminal to the communications controller through a communication network such as the Bell Telephone System. If an entry port is available, simultaneous utilization begins. The transmission of programs and data is uninterrupted: additions, corrections, and deletions can thus be made without delay.

The only time that delays are encountered occurs when multiple users request central processing in the same time frame. The executive monitor then puts the programs in queue, and processing is done according to the scheduling algorithm. This algorithm contains priority and timing considerations which depend on the system hardware and the type of system utilized. The microsecond speed of large-scale computers allows for a tremendous rapidity of throughput which helps create, among users, a growing sense of conviction that each has a computer of his own.

Immediate access, reduced turnaround time, conversational mode, and ease of operation are several of the attributes of a time-sharing system. The ability to get answers quickly can make statistical analysis feasible, as opposed to intuitive, off-the-cuff estimates. The language flexibility and simplicity give the man with the problem the ability to work directly with the computer instead of through programmers and operations units. Debugging, with the on-line capability for making modifications, is greatly simplified.

The first time-sharing system was made commercially available in July 1965 (GE 235 System). Since then a number of coast-to-coast commercial systems have been installed (GE 235, SDS 940), time-sharing systems are making their entry into the educational field (IBM 1500, RCA Spectra 70/45), and additional time-sharing systems are being set up for research centers (GE 645, IBM 360/67).

See accompanying illustration.

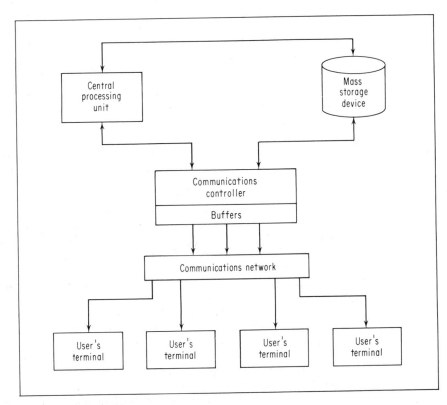

Basic time-sharing network.

time-sharing system, TSS/360 An operating system for large-scale 360 configurations having time-sharing features. Probably the most sophisticated, complex operating system being implemented at this time.

TSS/360 is designed primarily to allow many simultaneous users to interact with the computer in a conversational mode. These users are human beings with problems to solve or jobs to do, having access to a computer input/output terminal (which may be near the computer or many miles distant from it), and with the authorization to use the facilities of TSS. Conversational interaction means that the computer analyzes and acts on each input message as it is received, and if necessary responds immediately with error diagnostics, intermediate results, or requests for additional input. Each user feels that he alone is using the computer, for each active terminal appears to have the computer's uninterrupted attention. In reality, each of the programs or users receives frequent but very short intervals of service from the computer. The operating system and hardware allow rapid switching from job to job, thereby creating the illusion of undivided attention for each user and also fully utilizing the hardware capacity to perform multiple operations simultaneously. In addition, nonconversational, or background, programs are run on the computer as sufficient time, memory, and input/output devices become available. This automatically fills otherwise idle time with less critical computational tasks, avoiding waste of computer facilities and further increasing the total amount of useful work performed each minute.

The most important single design feature of TSS and its supporting hardware is the provision of virtual memory space through its memory-mapping facility. The memory map converts each program instruction address reference, or virtual address, into an actual hardware memory location, or real address. Each program appears to reside in an otherwise unused main memory having more than 16 million bytes of storage capacity. Any address that the program is capable of referring to will be converted by memory-mapping hardware into an actual address of a memory location within the computer, and the converted, real address will be used for storing and fetching of instructions and data. If the program's virtual address refers to data not actually resident within the main memory, the supervisor (TSS) locates the desired datum in external storage (drum or disk) and brings the datum into memory. Other programs execute while this I/O is taking place, assuring that no computer time is wasted. When the requested datum is in memory (read-in complete), the memory map is adjusted to show its new real location, and execution of the original program can be resumed.

This is actually accomplished by dividing the memory into pages of 4096 bytes. A virtual address is considered to be divided into leading bits (page address) and 12 rightmost bits specifying the location within a page. Memory-map hardware replaces the leftmost set of address bits with the bits designating the actual memory page to be used. The bits describing location within a page are not disturbed. This action enables 32-bit or 24-bit virtual addresses (4-billion- or 16-million-byte addressing range) to be executed on hardware having, for example, only 524,000 bytes of real memory. External storage used for back-up or extension of main memory is similarly divided into 4096-byte pages, and special hardware facilitates moving these pages into or out of main memory as integral units. The accompanying diagram explains this organization graphically.

A person becomes eligible to use TSS services by being assigned an identification code, a password, charge numbers, and a privilege class, and having these made known to TSS via a JOIN command. The JOIN command defines the person, his right to use the system, and his restrictions on usage to the operating system. One individual, the system manager, is automatically JOINed to the system when it is created. His power is absolute, and he can JOIN or QUIT (discontinue the permission to use TSS to) any other person. The system manager JOINs system administrators to the TSS. Administrators can use the system themselves, but usually they JOIN other individuals as users. In addition, a MAIN OPERATOR is JOINed at system generation time, and subsidiary operators may also be JOINed. The manager and administrators have financial and administrative authority over the system, the users, and the operators. Users are allowed problem-solving rights but few other privileges. Operators are not normally users, but are responsible for mounting tapes and disks, keeping the printer supplied with paper, reading and punching cards, etc. All JOINed persons communicate with the computer via consoles or prerecorded data sets similar in format to console inputs.

A person connects himself to TSS by finding a console, requesting ATTENTION, and giving a LOG ON (begin job) command when the computer responds to the attention request. During LOG ON the person must identify himself by giving his correct identification code and password. He may then communicate with TSS by giving COMMANDS, accepting or supplying data as required. When his session is over, he disconnects himself by giving a LOG OFF (end-of-job) command. In nonconversational mode, a background program begins with LOG ON and ends with LOG OFF, and uses commands similar to those of conversational users. Thus background programs are somewhat like prerecorded conversations but are handled in a lower-priority, noninteractive fashion. Also, a job begun in conversational mode may be continued in background mode if a suitable prerecorded remainder of the conversation exists.

TSS supports punched-card, printer, and magnetic-tape data sets similar to those of OS/360 and some lesser operating systems. However, direct-access-device storage organizations are quite different from those of other operating systems. Random-access storage is divided into 4096-byte pages and treated as nonresident extensions of memory. Thus a virtual sequential data set appears to the pro-

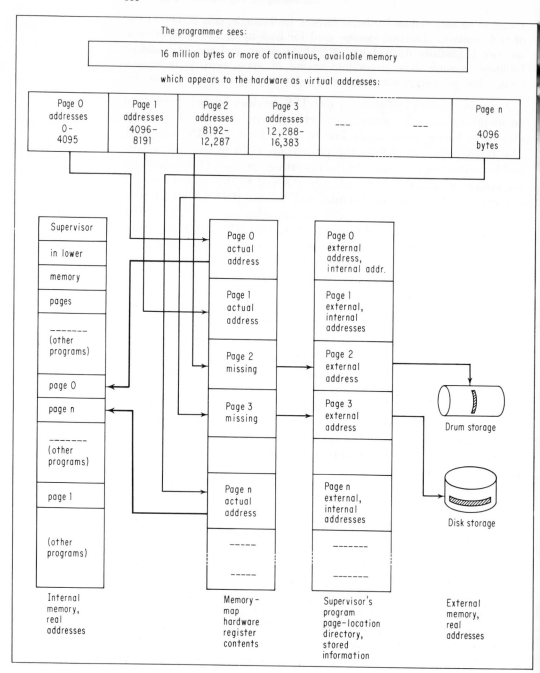

Operation of memory-map functioning: time-sharing system TSS/360.

grammer as contiguous records stored in an extension of main memory. A virtual index sequential data set is similar, but records are stored in ascending order by key, and an index gives direct access to any particular record. Program libraries of all kinds are virtual partitioned data sets, where each named member begins on a new page boundary but may extend into additional pages. Whenever less than 4096 bytes of data are stored in a page of a virtual data set, the remainder of the page is wasted. TSS also supports sequential data sets on direct-access storage devices, allowing compatibility with OS/360. Virtual and nonvirtual data sets cannot reside on the same volume of storage.

TSS includes an assembler and a FORTRAN IV compiler, with compilers for PL/1 and COBOL to be added later. Also, graphic access methods and sort/merge utilities will be added to TSS. The output of a compiler or assembler is an object module which can be executed immediately or united with other modules by a linkage-editor run. This ability to run without linkage editing surpasses the capability of OS, DOS, or TOS, while the option to use linkage editor makes available all of the flexibility of these other operating systems.

See: CONVERSATIONAL TIME-SHARING, DATA MANAGEMENT, INDEXED SEQUENTIAL DATA SET, MULTIPROGRAMMING, OPERATING SYSTEM 360, PARTITIONED DATA SET, REAL TIME, TIME-SHARING.

TOS (Tape Operating System). A powerful and flexible operating system for System 360 computers having at least 16K of memory, at least four magnetic tapes, and no random-access storage devices. TOS supports a flexible job control language, permits automatic job-to-job transition, and includes compilers for every IBM-supported language. TOS is a twin to DOS, the disk operating system.

Using TOS, every peripheral device is referred to by the programmer by means of a symbolic name. The operator, via console or control cards, assigns the symbolic names to actual peripheral devices at run time. In this way, any convenient tape station may be substituted for another tape or printer or card device as conditions require. If the data sets are properly configured, a printer or card device may be substituted for a tape. The distinction between actual and symbolic-device addresses permits this run-time substitution. It is made possible by dividing input control into physical input/output control system (PIOCS) and logical input/output control system (LIOCS). PIOCS is permanently resident, and contains one control routine for each kind of peripheral device attached to the computer. Thus PIOCS is very configuration-dependent. It deals only with physical records (with one exception—it detects end-of-file delimiters on SYSIPT and SYSRDR, the regular input streams, to prevent any job from accidentally reading too far and ruining the following job). The actual manipulation of data within the records is the responsibility of LIOCS. LIOCS handles buffering and overlap, blocking and unblocking, and labels. The LIOCS routines are job-dependent, and are included when needed in a program by linkage editor. Thus LIOCS occupies no more room than required, for only what is needed will be present.

Components of TOS and users' programs reside on a tape core image library, a collection of ready-to-run routines. In addition, compiled programs may be saved in object-module form in a relocatable library. This library permits the same routines to be linkage-edited into as many programs as necessary without having to be recompiled each time. An optional source-statement library supports the assembler macroinstruction library and COBOL external COPY library. Each library entry is preceded by a directory entry in the form of a header record. The librarian (a utility routine) supervises all three libraries.

In TOS, but not in DOS, it is possible to construct private libraries on tape reels that may be dismounted when not needed. This ensures protection of proprietary programs and also permits faster access by not having to read past unneeded (other users') library entries. Private libraries may be relocatable or source image (but not core image) and are made known to the system via control cards.

TOS supports FORTRAN (in 32K) which includes ASA Basic FORTRAN. Compile-and-go is available on four-tape systems. COBOL is available on 16-K computers (does not support direct-access devices). Compile-and-go operation requires five tapes; compile-only needs four. PL/1 is available (may require 65K). RPG and ASSEMBLER run on minimum TOS configurations. Autotest is a powerful system for debugging assembly-language (BAL) programs.

TOS will support multiprogramming on 32K or more. The background program (10K to 524K) comes from the job stream in the normal way. One or two foreground programs may be initiated by the operator in regions (2K to 524K) at the high-address end of memory. Memory protect is required for multiprogramming.

Teleprocessing may be conducted in background or foreground mode. Only BTAM is supported, giving low-level (close to machine language) access to a wide variety of remote I/O functions. Teleprocessing is available only in BAL (assembly language) but can be linked to other languages via linkage editor.

TOS is available on 16K memory computers having only four magnetic-tape drives. Almost all the power of TOS is available with 32K and five magnetic tapes, with memory protect if multiprogramming is desired. Normally, the system-resident routines occupy only 6 to 9K of memory (depending on configuration), leaving most of the computer available for programs. TOS can be run on any larger-scale computer up to 1024K, but few of the very large installations do not have direct-access storage devices. Installations having direct-access storage devices will use DOS or OS/360.

touching characters   See ADJACENCY.

trace   To provide a record of every step, or selected steps, executed by a program, and by extension, the record produced by this operation.

Tracing is a valuable debugging technique which is possible on many digital computers. Usually a trace printout is obtained for every traced instruction. This printout will show:

The location of the instruction

The instruction itself

The data in the operands of the instruction

The machine-register contents

A programmer may elect to trace some or all of the suspected sections of his program to determine why an error condition occurred. A tracing routine maintains control of the program. It examines each instruction before allowing it to execute, and ensures that control will return to the trace routine (and not the successor instruction) when the instruction is executed. It is important that the tracing routine leave intact the natural operation of the subject program.

Tracing is only practical on computers above a certain minimum size and power, since otherwise memory could not be spared for the trace routine and too great a slowdown would be entailed. Any sufficiently large computer can utilize tracing techniques. Tracing is necessarily slow, because it operates interpretively and generates a large volume of output. This is the major reason for selective rather than indiscriminate tracing. On large computers selective tracing is to be preferred to memory dumping because a dump (printout of the contents) of a large memory contains too much irrelevant data.

track   The portion of a moving memory medium (such as tape, disk, or drum) which passes beneath, and is accessible to, a particular read/write head position.

Tracks run lengthwise in tapes whereas tracks are circular in disks or drums.

With fixed-head devices, a track is 1 bit wide. On moving-head devices a track corresponds to one position of a particular read/write head assembly, and may be more than 1 bit wide if multiple-head assemblies are used.

On devices with circular tracks, the finite capacity of an individual track constitutes an important programming consideration. If the length of a data record is not a submultiple of the track length, wasted space results. For example, if the capacity of a disk-pack track is about 3600 characters, then four records 895 characters long can be accommodated on a track giving efficient utilization, but only three records 904 characters long will fit (giving nearly 25 percent waste of disk capacity). Contrast this with magnetic tape, in which any size record that will fit into memory may be chosen. Most magnetic-tape records are less than an inch long, or a few inches long. A full reel of tape is 2400 feet, which accommodates a large number of any-size records.

A partial solution to the fixed-track-length problem is hardware that permits track overflow, or automatic continuation of data from one track onto an adjacent track.

The grouping of tracks into cylinders (a collection of tracks that can all be accessed without moving the read/write head assembly) introduces considerations similar to those produced by finite track length, but less severely confining.

Certain rotating-device tracks are divided into fixed-length segments called sectors. If the hardware permits accessing only an integral number of sectors, certain programming techniques must be used for records of nonsector length. Example: to change part of a sector, one must read the entire sector, change a part, and write it all back into its old location.

transform To change the form of data in a specified way. In mathematics, a change of variables that completely alters the manipulation properties of a problem, while preserving the essential nature of the problem.

In ordinary algebraic manipulation, multiplication and division are considered to be more difficult than addition and subtraction. If these difficult operations are present in great numbers, it is possible to take logarithms of the ordinary numbers in the problem. This changes the rules of the game. The difficult operations may now be performed using addition and subtraction (although addition and subtraction now become impossible), and the more difficult operations of root extraction and exponentiation become the ordinarily difficult multiplication and division. To return to ordinary numbers simply requires the antilogarithmic transformation of the results.

In the same way, the Fourier and Laplace transforms alter the manipulatory properties of functions. The difficult operations of differentiation/integration are replaced by algebraic operations (the conventional multiply/divide operations become difficult in the transform domain). The inverse transformation must be made in order to display the obtained answers.

Human beings usually carry out both logarithmic and Laplace transformations, by looking up the items in tables. Computers can perform look-up operations, but can also be programmed to routinely calculate both kinds of transformations.

translate To convert from one language to another, or to convert characters from one representation set to another, and by extension, the computer instruction which directs the latter conversion to be carried out.

The need for translation from one character set to another arises often enough so that many computers provide hardware translation capability. The translation is performed as a multiple-table-look-up operation. Each source character is interpreted as a numeric value and used to calculate the address of its replacement character. The replacement character is moved from a table to either the original character location or a destination area. Sometimes it is possible to mark specific characters in the translation table so that special action may be taken in case one of the marked characters appears in the source text. This permits computers to scan for control characters or delimiters in the source text (in the IBM 360, the TRANSLATE instruction translates, the TRANSLATE AND SCAN instruction scans only; in the Honeywell 200, the MOVE ITEM AND TRANSLATE instruction both translates and scans).

Character-translation is required for:

1. Converting from 7-bit ASCII to 6- or 8-bit internal code
2. Converting from 5-, 7-, or 8-level paper-tape code to another paper-tape code or internal format
3. Converting from 8-bit EBCDIC to 6-bit BCD
4. Converting from Hollerith punch-card code to an internal character set
5. Converting from one computer's internal or external code to another (noncompatible) computer's code

Language translation is divided into two classes: natural language translation, and artificial language translation.

Artificial-language (programming languages, higher-level languages, problem-oriented or procedure-oriented languages) translation is the easiest-to-carry-out class because the artificial languages are already machine-interpretable. A large-scale conversion effort begins with writing a language conversion program, and usually ends with human editing of the final text (if necessary).

At the present time, natural language translation is more difficult. Complete conversion by computer has not been obtained (and may never be) but in certain cases workable translations have been produced without final human editing.

Most translating begins by looking up source-language words in a comprehensive dictionary to discover source-language parts of speech, tense, case, gender, and also target-language equivalents (kernels or roots of equivalent words).   There follows a phase of parsing, or analysis of interword relationships.   The final phase consists of target-language synthesis, construction of equivalent sentences of like meaning, tense, and organization.   In no case is it possible to deal with an extensive set of colloquialisms, slang, or nongrammatical constructs.

transmit   To cause a copy of some information to be created at one or more remote locations.

As a rule, the original data remains at the originating location except in the case of real-time transmission where no recording is made at the point of origin.

A temporary or storable copy of the information is generated, equivalent in utility to the original data, but not necessarily identical in form.   The means of transmission is commonly electrical; but radio, microwave, and optical signals are also used.   A broadcast type of transmission can result in multiple copies being created: information can thus be endlessly duplicated without losing its meaning.

Electrical transmission may be broadly divided in the following classes:

Narrow band: less-than-voice quality lines with speeds of 10 to 50 characters per second.

Voice band: voice-quality lines with speeds of 100 to 300 characters per second; voice bands are used by cathode-ray-tube terminals.

Wideband: large band lines with a speed of 5100 characters per second, usually used to transmit from computer to computer.

Synchronous: uniform rate of character flow.

Asynchronous: irregular rate of character flow, each character preceded and followed by frame bits.

To transmit also refers to physically moving the original data from the originating location to some other location.   This transmission may be carried out by mail, truck, pneumatic tube, and the like.   This type of transmission is always slower than the electrical transmission, but may result in fewer errors.

transport   Usually connotes tape transport, a mechanical device for moving magnetic or perforated tape past a stationary read or write head.

A modern magnetic-tape transport contains the following elements:

1.   A supply reel with its associated motor, brake, and clutches
2.   A vacuum column that holds a length of unreeled tape
3.   A capstan, that is, a rotating shaft used to control tapes motion

4. A read/write head, with mechanism for lifting away from contact during fast rewind

5. Tape cleaners—usually vacuum cleaners

6. BOT/EOT (that is, beginning of tape, end of tape) sensors—usually photocells

7. Another vacuum column on the take-up side

8. A take-up reel with associated motor, brake, and clutch

The tape transport functionally operates as three distinct devices:

1. The supply servo (reel, vacuum column) maintains a proper amount of tape in the vacuum column; optical or pressure sensors in the vacuum column activate the reel to wind or unwind the tape according to whether the low limit or the high limit has been passed; the reel is at rest when the amount of tape is within limits.

2. The take-up servo acts exactly in the same way, but only with respect to that portion of the tape which appears beyond the read/write head; it functions independently of other servos.

3. The capstan/head area contains the capstan or capstans with pinch rollers or vacuum to move the tape, BOT/EOT sensors to prevent the tape from winding off the reel, tape brakes, and cleaners for a rapid stop and contamination control, and guides to assure the correct alignment of the tape. The computer directs the capstan/brake to read, write, and space, etc. The reel servos ensure that a proper supply of loose tape is always maintained.

In the rewind operation, the capstan/head is out of tape contact and control: the supply reel is motor-driven at high speed to rewind, and the vacuum columns are empty. Optical sensors on the take-up reel slow the mechanism down to normal backspace speed when a tape-low condition is sensed, so as to prevent the tape from running off the reel: the motor stops when a BOT is sensed.

See TAPE TRANSPORT.

trap   An automatic transfer of control to a known location, this transfer occurring when a specified condition is detected by hardware. A trap is different from an interrupt in that it is caused only by the central processing unit (CPU), the program, or some internal event.

A computer may be provided with one or more automatic traps to enable handling of exceptional conditions. These traps are usually under program control; that is, they may be called for or called off by special instructions. Normal traps include overflow/underflow, divide check (arithmetic faults), exponent overflow/underflow (floating-point arithmetic faults), and transfer (branching—this trap enables writing diagnostic-tracing routines).

When a trap condition is detected and the corresponding trap is called for, a transfer of control to a hardware-designated location occurs. Simultaneously the location from which the trap occurred is recorded. This permits resumption of processing without unnecessary disruption. The hardware-designated location usually contains a transfer to the proper trap-handling routine, or it may contain an ignore-trap instruction (rare).

Without the trapping facility, every arithmetic instruction might have to be followed by an error test, resulting in a great waste of space and time: the omission of tests could result in garbage data generation.

A very useful trap is the invalid op-code interrupt. This permits software fulfillment of instructions available on a computer series but not installed on this particular machine. At the expense of execution time, this feature makes it possible to run any correct program on any computer of a series. If some op-codes are undefined, it is possible to utilize these for do-it-yourself instruction kits, or supervisor calls for particular purposes. If all else fails, this trap is useful for debugging.

See INTERRUPT.

troubleshoot   To find and correct errors and faults, usually in the hardware.

Troubleshooting hardware usually begins by isolating the trouble, thus finding the single circuit or component that is faulty. In complex systems like most computers, this can be an involved process. Once found, the faulty elements are repaired, readjusted, or replaced. Troubleshooting ends with a check-out, or verifying that the correct operation has been restored.

See DEBUG.

true complement   Same as RADIX COMPLEMENT: In the decimal system a ten's complement and in the binary a two's complement are true complements.

In fixed-numeral-length arithmetic (modulo arithmetic) a true complement has properties similar to a negation. Thus, in five-digit decimal arithmetic (arithmetic modulo 10^5) adding the complement of a number is the same as subtracting the uncomplemented number, except that a complement add produces a high-order overflow.

This statement holds only for fixed-length numerals (modulo arithmetic); otherwise contradictions occur. For instance:

$$
\begin{array}{rr}
120 & 120 \\
-\ 77 & +\ 23 \\
\hline
43 & 143
\end{array}
$$

where the 1 is really a failure in complementing the 0 in the numeral 077. With correct complementation, the example becomes

$$
\begin{array}{r} 120 \\ -\ 77 \\ \hline 043 \end{array}
\qquad
\begin{array}{r} 120 \\ +\ 923 \\ \hline 043 \end{array}
$$

In the addition of the complement, a true sum of 1043 is generated, but only three digits are allowed and so 043 is the result. A failure to generate a carry out of the leftmost position indicates that a change of sign has occurred, and the answer must be recomplemented if its true magnitude is needed. Example:

$$
\begin{array}{r} 077 \\ -\ 120 \\ \hline -\ 043 \end{array}
\qquad
\begin{array}{rl} 077 & \\ +\ 880 & \text{add complement} \\ \hline +\ 957 & \text{no overflow} \\ -\ 043 & \text{true answer} \end{array}
$$

truncate   To shorten a numeral by dropping digits, usually (but not always) at the least significant (or rightmost) end, and sometimes, to cut short an operation by terminating it according to some rule.

All digital computers must work with finite-length numerals as approximations to (or representation of) numbers. Results exceeding the chosen length are often generated (as in radix conversion, and more commonly, multiplication). It is then required to shorten these results by some rule. Truncation of least significant digits is the simplest rule to implement, although some form of rounding may preserve higher accuracy.

The errors introduced by truncation (loss of accuracy) propagate through further calculations, and may in extreme cases destroy the validity of obtained results. The study of truncation error and its propagated effect is a valid subject for numerical analysis. A common method of analyzing errors is to assume full accuracy, and at each truncation add a random number with value between 0 and 9 in the digit place retained. Experiments confirm that this model works with useful precision for most purposes.

It is sometimes possible to calculate a quantity by a process of successively better approximation. In most cases an unending sequence of operations results, taking theoretically an infinite time for completion. These must be stopped at a suitable point in time to provide for sufficient accuracy without consuming excessive time. A good rule is to stop when one approximation differs from the previous one by less than a preassigned amount. Truncation error is also introduced here, but it is under the direct control of the programmer or analyst. (In character or digit-oriented computers, variable-precision arithmetic may be used to optimize accuracy versus time trade-offs. This requires extra planning for proper truncation.)

truth table A tabular display of the definition of a logical operator which exhibits the value of the operation for every combination of argument values.

A logical, or Boolean, operator relates quantities that are either true or false, and produces a result that is either true or false. A truth table is a complete definition, or illustration, of a particular operator.

The following is an example of a truth table for the operator AND which is true only if all arguments are true, and false otherwise:

A / B	T	F
T	T	F
F	F	F

A truth table need not be square, or be limited to two arguments. For instance, the MAJORITY (A, B, C) is true if more than half the arguments A, B, C are true, and is otherwise false. The truth table for the operator MAJORITY would appear as follows:

A/B / C	TT	TF	FT	FF
T	T	T	T	F
F	T	F	F	F

In some instances, the symbols 0 and 1 are preferred to the symbols T and F. See EXCLUSIVE OR.

tube Usually connotes the cathode-ray tube, or CRT, at times called a display tube.

The display tube is similar in construction and appearance to the picture tube of monochrome television sets, and it is used for display of graphic and textual outputs from computers.

The display tube is normally capable of operating in two modes: the letter display mode and the vector display mode. The letter display mode is similar to typewriting in its versatility, but much faster and quieter. Expensive hardware associated with a display tube permits the simple programming of each letter (size, location, identity, and sometimes, brightness). On low-cost systems letter capability may be omitted. (On other systems it can be the only operating mode.) The vector display mode permits programmed display of points (dots) and straight-line segments (vectors) identified by their end points. This allows for the construction of any kind of display, at the expense of programming complexity. Some displays must be refreshed (or redrawn) 10 or more times per second, whereas others contain a form of local memory and can refresh themselves.

A light pen permits the user to talk back to the CRT for input to the computer. This device is actually a photocell which responds to abrupt rise in brightness as an electron beam passes its small viewing area. Through proper design, it ignores room lights, sunlight, etc., as being too steady (not abrupt enough). The computer notes time of detection, compares it with the position of the electron beam at that moment, and thus, deduces the position of the light pen (the pen may equally project a light beam to show the user where it is being pointed, but the computer ignores this light).

The electrostatic storage tube is an obsolete memory device for digital computers. It is similar to the CRT in appearance and function (but with a smaller viewing screen), and it stored and reread bits as charged or uncharged spots in an array on its active face.

The electron tube or vacuum tube was formerly used as a logical and operational element in digital computers. It occupies an intermediate position in speed and history between relays and transistors. Commonly used were the diodes (rectifiers), triodes (logical devices), dual triodes (two tubes in one glass envelope). They are no longer employed today because of high power consumption, limited life, and large size.

Turing, Alan Mathison (1912–1954) Alan Turing, British computer engineer, characterized the computer in abstract terms and showed this method to be academically significant. The most important of his abstractions, the Turing machine, is a precisely defined, generalized conception of a universal computer. Using this precise definition, Turing was able to express the criteria for computable problems and to prove that some problems are not computable in this sense. Turing studied the possibilities of machines teaching themselves through trial and error, and devised theoretically possible experiments such as the Turing identification game (given a conversation by means of typewritten messages between a person and a machine, how can an observer, analyzing the messages, determine which speaker is the machine?).

See TURING MACHINE.

Turing machine   A mathematical idealization of a computing automaton similar in some ways to real computing machines.

In general, a Turing machine has a finite number of distinct internal states and one or more potentially infinite tapes on which it can read, write, and perform shifting operations. It should be noted that in the Turing machine the read/write head, and not the tape, is shifted.

A Turing machine may be classified by the number s of distinct internal states that it has, and by the number n of distinct characters that it can recognize, the number n thus representing the size of its alphabet. The number of tapes available is less significant than n or s since all finite multiple-tape operations can be simulated on one infinite tape.

The Turing machine performs, according to a fixed rule, the operations of tape reading or writing, moving the read/write head, and changing to a new internal state. The rule selected for execution depends only on the present state and the unique letter of the alphabet currently being scanned on the tape. Thus, there are sn distinct rules, and the value of the product sn is often used as a measure of the complexity of the Turing machine design (this oversimplification is somewhat equivalent to that of rating cars by their horsepower, or computers by their access or cycle time).

Consider, for example, a Turing machine having three states, 1, 2, 3 (thus $s = 3$), and a two-letter alphabet 0 and 1 (thus $n = 2$). The product sn is equal to 6. The rules, which *are* the Turing machine, will be set to be:

State 1:
$$\begin{cases} \text{If scan} = 0 & \text{write 1} & \text{shift right 1} & \text{go to state 2} \\ \text{If scan} = 1 & \text{write 1} & \text{shift left 1} & \text{go to state 3} \end{cases}$$

State 2:
$$\begin{cases} \text{If scan} = 0 & \text{write 1} & \text{shift left 1} & \text{go to state 1} \\ \text{If scan} = 1 & \text{write 1} & \text{shift right 1} & \text{go to state 2} \end{cases}$$

State 3:
$$\begin{cases} \text{If scan} = 0 & \text{write 1} & \text{shift left 1} & \text{go to state 2} \\ \text{If scan} = 1 & \text{write 0} & \text{shift right 1} & \text{stop} \end{cases}$$

The stop instruction must be present, or computations would never come to an end.

These rules can be presented in a more compact fashion by means of quintuples of numbers:

(1,0:1,1,2)
(1,1:1,−1,3)
(2,0:1,−1,1)
(2,1:1,1,2)
(3,0:1,−1,2)
(3,1:0,1,0)

This form is essentially the one used by A. M. Turing in his 1936 presentation. Each quintuple is to be interpreted as follows:

First digit: the state.

Second digit: value of the currently scanned letter. The first two digits represent the inputs, or name of the rule: for instance, rule 2,0.

Third digit: the letter to be written in the current square.

Fourth digit: the movement director: -1 if the shift is to the left, 0 for no movement, 1 for a right shift (if multiple shifts are allowed, the magnitude of the digit will indicate by how many letter spaces the read/write head must be moved).

Fifth digit: the state to be entered before selecting the next rule; 0 denotes stop.

In a tabular form, this Turing machine can be presented as follows:

Letter	State 1			Letter	State 2			Letter	State 3		
0	1	1	2	0	1	−1	1	0	1	−1	2
1	1	−1	3	1	1	1	2	1	0	1	0

Suppose that the Turing machine is started in state $s = 1$; the tape will be represented by a section of itself, and below the part of the tape to be scanned will be indicated the internal state designator. Initially, the configuration will appear as follows:

0	0	0	0	0	0	0	0

1

This configuration calls for rule 1,0 which states that a 1 must be written in the square, the head must be shifted one place to the right, and the state $s = 2$ must be called. The configuration now appears as follows:

0	0	0	0	1	0	0	0

2

This configuration calls for rule 2,0 whch results in

0	0	0	0	1	1	0	0

1

Successively, then:

rule 1, 1:

0	0	0	0	1	1	0	0

3

rule 3, 0:

0	0	0	1	1	1	0	0

2

rule 2, 0:

0	0	1	1	1	1	0	0

1

rule 1, 0:

0	1	1	1	1	1	0	0

2

rule 2, 1:

0	1	1	1	1	1	0	0

2

rule 2, 1:

0	1	1	1	1	1	0	0

2

rule 2, 1:

0	1	1	1	1	1	0	0

2

rule 2, 1:

0	1	1	1	1	1	0	0

2

rule 2, 0:

0	1	1	1	1	1	1	0

1

rule 1, 1:

0	1	1	1	1	1	1	0

3

rule 3, 1:

0	1	1	1	0	1	1	0

0

This Turing machine has thus computed the number 111011.

No Turing machine has ever been physically constructed or realized in hardware as a device for its own sake, but general-purpose digital computers have been programmed to simulate Turing machines.   The purpose of such simulations has little, if anything, to do with real computers: Turing machines are used by mathematicians in defining the concept of computability. A well-defined number is said to be computable if some Turing machine can calculate this number in a finite number of steps; the number is noncomputable otherwise. Related to the concept of computability is the concept of decidability: a well-defined question will be nondecidable if an infinite amount of computation is required to answer it.

See UNIVERSAL TURING MACHINE.

turnaround system   In character recognition, a system in which the input data to be read are printed by the computer with which the reader is associated (see accompanying illustration).

An application of such a hardware-dependent system may be found in the area of invoice billing, and the subsequent recording of payments.

Synonymous with REENTRY SYSTEM. Contrast with OPEN-ENDED SYSTEM.

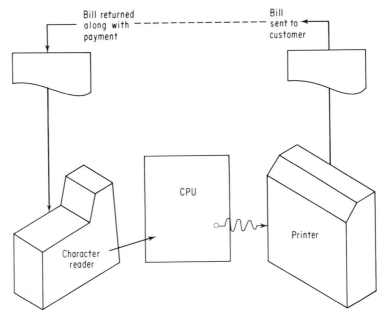

Document travel in a turnaround system.

turnaround time   The delay between submission of a job and its completion. Turnaround time can be measured fairly well, but may have various definitions.

To an individual user, it may include delays waiting to get on the computer and waiting until the output gets delivered to him. To a computer, it is time-off minus time-on. If several computers are involved, as in a satellite doing off-line printing for a large computer, turnaround time definition becomes even more involved.

Time-sharing is one means of reducing turnaround time while also possibly reducing throughput. See discussion under THROUGHPUT.

TV camera scanner   In optical character recognition (OCR), a device that images an input character onto a sensitive photoconductive target of a camera tube, thereby developing an electric charge pattern on the inner surface of the target. This pattern is then explored by a scanning beam which traces out a rectangular pattern with the result that a waveform is produced which represents the character's most probable identity.

One unique aspect of camera tube scanners is the ability to store a pattern for scanning subsequent to the exposure of the target. (This is possible because the removal of incident light on the outside of the tube does not affect the pattern on the tube's inner surface.) This obvious advantage has been applied in the area of moving documents where a high-intensity flash of short duration makes it possible to effectively "freeze" all motion. The resultant brief exposure can then be stored on the photoconductive target for eventual scanning.

The field of TV camera scanning is still in its infancy with most of the experimentation being conducted with regard for the target materials utilized.

two-out-of-five code   An encoding of the decimal digits using five binary bits and having the property that every code contains two 1's and three 0's.

There are exactly 10 two-out-of-five code combinations, so that every possible code must use the following patterns:

```
0 0 0 1 1    0
0 0 1 0 1    1
0 0 1 1 0    2
0 1 0 0 1    3
0 1 0 1 0    4
0 1 1 0 0    5
1 0 0 0 1    6
1 0 0 1 0    7
1 0 1 0 0    8
1 1 0 0 0    9
```

The order in which the patterns are assigned to digits is somewhat arbitrary, for in not more than four cases can a digit be expressed as its true binary value.

It is obvious from the above table that no systematic means of performing arithmetic with these codes exists, and so any arithmetic must be performed by a process equivalent to a table look-up of two digit sums and differences.

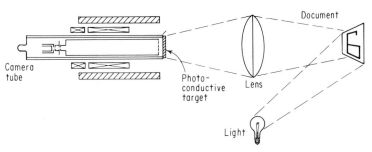

TV camera scanner.

The virtue of two-out-of-five codes is their adaptability to hardware detection of errors (invalid codes). The check circuit can merely count 1-bits, without regard to pattern or value. This check can detect all 1-, 3-, or 5-bit errors, 19 out of 25 of all 2-bit errors, and 2 out of 5 of all 4-bit errors.

A disadvantage of two-out-of-five codes is the requirement of five bits per digit, where four bits are normally sufficient.

The two-out-of-five code was first used in the Bell Labs Model II computer (1943), the first computer to employ built-in checking facilities. It is also used in the IBM 7070 series (transistor and core replacement for the tube and drum biquinary IBM 650).

two's complement In binary notation, a two's complement is a numeral obtained by changing each original 0 to 1, each original 1 to 0, and adding 1 to the rightmost position of the resulting numeral, while in binary arithmetic, a two's complement is a number derived from a given n-bit number by requiring the two numbers to sum to a value of 2^n.

The two definitions are equivalent, as may be observed from the following example:

1 0 1 1 0 1 1	original numeral
0 1 0 0 1 0 0	each bit complemented (one's complement of numeral)
0 1 0 0 1 0 1	add one for two's complement
1 1 1 1 1 1 1	sum of original + one's complement
1 0 0 0 0 0 0 0	sum of original + two's complement

Suppose that only n bits were retained in any numeral (fixed-length arithmetic). Then any binary number and its n-bit two's complement would sum to zero (with high-order overflow). This means that the two's complement has some properties similar to the negative of a number (overflow properties excluded). This permits many binary computers to use two's complement to represent negative numbers.

When using two's complement for negatives, the leftmost bit is interpreted as a sign bit ($0 = +$, $1 = -$), and the most significant bit is the leftmost bit with value different from the sign bit (that is, positive numbers are left-filled with 0's but begin with leading 1, while negative numbers are filled with leading 1's, but begin with leading 0). Note that it is impossible to represent -0 in this way, and that the largest magnitude of a negative number is one greater in magnitude than the largest positive number.

See TRUE COMPLEMENT, ONE'S COMPLEMENT.

type face   In character recognition, a physical unit of printing type, on which appears a character of particular size and style.

type font   In character recognition, a collection of type representing a complete character set, each member of which is constructed from the same style and size.

U

U format   A record format which the input/output control system treats as completely unknown and unpredictable.

When manipulating U-format records, the operating system or input/output control system (IOCS) merely moves data without attempting to examine or interpret them.   For output, it causes a record of specified length to be written, where the length of each record must be independently indicated by the program.   For input, one entire record is read and its size is noted.   If the input record exceeds the buffer size, the excess characters are ignored, and a long record indication is made available to the program.   The interpretation of the record, blocking and unblocking, must be performed by the problem program.

unary operation   An operation in which only a single operand is required to produce a unique result.

Examples of unary operations are: negation, complementation, square root, transpose, inverse, conjugate.

Most operations of mathematics, however, are binary (not to be confused with binary arithmetic) or dyadic (same as binary). A dyadic operation normally needs two operands.

Synonymous with MONADIC OPERATION.

underflow A condition that prevails when the result of an arithmetic operation is smaller in magnitude than the smallest nonzero quantity that can be represented in the intended result storage area.

A digital computer will almost always replace the result by zero when an underflow occurs. In most cases this causes only a small error, or no error at all if the result is used in addition or subtraction. In some other cases, multiplication or division, this approximation by zero completely destroys the validity of further calculations.

Some computers cannot recognize underflow as a possible error condition: this denies the programmer the opportunity to recover from an error.

In floating-point arithmetic, two kinds of underflow can occur: mantissa underflow (loss of all significant digits as with subtraction of equal nonzero numerals), and exponent underflow (attempting to develop an out-of-range exponent without loss of mantissa digits, as in multiplication of two small-magnitude numbers). Some computers distinguish these two cases, others don't.

Exponent underflow can be prevented (or cured) by scaling, but mantissa underflow can be cured only by double-precision (or higher-precision) arithmetic.

Compare with OVERFLOW.

universal Turing machine A Turing machine that can simulate any Turing machine.

A Turing machine is, in fact, not a machine but a set of mathematical rules and conventions which, taken together, have certain computer-like properties. A Turing machine has s distinct internal states and recognizes an alphabet of n distinct letters. It has one or more potentially infinite tapes or linear sequences of cells which can be written onto or read from. For each combination of internal state and letters read from the tapes, a specific rule spells out what letters are to be written on the tapes, what parts of the tapes must be read next, and what state is to be entered next.

It is possible to visualize a Turing machine as a computer having s central memory addresses, each address holding n different conditional instructions, and only one instruction per address to be executed, depending on the value of the letter currently scanned.

It is clear that any sufficiently complex Turing machine can be programmed (by properly preparing the initial contents of the tapes) to simulate any other Turing machine. There is, therefore, little interest in general-purpose Turing machines. The challenge is, rather, to design the simplest Turing machine that can simulate all other Turing machines, and in particular, one other universal Turing machine. Normally, the designer tries to minimize the product sn of his machine, but minimum s designs are also attempted (the lower bound of n being 2 when using binaries). For example, minimizing sn can be achieved by replacing many tapes by one tape on which the original tapes are interleaved, or by encoding large alphabets (that is, a large n) in smaller alphabets by using combinations of letters to represent each original letter. Reduction in the value of s or n will normally correspond to an increase of n or s, so that judicious thought must be given to such modifications.

As a rule, every simplification brought to a Turing machine will result in a longer running time (that is, in a greater number of steps required to do the problem). But, a Turing machine being an abstraction, each step can be theoretically performed in a theoretically vanishing time. As it seems to appear, the search for the simplest universal Turing machine is an academic exercise of uncertain value (at this time) in the concrete computer world.

unpack   To recover the individual data items contained in packed data, and more specifically, to convert a packed decimal number into individual digits (and sometimes a sign).

A digital computer memory is organized into fundamental units of equal size. Units of 5, 6, or 7 bits are called characters; 4 bits may be a digit, 8 bits a byte; 12 or more bits may constitute a word which may or may not be accessible in less than full-size subunits.

The size is always a compromise, balancing various factors. Short-word-length machines (24 bits or less) must often use two or more words per number or instruction. Long-word-length computers (36 bits or more, especially 48 or 60 bits) can often hold several numbers or instructions in one word. This use of multiple data per word is called packing, and saves space in memory. Unpacking is required to recover an individual item from memory.

For instance, to unpack a 48-bit word (Honeywell 800) with three 16-bit items of data, the word must be loaded into a register, and the register shifted right 0, 16, or 32 bits, the register then containing the desired item. In the case of the CDC 6600 with two, three, or four instructions (15 or 30 bits) per 60-bit memory word, the words are unpacked by hardware.

A packed decimal is a particular example of this principle. As read in from a punched card or tape, each digit normally fills an 8-bit byte: This, however, is an unpacked decimal, and is wasteful of space. Four bits could represent any of 10 digits, 2 signs, or 4 other special characters. Consequently, 2 digits or a digit and a sign, could be packed into each byte. To unpack such a word, the program extracts the upper 4 bits, shifts right 4 bits, stores in location A, and stores the remaining 4 bits in rightmost 4 bits of location A + 1. If digital values are found, the program adds to A and A + 1 the upper 4 bits (zone bits) of the required EBCDIC or ASCII code; then the sign is converted to the proper sign byte.

Also, a computer instruction directing that a packed decimal datum is to be converted to unpacked (display) format.

utility routine   A program or routine of general usefulness, usually not very complicated, and applicable to many jobs or purposes.

There are tasks that any data processing center must perform, such as card-to-tape conversions. A program for this purpose can be written once and used by every program-compatible computer.

Other utility routines include memory dumps, tape dumps, and routines to write header labels on new tapes and disk packs.

On small-scale computers, the utility routines are normally stand-alone programs (not used with an operating system) and must be individually loaded by the operator. On large-scale computers, the operating system generally provides most or all utility routines, which can be called (or activated) by the operator by various simple procedures such as a console call card, or by typewriter key-in. Intermediate-scale computers use a combination of both types.

V

variable A data item, or a specific area in main memory, that can assume any of a number of values.

A variable is a number, item, or field of storage that is expected to have several values during the execution of a program. The simplest example of such a variable is a counter, incremented by one for each item processed, and used to count and generate sequence (or serial) numbers. Such a counter must change its value, or it would be useless as such.

The ability to change the contents of memory is the keystone of the power of stored-program digital computers. Without this power, memory would be nearly useless, and not much better than a giant plugboard. Variable data permit adapting to changing conditions, processing multiple types of data records, modifying instructions, and so on.

variable-cycle operation An operation that requires a variable number of regularly timed execution cycles for its completion.

Most computer instructions that are data-dependent require different times for complete execution, depending on the value of the datum being manipulated. Arithmetic, logical, and testing operations usually fall into this class, and so do variable-cycle operations. Computer instructions that manipulate data without examining them are normally completed in a constant time, and so are fixed-cycle operations (which see). Data-moving operations are usually in this latter class.

variable-length record   A data or file format that does not specify exactly the size of each individual record, but allows each record to be exactly as long as needed, up to a fixed maximum size.

The length of a variable-length record may be indicated by a character count or size indicator, at the beginning of the record itself, or it may be delimited by record gaps without an explicit count field.   Blocked variable-length records must have size-indicator fields. If there are variable numbers of records per block, a block record count must also be given.

The use of variable-length records conserves storage space, especially on magnetic tape (on disks and drums, a variable-length record makes it difficult to predict the location of the next record, and it may cause wasted space by unevenly filling the tracks).

variable point   A system of numeration in which the location of the decimal point is indicated by a special character at that position.

If it is not practical to have the radix point (for instance, the decimal point in the decimal system) at the same location in every numeral during some process, provision must then be made for marking a variable-point location for every numeral.   Two alternative methods may be used: floating point or variable point.

The floating-point method uses an auxiliary (small) numeral to designate the location of the point.   This permits calculation of the point-aligning shift requirements and allows points to lie well beyond the numeral itself.   Thus floating point is used when many calculations are to be performed, as in scientific work.

Variable-point numerals are easily converted to (or are already identical with) the common, human-understood numerals (for example: 18.75, 0.98, 212.).   However, point-alignment shifts must be calculated by scanning both numerals, which is time-consuming.   Also, it is difficult (but rarely necessary) for the point to lie beyond the limits of the represented digits.

Venn diagram   A graphical means of showing relationships between mathematical sets.   The diagrams are symbolic or representative, and usually bear no physical resemblence to the sets under discussion.

Commonly, a Venn diagram is contained within a rectangle (which represents the universe of discourse, the totality of all members of all sets under examination). Each set is represented by a circle, enclosing a letter naming the set. Shading or crosshatching is often used to enhance clarity.

See accompanying illustration.

Examples:

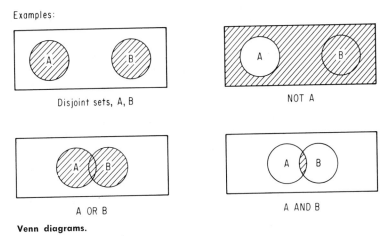

Disjoint sets, A, B

NOT A

A OR B

A AND B

Venn diagrams.

verb In COBOL, the action indicating part of an unconditional statement.

A statement in COBOL specifies an action to be performed and the data to be operated on. Each statement of the PROCEDURE DIVISION (except conditional IF statements) begins with a verb, and each verb marks the beginning of a statement.

For example:

ADD A TO B GIVING C
GO TO NEXT-STEP-TEST
WRITE LISTOUT BEFORE ADVANCING TWO LINES

The similarity to English verbs is evident. Note that ADVANC-ING, GIVING, are not verbs, but reserved words with special meanings. (They are not called adverbs, but are used to modify verbs.)

verify To determine whether an operation has been completed correctly, and in particular, to check the accuracy of keypunching by using a keypunchlike, nonpunching but card-reading verifier.

In EDP operations, it is assumed that the computer makes few mistakes (on checked-out programs) but will certainly produce erroneous results if fed incorrect input (GIGO: garbage in, garbage out).. As most input is prepared by human beings, great care should be taken to ensure correctness before the computer gets the data.

Today, most computer input begins as manually punched 80-column cards. A device called a verifier has been developed for checking card punching semimechanically. This device mimics key-punch machine operation, but reads prepunched cards without punching any new holes. If the card does not agree with keyboard input in some column, the verifier lights up, buzzes, and stops to alert the operator. If an error is discovered, a shallow notch may be punched above the suspect column, to pinpoint corrective activity later. When no error is found on a card, a notch may be cut on the edge (alongside column 80) to indicate a correct card. When a deck is removed from the verifier, the edge notches form a groove in which the un-notched cards are conspicuous. The error cards are repunched, verified, and placed in the deck. An uninterrupted groove signals that a deck is correct. The notches do not affect card-reading devices.

V format   A data record format in which the logical records are of variable length and each record begins with a record length indication. If V-format records are blocked, the block must begin with either a number-of-logical-records indicator or a total-length-of-block indicator.

The size indications at the beginning of logical and physical records are used by the input/output control system or operating-system service routine for blocking and unblocking. Unblocked V-format records are handled in a manner akin to that of U-format records except that the size indication is known to appear at the front of the record.

V-format records always save time and space on tape storage media, for every physical record on a tape can be written at its own true length. On external storage devices having tracks of known and finite capacity (disks, drums, magnetic cards, data cells), it is possible to waste storage by poor utilization of track capacity. Fixed-format records can often be adjusted in size to properly fill each track, and thus result in more efficient processing.

void   In optical character recognition (OCR), an island of insufficiently inked paper within the area of the intended character stroke.

A void is measured by its largest dimension.

The number and maximum permissible size of voids are functions of the overall character stroke length; with the allowance varying between optical scanners, the individual characters themselves, and even between the component elements of a given character.

Contrast with BREAKTHROUGH.

volatile storage A storage device that must be continually supplied with energy, or it will lose its retained data.

Electrostatic CRT, acoustic delay line, capacitor-stored voltage, transistor flip-flop are examples of volatile storages.

The disadvantage of volatile storage is that data will disappear if the power is accidentally, or intentionally, removed. In spite of this, volatile storage is used because of its very fast access time, low cost, or both.

Nonvolatile storage (almost all magnetic; some optical and some punched-hole media) will hold onto its data through any mishaps.

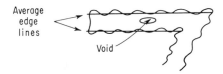

Example of void.

volume A single unit of external storage, all of which can be read or written by a single access mechanism or I/O device.

A volume usually is an entire disk, tape, or drum. Some disks are divided into several concentric sectors, each sector being provided with its own read/write head, its own rate of data transfer, and track capacity. In this case, each sector is a volume, and the volumes may be treated as logically independent.

When a portion of recording medium is dismountable, each mounting unit is a volume. Thus a disk pack is a volume, but a disk-pack drive is not. Dismountable volumes are identified by labels, both recorded and operator-readable. Nondismountable volumes are usually identified by their hardware address.

volume table of contents (VTOC) An index record near the beginning of each volume, which records the name, location, and extent of every file or data set residing on that particular volume. Usually not found on magnetic tapes, but often required on all disk packs and drums.

See INDEX, VOLUME.

W

wait A condition which indicates that a task cannot continue execution until some specified event or combination of events occurs. Also, a macroinstruction used by a task to place itself in wait state, and to indicate the event(s) being waited upon.

In a nonmultiprogramming environment a wait means that a computer must mark time or loop endlessly until an interrupt signals the occurrence of an event. When the required events are all noted, the operating system returns control to the program.

In a multiprogramming or multitasking computer a wait state enables other, ready or nonwaiting, tasks to execute while the waiting task cannot proceed. The task dispatcher keeps track of the wait/ready status of all tasks, and gives control of the central processing unit to the ready task of highest priority.

A hardware wait (no instructions are being executed) is known as a pause, halt, or stop, but is not called wait.

See MULTIPROGRAMMING, MULTITASK OPERATION.

weighted area masks In character recognition, a set of characters (each character residing in the character reader in the form of weighted points) which theoretically render all input specimens unique, regardless of the size or style.

Weighted area masks are invoked during the property-detection phase of character recognition. At that time the identity of the input specimen is determined on a continuous probability basis according to their effectiveness in the discrimination of the various type fonts.

The more obvious advantages of the weighted area mask result from less stringent requirements on the paper and printing ink employed, as well as its facility to process various document types.

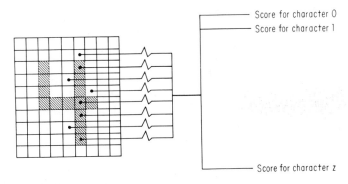

Score for character 0
Score for character 1

Score for character z

Weighted area mask.

Wiener, Norbert (1894–1964)   American cyberneticist and computer engineer.

Wiener originally developed the concepts by means of which simple analog computers which solved ordinary differential equations could be expanded to handle partial differential equations. To increase the number of data that the machine could deal with, Wiener devised televisionlike scanning techniques to represent functions of more than one variable.

He designed the central arithmetic unit to be digital rather than analog in order to reduce cumulative errors induced in repeated elementary operations. His concern with speed led him to replace electromechanical devices by vacuum tubes, and time-consuming logical decisions made by the operator by programs—that is, feeding into the computer the entire sequence of operations and decisions to be performed. Wiener pointed out that binary arithmetic is more economical than decimal arithmetic.

He is probably best known through his coinage of the word CYBERNETICS (which see).

word   The fundamental unit of storage capacity for a digital computer, almost always considered to be more than 8 bits in length.

Computers with words less than 9 bits long call the words bytes, characters, or digits (decimal).

In almost all cases, words are of fixed length. Today sizes of 12, 16, 24, 32, 36, 48 bits are common (multiples of 6 or 8), but odd sizes (18 bits, 51 bits, 60 bits) are also used. Each cycle of memory stores or retrieves one (and occasionally two) words. The size of the word indicates the power of the computer. Short words are cheaper, but they limit instruction, address, and data accuracy capability.

Long words admit powerful instructions, many addresses, higher-accuracy numbers or packed data items, but they cost more to store and to process (the cost of memory per bit is insensitive to word length, but higher-multiplicity data paths must be used for longer words).

Some computers feature variable word length. This concept treats memory as individually addressable characters (bytes, digits). A word is denoted by addressing the character at one end, and specifying its length (in positions) or denoting the other end by a punctuation bit (word mark).

word length   The number of bits, digits, characters, or bytes in one word.

There are two distinct cases to be observed: fixed-word-length computers, and variable-word-length computers.

In fixed-word-length computers (the majority of the second-generation designs), a word length is fixed by the designer of the hardware. Long words increase both power and cost of processor, very short words (12 bits) give trouble addressing large memories in short-length instructions. Every memory cycle delivers one (sometimes two) words. Fixed-word-length computers almost always have accumulators or registers one word long in which arithmetic is performed.

Variable-word-length computers require definition of operand size with every instruction that they execute. Either the data contain size-delimiting punctuation (word marks, group marks, etc.), or the instructions contain length-specifying fields. Word length has meaning for variable-length computers, but it is subject to programmer redefinition at any time.

word mark   A nondata punctuation bit used to delimit a word in a variable-word-length computer.

Each character typically consists of 6 data bits, a check or parity bit, a word-mark bit, and possibly additional bits (item-mark punctuation bit in the Honeywell 200).

The data bit holds information, the parity bit verifies accuracy, and the word mark stops move or arithmetic operations. Each instruction must begin with a word mark, for instructions may be of variable length, too.

word time   The time elapsed between the moment that the first bit of a word is read and the moment that the first bit of the next word is read from a storage device of a cyclic access type (such as from a drum, disk, or circulating delay line). This time is composed of the time required to read the entire word and the time required to cover the interword gap.

Word time plays the same role in drum-type main-memory computers that cycle time does in core main-memory computers. This time forms the fundamental pulse beat, or rhythm, of the computer, and all activities must be calculated in multiples or submultiples of word time or cycle time.

On some computers, medium-speed logic is interfaced with very high-speed delay-line storage. The delay line interleaves the bits of all the words that it contains, so that the same time is essentially required to read all of any one word. This gives the cyclic memory most of the characteristics of random-access main memories.

working storage   An area of main memory that is reserved by the programmer for storing temporary or intermediate values. In COBOL, WORKING STORAGE is a section in the DATA DIVISION used for describing the name, structure, usage, and initial value of program variables that are neither constants nor records of I/O files.

The size and contents of working storage are dictated by the immediate needs of the program. They will usually be in different places from program to program, and may change size or usage during the execution of any one program.

The working storage contains such intermediate variables as subtotals and working sums, indicators showing actions to be performed or options to be used, line counters for page-skipping purposes, and the title on the most recently read header card.

write   To transmit data from any source onto an external storage medium. In COBOL, FORTRAN, and many other languages, WRITE is a command directing that an output operation be performed.

The most common usage of write means to record on a moving magnetic surface (tape, disk, drum, cram-type device); whereas print is used for recording on paper with ink; punch is reserved for card or paper-tape recording; and recording into static memory (core, etc.) is called store or write, but more usually store. An electron beam writes on the phosphor screen of a CRT display.

If an arbitrary output medium can be used, write is the preferred verb.

X

X punch In an 80-column punched card, the hole in the second row from the top.

An X punch is used to denote a minus sign on an arithmetic quantity, and in specified nonarithmetic columns, to differentiate various types of cards intermixed in a deck. The combination of digit punches 1 through 9 and X punch forms the Hollerith codes J through R.

A standard card has 12 rows and 80 columns. The rows are named (and corresponding punches called) from top to bottom:

12 ROW or Y ROW or R ROW
11 ROW or X ROW
 0 ROW
 1 ROW
 2 ROW

  . . . .
 8 ROW
 9 ROW

The X and Y ROWS (and sometimes, when in combination with a

numeric punch, the 0 ROW) are called zone rows. Punches 1 through 9 are numeric punches. Zero is either numeric or zone, depending on whether it is the highest punch in a multipunched column or not.

Care must be taken to distinguish X overpunches from alphabetic (Hollerith) X punches. Alphabetic X has a zero-zone punch but no X overpunch.

See PUNCHED CARD.

Y

Y punch   In a standard punched card, a hole in the topmost row.

In numeric fields, it is used to indicate + sign, and in nonnumeric columns the presence or absence of a Y punch can be used to distinguish various kinds of cards in a deck.

For instance:

A master card may have a Y punch in column 5.

A submaster card may have a Y punch in column 12.

A detail card may have a Y punch in column 80.

The Y row is also called the 12 row (the opposite edge is the 9 row) or, sometimes, the R row.

See x PUNCH, particularly the last paragraph which applies equally well to Y overpunches.

Z

zero-level address   The operand contained in an instruction so structured as to make immediate use of the operand.

In the majority of digital computer instructions, the required operands are referred to by their locations or addresses. Thus, to add the quantity 1 to some number X, the required instructions would appear basically as follows:

PLACE CONTENTS OF 3212 IN ACCUMULATOR
ADD CONTENTS OF 4333 TO ACCUMULATOR

The computer, after interpreting these instructions, must fetch the content of location 3212 (the value X), place it in the accumulator, and then fetch the content of location 4333 (the value 1) which it then adds to X. But the operand 1 is a datum smaller (that is, more compact) than the address required to identify it.

Zero-level addressing, when used with the second instruction in the above example, would result in the following instructions:

PLACE CONTENTS OF 3212 IN ACCUMULATOR
ADD 1 TO ACCUMULATOR

Two immediate benefits are obtained from zero-level addressing:

1. Memory space is saved by not having to store small constant operands.

2. Time is saved by not having to cycle the memory to gain access to small constant operands.

The computer must be advised that zero-level addressing is being used. This is generally done in either of two ways: by means of special operation codes, or by means of indications stored in the address part of the instruction.

Some computers, such as the IBM 7090, provide zero-level addressing for index-register operations but not for general arithmetic usage. This is justified by the index-register capacity being exactly equal to the instruction-address-part capacity. As a consequence, the same program will perform address arithmetic in the index registers and refer to the arithmetic registers only for multiply/divide operations.

zero suppression A process of replacing leading (nonsignificant) zeros in a numeral by blanks.

Zero suppression is an editing operation designed to make computable (machine-format) numerals into human-readable format.

Users can be confused and mislead by leading zeros: they may hide the true size of the numeral and make it harder to grasp at a glance. Computers, on the other hand, are confused (?) by leading blanks since they are not computable digits (certain computers, the Honeywell 200 for example, are so constructed that blanks have the arithmetic properties of zeros).

example:

Internal computer form	After zero suppression
0 0 0 0 0 1	1
0 0 3 1 4 4	3144
9 8 2 7 0 6	982706
0 0 0 0 2 0	20

zone punch In a punched card, the 11 or 12 punch according to any code, the zero punch if another numeric punch is present in the same column, and sometimes the 8 and 9 punches in EBCDIC-coded cards.

The rows on a punched card are named as follows:

$$\left.\begin{array}{l} \text{12 or Y punch} \\[2em] \text{11 or X punch} \end{array}\right\} \text{zone punches}$$

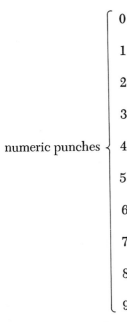

numeric punches $\begin{cases} 0 \\ 1 \\ 2 \\ 3 \\ 4 \\ 5 \\ 6 \\ 7 \\ 8 \\ 9 \end{cases}$

Multiple-punch coding, using zone punches and numeric punches in the same column for the representation of nonnumeric characters, began long before computers used cards as input/output media. The codes were designed for EAM equipment. The sorter could pick up all alphabetic characters by selecting 12, 11, 0, and no-zone cards and dumping into one of four different pockets. Each stack was then selected on the basis of the 1 to 9 punches. Thus, four groups of nine subtypes each produced 36 characters (alphabet and digits). In addition, blank, 11 only, 12 only, and 0–1 for the / symbol were recognized as special cases. As the need arose for new characters, these new characters were created by adding an 8 punch to existing combinations, resulting thus in additional double and triple-punched columns.

When computers appeared on the market, manufacturers were faced with the problem of converting the 12-row codes of punched cards into either 6-bit or 8-bit internal representation. So as not to increase the complexity of the hardware, and at the same time be compatible with existing code conventions, almost all codes were translated by placing the binary value of the numeric punches in the rightmost 4 bits of the internal character, and by translating each zone punch into the leftmost 2 or 4 bits of the code group. For instance, the Y punch could be represented by 1100000. The accompanying table shows a possible coding for card and computer of a standard character set.

Character	Card Code	Binary Code		Character	Card Code	Binary Code	
0	0	00	1010	O	11-6	10	0110
1	1	00	0001	P	11-7	10	0111
2	2	00	0010	Q	11-8	10	1000
3	3	00	0011	R	11-9	10	1001
4	4	00	0100	S	0-2	01	0010
5	5	00	0101	T	0-3	01	0011
6	6	00	0110	U	0-4	01	0100
7	7	00	0111	V	0-5	01	0101
8	8	00	1000	W	0-6	01	0110
9	9	00	1001	X	0-7	01	0111
A	12-1	11	0001	Y	0-8	01	1000
B	12-2	11	0010	Z	0-9	01	1001
C	12-3	11	0011	&	12	11	0000
D	12-4	11	0100	.	12-3-8	11	1011
E	12-5	11	0101	(	12-4-8	11	1100
F	12-6	11	0110	-	11	10	0000
G	12-7	11	0111	$	11-3-8	10	1011
H	12-8	11	1000	*	11-4-8	10	1100
I	12-9	11	1001	/	0-1	01	0001
J	11-1	10	0001	,	0-3-8	01	1011
K	11-2	10	0010	)	0-4-8	01	1100
L	11-3	10	0011	#	3-8	00	1011
M	11-4	10	0100	@	4-8	00	1100
N	11-5	10	0101	Blank		00	0000

Bibliography

This bibliography does not contain hard-to-find books, out-of-print books, trade magazines, or the vast amount of literature issued by computer manufacturers. To have included such items would have doubled the size (and the cost) of this volume and defeated the very purpose of a practical bibliography.

The bibliography has been divided into three sections: systems, computers, and programming. An attempt was made, in each section, to select the work best representative for the whole section. This attempt should not be construed as an endeavor to select the best book out of many good books but, rather, as an endeavor to single out the one book which appeared to cover the whole sections under consideration.

SYSTEMS

Johnson, Kast, Rosenzweig, *The Theory and Management of Systems,* McGraw-Hill, New York, 1967.

A remarkably well-planned and well-written book covering systems concepts, applications, implementations, and what trends such systems are taking for the immediate future. The last pages of the book (pp. 432–488) cover the work involved in setting up a fully integrated system in an actual case:

the Weyerhaeuser Company. A lucid presentation takes the reader through the maze of evolution, feasibility study, responsibilities, conclusions, recommendations, phases of implementation, detailed system design, and inevitable organizational adjustments. A fascinating bird's eye view of the complete system is offered on a double-page spread (pp. 464–465) by means of a streamlined chart aptly entitled "Whole Cotton Pickin' Mess."

ALBERS, H.: *Organized Executive Action*, Wiley, New York, 1961.

ANSHEN and BACH: *Manager and Corporations 1985*, McGraw-Hill, New York, 1960.

AWAD, E.: *Automatic Data Processing*, Prentice-Hall, Englewood Cliffs, N.J., 1966.

AWAD, E.: *Business Data Processing*, Prentice-Hall, Englewood Cliffs, N.J., 1965.

BECKER and HAYES: *Information Storage and Retrieval: Tools, Elements, Theories*, Wiley, New York, 1964.

BEER, S.: *Cybernetics and Management*, Wiley, New York, 1964.

BITTEL, MELDEN, RICE: *Practical Automation*, McGraw-Hill, New York, 1957.

BONINI, JAEDICKE, WAGNER: *Management Controls*, McGraw-Hill, New York, 1964.

BOULDING and SPIVEY: *Linear Programming and the Theory of the Firm*, Macmillan, New York, 1960.

BRANDON, D.: *Management Standards for Data Processing*, Van Nostrand, Princeton, N.J., 1963.

BUCHHOLZ, W.: *Planning a Computer System*, McGraw-Hill, New York, 1962.

BURCK: *Computer Revolution*, Harper & Row, New York, 1965.

CHERRY, C.: *On Human Communications*, MIT Press, Cambridge, Mass., 1966.

DESMONDE, W.: *Real Time Data Processing Systems*, Prentice-Hall, Englewood Cliffs, N.J., 1964.

ECKMAN, D.: *Systems: Research and Design*, Wiley, New York, 1961.

ENRICK, N.: *Management Planning: A Systems Approach*, McGraw-Hill, New York, 1967.

FISHER and SWINDLE: *Computer Programming Systems*, Holt, New York, 1964.

FRIELINK, A.: *Auditing Automatic Data Processing: A Survey of Papers on the Subject*, American Elsevier, New York, 1961.

GARRITY, J.: *Getting the Most out of Your Computer*, McKinsey, New York, 1963.

GREENBERGER, M. (ed.): *Management and the Computer of the Future*, MIT Press, Cambridge, Mass., 1962.

GREENBERGER, M. (ed.): *Computers and the World of the Future*, MIT Press, Cambridge, Mass., 1964.

GREGORY, VAN HORN: *Automatic Data-processing Systems*, Wadsworth, Belmont, Calif., 1965.

HAIMANN, T.: *Professional Managements: Theory and Practice*, Houghton-Mifflin, Boston, Mass., 1962.

HEIN, L.: *An Introduction to Electronic Data Processing for Business*, Van Nostrand, Princeton, N.J., 1961.

HODGES and ZIEGLER: *Managing the Industrial Concern*, Houghton-Mifflin, Boston, Mass., 1963.

KAUFMAN, F.: *Electronic Data Processing and Auditing*, Ronald, New York, 1961.

KENT, A.: *Textbook on Mechanized Information Retrieval*, Wiley, New York, 1962.

KENT, TAULBEE: *Electronic Information Handling*, Spartan, Washington, D.C., 1965.

KOZMETSKY and KIRCHER: *Electronic Computers and Management Control,* McGraw-Hill, New York, 1965.

LADEN and GILDERSLEEVE: *System Design for Computer Applications,* Wiley, New York, 1964.

LUXENBERG and KUEHN: *Display Systems Engineering,* McGraw-Hill, New York, 1968.

MALCOLM and ROWE: *Management Control Systems,* Wiley, New York, 1960.

McDONOUGH, A.: *Information Economics and Management Systems,* McGraw-Hill, New York, 1963.

McDONOUGH and GARRITT: *Management Systems, Working Concepts and Practices,* Irwin, Homewood, Ill., 1965.

McDONOUGH and GARRITT: *Management Controls in Systems Analysis,* Holt, New York.

McMILLAN and GONZALEZ: *Systems Analysis: A Computer Approach to Decision Models,* Irwin, Homewood, Ill., 1965.

McNERNEY, J.: *Installing and Using an Automatic Data Processing System: A Case Study for Management,* Boston: Graduate School of Business Administration, Harvard University, 1961.

MEADOW, C.: *The Analysis of Information Systems,* Wiley, New York, 1967.

OPTNER, S.: *Systems Analysis for Business Management,* Prentice-Hall, Englewood Cliffs, N.J., 1960.

PARKHILL: *The Challenge of the Computer Utility,* Addison-Wesley, Reading, Mass., 1966.

SCHMIDT and MEYERS: *Electronic Business Data Processing,* Holt, New York, 1963.

SCHMIDT and MEYERS: *Introduction to Computer Science and Data Processing,* Holt, New York, 1965.

SPRAGUE, R.: *Electronic Business Systems: Management Use of On-line-real-time Computers,* Ronald, New York, 1962.

VON HANDEL, P. (ed.): *Electronic Computers: Fundamentals, Systems and Applications,* Prentice-Hall, Englewood Cliffs, N.J., 1961.

WALLACE, E.: *Management Influence on the Design of Data Processing Systems: A Case Study,* Boston: Graduate School of Business Administration, Harvard University, 1961.

WIENER, N.: *Cybernetics,* Wiley, 2d ed., New York, -1961.

WILSON, I., and M. WILSON: *Information Computers and System Design,* Wiley, New York, 1965.

COMPUTERS

RICHARDS, R. K.: *Electronic Digital Systems,* Wiley, New York, 1966.

An encyclopedic work on computers with a wealth of details on little known facts about the origin and historical development of computers and computer components. This book should be considered as a must by anyone seriously interested in learning about computers or just simply interested in reading about computers. The mathematics encountered in chaps. 5 and 10 can be omitted by the lay reader without loss. An extensive bibliography, broken down by subject, is given at the end of each chapter.

ALT, F. (ed.): *Advances in Computers,* Academic, New York, 1963.

BARTEE, T.: *Digital Computer Fundamentals,* 2d ed., McGraw-Hill, New York, 1966.

BARTEE, LEBOW, and REED: *Theory and Design of Digital Machines,* McGraw-Hill, New York, 1962.

BELL, D.: *Intelligent Machines,* Blaisdell, New York, 1962.

BRITISH COMPUTER SOCIETY: *Optical Character Recognition,* 1967.

BUCHHOLZ, W.: *Planning a Computer System: Project Stretch,* McGraw-Hill, New York, 1962.

BUCKINGHAM: *Automation,* Harper & Row, New York, 1961.

CHAPIN, N.: *An Introduction to Automatic Computers,* Van Nostrand, Princeton, N.J., 1957.

CHU, Y.: *Digital Computer Design Fundamentals,* McGraw-Hill, New York, 1962.

CROWDER, N.: *The Arithmetic of Computers,* Doubleday, Garden City, N.Y., 1960.

DESMONDE, W.: *Computers and Their Uses,* Prentice-Hall, Englewood Cliffs, N.J., 1964.

ENGLEHARDT, S.: *Computers,* Pyramid Books, New York, 1962.

FEIGENBAUM and FELDMAN: *Computers and Thought,* McGraw-Hill, New York, 1963.

FLORES, I.: *Computer Logic,* Prentice-Hall, Englewood Cliffs, N.J., 1963.

FOSTER, D.: *Modern Automation,* Pitman, New York, 1963.

FREIBERGER and PRAGER: *Applications of Digital Computers,* Ginn, Boston, 1963.

GRUENBERGER and McCRACKEN: *Introduction to Electronic Computers,* Wiley, New York, 1963.

HALACY, D. S., JR.: *Computers, the Machines We Think with,* Harper & Row, New York, 1962.

HOFFMAN, W.: *Digital Information Processors,* Wiley, New York, 1962.

HUSKEY and KORN: *Computer Handbook,* McGraw-Hill, New York, 1961.

INMAN: *Fundamentals of Electronic Data Processing,* Prentice-Hall, Englewood Cliffs, N.J., 1964.

IRWIN, W.: *Digital Computer Principles,* Van Nostrand, Princeton, N.J., 1960.

MARTIN, E. W., JR.: *Electronic Data Processing: An Introduction,* Irwin, Homewood, Ill., 1961.

McCORMICK, E.: *Digital Computer Primer,* McGraw-Hill, New York, 1959.

PHISTER, M.: *Logical Design of Digital Computers,* Wiley, New York, 1958.

POSTLEY, J.: *Computers and People,* McGraw-Hill, New York, 1960.

RAISBECK, G.: *Information Theory: An Introduction for Scientists and Engineers,* MIT Press, Cambridge, Mass., 1965.

TAUBE, M.: *Computers and Common Sense,* Columbia University Press, New York, 1961.

VON NEUMANN, J.: *The Computer and the Brain,* Yale University Press, New Haven, 1958.

WEINSTEIN and KEIM: *Fundamentals of Digital Computers,* Holt, New York, 1965.

PROGRAMMING

KLERER and KORN (eds.): *Digital Computer User's Handbook,* McGraw-Hill, New York, 1967.

A programmer's vade mecum with its four main divisions covering programming and programming languages, numerical techniques, statistical methods, and computer applications. Chapter 1.6 by H. Bottenbruch,

Structure and Use of ALGOL 60, pp. 1.181–1.238, contains one of the most lucid and clear presentations of ALGOL to be found anywhere. Anyone with access to a computer, or even a time-sharing device, can experience the pleasure of learning ALGOL quickly and with all the depth desired. This handbook will prove to be a boon for all programmers, neophytes or professionals, and its programming language section can be read fruitfully by readers who have no desire to become professional programmers but who would like to understand the art of programming.

ANDERSON, D.: *Basic Computer Programming; IBM 1620 Fortran*, Appleton-Century-Crofts, New York, 1964.

ARDEN, B.: *An Introduction to Digital Computing*, Addison-Wesley, Reading, Mass., 1963.

BAUMANN, FELICIANO, BAUER, and SAMELSON: *Introduction to Algol*, Prentice-Hall, Englewood Cliffs, N.J., 1964.

BROOKS and IVERSON: *Automatic Data Processing*, Wiley, New York, 1963.

CHAPIN, N.: *Programming Computers for Business Applications*, McGraw-Hill, New York, 1961.

COLMAN and SMALLWOOD: *Computer Language: An Autoinstructional Introduction to Fortran*, McGraw-Hill, New York, 1962.

COMMITTEE OF THE CONFERENCE ON DATA SYSTEMS LANGUAGE: *Cobol—1961 Extended*, GPO, Washington, D.C., 1961.

CORBATO, F. and OTHERS, *Advanced Computer Programming: A Case Study of a Classroom Assembly Program*, MIT Press, Cambridge, Mass., 1963.

DEPARTMENT OF DEFENSE: *Cobol 65*, GPO, Washington, D.C., 1965.

DIJKSTRA, E.: *A Primer of Algol 60 Programming*, Academic, New York, 1962.

ENTWISLE, D.: *Auto-primer in Computer Programming for the IBM 1620 in Fortran*, Blaisdell, New York, 1963.

EVANS and PERRY: *Programming and Coding for Automatic Digital Computers*, McGraw-Hill, New York, 1961.

FENVES, S., and OTHERS: *Stress: A Reference Manual; A Problem-oriented Computer Language for Structural Engineering*, MIT Press, Cambridge, Mass. 1965.

FLORES, I.: *Computer Software*, Prentice-Hall, Englewood Cliffs, N.J., 1965.

GALLER, B.: *The Language of Computers*, McGraw-Hill, New York, 1962.

GARVIN, P.: *Natural Language and the Computer*, McGraw-Hill, New York, 1963.

GERMAIN, C.: *Programming the IBM 1620*, Prentice-Hall, Englewood Cliffs, N.J., 1962.

GREGORY and VAN HORN: *Automatic Data-processing Systems*, Wadsworth, Belmont, Calif., 1965.

GRUENBERGER and McCRACKEN: *Problem Solving with the IBM 1620*, Wiley, New York, 1963.

HALSTEAD, M.: *Machine-independent Computer Programming*, Spartan Books, Washington, D.C., 1962.

IVERSON, K.: *A Programming Language*, Wiley, New York, 1962.

LECHT, C. P.: *The Programmer's PL/1*, McGraw-Hill, New York, 1968.

LEDLEY, R.: *Programming and Utilizing Digital Computers*, McGraw-Hill, New York, 1962.

LEEDS and WEINBERG: *Computer Programming Fundamentals*, 2d ed., McGraw-Hill, New York, 1966.

LEESON and DIMITRY: *Basic Programming Concepts*, Holt, New York, 1963.

LYTEL, A.: *ABC's of Computer Programming*, Sams, Indianapolis, 1964.

McCRACKEN, D.: *A Guide to FORTRAN Programming*, Wiley, New York, 1961.

McCracken, D.: *A Guide to ALGOL Programming*, Wiley, New York, 1962.

McCracken, D.: *A Guide to COBOL Programming*, Wiley, New York, 1963.

McCracken and Dorn: *Numerical Methods and FORTRAN Programming*, Wiley, New York, 1964.

McRae, T.: *Introduction to Business Computer Programming*, Gee & Co., Ltd., London, 1963.

Metzger, R.: *Elementary Mathematical Programming*, Wiley, New York, 1958.

Nathan and Hanes: *Computer Programming Handbook: A Guide for Beginners*, Prentice-Hall, Englewood Cliffs, N.J., 1961.

Oakford, R.: *Introduction to Electronic Data Processing Equipment*, McGraw-Hill, New York, 1962.

O'Neal: *Electronic Data Processing Systems: A Self-instructional Manual*, Prentice-Hall, Englewood Cliffs, N.J., 1964.

Organick, E.: *A FORTRAN Primer*, Addison-Wesley, Reading, Mass., 1963.

Pennington, R.: *Introductory Computer Methods and Numerical Analysis*, Macmillan, New York, 1965.

Plumb, S.: *Introduction to FORTRAN*, McGraw-Hill, New York, 1964.

Ralston and Wilf: *Mathematical Methods for Digital Computers*, Wiley, New York, 1960.

Saxon, J.: *Cobol: A Self-instructional Manual*, Prentice-Hall, Englewood Cliffs, N.J., 1963.

Scott, T.: *Basic Computer Programming*, Doubleday, Garden City, N.Y., 1962.

Sherman, P.: *Programming and Coding Digital Computers*, Wiley, New York, 1963.

Smith and Johnson: *FORTRAN Autotester*, Wiley, New York, 1962.

Swallow and Price: *Elements of Computer Programming*, Holt, New York, 1965.

Wegner, P.: *An Introduction to Symbolic Programming*, Hafner, New York, 1963.

Wegner, P. (ed.): *Introduction to System Programming*, Academic Press, London, 1964.

index program

As a matter of interest, and because this is a book on computers, the INDEX for the CONDENSED COMPUTER ENCYCLOPEDIA was generated by a computer. The program was written in FORTRAN IV for an IBM 7094. The program, as such, can be run on other computers with little modification work. For the reader wishing to make use of such a concept, the program is reproduced on the following pages.

```
C
C
C      ****************************************************************
C
C
C          THIS PROGRAM WILL GENERATE BOOK INDEX DATA. THE INPUT CARDS
C              MUST FOLLOW THE PROGRAM AS DATA CARDS. THE OUTPUT WILL
C              BE ON UNIT 06 (SYSOU1).
C
C                      ***   INPUT  CARDS  ***
C
C              CARD1 =  COLS 1-10  NUMBERS  0-9
C                            11-36  ALPH     A-Z
C                            37    BLANK
C                            38    SLASH     /
C                            39    COMMA     ,
C                            40    DASH      -
C                            41    STAR      *
C
C
C          CARDS 1-N=COLS 1-69 ALPHANUMERIC HEADER ENDED BY 2 BLANKS
C          (PRE-SORTED)              OR COL 69 WHICHEVER OCCURS FIRST.
C
C                      70-80 PAGE NUMBER IN FREE FORM XXXA-XXXA,
C                            WHERE X IS 1-4 DIGITS, A IS A OR B
C                            , FORMS ARE   XXXX   XXXXA XXXX-XXX
C                            XXXXA-XXXX XXXX-XXXXA , ENDED
C                            BY 1 BLANK OR COL 80.
C
C          LAST CARD=COLS 1-6  ZZZZZZ
C
C                      ***   OUTPUT  ***
C
C          A KEYWORD WILL BE COL 1 TO FIRST BLANK. SLASHES ON INPUT
C              WILL BE PRINTED AS BLANK. FOR SUCCESSIVE CARDS WITH
C              EQUAL HEADERS - PAGE NUMBERS WILL BE SORTED ( TO A
C              MAX OF 100) AND PRINTED AS,XXXXA-XXXXA . FOR
C              UNEQUAL HEADERS BUT EQUAL KEYWORDS, THE KEYWORD WILL
C              BE STRIPPED OFF AND THE REST OF THE HEADER PRINTED.
C
C
C      ****************************************************************
C
C                      ***   ERRORS  ***
C
C          IF AN ERROR MESSAGE IS PRINTED, THE PROGRAM HAS ATTEMPTED
C              TO RESTART. AFTER 15 ERRORS IT WILL GIVE UP. IF AN
C              ERROR OCCURS SEVERAL CARDS WORTH OF DATA MAY BE LOST
C              . TO BE SAFE THE ENTIRE ALPHABETIC GROUP SHOULD BE
C              RERUN.
C
C      ****************************************************************
C
C
C
       0INTEGER  ALPH(50),
      1      NEWCD(80), OLDCD(80), NEWKEY(69), KEY(69), PRTIMG(132),
      2      LIST(200), PGARY(1100)
```

```
      0INTEGER CARDNO, PAGE, KEYSZ ,BLANK, SLASH, HDRSZ, COMMA, A,B,Z,
     1  DASH,SUM,TEMP,RVCNT,TWO,DIV
       INTEGER STAR
       LOGICAL FIRST, MATCH, END, ENDRUN
       EQUIVALENCE (STAR,ALPH(41))
       ENDRUN = .FALSE.
       CARDNO = 0
       FIRST = .TRUE.
       M = 0
C          DIVISOR OF 2**30 TO POSITION LEFTMOST CHAR TO RIGHTMOST
C          USEFUL ONLY FOR NON NEG NUMBERS FOR 7094
       DIV = 64*4096*4096
       PAGE = 1
       WRITE (6,1070) PAGE
       LINE = 1
       READ (5,1005) ALPH
  1005 FORMAT (50A1)
       A = ALPH(11)
       B = ALPH(12)
       Z = ALPH(36)
       BLANK = ALPH(37)
       SLASH = ALPH(38)
       COMMA = ALPH(39)
       DASH = ALPH(40)
    10 READ ( 5, 1000) NEWCD
  1000 FORMAT (80A1)
       CARDNO = CARDNO + 1
C
C     CHECK FOR END (6Z'S)
  5000 CONTINUE
       DO 20 I = 1,3
       IF ( NEWCD(I) .NE. Z ) GO TO 25
    20 CONTINUE
C     END OF RUN --- ALL CARDS READ
       ENDRUN = .TRUE.
C          IF FIRST CARD, EXECUTE SPECIAL ROUTINE
    25 IF (FIRST) GO TO 40
C     IF HEADING ARE NOT THE SAME, SORT PAGE NUMBERS AND PRINT
       DO 30 I=1,69
    30 IF (NEWCD(I) .NE. OLDCD(I)) GO TO 220
C     HEADINGS ARE THE SAME, ADD PAGE NUMBER TO THE LIST
C
C
C          COPY NEW PAGE NUMBER TO OLD PAGE NUMBER
    33 DO 35 I=70,80
    35 OLDCD(I) = NEWCD(I)
       GO TO   135
C              **         **         **         **
C
C     IF FIRST STORE NEW KEYWORD
    40 FIRST = .FALSE.
       DO 50 J = 1,69
       IF (NEWCD(J).EQ. BLANK ) GO TO 60
    50 NEWKEY(J) = NEWCD(J)
C     NO BLANKS, ERROR
    55 WRITE(6,1020) CARDNO, NEWCD
```

```
10200 FORMAT (1H1,45H *** NO BLANKS IN 69 COLS ON INPUT CARD NUMB ,I6/
     1          1H0,12H CONTENTS = , 80A1 )
      GO TO 400
C
C                **        **        **        **
C      BLANK FOUND IN 69 COLS, STORE SIZE
   60 NKEYSZ = J - 1
      GO TO 75
C      STORE NEW KEYWORD
C           *         *         *         *         *
C
C          ENTER HERE AFTER PRINTING LAST CARD. IF NEW KEYWORD IS UNEQUAL
C          TO THE OLD KEYWORD (OR FOR FIRST CARD, AFTER NAME CHECK).
C          NKEYSZ POINTS TO THE LAST CHAR IN KEYWORD.
C
C          IF NEW ALPHABETIC GROUP - SPACE PAPER
   70 IF (OLDCD(1) .EQ. NEWCD(1)) GO TO 75
      WRITE (6,1025)
 1025 FORMAT(1H0)
      LINE = LINE + 2
   75 DO 80 L = 1,NKEYSZ
   80 KEY(L) = NEWKEY(L)
      KEYSZ = NKEYSZ
C      CLEAR PRINT IMAGE
      DO 90 I = 1,132
   90 PRTIMG(I) = BLANK
C      K  INDEXES CARD,N1 INDEXES PAGE NUMBER ARRAY (PGARY), N  -- LIST,
C      L1 INDEXES PRINT IMAGE, STARTS AT CHAR 2
      L1 = 2
      K = 1
C           *         *         *         *
C
C
C          ENTER HERE TO MOVE HEADER TO PRTIMG.
C              K = CHAR1 OF HEADER TO MOVE (MAY BE AFTER KEYWORD)
C              L = PRINT POSIT. TO START STORAGE
C
  105 N1 = 1
      N = 1
      TWO = 0
C          MOVE NEW CARD IMAGE TO OLD CARD IMAGE
      DO 107 I=1,80
  107 OLDCD(I) = NEWCD(I)
  110 IF ( OLDCD(K ) .EQ. SLASH ) GO TO 120
C      TEST FOR 2 BLANKS MEANING END OF HEADER
      IF (OLDCD(K) .EQ. BLANK ) GO TO 125
C      NOT BLANK CHAR - ZERO TWO CNT
      TWO = 0
C      MOVE CHARACTER TO PRINT IMAGE
  115 PRTIMG (L1)   = OLDCD(K )
  118 L1 = L1 + 1
      K = K + 1
      IF ( K  - 69 ) 110, 110, 130
C      PRINT IMAGE STORED, STORE SIZE, STRING ON PAGE NUMBER
C
C      SLASH DETECTED, MOVE BLANK TO PRINT IMAGE
```

```
   120 PRTIMG(L1)   = BLANK
       GO TO 118
C
C     BLANK DETECTED INCREMENT AND TEST COUNT FOR 2 SUCCESSIVE ONES
   125 TWO = TWO + 1
       IF (TWO .LT. 2) GO TO 115
C          TWO BLANKS DETECTED, BACK UP POINTER
       L1 = L1-1
C     2 BLANKS OR 69 COLS STORED, HEADER NOW IN PRINT IMAGE
   130 HDRSZ = L1
C         HDRSZ HAS 2 BLANKS IF 2 DETECTED,
C                    NO BLANKS IF 69 COLS DETECTED
C
C***   PAGE NUMBER ROUTINE FOR STRINGING     ***
C         FORMAT =  XXXXA-XXXXA, WHERE X IS NUM, A IS ALPH OR NULL
   135 I= 70
C     START AT CARD COLUMN 70
       END = .FALSE.
   140 IF ( END ) GO TO 190
C
C          TEST FOR A,B, OR DASH. IF ANY OF THESE-END NUMBER FIELD.
      0IF((OLDCD(I) .EQ. A) .OR. (OLDCD(I) .EQ. B) .OR. (OLDCD(I) .EQ.
      1     DASH) .OR. (OLDCD(I) .EQ. STAR)) GO TO 150
C     CHECK FOR BLANK
   145 IF ( OLDCD(I) .NE. BLANK ) GO TO 190
   150 END = .TRUE.
       IF(( I .GT.70 ) .AND. (I .LT. 76 ))GO TO 160
   155 WRITE (6,1030) CARDNO, OLDCD
  10300FORMAT (1H1,57H PAGE NUMBER PUNCHED INCORRECTLY, NOT OF FORM XXXXA
      1-XXXXA  ,10HCARD NUMB ,I6 /1H0, 12H CONTENTS= , 80A1)
       GO TO 400
C              **         **        **         **
   160 SUM = 0
       I2 = 70
C         COMPUTE DECIMAL PAGE NUMBER FOR SORTING
C          RIGHT ADJUST PAGE DIGIT, SHIFT SUM, AND ADD TO SUM
   170 SUM =(OLDCD(I2)/DIV)+ SUM*10
       I2 = I2 + 1
       IF ( I2 - I )  170, 180, 180
   180 SUM = SUM * 10
       IF( OLDCD(I) .EQ. STAR ) SUM=SUM+1
       IF ( OLDCD(I) .EQ. A ) SUM = SUM + 3
       IF ( OLDCD(I) .EQ. B ) SUM = SUM + 7
C     STORE DECIMAL NUMBER FOR SORT IN FIRST SLOT OF LIST COUPLET
       LIST(N) = SUM
C     STRING CHARACTER ONTO PAGE NUMB. ARRAY
   190 PGARY(N1) = OLDCD(I)
C     INCREMENT PAGE ARRAY COUNT
       N1 = N1 + 1
C     INCREMENT CARD COLUMN COUNT
       I = I + 1
C          TEST FOR BLANK   OR  COL 80 AT CARD END
       IF (  OLDCD(I-1) .EQ. BLANK ) GO TO 210
C     IS CARD DONE..
       IF ( I - 80 ) 140,140,200
C     CARD IS DONE, MOVE BLANK TO LAST 20C., IF NOT THERE
```

```
  200 PGARY(N1) = BLANK
      N1 = N1 + 1
      I = I + 1
C     SET SECOND SLOT OF COUPLET TO START OF PAGE STRING (POS - NO. CHS)
  210 LIST(N+1) =  N1 -( I-70)
      N = N + 2
      IF ( N - 198 ) 10, 10, 215
C     STORAGE EXCEEDED
  215 WRITE (6, 1040) CARDNO, OLDCD, LIST
10400FORMAT (1H0, 46H***PAGE NUMB STORAGE EXCEEDED ***   CARD NO. = ,I6/
     1    16HCARD CONTENTS =    ,80A1/ (18I7))
      GO TO 400
C                  **         **         **         **
C     NEW CARD HEADER NOT THE SAME AS OLD ONE, SORT PAGE NOS THEN PRINT
C     BUBBLE  SORT
  220 RVCNT = 0
  223 DO 230 J2 = 1,N,2
  224 CONTINUE
      IF ((J2 + 2) .GE. N ) GO TO 230
      IF (LIST(J2) - LIST(J2+2)) 230,227,225
  225 CONTINUE
C     SWAP THEM
C     ORDER LIST IN ASCENDING ORDER.
      TEMP = LIST(J2)
      LIST(J2) = LIST(J2+2)
      LIST(J2+2) = TEMP
      TEMP = LIST(J2+1)
      LIST(J2+1) = LIST(J2+3)
      LIST(J2+3) = TEMP
      RVCNT = RVCNT + 1
      GO TO 230
  227 CONTINUE
C     PAGE NUMBERS ARE EQUAL, REPLACE SECOND ONE WITH LAST IN LIST
      LIST(J2+2) = LIST(N-2)
      LIST(J2+3) = LIST(N-1)
      N = N - 2
      GO TO 224
  230 CONTINUE
      IF (RVCNT) 250,250,220
C
C     END OF BUBBLE SORT
C     MIGHT ADD STAT ANAL -- LATER *** ---
C
C     PRINTING SECTION
C     HEADER IN PRTIMG, SIZE IN HDRSZ, PAGES IN PGARY, ORDER IN ODD LIST
C     ,NUMBER OF PAGES IS N/2.
  250 N5 = 2
C     TEST IF ROOM FOR A NEW PAGE NUMBER ON LINE
  255 IF ( L1    .GE. 119 ) GO TO 350
C     ROOM FOR PAGE
      PRTIMG(L1) = COMMA
      PRTIMG(L1+1) = BLANK
      L1 = L1 + 2
  260 NDX = LIST(N5)
      NDX1 = NDX
C     BLANK SEPARATES PAGE NUMBERS
```

```
  270 IF (PGARY(NDX) .EQ. BLANK) GO TO 290
C     NOT BLANK - CONTINUE FORMING PAGE
      PRTIMG(L1) = PGARY(NDX)
      L1 = L1 + 1
      NDX = NDX + 1
      IF ( NDX -(NDX1+13))270, 280, 280
  280 WRITE (6,1050) CARDNO, PGARY
 1050 FORMAT (1H0, 49H MORE   THAN 11 CHARS IN PAGE ARRAY, CARD NUMB =  ,
     1 I6/ 1H0,   6H ARRAY / (1H ,131A1))
      GO TO 400
C                      **        **        **        **
C     GO TO NEXT COUPLET
  290 N5 = N5 + 2
C     TEST FOR END OF LIST
      IF ( N5-N ) 255,292,292
C     ARRAY DONE, PRINT LAST LINE
  292 WRITE (6, 1060) PRTIMG
 1060 FORMAT (132A1)
      LINE = LINE + 1
C     IF OK GO TEST FOR EQUAL KEYWORDS
      IF (LINE .LT. 50) GO TO 295
      PAGE  = PAGE + 1
      LINE = 1
      WRITE (6,1070) PAGE
 1070 FORMAT (1H1, 60X, 10HBOOK INDEX ,42X, 5HPAGE  ,I3/1H0/1H )
  295 IF (ENDRUN) GO TO 380
C
C     TEST FOR KEYWORDS THE SAME
      MATCH = .TRUE.
      DO 300 J = 1,69
      IF (NEWCD(J) .EQ. BLANK ) GO TO 310
      NEWKEY(J) = NEWCD(J)
      IF ( NEWKEY(J) .NE. KEY(J) ) MATCH = .FALSE.
  300 CONTINUE
C     NO BLANK IN 69 COLS, ERROR
      GO TO 55
C     BLANK FOUND
  310 NKEYSZ = J - 1
C     TEST FOR NEW KEYWORD
  315 IF (  (NKEYSZ .NE. KEYSZ) .OR. ( .NOT. MATCH) ) GO TO 70
C                      ***        ***        ***
C     SAME KEYWORD, INDENT, STRIP IT OFF
  330 DO 340 I = 1,132
C     CLEAR PRINT IMAGE
  340 PRTIMG(I) = BLANK
C     INDENT  5  SPACES
      L1 = 5
C     START AT END OF KEY TO LOAD IMAGE
  .   K = KEYSZ +1
      GO TO 105
C     MORE THAN 119 COLS FULL, PRINT IT
  350 PRTIMG(L1) = COMMA
C                   *          *          *          *          *
      WRITE (6,1060) PRTIMG
      LINE = LINE + 1
      IF ( LINE .LT. 50) GO TO 360
```

```
      PAGE = PAGE + 1
      LINE = 1
      WRITE (6,1070) PAGE
  360 DO 370 I = 1,132
  370 PRTIMG(I) = BLANK
C     INDENT TO POSITION OF PAGE NUMBER ON PREVIOUS LINE
      L1 = HDRSZ + 2
      GO TO 260
C             *         *         *         *
  380 STOP 10
C
C         ERROR ROUTINES
C         TEST NUMBER OF ERRORS, IF LESS GO TO SAFE POINT, IF MORE STOP
  400 M = M + 1
      IF (M .GT. 15) GO TO 380
C         RE-INITIALIZE TO START AGAIN
      FIRST =  .TRUE.
      GO TO 10
C
      END
```

index